I0760187

Winner of the Jules and Frances Landry Award for 2017

Reconstruction in Alabama

From Civil War to Redemption in the Cotton South

MICHAEL W. FITZGERALD

Louisiana State University Press
Baton Rouge

Published by Louisiana State University Press

Manufactured in the United States of America
First printing

Designer: Laura Roubique Gleason
Typeface: Miller Text
Printer: McNaughton & Gunn
Binder: Dekker Bookbinding

Library of Congress Cataloging-in-Publication Data

Names: Fitzgerald, Michael W., 1956–
Title: Reconstruction in Alabama : from Civil War to redemption in the cotton South / Michael W. Fitzgerald.
Description: First printing. | Baton Rouge : Louisiana State University Press, [2017] | Includes bibliographical references and index.
Identifiers: LCCN 2016042879 | ISBN 978-0-8071-6606-2 (cloth : alk. paper) | ISBN 978-0-8071-6607-9 (pdf) | ISBN 978-0-8071-6608-6 (epub) | ISBN 978-0-8071-6609-3 (mobi)
Subjects: LCSH: Reconstruction (U.S. history, 1865–1877)—Alabama. | Unionists (United States Civil War)—Alabama. | Ku Klux Klan (19th century)—Alabama—History.
Classification: LCC F326 .F7545 2017 | DDC 976.1/06—dc23
LC record available at https://lccn.loc.gov/2016042879

The paper in this book meets the guidelines for permanence and durability of the Committee on Production Guidelines for Book Longevity of the Council on Library Resources. ♾

Contents

Acknowledgments vii

Introduction 1

PART I

1. A Mere Lapsus: Unionists and Conservative Dissidents during the Civil War 13
2. The Last Relicks of Barbarism: Army, War, and Reconstruction 33
3. Presidential Reconstruction: Unionism and the Politics of Definition 55
4. The Premature New South of Governor Robert Patton 83

PART II

5. Black Liberation: Freedom and Political Mobilization 107
6. Implementing Reconstruction: Governance and Biracial Politics 143
7. The Difference between Whaling a Freeman and Pounding a Slave: Terrorism and Resistance in the Klan Era 174
8. Railroads, Race, and Reconstruction: The Curious Legacy of Governor William H. Smith 205
9. Bipartisan Disaster: The Advent of Governor Robert Lindsay 229
10. False Dawn: The Promise of Reconstruction in the Early 1870s 257

PART III

11. Beneath the White Banner: Depression and the Overthrow of Reconstruction 285
12. "It Only Requires a Little More Figuring": Redemption's Aftermath 316

Notes 339
Select Bibliography 415
Index 443

Illustrations follow page 132

Acknowledgments

This work has had, alas, a substantial gestation period. Thus it is nearly impossible to remember all the people who have assisted and encouraged me along the way. In the interest of avoiding an Oscar-length list of thanks, only the most outstanding and recent debts can be mentioned here. If I overlook anyone, I hope my friends will forgive the omission.

Several scholars read drafts of the entire manuscript, a selfless act if one exists. I should thank Bertis English, Chris McIlwain, Terry Seip, and Mills Thornton. In Minnesota, David Willard lives nearby, and repeated conversations on the manuscript over coffee have been invaluable. But beyond all else, I should acknowledge the exhaustive critiques provided by Mark W. Summers. His daughter attended my institution, and given the usefulness of his occasional visits, I should have subsidized her tuition. Several individuals performed similar feats of kindness. Steve Chicione, for example, let me drive to his home after an Internet contact, and examine his photocopies from the National Archives. Several others behaved similarly, and I could scarcely credit the generosity with which I have been treated.

Various historians read portions of the manuscript, often quite extensive ones. Several are good friends, but such distinctions seem invidious. I should mention Bruce Baker, Hilary Green, Elaine Parsons, Rob Riser, Mitchell Snay, and Kidada Williams. Joan Waugh read one chapter, and Eric Foner read earlier versions of others. Professor Foner in particular provided a scholarly model and much encouragement over the years. Chris Waldrep provided commentary and assistance, as did my former undergraduates Max Grivno and Sarah Silkey. I'm not sure I ever persuaded Sarah Wiggins to read any of this manuscript, but conversations with her over the years were instructive. All these scholars have my thanks, but of course the book's errors are entirely my own.

This project involved repeated trips to the South, mostly involving the Alabama Department of Archives and History. Both the former director of the archives, Ed Bridges, and his successor, Steve Murray, have been abundantly helpful in making facilitating the process, and in providing insights during my extended stays in Montgomery. Norwood Kerr and numerous others were generous as well. I should also thank Carol Ellis at the University of South Alabama archives for expediting access to the excellent Pickens Collection. Nearby, at the University of Mobile, Lonnie Burnett facilitated making the special collections there available as well, and was helpful in other ways. And I should acknowledge the library staffs at the University of Alabama, Auburn University, and the Birmingham Public Library, along with public libraries and county courthouses along the way.

I profited intellectually from the scholarly documentary editing projects in the field. At the University of Maryland, Leslie Rowland at the Freedom and Southern Society Papers Project provided me access to that matchlessly organized collection, and she generously talked through my project and even assisted with citations. I received a short-term fellowship to the Grant Papers project at Mississippi State, and I should note Professor John Marszalek's role in securing it. A short-term fellowship at the Gilder Lehrman Center at Yale University, a seminar with Professor Richard White at Stanford, and grants from the National Endowment for the Humanities enabled this research too.

One of the pleasures of teaching in a liberal arts setting like St. Olaf College is seeing a profusion of fine students at an early, candid stage of their intellectual lives. A decade ago, Adam Lozeau and I coauthored a paper on the Ku Klux Klan, which we presented at the Alabama Historical Association. More recently, I benefited from the research of Cynthia J. Zapata and the statistical assistance of Ben Bayer. Sarah Paulson shared her internship research from the University of South Alabama, and two recent students read this manuscript in its entirety, Tim Klustner and Evan Holmstrom. I have been edified by the commentary of all three. Also, I have benefited from my colleagues with statistical skills. Decades ago, Catherine Fitch studied at my college, and I would like to acknowledge her associates at the University of Minnesota demographic history project. Utilizing their online IPUMS database, statistics Professor Paul Roback and his students Thomas Hegland, Eric King, and Charlotte Sivanich received a National Science Foundation grant (DMS-1045015) to support my research. His St. Olaf colleague Dick Brown and students

Rodney LaLonde and Omar Shemata worked on statistical mapping programs, and their skills are on display in this manuscript. More broadly, I should acknowledge the librarians at the University of Minnesota and St. Olaf College, specifically Kris McPherson and Kasia Gonnerman, among others. And of course all my departmental colleagues lived with the project much as I did, and I thank them all.

Over the years I shamelessly exploited friends and their families for housing in expensive places. The economist Don Davis, a fellow Canoga Park High School alumnus, assisted my research with extended stays at Harvard and Columbia, as did Parke Skelton in Los Angeles and my sister, Cheryl Fitzgerald Berriman, in the Bay Area. My late in-laws, John and Alexandra Kutulas, and Janet Kutulas and Peter Simcich did the same.

Finally, I should thank my spouse and colleague, Judy Kutulas, and my sons, Alex and Nate, for enduring conversation on this topic for much of their lives. My parents are gone and their absence is felt, in part because they both loyally read my books. My mother, a southern native, could never hear of my visiting Alabama without expressing her horror of the Birmingham church bombing. It got old, but I miss her now. In closing, I should note the origin of my interest in this subject in the UCLA History Department of the late 1970s. Armstead Robinson gave his early benediction to Alabama as a topic. He and Alexander Saxton are no longer around, but Margaret Washington is, and all three deserve my thanks for their guidance. I hope this work repays their pains, and I am grateful for the memories of that place and time, which gave me a kind wife and a career.

Reconstruction in Alabama

Introduction

Books seldom have a brief rationale, especially of a numerical sort. This one does—1905—the date of Walter Lynwood Fleming's *Civil War and Reconstruction in Alabama*. Of course more recent, sensible studies exist, but the standard account of the postwar period dates back over a century and shares the racial presuppositions of the Jim Crow era. "The negro was as wax in the hands of a stronger race," Fleming confides in a footnote, decrying the influence of northern carpetbaggers.[1] At the most obvious level, his dated beliefs justify a reexamination with contemporary eyes and different assumptions. A pedestrian place to start, perhaps, but Alabama provides a vantage point for broader reflection on the state of Reconstruction scholarship, and on its meaning for contemporary America.

Scholars well know the limitations of Fleming's major work, though the eight-hundred-page volume was well received by the profession at the time.[2] It established him as one of the exemplars of the Dunning school, which depicted Reconstruction as an era of profligate spending, corruption, and egalitarian excess. Reading Fleming today provides a cold bath of retrograde racial assumptions. Of the notorious Black Codes, he wrote, "it would have been well for the negro if they had been passed into law and enforced." Fleming depicts a widespread social and political challenge to white supremacy, an emphasis with some merit, but the insights in his work are overwhelmed by his overarching bias in sources and interpretation. Enthusiasm for the Ku Klux Klan presents his most troubling aspect. He saw organized violence by Democrats as the necessary response to the multifront egalitarian challenge. Fleming promoted the positive legacy of the Klan in public venues, and he served as an apologist for disfranchisement. He even excused lynching in print, if obliquely.[3]

It was inevitable that such views would come under later scrutiny. As early as the 1930s, W. E. B. Du Bois denounced Fleming's monograph as "pure propaganda," and the African American scholar Horace Mann Bond—the father of SNCC's Julian—produced a study of black education which anticipates some of the themes of this work.[4] In the 1960s, legions of Revisionists overthrew the entire Dunning school, and few now reference Fleming's scholarship except to deplore it. During the 1970s, revisionist scholars produced refutations of portions of his argument, from Peter Kolchin's study of emancipation to Sarah Wiggins's rehabilitation of moderate native white Republicans.[5] The trend shows no sign of relenting, with the war-related topics receiving more coverage than Reconstruction as a whole.[6] However, Fleming's scope, and perhaps the sheer heft of his volume, deterred imitators. "Fleming had the courage to tackle a survey of the entire Civil War and Reconstruction period in Alabama, a feat none of the rest of us have had the nerve to attempt," Wiggins notes.[7] Fleming's book remains a "starting point" for scholars, despite its dated premises and factual inaccuracies. One objective of this study is simply to rectify that, to provide a reliable, modern account.[8]

But there is bigger game afoot. The impetus of the revisionist wave was the Second Reconstruction of the 1960s, especially the political and constitutional conflicts over states' rights and federal authority. The analogy with the modern struggle over civil rights provided revisionists with their élan, their sense of egalitarian mission.[9] The rehabilitation of Radical Reconstruction deemphasized issues peripheral to that endeavor, making racial justice the central concern. The current historical moment is opportune to place African American aspirations in broader context. In the emerging literature on slavery, global capitalism appears as a major force in the financing, expansion, and marketing of cotton and other staple crops. Enslaved people were buffeted about and brutalized by this globalization, but slavery's demise eliminated their status as valuable property, along with masters' interest in their preservation. Emancipation exposed former slaves to the unmediated force of the world market, as small producers confronting landlords and more distant economic forces. The price of cotton, access to credit, foreign investment in American infrastructure, all these transformed the relationship of African Americans to the world. Thus liberated slaves entered the international economy, as individuals, at the moment they entered political life as enfranchised citizens.[10]

Alabama has as much claim to representativeness in this process as anywhere, at least in the cotton South.[11] The state's social geography is not unique, and the political trends have obvious analogues elsewhere. Fleming saw it as the model southern state.[12] State-level examinations tangibly integrate the racial politics of liberation with the broader currents of the mid-nineteenth century. But the revisionism-inspired wave of such studies dried up decades ago, somehow bypassing the state. *Reconstruction in Alabama* provides a fresh opportunity to look at emancipation in a productive framework, because economic-policy decisions often occurred at the state level. To take one fatal example, Alabama like other southern states embarked upon a program of public subsidy for railroads, which channeled northern and European capital toward the state. This was one of Reconstruction's signature initiatives, and when it brought bankruptcy, African Americans received most of the blame. This association of black suffrage with big government, high taxation, and corporate corruption buttressed racial reaction thereafter. There was enough substance to this half-truth to make it plausible to those who preferred to believe it. But the railroad program had roots in the antebellum history of the state, and a large bipartisan constituency that drove it to fruition.[13]

Over the decades, some scholars have suggested that the revisionist identification with the Republicans as protagonists obscures the economic divisions among whites.[14] Michael Perman, for instance, made the distinction between Whiggish centrists and Democratic small-government fundamentalists the central theme of his work, *The Road to Redemption*.[15] J. Mills Thornton suggested the revisionist emphasis on race has been overstated, because Republican fiscal policies drove white small farmers into the arms of the Democrats. Taxation thus offers "a persuasive explanation" of their behavior, as opposed to one based "merely on unvarnished racism."[16] And, as Samuel L. Webb makes clear, lingering Jacksonian-style misgivings against corporate subsidies proved prescient during the postwar years.[17] By no means does this book downplay the centrality of racial reaction in Reconstruction politics. Rampant murder and brutality make that fact indelible. But sharp divisions among whites over development policy, and subsequently over how to avoid state bankruptcy, opened avenues of political influence to African Americans. These circumstances simultaneously spread a battleground of heated policy disputes before the new voters, making them a convenient racist scapegoat for everything gone wrong.

Of course, railroads and development were not the salient economic issues to the freedpeople. The evolution of the postbellum plantation system mattered much more, and modern revisionist scholarship affirms that insight. Eric Foner's *Reconstruction: America's Unfinished Revolution* (1988) remains the field's indispensable work. Foner's achievement was to restate the basic revisionist political formulation and integrate it with the social history of emancipation, specifically the struggle for effective freedom on the plantations. This feat of synthesis gets a great deal right. Still, *Reconstruction*'s account is more incisive on the years just after the war, when the agricultural order was in chaos. The politicization of the freedmen intersected with labor unrest, and planters reacted violently against enfranchisement. But the mass mobilization ebbed, in part because laborers' discontent forced concessions. Landowners found ways to get freedpeople back to the fields more willingly—through "sharecropping" and other forms of tenant farming—and planters gleefully appropriated much of the resulting profit. Economic recovery gave rich planters something to lose, especially those in the middle of the black belt. Under the circumstances, the revisionist emphasis on white unity, on a unified sense of racial grievance, oversimplifies the reality of class divisions.

I find Foner's focus on the postwar collapse more compelling than his delineation of the plantation recovery that followed. Properly he depicts "the planter class" as benefiting from Klan-style terrorism, and he emphasizes the movement's elite direction. But it is worth cautioning that in Alabama freedpeople lived highly concentrated in areas where organized violence was short-lived or sporadic.[18] Racial supremacy as an idea was nearly universal among whites, but actual behavior differed depending on time and place. Foner depicts a discontented planter class as the 1870s dawned, presiding over "a kind of stalemate on the plantations" and frustrated with sharecropping. Planters resented the freedpeople's sense of quasi-proprietorship that came with the arrangement, Foner observes.[19] These twin contentions, of planter leadership in terrorist violence and their abiding discontent, make logical sense paired interpretively. But when cotton planting paid well, after years of losses, the elite mood brightened. Once Reconstruction became established, a substantial constituency of black belt "conservatives" benefited from labor peace and abundance. Economic recovery simultaneously inclined them toward optimistic collaboration with railroad initiatives, which encouraged a measure of bipartisan cooperation. Conservatives mostly remained housed in the opposition "Democratic and Conservative" party, as it was officially named, but they were prone to pragmatic accommodations with local Republican majorities. For years, these tendencies inhibited terrorism in the heart of the black belt, as empowered freedpeople used overwhelming numbers, arson, and bluff to discourage raids and force outside intervention.

Racial violence never vanished entirely. But in the early 1870s one might reasonably have concluded that a crisis had passed. For two and a half years, no large race riots or armed battles occurred in Alabama.[20] A competitive biracial democracy functioned across much of the state, as adversaries negotiated their way toward a different future. Only the depression of the mid-1870s changed this trajectory, swiftly and terrifyingly. Cotton prices collapsed, and international channels of credit ceased for merchants and planters, and through them, their tenants. Labor became superfluous, sharecroppers suddenly went without food, and social turmoil spread. All this thrust elite opinion back toward racial extremism, and into the violent White Line campaign that decisively ended Reconstruction. The interpretation here of Democratic politics is thus reminiscent of Michael Perman's work on Reconstruction, in that it emphasizes persistent "Whiggish" moderation by black belt planters. The crucial intent, however, is to take Foner's core insight of the centrality of plantation production and extend it fully through the 1870s.[21]

A more recent, broad reconceptualization of the field is Steven Hahn's *A Nation Under Our Feet* (2003). In some respects, Hahn replicates the sympathies of the modern scholarship, along with Foner's emphasis on plantation labor. Hahn is less appreciative, however, of what Reconstruction governance could bring to the landless poor; he sees even black Republican officeholders as shaped by their "petit bourgeois notions of respectability" and the needs of electoral politics. The social distance between legislators and their rural constituents limited change. His work critiques the individualistic presuppositions of revisionist scholarship, instead emphasizing the collective grassroots struggle for land and self-determination. This approach has much to commend it, particularly the emphasis on "Paramilitary Politics" of the era, and of the scope of the Klan and White League mobilizations. For freedpeople, electoral participation utterly depended on communal self-defense, and their ability to deter terrorist violence.[22]

Hahn's work nonetheless raises some of the structural questions evident elsewhere. The apocalyptic conflict of early Reconstruction receives stress, the more ambiguous middle period of agricultural recovery less so.[23] But the plantation system's evolution matters, and what employers were offering influenced how class struggle proceeded. For example, Hahn comments little on the shift toward tenant farming and its role in mitigating conflict.[24] For several prosperous years, if Alabama is any measure, relative labor peace descended on the cotton belt. There were labor conventions aplenty, as Hahn notes, but is difficult even to *find* a strike by agricultural laborers or sharecroppers, this at a time of declining terrorist repression. Hahn rightly depicts a baseline struggle for land and autonomy, from slavery to the Garvey agitation, but the shifting fortunes of landowners influenced laborers' collective response.

Both of these scholars place black aspirations for meaningful freedom at the center of their political narratives, explicitly.[25] Racial equality is indeed the central issue of the era, the aspect that makes Reconstruction's bygone struggles matter now. That said, the distinctive feature of Reconstruction is the entrance of black voters into the world of formal politics, inhabited by a white majority shaped by slavery and its loss—that is to say, racists of one stripe or another. Readers of this book need not seek a rehabilitation of the dominant wing of the Democratic Party—the states' rights, secessionist, and resolutely Confederate wing—save for an admission of how determinedly they pursued the chilling logic of racial extremism. The intellectual challenge is posed by those conservatives who resisted this emphasis, who preferred, at times, not to follow such premises to their full fruition. In Alabama, at least, the term "conservative" commonly described this cautious dissident tendency.[26] The revisionist literature often lumps uninhibited Democratic partisans together with their more pragmatic peers, in apparent distaste for parsing subtle distinctions in their racism.[27] This makes sense, morally, and perhaps interpretively too. Ultimately, they were likely to reunite when northern commitment lapsed, because the bulk of the white population shared so many common racial beliefs and grievances. But in this era of difficult choices they were tactically divided, and there were shades of racial intransigence. Besides, in pondering these events of 150 years ago, one wonders if today there is any benefit to highlighting a monolithic racial reaction.

Freedpeople did not have the luxury of ignoring distinctions of interest or sentiment, given that some opponents were prone toward murder. The black political class indeed had concerns distinct from the mass of agricultural laborers, but that was not entirely to their detriment as politicians or lawmakers. The skill with which leaders negotiated dangerous terrain, their growing sophistication, constitutes one of the overlooked elements of Reconstruction. The revisionist literature, with its identification with racial-justice demands, downplays the pragmatism with which black leaders operated. In Alabama, they made tactical retreats, and they pressed some issues only half-heartedly on their coalition partners. Flexibility often marked their conduct. For example, black leaders supported the railroad program, but primarily at the instance of their party's most conservative leaders, in hope of outreach to saner opponents. This conciliatory inclination partly explains the state's unusual trajectory under Reconstruction rule. Alabama's Republicans never elected an African American to state office, never integrated the public schools or colleges, never passed a civil rights bill; nor did they elect the numbers to local office common elsewhere. Civil rights demands expanded, but black leaders long finessed the steamroller of racial hostility, and thus allowed the cleavages among whites full reign, more effectively than one might think possible.

The profusion and class diversity of native white Republican allies partly explains this deferential pattern, as these "scalawags" provided the black minority the only route to democratic control. A substantial Unionist constituency existed in the hill country, profoundly alienated from the states' rights Democratic majority over class-tinged issues relating to secession, along with those embittered by the Confederate war. These Unionists, of various stripes and degrees of commitment, were joined by a trickle of Republican converts from conservative ranks, along with more circumspect collaborators. These were often established political figures, acting from some mixture of personal opportunism or flexibility. Means and experience smoothed their path to office, as it did the newly arrived "carpetbaggers," infused with the passions of the northern war effort. None of these coalition partners served African American interests all that well, but this was the hand circumstances dealt. Alabama's previous history thus scattered white dissidents and newcomers across the political landscape, making them essential players in Radical Reconstruction. All of this serves to explain the substantial attention to antebellum and wartime developments in the pages to come.

The structure of the book is broadly chronological, composed of topical chapters following the sequence of events. The book's interpretation forces one organizational quirk: an early emphasis on divisions within the existing political structure, so African Americans as actors receive sustained attention only as suffrage approaches. The first chapter deals with the prewar sources of dissident sentiment among white Alabamians on economic policy, class, and regional tensions and over the issues of secession and war. The second chapter examines the Union military and federal occupation, and the early wartime Reconstruction efforts and the transition to peace. This initial section concludes with the Presidential Reconstruction regime, especially the efforts to salvage the state's finances and thus secure outside capital, to implement public subsidies for railroad construction. This priority highlights the conservative desire to avoid provocative behavior on race, and thus escape all-out conflict with the North, a pattern which recurred through the Reconstruction era.

In the second section, the freedpeople receive sustained attention. We trace the evolution from slavery to enfranchisement, and the installation of the Republican Reconstruction government. One chapter examines the Ku Klux Klan, its antecedents, composition, and tactics, while the next examines the intertwined topic of the Republican railroad program. *Reconstruction in Alabama* then turns to the temporary Democratic victory in 1870 and its consequence, the collapse of state finances in a morass of corporate corruption. The section's concluding chapter examines the surprising fruits of hobbled Democratic rule, as the recovering plantation economy permitted an interlude of relative civility. The central argument is that persistent white divisions over finance and ideology, and the practical value of labor peace in a recovering economy, gave freedpeople real leverage. This theme appears recurrently, in part because the evidence of interracial accommodation in the black belt is so profuse.

And then the gears shift back. The final section deals with the economic collapse of 1873, the cessation of outside credit to plantations, the resurgence of racist violence, and the overthrow of Reconstruction. Long ago, C. Vann Woodward described the great Whiggish planters and New South investors as the victors in the Redemption settlement.[28] This book concludes with how Redemption came about: how extremist Democrats, stung by the recurrent defections, made white supremacy the centerpiece of the 1874 counterrevolution. They promised skittish rich landowners complete deliverance from local majorities, and once in power, they lived up to these pledges. The Redemption settlement permanently empowered the planter minority of the black belt, previously the perennial also-rans of Alabama's popular politics. Redemption handed them a reservoir of captive black ballots, providing a legislative stranglehold all the way to the Populist revolt and beyond. Whiggish visions of activist government fell by the wayside, but low taxes and negative government now served planters' interests well. Black belt planters emerged as major players in the "big mule" coalition with industrialists, at the expense of their own labor force, but also the legions of upland farmers who had handed them permanent control. One may discern some poetic justice, as the more restrained racists were rewarded at the expense of their more partisan comrades, but the benefits of planter domination for the former slaves are hard to find. It is poor consolation that the post-Redemption settlement could have been worse: in a generation it would be.

This book emphasizes formal politics and the plantation economy, and how they influenced African American choices and possibilities. Recent literature on the Civil War and Reconstruction gives more attention to the cultural and behavioral aspects of the era, from the imagery of terrorism to ideas of masculinity. The literature on the mayhem of the Klan, its abuse of women and children, and its symbolism, will certainly find no dissent here.[29] The cultural emphasis opens up fresh vistas as scholars move beyond the issues that long occupied revisionist writing. This study engages such topics as appropriate, as Alabama's experience complicates the emerging literature, especially the tendency to read Jim Crow's ossified order back into Reconstruction's more fluid alignments. The emphasis on Reconstruction's vivid horrors can overshadow the rest of the picture, because some people were situated to do more than testify bravely about atrocities after the fact. What *Reconstruction in Alabama* adds is illustration of how widely freedpeople deterred violence, how normal life appeared for years in wide sections of the black belt. This work's gestation period, as the fruit of a lifetime of research and reflection, gives it a long historiographic reach, reexamining the emphases of the revisionists in light of the recent literature. It reflects upon the origins of the unbridled rule of property in the New South, which cast a long shadow in the class-tinged violence of the later era of fire hoses and church bombings. This is, after all, the land of Booker T. Washington and Martin Luther King, of Montgomery and Selma. What happened in this "heart of Dixie," and how people chose to misremember it, set the stage for what was to come.

PART I

1

A Mere Lapsus

Unionists and Conservative Dissidents during the Civil War

. . . [I]t never made a serious impression on my mind that secession would produce war.

—James Pugh, Secessionist Congressman

To most modern eyes, emancipation and racial equality appear as the overriding concerns of the Reconstruction era. For this reason, native white Republicans raise disquieting issues given their unenthusiastic position on egalitarian issues. Without an antislavery grounding, Unionism is difficult to take seriously now as a moral commitment. And still less attractive, perhaps, are the elite "conservatives" who foresaw that sectional extremism promised ruin, becoming dissidents by virtue of losing their slaves to secession.[1] But these were precisely the concerns that mattered for dissenting whites, creating Alabama's premier apostates, the postwar "scalawag" Republicans. A constituency existed for transformative postwar change, or rather diverse constituencies, with deep roots in the political history of the state. Even among those who later opposed Reconstruction, there were fissures based on prewar politics, and over the secession crisis and the war. This background mattered little to the black population, as yet, but it structured the world of formal politics they would soon enter.[2]

Two facts stand out about Alabama's prewar political structure. First, the overwhelming majority of the free population favored slavery; they fully participated in the system of racial attitudes, fears, and controls that slavery spawned. These were widely shared norms, rather than being an imposition of the slaveholding elite. But slavery also highlighted the dividing line between the interests of the wealthy and the rest of the free population. Overlapping patterns of class and regional division undergirded Alabama's formal politics from statehood on. The consequence was a schizophrenic political order. Slavery went unchallenged, but libertarian hostility to the designs of wealthy planters became the dominant political value.

An antielite, proslavery impulse shaped antebellum political development, and for the purposes of understanding Reconstruction, we must briefly trace that evolution. Tennessee Valley founding elites initially dominated the state's politics, and in the 1820s they pursued banking and transportation measures, particularly river improvements and a faltering canal project around Muscle Shoals. Opposition to the "Royalist" economic dominance led to creation of a state bank which collapsed, taking the state's federal education endowment with it. Responsibility was mixed, but disaster fed the antielite, antistatist backlash among farmers in the poorer and more isolated areas.[3] Alabama thus became a "particularly Jacksonian state."[4] Democrats carried every presidential and gubernatorial election in the three decades before the Civil War. One consequence was a progressive revenue system that targeted slave property, leaving smaller farmers' land lightly taxed.

Geography structured these patterns. The black belt stretched across Alabama's south-central portion, from Montgomery to Selma and beyond, a densely populated region dominated by cotton plantations. In the richest counties like Dallas, the population was three-quarters enslaved or more. Such areas, fully integrated into the international economy, possessed the preponderance of Alabama's wealth. The Whig Party carried the region, favoring government promotion of banking, corporations, public education, and internal improvements. Some prosperous areas surrounding the black belt voted with them, like the river counties of the southwest part of the state. Finally, the few urban outposts supported the Whigs on the assumption that river improvements, and, eventually, railroads would bring commerce to their doors. These same areas backed Protestant-tinged uplift initiatives like temperance and state asylums for the disabled, along with a more widely dispersed tax structure to pay for it all.[5] Elite Whigs had the singular experience of being locked out of formal power by the agrarian masses, immune to their hopes for social progress, and, they thought, reckless.

The mountainous north-central portion of the state, and piedmont areas to the south of it, bore little resemblance to the plantation belt. The Appalachians petered out here from the northeast, providing a region of mountain ridges and plateaus interspersed with narrow fertile valleys. The population was overwhelmingly white, and small farms predominated, growing food and raising livestock. Hill country farmers were

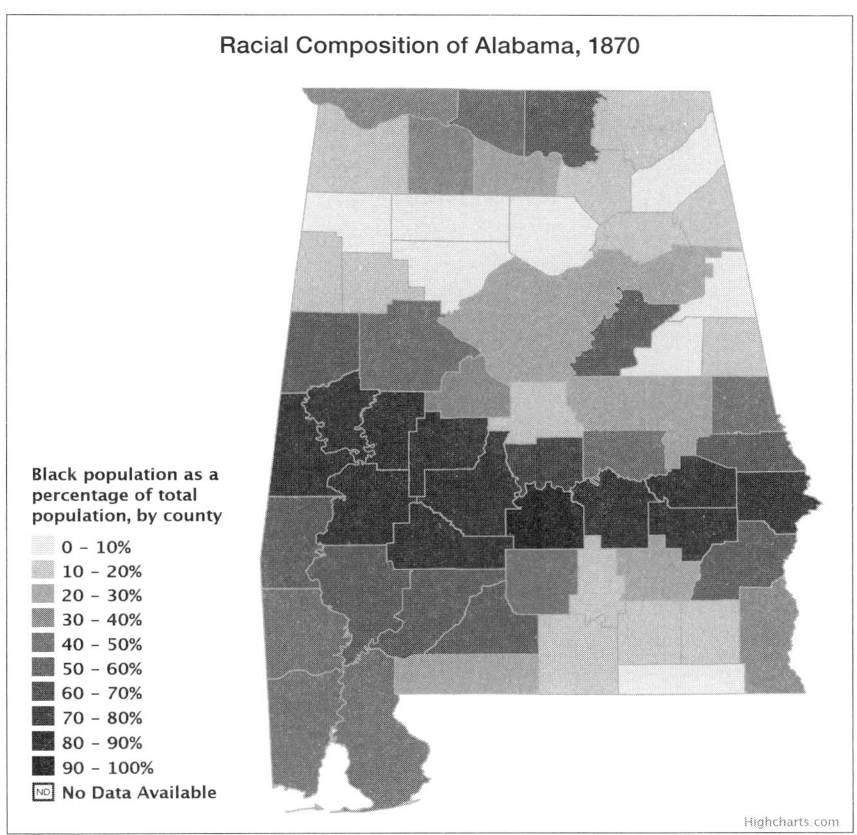

sometimes prosperous and might even own a few slaves in the valleys, but they were geographically isolated and less dependent upon the cash economy. They voted for the low-tax Jacksonians, which provided the basis for the prevailing Democratic majorities. The few sparsely populated "wiregrass" counties of the southeast had much the same social profile, though their politics were less reliably Democratic. The commercial patterns of the state heightened these regional differences. The wiregrass counties traded with the cotton belt or the Gulf Coast, while the prosperous Tennessee Valley at the extreme northern tip of the state dealt northward. This solidified northern Alabama into a democratic bloc, at least in the popular consciousness, opposed to the rich cotton belt of southern Alabama.

With the Mexican War, the growing salience of slavery challenged the regional rivalry over economic issues. Though the power structure united on defending the institution, divisions opened over how best to protect it. Whigs attended more to external constituencies, and they feared allowing territorial disputes to imperil more practical concerns. They favored compromise as opposed to states' rights constitutional abstractions. Democrats, on the other hand, favored national expansion to benefit the (white) common man. Small-government Democrats benefited from growing fears of Washington, but they also became more identified with states' rights extremism, which hurt them on occasion. For example, during the crisis of 1849–50, Alabama's Democrats rejected compromise measures, a position widely interpreted as threatening disunion. North Alabama recoiled, and a Unionist coalition subsequently triumphed. This reversal, however, only interrupted Alabama's path to secession. The disintegration of the national Whig Party over slavery cast voters adrift, with most heading to the Know-Nothings in the mid-1850s and subsequent ultra–states' rights Opposition groupings. But with the emergence of a northern antislavery Republican Party, Whiggish sectional moderates lost influence.[6]

The sectional controversy drove political development, but other policy disputes would linger into Reconstruction. During the prewar decade, prosperity and the possibility of conflict encouraged government activism. With the disruption of the political system, elite former Whigs poured into the Democratic leadership, which strengthened their bipartisan policy influence. At mid-decade, the legislature passed public-school laws creating an administrative structure under state control, to extend access into rural areas. More contentious were struggles over transportation policy. Railroads had emerged as the technology of the future, and neighboring states were subsidizing or building lines. Alabama, a "singularly unprogressive" state, resisted the trend, and it long required crossing three state lines to travel from Huntsville to Montgomery.[7] Geologists extolled the mineral region around modern Birmingham, but only railroads could unlock its potential. In 1850, Congress at Senator Stephen Douglas's initiative bestowed federal land grants to build the Mobile and Ohio Railroad, but this line bypassed Alabama almost entirely. Mobile's urban rivals then began securing land grants and pursuing their own projects.

Future Reconstruction-era leaders played major roles in the railroad boom, with Robert M. Patton being the most important. As a Whig merchant, Patton had been instrumental in creating the Memphis and Charleston line through the Tennessee Valley. Now a converted Democrat, Patton became equally prominent in promoting railroad legislation for a line into the mountains. The Alabama legislature passed subsidy proposals with a free hand, but unfortunately for proponents, Governor John Winston opposed general-aid laws. Winston's bold stand for traditional Democratic beliefs converted him into a hero in the hill country—Alabama's version of Old Hickory—and he was triumphantly reelected. The "veto governor" disallowed some thirty-six enactments in one session.[8] After he left office, proponents again mobilized to pass an ambitious aid law, but the crisis timing prevented implementation—and the secession process revised the state constitution to inhibit state subsidy.[9] Onetime Whigs and modernizing Democrats remained deeply frustrated. When circumstances allowed Patton as postwar governor to revisit the issue, the consequences would be dramatic.

Divisions over the 1860 presidential campaign overshadowed all such issues, as the national Democratic Party split on sectional lines. Longtime secessionist William Yancey led a platform walkout at the Charleston convention over federal protection of slavery in the territories. The underlying issue was the nomination of Senator Douglas, the northern favorite. In Alabama, the division was bitter, as an ad hoc Douglas delegation helped bar the walkout delegates from reentering the convention. Southern Democrats then nominated Vice-President John C. Breckinridge, while the national Democratic Party nominated Douglas. Ex-Whigs and border-state moderates nominated John Bell of Kentucky under the Constitutional Union Party banner, setting up a three-cornered race in Alabama which Breckinridge won with 54 percent of the vote. Bell received 31 percent, mostly in the former Whig counties of south Alabama, while Douglas took 15 percent, carrying Mobile and four Tennessee Valley counties.[10] The Southern Rights Democrats thus won a sizable majority over the two opposition candidates, whose followers were often termed "conservatives."

Breckinridge's statewide victory largely unfolded in the traditional Democratic strongholds of the hills. Voters here did not understand themselves to be endorsing disunion, for they would soon reject immediate secession, but in terms of future Republicans, Alabama's ultimate white dissidents, several points emerge. Postwar "scalawags" often were accused of opportunism, but on the Union issue in 1860, it was not true. Douglas voters in particular cast an emphatic Unionist ballot, and the Douglas victories in the Tennessee Valley were unusual so far South. This vote represented a public statement against sectional extremism.

Of grassroots Republicans testifying before the Southern Claims Commission in the 1870s, twenty-one reportedly voted for Douglas, and only two for Breckinridge.[11] This association seems stronger still among Republican leaders. Prominent later scalawags figured in the convention dispute, including Nicholas Davis and D. C. Humphreys. Others served as Douglas spokesmen, among them future provisional governor Lewis Parsons, Governor William H. Smith, and congressmen Alexander White and Charles Hays.[12] Republicans clustered in Huntsville, like the anti-secession militant Joseph C. Bradley. Of course, many other Douglas supporters became Democrats after the war, so the pattern is more an enhanced probability than a unified Republican tendency. Still, this pro-Douglas stand marked one at the decisive moment as a nationalist outlier.

Given the centrality of race in Reconstruction, the inevitable question is whether these future Republicans harbored misgivings about slavery. The obvious answer is no, because Unionists' strongest public argument was that secession imperiled slavery. Little relationship existed between the abolition heresy and later white Republicanism, no real indication of relative racial enlightenment. That said, one could discern fissures over the urgency of slavery's defense, especially in the nonslaveholding mountain enclaves, and resentment of the slaveholders' war turned many against the institution. Even within the elite, one can find scattered evidence of heterodox beliefs among future Reconstruction leaders. John Calvin Goodloe purchased a northern-origin kidnapped "slave" of some notoriety, one of the inspirations for *Uncle Tom's Cabin.* Goodloe allegedly bought the light-skinned victim from jail as a runaway, intending to allow self-purchase.[13] During the war Goodloe spied for the Union troops, and in 1862 he claimed "I have b[e]en an emancipationist all my life."[14] Similarly, Thomas M. Peters opposed secession ferociously. He later recalled that, as a Henry Clay Whig, he had never believed in slavery as a permanent institution and favored colonization. His fellow Supreme Court justice, E. W. Peck, was a colonization-society officer, reportedly suspected of antislavery beliefs. Possibly those holding private doubts were open to other resentments against slaveholding secessionists.[15]

Events moved swiftly with the Republican victory in November 1860. Alabama voters viewed Lincoln's election as the culmination of northern aggressions, and those tarred as craven "submissionists" operated on the defensive. South Carolina forced the issue by leaving the Union, just as Governor A. B. Moore called a popular vote. A vigorous campaign ensued between two contesting positions. In keeping with states' rights principles, "immediate secessionists" contended Alabama should instantly leave the Union. The opposite position was less clearly defined. "Cooperationists" or "cooperative secessionists" sought delay, or presenting an ultimatum, or simply conferring with other states to secede as a unit. The scalawag Milton Saffold later claimed that "it was well known that the co-operationists hoped to defeat secession by advocating a co-operation of all the Southern States, which they knew to be unattainable."[16] Whatever the precise intent, cooperationists lost by a substantial popular majority at the polls, though by a lesser margin among the convention delegates.

In that vote partisan loyalties dissolved, but the underlying regional divisions intensified. Virtually all of south Alabama voted for immediate secession; nearly all of north Alabama voted against it. That is to say, the traditionally moderate Whig section of the state voted for secession, while the Democratic northern enclave voted for relative caution—a reversal of longstanding patterns prompted by Lincoln's election. In the black belt, the threat to slavery overcame traditional Whiggish restraint, and public pressure forced skeptics into line. Former Bell voters sat out the election in large numbers, dispirited but acquiescing to secession.[17] Even the few cooperationist candidates there sounded more like cooperative secessionists than outright opponents.

In north Alabama, however, things unfolded differently. The Tennessee Valley, on the potential border of a southern nation, rejected immediate secession. In the mountain counties the margins were overwhelming: Walker County voted five to one, and in Winston the vote was unanimous. At least twelve delegates elected as cooperationists later supported Republican Reconstruction.[18] The sweeping majorities for cooperationists must represent something beyond conditional secessionism, more like outright Unionism. Mingled with this sentiment was the regional distrust of the rich planters of the black belt. The perception spread that north Alabama's small farmers, and the exposed residents of the valley, were being dragooned into conflict to protect somebody else's slaves.[19]

By the time the convention met on January 7, 1861, Mississippi and Florida had seceded, while Governor Moore seized the forts outside Mobile with state troops. These developments undermined the cooperationist position. On test votes, immediate secessionists demonstrated a firm fifty-four to forty-five majority, and tempers flared. Yancey threatened that, once the convention voted secession, holdouts became traitors. In

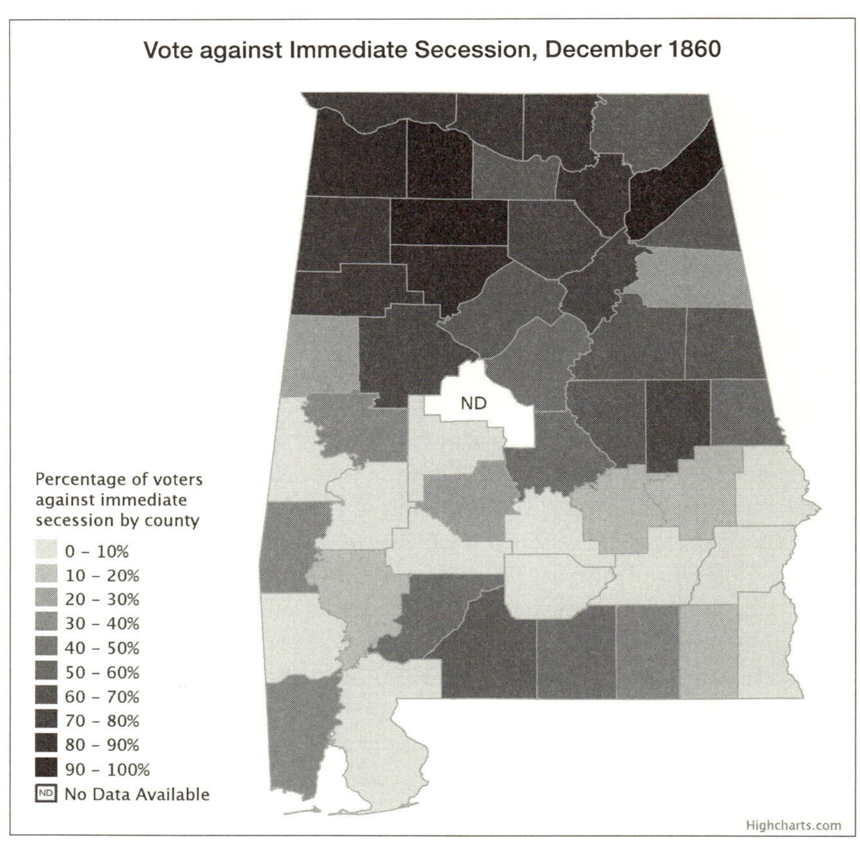

response, Nicholas Davis demanded a referendum, and he offered to fight Yancey and his secessionists at the foot of the mountains.[20] An alarmed secessionist editor wrote, "The people have been so aroused by Red republican harangues, that they are *in advance of their leaders* & prepared for anything."[21]

Faced with raw divisions, pragmatists tried to smooth things over. Cooperationists of standing came under pressure to demonstrate their loyalty to their kinsmen, to their society and the slaveholding order. Most of the wealthy cooperationists of the Tennessee Valley bowed to this as inevitable. War was not certain, and holdouts faced political irrelevance in the new Confederate state, possibly exile. Thus few future Republicans of prominence could claim uncomplicated records of loyalty. Some explained that, since secession was legal, they bowed to the popular will, and when the final vote came, the secession margin swelled. Several of those elected as cooperationists voted for the ordinance, while others signed it. Afterwards, thirty-three non-signers issued a statement that they were with Alabama, whatever ills befell. Only a handful followed Christopher C. Sheats in rejecting nominal acquiescence to secession.[22] Years later, Unionists recalled specific betrayals, like the ordinance signature of Reconstruction governor David P. Lewis. But for such eventual Republicans, it was difficult to know where to draw the ethical line. If shooting did not start, the passions of the masses would ebb, and negotiated reunion might yet be possible. Many in the Confederate capital of Montgomery, like Mary Chesnut, heard talk of a political structure honeycombed with "reconstructionist" sentiment.[23] The pressure for acquiescence was strong, for fear disunity would encourage northern coercion.

Secessionist leaders sought conciliation. As John T. Morgan recalled, "I was resolved that North Alabama should neither be driven nor permitted to make an issue with South Alabama, in the Convention. . . . Otherwise some of her people might have been driven to take up arms against us."[24] Delegates appointed cooperationists to the Confederate Congress, like David Lewis, though he quickly resigned. Joseph C. Bradley accepted a position as Confederate war tax collector. In his telling he stocked his department with cooperationists and then resigned without taking a salary. His rationale was to maintain his patronage network to make peace. Such nuanced stories characterized prominent cooperationist leaders. Former US senator Jeremiah Clemens voted for the secession ordinance while saying he would not cast the decisive vote for it. A fellow delegate "denounced Jerry as a traitor, and said that he had sold his constituents for a Major-General's commission." But this Unionist holdout, Nicholas Davis, accepted appointment to the Confederate Congress himself.[25]

Coerced Confederates abandoned the Union cause hesitantly. In March, Bradley wrote Andrew Johnson that, if peace held, conservatives might "start a candidate for Gov & try and get our state out of the hands of the Secessionist."[26] If cooperationist leaders could be co-opted by office and circumstance, the more emphatic Unionists resisted. Just after secession, Thomas M. Peters invited the national administration to maintain its authority, militarily, in northern Alabama.[27] Even after the war began, future Republican D. C. Humphreys reportedly issued a revealing pamphlet. Though he now professed southern loyalty, he emphasized that because Alabamians hated tyranny they did not "love the new order."[28]

cult to escape service, especially if local opinion offered protection. The draft-induced spike in deserters augmented their numbers. As enforcement intensified, farming became impossible, and layouts in the woods became dependent on family and neighbors for food. Frustrated enrollment officers pressured residents while seeking out Confederate sympathizers for information. Overstretched government officials moved toward harsher measures in areas where Confederate loyalties were fragile.

As the draft took hold, military events reshaped facts on the ground. Union victories at Fort Henry and Fort Donelson opened the Tennessee River to raids up to Muscle Shoals in the state's northwest corner. In April 1862 an overland offensive suddenly seized the entire Tennessee Valley, and the Union held the region north of the river most of the time thereafter. In the following chapter, we will analyze the impact of military occupation and guerrilla warfare on that region's politics. Here, we examine what the nearby Union presence meant in the areas still subject to Confederate authority, south of the occupied valley. For draft evaders escape through Confederate lines became a real if dangerous possibility. Union arms, raids, and information offered encouragement to these varied groups who collaborated in resistance. Confederate authorities ratcheted up repression accordingly.

One action by Governor Shorter highlights the resulting conflict. He commissioned a leading cooperationist, Robert Jemison of Tuscaloosa, to investigate his former allies. Jemison found great disloyalty in mountainous Winston, and in parts of Fayette and Marion counties.[31] It appears a Hard-Shell Baptist preacher had died in the course of arrest for Lincolnite sympathies. Hundreds gathered to avenge him; they staked out the roads, intimidated citizens, and even reportedly manufactured gunpowder. Jemison sent ministers and spies, finally ordering the simultaneous arrest of fourteen leaders across four counties. He viewed these impoverished men as Tories by conviction, recommending the "arrest or killing" of still more.[32] Jemison hoped he had made his point to draft evaders, but the federal capture of Corinth undermined his efforts. The Tennessee River frontier could be patrolled, but with a porous border to the west, the mountaineers became less tractable.[33]

Such clusters of early Unionists likely gravitated to postwar Republican politics more readily than the later flood of individual deserters. The evidence in Southern Claims Commission records fits the traditional view of "scalawags" as impoverished. Among the grassroots Republicans located, family wealth and slaveholdings were a fraction of that of the average white Alabamian. Shadrach Bray "was one of the poorest of the poor, living on Sand Mountain, where all were, and are, very poor."[34] Several claimants referred to themselves as impoverished, and later white Republican votes demonstrably concentrated in the poorest mountain enclaves.[35]

This plebeian profile likely contributed to the arbitrary treatment so many claimants reported at the hands of Confederate officials. John McBride thought that his fellow Unionists were not in as good repute as blacks.[36] In a slaveholder republic, socially peripheral farmers could not expect to fare well if perceived as seditious, especially by draft enforcers in isolated places. Jacksonian-tinged commentary on the Confederate elite pervades these sources, a distillation of decades of northern Alabama resentment.[37] One eventual Republican thought that "if the rebels were successful the large slave holders would get possession of all the good land in the South, and push all the small farmers out on poor nobs," that is, the barren hilltops.[38] Such emphatic statements owed something to class and educational background, because men of modest origin voicing transgressive views might well express themselves vigorously. Neighbors called J. R. Jack a noisy Union man, blunt and straightforward.[39] Uninhibited verbal behavior often reinforced the status of community outsider. Planter dissidents might vent harmlessly in relative isolation, but modest farmers' insurgent talk resulted differently, depending on the neighborhood. One old man reportedly defied the threats because he had so few years left. He dared the authorities to come get him.[40]

Even allowing for exaggeration, repression appears severe among over a hundred future Republicans named in the claims testimony. About half were threatened with death or grave injury. Nearly a quarter recalled arrest by Confederate authorities, and most of these were held by draft agents to clarify their status or to pressure them to report. Some men were seized by undisciplined cavalry and guerillas, and a few escaped at evident risk of their lives. Republican outrage at this treatment seldom suggests entire innocence. Loyalist talk got people into trouble, but conscription inspired most of the conflict. Many either lay out themselves, fed draft evaders or their relatives, or led men through the lines. Some deserted; others had sons who did so, which embroiled whole families. Several men appear in multiple categories, which itself emphasizes the searing nature of their wartime experience.[41]

These postwar Republicans, with proven claims, look like consistent Unionists. Loyalists lived primarily in the hills and mountains, areas where they were joined by larger numbers of deserters with more nebulous motivation. As the Confederate Army retreated toward northern Alabama, soldiers could return home temporarily or overstay their leaves, expecting to return when the authorities gathered them in. But as the carnage continued, many fled into the hills and swamps with no obvious means of provision. Armed bands solidified for self-protection, and some resorted to raiding richer farmers for food or driving suspected informants out. From St. Clair County, for example, Confederates received reports of widespread looting. Cavalry was ineffective on the rugged hillsides, and bandits lay in wait for government agents. Confederate officers urged stern measures to forestall desertion by the alarmed family men stationed nearby. "Immediate death if they flee, and the halter if they surrender, should be the only alternatives offered to tories and traitors," one colonel urged, and citizens lynched at least two deserters in custody.[42] Not surprisingly, the mountain districts of St. Clair remained an open sore long after war's end.

Untangling which motives facilitated later pro-Reconstruction sentiment is difficult, but southeastern Alabama's contrasting trajectory provides one clue. The lightly populated southeastern wiregrass counties were poor. Federal raids from the coast provided encouragement for draft evaders, and many Alabama men joined the First Florida Cavalry (Union). Even within Confederate ranks, the quasi-conscripts of General James H. Clanton's brigade mutinied under the inspiration of a shadowy "Peace society."[43] In Henry County, captured deserters were liberated by comrades after a gunfight.[44] The level of conflict thus resembled that in the mountains, but the wiregrass region never developed much of a Reconstruction following—in terms of the proportion of white votes, about a seventh as many. The wiregrass lacked north Alabama's regional animosity to the black belt, and it also voted for Breckinridge and secession. Antecedent Unionism in the northern hills, rather than draft resistance alone, solidified a later Radical Republican constituency.[45]

Alabama's erosion preoccupied Jefferson Davis's government. In early 1863, General Gideon Pillow arrived to enforce the draft, and he reported eight to ten thousand mingled deserters and Tories present. Pillow's stated policy was to disregard previously granted legal exemptions.[46] His superior, General Braxton Bragg, lauded his rigor, but Richmond authorities soon relieved Pillow for antagonizing public opinion and civil authorities. The desertion problem then worsened, given bad news from the front, so General Pillow returned. His figures showed half of the troops in the western armies absent after the surrender at Vicksburg. He termed Alabama's mountains a disaffected region with deserters resisting companies of cavalry, sometimes successfully.[47] Pillow sought overpowering force, because "Men would not leave the Army when they knew they could not stay at home."[48] His exertions gathered five thousand soldiers in a few weeks, but he also turned Alabama's home front upside-down.

Pronounced Union men often dropped out of the formal electoral process, a saving grace for Confederate loyalists, but gathering opposition at the ballot box posed pressing issues in Montgomery. In August 1863, Governor Shorter ran for reelection, having compiled a record of support for the Davis administration. But the mood of the electorate had soured; the demands of the central government for taxes, and for impressment of slave labor, infuriated even the planters. Furthermore, Alabama did not allow absentee voting, disfranchising thousands still serving in the ranks.[49] The elections followed the defeats at Gettysburg and Vicksburg, with demoralized captives streaming home in time to vote, just as General Pillow resumed his draft-enforcement exertions.

Governor Shorter's defeat loomed, a Coosa County supporter warned. Deserters were everywhere, and the shadowy peace organization spread. One opposition candidate, William Garrett, denied "all knowledge of them, disclaims Reconstruction. . . . But is for an entire change in our State Government from Govr. down."[50] Such candidates could run straddling the gap between former anti-secessionists and outright supporters of negotiated reunion. Governor Shorter lost nearly every county, by a margin of 28,221 to 9,664.[51] Voters crushed ex-secessionists and states' rights Democrats, like Congressman J. L. M. Curry. Even Williamson R. W. Cobb went to Congress, later to be expelled as a traitor. That fall, the legislature would defeat the secessionist Senator C. C. Clay, in favor of the flexible ex-cooperationist Robert Jemison. According to Joseph Bradley, the new senator intrigued with him in support of peace negotiations.[52]

It was not clear what the electoral mandate meant beyond repudiation of ex-secessionists. In the absence of a formal party structure and platforms, political discourse referenced obsolete landmarks. Decried by opponents as a treasonous peace party or grumbling croakers, the victors called themselves "conservatives," a loose term that harkened back to the Bell and Douglas voters, and more vaguely to Whiggish moderates before that. The label also referenced the formally organized wartime movement in North Carolina, along with the anti-administration faction in Richmond and civil libertarians everywhere.[53] One dissident later claimed, "The object of the Conservative Party was to wrest the control of the State from the hands of the supporters of the Confederate Government & place it again under the Federal Government."[54] In 1863, this understanding was more indistinct, but furtive antiwar men influenced the lower house of the legislature, their politics shielded by prior obscurity. Legislator Lewis Parsons became the most publicly known of these leaders.

The nebulous peace society was centered at Parsons's Talladega vicinity, but expressions of this sentiment existed elsewhere.[55] Planters could see society unraveling under the pressure of war, with the demands for supplies and the impressment of slaves.[56] Governor Shorter warned about sections of the black belt where, he claimed, slaves outnumbered white men a thousand to one.[57] A correspondent feared a new militia law would leave families "exposed to the ravages of the colored race."[58] As Union victory appeared more likely, anxious planters turned on their faltering government. Optimistic expectations of the North's terms on slavery increased the appeal of a separate peace.

"Conservatives" found the chaos of war temperamentally difficult, as the choice of name might imply. Firm numbers come hard because few within Confederate lines willingly courted treason charges, but a dissident network congregated in the legislature and government bureaus. Given the election results, they presumably spoke for somebody, especially influential planters and merchants who found a way to avoid military service. In November 1864, with the army desperate for men, some 1,315 "overseers and agriculturalists" still legally avoided conscription, presumably under the twenty-slave exemption. They represented a substantial portion of Alabama's 6,000 planters.[59] If postwar accounts can be believed, Vicksburg persuaded much of the conservative leadership that the conflict was lost. Joseph Bradley fled the Union occupation of the Tennessee Valley and made negotiated peace his mission. He was joined by Milton Saffold and Lewis Parsons, all three of whom would become postwar Republicans. Longtime legislator J. J. Seibels became the faction's fulcrum in Montgomery, identified to Lincoln himself as the leader of those who sought negotiated peace.[60] Confederate spies reportedly overheard Seibels speak of passing through the lines, to offer surrender in exchange for a protracted emancipation process.[61]

People atop the social pyramid seldom defy community opinion recklessly. Circumstances required a deft touch. Elite dissidents generally had the connections to avoid army service, or to resign commissions and come home, often securing positions in the government. They sheltered open Unionists from prosecution, or tried to get them out of jail, to open bridges to the federal authorities. They also had contacts in Richmond, like former Supreme Court justice John A. Campbell, a known advocate of negotiations. To escape the draft, Milton Saffold took appointment by Campbell as a sort of ombudsman for political prisoners. By his account he liberated as many as he could. These elite dissidents disavowed open treason to the Confederacy, or betrayal of their neighbors—or the racial order. Such measures were suicidal anyway, with the army at hand, but the expectation was that Union troops would soon overrun the state. Conservatives could then treat for terms rather than allow devastation of Alabama's still-intact plantation region.[62]

However, the same electorate that had elected peace men to the legislature also elected Thomas H. Watts to the governorship. Decorous campaigning and the absence of formal parties delivered a blurred mandate: the electorate voting for him as a vague "conservative" misunderstood what they were getting. Watts had been a states' rights Whig who backed secession after Lincoln's election. After losing to Shorter in 1861, Watts served as attorney general under the Davis administration. Shorter's opponents unified on Watts to defeat the secessionist governor, but once elected, Watts proclaimed himself a loyal Confederate, to the surprise of his sponsors. He once urged that Mobile should become "a heap of ashes, before the Yankees pollute it with their footsteps!"[63] He issued shrill periodic reminders of the racial nightmare that awaited federal rule.[64] The governor was, however, more attuned to public frustration than his predecessor and prone toward a peppery defense of states' rights against the Davis administration.

Any formal state peace initiatives depended on Governor Watts's cooperation, so the impasse with his erstwhile supporters intensified. The governor admitted he presided over a deadlock: "The Militia Laws—as they now stand—are, almost, worthless. I would call the Legislature together, if I had any assurance, that any thing good would be done."[65] In military terms, central and southern Alabama long enjoyed deceptively good fortune, as the Union armies pursued opportunities elsewhere. Bragg won the only major Confederate victory in the west at Chickamauga in September 1863, and even subsequent reverses did not result in invasion, though deserters streamed home by the thousand.[66] Sherman's 1864 Atlanta campaign mostly bypassed the state, but this subjected Alabama to the demands of a desperate government. One civilian complained that the Union troops constantly raided them, while Confederate cavalry units were seizing supplies from the other direction: "What men they have are deserters from other commands. How long are we to be thus oppressed and ruined by our own soldiery?"[67] Where Union men congregated, the situation was worse. Irregular Confederate cavalrymen killed the Winston County probate judge in custody, reportedly in atrocious fashion. Local notables warned of a second civil war in the offing.[68]

In 1864, these predictions proved true. In sparsely populated Coffee County along the Florida border, residents fled to the Union Army, then filtered back home as deserters twice over, raiding prosperous neighbors for supplies. Once they killed several Confederate officials pursuing them. A judge called them a continual terror, and another feared to try cases in the area.[69] In northern Alabama, these complaints spread from the mountain fastnesses into the surrounding piedmont. From Shelby County came the complaint that numbers of draft evaders, with neighborhood support, were raiding Confederate sympathizers, and similar reports came from Autauga.[70] A politician wrote that, in half a dozen insecure northern counties, "the Tory element has already the ascendancy in point of Military strength over their loyal neighbors," because the federals supplied their organizations with arms.[71]

Complex political effects resulted. Draft resistance came harder to prosperous people, and their property made their families targets. The raids therefore solidified much of the threatened home front behind the authorities. Confederates depicted the Tory bands as violent outlaws, with enough justification to make the view plausible. Even a northern general feared Unionist refugees would be "driven by want into brigandage" unless recruited quickly.[72] Alabama provided food relief to the families of Confederate soldiers, but not deserters, which further polarized the scourged countryside. Finally, as numerous historians have argued, all the death and destruction at northern hands bound most whites to the cause, as did solidarity with men at the front.[73] So did the slavery issue, because emancipation guaranteed transformative racial consequences if the North won. Most white Alabamians remained loyal to the underlying values of the society, though circumstances forced many into practical opposition to the Confederate authorities. But defiance had innumerable gradations, and an array of class-tinged local animosities lingered into the postwar era.

After Atlanta fell, conservative leaders moved toward open opposition. Governor Watts had concluded that the militia laws were defective because he could not order militiamen to leave their home counties. Alabama could not even repel a raid, but leaving white men on the plantations mattered, too, so the legislature passed nothing, indulging in an acrimonious exchange with the governor.[74] Conservative leaders used the session to force peace negotiations onto the agenda, as northern presidential politics provided the opportunity. The Democrats nominated General George B. McClellan on a "copperhead" platform of negotiated reunion—with slavery presumably intact. Therefore Lewis Parsons proposed a double-edged response: if the Democrats won, Alabama should be "willing and ready to open negotiations for peace on the bases indicated in the platform," if other Confederate states agreed.[75] The resolution suggested reunion, but the indistinct proposal could be defended as a maneuver to weaken Lincoln. Parsons disavowed personal belief in the possibility of Reconstruction; he contended that, if negotiations failed, Confederate resistance would be stronger. Most southern observers instead smelled treason, by those representing as yet undamaged large property holders. President Davis rebuked the initiative while in Montgomery, and there were threats of mobbing Parsons. Most southern newspapers did not even report Parsons's speech, because "No man not willfully blind can be ignorant of the mischievous effects of these resolutions."[76]

After behind-the-scenes controversy, the peace resolutions were buried. Because candor courted dangerous backlash, it is difficult to untangle the proponents' actual goals. According to one account, all of the House supporters disavowed Reconstruction on the floor.[77] Parsons's intentions still are not clear, and he never talked much about them, even after Andrew Johnson made him provisional governor. Still, there are prior indications that he held antiwar views. Confederate spies had identified Parsons as the leader of the peace society, aided, perhaps, by Seibels.[78] Agents claimed to have infiltrated an oath-bound organization of indistinct goals. The conspiracy claims are difficult to evaluate, but two of those named, future Republican Congressman R. S. Heflin and legislator A. A. West, soon fled to the North to sign a Unionist manifesto.[79]

Open controversy subsided after Lincoln's reelection dissolved the peace initiative's rationale. Still, some conservatives had long anticipated that Sherman's hosts would move toward Montgomery, so then they could conclude peace.[80] After losing Atlanta, General J. B. Hood had circled his army westward behind Sherman, harassing supply lines from northeastern Alabama, so this seemed a reasonable scenario. Instead, Sherman marched eastward to the Atlantic, and rather than racing to catch up with him, Hood determined upon an offensive. Luck again spared central Alabama from devastation, but an undersupplied Confederate Army again traversed northern Alabama. Few civilians welcomed them.[81] Even Confederate generals reported soldiers "roaming over the country engaged in the pillage and robbery of defenseless women and loyal citizens. . . ."[82] Hood battered his way northward and, in mid-December, he lost decisively at Nashville. Terms like "disastrous" litter official Confederate descriptions, and Union generals boasted of destroying half his army.[83] Demoralized troops then filtered back through the Tennessee Valley. This time, many simply went home, persuaded their war was over, while others stayed on in guerrilla enclaves. Now chaos truly came to the northern region.

Black belt planters had dodged the bullet once again, but now time ran out. Union generals envisioned sweeping into central Alabama *unopposed*. Conservatives pleaded with the governor to press negotiations on the Davis administration, but Watts vowed to fight on.[84] He spoke of treason readily with rhetoric that still intimidated would-be peacemakers. Who would govern defeated Alabama? "Some flat-nosed, thick-lipped sons of Africa, appointed by your conquerors," Watts fumed.[85] The prospect of emancipation, given the shared racial beliefs of the white population, made for effective speeches despite the military situation. The governor's racial animus remained consistent, and even when the Davis administration endorsed black troops in the war's last weeks, Watts declared such measures illegal under Alabama law.[86]

Conservatives thought the governor insane. Joseph Bradley had long since confronted Watts, telling him he intended to cross the lines to negotiate, but the governor threatened to jail him.[87] Such contacts did occur, and Bradley fed information of Hood's whereabouts to Union officers.[88] Peace negotiations proceeded within the military itself. Before Hood's defeat, General P. D. Roddey, commanding undisciplined cavalry in northern Alabama, negotiated via intermediaries with Union authorities. Roddey offered surrender if some reasonable accommodation could be made regarding slavery. Gradual emancipation after, say, fifteen years would insure compliance. His Unionist emissary, the German immigrant J. J. Giers, went north to consult General Grant and even President

Lincoln himself, but Washington offered no such terms. Still, the negotiations suggested that someone besides Confederates would soon assume the reins of power.[89]

By the spring of 1865, conservatives or "Reconstructionists" openly awaited the next opportunity to contest local races or to vote Governor Watts out of office.[90] They still hoped for unrealistic terms but favored immediate capitulation regardless. Bradley proposed himself as an opposition candidate, but the anti-secessionist leader and Gettysburg veteran M. J. Bulger had wider support. Military events overtook this leisurely schedule as Union cavalry ripped through the black belt in April. Taking advantage of the opportunity to get a message through the lines to Lincoln, J. J. Seibels explained the hopes of conservatives. He urged that federal authorities retain the existing state structures. If the scheduled elections could be held, peace men would rally around Bulger and sweep all before them. Representation in Congress could soon resume "as if nothing but a mere lapsus had taken place within the last four years." Seibels sought to protect the remaining possessions of those who now wanted peace, including most of the plantations of the cotton belt. But he called for "exemplary punishment" of the secessionist leaders who had led the wicked disruption of the government.[91]

Seibels backed stern measures as "necessary for future reference, should such an attempt ever be contemplated again." Seibels's endorsement of further punishment and perhaps executions echoed into the Reconstruction era. While north Alabama's Unionists and draft resisters provided the bulk of the white votes for Reconstruction, former conservatives provided many of the officeholders and spokesmen. A substantial portion of the antebellum political class became Republicans, eventually accepting black suffrage and alliance with the victorious North. They were perhaps as devoted to white supremacy as their peers, and personal opportunism encouraged many, but much else was involved. For years, conservatives had predicted that sectional extremism and secession would destroy the slave system. These men saw themselves as the real victims of the Civil War, losing their fortunes in a cause they never really believed in. Having been proven right, they were in no mood to join hands with those states' rights Democrats who had brought them ruin. The alienation within the Alabama ruling class became a fundamental reality, as Union military occupation brought unfamiliar players to the political table.

2

The Last Relicks of Barbarism

Army, War, and Reconstruction

Every dog must have his day, and it is time De Cuffys should have fair play.

—Union Recruiter JAMES T. AYERS

Historians seldom dwell on the connection between wartime military strategy and Reconstruction.[1] Revisionists have primarily criticized postwar Union forces for weakness, and for being co-opted by racists. However, military behavior affected Alabama's Reconstruction in a different fashion. The areas longest under Union control experienced a uniquely violent social trajectory. The northern portion of the state underwent federal occupation and ruinous forms of warfare, while the southern two-thirds saw relatively uninterrupted Confederate sway. Geography thus determined what kind of experience white civilians and enslaved people underwent at military hands. The Union Army became so efficient a mechanism of destruction that it proved an imperfect vehicle of pacification. Since the postwar political issues centered on the federal government's role, and army occupation both enforced emancipation and empowered Unionists, the behavior of that government's army mattered.

Regional divisions over secession made no military difference for the first year of the war, because the Union Army only threatened the state in the spring of 1862. U. S. Grant's capture of Fort Henry opened the Tennessee River up to Alabama's northwest corner. Then Union General O. M. Mitchel avoided the rail routes to the valley and simply marched overland, achieving complete surprise. As distracted Confederate forces recovered from Shiloh, Mitchel entered Huntsville early on April 11. Seizing fifteen locomotives, Mitchel's troops rode the Memphis and Charleston rail line for 150 miles. The state's northern plantation district came under federal control from Tuscumbia to Stevenson.[2]

Invasion changed the nature of the conflict. Initially both sides fought by quaint, courtly rules; there are accounts of prisoners from Shiloh strolling through Cahaba on their honor, or with escorts, buying foodstuffs.[3] The early occupation of the Tennessee Valley fostered a brutal form of warfare, which anticipated the terrorist violence that engulfed the region after war's end. Behavior swiftly changed as plantation areas came under occupation. Scholars have frequently noted the emergence of a federal "hard war" policy of targeting noncombatant property in mid-1862. The plantation area and hills just north of the river figured prominently in this strategic evolution, as Confederate sympathizers and small guerilla units began hit-and-run attacks. Picking off individual soldiers struck Yankees as unsporting and brutal, and anger toward these hidden enemies intensified. As John Large wrote, the soldiers resolved "to take no more prisoners but shoot every man they see in the woods."[4]

Guerilla warfare and bushwhacking would become a constant feature north of the Tennessee River. Union troops worked out anti-guerilla measures. Much of this activity targeted noncombatants, including loyalty oaths and selective expulsions. General Mitchel, for example, seized civilian suspects along the telegraph lines, on the strength of slave testimony. Otherwise normal-sounding soldiers started saying startling things. As early as May 1862, Lieutenant Colonel John Beatty threatened the residents of Paint Rock. "Hereafter every time the telegraph wire was cut we would burn a house; every time a train was fired upon we should hang a man," he warned, even if it meant killing every male between Decatur and Bridgeport. He then set fire to the town, with the reported approval of General Mitchel. Officers adopted progressively more drastic responses. One sought information by arresting civilians, adding that, if needed, "use force in getting what is desired."[5] After months of fighting guerrillas in northern Alabama, Colonel Edward Wood wrote from Georgia, "we hang them, burn their houses, & lay waste their arms," but still they persisted. Only extermination and depopulation could bring victory, he concluded.[6]

Strategic choices in the summer of 1862 exacerbated these trends. As numerous historians have observed, General Don Carlos Buell's slow progression from Corinth eastward toward Chattanooga transformed his soldiers' behavior.[7] Like General McClellan in Virginia, Buell protected civilian property in the hope it would encourage pacification and surrender. He rebuilt the railroad through the valley as he went, in order to shield the surrounding plantations from his soldiers. When raids cut the rail line, the army was reduced to half-rations, as they marched through one of the South's premiere grain-producing regions. The troops rebelled. "The boys is stealing everything they can get their hands on," one soldier wrote.[8] Infuriating rumors spread that their rations were distributed as relief, or corruptly sold, to the dependents of Confederate soldiers. One Illinois soldier wrote, "I hope that Abe Linlcon will issu the orther that our Army shall go Thrugh and swepe the County and save nothing but take evre thing that they can com to and kill evre man that is in arms. . . ." Another soldier envisioned Rebel civilians being shot down like dogs.[9]

Brutality escalated on both sides. One Confederate prisoner reportedly bore a ring made from the shin bone of a Union soldier; his captor claimed it as "one of the last relicks of Barb[a]rism."[10] The spectacular "sack of Athens" revealed converging pressures toward harsh behavior, given the injustice of what occurred from the point of view of residents. If there was a community in Alabama where the elite resisted secession, this would be the place. Union flags fluttered there after secession.[11] However, outside town, the sabotage of a railroad bridge killed many soldiers. Union troops blamed the locals who had not warned them of the peril, some apparently acting as guerillas. Colonel John Turchin then informed his command that he would be off reconnoitering for two hours, an invitation to wreak havoc. Soldiers broke into the downtown stores, appropriated the contents, damaged property for sport, and even raped one enslaved woman.[12] Afterwards, Buell had Turchin court-martialed, but he became a hero in the northern Republican press for rejection of a "kid gloves" approach to warfare. Turchin also assailed slavery, asserting that African Americans were the Union's only friends in Alabama.[13] Lincoln soon pardoned him, and the president soon replaced the unsuccessful General Buell even as he removed McClellan, indications of a shift in federal policy.

The relationship between such wartime events and the Reconstruction era is indirect, but in this case, suggestive. Thirty miles from the Ku Klux birthplace of Pulaski, Tennessee, Athens was allegedly the first community in Alabama to found a Klan, one demonstrably dominated by elites. One of Alabama's Radical Republican firebrands, Daniel H. Bingham, also emerged from this traumatized setting. Originally from New York, this editor and local politician was a Unionist in the secession crisis. When Union troops arrived, he sought a mediator role, pleading with Turchin's troops to stay the destruction. His pains identified him with the now-hated Yankees, generating threats and then the first of the beatings Bingham experienced. By 1863, he fled to join the Union exiles in Washington. He would soon become an avid opponent of slavery and proponent of Reconstruction efforts.[14]

Abuse of civilians and property seizures became far more pronounced over time. These issues became entangled with defiance of superiors' orders—and the politics of slavery. On July 4, Kentucky officers extolled the Union and denounced abolitionists. Tiring of this rhetoric, enlisted men loudly demanded to hear an antislavery officer. Among frustrated and hungry troops, all forms of social restraint eroded simultaneously: "One woman spit upon a soldier, and he hit her a back-handed slap that made her squall."[15] Captain S. S. Canfield seemed untroubled by this, more irritated that civilians courted officers to get their runaways back. After one such episode, he reported, "the men of Company K declared if another man came into camp hunting slaves, they would throw him into a slop hole." This former Douglas Democrat saw Huntsville as undemocratic, because residents graciously welcomed proslavery officers while excluding more common soldiers from their hospitality.

The "hard war" strategy encouraged emphatic ideological responses. While soldiers encountered many neutral experiences with civilians, the negative ones made a stronger impression. Hostile interactions in guerilla-prone areas readily congealed into political convictions, with the circumstances of occupation encouraging endless camp discussions. The free-labor critique of southern society thus took angry root among the rank and file. "Liberal institutions and improved cultivation would make this an earthly paradise," Jenkins Jones wrote.[16] Just about everything furnished grounds for social criticism. One officer jibed at Alabama's place names, admittedly from Greasy Cove.[17] Another thought that Tuscumbia was a small, dilapidated village, and as for "public improvements, that idea had not reached so far south!"[18] A. C. Weaver similarly described Decatur as a "shackly dirty little town," even before the army leveled it.[19]

Despite the beauty of the northeast Alabama's mountains, its utilitarian camps and depots inspired distaste. Several decried the mud and poverty around Stevenson.[20] One soldier concluded Alabama was God's rubbish yard, thinking Bridgeport the ugliest spot around.[21] Another thought that town had economic promise, though it suffered under sorry southern enterprise. Ten thousand people reportedly lived in tents in the vicinity. One Republican colonel, John Geary, complained, "the lazy, good for nothing *white-trash* live in their miserable excuses for houses . . . starving to death. Except such things as they can beg from the soldiers, they have nothing to eat."[22] Of course, traumatized farmers fearing expropriation seldom manifest a work ethic. As destruction became prevalent, soldiers found the region ever more depressing. Huntsville was the exception, because the mountains and the spring downtown won aesthetic admiration. Chauncy Cook wrote his parents of its beauty, though he saw little life nor business. The federal occupation centered there, making the city a relatively safe preserve with some Unionist sentiment, nearly undamaged by troops.[23]

Slavery provided occasion for moral criticism, as part of this wider revulsion. One wartime account observed, "All through the Southern States, but no where so apparently as in Northern Alabama, the octoroons, quadroons, and mulattoes seem to constitute the greater portion of its slave population."[24] Huntsville in particular inspired sarcastic commentary on the profusion of light-skinned domestics, it being "a verry fast place in the days of Slavery the King when the rich were rocked in the cradle of luxury, vice, idleness, and crime," according to one private.[25] Such wealthy enclaves appeared suspect in relation to the surrounding misery, and John M. King found precious little to admire, not even in Tennessee Valley agriculture. The fences were old-fashioned, worm-style wooden ones. He had heard much about the cotton gin, but it was "the simplist little thing in all creation." Even on the plantations, he found cultivation painful to watch, fifty years behind the times: "If the head of a long-nosed hog were to have handles attached and chained fast to a small log it would give as good an idea of an Alabama plow as anything I might describe."[26]

Inner certainty of northern superiority, sharpened by the occupation, had lasting significance because many Republican leaders had spent time in the area—including both eventual US senators. During Radical Reconstruction, northern veterans helped politicize the newly enfranchised freedpeople, and their ideology grew straight out of the passions of the war. The negative "carpetbagger" stereotype connoted defiance of southern mores on race and behavior. As outsiders, newcomers, they were less amenable to community pressure than native-born Republicans. Alabama's most disliked carpetbagger would be General George E. Spencer, and he did not exactly exude idealism. Still, even Spencer denounced the institution in terms suggesting conviction. His wife, Bella, joined him in camp, and she wrote a novel referencing the "revolting details" of slavery and its sexual enormities. General Spencer thought the north Alabama contraband camps proved the success of free labor, and he lobbied superiors to issue them rations. Spencer considered investing in a planta-

These examples notwithstanding, the outbreak of war in April changed everything. With Fort Sumter, a popular surge rallied behind President Jefferson Davis's government, and volunteering was substantial even in northern Alabama. In the Tennessee Valley, and among conservatives in the black belt, slaveholders understood that, whatever they had thought previously, losing the war meant disaster. Early battlefield successes, like Bull Run in July, encouraged belief in Southern victory. In 1861 secessionists swept the polls. John Gill Shorter, a longtime secessionist per se, was elected governor easily over a former Whig, Thomas Watts. With secession resolved and debate over the war in abeyance, the election map reverted to its traditional geographic pattern. Northern Alabama voted overwhelmingly for the former secessionist Democrat, Shorter, while the cotton belt voted heavily for his ex-Whig opponent. Amid the wartime cessation of a formal party structure, people clung to familiar landmarks in an unrecognizable landscape. This pattern persisted into the Reconstruction era.

Some Union men remained unreconciled to secession, and they matter here because they provided most of the white Republican voters later on. The "unconditional Unionists," perhaps a tenth of the white population, generally went silent.[29] For about a year, it was somewhat feasible to sit out the war as neutrals. Dissenters mostly contented themselves with venting at friends and family, sometimes even slaves. In the isolated mountains, though, open opposition remained more possible, as the war drew committed Confederates away to the front. Some Unionists spoke of joining a "Nickajack" state modeled on West Virginia. In Winston County, around early 1862, a mass meeting occurred whose resolutions proclaimed the region's neutrality. Some men went beyond this. One peace candidate ran for the state senate from Walker County early in the war. Rumors spread he would be mobbed, but he stood his ground, nervously turning a penknife over and over in his hand as he orated away.[30]

As casualty lists mounted, Confederates became less tolerant. In wealthy areas, southern patriots sought to commit their lukewarm neighbors. Civilians were pressured to accept Confederate money, buy bonds, or otherwise promote the cause. The passage of conscription in the spring of 1862 put far more pressure on Unionists, or those who for other reasons proved unwilling to fight. Neutrality became impossible for able-bodied men to age forty-five, and then up to fifty, especially those who lacked the connections to find alternate service. Either they would volunteer, or wait to be drafted, or evade conscription. In the hills, it initially was not diffi-

tion near Athens, hoping to make money and do the country some good. However misplaced Spencer's optimism was for cotton production, his expectation of entrepreneurial success was shared among his comrades who stayed on at war's end.[27] Integral to this attitude is northerners' war-born certainty of the superiority of the civilization they embodied. They brought a well-honed, anger-fueled critique of the society they had just vanquished on the battlefield. Their racial views were likely not that dissimilar to those of other Americans, but they disdained the slaveholding society that created secession. Soldiers took pride in having wrecked a corrupt social order, dominated by rich traitors. This bound them to the freedpeople, whose perception of that society paralleled that of the veterans.

To be sure, one can find racism aplenty among northern soldiers. The term "nigger" was in widespread use, even among soldiers backing emancipation like the antislavery recruiter James T. Ayers.[28] Patronizing or worse attitudes toward escaping slaves were common. One Minnesota soldier wrote, "I believe in *confiscating all rebel property,* but 'Good Lord deliver us' from the negroes." He compared the average field hand to "an orang-outang."[29] Given the undisciplined demeanor of many of these young men, more repellent attitudes appeared, expressed with sexual bravado. From Huntsville, one convalescing Kentucky soldier wrote, "I tell you I had much rather stay around here in the shade & drink whiskey & fuck niggers than to be up with the regiment and be on guard every other night."[30]

Most Union soldiers nonetheless directed their hostility away from the slaves. It made emotional sense to view themselves as an army of liberation. By their lights, most sympathized with the woes of the black population. Given that they confronted guerilla warfare from a hostile slaveholding population, they turned to the slaves. Soldiers frequently acted on tips from runaways and frequently worked them around camp, often without pay in exchange for protection. As one Democrat wrote, "Their friendship for us is general, and unmistakable. They meet with little encouragement, but will run any risk and ask for no reward except sometimes a chew of tobacco."[31] Antislavery views became prevalent in the ranks, partly in protest against the efforts to protect civilian property. But it also had to do with what they saw of slavery. Midwestern farm boys witnessed enough to shock them. One young man wrote in his diary of an experience outside Decatur. A mulatto women came into camp with her two flaxen-haired, blue-eyed children. The four-year-old bore a "perfectly blue" back, having been beaten by an overseer. "Such sights are fast abolitionizing our army," he concluded.[32]

There were other such occasions of moral insight. One soldier inspected hundreds of recruits for an Alabama regiment, and "Some was white as you or I." Most bore indications of flogging, and he saw some with their Achilles tendons severed to prevent escape. He avowed himself an abolitionist, and he concluded that black troops would form the only possible standing army in the South.[33] Similarly, Chauncey Cook witnessed things reminiscent of *Uncle Tom's Cabin,* his attitude hardening as he traveled southward. He sat for two hours listening to an elderly runaway whose wife and children had been sold to Alabama. In Mooresville, civilians taunted that the Yankees sought emancipation, and he mused, "to tell the truth, that is about all I care for." Cook described an episode in which recovering Union soldiers harassed a female hospital employee. They jokingly asked if any of her children had been sold, and indeed another Alabama trader had bought three, nearly as white as the soldiers were. In tears she asked the chastened young men, had they no mothers themselves? "To think that these slave holders buy and sell each others' bastard children is horrible," Cook wrote home.[34]

The unstable military occupation encouraged all these trends toward harshness. Union troops evacuated the Tennessee Valley in the fall of 1862. Mild federal policies had delivered an intact crop to their Confederate successors. The obvious response was to strip contested areas of productive resources. When Union forces regained the region again in the fall of 1863, emancipation was federal policy, and the army welcomed runaways and recruited black soldiers. Antislavery views increasingly ran rife in Union letters and diaries. One USCI officer wrote that veteran troops cheered his men as they marched from Stevenson, adding that all the old soldiers welcomed them.[35] These developments antagonized prosperous whites, but military policy forced residents and refugees to make difficult choices. The army required loyalty oaths of those within Union lines, and nearly 7,400 civilians signed.[36] To combat guerillas, federal forces armed "home guards" and recruited scouts. Such measures polarized the Tennessee Valley population, in both political and class terms. Furnishing information to one side or the other became a matter of life or death. Most everyone in Alabama seemingly knew their neighbors' politics, so wartime choices cast a long shadow into the postwar world.

A harsher counterinsurgency strategy emerged, designed to punish civilians south of the river who sheltered guerillas or those who lived anywhere near them. Depriving the Confederates of food supplies would inhibit cavalry operations, horses requiring large amounts of grain and forage. Solidifying Union strength thus spread destruction to wider and wider areas. In May 1863, General Grenville Dodge ordered a raid through the Tuscumbia area. He left a desert behind, a soldier thought: "Our rear guard has this day laid waste with fire and sword, the country through which we passed. Houses, barns, cribs, mills, etc., all share one fate. At any time during the march, you could see two or three buildings burning."[37] One Kansas unit burned more than even the liberal amounts authorized. They joked that they carried grain in their pockets to toss into empty barns, thus rendering them liable for destruction under orders. The purpose was to depopulate the whole vicinity, so that enemy guerillas could not subsist there. Dodge himself thought they had rendered useless the garden spot of Alabama.[38]

General William T. Sherman, who commanded the theater in 1864, promoted this style of warfare. "To secure the safety of the navigation of the Mississippi, I would slay Millions," he wrote.[39] In one respect, though, Alabama benefited from Sherman's military leadership, because his attention mostly focused elsewhere. His recent raid through Meridian fortuitously spared the central Alabama black belt. Things were very different in the occupied northern region. Perhaps to speed Reconstruction efforts, Sherman warned the people of the Tennessee Valley that slavery was gone and that Confederate preferences would no longer be tolerated. Sherman passed along to Huntsville residents his threat of expulsion in favor of northern settlers: "tell them that it is for them *now* to say whether they and their children shall inherit" their beautiful lands. He asked that his warning be published.[40]

General Sherman inclined toward ferocious rhetoric, but his army on the march reveled in sheer destructiveness. After Sherman captured Atlanta in September 1864, the guerillas operating around Gaylesville troubled him. So he backtracked much of his army to the prosperous area, before marching to the sea. "We are eating out this valley good, so that it will not be necessary to come again," Sherman wrote.[41] Even some of his soldiers were taken aback. One reported that the day was spent robbing and foraging shamefully.[42] He stayed in camp, reflecting at length on the difficulties the situation posed for sensitive souls. Another soldier was less troubled: "what we can't use we destroy and thus lay the country waste. . . . These people are getting their *southern rights*."[43]

The agony of noncombatants only solidified the troops' aversions, as did shared complicity in their army's actions. One chaplain wrote of numerous ideologically tinged subjects, from "Southern Agriculture" to "Southern Treason." He wrote from Gaylesville without batting an eye, seeing humor in the mock bill of fare chalked up at an abandoned plantation.[44] Another soldier observed: "At one house we passed this morning we saw three of the ugliest-looking women imaginable. They sat on the porch step, side by side, hoopless, unkempt and unwashed." He delighted in stripping civilians' food, perhaps because Sherman intended "to use us to Christianize this country."[45] Such distaste extended to the refugees they had ruined. One soldier at Bridgeport depot reported that formerly prosperous women prostituted themselves for coffee and sugar. He mingled pity and disgust for those gathering fruits of their treason.[46] From Scottsboro, an immigrant captain wrote of the lowest people he had ever seen in term of intellect, morally abandoned beyond belief. Even J. T. Ayres, a minister no less, hoped that cutting off civilian rations would drive the "dirty sluts" away from Huntsville.[47]

By the end of the war, much of the Tennessee Valley and especially the plantations and farms south of the river were depopulated, the slaves having fled to freedom. Beyond the military efficacy of Union policies, this behavior had one positive aspect: it scrambled the practices of racial slavery. By early 1864, "The slave was actually free and he knew it, and there was a force present to remind him of it," one lawyer recalled. Numerous ex-slaves filed postwar damage claims on grounds that they had accumulated earnings during the occupation. Millie Richardson recalled her father as "a stirringy man" who had a thousand dollars when he died.[48] The military provided hundreds of jobs for willing workers, both black and white refugees, on transportation and fortifications. Contrabands frequently prospered as military laborers, the proceeds of which the Union Army often relieved them. Furthermore, whites often made plantation land available to those who were willing to farm on their own account, in hopes that cultivation would deter confiscation. Tennessee Valley planters thus harbored few illusions that slavery could be reconstituted, in contrast to slaveholders elsewhere.

Though federal policies toward civilians and their property were established by early 1865, it was only then that the impact spread throughout Alabama. The central plantation belt had providentially escaped damage, and General Thomas in Nashville preferred restrained measures, like permanent occupation. He envisioned negotiated Reconstruction, and a rumored role as military governor, as contacts proceeded through his lines.[49] Instead, General Grant ordered the largest cavalry raid in American history. General James Wilson's force of 13,500 would sweep southward, to join Sherman's army in the Carolinas. "Our instructions were . . . to take with us or destroy everything that would be of any service to the rebel cause," one soldier recalled.[50] These measures represented effective war-making, but they also spread hard war techniques into the plantation belt a week before Lee surrendered. Wilson's cavalry force lived off the nearly stripped land, without sparing the Unionists of the mountains they traveled through. Given the approach of peace, and the interplay between military measures and the pacification task, federal decision makers might have avoided the raid strategy.[51] A permanent occupation would have fostered the conservative leadership in Montgomery that had been seeking to negotiate Alabama's surrender. These measures would have yielded different social consequences than the Dantesque exercise that occurred.

Instead, all of the skills and attitudes derived from the northern Alabama experience descended on the black belt. General Wilson's target was one of the South's last remaining industrial complexes, Selma and the mines supplying it. Cavalrymen scattered southward across the mountains, destroying mining operations and foundries. Wilson detached General John Croxton's raiders toward Tuscaloosa to distract Confederate attention. He targeted the University of Alabama, a memory that still rankles: the landscaped rubble mound remains a gathering place on campus.[52] The strategy worked, however. General Forrest's outnumbered cavalrymen were out of position as Wilson's force concentrated on Selma. Wilson's men took the fortifications with few casualties, capturing much of the adult white male population enrolled as last-minute defenders. Victorious troops swept into Selma on April 2, the very day Richmond fell. John Hardy, a Unionist dissident and future Republican, recalled that "terrible scenes of plunder and outrages were witnessed in every direction." Soldiers found liquor and rampaged all night long. One colonel tried to keep his men away, but the general example was too strong. Here as in Tuscaloosa the troops had local assistance. As General Wilson recalled it, "the negroes broke loose and began to plunder the shops and stores." This conduct reportedly cost several African Americans their lives after the army left.[53]

Over the next several days, Wilson impressed black laborers and methodically demolished over sixty buildings. "This tickled the darkies wonderfully," one soldier recalled.[54] Given the munitions present, destruction on this scale meant incinerating most of the town. One soldier on provost duty wrote, “Thirteen large buildings are now burning, while the noise is almost deafening.”[55] In the midst of this chaos, Union forces recruited a regiment of black troops, who were followed by liberated slaves who could not keep up with the fast-moving Union forces.[56] African Americans were left scattered on the roads, exposed to the retaliation of demoralized Confederates. Furthermore, Wilson marched his Selma captives eastward, freeing them in small groups as he went. If the design had been to spread social conflict across the countryside, Wilson could not have done better. The sheer destructiveness of the cavalry compounded the effect. One Union soldier could trace the path of the army by the smoke; another saw a line of continuous devastation.[57]

Effective opposition ceased. Confederate forces evacuated Montgomery before Wilson’s host, but only after torching 97,000 bales of cotton, incinerating much of the warehouse district. Wilson paused to demolish a few military targets, then headed to Columbus, Georgia, for more ruination.[58] Ultimately neither Grant nor Sherman needed Wilson’s assistance or his destructive raid. After Wilson left Alabama, desultory Confederate control resumed briefly, while Union infantry marched inland. Before leaving Mobile, they dumped a statue of a slave in chains into a fountain, and they burned a reported slave mart in Claiborne.[59] On April 25, General E. R. S. Canby’s infantry arrived in Montgomery, finally establishing a permanent occupation. Liberated slaves pitched handfuls of Confederate money at them, reportedly millions of dollars’ worth. This much enlivened the camps thereafter, since gambling with US money was prohibited.[60]

Another shipboard force, coming upriver with a contingent of General Steele’s black troops, received an uproarious welcome from the African American population. “They would all dance, clap their hands, sing and holler. Then the troops from the boats would cheer,” one soldier observed.[61] After days of negotiation and armistice, General Richard Taylor successfully surrendered the main Confederate army on May 4. Some units remained operating through May, especially in the north, as smaller bands of cavalry and guerillas surrendered. The army’s task then became pacification and enforcing emancipation, a function that by weight of numbers they performed effectively at first. In June, there were 35,000 Union troops in Alabama, enough to overawe resistance and compensate for the lapse of civil law.[62] That said, the army and the national government acted in ways which would embitter the Reconstruction process needlessly. The government had created a mechanism that could not be adapted readily for peacetime functions. Union volunteers were like a force of nature; they deterred violence against the new freedmen and repressed some forms of crime, but they also spread disorder. The impact of the federal presence was thus double-edged, imperiling the crucial function of enforcing emancipation by undisciplined conduct.[63]

The occupation started smoothly enough. As they marched into the interior of the state, greeted with white flags as they went, General E. R. S. Canby's infantry knew the war was ending. In Greenville, they satisfied themselves with seizing the local printing press and issuing a newspaper; the whites were apparently surprised at their behavior, expecting worse.[64] When rumors reached them of Lincoln's assassination, many soldiers mused upon revenge. As Wyman Folsom observed, "One word from our Comdg. Gen[eral]. and the whole state of Ala would be laid waste. I could have killed every man in the Confed[eracy]."[65] But at the moment, Canby's force marched through wilderness with few victims at hand. By the time they reached Selma and Montgomery, the troops recovered their composure, happily before encountering the thousands of paroled Confederates from Lee and Johnson's armies. Surrendered Confederates avoided provocative celebration of Lincoln's fate.[66] Union soldiers frequently noted the resigned humor of their defeated foes. One soldier in Mobile found them friendly, happy to return home in peace.[67]

With peace at hand, one soldier described a new reality of pitching horseshoes, swimming, and picking berries.[68] Relief soon passed, and once rested, routine duties and drilling bored soldiers. One complained that soldiers literally sickened doing nothing that summer, in a state of nervous restlessness.[69] "No news, no money, no war. . . . I want to go home," another wrote.[70] The volunteers had been in the field for up to four years. They were desperate to resume lives and reestablish peacetime careers. Rumors of discharge undermined regiments' capacity to function: it proved difficult for officers to discipline their restive commands, or to restrain alcohol abuse.[71] A sergeant commented on lawless behavior, adding "WE WANT TO GET OUT." In an Iowa regiment, hundreds mutinied, demanding back pay and officers' efforts to get them discharged.[72]

These difficulties occurred amid rapid reductions in force levels to accommodate the policy decision to shift troops to the Mexican border to undermine the Emperor Maximilian. Disorder followed in Alabama as soldiers suddenly found themselves bound for another potential war. One private noted that his whole corps were indignant. He doubted whether

General Canby had any authority to send them there.[73] Regiments spoke of mutiny, and they put strong pressure on home-state politicians to secure their release. The departure of many regiments, moreover, denuded the state of the overwhelming numbers that inhibited most lawlessness. By the late summer of 1865, most of the occupation army had already left, and because white regiments had served longest, the troops available were primarily African American regiments and the First Alabama loyalists. As a shock treatment for slaveholders, this reality might have some appeal, but it complicated pacification, and the pressure from white veterans encouraged this policy.[74]

The cotton trade exacerbated disorder. Even during the war, as federal commanders used wartime controls to encourage Unionist sentiment, permits to undertake the lucrative trade northward gave off a strong odor of peculation. Upon arriving in Huntsville, General Mitchel asked permission to supplement his funds with cotton profits. The area's leading Unionist, Federal Judge George W. Lane, thought that 20,000 bales could be purchased, some 200 of them from ex-senator Jeremiah Clemens, the cooperationist leader.[75] Within three weeks, speculators were on the scene with the cooperation of Mitchel, including a son-in-law who was captured en route with business associates. Embarrassing as that was, the cotton issue was larger than Mitchel's conflict of interest.[76]

Wartime cotton prices spread corruption, but the problem grew exponentially after Appomattox. Though Dunning-era scholars wrote on the topic at length, and more recent historians have examined the wartime trade, revisionists have understated the topic's relevance to Reconstruction.[77] The state's experience is admittedly atypical because, "as the rebel Territory became contracted, the [Confederate] property was concentrated mostly in Alabama."[78] Planters had pledged cotton to the Confederate government, as a coerced investment or in payment of taxes. Surrendering Confederates turned the list over to the Union forces, reportedly 150,000 bales worth.[79] The cotton was considered a prize of war, and northern taxpayers expected the proceeds. But planters were hardly going to hand over the cotton voluntarily, and the Confederate government had never taken possession, so they felt justified. Treasury agents needed to seize the bulky bales before planters could hide them or disguise their origin. A repossession scramble thus was superimposed on the emancipation transition at this very moment.

Federal authorities had the legal right to the cotton, but the seizures might have been counterproductive. Nineteenth-century government had a fiscal leakage problem, and these conditions were less than optimal. Cotton agents received a full quarter share, which encouraged unscrupulous men to declare all cotton that crossed their paths Confederate. Numerous opportunities existed for government officials or army officers to interpose themselves in the marketing of cotton, in sort of a politicized protection racket. One chaplain noted that Union officers were offering to buy Confederate cotton on their own account, threatening seizure if the planters refused. Outraged, he offered testimony to superiors who found other matters to pursue.[80] Treasury agents also could operate with northern cotton buyers, and if Confederate cotton was sold to third parties, with the accompanying proof of ownership, it was worth considerably more. These practices encouraged other kinds of leveraged transactions. Ex-colonel George E. Spencer went into the cotton business predicting vast profits. He persuaded one impressionable merchant that, under federal confiscation acts, the private cotton he held could be seized. Spencer bought it for perhaps a third of its value, to the astonishment of the co-owners of the bales.[81]

According to a grand jury, less than a seventh of the cotton seized wound up in government hands.[82] This is difficult to confirm because the corruption tales are so profuse. The US Treasury official in Mobile, T. C. A. Dexter, was charged with theft in early August. He responded that numerous agents were scattered throughout the cotton belt, responsible only to the secretary of the treasury. Dexter agreed that only a small portion of the proceeds found its way into government coffers.[83] The official sent to replace him claimed he saw Dexter with a huge stack of bonds, apparently in the act of bribing someone.[84] But that officer, T. M. Tomeny, was also convicted of theft, only to be pardoned by Andrew Johnson. All of these officers accused each other in lurid detail, a complicated saga that must have had considerable basis, and at least one other officer confessed outright. Even visiting reporters noticed the suspiciously elegant clothes and diamond rings of one treasury official.[85]

In the cotton belt, these fiscal issues engendered lawlessness. Widespread theft demoralized those planters inclined toward pragmatic cooperation with the US army and government. One planter feared losing all his cotton after armed men took three wagon loads. "It seems the citizens, soldiers, & darkies unite to plunder the planters," he wrote.[86] Another planter had several soldiers arrested, and immediately military agents arrived, looking for stolen government mules. His complaints risked everything because "if this garrison at Uniontown knew what I have here written my plantation would be burned up in 24 hours."[87] Cotton theft was pervasive if soldiers' own letters are to be believed. A provost guard in Selma reported that almost everyone was doing it.[88] A soldier in Marion likewise found an enormous amount of cotton stealing going on, blaming a Union colonel.[89] Civil government had ceased to function after surrender, so the only recourse was to the army itself for redress.

One of the state's less-known contributions to American literature illuminates this illicit trade. The humorist Ambrose Bierce was stationed in Selma, on duty connected with the cotton agents. His "Way Down in Alabam'" recalled a wide-open scene, with his treasury colleagues accumulating fortunes. The work was dangerous because martial law was effective only near army posts. Cotton on plantations was immobilized but well hidden, and the finders' fee he thought none too generous given the number of officials already assassinated. Freedpeople were the main reliance for finding cotton, they being "zealous" to repay the Yankees, but "many poor devils among them forfeited their lives by services performed with more loyalty than discretion." As for Bierce, he fended off a bribe to approve a large shipment of cotton downriver by certifying it as private. Two well-dressed men plied him with food and alcohol while he tried to wheedle information out of them. Bierce felt in danger until he befriended some ex-Rebel comrades in drink, "glorious fellows" whose reputation for violence secured him protection.[90]

Soldiers found the entire situation sordid. One wrote, "all we are kept here for is to guard these cotton speculators & Government thieves," and when they were done, he figured he could probably head home.[91] The complaints died down late in the summer, as the cotton disappeared, but other damaging federal interventions ensued.[92] President Andrew Johnson's initial law enforcement appointees had Unionist backgrounds and became prominent Republicans. District Attorney James Q. Smith had been jailed as a political prisoner and then exiled, while his marshal, John Hardy, opposed secession and had been repeatedly indicted for disloyalty.[93] Both believed that leading secessionists deserved punishment and that the president would provide it. As Johnson's surprisingly lenient policies emerged, these federal officials sped confiscation proceedings against as-yet-unpardoned Confederates.[94] Johnson's eventual action relieved all their penalties, but the fees they accrued in the meantime would go to court officials, which Smith calculated as a minimum of $150 per dismissal. The procedure looks lucrative, but Smith's motivation is indistinct, likely a combination of opposition to presidential policy, harassment of impenitent traitors, and personal payback. Still, these actions were decried as an exercise in profiteering. The episode initiated years of controversy involving the court of Federal District Judge Richard Busteed, whose unsavory reputation would overshadow those of his subordinate officers.

These failings pale in comparison to the good the army was doing in repressing violence.[95] Slavery engendered racial mayhem, and now emancipation both intensified white frustration and eliminated what self-interested checks slaveownership provided. As one Union soldier reported from Selma, "The Negroes are flocking in by hundreds and say the Rebs are shooting them down like they would a sheep killing dog."[96] Appallingly graphic reports followed, which made protecting freedpeople's lives a national responsibility of a high order. But the scramble for cotton proceeds, legitimate or otherwise, and the other distractions caused by federal officials hurt the capacity of the army to protect anyone. The cotton losses made it difficult for planters to resume production. These complications also undermined the moral legitimacy of the army presence, which was going to be necessary for a long time. Most whites in Alabama wanted the soldiers gone, for a variety of reasons, and the frauds provided justification.

Securing order would have been difficult under any circumstances. In north Alabama, the chaotic Union occupation had demolished slavery in stages, but in the cotton belt, emancipation descended suddenly. Slaveholders did not want to believe that northerners would insist on immediate, uncompensated emancipation. There was always the possibility of a favorable Supreme Court decision, an overseas war, something to forestall the inevitable. At the least, hard-pressed planters hoped to get a crop in the ground, to secure a last springtime of slave labor. For these reasons, slaveholders in yet undisturbed areas seldom spontaneously freed anyone. Or, if they did tell the hands they were free, they did it in veiled terms that made its exercise less likely. The slaves, facing violence from emotionally overwrought owners, often feared to depart. To feel really liberated, many slaves wanted their masters to acknowledge it as a fact, preferably in the company of bluecoats. This duty many gleeful soldiers initially relished, as one response to Jefferson Davis's capture suggests. Someone displayed a caricature of "the Traitor President" with a noose around his neck, with the rope held by "an over-grown negro woman clad in expensive crinoline."[97] Despite the dubious racial politics on display, the episode certainly indicated preference for the ex-slaves over their late masters.

The army had to repress disorder during the emotionally fraught transition to freedom, and soldiers spent much of their time gathering up civilian arms. The civil courts were not functioning during the interregnum, and even if they were, the laws were not designed to punish violence against African Americans. Whatever racial limitations northern soldiers had, the force directed at slaves shocked them. For example, an overseer attacked a party of runaways while asleep, killing a man and a women. Along with a maimed man, four women came into camp in Montgomery with their ears hacked off. "This is a nice specimen of Southern chivalry," a soldier observed.[98] When freedmen reported assaults or whippings with physical evidence to back them up, federal soldiers normally tried to punish the perpetrators. Even random enforcement was sufficient to make an impression throughout the state. On the other hand, sometimes planters feared violence from slaves that they had not yet freed. Some freedpeople reportedly refused to work but expected planters to continue to feed them. Union troops prevented a good deal of conflict simply by being present on the plantations, or nearby in case of trouble.

For weeks after the surrender, planters entered Union camps cluelessly seeking to retrieve runaways. It took some time for reality to set in, that refugees were not going to be sent back, and this occurred first near concentrations of the troops. The army's presence changed everything, because once slaves left, planters recognized that the institution was much less likely to ever be reconstituted. Thus, as the Union presence spread, the first order of business was to visit plantations, sometimes in force. This process took longer than one might think possible. In Greene County, for example, one planter's agent called the hands together and explained they would "likely be legally free in time," so he suggested they keep working in the meantime. Only in early June did "abolition preachers" arrive. The freedmen immediately ceased labor, refused to sign a contract, and insisted that the overseer be fired. It took the army to get them under contract and back to work, to explain what they could and could not expect of former masters. The pattern is crucial, because the Union Army had a mixed role. Officers projected the emancipation policy into the countryside, while exerting themselves to minimize its disruptive effects.[99]

At the moment of transition, planters sometimes found the army a useful presence. Chaplain Henry N. Herrick, "sort of an extemporized

Supt. of Freedmen" at Demopolis, exemplified this dual duty. Herrick hated slavery, writing his wife of fearful escapee stories, and he certainly tried to implement emancipation starting in mid-May. As a Baptist minister, Herrick spent much of his time on moral preachments, enlightening the freedmen on the evils of frequent divorce and other failings.[100] Herrick nonetheless found them appreciative, reflecting, "I never was used to such homage before."[101] Despite his egalitarian commitments, Herrick pressed freedmen to return to their plantations and go back to work. He found himself popular with the planters, and he visited these "humbled nabobs" alone by carriage. They reportedly treated him splendidly.[102]

These mingled priorities reflected those of the army more broadly. Despite their settled distaste for slavery, soldiers settled into a complex interaction with the freedpeople. Soldiers understood their role in bringing freedom as part of the pacification process, but the holdouts tended to be in out-of-the-way places, easily overlooked. Around military camps, which were concentrated in the black belt, the intimidated planters generally were not the problem: the accumulating freedmen increasingly were.[103] Once emancipation looked to be accomplished, the task became getting society functioning. Soldiers' free-labor beliefs suggested that the ex-slaves could be usefully instructed in the behavior patterns of the new order. The occupation army also followed wartime precedents designed to minimize disruptions to military operations. In mid-May, General Canby extended the labor codes in operation in Louisiana to most of Alabama. The labor code provided wage levels and hours, on terms that resembled the gang-labor system of slavery but without authorizing physical coercion. Freedmen were also made subject to wartime vagrancy statutes and a racial pass system, all enforced by the military authority of their liberators.[104]

The Freedmen's Bureau was just being organized in Washington; in the meantime, Rev. Thomas W. Conway, superintendent of freedmen's affairs in Louisiana, arrived to take charge. In late May, Conway established subordinate agencies in Mobile, Selma, Demopolis, and Montgomery. All four of the officers he chose had served in the US Colored Infantry; he sought superintendents with relevant experience who presumably had their hearts in the work. As he traveled, he called public meetings to announce emancipation, to the dismay of slaveholders. That said, he brought with him his experience formed in wartime Louisiana. Conway's officers understood that "idleness would be considered a crime and could not be tolerated." These are stern words, and tough love seemed to be the watchword toward the freedpeople. "Hire them out! Cut wood! Do anything to avoid a state of idleness," he directed.[105]

Conway's assistants followed his lead. In Selma, Chaplain S. S. Gardner had abolitionist convictions. Despite this, he feared that in the ruined vicinity, planters would simply abandon production for the year, causing a humanitarian nightmare. Planters might evict multitudes, handing them to the army for support. For these reasons, Gardner approved many contracts with no wages provided beyond food and housing. Literally free labor of this sort implied coercion, and Gardner sent out military guards to maintain authority on plantations and enforce tolerable labor. Heeding complaints of poor work, he even concluded that, in some cases, "such discipline as would be considered mild and humane under the old plan might be used, especially with the young and thoughtless." He thus authorized whippings for some weeks, to his subsequent embarrassment. To a striking extent, this future Radical Republican firebrand became thoroughly enmeshed in the labor practices of the old regime.[106]

The flood of liberated slaves to the refugee camps and army installations redoubled these repressive inclinations.[107] Many thousands of fleeing slaves followed the Union Army about central Alabama, seeking freedom. Even after the conflict wound down, freedpeople sought out the safety of the camps. Chaplain C. W. Buckley had much the same political profile as Gardner in Selma. He would be elected to Congress, and a leaked letter endorsing confiscation would cause him and the Freedmen's Bureau substantial embarrassment. Despite these evident loyalties, he had over three thousand people in his refugee camp in Montgomery. The army felt overwhelmed, and the camps were disease-ridden and deadly places. Buckley too resorted to stern measures to stem refugees. He affirmed a "persistent and unyielding determination to make every Negro remain on the plantation," and he added that his pass system had cleared the city of idlers. His superior, Conway, approved this policy. Buckley sent guards to enforce order on the plantations, despite his awareness that many hands were working for nothing more than food.[108]

The men assigned to working with the freedpeople were more patient than officers and enlisted men in general. In all the camps, soldiers felt overwhelmed by the flood of liberated refugees. One newly arrived soldier reported talk that blacks outnumbered whites in Montgomery by twenty-five to one, an exaggeration that conveys a sense of unease.[109] Military superiors saw the migration of freedpeople to the cities as inconsistent with pacification, and they naturally inclined toward authoritarian responses. As for the common soldiers, the freedpeople ran afoul of their desire to go back home. For example, Wyman Folsom expressed vigorous hostility to slaveholders, slavery, and southern women especially. But after arriving in Selma, new concerns intruded on his mind, because "Negroes are coming in by the hundred and they keep coming round to hire out every five minutes. . . ." Within two weeks, he was fed up and expressed his frustration in racial terms: "I will jump ten foot high and crack my heels nine times when I get out of this land of *Negroes*. I am heartily sick of them and they are very much degraded, especially the female population."[110] Frustration increasingly turned soldiers against the freedpeople, who they blamed for their detention in Alabama's summer heat.

Urban environments fostered the harshest policies to deter refugees, and Alabama's largest city exemplified them. On May 1, with the war all but over, the army ordered all unemployed men in Mobile to report for work on fortifications or face arrest. The army issued certificates of employment so that jobless blacks could be readily impressed. Later that month the army ordered the arrest of all persons without visible means of support; they were to be formed into gangs and worked on the streets.[111] One appreciative woman wrote that "the negroes are kept in order not a loiterer is to be seen."[112] In Montgomery, post commander Charles Turner received a warm welcome from local whites, who plied him with invitations and strawberry shortcake. Turner agreed that many of the migrants were "worthless vagabonds." He anticipated trouble if the army did not keep "some sort of stringent control."[113]

Planters were not inclined toward praise of the Union forces, but they noticed these policies. It did not take long for planters to allege abusive behavior by Union troops. In early June, one general in the interior reportedly told a planter to strap his hands "like hell" and make them work.[114] Later that month, a planter reported that perfect order had been restored. This was no racist fantasy. One order decreed that "Negroes will not be allowed to congregate in large numbers and remain in Demopolis." Soldiers sent freedmen home on pain of forced labor, and guards were stationed on the roads to arrest those without passes. One nearby planter reported that soldiers "used persuasion & finally (in the last few days) their bayonets to make the negroes enter into contracts with their former masters & return to their work."[115] All these reports served to diminish the moral luster of the victorious Union cause, but they had basis in reality. These were temporary measures, and the soldiers clearly intended that the freedmen would soon become free workers in the sense northerners understood that term. But the repressive practices bolstered the plantation system at a crucial time, and their precedents would be seized on to reestablish a labor repressive regime on an altered basis.

For these reasons, the role of the Freedmen's Bureau that took over the task is probably misunderstood. The literature on the bureau, and in Alabama specifically, has tended to be critical, viewing it as an agent of social and labor control. General Wager Swayne in particular appears as more "pro-planter" than most of his bureau associates.[116] One historian concluded that he pursued policies often "fatal to the interests of the freedmen."[117] These claims had some basis. Upon arrival, Swayne inclined toward rigor, and he always sought cooperation of Alabama's civil officials. He quickly rejected the idea of confiscation, and he expressed worry that the freedpeople believed the "forty acres and a mule" talk. He seemed at first to credit the rumors of a possible uprising. Swayne did have earnest Protestant convictions, which inclined him toward the sort of moral preachments common among those working with the freedpeople. He initially countenanced discriminatory prohibition laws, because freedmen were "at present an unsettled, numerous and excited people."[118]

But in the context of what the army was already doing in Alabama, Swayne's conduct looks different. By the time he arrived in late July 1865, army policies had already developed in an authoritarian direction. Simply removing freedmen's affairs from the purview of the regular command probably improved their welfare. He found the contract system "established here, practically and in orders," so Swayne's labor code, General Orders No. 12, mostly ratified the existing guidelines. The changes he made benefited the laborers by implicitly banning whipping, a provision soon spelled out. The code abandoned the pass system as well, finally granting freedpeople the right to move around freely so far as the federal government was concerned. He disavowed coercing anyone to sign a contract, and he soon suggested the whole idea of annual labor agreements undermined the bargaining position of the freedpeople. Admittedly, all these changes were encouraged by his bureau superior, O. O. Howard in Washington, but it is difficult to see Swayne's intervention as anything but an improvement.[119]

In sum, Union troops left a decidedly mixed legacy as an army of liberation. In northern Alabama, guerilla warfare and harsh occupation policies scattered social chaos that surely encouraged the region's later Klan eruption. Wilson's raid spread ruin through the cotton belt just as the war was concluding. The war created a human engine of destruction and appropriation that was difficult to halt after Appomattox, as the cotton thefts indicated. As for the soldiers themselves, they manifested a war-charged hostility to the slaveholding society. They were undisciplined agents of liberation, spreading disorder through the region, much of it unnecessary or counterproductive. The army's emphasis on pacification did not always work to the advantage of the freedmen, as military exigency and convenience held sway. Still, the soldiers of the victorious Union Army were on scene, and they were able and disposed to superintend the transition to freedom. The liberated slaves saw them as friendly, at least relative to their ex-masters and to the temporarily compromised power structure of white Alabama. That looming presence in the process of Reconstruction would present the real threat to African American freedom as emancipation dawned.[120]

3

Presidential Reconstruction
Unionism and the Politics of Definition

You went into the rebellion *con amore*. I did not. You forced my complications.

—Milton Saffold, conservative leader

Harsh wartime occupation colored the fate of those civilians identified with the Union cause. As eager as the conservatives in Montgomery were to negotiate peace, their location precluded effective cooperation with federal authorities. Other actors would be far more advantageously situated. Thus the residents and refugees in the Tennessee Valley dominated the wartime gestures toward Reconstruction, and the unpopularity of the northern occupation spilled over to those operating under its auspices. Nothing concrete came of the Unionists' efforts, but their frustrations set the stage for the conflicting agendas of the Presidential Reconstruction era. How could those identified with the Union protect themselves, and what could be done to guarantee the results of the war from the inclinations of the electorate?

Before the war, Alabama had "drifted to the very verge of a lawless democracy," as one conservative recalled.[1] Because states' rights Democrats were the long-dominant political tendency, varied opponents dreaded the postwar reassertion of that established supremacy. As the outcome of the war became evident, disaffected elements looked to the army and to Washington to strengthen their hand, for moral validation or simple protection. White dissidents proved a heterogeneous lot, frequently lumped together terminologically as Union men, and many opportunistically adopted the term to obscure more recent Confederate loyalty. But "Union" could mean anything, creating a linguistic morass which still complicates the writing on Reconstruction.[2] It could mean nothing more than opposition to the states' rights Democratic tendency—Unionism relative to whatever scale seemed locally or socially appropriate. It could mean ex-Whigs or Douglas Democrats, anti-secessionists, or wartime defeatists. It took in collaborators in occupied areas, draft evaders, even former Union soldiers.

Few could meet a legal standard of consistent loyalty, particularly politicians of any note. Still, the Union name meant something real, though imprecise. For some wealthy men, Unionism meant private qualms and draft evasion eased by social connections, while for poorer farmers it often meant risking death at the hands of the Confederate authorities. In any case, the white potential constituency for Radical Reconstruction was less ideologically and socially compact than the Democratic opposition—even without the eventual addition of the freedmen to their ranks. The Union following quarreled over degrees of complicity with Confederate rule, and minute distinctions in behavior during the secession winter cast a long shadow. These divisions emerged most intractably in the portion of the state under federal control the longest.

Talk of reconstructing Alabama commenced immediately upon Union occupation of the Tennessee Valley in April 1862. Unlike Joseph Bradley, who fled to promote peace negotiations, most prosperous white residents chose to stay on, to protect their property and slaves. Most lapsed into effective neutrality, whatever their private loyalties, but the more emphatically anti-Confederate or boldly self-interested cooperated with the occupation, especially those who sought army permits to trade cotton northward. This association proved unpopular as troops respected civilian property less. The Emancipation Proclamation embittered slaveholder opinion, making open collaboration a bright red line of class betrayal.

South of the Tennessee River, Union sympathizers remained at the mercy of Confederate retaliation. But in the four counties mostly north of it, and especially in administrative centers like Huntsville, Union forces guaranteed relative safety much of the time.[3] There open loyalty to the United States was possible, intermittently. Jefferson Davis himself heard that Confederate sympathizers were fearful to speak openly in front of neighbors.[4] For those identified with the Union occupation, the nightmare came when the fortunes of war periodically drew Federal troops elsewhere. Collaborators were "really criminals who ought to be arrested," as Confederate general Braxton Bragg observed.[5] The Huntsville hotelkeeper James Hickman, who had entertained Union officers and secured permits for trading cotton northward, got into in legal trouble with both sides. He was repeatedly seized by the Confederate military, jailed by civil officials, and eventually put on trial for treason.[6] Confederate raids and guerillas frequently targeted the property of collaborators and occasionally tortured or killed them, or simply conscripted them on the spot. Thus pronounced Union men often fled, like D. H. Bingham of Athens. That course thrust them as exiles into ever greater visibility and dependence on the Lincoln administration.

Huntsville became the hub of elite Unionist activity, with ex–US Senator Jeremiah Clemens as the central figure. He had taken a convoluted path as cooperationist leader who voted for the secession ordinance while calling it treason. "The majority is against us—we must go with the State, or create civil disturbances of the most dreadful character at home," he observed.[7] For this betrayal, Unionist holdouts reportedly burned him in effigy.[8] With the Union Army's first occupation of north Alabama, Clemens changed his politics yet again. He resigned his commission in the state militia to become an emphatic supporter of Lincoln administration policies. When the Confederates temporarily regained possession, he fled. He relocated to Philadelphia to write a loyalist novel—he was a relative of Samuel Clemens—and to lobby for appointment as military governor.[9]

Elite figures like Senator Clemens and the future scalawag David C. Humphreys hoped to induce the Lincoln administration to initiate the reunion process immediately. Refugee politics became a factional morass, with personal rivalries amplified by the national press. For example, in mid-1862 the refugee Robert S. Tharin warned Washington against cotton planters like Clemens, a class that had "reduced the non-slaveholding population to a level with the despised negro."[10] Tharin sought appointment as military governor, but unfortunately his emergence coincided with Lincoln's shift toward emancipation. The embittered Tharin then spoke at Democratic rallies and wrote a loyalist memoir, but he reportedly ran into trouble with the authorities and returned to the South.[11]

The Republican administration resisted action, presumably believing the military situation too unstable for a mini-state to prosper. Still, once Lincoln proclaimed his 10 percent plan in December 1863, the omens looked more promising. General Sherman's fearful threats of impoverishment were meant to jump-start the Reconstruction process. "If the People of Huntsville think differently," he warned, "let them persist in this war three years longer and then they will not be consulted."[12] Though the occupied region north of the river did not meet the plan's numerical threshold, leaving actual implementation beyond reach, the logic of events encouraged reunion gestures.[13] Public meetings might secure presidential favor or induce the Union command to defend the region more consistently. In March 1864, Clemens and Humphreys addressed reunion rallies in Huntsville, the first such substantial gatherings in Alabama.[14] Clemens utilized unsettling arguments: "We had rebellion, and the consequence now is that not one man in the State of Alabama who can say he has the title to a single nigger."[15] Nothing came immediately from the gatherings, perhaps because Sherman's main force marched away to Georgia, and subsequent events justified Lincoln's caution. Late in 1864, General Hood's offensive through the Tennessee Valley prompted mass flight by contrabands and prospective Unionist officeholders alike.[16] Only victory at Nashville and the dispersal of Hood's army prompted the Huntsville cohort to try again.[17]

As these events transpired, an entirely different constituency sought the Unionist mantle, in numerical terms a much larger one. "Unconditional Unionists" or loyalists, those who could claim something resembling consistent adherence, underwent distinctively harsh experiences at Confederate hands. In the hill and mountain regions south of the river, refugees escaped into the Tennessee Valley as soon as opportunity allowed, becoming vigorous players in Reconstruction politics. "They say they are going back to kill every reb in their country," one northern soldier observed.[18] In all, an estimated three thousand white loyalists joined the Union Army from Alabama.[19] Governor Shorter asked permission to try captured Alabamians as citizens for treason and "instigating slaves to rebellion," so Union soldiers knew just where they stood.[20] The state's sole white federal regiment, the First Alabama Cavalry, became the institutional focus for loyalist veterans. It was primarily composed of refugees from the hill country, the center of white Republican support later, and its Colonel George Spencer became Alabama's much-reviled carpetbagger senator.[21] The regiment fostered the refugee William Hugh Smith, who later became the state's first Republican governor. In December 1862, Smith and several brothers fled Randolph County to escape military arrest.[22] He then recruited and spied for Spencer's regiment. In October 1864, he and fellow exiles acquired notice with a public letter, emphatically Unionist though indistinct on Lincoln's reelection and slavery.[23]

The wartime aspirants for Reconstruction leadership were disparate, but the more prominent leaders had one thing in common. Prewar politicians often based their anti-secessionism on the effective defense of slavery and white supremacy. Their arguments, however prescient, promised less well when circumstances thrust them into electoral alliance with the freedmen. Future scalawags said and did profoundly inconvenient things. Republican Attorney General Josiah Morse, for instance, figured in a late antebellum legal case in which he tortured a confession out of a slave.[24] Congressman Alexander White became notorious just after the war for opposing state action abolishing slavery. Likewise, when D. C. Humphreys urged surrender, he anticipated federal "political cooperation so as to secure the management of that labor by those who were slaves. There is really no difference, in my opinion, whether we hold them as absolute slaves, or obtain their labor by some other method."[25] To be fair, he then faced up to emancipation's implications sooner than most. But if even Humphreys could thus anticipate the Black Codes, what reason would the freedmen have to trust any native Republicans of the leadership class?

Perhaps one reason existed, and at the moment it mattered. Pronounced Unionists accepted or even sought the extinction of slavery well before war's end. The loyalist element in the hills traditionally voted Jacksonian Democrat. They embraced class-based resentment of wealthy slaveholders, who they blamed for war. Dissidents sometimes depended on slaves for information and aid, and conscription agents even hunted draft resisters with bloodhounds. Many ex-slaves testified about wartime collaboration with Unionists, such as the future Republican J. C. Goodloe. Furthermore, even among more prosperous Union men in the Tennessee Valley, prolonged occupation made the survival of slavery look unlikely.[26] Some discovered Unionist politics could encourage voluntary wage work from their nominal slaves, just by acquiescing to liberation. And for the political class, there was the evident sense that everything depended on the administration's pleasure. If Union men hoped for protection and sponsorship by the victorious North, they would have to be forthcoming on emancipation.

The last throes of the Confederacy galvanized Reconstruction activity. Wilson's cavalry raid in April 1865 persuaded most Alabamians that the war was indeed over. And Lincoln's assassination convinced even ex-Confederates that a show of contrition might be politic, so resolutions proliferated welcoming peace. Given Andrew Johnson's record, contemporaries assumed that pronounced Unionists would now prosper. As military governor, he had presided over the creation of a new Tennessee constitution, which abolished slavery and disfranchised numbers of ex-Confederate soldiers. He was the South's best-known loyalist leader, and just after Richmond fell he observed that "death is too easy a punishment. My notion is that treason must be made odious and traitors must be punished and impoverished, their social power broken. . . ." Even after Lincoln's assassination, he talked this way.[27] At first, he appointed Alabama Unionist exiles to office, and the Huntsville contingent expected his support, for they had courted Johnson for years.

These expectations were not borne out, partly because of the number of aspirants, and partly because prominent defecting Confederates finally offered cooperation. After Hood's defeat, a delegation called on commanding general George H. Thomas for guidance. Without apparent direction from superiors, he suggested that they call a convention from the area north of the Tennessee River. If the convention declared slavery dead, leaders could bear these resolutions to Washington and ask for presidential recognition.[28] In April, Thomas urged that the existing courts resume doing business on the basis of the existing Alabama Code, without even mentioning any modifications required by emancipation. J. J. Giers bore this offer across the lines into Morgan County, holding a public meeting with Confederate soldiers.[29] They equivocated on surrender, but it increasingly looked like reunion might be swift. These ad hoc decisions made sense in pacification terms with guerillas still in in the field, but as a blueprint for peace they had consequences. Existing Confederate officials would govern the transition, which frightened Unionists of longer standing, like Clemens: "These men ruled & oppressed us when treason was in the ascendant, for God's sake do not let them lord it over us now when the Union cause is triumphant. Give their offices to Union men."[30]

Here chance took a hand. Ex-senator Clemens was the best-known Union exile and an obvious possibility for provisional governor. President Andrew Johnson's policy was still in flux, but he promoted some men elsewhere with similar profiles. By this point, Clemens saw his strong suit as support for an emancipation agenda. In preference to seeing ex-secessionists regain power, or even the vote, Unionists would prefer "to treat every black man as a free man and without further legislation & allow him to vote as if fully entitled to do so."[31] His appointment might have changed Alabama's trajectory, but in May, Clemens died.

The disarray in north Alabama shifted the initiative to the other large group of aspirants for leadership, the conservatives centered in Montgomery. John J. Seibels emerged as the spokesman for this group, which included Joseph Bradley and Lewis Parsons.[32] Late in the war, these men had been nudging the state toward surrender.[33] These so-called "Reconstructionists" planned to field peace candidates, but Wilson's destructive raid overtook them.[34] From still-smoldering Montgomery, Seibels wrote President Lincoln on April 14 recommending precisely the opposite approach to that projected by Clemens. There was a better—elite ex-Confederate—element for peacemaking in Alabama than elsewhere. The federal government could halt bushwhacking by "at once organizing the local militia as a police patrol & c." Scheduled elections could be held and representation in Congress soon resume as if nothing had occurred. Thus Alabama might be purged of secessionist leadership, but be readmitted with the forms of existing governance intact. Slavery could then be abolished "by a well digested gradual system of emancipation, of say, from fifteen to twenty years."[35]

When the permanent federal occupation of Selma and Montgomery began in late April, ill-supplied Union troops kept seizing food from nearby plantations. Seeking an end to all resistance, Seibels and his allies sought permission to have the legislature meet. Union generals tacitly encouraged them.[36] Action awaited the final surrender of General Richard Taylor's command on May 4. Several days later, a modestly attended public rally was held in Montgomery, with Seibels, Bradley, and Milton Saffold on the resolutions committee, along with prominent secessionists like ex-governor Shorter. The resolutions deplored the assassination of President Lincoln and proclaimed loyalty. The term "conservative" went into temporary eclipse: everyone now called themselves "Union," even ex-Confederates who were Union in the sense of understanding that resistance must cease.[37]

The gathering was not harmonious. Two rival petitions were sent to the president, one signed by nearly sixty names, and the apparently revised majority statement signed by over seventy. A participant recalled the prominence of ex-secessionists and ex-Confederates as the underlying issue. Differences arose over whether federal recognition of the existing legislature should be sought, so that it could call a convention to revoke secession legally. Bradley recommended that alternative, but most of the platform group, and most of the conservative signers, preferred the more deferential approach of Seibels. A military governor could be appointed, if President Johnson thought necessary, with a state convention to be elected under his authority. This untainted body would adapt the state's existing laws. Lewis Parsons, the longtime proponent of peace negotiations, suggested sending both sets of resolutions. A delegation would accompany them to Washington comprised of the more peace-identified leaders, including Parsons, Seibels, Bradley, and Saffold.[38] Significantly, neither of the two statements mentioned slavery. Before the rally, a reporter suggested that Lincoln's emancipation proclamation had been "transcended" by the surrender. Those most directly involved—presumably large slaveholders—thought emancipation "intended as a war measure, and not as a peace policy."[39]

It took until early June for the delegation to reach Washington. On route, Parsons and Bradley gave a speech in Huntsville, consulting with Nicholas Davis and other northern Alabama leaders who preferred leadership with better Unionist credentials. Davis demurred at recognizing the existing Alabama government for any purpose, and he was more willing to renounce slavery.[40] In addition, economic issues were in contention, like whether poorer taxpayers would have to pay wartime state debts for the benefit of south Alabama's wealthy bondholders. Thus Davis, J. J. Giers, and other north Alabamians proceeded to Washington too. By the time everyone arrived, fifteen or more in all, President Johnson's policy had taken shape under his North Carolina proclamation of May 29. Confederate legislatures would receive no recognition, and Johnson insisted on new constitutional conventions. Several of the Montgomery delegates thus arrived to find their central proposal repudiated in advance. Members started heading home, some pausing to apply for presidential pardons, while Johnson sought a recommendation for provisional governor. Some suggested Seibels, but Johnson hesitated, seeking a figure less identified with the former regime.[41]

If Johnson anticipated his future policy, these delegates made a counterweight to more emphatically loyal aspirants. Already in Washington, the exile Daniel H. Bingham presented himself as a true Union man. He envisioned a South "*yankeeized* by the introduction of free schools, free speech, and free labor."[42] From Alabama, letters also promoted D. C. Humphreys, fresh from incarceration during Hood's raid.[43] Meanwhile, the First Alabama Cavalry veterans campaigned on behalf of William H. Smith. Of approximately 150 names on one petition, nearly a third signed with an illiterate "X." Their emissary, Colonel Spencer, met repeatedly with the president before the Montgomery delegates even arrived, but Johnson evidently preferred a candidate more acceptable to white opinion.[44] It appears the more moderate north Alabama leaders, like Nicholas Davis and George S. Houston, warily made common cause with the

Montgomery delegation against the more emphatic Unionist exiles. After nearly three weeks' reflection, President Johnson chose Lewis Parsons, the best-known peace man operating within the Alabama state government.[45] Bradley, for one, expressed satisfaction. "I believe Parsons will do any thing for me that is right and I will ask for nothing that is [w]rong," he wrote.[46]

Flexibility marked Provisional Governor Parsons's prior career. A Whig turned Douglas Democrat, and an anti-secessionist, he went with his state in 1861. The point about Parsons, and the conservatives like him, is that it is difficult to tell how far his opposition to the Confederacy went, working as he did within the establishment. In August 1863, his protégé Marcus Cruikshank was elected to the Confederate Congress, and Parsons went to the legislature with a large cohort of reputed peace men. Confederate agents accused Parsons of leadership in an antiwar conspiracy.[47] In the fall of 1864, Parsons proposed the resolutions offering to negotiate peace on the basis of the Democratic platform. The rationale was that the tactic would help defeat Lincoln, so it was not exactly treason. Such fluid politics suited Johnson's as yet indistinct policy of conciliation of ex-Confederates.[48]

Conservatives supported Parsons's appointment, and even ex-secessionists seemed relieved. He was fully identified with the state rather than an exile. Parsons's initial proclamation affirmed, "The appeal to arms has been made and decided against us," the pronoun being a rhetorical nod toward his onetime Confederate loyalties. He extolled Alabamians' courage fulsomely enough to inspire northern aspersion, but he also bluntly stated, "There are no slaves now in Alabama."[49] As Governor Parsons assumed his duties in July, restoring public order represented the obvious priority. He cooperated with the Union soldiery and federal officials. There were grounds for complaint in that summer of cotton seizures, but he avoided confrontation, aware that his own authority had no legal basis beyond presidential appointment and army bayonets.

To the extent that Governor Parsons sought to reshape the polity, the pardon process provided a vehicle. President Andrew Johnson's amnesty proclamation exempted fourteen classes of individuals: those worth more than twenty thousand dollars, various categories of secessionist leaders, high Confederate officers and civil authorities, and those guilty of war crimes. These men had to seek individual pardon from the president, a process protracted enough to prevent their voting in the elections for a state constitutional convention.[50] At first, everyone expected the president to be a stern taskmaster, which Parsons could use to minimize elite ex-secessionist influence, in order to guarantee emancipation and the other essential results of the war. Even among those not in the exempted categories, the oath of loyalty deterred ex-Confederate participation, as would the explicit obligation to abandon all title to slave property. Presidential Reconstruction thus effectively disfranchised, and barred from office, far more ex-Confederates than the much-decried Radical Reconstruction measures ever would.

Military guidelines directed that that the individual pardons would be routed through the governor before being sent on to Washington. To the president's questionnaire of applicants, Parsons added other queries. Had they served on vigilance committees? Hung or hunted Unionists with dogs?[51] The evident intent was to impress upon ex-Confederates the enormity of their crimes. Expectations of a rigorous process bound Parsons to the fellow conservatives who had supported his appointment, especially Bradley, who acted as if responsible. They envisioned Parsons playing "good cop" to the presidential "bad cop." Bradley anticipated that the more modest offenders would be pardoned first, especially those abused by rampaging Confederate troops, who would fare ill. As Bradley wrote Johnson, "I want to strike *terror* in the heart of these vile wretches. We intend to have every one of them tried for their misconduct as soon as Law is restored."[52] Union men first was his pardon policy, defined primarily on political behavior in the winter of 1861. Bradley explicitly preferred Douglas Democrats and poorer men over rich secessionists, along with those who seemed "badly whipped."[53] He assumed that his extensive network of political contacts were the obvious leaders in the work of Reconstruction.

For those under ban, speedy pardon was a matter of urgency. Considerable plantation land owned by leading secessionists in northern Alabama had been seized, some of it occupied by the army or for refugee camps. Pardon might facilitate recovery, and it would permit men of means, like railroad executives, to conduct business. Furthermore, wartime confiscation legislation authorized prosecutions to strip wealthy and unpardoned ex-Confederates of their possessions. In late July, Governor Parsons was still fielding questions about the twenty-thousand-dollar exclusion, whether it indicated that the unpardoned were to face dispossession. As it turned out, federal District Attorney James Q. Smith attempted to do precisely that, apparently in pursuit of court fees as well as punishment. This raised the nightmare scenario: treason trials and hangings, as authorized by wartime law.[54]

An exacting pardon process would benefit Parsons's newfound colleagues in several ways. Milton Saffold and D. C. Humphreys set up shop as lobbyists in Washington, loyalist intercessors for hire. Saffold's career move turned out miserably, he being excluded from practicing law by the federal ironclad oath; soon he was begging officials for jobs and personal loans.[55] Others benefited better financially from the pardon business, and there were political advantages besides. Joseph Bradley anticipated an expansive role, smoothing frayed personal ties with the penitent secessionist elite. He forwarded detailed listings of who deserved pardon first, assuring Parsons that this would promote the president's agenda.[56] Bradley took this retail approach to politics to extraordinary lengths, urging pardons to secure individual ballots at the next election.[57]

Initially barring prominent ex-Confederates looked conducive to a goal most white Alabamians shared, the swift resumption of civil government.[58] Gov. Parsons's pardon questionnaires would only make sense if he intended to discriminate on the basis of the information.[59] He resisted pardons for leading secessionists, especially those whose records he knew well. In the case of Eli S. Shorter, the brother of the ex-governor, Parsons reportedly withheld his approval. When told of this, Eli Shorter expressed studied skepticism that the governor could be "influenced by his old party prejudices to do an injury to any one." After prodding, Governor Parsons endorsed the petition, but only on the grounds of prospective rather than past loyalty.[60] A selective pardon policy, Parsons concluded, would minimize ex-secessionist control of offices and provide leverage to enforce emancipation.[61] Unfortunately Parsons's pardon plans were tripped up by the discovery that his secretary of state, W. E. Garrett, solicited payments for expedited processing. Investigation and his resulting resignation halted approvals for some weeks.[62] By the time consideration resumed in September, it was clear that President Johnson intended widespread pardons of the ex-Confederate elite.

Parsons's policy toward existing officeholders evolved along similar lines, from initial rigor to laxity, tempered by confusion. As Johnson's agent, Parsons enjoyed sweeping authority, and he quickly removed most of the higher state-level officeholders. His stated policy was to appoint (or reappoint) probate judges and sheriffs individually, but he primarily concentrated on vacancies. Several occurred where the army or loyalists drove out the Confederate officials, so Parsons presided over a hit-or-miss micropurge with wildly divergent results.[63] In eastern Alabama, near his Talladega home, he often appointed anti-Confederate dissidents. Farther afield, though, he preferred selective appointment of opponents of secession, or, in the black belt, former Whigs or wartime conservatives. In lesser positions he removed almost no one, either because of concerns for repressing lawlessness or the simple numbers involved. Wartime officials thus predominantly remained in place, to influence law enforcement and relief policies, and numerous complaints of discrimination resulted.

This reality redoubled the significance of appointing circuit judges and others who ran the court system, and it initially proved difficult for Parsons to disregard pleas for restitution from former supporters. From Talladega, poorer Unionists demanded prosecution of draft officials and vigilance committee members, especially one who had already captured Parsons's attention: "By hanging shooting & c. there are no less than nine men's bones lying in two miles of Silver Run . . . the victims of his black heart!!"[64]

Governor Parsons's appointments enabled some exemplary prosecution of the worst offenders. In Randolph County, ex-Confederate local officials fled pursued by armed loyalists and Union veterans. The governor appointed his recent Unionist rival William H. Smith as circuit judge.[65] Smith's court indicted numerous ex-Confederates. There were also reports that the grand jury disregarded continuing violence by the ex-Unionist bands. Parsons's close associate Marcus Cruikshank complained that perpetrators of a grave assault on an ex-Confederate official had been found guilty, but they were fined one cent in Judge Smith's court. In another case, apparent Unionists had killed an old man, and after several escaped, Cruikshank feared Judge Smith still intended to bail one of the remaining accused.[66]

Parsons initially feared disappointing unconditional Unionist allies, but he distanced himself from their conduct. Given presidential policies, and Parsons's desire to diminish conflict, he preferred not to promote such prosecutions. More striking, though, is the speed with which he disappointed his former conservative allies. Initially, men like Bradley wrote the governor confidently, as if they had an understanding on appointment policy. In one revealing example, from Sumter County came a conservative petition demanding wholesale removals. The future scalawag A. W. Dillard wrote, "If there are only half a dozen true men in a county, they should be appointed to office in preference to secessionists."

Seibels endorsed this over to the governor with the request that he read it carefully. This was not advice, however, calculated to widen the circle of Parsons's political friends, and in August, Seibels died, cutting one tie with the governor's former political sponsors.[67]

As a practical matter, administering a rigorous purge may have been difficult. The president pressed for speed in Reconstruction, to present Congress a fait accompli. This encouraged cosmetic replacement of positions already vacated by ex-Confederate officials, rather than wholesale removals. Parsons was also getting respectful mail from the former Confederate elite, ex-secessionists included. Pardon seekers in Washington sought cooperation with President Johnson and his appointees. Beyond this, Parsons's underlying racial loyalties and social position remained. Ultimately, his disagreement with the secessionists and wartime Confederates was tactical, over how best to save the social order. He and other conservatives shared with the old slaveholding elite a desire to rid Alabama of the military presence, to recover what might yet be salvaged from the wreckage of Civil War. Personal popularity beckoned as the likely result of Alabama's restoration, and for a politician recently reviled as a covert traitor, his growing stature was seductive. Parsons distanced himself from conservative sponsors, backing away from the pronounced Unionists even more.

Parsons's former allies expressed growing unease. Bradley's importunities were emphatic: "all the men I recommend are Union men & must fill the offices, you understand me in this."[68] In August, Bradley aired his misgivings publicly, utilizing the one Unionist editor in the state, William Figures, and his Huntsville *Advocate*.[69] Figures and Bradley contended that Parsons's policies emboldened secessionists, rightly, but the process yielded a constitutional convention that proved amenable to Parsons's suggestions, and to those of President Johnson as well.

While the process of oath taking, voter registration, and election of constitutional delegates proceeded, Parsons's preoccupation was restoring order and avoiding conflict with the military authorities. Parsons announced that the existing criminal and judicial apparatus was in operation, that all prewar laws were now operative save for those relating to slavery. But General Swayne of the Freedmen's Bureau responded with a learned legal memo, demonstrating that the provisional governor had no more legal standing than he did; they were creatures alike of the commander in chief's powers. Other army men felt the same way, with General Arthur McArthur threatening to shut down the Selma *Messenger* for treasonous editorials.[70] As one lawyer warned Parsons of the military, "you will have trouble, they rather think that you are subordinate to them."[71]

Given what occupation did to Union soldiers, tension with civilians was predictable. Even the churches prompted sharp civil-military confrontations. During the war, Union troops frequently seized buildings from the pro-Confederate Southern Methodist and Southern Baptist denominations, turning them over temporarily to their national counterparts. After Appomattox, the army attempted to convey buildings built for dependent slave congregations to the burgeoning African American denominations. In Mobile, this would generate litigation and repeated arson. But the most publicized conflict involved the Episcopal Church, whose ritual contained an explicit prayer for the president of the United States and all others in civil authority. In late June, Bishop Richard Wilmer advised that the prayer ought to be dispensed with, representing as it did a plea for continued occupation. Even the initiation of Presidential Reconstruction did not modify Wilmer's policy, so General Thomas directed that the clergy in Alabama be "forbidden to preach or perform divine service." Wilmer relished martyrdom, but his churches remained closed for some time.[72]

A gut distrust of the Alabama power structure found intermittent expression within the army ranks too. Soldiers scoffed at the loyal pretensions of all ex-Confederates, even the conservatives who now presented themselves as morally entitled to rule. On July 4, US soldiers arrived for festivities in the capital sponsored by Seibels among others. The featured orator, Milton Saffold, somehow avoided reference to secession, war, or slavery. One soldier thought the old-fashioned patriotic rhetoric was ludicrous, given its source. "We felt insulted, outraged by him," a chaplain recalled.[73] This sentiment lingered among the soon-to-be "carpetbaggers," long after the bulk of their comrades returned home.

The army was not to be trifled with, and for the moment solders were politically invulnerable. The northern public would not tolerate resistance to federal authority, not by ex-Rebels. There were no state forces, the white public was largely disarmed, and only the army remained to enforce order. The future trouble-spot of Greenville demonstrated this after one company relocated; two robberies and several outrages occurred in the interregnum of one night.[74] Wartime chaos reportedly freed the entire population of the state prison, though this seems to have contributed only modestly to the prevalence of crime.[75] Given the continuing violence in the mountains, lack of an effective state force was no small matter. One group of Talladega County neighbors petitioned for a few federal soldiers "for the purpose of keeping the Freedmen in subjection, & restraining bad white men from horse stealing etc."[76] But getting along with the occupation force was no mean feat, because thousands of young soldiers remained unwillingly in Alabama, bored and drinking and desperate to go home.

The most unsettling thing the army did, from the point of view of Alabama's power structure, was probably its imperative role in enforcing emancipation. Soldiers' brusque presence and random policing presented the only real deterrence toward racial violence, which was by all evidence rampant and practically unpunished by civil authority. One former legislator, S. S. Houston, wrote of the southwestern river region that no effective law existed for freedmen. Residents half-expected to retain them as property, and murderers strolled about with impunity. "Sometimes all is quiet and the people seem satisfied," the future Republican observed, "and then again . . . news will come that so and so killed a negro[,] served him right *say they etc.*" The responsible classes would not exert themselves to impose order.[77]

Circumstances thus made the relationship with the Freedmen's Bureau critical, and, conveniently, General Wager Swayne sought cooperation. The son of Supreme Court Justice Noah Swayne, his patrician background made him a persuasive advocate. Swayne's situation encouraged conciliation, because his predecessors had already put his agency into substantial debt. Congress provided revenue from confiscated lands for the bureau, but his domain of the southern three-quarters of Alabama was occupied so late that that few such lands existed.[78] Swayne arrived late enough for him to realize that further confiscation was unlikely, if he ever approved it at all. Lacking the wherewithal to establish a network of agents, Swayne hit upon the expedient of appointing civil officials as subordinate bureau agents. Swayne abjured creation of separate freedmen's courts on condition that magistrates accept black testimony and avoid obvious bias.[79]

One Alabama newspaper called the freedmen's courts the worst single thing about the bureau.[80] Therefore Governor Parsons endorsed civil jurisdiction, though Swayne himself concluded his policy did not serve freedpeople well. Still, allowing black testimony—slave or free—contravened prewar laws. Swayne pointed out that everything about the state's situation was extralegal, but that freedom implied access to the court system, and anything less would antagonize the northern electorate. Parsons canvassed several leading lawyers, who mostly agreed on the necessity. Parsons nonetheless demurred on political grounds, forcing Swayne to issue the order, but the governor then urged local officials to accept the terms.[81] When Mobile's wartime mayor refused to accept black testimony, the governor again declined to act, but he backed Swayne once he removed the intransigent official.[82]

A northern reporter concluded that the governor had a reputation for promising much but doing little.[83] Still, Swayne thought him trustworthy, and the two men worked out a de facto collaboration. Swayne sought and often received civil authorization for military arrests. On more sensitive issues, the general would press the governor, who generally did nothing, forcing the military to order redress. Once the political heavy lifting occurred, the governor could then urge realism on the public. The governor was honestly endeavoring to carry out presidential policy, but he feared aggressive action could be "used in a political canvass, as to return to the Convention bad men, who would cast the constitution in an impracticable mold."[84] On slavery, on industrial education, and on black testimony, Parsons was reportedly flexible. A northern reporter heard the governor say that, for everyone's safety, the freedpeople must be brought within the pale of civil law.[85] Carl Schurz claimed that the governor had spoken to him of the possibility of black suffrage, or at least suggested the convention might refer the topic to the legislature.[86]

Parsons carried out the Presidential Reconstruction policy effectively enough, given the volume of logistical obstacles. The office bribery scandal slowed implementation, and the governor's initial proclamation did not help matters by getting dates wrong.[87] Under President Johnson's general orders, all prospective voters and jurors had to take a loyalty oath. Governor Parsons assumed oaths could occur before newly sanctioned local officials, but this violated the military's interpretation of their orders. The army sent agents, but in some places they never arrived. Bibb County did not hold elections and went unrepresented, while Coosa officially tallied one vote. In addition, the prospect of taking an oath before an army officer discouraged participation.[88] Press reports and some subsequent historians suggested some 56,000 white men voted in the elections for the Constitutional Convention, much below the approximately 90,000 that voted in the election of 1860.[89] Even this figure exaggerates the number, being the registration total. The true vote was under 30,000. This would represent a third of the prewar vote, and the imprecise reporting itself suggests official confusion. Fragmentary voting tilted the electorate away from the states' rights Democratic constituency.[90]

This likely was intentional, because Parsons sought to restrain the coming convention. Governor Parsons's orders specified taking loyalty oaths twice, once before the military, then before civil officials.[91] Parsons's close collaborators operated on the assumption that he used the pardon process to build a pro–Johnson administration party or faction. He actually sped his processing so that several of his unpardoned supporters could serve in the convention, though allegedly some delegates did so regardless.[92] The better-known secessionists did not participate, for they would likely draw unpleasant attention and impede Alabama's readmission. The Montgomery *Advertiser* urged against contested elections: voters should simply send their most prominent men as delegates.[93] Circumstances thus weighed against uninhibited discussion of the issues. "We are . . . forced to swear that we will abolish slavery—or have all else we have got confiscated—and [be] ruled by a military force," one delegate observed.[94]

When the convention gathered in early September, the inclinations of the delegates were not readily apparent; the majority reportedly had not been in public life before, with planter or farmer being the leading profession. Nearly half the delegates were over fifty years of age, and one account thought them mostly former Whigs.[95] According to an analysis in the press, some forty-five had voted for John Bell, along with thirty who voted for Stephen Douglas; a mere twenty-four had voted for the winner in Alabama, John Breckinridge. Thus 1860 "conservatives" outnumbered southern-rights Democrats by over three to one. Eleven delegates had served in the secession convention, but only one had voted for the ordinance. Among the delegates as a whole, eighteen of the ninety-nine had voted for immediate secession. The rest voted for cooperation, and "many of them were Union all the time." Five or six reportedly had long been within the federal lines and were considered outright loyal.[96]

All the same, older landmarks were not that all that relevant. In the Tennessee Valley, everyone called themselves Union, but beyond this "a hundred undefined shades of political complexion are visible."[97] All delegates endorsed President Johnson's leadership. All sought readmission of Alabama with minimal preconditions. A *New York Times* correspondent discerned three factions in the convention, the largest perhaps being the north Alabama anti-Confederate contingent, over a third of the delegates. These men sought redress of both regional and class-tinged grievances against south Alabama's planters. The other two groupings represented primarily the black belt, the conservatives who had been Parsons's original sponsors, and those still identified with the Confederate legacy. On economic issues, these latter two groups tended to align, but no consistent majority dominated proceedings. The situation thus enabled Governor Parsons to broker between the factions.[98]

The northern Alabama bloc pursued symbolic Unionist affirmation more than concrete policies to perpetuate their influence. The dozen unconditional Unionists and federal veterans in the convention showed little inclination toward the proscriptive measures of neighboring Tennessee.[99] The constitution limited the formation and recharter of banks, noteworthy in a state currently lacking solvent financial institutions. The delegates also turned back a proposal to eliminate direct election of judges, or to award them lifetime tenure or ten-year terms. One major decision was retention of the "white" basis for representation. The proponents argued that anything else opened the door to congressional enactment of black suffrage, and their position somewhat surprisingly prevailed.[100]

The most heated issues grew out of the repudiation of the state's wartime debt, officially reported as over four million dollars.[101] Most north Alabamians resisted further taxation to benefit black-belt and urban bondholders. South Alabama delegates, on the other hand, objected to anything resembling repudiation. The majority hoped to leave the issue open until the legislature could deal with it, but the northern press response was instructively sharp. A telegram from prominent pardon seekers then in Washington warned of presidential displeasure. A lopsided reversal occurred, sixty to nineteen, though with numerous abstentions. A northern reporter marveled at the prompt turnaround.[102]

Two concerns were of overriding political significance, the first being how to retract disunion officially. Bearing the Confederate debt issue in mind, the northern Alabama bloc disavowed secession variously as unconstitutional, unauthorized, or illegal from the beginning. One early resolution denounced "the leaders of the rebellion, who have caused the earth to be drenched with blood. . . ."[103] The convention settled for declaring secession null and void, and though the northern Republican press commented on the grudging tone, the vote was comfortingly unanimous. The president and the nation expected an equally clear renunciation of slavery, but it proved difficult to prevent *all* of the delegates from articulating honestly held beliefs, ones which resonated with their constituents.

A former congressman, Alexander White, presented a detailed updating of the proslavery argument. Any concessions now would lead to full political equality at the hands of Congress. The Radicals would let freedmen "vote at the polls, sleep under our roof . . . mingle in our social intercourse and marry our daughters." White proposed simple acquiescence to Lincoln's proclamation, subject to adjudication by the Supreme Court. Even the deluded North would see emancipation's folly eventually, and he preferred to keep the door open for eventual reconsideration. If emancipation had to come, "let it be done by others, and not by our own act."[104]

Alex White wanted his speech to be reprinted widely. From Calhoun County, the governor heard that everyone now thought that former slave owners would win compensation, or that they would have forty years as a grace period.[105] The correspondent suggested that White would be elected to Congress, and he eventually was—as a Republican! This unsettling insight into the future Reconstruction biracial coalition has broad application. At this point, none of the varied factions showed any consistent willingness to defend the freedmen. The Union delegates were not yet threatened enough to do so; nor did the future Republicans present distinguish themselves with support for civil rights. Some delegates even surpassed White's proslavery eruption. A former Confederate captain decried emancipation, referencing "the most unheard-of immoralities" being practiced in Haiti. He inspired satire even among sympathetic reporters, and there was a rumor that Andrew Johnson, in dismay, stopped processing pardon applications.[106]

Delegates expunged the more unrestrained motions from the record. Learned lawyers affirmed that the laws of war allowed emancipation, even if the constitutional mandate was less secure. The Supreme Court would uphold emancipation on one of several grounds, and even if they did not, what earthly power could reenslave the freedmen?[107] The vote on the emancipation provision was eighty-nine to three, but the text raised issues. The wording simply declared that the institution of slavery had been destroyed, that henceforth servitude would no longer exist. The legislature was enjoined to protect the freedpeople while guarding against "any evils that may arise from their sudden emancipation."[108] What evils, critics asked, and what did lawmakers propose to do about them? White's uninhibited speech was "worth more than a dozen acts which the Convention passes as measures of expediency," the New York *Tribune* concluded.[109] It raised the issue of what the status of freedpeople would be, once readmission occurred.

Other disquieting racial issues arose. An African American petition requesting the suffrage was tabled—unanimously. One delegate, future Republican Tollifer Towles, was troubled by the migrants moving into the state. He proposed expelling all free blacks who had entered Alabama since 1861. Delegates buried the notion, but it reflected their rising alarm, real or feigned, at the possibility of an insurrection. In terms of press attention, black testimony in court proved the most difficult issue. Antebellum laws banned both slave and free black testimony, but General Swayne had reversed this. Testimony looked like a minimum condition of freedom, unlikely to do any practical harm before all-white courts and juries. But delegates would not write this provision into permanent law, and a complicated compromise adopted the bureau practice temporarily. Freedpeople could testify in cases involving themselves, but not in those in which whites sued or prosecuted each other. This peculiar provision—soon reenacted on a permanent basis—encapsulated the half-hearted liberation that disquieted the northern public.[110]

Governor Parsons looked to President Johnson to press for moderation. No such guidance came, and the president did not even keep in close contact. At one point, Parsons wrote that, if black testimony was absolutely necessary, Johnson should telegraph the warning explicitly, but none arrived.[111] On a more dramatic issue, just before the convention met, Parsons wrote requesting more federal troops to repress disorder.[112] Instead, Johnson suggested organizing civilians as an armed, mounted posse, an alternative the governor had not even raised. Johnson thought it "preferable to give this natural impulse a proper legal shape and control" rather than leave it entirely unrestrained.[113] Confederate soldiers and sympathizers had been commonly disarmed by federal troops, and all militia activity was banned, so this promised a shift in power on the ground.[114] Parsons chose not to resist the suggestion, that being political suicide. Parsons appointed officers for each county, and his instructions sounded restrained, but the militia discourse took on an unsavory familiarity.[115] In Coosa County, a leader requested the removal of federal troops, despite his admission that a terrorist organization, the Black Cavalry, operated there.[116] One of Lee's former officers even referenced a repulse of black troops before Richmond. "I mention this to show the effect of artillery operating against heavy masses," he wrote. He recommended mobilizing fourteen cannon units with thousands of rounds of ammunition.[117]

Whatever the ill omens, the constitution had been quickly revised, and the delegates went home. Governor Parsons reported the successful outcome of the constitutional convention in a long letter to the president. As he pointed out, the freedpeople had been secured in the family relation, granted the right to acquire and hold property, and had been given access to the court system and granted the right to testify with only limited exceptions.[118] The Alabama convention caused the president less embarrassment than elsewhere, and it was more enlightened than the subsequent Alabama legislature. General Swayne found no fault with the governor.[119] President Johnson declared the proceedings "met the highest expectations of *all* who desire the restoration of the Union."[120] Governor Parsons followed this endorsement with a trip to Washington, to speed readmission. He asked General Swayne along, thus mutually reinforcing the reputation of both men. Swayne hoped to add the Tennessee Valley into his Freedmen's Bureau domain, which had been administered from Nashville. Swayne also sought bureaucratic changes to assure a secure source of funding for his agency from captured Confederate property. Parsons endorsed these requests, while Swayne supported favorable federal treatment on state bonds. Both men had collaborated extensively on famine relief, and their cooperation furthered this goal too.[121]

As Provisional Governor Parsons's term drew to a close, the outcome must have seemed curious. Six months previously, he was reviled as a covert traitor. The Union Army reportedly broke up an attempt to bushwhack him in August.[122] He had entered office with the endorsement of conservative leaders, but it dawned on him that their constituency was not that large. Despite their social standing, upper-class draft evasion and covert peace activities left them resented as "croakers" by resolute Confederates; nor were they loved by more emphatic Union men. In response, Parsons's politics had evolved. He followed Johnson's shift toward conciliation of ex-Confederates, lagging rather than leading, seemingly surprised at how liberal it proved to be. To pursue the earlier metaphor, Parsons could hardly play good cop if the bad cop demurred. He disappointed the expectations of those who supported him. Still, by preventing the ills that the elite had feared, and in securing the restoration of Alabama, he rendered himself the most popular political figure in the state.

Suggestive evidence bears on his motivation. In early November, his wife, Jane, wrote their daughter to discourage a romantic relationship. She was too young, and her choice of beau no longer seemed fitting. Her father would be sent to the Senate in Washington, and he would probably occupy high office for the rest of his life. Mrs. Parsons marveled at the change in his standing: "being a northern man can no longer be used against him, as has been done for years by *Southern Chivalry* the same are now loudest in his praises; and proclaim him good and great." Therefore, Jane Parsons warned the daughter to take her time, and to "be prepared to take her place among the very first in this country or any other."[123] Parsons illustrated a problem that would bedevil the Unionists, and after them, the Republicans. Elite opinion and the Democratic press could turn social approval on like a spigot, and white southerners found it nearly irresistible.

Back home, Parsons's late conservative allies had less to be pleased about. Joseph Bradley wrote Andrew Johnson three times on September 8 alone, on the mistaken presumption that the president still cared what he thought. To Bradley, "the wholesale appointments of State officers made by my friend Govr. Parsons" had not worked well, and Union men fared poorly at the polls.[124] Furthermore, Parsons had recommended pardons for men that ought to have been kept in the cold until Alabama was rehabilitated.[125] These trends looked bleak to those who saw themselves as Union men, however defined. Johnson's evident approbation convinced white Alabamians that their probationary period was over. The militia talk encouraged a martial assertiveness that boded ill for Union veterans and others in armed resistance to the Confederacy. The Freedmen's Bureau at least promised the ex-slaves some level of ongoing oversight. But what protected the hated unconditional Unionists once the army left?

Then there was the resumption of the circuit courts, which occurred regularly each fall. Outside of the isolated mountains, ex-Confederates were the majority, which meant that the unconditional Union element provided the victims.[126] Appomattox returned dedicated Confederates home, which changed the political composition of much of northern Alabama. With Parsons's reappointments, former Confederate officials were in a position to seek indictments for wartime thefts and violence by Union men, and sometimes even by soldiers in arms. In Marshall County, a reported forty of seventy-one grand jury indictments were reportedly of discharged Union soldiers or scouts.[127] In Lawrence County, one former Federal captain complained that only Union men had been indicted. "If this is justice loyal men will have to leave the country," he wrote.[128]

This redoubled the shift in election results. Once Andrew Johnson declared his approbation of Alabama's constitution, he sanctioned elections for the legislature and Congress. In the mid-war statewide elections, opponents of the Davis administration had swept the state. And in the recent elections to the constitutional convention, circumstances biased the result away from the hard-line Democratic position. For a time, Milton Saffold recalled, Union men thought the Rebels' power was "entirely broken and gone."[129] At the convention, they acted with the confidence that they would exercise political influence for some time. Beyond the white basis for representation, they did little to assure even temporary control. The notion of ex-Confederate disfranchisement does not appear to have been raised. Everyone seemingly agreed that Governor Parsons's goal of rapid restoration of Alabama, the removal of Union troops, and the remobilization of the militia were fine ideas.

Governor Parsons therefore concluded that, with the state restored to civil law, all citizens could vote, oath or no oath, pardoned or not.[130] At the top of the ticket, the effect was not dramatic. Perhaps for prudential reasons, none of the three candidates for governor was a strong secessionist. One, W. R. Smith of Tuscaloosa, was among the most open peace men in the Confederate Congress; he stormed out of Richmond after being accused on the floor of treason. The second candidate was M. J. Bulger, an opponent of secession who went into the Confederate Army but had been expected to be the peace movement's candidate in 1865. Both men had strong credentials as antiwar conservatives. They were easily beaten by the third candidate, Robert M. Patton of the Tennessee Valley's Lauderdale County, who had less of a Unionist profile. He ran strongly in the black belt and won by a substantial plurality, receiving 23,042 votes, trailed by 16,713 for Bulger, and Smith with 9,219.[131]

Many more voted than in the previous constitutional election, by about half, and ex-Confederates won sweeping victories. "Politically our State had gone wild," Bradley wailed, noting that three-quarters of the legislature were former Confederate soldiers.[132] In Huntsville's vicinity, the Unionist David C. Humphreys was beaten for the legislature, losing badly in the plantation precincts.[133] Each of the six congressional races had Union candidates running. Five of them lost. The sixth, future Republican Burrell T. Pope, won narrowly. The winners had generally been former Whigs who opposed secession, but only Pope could take the "iron clad" oath, and several victors ran on their ineligibility as a positive credential. It worked in Alabama, but the Republican majority refused to seat any of the southern congressmen, on the ground that the ex-Confederate states had not yet been reconstructed.[134]

After the November 1865 elections, Union men of all stripes recalibrated their voting strength downward. Several would testify before Congress that they had between ten and fifteen thousand of what they termed genuine Unionist voters, a fifth or less of the white electorate. They conceded they could not even poll that many, so absent outside intervention they were a hopeless minority. As W. H. Smith later recalled, only in a "very few localities" had a majority been loyal during the war.[135] The speed of restoration alarmed him, and Smith told the governor it was high time to "make war on these rebels. . . ."[136] The status quo, with federal troops near at hand, looked better than immediate control by well-armed enemies. Delay might let wartime animosities cool. Though slow to break with Andrew Johnson, dissidents looked toward outside assistance, especially Republicans in Congress, to bolster their waning political influence.

Wartime "tories" and strong Unionists were the most alarmed, but more temperate wartime conservatives felt little better, though their concern was more political marginalization than outright fear. After all, Alabama had "never had a Whig governor, a Whig Senator in Congress or a Whig legislature . . . until all party distinctions were whelmed in the Confederacy."[137] From the conservatives' point of view, events had proven them right about extremism, secession, and the war's likely outcome. States' rights ideologues had killed slavery and ruined the South, and conservatives had suffered grievous loss in a conflict they felt little responsibility in bringing on. But Cassandras do not necessarily fare well before the voters. Now, the electorate rejected those who had been demonstrated correct all along. The masses preferred Confederate war heroes, albeit reluctant ones. For conservatives with political aspirations, this was too much to be borne. They too looked for Washington to provide consequences that would sober the public, though they were reluctant to court northern intervention openly.

Conservatives had little to offer Republicans in Congress. Their complicated records as unenthusiastic Confederates hardly entitled them to northern sympathy. Pronounced Union men deserved more, but their limited numbers and modest socioeconomic standing made them less of a priority. Union men of all stripes could benefit from the perception that ex-Confederate rule menaced them and the freed slaves too. So Joseph Bradley, utterly antagonized, embraced civil rights. In September, he lobbied to retain black troops locally. He also sought to "elect men to our legislature, who will vote for the amendment to the Constitution forever abolishing slavery in the United States, and who will vote for a law giving a Negro equal legal rights with the whites, who will not vote for any Law to oppress the Freedmen."[138] The following month he endorsed basic constitutional rights, to none other than Andrew Johnson. Though he thought freedmen were not yet suited to the ballot, he also indicated their behavior and his own democratic principles might change his mind.[139] Bradley misread the president, but such pleas would soon be directed to Congress with more effect.

After Congress turned away the southern claimants, more pronounced Union men followed this path. From Washington, as a lobbyist, D. C. Humphreys wrote that it was time to act on true Jacksonian principles: "I think we will not have a settled community till laws are made in accordance with the spirit of freedom." The freedpeople were law-abiding, and whites would benefit if they prospered as free agriculturalists. Humphreys even suggested it would disarm northern criticism to accept freedmen into the militia![140] Civil rights advocacy became the vehicle for preventing premature readmission on the terms of the ex-Confederates. This fell far short of demanding black suffrage, but de facto alliance with congressional Republicans would propel dissidents in that direction, faster than most would have dreamed possible. Here was the effective genesis of the Reconstruction alliance in Alabama: Unionist leaders claimed the political experience and moral legitimacy to speak for the freedmen to Congress.

In January 1866, a cohort of unconditional Unionists arrived in Washington. In congressional testimony, they forthrightly linked their imperiled situation to that of the freedpeople. William H. Smith testified, "They still persecute Union men and negroes. They whip the negroes, shoot them, hang them, kill them. . . ." D. C. Humphreys testified that landowners were refusing to rent land to blacks around Huntsville, but the stationing of black troops there corrected problems. General Spencer of the First Alabama regiment, as a northerner, emphasized the freedmen's needs more, but he too connected their fate with that of his Union veterans. Local testimony reinforced the sense that things had gone seriously amiss in southern race relations. These pleas were difficult for Congress and the northern public to ignore.[141]

This constituted the Achilles heel of President Johnson's policy. Johnson had undermined his late Unionist and conservative allies by his appeal to the former secessionist, Democratic base. In response, Governor Parsons did as bidden, but nothing in Presidential Reconstruction guaranteed the safety of the ex-Unionist element. Presidential support tempted ex-Confederates to believe that their probation would be short, and that Congress's wishes could be safely overlooked. They assumed that the outright alarm of the unconditional Unionist minority could be disregarded with impunity. But as the Unionist leaders seized upon the grievances of the ex-slaves, they made the freedpeople politically salient in a way they could not yet do for themselves.[142]

It took some months of persuasion for the broader unconditional Unionist following to seek alliance with the Congressional Republicans. By 1866, though, these "Radical" leaders increasingly spoke for alarmed loyalists in the mountain and upper piedmont regions. In the highland enclaves, once beyond effective Confederate control, Unionism went from dominant opinion to imperiled minority overnight. Everyone seemingly had wartime scores to settle, at least to the extent of driving opposition away. Meanwhile, a truly doleful economic situation developed, disastrous food crop failures in 1865 and 1866, which afflicted the huge numbers of widows and their children in the hills. During the war, Alabama's government had distributed provisions in bulk to the families of Confederate soldiers, while intentionally not feeding the families of deserters and those who fled. These existing networks became the basis for food distribution when peace returned. Unionists and draft evaders generally lived in the most isolated areas, where it was difficult to send relief, and several counties were too financially strapped to transport supplies. Furthermore, General Swayne preferred to work through state commissioner Cruikshank, as did most of the northern benevolent societies. These institutional realities underscored the relevance of politics to the relief process, when one's partisan loyalties could determine who had food.[143]

Between control of civil courts and law enforcement, the looming withdrawal of federal troops, and the politicized nature of food distribution, open Unionists moved toward armed resistance. Guerilla conflict escalated with their ex-Confederate neighbors. The unconditional Unionist element was not vast in extent, comprising a dominant majority in perhaps two counties, Winston and Randolph. But throughout northern Alabama's mountains and highland plateaus, they were sizable enough to pose a problem for the Presidential Reconstruction government, both in terms of public order in Alabama and in Congress.

Governor Patton and his state establishment minimized the political dimension of these disorders, even to Swayne and his bureau. Political and class bias obscures much beyond the fact of conflict. Still, a host of confrontations occurred in 1866. In rural Tuscaloosa County, Union

Leaguers were meeting in a school and church, and someone torched the building. Perpetrators then issued death threats against both Unionists and the black witnesses to the arson. One official thought the Union men would fight back.[144] Such instances mostly reached the public in the form of disputed trials and jailhouse raids.[145] In Fayette County, a man who shot a deserter in wartime was threatened and eventually jailed by a mob; he was charged with murder, but he was then released by a another mob. Similar obscure disturbances were alleged over prosecution of ex-Confederates in Walker County.[146] From Bibb and Shelby counties, complaints came that "Tory & deserter bands" were killing and driving out citizens, forcing them to sacrifice property and move into the more settled regions.[147] The backstory, according to a bureau officer, was that a Union man's sons avenged his death when one of the perpetrators returned home. The sons were arrested for murder, but some two hundred sympathizers liberated them from jail in Columbiana.[148]

Political motivations are difficult to untangle from simple brigandage. From Monroe and Baldwin counties came reports that former Union veterans had joined with "half-breeds" as livestock thieves.[149] In Randolph County, there were complaints of armed bands driving out elite ex-Confederates. Unionists there so dominated local government that punishment proved impossible. In Winston County, the wartime mountain stronghold, Unionists prevented civil law from functioning. When Circuit Judge W. B. Wood prepared to hold court late in 1866, he received multiple death threats, likely as a representative of the reconstituted "Rebel" state government. The judge stayed away.[150]

Conflict had a random element, because political agility sometimes disarmed opposition.[151] On the other hand, the borderlands of Blount and St. Clair counties bled profusely. State officials preferred to emphasize simple lawlessness, but the partisan dimension seems overt.[152] It appears that, as the federal occupation began, in St. Clair County a Unionist named Baggett volunteered to help disarm opponents. In mid-1866, he and one of the Confederate sympathizers, named Kendrick, had some roadside confrontation. A group attacked Kendrick's home, in the course of which a Union man was killed. A reported forty to one hundred Unionists burned the home and then turned to beatings and burning gin houses—presumably a class marker—in the vicinity of Ashville. One reportedly threatened that, if resisted, "they would have 200 Negroes in arms in two hours to destroy & ruin the county."[153] The truth is obscure, but one Unionist politician thought that some ex-Confederates *were* in danger if they returned. Marcus Cruikshank investigated and concluded that two parties struggled for supremacy, and that everything grew out of wartime strife.[154]

Conflict pushed some Unionists toward the freedpeople as allies in arms. Blount officials complained that, in the border area, Unionists "forewarned the Tax Collector, not to shew himself in that region, and have boldly avowed that they would pay no tax to the 'rebel state,' as they call the State of Alabama."[155] The officials requested federal troops to enforce the law, strong indication of the severity of the situation. In 1867, similar complaints recurred in neighboring St. Clair County. The tax collector advertised delinquent lands for sale, but the dissidents were threatening to bushwhack anyone who bid on the land. They allegedly hired a freedman, Brown Abe, to assassinate the collector. The hotbed of resistance, Branchfield Precinct, was just 7 percent black, which made it the whitest and presumably poorest area in St. Clair County. According to a furtive official, the resisters were "mostly the persons who gave the country so much trouble in time of the war you know who I mean."[156]

Wartime vendettas, in isolated frontier-like conditions, encouraged violence, and some destitute highland farmers resisted paying taxes. Fear of retaliation, of change, was pronounced among former "tories," Union veterans, and others known for unpopular wartime choices. For example, William Looney of Winston County, who had recruited hundreds of federal volunteers, faced indictments for murder in three counties and was hiding in the mountains once again.[157] By the spring of 1867, one army official claimed that he was overwhelmed by the violence. An ex-Confederate colonel had reportedly killed six Union men for their politics, and they were fed up. "The Union men are determined to form a band for self protection, and if they fail to reach the guilty party they will hang his nearest relative," the approving federal officer reported.[158]

The presence of the military looked like the only protection. As things stood, the army effectively barred all prosecutions against Union veterans or sympathizers for acts committed under orders and, in practice, for nearly everything they had done.[159] The Unionists' fate was unclear once their ex-opponents dominated a restored militia and the courts. Governor Patton attempted to reduce the anxiety on both sides by pardoning all wartime crimes save murder and rape, but this still left ample room for criminal prosecutions and civil suits. Small wonder that the unconditional Unionists opened the door to congressional intervention, even if the terms included black suffrage.

4

The Premature New South of Governor Robert Patton

I have confidence in the future prosperity of Alabama.

—Robert Patton, May 1867

In most ways, Alabama's development during this era unfolded like that of other southern states. During Presidential Reconstruction, however, the state's political leadership took a distinctive path. Provisional Governor Parsons established this pattern of conciliation, and he succeeded politically enough to win unanimous selection to the US Senate. His elected successor, Robert Miller Patton, pursued this policy even more urgently, becoming one of the few Presidential Reconstruction governors to back implementing black suffrage. Patton's priority was righting the state's finances to facilitate economic development. This meant seeking the support of northern elites, especially investors and congressional leaders, Republican though they might be. For liberated African Americans, the benefits were indistinct, but Patton's leadership little resembled the executive intransigence unfolding elsewhere.[1]

Patton's overriding problem was the southern states' anomalous status, having governments that were recognized by the president but barred from Congress. Until full readmission, Alabama's economic recovery could only be hobbled. The solution was to persuade Congress that the state meant to do justice to the freedmen. Quasi-Senator Parsons, seeking admission to Congress, endorsed something approaching equality before the law, short of suffrage. The freedmen "should receive the same protection which our laws secure to our non-voting population," that is, a civil status resembling that of white women and children, rather than suffering under specifically racial legislation. Parsons's stand, which won General Swayne's euphoric endorsement, bolstered his successor's moderate inclinations.[2] Governor Patton assumed office under circumstances that highlighted his conditional status. He remained in limbo until Alabama's provisionally recognized state legislature ratified the Thirteenth Amendment, abolishing slavery. This experience, and his frequent trips to Washington and New York City, underscored the importance of external constituencies.[3]

Robert M. Patton's long decades in commerce and political life pointed him in a moderate direction. Born in Virginia in 1809, the son of a successful Irish Protestant immigrant, he trained as a merchant in his father's dry goods establishment in Huntsville. His limited formal education may have contributed to his distaste for constitutional abstractions. Also, his father and then his brother were partners in one of the first successful textile mills in the South, giving Patton unusual exposure to industrial pursuits. Removing to Florence, he was elected in his mid-twenties to the legislature as a Whig, serving there for decades despite local Democratic majorities. He maintained a reputation for competence and official probity. He prospered nonetheless by the onset of the Civil War, as a retired merchant worth over $250,000. He was rich by any standard, owning a plantation with 118 slaves, though he never much emphasized paternalist rhetoric.[4] Patton pursued diverse financial interests, taking the lead in the construction of the Memphis & Charleston Railroad project through the Tennessee Valley, an interest in railroad development that would mark his executive leadership.[5]

During the mid-1850s, he shifted from the disintegrating Whigs toward the Douglas Democrats, serving as a delegate to the ill-fated Charleston convention, hoping to prevent a split in the party. Living on Alabama's northwestern border, Patton was thus a proslavery "conservative" seeking sectional compromise. In the secession crisis, he followed a common pattern of opposing disunion irresolutely after Lincoln's election, then defecting, thus infuriating more decided Unionists. Early in the war, he served as a civilian agent for the Confederate cotton loan, and he sacrificed two sons to the cause. But when the Union troops arrived, he resigned his position as president of the Senate. He returned home and farmed with the aid of a single "faithful negro," periodically interrupted by the sacking of his estate.[6] After his return, Patton said, he took no active part in the war. He thus deftly disengaged from the failing Confederacy without antagonizing its adherents. He then served as delegate to the 1865 Constitutional Convention, and he was prominent in the nebulous north Alabama bloc lumped together as Unionists. He won election as governor precisely because his two opponents had stronger credentials as peace men, which made Patton more acceptable to the ex-secessionists reentering the electorate that November.

Patton's winning political profile was as a realist: he later said he suspected the Confederacy was doomed, but went with his state anyway and took no role in wartime Reconstruction efforts. Patton's personal wealth and its near-total loss determined his perspective, as did his own self-confident sense that he knew what Alabama needed.[7] Patton believed freed slaves were unlikely to work well as plantation hands, and no one would call him racially enlightened. Announcing his bid for governor, he intoned: "This is a white man's government, and we must keep this a white man's State." He once slipped "free niggers" into a veto message, at least as published.[8] Patton mustered far more compassion for lower-class whites, being known for his Sunday school efforts among millworkers.[9] His government facilitated the distribution of large quantities of food across stricken northern Alabama.

Patton saw economic diversification as more important than racial legislation designed to reconstitute plantation agriculture. In Patton's words, "we could no longer depend upon the cultivation of cotton in the South. . . . [T]he people of the State must now turn their attention to another channel of industry—manufacturing."[10] Cotton production would certainly be less profitable than previously, and using white labor was an untried experiment. In a widely noticed piece in *DeBow's Review*, Patton anticipated the New South creed. During slavery, manufacturing never got the attention it deserved, but necessity now dictated a diversity of pursuits. "In the streets of our beautiful capital, you will not find a single carriage, barouche or buggy that is not of foreign build," he complained. Importing northern goods enriched "New England nabobs," who strove to tax the cotton planter and his workers, and thus degrade them to subservient status.[11] In thus stoking southern resentments, though, Patton contradicted the interregional collaboration he sought to make his priorities a reality.

Textile production occupied pride of place in his vision. As governor, Patton spoke repeatedly at newly constructed cotton factories, even outside the state. He once spoke in the morning at one mill, then resumed his speech in the afternoon at a nearby one.[12] Southern redemption comprised a central theme in his orations. "We will yet become prosperous, independent and rich," he pledged, but only by curtailing importation of northern goods and luxuries.[13] These statements implied welcoming outside resources, entrepreneurs, and skilled workers, even from overseas.

Patton extolled these measures as the means by which Alabama could rise from the ashes. The irony of seeking northern investment did not escape listeners. As one admirer enthused, "We shall not as 'Bob Toombs' once said, call the roll of our slaves at the base of the Bunker Hill Monument, but we will supply Boston and even Lowell with cotton goods."[14] Patton himself fostered no such illusions but looked toward northern cooperation to build a different future.

Factories required transportation, and Patton eagerly devoted himself to railroad projects and other forms of infrastructure improvement. Alabama's railroad network was badly damaged by the war and incomplete. No direct route existed from Montgomery to Selma; nor could one get to Huntsville without crossing into neighboring states. More crucially, the coal and iron region around what would become Birmingham had scarcely been penetrated, even though geologists had long since demonstrated its economic promise. For heavy industry to develop, the mountain region needed railroads, but where was the capital to come from? Southerners had no money, banks were mostly insolvent, and northerners were not pursuing investment in a ruined region. As a longtime Whig, Patton saw government aid as the answer. Loan guarantees and subsidies could channel private capital toward Alabama. But government promotion required solvency, and Alabama had nothing in its treasury and had not paid bondholders since the war began. The state stood on the brink of default. With his financial background, Patton felt himself competent to address the crisis.

His priorities were not universally shared. As elsewhere in the South, defeat, loss, and fear encouraged many whites to focus on the race issue. Patton faced a legislature with a resurgent presence of states' rights Democrats, composed largely of ex-Confederate soldiers.[15] Lawmakers determined to reverse the concessions previously made, both for practical and emotional reasons, the enforced discretion on display in the Constitutional Convention having grown tedious. Late in 1865, the legislature considered a host of "Black Code"–style provisions, explicitly racially discriminatory, prodding freedpeople to sign labor contracts for the new year. One proposed vagrancy law was stringent enough, but hard-liners amended it to make the penalty ten days labor for whites and six months for freedpeople. Another provision declared African Americans without work for ten days at a time vagrants, without even mentioning white offenders. In the course of one day, the Senate approved bills outlawing non-medicinal sale of alcohol to freedpeople, and outlawing all sale or use of pistols. Those seeking discretion were taunted as "dirt-eaters" by their colleagues. As one intransigent observed, "Heaven itself had made a [racial] distinction and the Federal bayonet and Federal authority could not break down that distinction."[16]

Alarm in the black belt encouraged these measures. For months, rumors circulated among freedpeople of "forty acres and a mule." As a justice of the peace wrote, "It seems to be a general opinion with them that there will be a division of lands and other property about Christmas."[17] It is difficult to distinguish between loose talk by freedmen, actual plotting, and nervous overreaction. Still, freedmen were disillusioned by the results of their first year's labor and troubled by the ferocious laws. Gang labor, overseers, and the like bore an uncomfortable resemblance to slavery, and some fantasized that outside deliverance might be at hand. In the fall of 1865, planters tried to sign hands to early contracts with no success, laborers preferring to see their year's pay first. This alarmed planters who feared insurrection, and Freedmen's Bureau officials believed trouble possible. General Swayne reported that confiscation talk was well-nigh universal among freedpeople, and he exerted himself to dispel the rumors.[18]

Planter anxiety rose as the new year approached. A public meeting at Notasulga warned of an uprising, perhaps soon.[19] The locals sought guns and ammunition from Governor Patton, and the press reported the wild rumor that seventeen families there had been killed. The Mobile *Advertiser and Register* discounted the talk, but added "it is at least prudent for our people to be prepared and on their guard."[20] Federal veterans caused particular anxiety, and local whites sought authority to disarm them. More alarming still were the actual USCI troops, perhaps half the federal force, still stationed in the Tennessee Valley and elsewhere.[21] In December, an obscure armed confrontation occurred in Choctaw County, after reports of night-riding, whippings, and arson. Army officers sent a USCI detachment to Bladon Springs, to prove a point. The force soon departed, but they left Lieutenant W. B. Cheatham behind to tend to his sick wife, along with two of his men. Afterwards, a public meeting warned those who had provided medicine or fraternized with the soldiers to leave town. Someone shot into the Cheathams' tent, and threats were made. Their army comrades returned in force, reportedly killing a white man who was apparently one of the night-riders. This perplexing episode entered into the political discourse of white Alabama as an alarming atrocity—by black troops.[22]

Thus Governor Patton confronted both rising popular anxiety and legislative intransigence. By the time he returned to Montgomery, Black Code provisions were passing readily. But Patton's consultations with congressmen and northern financiers persuaded him that confrontation was folly, with Alabama's representatives in limbo and the refinancing of its debt under negotiation. The electorate demanded repressive measures, but Patton feared the consequences. In resisting the popular will, Patton turned to a double-edged resource, the state's military command and specifically the Freedmen's Bureau. Patton found that Assistant Commissioner Swayne backed his policies, and the two men moved toward each other as functional allies.

John Wager Swayne took his duties on behalf of the freedmen seriously, but he was no bomb-thrower. The Yale-educated son of a Republican Supreme Court justice, he was well connected, and he used his legal training and polish to advantage. His background perhaps made him disdainful of financial chicanery and especially Judge Busteed's court. General Swayne's religious views endeared him to O. O. Howard, the head of the Freedmen's Bureau, and his missing limb enhanced his moral authority. Swayne inclined toward behind-the-scenes lobbying, which meant using his influence in Washington on behalf of Alabama's officials. It also meant picking his fights and distancing himself from the unconditional Unionist element. Also, upon arrival in Alabama, Swayne inclined toward a "tough love" approach toward the freedpeople, which credentialed him with the landholding elite and somewhat explains his good press. The ultimate question is whether the general was manipulating the Alabama power structure more than it was using him. His lobbying, to the extent successful, increased the likelihood that federal oversight of Alabama's racial policies would soon cease. Still, Swayne never doubted his proper course. In the fall of 1865, he encouraged the tactical moderation of the constitutional delegates. As Swayne wrote, "During the meeting of the Convention, a few of the members kept aloof, but between the greater number and myself entire cordiality existed, and we seemed to be working harmoniously together for the common good."[23] Thus by the time Governor Patton appeared on the scene, Swayne's record as a legislative lobbyist was extensive.

The two had met before the war, and Swayne discerned "a practical, conscientious, economical old merchant, who, I thought, would neither deceive nor be deceived."[24] Swayne bolstered Patton's moderate inclinations, and the two men could play off one another before lawmakers.

Summoned to a private meeting with Governor Patton and legislative leaders, Swayne decried a proposal to extend prewar slave-code provisions to the freedmen. The general "simply opened the Statute book and pointed out provisions which required all free negroes to leave the state, and others of the same or worse tenor."[25] He asserted his legal authority and intent to void discriminatory legislation. Swayne thus posed the practical issue of whether lawmakers wanted their racial legislation overruled by military edict. This meant a black eye before the national public, something Governor Patton preferred to avoid given the possibility of congressional intervention.

Anticipation of a Christmastime black insurrection drove the legislation. Once New Year came with no disturbance at all, the sense of public relief made the fears look foolish. As Patton observed, the freedmen were everywhere "making contracts for the present year upon terms that are entirely satisfactory to their employers," and they apparently worked well.[26] Furthermore, Patton had ventured to Nashville to secure a promise from General Thomas to arm the prospective state militia with six thousand surplus federal guns. These pledges reassured nervous whites and promised the quick withdrawal of army troops.[27] In this context, some of the Black Code legislation looked dubious, even to most whites. Following Swayne's suggestion, Governor Patton opposed the act "to extend the criminal laws of this State applicable to free persons of color, to freedmen, free negroes, and mulattoes." One proposed section punished all free Negroes who preached without five slaveholders present, while another criminalized black preaching before slaves—both invalid on their face with slavery abolished. Another provision barred entry into the state on pain of two years' imprisonment. The mere recital of these provisions, Patton thought, demonstrated the danger and injustice of enforcing them.[28]

Governor Patton seized the moment to sweep away the most destructive proposals. He vetoed vagrancy laws and other discriminatory legislation, including one that he apparently signed but now explained away as a clerical error.[29] In his January 1866 message he articulated his thinking. The freedmen were behaving so well that the common law of contracts sufficed. No good could result from having "one Code of laws for the whites, and another for the blacks, in their new relations, so far as concern the rights of persons and property."[30] These were strong words in an Alabama context, but efforts to override his vetoes failed. It appears Patton drew upon Jacksonian strictures against legislative favoritism toward planters, and northern Alabama sustained his position. A change in tone was evident statewide. The Montgomery *Advertiser* initially supported discriminatory laws, but the editors backtracked: "We trust there is too much good sense in the Legislature, to occupy much time discussing these measures, or any difference gro[w]ing out of them between the members and the Governor." Patton's mail was also favorable. A Tuscaloosa lawyer wrote assuring him of widespread support, agreeing that discriminatory laws were absurd as Alabama was situated.[31]

Patton's intervention can be viewed as an unusual instance of pragmatic leadership on racial issues. Though numerous statutes targeted freedmen in practice, the state mostly avoided the explicitly discriminatory laws that inflamed northerners, undermined President Johnson, and eventually yielded the Fourteenth Amendment. General Swayne welcomed this ambiguous outcome, and thereafter he and Patton collaborated closely. Patton agreed with Swayne's suggestion that he announce a blanket pardon for all acts save murder or rape that occurred before war's end. Swayne enthused that with Patton's help he had liberated hundreds of jailed freedmen, with few negative consequences. Patton's actions won him a reputation among attentive northerners as a sensible fellow.[32]

Bolstered by this outcome, Governor Patton pivoted to the issue he cared most about, the economic welfare of the state. With no funds in hand, Patton faced the threat of widespread starvation. During the last months of the Confederacy, state authorities provided provisions for well over a fourth of the white population.[33] After Wilson's raid, thousands of destitute people needed food. Most were white widows and children in northern Alabama, but liberated slaves added to their numbers. One of the Freedmen's Bureau's legal responsibilities was provision of relief to white refugees. The congressional intent was to feed Unionists, but Swayne interpreted this provision widely, distributing supplies through local officials who were generally former Confederates. In 1865, 1866, and 1867, vast quantities of government and private relief supplies flowed through the bureau's hands into the state. In January 1866, for example, Swayne provided rations to feed twenty thousand people daily. O. O. Howard worried about the northern political impact, and Swayne and Patton actually collaborated on avoiding publicity.[34] With legislative approval, Patton appointed former peace-faction congressman Marcus Cruikshank to cooperate with the bureau and private efforts. Cruikshank agreed to a nondiscriminatory basis, though some local officials disregarded that provision. For example, early in 1867, white recipients predominated nearly ten-to-one in Butler County.[35] Whites received a disproportionate share of the relief supplies, two-thirds or better, but freedpeople got some of the food nearly everywhere, reinforcing the precedent for public aid. From Governor Patton's perspective, the political results were favorable. The aid endeared him to the recipients, and it favorably portrayed his positive relations with the bureau.[36]

The governor acted upon the financial woes of his white constituency. During the war, the federal government enacted a direct tax on Alabama and other states, and the sum remained unpaid and accruing penalties at war's end. Despite the state's financial straits, Patton assumed responsibility rather than oblige the destitute multitudes to pay up.[37] Patton assisted his popular constituency in other ways, observing, "The industrial and business interests of the people are so much deranged that I think some legislation is necessary in relation to the collection of debts."[38] He promoted legislation to stay enforcement of private recovery efforts, or at least spread them out over time. For a former Whig, devoted to the sanctity of debts, this represented a major departure. It promised to benefit farmers in ruined areas, at the expense of creditors—and laborers. The legislature enacted relief measures, though the Alabama Supreme Court quickly found them unconstitutional.[39] Even so, Patton at least discouraged debt collection, and Military Reconstruction would later allow proponents to revisit the issue.

All the governor's initiatives depended on state credit, which required agility on complex, technical issues. Legislators trusted him on such matters, one banker wrote, and state finance was potentially a matter of life and death. One telegram implored, "Will you authorize us to sell state bonds for the starving poor in Marshall Blount & DeKalb & what amount."[40] The legislature enacted nearly all the fiscal measures he asked for, but the devastated state could not raise funds directly. As Patton reported, "no State taxes were collected, since the close of the war, until the last calendar quarter of 1866." Leading banks had little money to lend, so no alternative existed to outside borrowing.[41] Even so, Alabama enjoyed better prospects than other southern states. Prewar Alabama had enjoyed strong credit, and unlike neighboring Mississippi, the state had never defaulted. The repudiation of the Confederate debt insisted on by President Johnson paradoxically eased existing obligations. But the interest on bonds had long gone unpaid, and the total now amounted to over four million dollars, owed mostly to northern and British bondholders, plus another two plus million owed to its own borrowed school and university endowments. External creditors were willing to extend the loan on reasonable terms rather than risk repudiation.[42] All the state needed to do was to cover the semi-annual interest payments. For the moment, the demand for new Alabama securities was nil, so Patton borrowed yet more money from northern financiers, to tide the state over. Political instability, however, threatened everything. Patton needed to prevent the conflict between President Johnson and Congress from collapsing creditor confidence.

Restoring the state's finances meant resuming the normal functions of Alabama's government, and as a former Whig, Patton pursued these goals with zeal. Securing loans allowed the state partly to reopen the existing public school system, though it remained for whites only. Patton recommended measures to equalize state funding in favor of poorer districts, and he was solicitous of the destroyed university. Passing a rebuilding loan from the legislature was easy, but securing actual funds was another matter. It took years, but the university at Tuscaloosa reopened in 1869. Patton also provided funding for the nearly bankrupt state asylum, still functioning under the well-regarded leadership of Dr. Peter Bryce. Another gubernatorial initiative looks perhaps less attractive, growth of the state's penitentiary through expanding the practice of prison labor. The prison population of fifty-one was now mostly composed of freedmen, and Patton expected more prisoners once the courts recovered, so he hoped to make incarceration profitable. Among other things, he proposed the convict lease, so that "the labor of convicts may be so directed as to aid in developing the mineral and other resources of the State."[43] Appalling measures, perhaps, but the priority on economic development was clear. Businessmen approved.

Patton's financial gyrations underscored his efforts to portray Alabama as a plausible place to invest. Several thousand northerners had moved to the state, many of them buying plantation lands.[44] These purchasers Patton encouraged, despite the growing popular resentment of the northern presence. He envisioned a white working class, thinking freedmen unsuited to industrial pursuits. He therefore welcomed immigrants: "We have ample field for the employment of all industrious classes, who may be desirous of identifying themselves with our interest and destiny. Let them come. . . ."[45]

Railroad promotion figured centrally. The war damaged existing railroads, and insolvent half-completed projects littered the state. In the mid-1850s, several had received large federal land grants on condition of completion within ten years, but time was up and they stood to lose them. Patton fended off Radical Republican initiatives to distribute the forfeited land as homesteads to freedmen and poorer whites. At the state level, several railroads owed large prewar loans which they were unable to pay back. Patton deferred repayment of the loans, with one crucial exception. He used the threat of bankruptcy to force consolidation of the two lines he thought particularly crucial to Alabama's economic development.

All these varied measures displayed Patton's preferred emphasis on economic issues. His conciliatory approach toward national demands delivered benefits to his white constituents, at least. They appreciated Patton's success, and they valued his prying supplies from northerners, but they did not care to see the sectional moderation his approach relied upon. Finance was not the issue that engaged the electorate. In April 1866, a Freedmen's Bureau agent in Talladega highlighted the emotional concerns that did. At the close of the school year, "the Teacher's wife, while singing 'The Conquered Flag' displayed to the assembly a Confederate Flag which was received with vociferous cheers and numerous rounds of hip, hip, hurrahs, etc."[46] At Huntsville, a northern benevolent society carefully requested permission to open a freedpeople's school. The governor duly forwarded the request, but future congressman W. W. Garth feared "pandemonium" after a black influx. "You can say to your Philadelphia correspondents that we deny their right to inflict upon us such a curse, and that we are to a man most decidedly opposed to their project, at least we are opposed most decidedly to its location here," he wrote.[47]

Agricultural turmoil encouraged confrontation. The year 1866 would be one of the worst for crops in Alabama's history, partly because of unusual flooding and residual wartime damage, but largely because labor relationships remained unsettled. Landowners blamed the freedpeople, and the wretched crop combined with rising political enthusiasm to encourage mayhem. In the east-central part of the state, the terrorist Black Cavalry expanded, targeting the African Methodist Episcopal Church and other newly arrived black denominations.[48] In Tuscaloosa, as soon as the garrison left town in April, the upper-class "Chivalry" went on a rampage, mobbing an agent for the Mobile *Nationalist,* a freedmen's newspaper. At a concert at a freedmen's school, the "demonstrations there ridiculed the 'Freedmen's Bureau'" while they "exalted the . . . Confederate

Govt. and Army & insulted every Loyalist present." Before long, assailants were breaking up religious meetings and burning schools, with the leading spirit being a prominent merchant.[49]

One coarse example conveys the climate in a future Klan stronghold. With Freedmen's Bureau encouragement, Ben Hildreth, a local white, announced plans to open a freedmen's school in Greenville. Three "Independent Characters" informed him he was a "dam low down old rascal" who ought to be tarred and feathered. Threatening arson, they suggested he save his family of "whores and rogues" from homelessness. The anonymous authors, supposedly former schoolmates, concluded with startling vividness: "a man that would do as you are doing would steal the grease off a dead negroes cunt to fry eggs in and steal the eggs."[50] Facing this demented venom, Hildreth dropped his plans, but the bureau could not endure such a challenge. A small detachment arrived, and a school opened within weeks. This pattern of escalating conflict marked bureau operations as the year wore on.[51]

The struggle between President Johnson and the Republican majority in Congress transfixed Alabama. For all voters save the conflicted Unionist minority, the president appeared as the South's savior. States' rights Democrats identified with his rhetorical struggle for their core values, and they tired of enforced caution. Some resented Patton and his conservative colleagues as Cassandras on secession. "They incessantly fatigue our ears with the burthen of their superior prevision and wisdom, and point, with affected sorrow, to our past predictions," one newspaper complained. This sentiment found political expression in Mobile. Confederate Admiral Raphael Semmes sought election as probate judge, despite his having just been released from jail. Conservative leaders opposed the still-unpardoned commerce raider, thinking his prominence damaged the South, and Patton and even the president concurred. The Mobile *Times* demurred at such pussy-footing, because "we—the original, uncompromising secessionists—were right before God—before law—before man" in Constitutional matters.[52] To their browbeaten targets, Semmes's allies "seemed determined to overawe and proscribe every man who dared oppose their candidate." After the admiral's uncontested election, General Swayne wrote him that he could not assume office and was liable to arrest. The position remained vacant for months, in a show of intransigence by Semmes and his supporters.[53]

Governor Patton understood what this meant for the struggle against congressional Radicals. Alabama had informal lobbyists in Washington who pressed the point. Lewis Parsons, still unadmitted to the Senate, warned that southerners had no choice but to remain inactive. "If our people are wise they will not toast Jeff Davis unless they wish to aid our enemies & his to roast him & us. Do my dear Governor impress this on the people," he emphasized.[54] Alabama managed to avoid the headlines, but the bloody Memphis race riots in May, and in New Orleans in July, undermined the president's case. Patton's recurrent trips northward on financial and relief errands reinforced the urgency. "No one will invest in such a country; State Stocks, Rail Road Bond or stocks paying large dividends are no inducement long as the hatred of the people of the North exist," one New York contact warned.[55] But Patton had been elected by the white voters of the state, and he was testing their patience.

Patton had endorsed the president against Congress, but now his close association with Swayne became problematic.[56] The Mobile *Times* decried the Freedmen's Bureau as an engine of tyranny, this as early as May.[57] As the 1866 congressional campaign proceeded, with Alabama on the sidelines, Swayne saw that the climate had changed. "A scurrilous newspaper . . . has found no readier way of obtaining large circulation than by filling its columns with abuse of me," he wrote.[58] In September the governor wrote President Johnson that it was time for the bureau to leave. Patton praised the general, but his agency had "a bad influence upon the Freedmen, and an injurious effect upon the politics of the state."[59] Swayne, though personally wounded, concluded that Patton's comments would "keep him straight with the public." Besides, the political tidings looked favorable, so Swayne awaited deliverance by Congress.[60]

After the northern election returns repudiated Johnson, Patton initially stood his ground. The Republicans had run and won on the proposed Fourteenth Amendment, which outlawed discriminatory Black Codes and provided for equal civil rights short of suffrage. The first section decreed natal citizenship, and it guaranteed "equal protection of the laws" and the "privileges or immunities of citizens" against state action. States would lose representation for the male citizens they disfranchised, save for rebellion, which would reduce the numbers of southern congressmen. Former officeholders who had backed the Confederacy lost the right to hold public office, until their disabilities were removed by congressional vote. None of this attracted the governor, for the amendment barred him from office. Patton opposed ratification, at first, and in November the legislature crushed it. But lopsided refusal by the southern states ensured further congressional measures. Unless they meant to abandon the freedmen, and all influence over the ex-Confederate states, the newly victorious Republican majority had to transform southern governance.

Patton's financial house of cards now faced a windstorm. Governmental uncertainty unraveled all his labors. During the election campaign, financiers reported that no market existed for Alabama bonds any longer. In December, Alabama's leading creditors demanded immediate repayment. Patton had ignored a previous warning, and now they threatened to dump all the bonds they held as collateral.[61] Among other disasters, this threatened default on Alabama's approaching interest payments. Patton again hurried to New York, to find resistance to loaning money to a potentially ephemeral government. Patton finally found help from "a company of capitalists" who were "interested in Railroads in this State and in the development of mineral resources."[62] Doubtless they sought to preserve the credit of a state they soon hoped would award them subsidies. Still, the experience highlighted the peril. The "bankers and moneyed men of this City" said that when Congress readmitted Alabama confidence would return, but until then bonds could only be sold at ruinous discounts.[63]

Patton's other news proved equally grim, because rejection of the amendment galvanized Unionist dissidents. All that fall, D. H. Bingham and his comrades had toured the North, speaking out for black suffrage even before Republican congressmen thought it expedient. During the winter, large unconditional Unionist meetings in northern Alabama endorsed drastic change. Alabama leaders gathered in Washington, including W. H. Smith, D. H. Bingham, and Milton Saffold. J. J. Giers participated too, feeding information to his relative, Governor Patton. These leaders helped create a Southern Republican Association, even opening an office. As embattled Unionist emissaries, congressmen consulted with them rather than with spokesmen for the still-theoretical African American electorate.[64]

Congress pondered two templates for Reconstruction all that winter. The first was simply to sweep away the existing governments with military rule. This took the form of a proposal to abolish ten ex-Confederate state governments and subject them to army oversight, likely manning these territorial-style governments with loyal appointees. The other proposal installed a loyal interim government in Louisiana and gave African Americans there the right to vote, and by precedent, elsewhere. In Alabama, blacks comprised 48.1 percent of the voting-age male population, which could in theory make strong Unionists a permanent majority.[65] Looking toward a lasting transformation, Congress eventually blended these approaches into the First Military Reconstruction Act. Transitional implementation of equal suffrage seemed more democratic, and potentially more stable, than widespread disfranchisement or indefinite military rule.

While lengthy debates transpired, the southern Republican cohort grew frustrated. By February, some were speaking of impeachment and confiscation.[66] Increasingly, published statements endorsed black suffrage, though this occasioned debate.[67] To act, congressmen wanted the political cover the southern Republicans provided, and Unionist Tennessee's voluntary enfranchisement provided additional encouragement. But endorsing the measure in Washington and then returning to live in Alabama presented no small challenge, and some future Republicans sought passage without their fingerprints. It was one thing to be seen as accepting Congress's terms, but quite another to be recommending equal suffrage per se. As Congress hurried to complete a Reconstruction bill before adjournment, D. H. Bingham, the association's secretary, circulated a petition endorsing the Louisiana bill which included equal suffrage.[68] J. J. Giers and William H. Smith promptly disavowed their signatures as unauthorized.[69] But Smith did not explicitly oppose black suffrage, a studied imprecision that typified his racial politics thereafter.

Smith nonetheless sought dramatic change. His angry complaint about military conduct makes that clear. Smith sought Swayne's replacement with an earnest Radical, preferably Milton Saffold. Freedmen's Bureau agents should be chosen from the "unswerving radicals" of Alabama, and they should use food distribution to extend the government's influence. In this context of emphatic white loyalty, Smith's attention to railroad matters was also noteworthy. Presidential pardons had left control of railroads in the hands of "Secession capital." But the vast federal land grants bestowed to these companies had lapsed, and he sought legislation putting the land in the hands of new railroad corporations with loyal directors. Unionist control would promote Alabama's "mineral & Lumber regions," while secessionist directors had ignored these free-labor enclaves. These strictures anticipated the railroad zeal which would later characterize Smith's governorship, and they aligned him with the development priorities of the beleaguered Governor Patton himself.[70]

Back in Alabama, ruling circles assumed Congress had done its worst by leaving southerners unrepresented, but they were going to be disabused. Northern contacts made Patton uncomfortably aware of the omens. Up till now, only the pronounced Unionists in northern Alabama recommended ratification of the Fourteenth Amendment, as a way of securing readmission and barring ex-secessionists from office. In early December, Patton suddenly endorsed their position. He told the legislature that, while he still disapproved in principle, Alabama had to act "lest the stability of our affairs be suddenly broken up." One immediate result was to smooth his relationship with Wall Street: "Since the threatenings from Washington all persons [in New York] think it will be proper to Ratify the Amendment, as a finality. . . . [S]everal gentlemen have called upon me fully approving my suggestions to the L[egislature]." Financiers told him the amendment was the least they could expect from Congress, so Patton hoped the president might back his position on pragmatic grounds. He misunderstood Johnson's viewpoint, and that of his own former ally, Lewis Parsons. They and their intimates spent the winter crafting race-neutral alternatives to mass enfranchisement, without securing agreement even from supporters, and Congress easily brushed their half-measures aside.[71]

With the governor frequently absent, General Swayne presided over a full-court lobbying effort in Montgomery. He believed the public was too ignorant to understand their situation: only "the threatening programme of a territorial government with indefinite results" would move lawmakers. Conservatives had some political influence, and they now were truly alarmed. One prominent politician and railroad promoter privately feared confiscation.[72] Swayne thought "the coast was almost clear" for enactment, but a telegram came from ex-governor Parsons telling legislators to stand by the president.[73] The Senate defeated ratification by the margin of twenty-seven to two, and the House by sixty-nine to eight. Proponents tried again in January, only to be stopped cold by a telegram from the president himself. Insiders believed it might have passed, that supporters waited in the wings had the result been close. Modest as it was, this was the best showing in any of the states to undergo Congressional Reconstruction.[74]

If legislative leadership balked, Patton's endorsement of the Fourteenth Amendment braved a popular firestorm. One admirer called Patton's audacious stand "political death" for the moment.[75] The regional press rose up in righteous anger. "A Southern Governor Cowers under Radical Threats," one headline read. More revealing was the meek response of the Montgomery *Advertiser,* which enjoyed the public printing and served as the governor's personal organ. It reported a Washington rumor that Patton had never personally endorsed the amendment, but only brought it to the legislature's attention. The paper defended Patton's motives, though conceding that nine-tenths of the southern electorate opposed ratification.[76] One ex-secessionist leader, former senator C. C. Clay, rejoiced at "A glorious rebuke to Gov. P. The papers are terribly severe on P. & he must feel that he has played a foolish game and lost."[77]

Or maybe not. In a speech at Huntsville, Patton articulated his core conservative values. Southerners needed to stop acting like the Confederate leadership that kept fighting two years too long. If President Davis had made peace, "my two sons would have been saved," he stated with emotion. Patton estimated that the Fourteenth Amendment would render just 3,000 or 3,500 men ineligible for office, less than 5 percent of the white electorate. Their status was not worth further conflict, he thought, and the governor stood his ground gamely before the crowd. An unhappy reporter "left him arguing and explaining the amendment section by section."[78] Patton thus pursued the economic emphasis and pragmatism that he thought rightly animated political life. The state had been fatally unrepresented in Washington for six years. Alabama needed readmission on the terms Congress prescribed: the state's economic health demanded it.

The economic emphasis made sense that winter. The same legislature that voted down the constitutional amendment made a fateful departure in policy, one dependent on the state's credit. In February, the legislature overwhelmingly passed a general aid program of railroad subsidies. Any railroad of over twenty miles built in the state would receive state guarantees for its stock of twelve thousand dollars per mile, or much more, depending on terrain. This endorsement would enable projected companies to seek funding on Wall Street and overseas. The governor does not seem to have been the central player in this policy; he did not aggressively promote the proposals in public. Still, as a former Whig with railroad connections, he could be expected to favor aid. One railroad enthusiast thought him among the most liberal men in the state on development matters.[79]

Alabama's political class thus acted impetuously at this moment of truth. They embraced economic policies dependent on the good will of Wall Street even as they sailed into confrontation with Congress. With state government passing out of their hands, inaugurating vast subsidy measures for others to implement—well—the recklessness merits emphasis. Even before this, Alabama faced pressing financial troubles, and one Mobile banker dreaded passage as a calamity, saying "good bye to its Credit." Another creditor denounced the idea, certain that enactment would undermine existing bonds.[80] But given how invested Patton was in economic growth, and how central railroads were to that growth, his backing was predictable. Whigs like Patton pushed such measures fruitlessly for a generation, and he had righted the state's credit for the moment. Who knew when enactment might be possible again? Patton hoped to implement the aid program, and he devoted himself to maintaining the power to do it.

But how? The next state elections were scheduled for August, and the governor already was a candidate for reelection. "I may have opposition yet have no fear any man can beat me before the people," he wrote. He had a point because, as one supporter assured him, "there were too many corn sacks yet in his neighborhood marked 'Gov. Patton' for the people to forget you."[81] Patton expected that his endorsement of the amendment meant Congress would restore his officeholding eligibility quickly. The governor felt his predictions, however unpopular, would be demonstrated correct. And so it proved. In early March 1867, Congress set forth how ten ex-Confederate states would be restored to the Union. The army would oversee balloting under black suffrage, while temporarily disfranchising those barred from office under the pending amendment. This electorate would choose delegates to write new state constitutions. Existing governments were declared provisional, with officeholders subject to military removal. Patton took comfort in his swift vindication, but the only way to take practical advantage was to implement the terms.

Unwelcome as it was to him, black suffrage promised a solution to Patton's varied problems. Instead of indefinite military rule, the Reconstruction acts only provided for temporary implementation of equal suffrage, followed by full state readmission. Reconstruction offered escape from Alabama's fiscal netherworld, and Patton laid out his thinking to a relative that summer. The material interests of the state required restoration, especially the university and mental institutions, and he had secured the outside resources to do so. So long as Alabama remained excluded from Congress, all these initiatives remained in peril. Furthermore, "It is a fixed fact that the Negro is now free and will be enfranchised. No powers or influences can prevent this." He was confident that under General Swayne and his superior, John Pope in Atlanta, he could retain some influence. Noncooperation instead risked disastrous misrule. He warned of

Brownlow's Radical regime in neighboring Tennessee, with disfranchisement of most of the white population. Action would preserve Alabama's "Good White Citizens" from disfranchisement. All that was needed to satisfy Congress was to strike "white" from the state constitution, and he hoped this would be all that the Reconstruction lawmakers attempted. Alabama had the best terms they were ever going to get, so Patton endorsed "capitulation without delay."[82]

Thus, depending on definition, Patton became the leading Republican "scalawag" among the governors elected under Johnson's Presidential Reconstruction plan. In evaluating his motivations, one can note his hopes for being relieved of disabilities and thereby retaining his position. His personal finances were more exhausted than the state treasury, he said, but it would seem public spirit and sheer ego motivated him to persist. "No child with its doll was ever more infatuated than this man with his present office," one Unionist complained.[83] Patton sought political vindication from the social elite that had so criticized him. One suspects that idealistic intentions toward the freedmen played little role, and enthusiasm for the unconditional Unionist element none. Given the pains he lavished on finance, and his surprising success, Alabama's economic health was his evident goal. For the last half-century, revisionist historians have not been much drawn to fiscal issues in explaining the admittedly more important aspects of Reconstruction. In the case of Alabama, however, the development aspirations of the leadership colored its racial politics, a pattern that survived Governor Patton.

Even during the tumultuous subsequent implementation of Military Reconstruction, the state's financial condition consumed Patton. All through 1867 and early 1868, the governor warded off testy creditors demanding repayment, some claiming he had misled them with optimistic predictions or paying other bondholders first.[84] He left legions of teachers unpaid, and, more happily, hit on the notion of emitting tax anticipation certificates, to serve as a circulating medium for a cash-poor state.[85] With Swayne and Pope's help, he induced the Treasury Department to approve the notes, despite their iffy legal status. Uninhibited Democratic newspapers tried to undermine the notes, but he carefully issued them in small quantities and persuaded the state's bankers to circulate them.[86] Two hundred thousand dollars of "Patton money" tided his treasury through the Military Reconstruction process. The notes circulated for years, buoying his government with an interest-free loan.

Patton's fiscal expedients proved successful, which enabled his further exertions to aid railroads. Despite the Reconstruction process, Patton assumed the railroad legislation was operative, and he negotiated over the debts existing railroad projects owed the state, so that they would benefit from its provisions.[87] With government in limbo, no one would consider investing in railroad bonds, state endorsement or no. Still, as Patton wrote in May, Reconstruction's swift progress would improve the prospects. Patton was "very sure by this time [in] twelve months Alabama will be fully reestablished in her relations with the Federal Union; and in consequence, her 8 percent bonds as an investment; will be sought at a premium."[88] This prediction proved true. Alabama's bonds soared with readmission, enabling Patton's Republican successor to implement the state aid policy his Presidential Reconstruction government had passed.

In the meantime, Patton helped several of the railroad investors who had loaned the state money in other ways. He induced General Swayne to urge superiors to allow favorable corporate privileges to the Wills Valley railroad.[89] More dramatically, his intervention also helped that line absorb a crucial neighboring project.[90] Two lines were projected to bisect the mountains of central Alabama, the Wills Valley road building southwest out of Chattanooga, and the North East & South West line linking up to it from Meridian through Tuscaloosa. But along with several other railroads, the latter line was in debt to the state for previous loans now overdue. Patton induced the two lines to combine by forcing the latter railroad into bankruptcy. This yielded the first railroad to penetrate the mineral region surrounding modern Birmingham. Here was Patton's premiere contribution to the eventual New South.

Northern investors, in turn, appreciated his leadership. As his position as governor disappeared in mid-1868, Patton became president of the Wills Valley line. At least one railroad executive discerned a conflict of interest. Robert Jemison of the North East & South West Railroad "found Govr. Patton more exacting than I had immagined. He was very anxious to get hold of our Road for his Boston Company on the most favorable terms & this I fear may have unconsciously influenced him in his views & policy."[91] Jemison all but called him a crook, but Patton's successor, William H. Smith, supported his financial policies. Patton's augmented Wills Valley line would soon become the state's most important railroad project, the Alabama & Chattanooga through the coal and iron region. The railroad's creation, and Patton's salvation of the state's credit, would have dramatic consequences as Republican Reconstruction unfolded.

To anticipate subsequent developments, none of Patton's efforts had the political results he sought. His reelection hopes met only frustration, despite all his lobbying in Washington, as Unionist opponents leaned on Congressional Republicans to oppose him. Congress delayed lifting his disabilities, determining on a wider policy of leaving prewar officials under ban until after new governments were established. This failure notwithstanding, Patton's unique intervention colored the implementation of Military Reconstruction. For nearly a year, Patton induced much of the political structure to collaborate, or at least remain inactive. Alabama was the first state to undergo Military Reconstruction, giving it a unique national importance. Patton's position, with the active encouragement of the Freedmen's Bureau, encouraged the politicization of the former slaves. But Patton's tissue of financial expedients mattered nothing to them. It is to the plantation origins of their social insurgency, and its partisan expression, to which we now turn.

PART II

5

Black Liberation

Freedom and Political Mobilization

> Ten thousand vagabonds turned loose to roam
> 'Mong honest people without bread or home
> Their hearts as impious as the imps of hell
> Seek to intrude where love and virtue dwell.
>
> Poem—"Glory of Gainesville Departed"

The intricacies of Alabama's white political structure have dominated discussion so far, but other actors waited restlessly in the wings. Liberated slaves' advent into formal politics defined the Reconstruction era. Scholars sometimes emphasize consistent grassroots pressure for rural change, rooted in the hopes for land redistribution. But armed suppression initially stifled labor agitation on the plantations, which shifted black aspirations to safer venues, like churches and schools, and to the more complex class terrain of the cities. Certainly "separatism, self-help and racial solidarity" are important themes in black politics, but only with Radical Reconstruction did rural politicization emerge, as enfranchisement enabled a challenge to the plantation regime.[1] Mass agitation pushed agriculture toward a new equilibrium, as the practices of slavery yielded to other forms of commercial exploitation.

As Steven Hahn suggests, to understand black politics one must start with the centrality of slavery, and the oppressions and solidarities it created.[2] Slavery was a system of labor exploitation, premised on force, which shaped everything black people thought or did. "Back in the slavery days dey didn't do somefthin' and run. Dey run befo' they done it," Randolph Johnson recalled.[3] Such calculations of resistance and retaliation characterized slave life, and racial oppression marked them in numerous other ways. Nearly all African Americans appear as landless and illiterate in the federal census five years after the war. Over 93 percent of adult males officially could not read, and freedpeople otherwise were scarred by slavery's traumas and disruptions.[4] Still, their collective experience guided them as they groped toward a different future. They possessed the skill to grow cotton, work that they performed better and cheaper than anyone else. They also had a consciousness of common racial oppression; they shielded each other as an endemic reality of the slave system. They shared a democratic inclination that served them well in their collective struggle for freedom. Their unity was a central reality of the Reconstruction era, and slavery largely explains it. All shared common racial oppression, and nearly all shared similar material deprivation as well.

Nevertheless, there were fissures within this racial experience which encouraged later political factionalism, once their voices mattered politically. The bulk of Alabama's enslaved men and women labored in the cotton fields of the south-central black belt, generally in gangs under planters, overseers, or black slave "drivers." Supervisors were generally armed with the whip, and it was commonly used, given the difficulty of extracting work for five and a half or six long, hot days a week. Facing these forms of discipline, field hands often forged common behavior patterns, concentrated as they were in the slave quarters. As Alabama's Daniel R. Hundley saw it, the slaves on wealthy plantations lacked "the advantages of daily intercourse with educated white persons," and they were thus less "moral and tractable" than their peers.[5] They may not have resented slavery more, but plantation hands were more capable of maintaining shards of their past, fused into a wider countercultural identity. These distinctive cultural aspects ranged from speech patterns to "hoodoo," as whites gleefully discerned evidence of African-derived barbarism. Victorian gender norms, especially the expectation of female passivity, ill comported with the strenuous work regime. Martha Bradley, a slave at Mount Meigs, recalled that the "overseer he come 'round and say sumpin' to me he had no bizness say. I took my hoe and knocked him plum down." Charity Grigsby told a similar story of another woman, save for a fatal result.[6] Common oppression in the fields, living together, fused workers even across gender lines. Collective resistance was more possible, more spontaneous, among agricultural laborers who shared so much.

These strengths carried a stigma, and an interviewer, decades later, noticed that former field hands seldom admitted it.[7] Even a northern schoolteacher thought field hands "extremely brutish and groveling."[8] Whites broadly attributed negative cultural traits to the predominantly unmixed ancestry of the field hands, as a sort of social shorthand for an Africanized majority population. One ex-secessionist firebrand described a freedwoman "who says an old African hag put a snake in her four years ago, and the Obi doctor has gone to deliver her."[9] In Alabama, "blacks" as opposed to "mulattoes" represented over 90 percent of the entire African American population.[10] This made stereotypes toward everything from voodoo down to speech patterns racist weapons. That reality of the public sphere encouraged the leadership pattern which emerged after emancipation: a uniquely situated minority with the African American community stepped to the fore.

Alabama's few urban enclaves evidenced this pattern strongly. In 1870, just 5 percent of African Americans lived in cities of 2,500 population, but they had experiences that made them politically influential beyond their numbers.[11] Here those with mixed racial background congregated; they were about twice as likely as those described as black to live in cities.[12] In urban areas, physical brutality was less pervasive, the work and surroundings more varied, and literacy was more common. Also, in the cities enslaved people encountered the state's few nominally free blacks. Free blacks represented under 1 percent of the black population, with almost half living near Alabama's one substantial city, Mobile. They prospered in occupational and material terms, often literate and functioning as middle-class tradesmen. Color distinctions mattered: in 1860, seventy-five of the eighty wealthiest free black families in Mobile were headed by "mulattoes."[13]

Most free blacks shared a sharp consciousness of racial oppression with their enslaved comrades. Nearly all had spouses, relations, or close associations within the slave population; they socialized with the urban domestics or laborers, worshipped with them in Protestant churches. Government policy increasingly reinforced this identification. For many decades, it was illegal to teach either slaves or free blacks to read.[14] As the Civil War approached, Alabama moved toward harsher legislation against free blacks, thinking them a threat to the slave order. Public policy discouraged manumissions and pushed freed blacks into exile. During the secession crisis, Alabama legislators pondered forcible reenslavement, and several individuals in Mobile petitioned the government for a choice of masters.[15]

There is one exception to this pattern. In Mobile's vicinity, several hundred mixed-ancestry French speakers lived in an intermediate racial category. "Creoles," as they were termed in local parlance, descended from relationships between French or Spanish planters and women of African descent, inheriting their Catholic religion from their male forbearers. "Many of them are wealthy," a contemporary observed, and some owned plantations—and slaves. They enjoyed a separate legal status dating back to the Louisiana Purchase and Adams-Onis Treaty, enjoying civil rights short of suffrage. As one newspaper recalled, "they could stay out as late as they pleased at night, could smoke cigars on the streets, could testify in courts of justice, etc."[16] When the crisis of slavery came, they had something to lose. One general even sought to use Mobile's Creoles as Confederate soldiers, because "they do not stand here upon the basis of negroes."[17] Emancipation swept their niche away, and the issue became whether to cling to a disappearing status or embrace emancipation. Some took the plunge.

The Creoles, free blacks, and even the urban slaves were numerically negligible, but Reconstruction placed them in a strategic role. Men with extraordinary attributes dominated the black political leadership. Of prominent Republican activists or officeholders with known background, over a third had been free, a thirtyfold overrepresentation of their numbers. Almost half were reported as of mixed ancestry.[18] This pattern prevailed among prominent officials. Congressman James T. Rapier had been educated at a black settlement in Canada with utopian overtones. The Mobile Creole Philip Joseph was raised to a life of leisure, but the war badly disarranged his life plans.[19] John Carraway's father freed him, but when his white relatives contested the will he fled northward. Shandy Jones, similarly liberated, prospered as a barber in Tuscaloosa, but he developed an indiscreet enthusiasm for African colonization.[20] The slave prodigy Horace King fared better: his renown as a bridge architect and powerful sponsors facilitated his self-purchase.[21]

Such tales had echoes even among longtime slaves. Representative John Dozier reportedly had been owned by a college president and learned to read Greek as a slave, on his way to a ministerial career.[22] Congressman Benjamin Turner was an enslaved entrepreneur, running a stable and Selma's omnibus line while hiring his own time. Turner recalled "he had $1600, in gold & offered it to his master to buy his freedom," but his owner replied that $5,000 would not be enough, and the laws inhibited such liberations. When the Union Army captured Selma, Turner protested the seizure of his horses and had a gun leveled at him, but he put on some blue clothes and enlisted anyway.[23] The evidence suggests enfranchised freedmen sought conspicuously successful representatives, even more than their white counterparts did.[24]

Sectional crisis fused these disparate strands as legal repression escalated, and the crisis touched even the field hands. In May 1860, arrests for conspiracy occurred at Selma, and in August an arson scare broke out in Talladega. One white resident was hung, and a planter warned of the "general opinion amongst the slaves that they were to be free sometime this year."[25] In the Tennessee Valley, insurrection rumors and illegal liquor sales inspired vigilance committees. Daniel Hundley rode patrol outside Huntsville. He wrote, "It seems that the negroes have concluded that Lincoln is soon going to free them all, and they are everywhere making preparations to aid him when he makes his appearance."[26] Vigilance committees whipped confessions out of suspects, and Hundley reported that four slaves were hung.

Escalating repression could hardly escape slaves' notice, but the best course was not obvious. More isolated slaves, away from the plantations or Union presence, had only an indistinct understanding of their situation. In Shelby County, Edmund Ross testified of the war, "We didn't know much about it, no'how until it got about to a close." David Neely similarly reported that people were afraid even to talk about it among themselves.[27] Elderly ex-slaves often told interviewers that as children they had feared the Yankee troops, suggesting their parents had not communicated the issues at stake.[28] Sources even mention an occasional "Rebel negro" but so explicitly as to highlight rarity.[29]

Enslaved people often spread information eagerly. In the Tennessee Valley, widespread anti-secession rhetoric brought slaves into the conversation. In Madison County, one Union white man talked emancipation "in the presence of others, colored men fifteen or twenty at a time."[30] John Jones heard a neighbor tell him repeatedly that the Union would free all the slaves.[31] One slave recalled that a mentally deficient white neighbor talked Union endlessly to him; Coleman Swoope did not believe the back-to-Africa promises, but he apparently enjoyed their conversations anyway.[32] Ex-slaves vouched for masters' loyalty, citing conversations during the war. Some testified they had protected their dissident masters, manifesting wartime political engagement.[33] Many took action when it seemed feasible. In the Tennessee Valley, just about everyone able-bodied could escape to federal lines and refugee camps. Five thousand black troops were credited to Alabama, some 6 percent of the male population of military age.[34] Soldiering provided a political education, and veterans came home armed. Within Confederate lines, on the other hand, only tantalizing evidence exists of formal organizing. Dudley Smith recalled, "A few of us colored men in Tuscaloosa had a club or society, which was for the purpose of communicating with the loyal white[s], & learning how the war was progressing, & for giving & receiving information generally on this subject." Several recalled predictions of federal victory. When rumors leaked out, whites talked of executions.[35]

Toward the end, everyone knew the score: one ex-slave recalled the war as the general topic of private conversation.[36] Even in the untouched black belt, slavery eroded. Able-bodied owners and overseers left to fight, which compromised both the stick of violence and the carrot of material incentives.[37] Slave concentrations grew, with relocations into Alabama's relatively safe cotton belt. One Tuscaloosa woman feared rampant theft from the hungry migrants into west Alabama. The Confederate government leaned on such secure areas to provide labor, which spread social confusion.[38] Officials impressed thousands, working them urgently in unhealthy conditions. Fortification laborers escaped, sometimes with the collusion of frustrated owners.[39] In October 1864, the Confederate engineer in Montgomery said that over two-thirds of his laborers escaped. There just were not enough soldiers to watch them.[40] In the war's last weeks, future senator John Morgan and other Confederates started recruiting black soldiers. Time ran out, but the evidence does not suggest success.[41]

Wilson's raid in April 1865 left a localized pattern of chaos, with strips of devastation along the roads from Selma eastward to Columbus. In the ruined areas, planters often ceased production for the year. "What am I to do with the Negroes that are driven off the plantations by their former owners," asked a federal colonel in Union Springs.[42] On the intact plantations, especially those remote from Union occupation, planters instead endeavored to maintain slavery for as long as possible. One returned Confederate defied emancipation until Big Frank had him arrested.[43] When freedom finally came, enslaved people celebrated with "as much exaltation as they dared," one white memoirist candidly recalled. But the realization gradually dawned that no one was obliged to feed or house freedpeople, not even the victorious army. Whatever sparse securities slavery provided were soon going to disappear, especially if they left their familiar homes and struck out for freedom.[44]

At war's end, engagement in wider political events ironically narrowed. Joining the army, providing information to Union forces, shielding escaping prisoners, all these actions allowed intervention in momentous matters. This was the moment of truth in their lives. Slaves understood their actions as having political, even millennial consequences. With peace, and the implementation of Presidential Reconstruction, the agenda changed. Emancipation put a premium on coping as individuals with the transformation of their status. Besides, limiting freedpeople's collective influence was a central goal of postbellum white politics, the point of all the militia activity. Even the US Army and the Freedmen's Bureau promoted work rather than fostering collective activism.

Former slaves had plenty to think about in the spring and summer of 1865. Vast numbers left the plantations, to assure their freedom, or to seek the relative security of army camps. Slavery had scattered black families across the South, and many felt the urgent desire to locate spouses, children, parents. Once Confederate resistance wound down and the embittered soldiers returned home, multitudes of slaves took to the roads. Many simply sought change, to guarantee against re-enslavement, or to seek the opportunities of the cities. Robert Jemison believed that "Some amongst them will hear to no [labor] terms offered to them, nor will they leave the premises to earn an honest support elsewhere; but skulk & hang around our plantations killing, our stock, depredating & stealing generally."[45] Jemison actually urged the army to garrison Tuscaloosa in June, thinking it would bolster the planters. However many liberated slaves intended to avoid labor, and for how long, Union officers feared permanence. The obsession with short-term work habits played into the hands of the planters. One woman counseled relatives, "Of course you will keep your negroes on your plantation & hire them. . . . I suppose the State will meet & make laws for their employment. Just keep yours together to make your crops but let them decide." From what she saw of the soldiers, she was confident they would keep laborers on the farms.[46]

Most freedpeople stayed put, or they briefly traveled and then returned to their former neighborhoods. Those bearing evidence of abuse could expect army protection, but soldiers resisted the flood of plantation hands into their camps. Into the summer, the army enforced a pass system designed to keep freedmen away from the cities, and soldiers sometimes enforced urban vagrancy ordinances. The army pressured freedpeople to sign annual labor contracts, and once assured that this was how freedom worked, the ex-slaves mostly complied. For their part, through their haze of loss and defeat, planters realized they had to try something, if only because open land invited federal seizure.[47] "No planter sees any way by the present lights to make useful laborers out of free negroes," but they would probably try, one Selma merchant concluded.[48]

Legislation might fix things. "Well," one diarist wrote, "we have the power to pass stringent police laws to govern the negroes. . . . For they must be controlled in some way or white people cannot live amongst them."[49] Ex-slaveholders knew how to produce cotton. Literal property in slaves might be gone, but they expected freedmen to farm much as they had. Planters hoped to maintain gang labor, tight supervision, women and children in the workforce, to exercise oversight over freedmen's lives. One earnest Episcopal minister even wrote church attendance into his labor contract.[50] All planters' prewar habits, their brand of Christianity and proslavery ideology, made this behavior natural. Anything less meant racial anarchy. Planters hoped annual labor contracts with a withheld wage could substitute for the loss of physical coercion. This loss proved crucial, however. Without the whip, it proved impossible to force people to work like slaves, which encouraged the planter violence cataloged so profusely in the Freedmen's Bureau records. The freedpeople were "sassing" employers, not acting in familiar ways, which affronted owners and managers. In August, a federal soldier wrote that whites took advantage of "Cuffy's ignorance by hireing and not [paying] him[,] cheating him in making change & in a thousand ways the poor black [is] kicked a bout, [and] in case of a quarrel or fight which is frequent the law is all on one side."[51] Things would only change, he thought, when the area's black majority stood their ground.

Freedmen found their former owners proceeding toward a defined goal while they themselves had barely taken stock. Liberation must have been utterly disorienting, and they were likely incapable for a time of laboring well. Ominous things contradicted their sense of how freedom ought to work, but freedpeople puzzled over where precisely to object. They could not control the contract terms, or rely on being paid, so they focused on the other aspects of their lives they could reshape. Freedpeople adopted surnames, sometimes even middle names as well, as being among the entitlements of freedom. Liberated into destitution, they pursued symbolic changes, challenging those practices they most hated. Family concerns inspired much of this activity, starting with the widely noted traveling to reunite scattered relatives. Missionaries and bureau agents eagerly promoted Victorian understandings of the gender relations of freedom, with some effect, but freedpeople selectively chose which practices merited acceptance. Vast numbers of couples legally married, thus sanctioning families and rendering children legitimate, while others preferred the more fluid norms of the old regime which distinguished between casual and serious relationships.[52] Circumstances thus brought the ex-slaves into friction with judgmental northerners; for example, bureau employees frequently noted the popularity of marriage, but they were less favorably impressed with the commonness of extralegal divorce.[53]

Changes in freedwomen's roles had economic implications. For domestics, living in their masters' homes complicated the dissolution of slavery. One elite woman reported that, when her friends met, servants were the major topic even six months after Appomattox.[54] Domestics socializing on site, and their child-care arrangements troubled employers. Servants quit jobs with little notice, sometimes telling employers off. Women's field labor presented the more crucial issue. The norms of freedom placed them near the home, away from white supervisors, attending to gardens and families.[55] A bureau leader reported one-third of the freed*women,* and just one-tenth of the freed*men,* out of compliance with their labor contracts in 1866.[56] Poverty prevented wholesale abandonment of the fields, but employers viewed freedwomen's labor as less reliable. Planters saw a mindless embrace of freedom's symbols, but one might instead discern adaptation to changed circumstances and to slavery's emotional residue.

Education inspired the most idealistic hopes for the future. Prewar Alabama had made teaching black people illegal, and once freed they actually paid poll—or head—taxes that went exclusively to white schools. Ignorance bore the stigma of slavery, and the ability to read and figure looked like practical necessities. There was a widespread sense that children, at least, belonged in schools and not in the fields. Their eagerness furnished a potent argument: a newspaper joked that the main economic activity in Gainesville was the sale of schoolbooks.[57] Education pointed to a brighter future, individually and collectively, and it also provided grounds for seeking northern sympathy and aid. Northern missionaries and teachers headed by scores to Alabama, but the bureau thought it unsafe to open schools in isolated places. In smaller towns, the task fell mostly to literate ministers in the emerging black churches.

For all freedpeople could do for themselves, they had to make free labor pay. The Freedmen's Bureau initially provided them only limited encouragement. Swayne conciliated the elite, on one occasion helping the secessionist ex-senator C. C. Clay recover confiscated land.[58] Swayne sought profitable free labor plantations, and he solicited northern migrants to demonstrate how they should operate.[59] General Order No. 12, his standard labor code, decreed that all substantial contracts be written down. The terms guaranteed food, housing, and medical attention for laborers and their families, without specifying a minimum wage beyond that. Husbands would sign the contracts, which embraced the labor of all those family members able to work. Swayne's code implicitly barred violence, but it allowed employers legal recourse against those who neglected their work, defined as missing more than one day or three days in a month without cause. Because Swayne believed "many persons" had not yet learned the binding force of a contract, the civil authorities could treat them as vagrants. They could be set to work on the roads, thus providing bureau sanction for the chain gang.[60]

Swayne's recognition of civil officials meant they oversaw contracts with only modest oversight. General Howard in Washington featured the policy as a model, while others were less impressed. Some abuse looks clear. A planter wrote, "My friend Robt. Christian is at the head of the Bureau (Magistrate) & ties up darkies by the thumbs & c. In time we will have order, but the Darkies wont work till compelled by want, & c, & c."[61] When civil officials saw their duties differently, things could fare ill. In 1866, near Perote, two magistrates liberated laborers of a planter who had whipped them and shot at them, according to white witnesses. The upright magistrates then found themselves arrested and tried under anti-enticement statutes. In Sumter County, an apparent civil Freedmen's Bureau magistrate disapproved a contract brought for his inspection. The outraged employer then killed his complaining laborer, escaping to Texas.[62] Swayne himself concluded that his policy of sanctioning civil officials did not work, and indeed he repented of his entire contract system as well.[63]

Swayne's policies bought him influence in Montgomery, but laborers had little immediate reason to appreciate them. Alabama's lawmakers avoided starkly discriminatory Black Codes, but the vagrancy laws served the same purpose. Worse still, whippings and other forms of physical violence remained prevalent. One bureau agent found his greatest problem was "the persistency of the planters in continuing their old habits of punishing or shooting those who in any way offend them." In the agent's own Demopolis office, a freedman made a charge against a prominent planter, whereupon the outraged Baptist layman assaulted him.[64] Whatever harms slavery did the freedpeople, its lingering influence on employers exacerbated them. The Unionist David C. Humphreys thought a lifetime of force made whites incompetent to acknowledge freedpeople's rights. "We must have time to accustom our minds to the change," he wrote, suggesting the bureau best remain close at hand.[65]

It was in this context that rumors spread of "forty acres and a mule" and of a Christmastime insurrection. Sherman's January 1865 order confiscating plantations along the Atlantic Coast, and the bureau legislation itself, suggested that some land distribution would occur. In July one bureau officer, Charles W. Buckley, suggested that the agency had better hurry and seize land for refugee farms. General Swayne stopped all such talk by subordinates, but the freedmen were another matter. Bureau agents sometimes suggested that freedpeople credited the rumors of property division.[66] Several thought the talk discouraged contracting, and one agent gave a speech proclaiming the rumors false.[67] Swayne himself feared trouble, but New Year's came and went with no sign of insurrection.[68]

Hopes for outside deliverance are not an actual uprising, especially not against the federal army that had freed them. What martial preparations did occur had little to do with confiscation. In October, a bureau agent reported a "spirit for bitter retaliation" in Tuskegee, prompted by substantiated reports of brutality in isolated Pike County. Individuals proposed to aid their relatives, reportedly drilling, and two freedmen called on the agent for his sanction and arms.[69] He dissuaded them, and he detained Henry Pinckard, the alleged captain; word leaked out, and panicky whites conducted other arrests.[70] Little indicates such activities elsewhere, but the reports had ramifications. One woman wrote, "Companies of Malitia are being raised to protect the country from any insurrectionary movement during the winter which gives confidence to us all."[71] By December 1865, the state had organized over one hundred militia companies, according to Governor Patton. Their primary function was seizure of arms, despite the lack of legal authority so far as the bureau was concerned. The wider threat of civil-military conflict was evident. One federal detachment operating under orders to seize government horses was confronted by a posse near Gaylesville in Cherokee County. A soldier was killed, for which the military imprisoned sixteen participants.[72] Likely as a result of such actions, as well as growing pressure from Congress, General Grant turned down Governor Patton's request for the removal of troops; nor would he give the state surplus arms.[73] Facing army opposition, formal militia activity apparently lapsed, but the mobilization served its purpose. It deterred whatever collective measures farmworkers might have taken, even strikes or other forms of pressure. After New Year's, multitudes of freedmen began signing labor contracts for the year, as called for under Alabama's vagrancy statutes. Within weeks the towns had been cleared of freedpeople.[74] Resigned laborers went back to work while their grievances festered.

Labor complaints could not be collectively addressed in this climate of rural repression. But the sense of community urgency persisted, which shifted energy into the safer environs of Alabama's few cities. Here, racial uplift efforts took precedence. All benevolent or self-help efforts had political implications: they combined crusading antiracism with skepticism of outside allies. Freedpeople fashioned a language of racial self-determination, though it existed in tension with the color-blind Radical Republicanism of the emerging political sphere. These views suited their situation: they depended on national aid and protection, which placed them at the whim of an array of white missionaries, teachers, soldiers, and bureau personnel. These varied actors answered to distant bureaucracies or the Republican Congress. At their best, these northern allies were principled paternalists who believed they had the answers for southern society, and at worst they were self-interested or outright racist. Before war's end, a chaplain in Decatur commented on the emotional style of black religion, the emphasis on Moses and liberation, as a "mass of religious *rubbish*."[75] Facing such attitudes, freedpeople sought independence, or at least some check on northern allies.

Under the old regime, slaves were incorporated in subordinate roles within the Protestant churches, especially the regionally dominant Southern Baptists and Southern Methodists. These denominations had split from their national bodies over slavery, and they held lingering proslavery views.[76] With liberation, Baptists suffered a wholesale exodus, as freedpeople sought alternatives in a free marketplace of religious ideas. Southern Baptist leaders feared a "troublous scourge" under outside—northern—tutelage, but most freedpeople preferred independent local control, which muted the sectional overtones.[77] Among the Methodists, however, centralized ecclesiastical structures encouraged outright conflict. The Methodist Episcopal Church offered financial assistance and schools to Alabama converts. Missionary Aram S. Lakin, a future Republican activist, secured a substantial following among both freedpeople and highland Unionists. Holding these constituencies together proved no mean feat. A local convert, Rev. J. B. F. Hill, opined, "All of them [freedmen] are ignorant, most of them are superstitious, and if left to themselves . . . will lapse back into some of the forms of heathenism."[78] Given such beliefs among Northern Methodist preachers, a niche clearly existed for an evangel of racial self-help, and two northern denominations obliged, the African Methodist Episcopal Church and the smaller AME Zion. Freedpeople thus confronted a choice between a well-funded, interracial northern church and two proto-black nationalist alternatives.[79] All three embraced Radical politics.

It took years for the religious situation to stabilize, but most African Americans migrated toward politically engaged churches that they controlled. The Southern Baptists acquiesced, for fear they would lose legal title of their own churches to black majorities. Their parting sometimes featured financial assistance, as Southern Baptists grappled morally with the emancipation they deplored. One leader, the ex-secessionist congressman and future educational spokesman J. L. M. Curry, endorsed black schooling before his state convention. In Marion, Baptists helped finance a school, and at Montgomery, several Baptists assisted Sunday schools, though missionaries suspected they came to counteract Yankee influence.[80] Methodists made similar declarations supporting black schools, but such subtlety initially eluded them where African Methodist evangelists were concerned. One preacher, Robert Alexander, was beaten by men who vowed that no schools or black ministers should exist in Auburn. Once the AME denominations became established, violence diminished, as southern leaders concluded that they made counterweights against their northern rivals. As one Republican warned, the promised northern subsidies had taught black Methodists to see "the Church North as their great enemy, and the Church South as their best friend."[81]

Analogous debates arose in education. One teacher asked, "Do the northern people understand how the golden moments for planting Yankee institutions in this fair land are slipping by?"[82] The American Missionary Association (AMA) financed several large urban schools and eventually founded Talladega College. Association leaders leveraged these investments to aid the sponsoring Congregationalists; they gained few black converts but benefited financially in mid-1866 at General Swayne's intervention. Bureau legislation authorized federal aid only for building schools, but Swayne diverted funds to staff them, and Howard acquiesced to his dubiously legal expenditure.[83] The northern societies only expanded operations gingerly outside the safety of major cities, which left an opportunity for the black churches or individual teachers to open privately run fee schools. These underfunded operations raised the issue of community empowerment versus formal academic preparation and outside money, which the AMA schools exemplified.[84]

Urban areas proved most hospitable to self-help efforts, a pattern which proved especially true in the fraught political sphere. Alabama's few cities were laden with migrants from the plantations. Officials harshly deterred in-migration, so distinctively urban grievances impelled early "Radical" activism. For example, Selma's mayor predicted trouble from the free Negroes that "infested" his community. Taxes and discriminatory measures drove many out of the recently burned town. That fall, Selma officials faced an outbreak of smallpox in the poorer neighborhoods, a problem evident in other cities. The city council barred most freedpeople from entering without an employer's permission.[85] Such issues were particularly pressing in Mobile, Alabama's one major city.[86] It possessed a unique concentration of propertied free blacks and Creoles, but after the war, interior towns stripped away the river cotton trade, which exacerbated racial ills. First the army and then the civil authorities adopted measures to stem the influx of ex-slaves. Vagrancy ordinances resulted in mass deportations of hundreds, as the city court auctioned them off daily to planters. That fall, several freedpeople were shot by army guards, and there was a battle on the streets between black soldiers and police. Racists torched black churches, as many as half a dozen, inspired by title disputes over prewar buildings.[87]

Goaded to protest, Mobile's activists summoned a statewide black convention in early November 1865, and some fifty-six delegates met, mostly from the vicinity. Delegates issued a politely worded call for rights and black enfranchisement.[88] When the legislature tabled their requests, they directed more emphatic protests to Congress.[89] While this transpired, the activists created Alabama's first black-owned newspaper. It struggled financially, but the Mobile *Nationalist* provided literate, egalitarian commentary. It counteracted the press blackout of inconvenient news, as one opposition paper candidly admitted.[90] Despite these successes, the paper endured controversy over the place of self-determination in a formally color-blind Radical movement. A northern missionary suggested the expediency of having a white editor, and after much debate the membership appointed John Silsby of the AMA. He quickly antagonized supporters with preachments over drink, swearing, and other lifestyle ills. His successor, Albert Griffin, instead emphasized political themes, but he too was beset by criticism from his governing board. His leading critic, the ex-slave Lawrence Berry, set forth for the interior to spread the Radical message.[91]

The newspaper controversy thus pushed race spokesmen, steeped in self-determination talk, into the cotton belt.[92] Their ideas remained influential in the churches and schools, among those founding black institutions. But the politicization of the countryside shifted attention to agrarian issues. A mood of black assertiveness persisted, but the approach of equal suffrage at the hands of Congress reshaped the agenda. Urban concerns of northern dictation, the frustrations with missionaries and the bureau, proved less worrisome than the prospective alliance with native, white, soon-to-be Republicans. Rural freedpeople distrusted the motives of scalawags more than they did the few northern newcomers, and this reality structured Republican factionalism thereafter.

These concerns lay in the future in 1866. In the meantime, *Nationalist* agents were among the first secular Radicals rural freedmen encountered. But would they even be permitted to hear emissaries preach racial equality? When Lawrence Berry reached Selma, nervous black leaders tried to deter him from speaking, though they conceded him a fundraising appeal at the end of a religious meeting. In Tuscaloosa, he unfortunately arrived just after an army detachment left.[93] Dozens of Chivalry searched for Berry, firing guns, though he eluded capture or injury.[94]

A distribution network nonetheless spread into the interior towns. Agents served as local correspondents, allowing prospective politicians access to a wider public. Benjamin F. Turner in Selma, Shandy Jones in Tuscaloosa, and Holland Thompson in Montgomery all served as sales agents.[95] Some encountered the harsh reception that Berry experienced. Teacher William V. Turner gave a public address in Wetumpka, reading from the newspaper's columns. A young magistrate threatened him with arrest during his speech, then broke a cane over Turner's head and drew a knife, for which he was duly convicted and paid a modest fine. As the Mobile *Tribune* editorialized, the Radical paper was "shocking to the sensibilities of our people" and likely to provoke riots.[96]

Other external influences with labor overtones reached the hinterland. Lawrence Speed, for example, had led a collective land purchase in southwestern Georgia with political implications. Radical discourse energized critiques of the plantation system, and the *Nationalist* devoted considerable attention to them. One letter suggested that "the free laborer will not long be content to continue in the relation of an employee, he will naturally aspire to become an independent operative."[97] The agricultural results in 1866 encouraged such reflections. Everyone in authority had assumed that the first peacetime crop would improve. These expectations were dashed, and by all accounts this was one of the worst crops of Alabama's history. In Demopolis, the bureau's Charles Pierce thought that freedpeople paid with a share had not made enough to clothe themselves, while those paid in cash mostly collected nothing at all.[98] The Freedmen's Bureau resumed issuing quantities of food early in 1867.[99] The disaster had any number of explanations: the price of cotton declined from its wartime highs, along with the destroyed fences, scarce plow animals, and damaged infrastructure. Unusual rainfall also caused flooding and insect devastation.

Ex-masters had a preferred explanation: "True the negroes are working better than was expected, but nothing like they use to, when we had the lash over them."[100] Planters could force freedpeople to sign contracts, by law; they could put them to work under gang labor with tight supervision; they could even dock their salaries for missed time. It did not matter; the army interdicted physical coercion, and without it people would not work like slaves. One bureau agent thought that freedpeople performed only two-thirds of the work they previously did, a figure close to modern estimates.[101] Planters complained freedwomen would collect their rations each week, but only came to the fields when they felt like it. Also, if the hands expected to lose money, they worked less. One overseer, W. W. Gwaltmey, experienced numerous woes but reserved his venom for laborers: "I tell all of them that $1 per day will be deducted from their wages in May & June for each day lost, but *nothing* in my opinion will make some of them work except the lash." Gwaltmey soon purchased a gun. Ex-slaves required twice the supervision, he thought, and that December he tried repeatedly to settle accounts with the hands. He evicted several but experienced difficulty replacing them.[102]

Every year, ex-slaveholders bridled at negotiating with their former slaves. "I am afraid I have paid too much to my negroes for hire. I am not fit to manage negroes now, at least as hired servants, I am too easy on them," the widow Otey complained in early 1866. She felt no more competent the following year, experiencing weeks of stress. The next year she was unable to pay off her employees until February. One confrontation with a field hand left her trembling. "It almost kills me to say unkind, unpleasant things to any one, however necessary," Otey wrote, but polite behavior could not be expected of unpaid workers, and it appears she paid off her white creditors first.[103] Without the plantation system finding a profitable equilibrium, frustration grew. One formerly rich veteran, E. Thornton Tayloe, reported widespread ruin. He blamed hands who were more interested in attending funerals and stealing than working.[104]

Freedpeople experienced graver ills. Their circumstances still resembled the old regime too closely for comfort. After signing coerced contracts, they went largely unpaid for a second harvest—that is beyond securing food and housing, the benefit package of slavery which they tended to disregard. Some were actually in debt for advances during the year, or for poor work. One rich black-belt planter kept a detailed tally; nearby planters had lost a staggering $149 per hand, which meant freedpeople received nothing.[105] All of the bureau's fine promises looked foolish; an official at Demopolis thought one-third of hands were swindled. Furthermore, the neo-Confederate resurgence encouraged harsh behavior, while army force levels declined from 7,832 to 831 over the course of 1866. Bureau ledgers groaned with complaints of nonpayment. For years, this followed the calendar's predictable rhythms as the native Republican J. H. Speed observed: "Many of the planters are driving off freedmen who have worked for a part of the crop, or who have worked for money wages for the year now that the crop is made and secure on the simplest pretexts. . . ."[106] Landowners could overlook poor work until the crop was laid by in mid-summer, then evict or frighten away the laborers unpaid. They could hire others for picking the cotton crop and pocket the difference. The numbers are difficult to quantify, but the complaints were widespread. Laborers were in technical noncompliance with contracts all the time, and they could often be legally deprived of their earnings.[107]

Alabama's laws enabled such behavior. To contest a contract resolution in civil court, laborers had to put up twice the amount in dispute.[108] This bonding provision was designed to prevent nuisance lawsuits. It protected planters right enough, but it also encouraged employer fraud. Another problematic aspect of the law dealt with leased plantations, many of them rented by northerners or poorer men willing to make concessions to freedpeople's preferences. If white lessees ran into trouble, as commonly occurred, the landlord legally seized the crop for his rent first, leaving laborers without recourse. In one instance, the bureau arrested fleeing lessees who had satisfied the landlord but left their workers unpaid, forcing them to pay up before leaving.[109] Then there was the simple matter of threats or violence. According to the tabulated bureau records in Selma, disputes were common, and it was mostly the employers being accused. If laborers then abandoned the crop, the planter had an excuse to withhold their share.[110]

At the end of 1866, freedpeople again proved reluctant to contract. They often sought individual escape, moving to cities, trying to farm unoccupied waste land, or seeking federal homestead land, poor and inaccessible as it was. The planters were again skittish about a possible uprising. This time, however, things were different: the army inhibited the white militia activity which had damped down rural activism the previous fall. All the agrarian grievances now converged on politics with the Republican victories in the congressional elections. Rural anger fed off these developments, and the political infrastructure was in place to amplify demands. Events in Washington pushed rural freedmen into national politics and Radical politics into the countryside.

One of the pragmatic arguments against black suffrage was the fear that former owners would command their votes. Until disproved at the ballot box, these claims were difficult to dismiss.[111] Moreover, in the Alabama legislature, some black-belt lawmakers proposed giving the ballot to some literate and property-holding freedmen, both for tactical reasons and to enhance legislative representation. This initiative failed, but the proponents appear to have been in earnest. For equal suffrage to become reality, Radical activists needed to persuade congressmen (and Unionists) that the unlettered ex-slaves could be trusted. Editor Albert Griffin anticipated that the southern states would reject the Fourteenth Amendment and force Congress's hand.[112] At his urging, the *Nationalist* activists called rallies to demonstrate that freedpeople sought the vote.

In the winter of 1867, their efforts were amplified by the cohort of unconditional Unionists in Washington. Black voting offered the prospect of loyal predominance in the southern states, without endless military rule. Congress heeded these pleas, providing a road map to reunion on the basis of universal suffrage. Implementing the Reconstruction acts meant three elections in Alabama in a bit over a year, which made the countryside a stew of political agitation. Having enfranchised hundreds of thousands with limited knowledge of formal politics, congressmen and Republican businessmen funded a southern organizing drive. The vehicle became an existing wartime Republican group, the Union League (or Loyal League). It was an oath-bound, clandestine body, which had absorbed existing unconditional Unionist clusters in the mountain South. These leagues had a self-defense function evident in the St. Clair County disturbances, among others. Republican politicians believed that both the secrecy and the fraternal aspect would be suited to the freedmen. Weekly meetings would enable organizers to instruc the new electorate on the goals and mechanics of voting, away from the intimidating presence of ex-masters.

During 1867 scores of organizers, white and black, traveled through the plantation regions establishing Union Leagues and other political groups. The prospective replacement of existing officeholders energized dissidents. Dunning-school historians frequently charged that the Freedmen's Bureau became a partisan engine promoting Union League activities. In Alabama, in 1867, these claims are accurate. General Swayne had tired of conciliating the power structure and welcomed a fresh start: "we have got the freedmen and the Union League, and more than these we have got truth and justice for our platform. . . ."[113] The league's state secretary, John C. Keffer, was Swayne's chief clerk, and the general's mail swarmed with reports from organizers. Official encouragement similarly emboldened the bureau-funded teachers and the northern benevolent societies. For their part, rural laborers welcomed these evangels of Reconstruction. "Although a good many of the Freedmen have not a very clear idea of what [voter] registration is, they know that they must go somewhere and do something and they have all made up their minds to go and do it," one officer observed.[114]

The Republican message was that political rights would transform their lives. One widely distributed pamphlet indicates the tenor. African Methodist minister Henry M. Turner reportedly authored the "Loyal League catechism," which was frequently read aloud by literate members.[115] The format was a short fictionalized dialogue between a white Republican and a freedman, which made sense given the racial composition of the initial league organizers. The dialogue pointed out that it was the Republican Party that freed the slaves and promoted equal rights, while it was fair to presume Democrats would reimpose slavery, given the chance. Thus freedmen should "shun the Democratic party as they would the overseer's lash and the auction block." After several pages, the fictional freedman professed himself satisfied: "You have clearly shown me my duty and I shall impart the information to my people."

Opponents claimed that the league organizers were promising the freedmen "forty acres and a mule." Read literally, the charge is mostly untrue. The congressional funders were party moderates rather than Radical Republicans, and the national leadership discounted such expectations. The Union League catechism confined itself to a call for legal equality. Nor did the politically active Freedmen's Bureau agents normally endorse confiscation talk. Still, discussions about land did occur freely, and talk of how little had changed since emancipation was an abiding feature of meetings. Activists critiqued the ills of the plantation system and explained how Reconstruction could facilitate a more democratic social structure. But whatever precisely the league organizers said, the freedmen heard land acquisition.

Millennial hopes infused the political sphere during 1867, and activists experienced the heady sense of presiding over a mass movement.[116] Future congressman Thomas Haughey organized eleven league councils in three weeks, averaging fifty members each.[117] He ran out of rituals and could not keep up with the paperwork. All across the Tennessee Valley and the plantation belt, leagues spread, though the penetration was less complete in the less populated wiregrass counties. The council membership mostly ranged from about fifty to several hundred, typically meeting on Saturday nights. A meeting in Gadsden had eighty-five freedmen attending and four whites, which seems the common proportion.[118] Secrecy prevented the opposition from breaking up the gatherings while assuring that African American voices would dominate proceedings. These meetings became a nursery of grassroots leadership and political discussion.

Rural self-defense measures spread. In Sumter County, whites counted ninety guns by moonlight in a nighttime militia drill.[119] From Perote in Bullock County, one freedman wrote Swayne: "Jeneral as I have d[r]il[le]d one time and is goin to drill againe to day I want to [k]no[w] of you whither wee are doing rite or not." His company met twice a month, and members swore "to protect an defend the United States against eney rebellion."[120] These efforts seem spontaneous, though sometimes it is difficult to tell. In Wilcox County, a cluster of northern veterans loaned their black supporters a flag for the Fourth of July. Afterwards, they took the fife and drum away and assured alarmed planters they meant no harm. But the Yankee planters previously exchanged gunshots with assailants, so their disavowals might have been less than heartfelt.[121] The freedpeople saw themselves as upholding the government, and even before Military Reconstruction passed, General Swayne asked permission to arm them. Ten such informal companies were already in the process of forming, he wrote.[122] His superior, General George H. Thomas, demurred, and the army thereafter discouraged such measures as provocative. Still, Swayne evinced a pragmatic awareness that self-defense might be essential to achieve suffrage. For freedmen, it was self-evident.[123]

Republican meetings provided instruction on the practices of parliamentary procedure. In May, Thomas Haughey requested the freedmen to select one of their own to recommend for voter registrar. "After a good deal of talk and some little feeling they at length decided to leave the whole matter to me," he reported, only securing his answer in private conversations.[124] Initially, such organizers had outsize influence, but freedmen soon gained more self-confidence. Radical speeches politicized the prevailing discontent over the labor system. The rhetoric spoke to their frustration over the holdovers of slavery. What could equality have meant to former slaves but the end of gang labor, tight supervision, and women and children in the workforce? These hated aspects of slavery remained part of their daily lives. Their material condition remained no better than slavery, and they faced more random violence. Democrats claimed that the league's re-enslavement rhetoric demonstrated the foolishness of the freedmen. But it instead furnished a charged metaphor for what remained unchanged on the plantations.

For the first crop season in southern history, the balance of fear shifted. The social levers by which planters intimidated black people suddenly failed. Opponents of Reconstruction could neither interdict, nor even locate, the shadowy Union League meetings. Reports of armed drilling spread, and landowners and overseers worried over the intent.[125] These predictions of aggression proved false, because self-defense was more about display than action. Freedmen almost never initiated open conflict, and there is no evidence of unprovoked attacks on whites by league members. What was different now was that they would likely fight back in the event of violence, which changed everything.

Planters responded vigorously: "The Negro will soon have to be disposed of in some way, perhaps as the indians were. They will soon become quite as savage, useless, and *more troublesome*."[126] Conflict escalated as the normal workings of a harsh plantation system became politicized. The postwar stream of evictions and beatings took on a collective dimension, threatening to escalate uncontrollably. Where blacks enjoyed predominant numbers, a display of force could evoke responses from those in authority. In Bullock County, in the eastern black belt, this process became almost routinized. One planter that spring had occasion to "correct by whip" a freedwoman, and Union Leaguers descended, bearing their prisoner to Union Springs for punishment. Similar events happened that fall, when a prosperous white shot John Keffer in the head after a speech. Armed leaguers again arrived, and the authorities arrested the perpetrator though he was swiftly bailed. Afterwards, freedmen staked out the roads to help an army detachment rearrest him.[127] These conflicts may explain the odd developments near Perote, which was already a scene of tension. A literate black activist, George Shorter, arrived from Montgomery claiming authority to govern the black population. According to a bureau investigation, Shorter established a league tribunal and issued divorce decrees. He apparently had community miscreants whipped, at least those who threatened disclosure, and someone, apparently white, burned down a black church. Alarmed civil authorities ordered the leaguers arrested, but an angry black crowd prevented it. The freedmen backed down once persuaded that they had been hoaxed, and the sheriff arrested ten or more, though Shorter soon escaped.[128]

These specifics may have been unique, but the wider circumstances were not. In wealthy Hale County, the *Nationalist* agent and voter registrar Alexander Webb returned from a statewide Republican convention. After threats, Webb was shot down in Greensboro by a storekeeper, the dissolute veteran John C. Orrick.[129] Leaguers descended in arms, some threatening to burn the town; the intimidated sheriff sanctioned them as a posse, while exasperated whites readied for battle.[130] "The country for miles around was in commotion, freedmen armed and hunting for Orrick, the roads leading to town picketed by Whites, to prevent Blacks from coming in, and in one or two cases shots had been exchanged."[131] All this occurred during the crucial plowing season, and planter John Parrish complained of pervasive league agitation: "The Negroes are told to ignore the Southern white man as soon as possible, not to work with or for him, or be controlled by him, but to set up for themselves."[132] Setting up for themselves, of course, meant renting or owning. A nearby overseer similarly complained that, after hands attended a rally, some said "they were to have the lands and the growing crop upon it, one or two said they understood now such things, they all belong to the u[n]ion leugue."[133] Small wonder that he was one of the first in the area to decide to rent land to squads of freedmen.

Such events, endlessly repeated, blasted the cotton crop. From Marengo County, E. T. Tayloe complained: "They have a Union League organized in the Old Methodist Church . . . where all our Negroes go Wednesday & Saturday nights, & get home only just before day, & then what are they fit for the next day."[134] According to planters, the freedmen dropped their labor for election rallies, drills, or any sign of trouble; their work habits both reflected their wholesale disaffection and increased the pressure on the plantation system. The upshot was a truly catastrophic crop in 1867, coming as it did after two losing seasons. One Selma lawyer thought that many planters were ruined and would lose their lands. He described a widespread conviction that nothing could be made growing cotton with free labor.[135]

Almost everywhere, the planters lost money. One wailed, "I owe the hands *nothing not a red cent,* for the simple reason there was nothing made not enough to defray the expenses of the place by considerable, &

they know it, the whole neighborhood also."[136] He thought he paid hands ten times more than they made. The freedpeople, on the other hand, believed work for whites pointless: "They will always get the oyster and leave us the shell."[137] S. S. Gardner agreed with them; other bureau agents were less sure the unpaid hands were being cheated, given the miserable crop, but freedpeople's embitterment was real enough. One woman sought to recover a seven-and-a-half-cent settlement, which looks more like a statement than an actual complaint.[138] Numerous causes for failure existed, but the political tumult certainly contributed.

"Property now sells for nothing," one Selma lawyer concluded.[139] The business model of plantation production was broken, and cotton factor J. A. Wemyss feared for his mental health.[140] As things stood, little likelihood of profitable operation existed. The Freedmen's Bureau predicted widespread eviction, with planters disinclined to contract for another year. Though labor was available, H. A. Tayloe feared freedmen would not work because the Yankee adventurers had filled their minds with politics.[141] The freedpeople showed little better temper. Nowhere around Demopolis were laborers contracting for cash wages, according to the bureau, because they figured that their chances for payment were greater with a share in the crop.[142] These complaints moved readily into the political realm. During the ratification campaign for the Reconstruction constitution, the bureau denied land redistribution plans for the umpteenth time.[143] From Selma came the report that no one at all had filed contracts with the bureau for the coming year, as of December 27.[144] Freedmen showed "a great indisposition to contract for part of crop unless the 'new laws' shall control them." The bureau agent in Montgomery reported that Republican speakers urged freedmen not to contract until after the next election.[145] Revealingly, the few contracts he had seen were for rental of land, and the only freedmen who made anything were those who had already done so.

At this moment of crisis, the price of cotton increased, offering planters the first promising news in some time. Fortuitously, a white boycott apparently defeated the Republican Constitution. E. T. Tayloe gloated that the outcome caused "great disappointment among the Negroes, that 'The new law has not come out' giving them lands, mules, etc. . . ."[146] Cotton factor Wemyss found his contacts more optimistic, but that only mattered if laborers went back to work in earnest.[147] Weeks were going by, and landowners needed to break the logjam, to offer something tangible. Planters also sought to limit their own financial exposure for the provisions they supplied their hands. What they needed, in short, was to retreat from direct, active management. In the spring of 1868, plantation owners increasingly began renting land directly to the freedpeople, either as individual families or in multifamily squads. From Greene County the bureau reported that a respectable number were renting and doing well.[148] The Union Springs *Times* observed: "Some few of them have saved enough to enable them to cultivate a little land on their own account, and these we most heartily wish to succeed." The rest were attempting to do so without sufficient means, and the paper denounced irresponsible whites who rented to them.[149]

Over the next years, tenant farming emerged on a large scale, in Alabama as throughout the cotton South. It looked like freedpeople would be able to acquire a measure of independence in due course. In October 1869, a planter wrote, "The Negroes are generally indisposed to work under white men, want to rent the lands & work on their own account," and some labor-poor landowners were caving in because freedmen would pay top dollar. The pattern spread, and by early 1870 renting land established itself as a common procedure for men with families. The Greensboro *Beacon* thought one hundred dollars was enough for them to make the attempt, wisely or not, and many apparently had that in hand after a good year's crop.[150] Tenant farming took various forms, but "sharecropping" became the most common. As normally practiced, the sharecropper would provide the labor while the landlord provided everything else—land, seed, and mules. The resulting crop would be divided in half, with the laborer's share reduced by whatever he had borrowed from the planter—or local merchants—for provisions during the year. Freedpeople now fed themselves, which meant less debt for planters and offered them new sources of profit. One planter observed that hands "invariably" spent their money "nearest home."[151] Tenants with some resources, like owning a mule, could negotiate more favorable terms, but widespread destitution made sharecropping prevalent.

The planters did not necessarily embrace the new order. In 1870, H. A. Tayloe wondered if Alabama now was "a fit country for a gentleman to live in. Overseers and the like are now the land renters and hirers. Having no principle they hesitate at nothing."[152] Someone had to watch the black population: this was the planters' belief after emancipation much as it had been under slavery. They assumed that widespread theft would result from the freedpeople feeding themselves, and that chaos and destitution would ensue. Planters never quite reconciled themselves to their loss of control, and whenever crops turned out badly, they complained that tenantry made things worse. The landlords were right that routine maintenance suffered, as did owners' capacity for ambitious projects, but these were long-term problems. Landowners were desperate by 1868, and rather to their surprise, tenant farming worked. At the crucial moment of insurgency, these changes finally restored profitability to cotton production.

Abandonment of centralized production persuaded the freedpeople to return to work. Numbers were "'gwine to farm fur derselves,'" whether they had any savings or not.[153] As tenant farmers, they could work under their own supervision. They could avoid gang labor, overseers, and the other aspects of plantation life that most resembled the slave regime. Wives and daughters could return to the field on their own terms, without being under the control of white supervisors, always a sore point. Renters broke up the old slave quarters, moving cabins to be near their individual crops and pigs and chickens. These changes tangibly removed them from the holdovers of the slave regime. Freedpeople long wanted their former masters out of their day-to-day lives, and circumstances now pointed in that direction. It looked like things were improving, that freedpeople might find individual escape. Change balkanized the collective agitation that had swept the black belt.[154]

A miraculous year of agrarian insurgency thus forced concessions, but it spent itself in the process. Constant turmoil became a more periodic excitement at election time, a pattern planters could live with. Tenant farming would solidify in much the form it would keep for the next half-century and more, the sharecropping regime. By all accounts, the freedpeople worked much better, and with cotton prices recovering the planters felt positive relief. Planters conceded that the freedpeople worked better now than they had ever expected. Free labor might not pay as well as slavery, but most planters would survive. In one factor's words, "cotton at 20 cts. without tax is a fair business, & they ought to kindly work every laborer in it, who will work at all. . . ."[155] Landowners soon realized that they could make money merchandising goods on credit. Planters after all kept the books, while the freedmen were illiterate; landlords could loan money to freedpeople more safely than others, lifting their profit margins. Plantation stores increasingly dotted the countryside, either owned by the landlord himself or merchants operating in combination with him. Landlords regretted the loss of control, but they could live with the changes. For the first time since the war began, ruin no longer stalked them.

Freedpeople had less cause to rejoice, but it took them a while to realize it. Their lives altered in ways that gratified their feelings, but their financial prospects did not much improve. In 1870, over 96 percent of Alabama's black families did not own land, though nearly a fifth reported over fifty dollars in property.[156] Sharecropping initially looked like a way station toward independent proprietorship, but when cotton production recovered, land prices did too, locking most into permanent landlessness. At the crucial moment, tenant farming stabilized the plantation regime and dissipated the frustration which fed the agrarian insurgency, making further concessions unlikely.[157]

The political consequences would be nasty, too. As day-to-day frustration ebbed, the political insurgency leached away. Plantation changes co-opted discontent, making the gut-level pressure driving black politics less compelling. Had widespread agitation persisted, labor relations and Reconstruction politics might have evolved differently, perhaps gaining further concessions. The insurgent wave had lasted long enough to create a new government under the terms of Congressional Reconstruction, but sustaining it with a popular movement was another matter. The end of the centralized plantation structure had another chilling feature, in that it changed the geography of rural spaces. Dispersal across the countryside left tenants increasingly vulnerable to night-rider violence. These changes exposed them to the worst terrorist outbreak in American history, the Ku Klux Klan, which turned the balance of fear back in whites' favor. It is to these worlds of formal governance and nightrider bloodshed to which we now turn.

Klan postcard. (Walter Lynwood Fleming Papers, New York Public Library)

Benjamin Turner, Republican Congressman, 1871–73. (Library of Congress)

Wager Swayne, Assistant Commissioner of Freedmen's Bureau. (Alabama Department of Archives and History, Montgomery, Alabama. Used by permission)

George E. Spencer, Republican Senator, 1868–79. (Library of Congress)

Robert M. Patton, Presidential Reconstruction Governor, 1865–68. (Alabama Department of Archives and History, Montgomery, Alabama. Used by permission)

Peace Faction Leader and Provisional Governor Lewis Parsons. (Alabama Department of Archives and History, Montgomery, Alabama. Used by permission)

Robert Burns Lindsay, Democratic Governor, 1870–72. (Alabama Department of Archives and History, Montgomery, Alabama. Used by permission)

George S. Houston, "Redeemer" Governor, 1874–78.
(Library of Congress)

Jeremiah Haralson, Republican Congressman, 1875–77.
(Library of Congress)

Nathan Bedford Forrest, Klansman and Railroad Promoter. (Alabama Department of Archives and History, Montgomery, Alabama. Used by permission)

6

Implementing Reconstruction
Governance and Biracial Politics

Alabama now stands redeemed from the rule of traitors and rebels.
—D. H. Bingham, October 1867

To modern observers, the status of the freedpeople is the overriding issue of Reconstruction. The mass of its eventual constituents certainly thought so, but the native whites who initiated the process in Alabama felt differently. From Governor Patton on down, dissidents of all stripes assumed that their interests, and not those of the freedmen, would shape the new order. Conservatives hoped to minimize economic damage, while the unconditional Unionists believed black enfranchisement would give them power. Their expectations drove Alabama's constitutional revisions, the South's first attempt to implement equal suffrage under congressional guidelines. As for the freedmen, the striking reality is the care the black leadership took not to disabuse their newfound white allies of these notions.

When Congress passed the First Military Reconstruction Act in early March 1867, no one knew what to expect. It was indistinctly thought-out for such landmark legislation, requiring several iterations. It was not clear who would even initiate the Reconstruction process, or how widespread disfranchisement was. To reenter the Union, states needed to hold elections in which all adult male residents would participate, save for those barred from office under the pending Fourteenth Amendment. According to Governor Patton's estimate, this provision disfranchised for the time being under 5 percent of Alabama's potential white electorate.[1] Voters had to sign an oath of eligibility and loyalty, and the resulting constitutions had to provide for equal suffrage. The law's ratification provisions were baffling: the conventions and the new constitutions apparently required a majority vote, in elections in which a majority of the registered voters participated. Given the arithmetic, approval required as few as 25 percent of those registered, though in practice passage needed much more. Once the electorate approved, and the new governments ratified the constitutional amendment, Congress would vote readmission to the Union. Military oversight would then end.

Alabama's loyalists had cause to be pleased, because they assumed that the freedpeople would be content to follow their leadership. Thus the exasperated Unionist constituency accepted or even sought black suffrage. As S. C. Posey reported from the Tennessee Valley, "There is not the slightest opposition manifested in this quarter to organizing under the Act of Congress."[2] Unionists acquiesced in the federal oversight and civil rights protections this implied, because they had urgent grievances. Across northern Alabama, Union League members petitioned for wholesale removal of ex-Rebel civil officials.[3] Combined with disfranchisement of ex-Confederates, such removals comprised the central demand of the Unionist Radicals, and defiant glee characterized the movement. In St. Clair County future constitutional delegate Jack Springfield presided over a Republican meeting which endorsed a presidential ticket of Thaddeus Stevens and Governor Brownlow. One flamboyant proposed resolution suggested exiling ex-Rebels to South Carolina, while another suggested constructing a moat once they got there.[4]

Unionist grievances trumped class grievances per se, but the regime transition inspired a host of complaints. Some Union enclaves had long resisted paying taxes to the "Rebel State." From Lee County came the grievance that the poll tax had quadrupled since the war while the land tax remained the same. Another constant complaint was ex-Confederate officials' control of relief provisions. There were more drastic proposals. Colonel George E. Spencer thought confiscation enjoyed majority support in several mountain counties.[5] Debt relief came up repeatedly. Many of those in desperate financial trouble were planters and former Confederates, but poorer Unionists in the famine-stricken mountains had special cause to back stay laws.

The Unionists' immediate obstacle was Robert M. Patton. He supported the Reconstruction process, but he hoped to channel it in a conservative direction. The governor sought to maintain office to preserve Alabama's threatened credit standing and his development initiatives. Though now disfranchised, he hoped that Congress would soon lift his disabilities. His northern financial contacts ventured to Washington on his behalf.[6] In the meantime, Patton encouraged his fellow conservatives to lead in reconstructing the state. Above all, Alabamians should "guard against the condition in which the State of Tennessee is now placed, by the disfranchisement of 7/10th of her best white citizens. This is as I conceive our greatest danger." Well into that summer, in the midst of agrarian insurgency, Patton depicted native white Radicals as his main worry.

Unionists resented Patton's influence with Swayne and his new superior John Pope, in command of the Third Military District in Atlanta. Thomas O. Glascock, the head of the state Union League, helped prevent congressional restoration of Governor Patton's right to hold office.[7] Glascock complained that Patton falsified his record as a Union man after secession, and that he "lent himself to the *fire-eaters* & became their candidate for Gov. vs. two Union candidates." Patton surrounded himself with secessionists at his inauguration, and his secretary, D. L. Dalton, had served in Richmond. George Spencer, colonel of the Unionist regiment, felt much the same way about amnestying ex-Rebels. "It is better the disability remain as it is," he wrote, "because the minute we place any of these men where they have power they will use it to the injury of loyal men."[8]

General Swayne perceived the governor differently, and he apparently distrusted the Unionist element as suitable allies for the freedpeople. Even before Congress enacted Reconstruction, Alabama's conservative political elite began making concessions on civil rights. The outgoing legislature repealed vagrancy laws, and there was a serious initiative to open schools, though separate ones. "Freedmen are now *free,* at least in form," Swayne observed.[9] With Military Reconstruction, Swayne suddenly gained the power to try wrongdoers directly. He had long complained that murder went unpunished, and now the threat of military incarceration temporarily deterred racial violence. One bureau official thought the courts were improving dramatically.[10] For its part, the military abolished the chain gang, inspected jails, and liberated many supposed vagrants. The army also released improperly apprenticed children, a longstanding grievance.[11] Reconstruction thus cut the Gordian knot, and something much closer to equal justice prevailed.

After years of frustration in Alabama, Military Reconstruction inspired Swayne to pursue big visions. He had political ambitions, and privately he expressed reformist views on capital punishment, women's suffrage, and even prohibition.[12] He was a "charming enthusiast" on the subject of education, one northerner wrote.[13] Swayne promised bureau aid for the AMA to establish Talladega College and other schools.[14] When the hard-pressed association hesitated, he hectored leaders. He also tried to continue the bureau's dubiously legal financing of teachers, because when freedmen were "actually represented, even in the Constitutional Convention, if need be, the State can be made to take on itself our whole school system, undiminished, which would be a gratification to ourselves, as much as it would be a benefit to them."[15] Swayne's superintendent, the zealous C. W. Buckley, made similar observations. With Buckley's encouragement, many teachers stayed on that fall in hope that a new government would make good their pay.[16]

The generals had differences with Governor Patton, but all resisted Unionist demands for an official purge. On this topic, Patton wrote, "Genl Swayne fully concurs with me."[17] Congress had left officeholders in place, provisionally, though in July the Third Reconstruction Act confirmed the military's power to remove them. But multitudes of Alabama officials were ineligible by the standards of the proposed Fourteenth Amendment.[18] Filling vacancies with men who could take the "ironclad" oath of wartime loyalty, as prescribed by Congress, presented a logistical nightmare. Particularly in the black belt, eligible whites with education and experience were rare, and widely appointing freedmen looked premature to Swayne's superiors. Just replacing resignations, deaths, and expiring terms proved difficult. Besides, Patton's support promised that officeholders might help, or at least not obstruct, Reconstruction. Swayne expressed annoyance with removal requests, deciding to act only for cause.[19]

Governor Patton professed confidence that "Reconstructionist" conservatives could guide the process of reunion. Much of the state's white press, and much of his incoming correspondence, initially agreed. Governor Patton spoke of Reconstruction as a nonpartisan movement, because forming parties could wait until restoration.[20] The league's spread among freedmen made this less plausible, and in early June, a statewide convention gathered to found Alabama's Republican Party. The governor urged his contacts to attend, but some were already alarmed.[21] Former secessionist governor A. B. Moore sent a letter of introduction for a delegate, the Republican J. H. Speed, but Moore urged reining in the north Alabama extremists: "The colored delegates will return home excited, call public meetings, address their people, poison the minds of the ignorant, & evil disposed & perhaps produce a conflict of races very soon."[22]

The Montgomery convention brought the discordant elements of the Republican movement together, and the carefully targeted assertiveness of the black majority proved instructive. Talk of District Judge Richard Busteed as a potential US senator provided the context. The judge's accession promised Republicans lucrative patronage jobs, but Swayne housed similar ambitions. Besides, Swayne loathed Busteed, calling his favorite John Hardy "the most rapacious person I had ever known in his official capacity."[23] Court officials had levied huge finders' fees on the bureau's revenue from Confederate property already in government hands.[24] The outraged Swayne helped secure Hardy's dismissal as marshal.[25] These measures pleased even Montgomery's elite community of lawyers, who pressed malfeasance charges against Busteed.[26]

Busteed irritated black leaders too. He had appeared at a conservative "Reconstructionist" rally in Mobile, distancing himself from the Republicans and civil rights. In Lowndes County, where he reportedly had a plantation, Busteed told freedmen not to bother with voting but just go to work.[27] These actions antagonized the well-informed Mobile delegates, led by John Carraway and the Creole leader Ovid Gregory. When General Spencer moved to invite Judge Busteed to a seat on the platform, it was "violently opposed by the negroes" and the meeting adjourned in disorder.[28] Delegates refused Busteed permission for him to explain himself, 146 to 25, with many abstentions. He was reduced to proclaiming his Republican bona fides outside the convention.[29]

Despite their numerical predominance, African American delegates deported themselves carefully. Unionist William H. Smith served as chair, and there were complaints that the various committees were seeded with non-league members, likely in a bid to moderate the resolutions.[30] Swayne himself believed he promoted success by balancing the various factions, defending his overt politicking as necessary, and it appears the freedmen tacitly accepted his advice.[31] Afterwards, Swayne predicted there would be no organized obstruction to reunion on Congress's terms.[32] A bright future beckoned, because "the colored vote if undivided will control this State in the election of all Legislative bodies. . . ."[33] The transition complete, equal suffrage would guarantee a more enlightened public policy.

Despite the Busteed dispute, the explicitly Republican convention otherwise achieved both programmatic unity and discretion. The unanimously adopted platform called for equal citizenship and for "free speech, free press, and free schools." It endorsed replacing the poll tax with fairer levies, so that the "tax paid by every man shall be exactly in proportion to his property, and none other." It called, somewhat vaguely, for election to office of those who had stood firm for the Union.[34] The civil rights theme was cautiously stated, and the resolutions did not suggest disfranchisement at all. The authors intended the document to be as welcoming as it could readily be, in contrast to previous league statements.[35] The dissonance reveals the underlying struggle for control of the Reconstruction process. Governor Patton promoted outreach to ex-Confederate conservatives, as opposed to Unionist demands for protection and office. What neither contending Alabama faction much noticed, however, was that the black delegates had not rallied to either group of native whites. Even now, it seems unclear who freedmen *ought* to have preferred. They contented themselves for the moment with an exemplary punishment of Busteed's misdeeds.

From the point of view of Patton, the convention's outcome looked successful, in that it had not embarrassed conservatives unduly. For the moment, shell-shocked Democrats, and especially former secessionists, preferred to let the process play out awhile. Many believed they were disfranchised under the vaguely worded Military Reconstruction acts, and several thousand actually were, which slowed organized opposition.[36] The lag confirmed for Patton and his allies that no pragmatic alternative existed. As Dalton observed, "Many good men, yielding more to feeling than judgment, are standing off and grumbling, but they will have to step into the current or be left high and dry."[37] An interregnum of black political influence, moderated by Patton's own retention in office, looked safer than continued limbo. As late as August, the governor predicted that four-fifths of the public would support reunion on congressional terms.[38]

Swayne was less sure, as hostility toward him intensified. Just after the convention, a doctor sent a youth "loathsome with ulcers from venereal disease" trooping through Swayne's hotel lobby, with a taunting note that the general could attend him.[39] Despite darkening omens, the military undertook black voter registration effectively that summer. General U. S. Grant viewed implementation as a congressional mandate, and Pope's letters manifest his own Republican politics, despite the prospect of removal if President Johnson's political fortunes improved. Pope directed that one-third of his local registration boards be freedmen.[40] Having oaths "administered by a darkie" would discourage participation, he thought, thus assisting the "out and out Union party."[41] These would become the first black public officials to serve Alabama. The league's John Keffer recommended several, which highlighted their political role.[42] They moved onto the plantations, encouraging registration and calling rallies. This projected Republican activity into previously untouched areas, like the sparsely populated wiregrass counties of the southeast.

W. H. Smith became head of the registration effort, as part of an apparent design to conciliate Unionist leaders. Swayne sought permission to hire Smith's brother, Colonel Robert T. Smith, along with another ally, at good salary. Swayne thought O. O. Howard would "appreciate my meaning when I say that they can each take care of several counties. . . ."[43] Swayne also temporarily appointed dozens of lesser agents.[44] Again, the native Unionist cohort predominated, like W. C. Garrison of Blount County and the onetime Confederate political prisoner C. C. Sheats. Overall, Swayne used bureau agents "pretty freely to instruct the freedmen of the existence and meaning of the work of registration, and with excellent results."[45]

These measures may have seemed necessary because of the perception that the popular following needed external direction. In Eutaw, the Freedmen's Bureau received reports of a Union League meeting with arms and alcohol present. The bureau threatened arrests, and the freedmen were ordered to desist from drilling.[46] The cities raised particular concern for social disorder. In economically depressed Mobile, for example, rural migrants surged into the suburbs. Passage of Reconstruction initiated a wave of grassroots activism, and a dock strike and occupations of segregated streetcars ensued. Swayne dispatched emissaries to rein in the Radical spokesmen. Unfortunately, a riot broke out on May 14, Alabama's first major postwar bloodletting and the first of several in Mobile. After days of inflammatory press criticism, Congressman William D. Kelley of Pennsylvania had addressed a downtown crowd. Upon being interrupted by whites, Kelley indelicately referred to the army regulars nearby as his guarantee of free speech. City police tried to arrest a heckler, a scuffle broke out, and dozens of bullets hit the speakers' platform, while alarmed freedmen mostly fired in the air. Two men died immediately, one white and one black, with several more injured. Pope then expelled the city officials, but he had difficulty finding white businessmen to accept military appointment. Swayne finally forced compliance with a threat to appoint freedmen.[47]

Reconstruction proceeded more smoothly elsewhere, and as of early September, black registrants outnumbered whites, 89,000 to 74,000. It appears that 15,000 or 20,000 whites failed to register, perhaps more.[48] While several thousand were clearly disfranchised under congressional legislation, thousands more thought they might be and feared legal consequences. But the rest refused out of indecision, alienation, or apathy. Even if these lopsided racial proportions proved temporary, they suggested no obvious way to derail the reunion process. White southerners were "prisoners of the accursed Radical, unconstitutional Rump Congress," one angry lawyer wrote.[49] Though opposition sentiment grew, they remained tactically divided on whether to register, whether to then vote or not, or whether to boycott the whole process. Then there was the issue of who should front the movement, former secessionist Democrats or the conservative minority who held the balance of power.

The precipitating factor was the approach of the election to authorize a constitutional convention and select delegates, scheduled for October 1–3. After private consultation, former Confederate general James Clanton called a "Conservative" convention in Montgomery in early September, but only thirteen of Alabama's counties were represented.[50] The keynote speech was given by M. J. Bulger, the former Unionist candidate for governor. Significantly, the gathering offered no tactical guidance on how to proceed in the coming elections. Instead, it settled for organizing itself for future measures. Members pronounced suffrage a state concern and urged freedmen to distrust political newcomers.[51] The core issue raised was how to approach the black electorate. Some participants resisted the very notion.[52] This would remain a contentious topic throughout Reconstruction, reinforcing divisions between states' rights Democrats and their conservative former rivals.

Editor Joseph W. Taylor of Eutaw, for example, made gestures in the direction of black participation in the convention, but his words offered no welcome. He elaborately painted a Reconstruction which would "destroy the white man's government which our fathers formed . . . to erect upon its ruin a mongrel, cross-breed government, a mulatto government, half white and black, a monster which nothing but the heats of fanaticism and the lusts of ambition could have engendered, to curse the world and shame the political degeneracy of the times, with its monstrous deformities." No potential recruits could have missed his true feelings. The process would end in a race war and perhaps extermination. To avoid this fate, intelligent freedmen should vote for the conservatives. It was only rational.

The more exuberant delegates, like the future Klan chieftain Ryland Randolph, requested that the newspapers print Taylor's speech entire. In theory, at least, Taylor appealed to black voters, but other delegates disdained that pose. One reportedly said that, "when the negroes became as intelligent as he was, then he was for letting the negro vote, and not before." These were not comments designed to flatter the African Americans present, and simple exclusion might have been more reasonable. The resulting resolutions offered assurances of good will, but they did not endorse black suffrage; nor did they mention public schools. Delegates instead proclaimed their desire to instruct the freedmen in their new responsibilities. They acknowledged freedmen as "inhabitants of a common country" without quite using the word citizen.[53]

The rhetorical escalation held real dangers for both sides, especially in migration-swollen cities like Montgomery. The conservative delegates commissioned black speakers, one named Joe Williams. Angry talk spread at league meetings, as some activists threatened Williams as a race traitor. When Holland Thompson intervened to defend free speech, rival black leaders accused him of spreading false rumors.[54] These denials backfired: Williams was attacked after a speech, and John Hardy, now a Republican editor, thought him in danger of being killed. White protectors intervened, along with cavalry, and opponents thereafter preened as defenders of black civil liberties. Clanton later claimed he held off a Radical mob at gunpoint.[55]

The growing polarization undermined Governor Patton's appeal to white pragmatism and the inevitability of Reconstruction. "I am really surprised that so many good citizens are refusing to Register, and many others Register (as they say) to vote against a convention," he wrote. He devoted himself to getting Congress to restore the franchise to conservatives.[56] Patton claimed that he had persuaded leading Senators to modify a wholesale purge of officials who could not take the "Ironclad oath."[57] As enacted, the Third Reconstruction Act merely buttressed the district commanders' authority to make removals. Congress thus enhanced the authority of General Pope in Atlanta, as opposed to Patton and Swayne, and Pope lacked Swayne's carefully tended ties to the elite.[58] That summer, Pope predicted sweeping margins for Reconstruction, three-quarters of the black vote and a majority even among whites. And with the support of General Grant, installed as interim secretary of war, Pope determined to finish the process whether obstructionists liked it or not.[59]

Pope's intervention had broad ramifications. In August, he directed that henceforth, civil juries would be selected from voter registration lists, thus allowing freedpeople access and redressing issues of court fairness. There was some voluntary compliance, and one could argue the precedent eased later service on juries.[60] But lawyers were professionally affronted. William Cooper decried "J. Pope Military Monster," and he sketched an eagle in his diary that he pronounced dead, dead, dead. Officials resisted on formally nonracial grounds, existing precedents granting preference for literacy or property possession. Legal vehicles for evasion were endless. Some circuit judges refused to convene courts at all, while other local officials resigned, creating yet more vacancies which the military could not fill for months.[61] These vacancies hobbled civil law enforcement at a time when lawlessness required no encouragement. Moreover, the previous legislature had created numerous new counties just before the registration process halted local elections, so Pope had to staff whole governments by appointment.[62] Together, the effect was chaotic.

Efforts to rein in the press had similar results. The provocation was real, as some newspapers encouraged harassment or violence. In his General Order 49, Pope ordered that no government advertising or legal notices could be printed in newspapers opposing readmission under the terms of Congress.[63] John Forsyth of the Mobile *Register,* the most powerful Democratic paper in the state, observed the policy was "starving many & pinching all of us."[64] Most newspapers nominally complied, while several lost their advertising which subsidized a fledgling Republican press. In one instance, Democrats simply rented the opposition their printing establishment to create the Moulton *Union.*[65] On the other hand, military intervention often made heroes of the most uninhibited editors. There were limits to what military pressure could achieve. Pope's measures antagonized the political elite, composed largely of lawyers and editors, many of whom would be barred from office by the proposed Fourteenth Amendment when Reconstruction concluded. In the meantime, many remained in position to hinder the process when they chose.

Race-drenched public abuse facilitated official obstruction. In Mobile, a news vendor strolled about in epaulettes belittling Mayor Gustavus Horton, the military appointee. Nettled, the mayor ordered the apparently unstable freedman from the city.[66] There were local precedents, but opponents brought charges for violation of federal civil rights statutes. Horton's case went before none other than Judge Busteed, who saw the opportunity to punish his Republican critics. Busteed jailed Horton, threatening a several-year sentence, though he eventually settled for a $250 fine.[67] But Busteed had little time to savor this triumph. District Attorney L. V. B. Martin, who replaced the judge's protégé J. Q. Smith, wrote a fifty-three-page complaint alleging gross cruelty. The judge held court without informing Martin and locked his office doors, mandating a several-floor detour on routine business. The exasperated Martin finally shot Busteed, which "suspended his persecutions for the present," as Horton's wife concluded.[68]

Violence loomed, but Reconstruction's opponents still could not settle on an electoral strategy. In some localities they fielded candidates for the convention, in most not. "It matters little to us what this body shall do," the Selma *Messenger* later explained; ". . . It can make no Constitution under which any white man can live."[69] The freedmen, however, were energized by casting their first votes. Daniel Larkins came from Elba to "see the great men" in Montgomery, about eighty miles distant. He asked a white Republican to give him "*some paper so that he could find the right one to learn it all from.*"[70] In the black belt, the core issue was how much to trust their late masters. In Dallas County, Benjamin F. Saffold, Milton's brother, had a Unionist record by central Alabama standards. He had led a ticket opposing immediate secession, and he endorsed allowing black testimony after the war. But did freedmen want to vote for a former slaveholding grandee? "That man Saffold I don't believe is to be trusted," one activist said. "I wouldn't trust him alone [as delegate], but Mr. Coon, Mr. Silsby, Mr. Jordan Hatcher and Mr. Strother are going too, and Saffold can go and *hold up* their coattails, and they can keep a watch over him, and I think he will be all right."[71] Freedmen might vote for such a Republican, but they intended to monitor him closely.

In the black belt, Republican mass conventions chose diverse convention slates. Most tickets were interracial, but in none were the majority African American. In the region, ten prewar southern whites, nine African Americans, and fifteen delegates of northern origin were elected.[72] Several of the southern whites were "Reconstructionists" of indistinct politics, so committed native Republicans were a distinct minority. In several locations, rival slates appeared, mostly composed of Republicans but sometimes opportunistically promoted by Reconstruction opponents. The freedmen voted as a bloc for those they understood to be the regular Republican candidates, and even Benjamin Saffold won overwhelmingly over northern-origin and black opponents.[73]

In the northern half of Alabama, native Unionists predominated. The electorate there chose four black delegates, three northerners, and thirty-four native southern whites, predominantly Radicals. It appears the demographics discouraged African Americans from assuming leadership. But in the Tennessee Valley, and especially Huntsville, there were so many Unionist tendencies and aspirants—and freedmen—that race-charged factionalism emerged immediately. Early in 1867, the elite ex-cooperationists around Joseph Bradley, especially Nicholas Davis and William Figures of the Huntsville *Advocate,* accepted Congress's terms as inevitable.[74] But unconditional Unionists and northern newcomers immediately challenged them, men who endorsed black suffrage per se. These Radicals viewed Military Reconstruction as desirable rather than a disagreeable imposition. An early factional controversy arose out of the reluctance of Bradley to promote blacks as voter registrars. While visiting Montgomery, his ally Figures was asked to recommend names of freedmen, but he had no idea who to suggest.[75] Onetime cooperationist leaders expected deference, but given the choice, the freedmen preferred open Radicals and some even heckled Bradley. Furious, Bradley decried the leagues and blamed northerners, especially the bureau's John Callis, for pandering racial appeals. Bradley supposedly even threatened "the assassin's knife" against his Radical tormentors.[76]

Historians emphasize Reconstruction's factional divisions between scalawags and carpetbaggers.[77] During 1867, however, native white "scalawags" scarcely existed as a bloc. The popular constituency of draft resisters and First Alabama veterans lined up with the freedmen as Radicals—hostility to ex-Confederates rather than civil rights being their defining issue. Leadership divided on ideological lines, reflecting a class-tinged resentment of Tennessee Valley planters with their complicated wartime records. One veteran wrote that Decatur was in "the most Loyal portion of the State and we do not consider it as coming with very good grace for Huntsville to suggest our appointees when her record for Loyalty is of so doubtful a character."[78] Bradley was particularly resented for having fled the Union occupation, and for his early influence with Provisional Governor Parsons and President Johnson.

Republican divisions notwithstanding, the fall campaign passed by in relative peace, the opposition being tactically divided and not yet having adopted violence as a strategy. However, in the future Klan stronghold of Calhoun County, whites violently dispersed freedmen walking to a Republican rally. There were reportedly threats against two Republican leaders, but a train conductor got his passengers through the mob without stopping.[79] These events occurred infrequently, and election day itself proceeded smoothly. The freedmen trooped to the polls peaceably, voted, and left for home—all ballots being cast in the county seats, to maximize official supervision and minimize intimidation. A Republican paper proclaimed the election "the most orderly and quiet ever held in Tuscaloosa," with no drinking and no fighting.[80] The constitution call passed easily, in part because over 5,000 perplexed whites cast ballots against it, many in the isolated wiregrass counties, which helped surmount the turnout threshold with 13,000 votes to spare. The vote itself was overwhelming, with a reported 18,553 whites voting to accept the terms of Congress, which would represent one-quarter of the approximately 74,000 whites registered. These numbers suggest a substantial north Alabama constituency. Two predominantly white counties polled majorities of those registered, Winston and Randolph, and others came close, like Blount, Fayette, and St. Clair. Almost all of the pro-convention votes went for Republican candidates, generally those considered the most Radical.[81]

The result notwithstanding, Swayne expressed misgivings: "We have carried the election, but not by such a vote as we felt sure of getting. The power of intimidation has been very great. The Union League is understood to have 43,000 white members, of which not one half can have voted."[82] With limited white participation, Swayne perceived that the appeal to elite pragmatism was in peril. The hundred delegates, by one count, contained five conservatives and only one in the Rebel interest. Circumstances empowered the most Radical of the native Unionists. Even in contested races, the league-backed candidates generally won, like the leading Radical D. H. Bingham, who received 1,997 out of 2,360 votes cast. Bingham sent Thaddeus Stevens his outline of a constitution, borrowing from progressive elements of other states. He wanted enhanced redress for wrongs done outside of military authority during the war. He sought to void all legislation touching property since January 1864, and to stop civil lawsuits until the new constitution became operational. Most crucially, "We shall restrict the elective franchise and the right to hold office in the State a little beyond the military bill—and sh[all] make the [ironclad] oath of July 2, 1862, the test of office."[83] That is to say, he sought a constitution barring some ex-Confederates from voting and virtually all of them from holding office. For the largest bloc in the convention, the native white Radicals, these were mainstream views.

Developments in the North made this profile problematic. That fall several state-level black-suffrage referenda were on the ballot. All lost. The results suggested that Republican voters were not overeager for Radical experiments in the South.[84] These electoral defeats sent a shock wave through the congressional leadership, and suddenly the presidential election in 1868 looked doubtful. No one knew how the electorate would respond to African American voters and lawmakers, and these innovations offered a target-rich environment for racist satire. Facing these headwinds, the Senate failed to modify the requirement for majority participation in the ratification vote, a fateful omission as it proved. As for Alabama, the election results emboldened hard-liners by undermining the inevitability of Congress's terms. If opponents forestalled the process, a Democratic national victory might make the whole nightmare go away. In Mobile, the rumor was that the freedmen had voted their last. Colonel Spencer observed, "the Rebels are very jubilant and talk of the time when they are again going to commence hanging."[85]

At Swayne's initiative, Alabama's convention met first, but these were dangerous times to seek the national limelight. Unconditional Unionists had long bridled at Swayne and Patton's retention of ex-Confederate officeholders: now delegates acted on their electoral mandate. When the convention gathered in early November, the native Radicals took the initiative. They chose as chair E. W. Peck, a former Whig lawyer who had been hung in effigy but escaped actual wartime harm. At least eight delegates had refugeed to the Union lines, some having served in the Union Army. Several had harsh wartime experiences, like the propertyless league-leader William C. Garrison. Garrison recalled plenty of experience of Alabama's Rebel courts, but "the only protection I could obtain was from my rifle, and from the bushes."[86]

The dominant figure early on was Bingham himself. He proposed that all minors whose property had been invested in worthless Confederate bonds, as wartime laws decreed, should be able to recover from their guardians.[87] Decrying wartime court decisions, he "wanted this Convention to give the people a chance to redress their wrongs." Bingham proposed that the railroads constructed by the Confederate government, and then given by President Johnson's order to companies with disloyal directors, be seized to fund the common schools. He defended a proposal to eliminate newly created counties, in part because they bore "the names of former rebel Generals and guerilla leaders." More crucially, he recommended the convention confer with General Pope on creating a provisional government within twenty days. This latter proposal was only narrowly defeated, on the tactical grounds that it implied criticism.[88] Thomas Haughey went further: the convention itself should organize a provisional government. Delegates would appoint a loyal governor who would choose subordinates who could take the "ironclad oath" and then conduct the ratification election.[89]

Delegates sidetracked the more startling ideas, like renaming a county after Tennessee's Brownlow. John Keffer warned of anarchy if most wartime court proceedings were voided. Still, the north Alabama Radicals were in deadly earnest on the disfranchisement provisions. Two proposals came from the Committee on the Elective Franchise, the first being a minority report calling for no disfranchisement beyond the temporary provisions under the Military Reconstruction acts. One black delegate, Thomas Lee of Perry County, signed the report on the grounds that "all I want is equal rights in the courthouse and equal rights when I go to vote."[90] The majority report, on the other hand, required all voters to take an oath to maintain the constitution and to "accept the civil and political equality of all men," refraining from interference with others. The proposal disfranchised nearly no one, but the expectation was that some ex-Confederates would find the oath distasteful enough to refrain from registering. The majority report also had an unusual provision designed to surmount the participation threshold. Anyone who registered and then refused to vote on the constitution would forfeit voting privileges thereafter. The moderately Republican *New York Times* called the notion extravagant, but proponents stood by their measure. "The only question is as to whether we have been too liberal," the majority members concluded.[91]

The delegates thought so, rejecting both proposals despite General Swayne's rumored support for the majority report.[92] A test vote upheld disfranchisement by sixty-three to twenty-two, a measure of the prevailing sentiment. In the up-country, this looked like a matter of survival. Several delegates received warnings not to return home. At the county level, enfranchising freedmen mattered little in areas where few freedmen lived: disfranchisement of ex-Rebels was what delegates came to do. On the other hand, Congress provided little encouragement. Former Confederate general Josiah Gorgas rejoiced, "Even the radicals seem to be awakening at the north to the insanity of placing these states under negro rule."[93] Reports of Washington's displeasure stopped the delegates in mid-debate, and they dispatched an emissary for advice.[94] When pleas to desist came, however, delegates largely ignored them. The convention jettisoned the proposal for punishing nonvoters but left the civil-equality oath intact. Voting provisions essentially reenacted in state law the Military Reconstruction acts, barring prewar officeholders who had voluntarily aided the rebellion. These limitations would remain until lifted by the Reconstruction legislature.

The convention was America's first lawmaking body with a substantial black presence, which makes the lawmakers' behavior worth some attention.[95] For these untested delegates, the disfranchisement fracas raised difficult issues. Their white allies offered inconsistent counsel, and hostile observers—and turn-of-the-century historians thereafter—burlesqued their participation. The New York *World* featured the "Black and Tan" convention and its "negro barbers, coach drivers, and valets." A reporter called the black delegates "simply automats," though his own column suggests otherwise.[96] Several delegates spoke up repeatedly or offered resolutions, especially those who had been free before the war. One observer conceded their "tolerably good grammatical language."[97] If some delegates spoke little, missteps could have ruinous consequences, and the issues that roiled their white colleagues were not the ones they cared most about. They reportedly functioned as a bloc, with some voting for frequent adjournment, which might suggest consultation. John Carraway sought to see legislative proposals in print, purportedly to help his colleagues inexperienced in debate, but perhaps to discourage legislative chicanery as well.[98] The delegates evidently puzzled out the issues for themselves.

African Americans had both the numbers and skills to influence proceedings, given the composition of the Republican electorate. Seventeen African Americans attended the convention, a significant minority of the ninety-six delegates who actually attended.[99] At least six were of mixed ancestry, and five were free before war's end. Several held substantial property by 1870, while only two were reported to be illiterate.[100] On the crucial disfranchisement issue, it appears that most distrusted restoration of voting rights to ex-Confederates without preconditions. Thomas Lee, who spoke in support of the mild minority report, came from Perry County, home of the rich planter J. H. Speed, who served with him on the franchise committee. After Lee's speech, Radicals hectored him in the halls for having thus betrayed the Republican cause. He modified his position thereafter, taken aback by the conflicting advice he was getting.[101]

Sympathetic historians have sometimes credited black lawmakers with opposing disfranchisement measures, perhaps motivated by the modern distaste for such policies.[102] In Alabama, it appears concessions to former slaveholders came hard. Most black delegates supported limitations, lining up with Bingham's faction repeatedly on test votes. John Carraway is perhaps representative. He disclaimed any bitterness but "simply asked, as a measure of self-protection, that the political power of the State be kept in the hands of loyal men."[103] As partisan Republicans, the black delegates distrusted the conservatives present. But unlike the north Alabama Radicals, they weighed tactical advice for moderation. James T. Rapier, for example, early proposed that Congress relieve all disabilities of ex-Confederates who supported the Reconstruction process, especially his neighbor, Patton.[104] Both of the contending native white blocs—Radicals and conservatives—had agendas at variance from those of the freedmen. Reconstruction's success depended upon the support of Congress, whose preferences the black delegates were indifferently situated to gauge. If they listened to anyone, it would be the northerners—especially the four Freedmen's Bureau agents who were on leave to attend, plus Keffer from the bureau office, who bore the wounds of his recent shooting.[105]

On other issues, the course seemed clearer. Conservative delegates moved to have magistrates and judges, and perhaps other local officials, appointed by the governor. A Republican journalist observed that the proponents did not dare to say what that really meant, that the new voters were "not the best judges, in all cases, of who should interpret law." This committee proposal initially had support from leading Republicans, perhaps on the grounds of expediency for the coming election. On the floor, however, Thomas M. Peters, a Unionist wartime refugee, denounced the whole notion as undemocratic—a popular position ever since Jacksonian days. Once the issue was raised openly, Rapier and other African American delegates perceived an insult. Peters's motion carried narrowly, and the constitution broadly provided for popular election of local officials.[106]

Black leaders kept a modest profile mostly because the direction of events suited them. The convention implemented the basic principle of equality before the law. Some members, even Republicans, proposed suffrage limitations based on education, possibly to take effect after a period of years. Delegates rejected all these proposals, but that implied no lack of enthusiasm for education. The constitution created a statewide system of free public schools, open to both races, till age twenty-one. An elected board was created, with full legislative powers over the schools. These measures passed surprisingly easily. The constitution provided a dedicated revenue stream, in theory, of over 20 percent of state revenues. One Freedmen's Bureau educational leader concluded that "*in no State* of the Union is there a *more liberal provision* for the cause of Common School Education than in the State of Alabama."[107]

For the more conservative delegates, the proceedings looked bleak. Without more white voters, and rapid restoration of the right to hold office, their future influence in a pro-Reconstruction coalition looked limited. At first, some assured skeptical outsiders thought they could rein in the more Radical delegates. Many soon reconsidered, especially because the Republican caucus concluded to elect officeholders at the ratification vote.[108] This spared Republicans another potentially violent campaign, and might help secure the needed voter participation, but it had political implications. The caucus determined to nominate statewide candidates—with Patton still disfranchised—even as congressional Republicans pondered a bill to relieve some disabilities. D. L. Dalton reported to the governor, off in Washington, "The moderate men of the Convention have lost all heart, and are now indifferent as to what is going on." North Alabama's Radicals evidently controlled the caucus, and so "Judge Smith and Gen. Swayne are much discouraged. They say they have little influence with the extreme men."[109]

By early December, the conservative delegates determined to defeat ratification. A sabotage strategy had been rumored for weeks. The former secessionist Henry C. Semple had been elected as a Republican, but he later claimed he came to draft a constitution, as pledged, and then oppose it.[110] To this point, civil rights demands had been modest. Alabama's black delegates were restrained relative to those elsewhere, most notably South Carolina and Louisiana, but Semple now pressed test votes on divisive racial issues. The constitution said nothing about integrated education, but Semple sought explicit guarantees against it. He also proposed segregation on transportation, on steamboats, railroads, and the like. For good measure, Semple sought an ab initio ban on intermarriage. This moved Carraway, the manumitted product of an interracial union, to satire. He proposed life imprisonment for any white man cohabiting with a black woman, to the amusement of delegates who detected a personal dig at Semple. More seriously, Carraway decried the "hurtful" intention. The law insulted his race without practical effect, as no such intermarriages were in evidence.[111]

All of Semple's proposals were soundly defeated. No doubt he expected nothing less. But Semple had a point, because the Republican majority's relationship to racial justice had been carefully left vague. Despite the caution of the black delegates, some pondered a less discreet approach. No one talked confiscation, but Alfred Strother, a propertyless farm laborer, offered a resolution to inquire into retroactive pay for freedmen since the Emancipation Proclamation. Delegates buried the proposal in committee, but some reportedly thought the idea had merit.[112] More serious was Keffer's proposal for an open accommodations law for public conveyances. "An unpleasant debate sprang up in which the colored delegates participated more generally than before," a reporter noted, inadvertently suggesting a rising trajectory of participation. The subject was postponed, and when Semple moved to resume consideration the black delegates unanimously voted to leave it in committee. They contented themselves with defeating all efforts at explicit legislation to separate the races.[113]

Toward the end of proceedings, economic issues came to the fore. The north Alabama cohort pressed debt relief. One committee proposal was for an 80 percent reduction on all pre-1865 debts owed within the state. Given the collapse of land values and the loss of slave property, the notion made sense, and the federal government passed an extensive bankruptcy law in 1867. But congressional displeasure loomed, as the fate of similar measures in Georgia would later reveal.[114] Delegates settled on more modest alternatives. The convention stayed all enforcement of debts until January 1869, partly as an incentive for ratification. Delegates also increased the exemption from debt execution to one thousand dollars in personal property and a homestead. None of these proposals much benefited the freedmen—perhaps the reverse, though no one apparently said so. The delegates did vote laborers a prior lien on the crop for their wages, and General Swayne implemented it immediately by military order.[115]

The sections relating to corporate enterprise were equally important. The constitution passed general corporation provisions while limiting special legislation on corporate charters, which reflected the Jacksonian inclinations of the north Alabama delegates. Delegates were also mindful of the state's previous difficulties in administering money. Federal land grants for education, and 400,000 acres in aid of Muscle Shoals improvements, had been lost or diverted long before the war. With this sorry record in mind, delegates banned the state undertaking internal improvements directly. The constitution did allow the state to loan its credit for private projects, but only after considerable debate. Chairman Peck came to the floor to denounce the whole idea. One Republican moved that grants should be authorized by two successive legislatures, while Albert Griffin thought proposals should be voted on by the entire electorate. Corporate power raised fears, and Henry Semple drew upon his relevant prewar experience in Montgomery. He warned of "the corrupting influences to which legislators are subject, and about the necessity of guarding the doors of the Treasury, & c."[116] Despite his personal unpopularity, delegates voted for Semple's proposal to require a two-thirds vote for aid, rather than a simple majority.

As time went on, criticism grew. The delegates abolished three recently created counties, by ordinance, leaving their legal status muddied. There were more pressing issues. Repeatedly passing individual divorce decrees seemed inappropriate, and the salary to be paid convention delegates also raised hackles. Eight dollars per diem, given inflation, was not far outside of previous standards, and Alabama paid much less in toto than other southern states. But this was the first Reconstruction convention, and depressed circumstances made the cost issue sensitive. "I cannot tell you what an unpleasant impression has been created by the newspaper reports on this subject," warned General Pope.[117] Horace Greeley criticized the delegates in print, while Senator Henry Wilson complained about Bingham's speeches.[118] Reflecting this pressure, General Pope urged swift adjournment in repeated, and highly partisan, telegrams. "I speak . . . for the interests of the political party, upon whose retention of power for several years to come the success of reconstruction depends," he wrote.[119]

The critics overreacted. Once the constitution was finished, most Republican newspapers deemed it competently drawn, even progressive.[120] Delegates rewrote the constitution in thirty-one days, the quickest such performance in the Reconstruction South. Neighboring Mississippi took over four months, and a deadlocked convention in Texas met for over six months. Patton's aid provided the convention means, as opposed to Georgia where officials cut off funds. Alabama's implementation thus proceeded smoothly, no fuss, no violence. Furthermore, the convention's Radical faction did not dictate the statewide ticket. Despite conservative abstentions, the more restrained Republican delegates turned Bingham down for governor.[121] He received just eighteen votes, and, bitterly disappointed, died some weeks thereafter of pneumonia. W. H. Smith's fifty votes meant that most freedmen backed him, and apparently the northerners did as well. Observers perceived Smith as the moderate alternative, "originally opposed to the Reconstruction Laws" and a bit "weak-kneed in reference to Rebels." Some declared him a reluctant candidate.[122] The other state nominations were divided between newcomers like Colonel Andrew J. Applegate for lieutenant governor and native southerners like Superintendent Noah Cloud for superintendent of schools. The latter group predominated. All three Supreme Court candidates were longtime residents with strong legal backgrounds—Elijah Peck, Thomas Peters, and Benjamin Saffold. The more pronounced native white Radicals were frozen out of nominations, as were the freedmen.

None of this satisfied the more conservative delegates, who struck back as the convention concluded. Only sixty-six delegates voted final approval of the constitution, and fifteen delegates denounced it, among them Semple, Speed, and other native whites. Their protest charged that Republicans had cultivated a "drilled phalanx" of black delegates by "trampling upon the pride of race of the old inhabitants of the State. . . ." At a mass meeting, one conservative delegate reportedly threatened armed resistance. The applause lasted for minutes. He was joined by James Clanton and Democratic editors, cheered to the rafters, with a few silent freedmen looking on.[123]

The logjam had broken. "We are beginning to stand as a Unit—the white People proper," editor Robert Tyler wrote. "We do not think there can be more than 2500 white men in the State who are with the Negroes."[124] He launched a formidable lobbying drive to remove generals Pope and Swayne. For months, Johnson's advisors had been urging restraint, to allow a northern reaction to develop. But the convention changed the situation, and Pope's order combining the ratification and candidate election infuriated the opposition. One of the Republican delegates, irritated by Pope's hectoring, leaked his indiscreet letter to the Democratic press.[125] Editor John Forsyth wrote that the general's removal was worth twenty thousand votes, and it would reverse the cruel wrong being done to Democratic newspapers.[126] Late in December, the president replaced Pope with the more conservative General George Gordon Meade, of Gettysburg fame. The still more conservative Colonel Julius Hayden replaced Swayne. By this point Governor Patton, still operating under disabilities, had enough, and his secretary Dalton wrote that Meade was "one of our sort of men," a decided Democrat.[127] Dalton exaggerated, but both appointees sought a nonpartisan profile. As things stood, several voter-registration officials were running for office, thus overseeing their own election.

Meade sought neutrality, favoring implementation of Congressional Reconstruction in some form, but crises in Georgia and Florida distracted his attention. Hayden thus exercised substantial latitude, and so his "Hd Qrs ceased to be a political Club House" once he took command.[128] He occasionally warned against political speeches—that is to say, Freedmen's Bureau agents were not to instruct enfranchised voters in their new duties.[129] General Grant thought this excessive, and Hayden soon left Alabama, but in the meantime Hayden removed some noncandidates as voting officials for partisanship. His registration head, W. T. Hatchett, explicitly preferred appointees from both parties. This meant last-minute replacement of election officials in the black belt, in areas where few whites could take the legally required test oath. Several appointees reportedly opposed ratification. One election official reportedly said, "No decent man can live under such a God-damned Constitution, and that he was going to oppose it, and that we would see that the whole damned thing would go to hell." If Pope and Swayne had promoted reunion under congressional terms, as Republicans, their successors moved some lesser distance in the opposite direction. The shift and the personnel changes it implied undermined the prospects for ratification.[130]

Bad omens shook Republican leaders. The Huntsville *Advocate* wanted the convention to reassemble and strike out some of the constitution's unpopular features. Smith disavowed even the limited disfranchisement provisions, also promising that the schools would probably be segregated.[131] However expedient such concessions looked, the core Republican constituency responded differently. Freedmen did not yet press for direct representation, but they apparently reacted to the native defections by rallying to northern newcomers. In December, district nominating conventions met, and of the six members to be sent to Congress, five were postwar migrants to Alabama. The sixth, Thomas Haughey, was a prewar resident born in Scotland. Prominent Freedmen's Bureau officials, like Charles W. Buckley and C. W. Pierce, received nominations. This occurred most dramatically in the faction-torn Huntsville district. After a divided convention nominated a moderate northern officer, J. W. Burke, the Radicals assembled separately. A freedman reportedly called on his comrades to abandon the native southerners and join their Yankee friends upstairs. A second gathering then endorsed the bureau's J. B. Callis as an "Independent Radical." Superiors removed Colonel Callis, but he won in absentia. Burke fumed that Callis had so riled the blacks that nothing could convince them of "the perversity of his designs."[132]

The state ticket posed fewer "carpetbagger" appearance problems, and the nominations for lesser office mostly went to prewar residents. Among the state senate nominees, they outnumbered northern newcomers twenty-two to ten, along with one African American. For circuit judges, the margin was ten to one.[133] Postwar migrants were overrepresented among Republican officeholders, but they never predominated anywhere but in Washington. Still, the highly visible congressional nominations lent substance to charges of a bureau takeover. Disfranchised former officeholders were livid, and native rivals were antagonized along with their following.[134] Unionists of all stripes viewed these nominations as an insult to their wartime loyalty, and a threat to their own control of the Republican movement.[135]

The initial surge of native white support for Reconstruction receded. Radical candidates in October received far more white votes than they would four months later, perhaps twice as many. The changes in the military must have contributed to the result. Pope's press policies were abandoned, encouraging open opposition. Furthermore, all the pragmatic arguments dissipated if Congress was backing off. The conservatives around Patton lapsed into inactivity or opposition, his financial priorities being overshadowed by events. Elite defections left committed Republicans isolated, exposed to press ridicule and social pressure. Once party selections occurred, the Unionist leaders not nominated found themselves uncompensated for all their pains. Numerous Reconstruction supporters defected at this juncture, often in racial bitterness.

Other substantive issues contributed to this result, among them the sheer novelty of this first Reconstruction constitution. In evanescent Baine and Jones counties, abolished by the convention, officeholders defected, perhaps land speculators in county sites too. On economic issues, delegates turned back sweeping debt-relief measures, and to avoid the stay law creditors sped proceedings, so the first fruits of the constitution hurt debtors. The election campaign occurred at the end of another wretched crop year, and that outcome embittered everyone. For unconditional Unionists who sought a Tennessee-style government, the proposed constitution offered little comfort. On disfranchisement and proscription, the demands that galvanized the Unionist upsurge, the strongest proposals met defeat. North Alabama Unionists had supported Reconstruction primarily because of the continuing conflict with ex-Confederates, for control of courts and juries and law enforcement. Now, wider issues swamped their parochial power struggles.[136]

These factors transformed the racial atmosphere. The absence of positive appeal for unconditional Unionists encouraged the salience of race. Black demands in the convention were modest by standards elsewhere. No one pressed for confiscation, and no positive integration measures passed on public transportation. Indeed, no broad integration measure ever passed under Alabama's Reconstruction government, period. Still, speculation on the constitution's open-ended provisions became a mainstay of the Democratic press. Delegates had rejected positive guarantees of segregation, and they enacted the oath to accept the civil equality of all men. These actions served as a racial hook for other alarmist misgivings against the constitution. The oath in particular was ambiguous, in that it was not clear whether voters thereby forfeited the right to modify the provisions, a plausible interpretation that struck most whites as unfair. One columnist termed the enactment worse than slavery itself. Furthermore, the press stoked fears of a black takeover by its estimates of numbers to be disfranchised. One newspaper estimated a third of the whites; other estimates ran thirty thousand or more. Since no firm count existed for the former officeholder exclusion and other provisions, these numbers metastasized. One planter, H. A. Tayloe, dreamed up nineteen-twentieths. Together, these fearful possibilities provided ample excuse for opposition.[137]

Congress ultimately bore responsibility for the Republicans' woes. Readmission under equal suffrage was congressional policy, but the details frustrated implementation. The Reconstruction acts said that, if a majority of the registered electorate voted in the ratification election, and if those voters gave it a majority, Congress would readmit if otherwise satisfied. This meant that, if half the electorate did not vote, the constitution was defeated. At least that was the strong implication of the law, a provision which became the gauntlet.[138] All the voters who died, moved away, or were deterred counted against ratification. Furthermore, if a boycott occurred, anyone who did vote in the election was publicly identified as a Reconstruction supporter. Convention delegates realized the implications, and they had pleaded with Congress to change the law to a simple majority approval. The House complied, but the Senate demurred. Black registrants outnumbered whites by fifteen thousand, and two subsequent elections would demonstrate that a Republican majority existed, but not under these rules.[139]

For the opposition, the tidings looked good, but their tone caused problems. Sympathetic editors and politicians nationwide had urged restraint, to avoid reanimating northern fears of the rebellion. Now, the rhetorical climate changed as empowered states' rights Democrats seized on race.[140] A manifesto claimed that ratification would bathe Alabama "in the darkness of ignorance and barbarism," leaving churches to be "desecrated by the foul rites of fetic[h]ism."[141] The campaign took on ugly overtones. James Clanton said that, if freemen voted Republican, "in less than six months their throats would be cut, and their carcasses would be rotting in the woods." The New York *Tribune* reported his Greenville speech as an obscenity-laced threat of extermination.[142] Some constitution opponents bridled at these expressions, preferring economic retaliation. The Mobile *Register* warned that it took voters' names, and the Mobile *Tribune* cited the wholesome example of a freedman who lost his fine job fifteen minutes after voting.[143]

If whites refrained from voting, and they thus frustrated the terms laid out by Congress, no one knew what would follow. The law's provisions provided no indication. Congress might vote readmission anyway. In that event, a boycott would give the Republicans control of every office in the state. National newspapers predicted that possibility, and one might have thought the scenario worth considering.[144] A safer alternative existed: if Democrats and conservatives fielded candidates but voted against the constitution, they might defeat it, as would happen in neighboring Mississippi. Failing that, they would still win local offices and control much of the legislature. Not attractive options, perhaps, but they might mitigate a Republican interregnum, and prospective governor Smith was not seen as fiscally irresponsible or egalitarian on race. The ambitious railroad aid law still awaited implementation, so any influence mattered. Disfranchisement was not likely to last long given tepid northern support, and whites remained a majority. In due course, the elite might have regained influence, given all the advantages wealth, education, and experience gave them. Participation could have avoided the chaos and violence to come. Nor was standing aside guaranteed to win friends. As one Maine newspaper nastily warned, "If they choose to lay down and let the niggers roll over them, they will have no claim to anybody's sympathy."[145]

When opponents gathered in Montgomery in mid-January, they had no idea how to respond beyond exhortations to uphold white supremacy. After heated debate behind the scenes, they determined on a boycott.[146] With three weeks remaining before the vote, they were poorly situated to run candidates anyway. At the urging of ex-governor Parsons, the assembled delegates called for non-participation in rousing terms. "We cannot come in contact with this leprous and noxious thing, without being defiled with its corruption," the activists wrote.[147] The numerous signers of this document included former secessionists who now reasserted their claim to leadership. "We are the lawful voters of the State; our right, the proud heritage of the white race, is guaranteed to us by the Constitution," or so the delegates affirmed. Ironies abounded: ex-governor Lewis Parsons, Samuel Rice, and Alexander White signed the defiant statement. All somehow became prominent Republicans after readmission occurred.[148]

The vote in early February played out as predicted. The freedmen provided ratification a huge majority, 70,815 to 1,005, in numbers the opponents could not match, but the turnout was not enough. At Grant's suggestion, Meade had lengthened the balloting period to five days and voided several fraudulent results. The vote still failed of the specified majority by over 8,000 votes, Meade concluded.[149] In black-belt counties, overall totals are close to those of the convention election, but with almost no white support. Greene and Macon counties returned 4 white votes apiece for the convention, Bullock none at all. In north Alabama the figures suggest a large drop off from the previous vote, by a third or more.[150] Overall, around 7,500 whites voted for ratification, 10 percent of those registered and a somewhat smaller portion of the overall white population. They concentrated in places like Winston County, where the vote almost reached half, and DeKalb with an apparent majority. In the mountain region as a whole, nearly 28 percent of those registered voted for the constitution. About half that proportion voted in surrounding areas of the Tennessee Valley and the piedmont. Elsewhere the percentages sagged, under 4 percent even in the impoverished wiregrass counties of the southeast. These voters should be viewed as the rock-solid residuum of pro-Reconstruction sentiment. Turnout among whites concentrated in the poorer counties of northern Alabama, but the geographic pattern points toward the wartime Unionist strongholds rather than toward poverty per se.[151]

"[T]he white men have proven themselves worthy of their names and lineage," a former secessionist enthused, because Alabamians had defied congressional pressure and voted their convictions.[152] Reconstruction opponents were jubilant. One Freedmen's Bureau agent wrote, "They crow over their victory exceedingly and I get to share the benefit of all of it alone. I am dreadfull sick of it."[153] Battered Republicans and a few conservatives sought a path to reunion. Some suggested revisions to the constitution, as did General Meade and some of the delegates.[154] Governor Patton preferred recommencing the process entirely, starting with new elections, and then separating the ratification election from a subsequent vote for officers. This offered Congress yet another opportunity to remove Patton's disabilities, with a chance to retain the governorship.[155]

These options have some plausibility, given what was to come. Some pronounced Republicans, especially the prospective officeholders, determined upon a different course. The Reconstruction laws left grandly in-

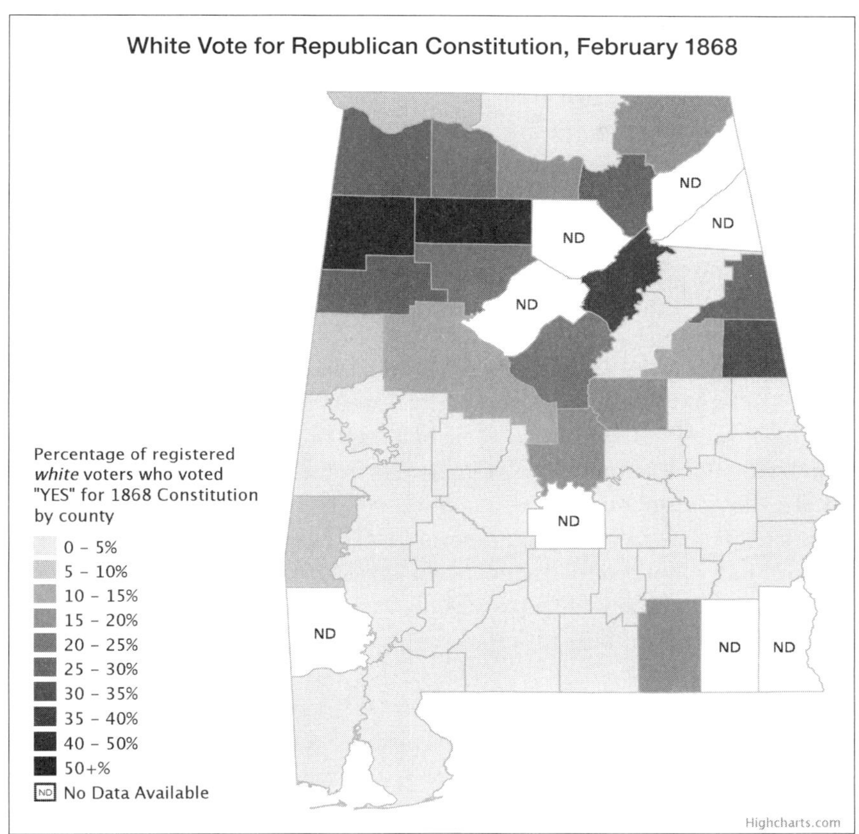

distinct what would happen if a majority refused to vote. Congress could just declare effective compliance, rather than delay readmission indefinitely. One delegate, Mark D. Brainard, saw this as a positive opportunity: "are not our chances much better with every office in radical hands than they would be with one third of the counties under the control of rebels in the Presidential contest?" Others talked in terms of political survival. J. L. Pennington thought Republicans had polled their maximum vote, so only actual control held any hope.[156]

Many Republicans thought the notion of reversing the apparent outcome unwise. William H. Smith did not endorse his own installation as governor, not under these auspices. George Spencer feared readmission would hand the electoral vote to the Democrats in November. He preferred keeping military rule till people tired of it, and then try again after a Republican national victory.[157] Faced with such conflicting advice, Congress showed little enthusiasm for readmission. Thaddeus Stevens initially disavowed the idea, and Congress satisfied itself with changing the subsequent approval requirements. Matters hung fire for months, while the presidential impeachment trial proceeded and other states ratified constitutions. In the meantime, proponents assembled evidence of a tainted vote and unfriendly military management. Having lured so many freedmen onto the firing line, proponents urged Congress not to leave them in the lurch. "Accept the constitution, and our legislature will take care of the State," Chambers County Republicans urged.[158]

Evidence of intimidation was not hard to find. A Wetumpka newspaper listed all the white voters by name, then predicted that "numbers of those who have voted will withdraw their ballots before to-morrow night." Five apparently did so, along with twenty-two freedmen. Colonel Hayden admitted that numbers of freedmen had been evicted, but increases in the price of cotton meant they found employers easily, no real harm done.[159] Hayden had a point because economic pressure never worked well electorally. Freedpeople widely disregarded economic threats, whatever the cost. Only force would prevent them voting Republican: the whopping margins proved it.

Testimony piled up. Over 120 freedmen filed affidavits that they had been fired.[160] In two counties, threats or destruction of official documents prevented elections from being held. In Lowndes County, ballot boxes were stolen. In Greensboro, a meeting reportedly resolved to incapacitate bureau agent H. G. Claus, who was then brained with a "slung shot." A messenger was shot at in Eutaw. Candidate William Miller reportedly fled town to save his life, while another nominee was knocked down and then shot. As yet, no one mentioned the Klan, which suggests limited intimidation relative to subsequent elections. But the canvass bore little resemblance to the peaceful previous vote.[161]

Alabama's readmission became the focus of national debate. The New York *Tribune* and the *Times,* both Republican, exchanged sharp editorials.[162] Congressmen proposed to square the circle, even as Meade spent months recalculating the votes and proposing fixes. The timing proved miserable: the Ku Klux Klan burst into view across Alabama in late March, promoted by the now-liberated Democratic press. The ashes of apparent victory probably strengthened Alabama's outbreak, though the Klan spread all across the region simultaneously. Regardless, after President Johnson's acquittal, Congress included Alabama along with five other reconstructed states in an "omnibus" readmission bill in June. Congressmen concluded readmission was within their discretion, thus reaffirming equal suffrage as part of Alabama's fundamental law. William H. Smith became governor in mid-July, his all-Republican government became operational, and military control finally ceased.[163]

Republican rule thus commenced in Alabama, and its subsequent development was correspondingly unique. Whatever criticisms one might make of Governor Smith's behavior, his hobbled advent to power explains much. So did his background, which mingled white social acceptability with stubborn Unionism. His Randolph County was a poor nonslaveholding enclave separated from the mountain region it resembled, though he himself was a slaveholding lawyer. Serving in the legislature, Smith moved away from the states' rights Democratic position, becoming as a Douglas elector in 1860 and opposing secession.[164] In late 1862, he found himself in the midst of local resistance against conscription. Smith testified he fled to escape the governor's order for his arrest. Several of his brothers joined Colonel Spencer's regiment, while Smith became a spy and recruiter, finally accompanying Sherman's march to the sea. At war's end, Spencer's comrades pressed to have him made provisional governor, and he subsequently accepted appointment under Governor Parsons as judge. He resigned in frustration because he "could not hold court without being insulted by the rebel lawyers. . . ."[165] As Military Reconstruction approached enactment, he resisted having his name associated with black suffrage. Smith possessed loyalist credentials aplenty, but he also had a trajectory as an episodic insurgent inclined towards personal pique. His nomination for governor was perceived as a success for moderation. He prided himself on his entrée into polite society, and he was reluctant to isolate himself further by espousing civil rights.

This inclination only intensified as governor under an arguably defeated constitution. Even with a monopoly of formal power, Republican rule looked fragile, and Smith evidently concluded that a predominantly black party had no future. Among all the Reconstruction governors, Smith moved most determinedly to conciliate the elite, especially former conservatives. Alabama thus never came under "Radical" Republican rule, certainly not under Smith. He backed away from his unconditional Unionist constituency, presenting himself as a "conservative Republican" and emphasizing his Georgia origin. Smith cultivated the image of a somewhat misplaced member of Alabama's lawyer elite. He would assail "carpetbagger" influence, most emphatically that of his former sponsor

George E. Spencer, elected to the US Senate by the new Reconstruction legislature.

In July, the Republican legislature gave the state a congressional delegation without a single native southerner, or African American, for that matter. Alabama's other senator, Willard Warner of Ohio, became an ally of Governor Smith's, but Spencer became his carpetbag nemesis. A personal issue generated the conflict. As Governor Smith settled into office, Alabama's established legal fraternity led by Henry Semple pressed impeachment charges against Judge Busteed, while he recuperated from his shooting at his home in New York for long periods. Smith backed impeachment, which pleased the legal community while potentially ridding the state of a corrupt official. Under the Bankruptcy Act of 1867, lucrative positions as registrar were to be appointed by the chief justice and commissioned by federal district judges. Spencer, Keffer, D. H. Bingham, and other Republicans received appointment, but Busteed reportedly expected a thousand-dollar payment apiece. To his "very intimate" friend Smith, and indeed everyone in earshot, Spencer denounced Busteed as "a villain, a rascal, and all that sort of thing."[166] But Spencer preferred not to testify that he had bribed Busteed, so he claimed he had given the money as "a gift," to compensate the judge for his increased workload. Other witnesses evaporated, and Congress refused to impeach the nominally Republican judge at the behest of ex-secessionist lawyers. The outcome infuriated Smith, who provided a list of witnesses to Spencer's previous statements. After hearing reports of the senator's negative comments, Smith informed him that it had become "a case of personal veracity between you and me," and he cut off ties.[167]

Smith's feud with Alabama's leading "carpetbagger" dovetailed with his policy moves. As newly installed governor, Smith dominated the scene for months after his inauguration, and the legislature then went out of session for nearly all of 1869. Smith exercised unusual influence, and his priority was to make the Republican Party attractive to former conservatives. The governor exerted himself to get several high-profile measures enacted within weeks. Smith persuaded the legislature to offer blanket relief for all those disfranchised under the constitution. He pressed the school board to decree segregation as state policy, which they did with equal dispatch. He had no intention of implementing the constitution's provisions for a state militia, fearing conflict would result from mobilizing the freedmen. He thus left his government all but unarmed, which reassured the opposition of his conciliatory intent while antagonizing Radicals. And he vetoed legislators' attempt to cast Alabama's electoral vote themselves that November.[168] The legislature acquiesced, but only after Smith journeyed to Washington to secure troops from President Johnson, to guarantee that the election could be held under military protection. That November, Grant and the Republicans actually carried Alabama by about four thousand votes. These political successes apparently confirmed the reasonableness of his strategy.[169]

Smith's search for a sensible middle ground, and sensible opponents, dominated public life. African American priorities carried little weight, and stiff-arming the freedpeople became his political strategy. As stated here, Smith's policies sound plausible, even inevitable. Concessions might give his wobbly government, or at least Smith himself, some legitimacy among most whites, and it won him praise in the press. But among Republicans his leadership promoted a factional backlash. On two crucial issues, Smith's policies shaped the state's evolution, his support for promotion of railroads being most important for the state's financial future. For most Republicans, though, far more immediate was Smith's response to the terrorist activity that engulfed the state. It is his interrelated efforts to conciliate the opposition on these two issues, the Ku Klux Klan and the railroads, to which subsequent chapters turn.

7

The Difference between Whaling a Freeman and Pounding a Slave

Terrorism and Resistance in the Klan Era

> We the Colard citizens of Coosa Co. . . . is a standing up to all Clans and obeyed the laws so far and yet we have not received our just wrights here as sittysons. . . .
>
> —Ziegler Chapman, October 1869

The Ku Klux Klan receives abundant emphasis in contemporary scholarship, for good reason. Everything from its performance aspect to its appearance in national discourse has received scrutiny; the movement's sexual license and abuse of women alone secure book-length treatment.[1] This emphasis suits the situation in northern Alabama, where terrorism was pervasive and uninhibited. Still, the scholarly attention to dramatic horrors can overshadow tangible issues on the ground, like what means of mitigation existed. Sometimes there were options: though Republicans never devised fully effective defenses, they had some success when numbers favored them, in areas where the bulk of the freedpeople lived. The prospect of black retaliation alarmed cautious grandees, sometimes to good effect. Moreover, the threat of uncontrolled escalation made the issue difficult for politicians to ignore. Across much of Alabama, popular resistance thus disrupted the pattern of night-riding without consequence.

Americans today tend to think of the Reconstruction Ku Klux Klan as distinctive. Indeed it was, but terrorist violence had numerous antecedents in Alabama, as elsewhere. Slavery and the racial controls it spawned were the overriding causes. Whites monitored enslaved people obsessively. The extraction of labor from unwilling workers lent itself to forceful behavior which the modest state structure subjected to few limitations. Masters and overseers whipped at discretion, forming habits that could not easily be overcome. Thus the antebellum South was notorious for its duels and knifings and its testy defense of personal honor. The overwhelmingly rural region retained a frontier ethos longer than similar areas elsewhere.[2]

The prevalence of whipping and similar means of discipline weakened respect for the rule of law. Citizens understood themselves as presiding over a dangerous, captive population. When trouble threatened, white men came running armed, and legal niceties looked irrelevant. Historians have found that slave defendants sometimes received surprisingly even-handed justice before the court system, but legal technicalities only intensified the popular inclination toward extralegal punishment.[3] The naturalist Philip Gosse spent a year as a tutor outside Selma in the late 1830s, and he identified a distinctive popular viewpoint, that the people were the source of law and therefore were above the law. In Alabama, every man was "his own law-maker and lawbreaker, judge, jury and executioner." The Britisher feigned a lack of curiosity, but he nonetheless got an earful of torture tales, literally hearing the whippings himself at day's end.[4]

The Klan's more direct predecessor was the slave patrol. An elderly freedwoman, Nancy Pugh, decades later, mixed the Klan and prewar patrols together indiscriminately in her memory.[5] Across the antebellum South, able-bodied white males were obliged to ride periodically on road duty. Though the wealthy often bought their way out, most men rode on overnight patrols.[6] They whipped local slaves without passes while arresting apparent runaways. The "paterrollers" tended toward drunken disorderliness, which only bolstered the authority of the masters by discouraging slaves from wandering. This widely shared experience underlay postwar behavior. Klan apologists would frequently depict themselves as "regulators," doing routine crime control; the reality behind this lay in the widespread sense that somebody white needed to be on guard. The difference was that planters lost their financial motivation to protect slaves' lives. Little restrained self-appointed patrollers after the war.

Political crisis intensified violence. Those opposing immediate secession often found themselves endangered by mobs. In the Tennessee Valley and especially in the mountains, communities remained badly divided even after war began. In Cherokee County, Ebenezer Leath heard that he and other Unionists were denounced by a secessionist preacher. Leath confronted the preacher at gunpoint and "kicked him until he begged like a dog." During the war, he threatened draft agent Bratch Porter. Leath's ferocious reputation deterred a postwar terrorist raid, while

Porter would be killed in Klan regalia.[7] Conscription yielded equally longstanding hatreds elsewhere. Outside Talladega, Union officers complained, poorer whites evened scores bloodily with neighbors who had enforced conscription too zealously.[8]

Northern Alabama became a petri dish of chaos. The early occupation prompted guerrilla warfare. Squads of nocturnal horsemen targeted individual Unionists or escaping slaves, acting in ways that anticipated postwar behavior. In Limestone County, the planter Sam Moore led a wartime guerrilla band on his way to federal prison as Klan leader.[9] Faced with widespread bushwhacking, northern troops responded with retaliatory destruction and the arming of Unionist home guards. The Tennessee Valley, with its unique wartime experience of elite impoverishment and profusion of refugees, became the incubator for Reconstruction-era night-riding. The organization appeared in north Alabama in 1867, nearly a year before it was common elsewhere.[10] Athens was just thirty miles from Pulaski, Tennessee, the origin of the organization, and Klans in the vicinity were prone to public displays. At Huntsville, for example, about one hundred Klansmen rode around the county courthouse to disrupt an election meeting.[11] On another occasion, a Union officer in Decatur found well-drilled Klansmen surrounding the train depot. Future congressman C. C. Sheets denounced Klansmen in a speech, only to find himself confronting them at his hotel.[12] To the extent that the Klan was an organized, centrally directed movement, it most resembled it here.

Presidential Reconstruction added another source of night-riding. When Confederate veterans returned home, they transformed upland neighborhoods previously dominated by draft resisters. The reinstallation of wartime officials left outnumbered Unionists infuriated, and contending bands sometimes came to blows. St. Clair's Union veterans, for example, openly resisted county officials, and in the inaccessible mountain areas conflicts persisted. Northern Methodist activities added a religious dimension: conflict was rife, and in mid-1866 one missionary in Huntsville feared widespread secret societies.[13] Furthermore, when Governor Patton tried to reorganize all-white militias, the army disallowed it, but that did not end extralegal night-riding and the disorderly seizure of arms.[14]

Vigilante groups operated locally prior to the actual Klan. Long before black suffrage, emancipation served as provocation. As early as 1865, something resembling Klan operations appeared in southwestern Alabama around Bladon Springs. At the same time, the "Black Cavalry" spread into the eastern portion of the state, in the vicinity of Clay and Coosa counties. Ex-Confederates were riding around with faces blacked, or in masks, burning homes and churches. They assaulted or threatened African and Northern Methodist ministers. Some also targeted blacks who farmed independently, a motive that occasionally appears elsewhere. The Black Cavalry functioned for over a year, and according to the Freedmen's Bureau, they once shot a magistrate who attempted to prosecute them.[15] Alabama's longest-lived Klan cluster, in Tallapoosa and Coosa counties, drew from this pre-existing movement. In Henry County, disguised riders called the Jay Hawk Rangers were reportedly trying to drive off black laborers, even threatening whites for hiring them. Such structured groups were rare in the plantation belt, though individual violence inflicted by former masters was rife. Ex-slaveholders and overseers had difficulty managing free laborers, if the bureau records are any indication, but organized vigilantism developed later.[16]

Only with Congressional Reconstruction did grievances coalesce into a broad resistance movement. Military implementation of black suffrage, combined with the shift to decentralized tenant farming, galvanized a mass response. In Alabama, the political motivation seems most immediate. Apologists blamed the Union League for provoking the Klan in self-defense, which had some truth in terms of inspiring white alarm, because race-war talk circulated widely. The Klan began operating in the Tennessee Valley just as blacks received the vote. It spread statewide during the impeachment trial of Andrew Johnson, in March and April 1868. This occurred while Congress debated readmitting Alabama, under the constitution most whites thought they had defeated by boycott. Unprecedented political developments thus enabled the Klan's spread.[17]

Early in the twentieth century, the Dunning-school historian Walter Lynwood Fleming defended the Ku Klux Klan, arguing that it was started by wealthy men, pillars of the community, and only gradually fell into the hands of lower-class troublemakers. More recently, Eric Foner's magisterial *Reconstruction* similarly emphasized upper-class direction over the movement.[18] Elite sponsorship makes sense, especially early on, because numerous factors promoted extremism among the political class. For one thing, anti-Reconstruction newspapers had lost their official advertising. This infuriated editors, and the press printed Klan notices widely, until prevented by yet another military order. Among lawyers, too, the new constitution stopped debt proceedings, exacerbating other interruptions in income. Judges and lawyers were antagonized by Pope's order mandating biracial juries, and the policy had to be implemented that spring. But the most pressing elite issue was the status of former officeholders. Readmission of Alabama coincided with the ratification of the Fourteenth Amendment. It barred from office all prewar officials complicit in rebellion, until Congress removed disabilities. Removal and indefinite exclusion encouraged harsh responses.[19]

Memoirs highlight the political elite in regulator activities. Given the approving public climate, later politicians often bragged about youthful exploits. Thomas McCorvey recounted his recruitment to the Knights of the White Camellia, apparently in Monroeville. The son of the prewar probate judge, and now as a legal clerk of seventeen, he was befriended by lawyers and courthouse officials. McCorvey rode with such comrades during the 1868 presidential election. The first Ku Klux Klan reportedly established in the state, at Athens, demonstrated a similar pedigree. Susan Davis recalled seeing her father, a lawyer, in his Klan garb. She wrote a dubious celebratory history, but her contacts identified the original officers of the county Klan. Several of the men named are conspicuous for family wealth. The "Grand Cyclops," Nicholas Richardson, was worth nearly $30,000 dollars in 1870. Three more Richardsons, apparently brothers, lived with a father worth nearly $200,000 in 1860. Davis's informants as well as McCorvey expressed clear motivation: night-riders rode to combat Reconstruction and punish infractions of the racial order.[20]

Similar evidence comes from all over the Tennessee Valley. Sartorial sophistication provides one indication. Legislator J. J. Hinds of Decatur recalled Klansmen wearing pasteboard funnel hats, long gowns, and red pants with white stripes up and down the seams, with full disguises for the horses as well. Other victims recalled equally ornate outfits, which must have involved expense, as did simply owning horses rather than mules. There are individual stories as well, one incongruous. A Klan founder recalled Captain A. H. Keller of Tuscumbia as the first man initiated in Alabama. That detail is questionable, but black testimony at the time identified him as a Klan chieftain too. Keller was a lawyer and future Democratic official, in a Klan-ridden locality, and his case seems exceptional in one only respect: the moral luster of his daughter Helen's career as a disabled-rights crusader.[21]

Ryland Randolph, Alabama's most notorious Klansman, vividly illustrates the theme. A Confederate captain with an undistinguished wartime record, he was the son of a wealthy former US naval officer. He served simultaneously as terrorist chieftain, editor of the Tuscaloosa *Independent Monitor*, and Democratic state representative. In Randolph's estimate, his company "did much good service to Tuskaloosa County in its capacity of Klan," and his editorials threatened victims who were then whipped the very same night. His venom surpasses belief: the military jailed him for "the carving up of a negro on the streets of Tuscaloosa," as he reminisced. Randolph engaged in several duel challenges, and he lost a leg in a street confrontation. He wrote his fiancée suggesting she carry arms, joking that she could use her pistol—his gift—against rival suitors.[22] One would hesitate to describe the fiery atheist Randolph as typical, but he represents the extravagant edge of elite feeling.[23]

Systematic examination of the evidence provides a social context for these individual examples. Various sources reveal nearly six hundred names of those plausibly accused, at the time, of being disguised night-riders or active Klan participants.[24] Those located in 1870 were mostly young, with a median age of twenty-four, and their median real wealth as individuals was exactly zero. A substantial minority were described as farm laborers, day laborers, and the like.[25] Many still lived at home, and their family means do not look prepossessing. Average household wealth of suspects is $1,975, with median wealth $500. Some evidence suggests the bulk of the property held by accused Klansmen was in livestock, particularly swine and cattle.[26]

In view of the war, these men's modest standing is not that surprising. The contrast with their prewar background, however, is startling. Most of these young men were dependents in parental households before the war. Of 147 men whose own wealth, or that of their parents' households, can be located, the average household wealth was $19,837, with a median wealth of about $5,000.[27] The evidence thus suggests a *tenfold* reduction in wealth during the war decade. Postwar formation of new households accounts for some of this contrast, but terrorist participants look prosperous before the war.[28] Slaveholding provides the revealing measure. Of those whose families could be located before the war, a majority appear in the slave censuses.[29] The average number reported is thirteen slaves, and if men of vast wealth were uncommon, planter families were well represented. Most names disappear from sight, but all the comparisons between prewar and postwar wealth suggest dramatic loss.

Another overlapping body of suspects looks similar. Republican Governor Smith received numerous reports of collective violence prior to November 1870, before the wave of federal indictments, and most apparently involved organized Klans or similar local offshoots. The names of fifty-one suspects appear. Those located possessed modest means after the war, with a median household wealth of about $1,000 in 1870. But their prewar median family wealth is vastly larger, $13,000. The devastated Tennessee Valley accounts for much of this decline, and the overall pattern holds even if one examines families of origin located both before and after the war. Both the age and the wealth of identified suspects declines by year of their reported involvement, from 1868 through 1870.[30]

The findings all point to drastic postwar impoverishment, a pattern that makes intuitive sense. If most night-riders came from prosperous families and they lost most everything, the trajectory of their lives shifted. This experience might well push young men toward reckless behavior, especially directed at targets identified with their Yankee foes. Emancipation embittered planter-class men, and now black suffrage outraged them. These changes encouraged racist violence across Alabama. In Greenville, for example, one grand juror sketched the Klan's social origins vividly: "Five sons of bankrupt planters (ex-cotton Kings) between 16 & 30 years of age and ten other[s] like ex-overseers from 30 to 80 years of age, make fifteen K.K.K.s. In some places they are organized, but in general they are not, nor is there more necessity for it than for so many rattlesnakes to organize to bite or for a vacuum to organize. . . ." That is the point: impoverishment and emancipation provided the underlying grievances, and political Reconstruction provided the spark. Elite social permission, by former slaveholders' sons, editors, and supplanted Democratic officeholders, allowed political violence to metastasize.[31]

Upper-class sponsorship provided the nucleus of wider support, as an incident in the black-belt town of Eutaw suggests. In March 1868, a group of planter-class men horsewhipped J. B. F. Hill, the native Northern Methodist minister and Union League leader. Some dispute occurred over appropriated firewood, and regulator episodes were often excused by such occurrences, difficult to untangle. Hill's flogging, lacking disguises, does not seem an actual Klan operation, but it otherwise resembled one. The army paraded the suspects through the streets in irons, and military justice sentenced them to years in the Dry Tortugas prison. But General Grant feared an appeal to Judge Busteed's court; so he ordered the defendants freed along with Ryland Randolph, then in jail, too.[32] The sequel is revealing: local leaders had prevailed upon business contacts to bail them in New Orleans, and the cotton factors did as requested, but they submitted a bill for their services. This provoked community outrage because back in Eutaw the men were heroes: "They were met about two miles from town by people from every adjoining county escorted by a train of vehicles of every kind with women children *every body* one mile long." Their lawyer, the reputed Klan leader John Jolly, greeted them with a speech. The young men became military martyrs, and a genuine terrorist campaign ensued against the witnesses. Greene County become a Klan hotspot, promoted by the Eutaw *Whig* and Randolph's nearby Tuscaloosa *Monitor*.[33]

In Alabama, the Klan's expansion followed a common pattern. During the spring of 1868, Klan organizers circulated printed rituals. General Forrest and his business partners were then promoting an insurance venture, and their travels facilitated the movement.[34] Klan placards started appearing, reprinted by sympathetic editors who were often themselves participants. The picturesque nature of the warnings, the array of ghouls and daggers, caught attention. Notices appeared even in towns where night-riding never caught on, and enthusiasts displayed little initial circumspection.[35] Mary Buford, near Eufaula, came from a prominent family: her brother once led proslavery settlers into the Kansas territory. That spring, she breathed a new optimism: "Cotton has advanced, the democrats are increasing north, and there is a Godsend known as the Ku Klux Klan. It is reported to be doing a great deal of good there is no doubt about it keeping in check the audacious proceedings of white and black radicals." She continued with a breathless recitation of their vivid costumes and headless pranks. "They have appeared in Clayton, Troy and I expect in most of the small towns of the State," she observed. Klansmen threatened the leading native Radical in the vicinity, Elias Keils, with political animosity the only motive Buford indicated.

Gleeful as Buford was, her kin did not exult over actual violence.[36] When a young relative began night-riding, they recoiled at the drunken beating of innocent freedmen, and the young man's father eventually evicted him. Supporters wanted to believe that regulators could ride without unseemly force. One Montgomery Klansman explained: "We organized to frighten the Negroes and have some fun. . . . We first thought of the organization to scare the negroes from the Loyal League meetings." The anonymous interviewee was a medical student, and he procured bones for dramatic effect. His comrades also once used fireworks to break up a Republican meeting. The political intention is evident, and there was just enough "danger to make it enjoyable," though eventually the novelty paled. Bad men began to do real mischief, he said, so his comrades disbanded their organization.[37]

Force escalated as participants became accustomed to transgressive behavior. Picturesque threats seldom worked for long, and whippings were long-familiar conduct, the default mode of Klan intimidation. Whatever the initial involvement of lawyers and editors and planters, continuous night-riding fell to less prosperous men, much like the prewar patrols. Only young men seeking excitement would ride around night after night. Such participants were less disciplined, less concerned about the political impact or cotton production, and more inclined toward seizing victims' property. They also had their own grievances against the freedpeople, and they frequently acted upon them without restraint. Finally, as arrests accelerated, it became expedient to silence witnesses. One man's testimony might unravel a whole chain of participants, especially when federal prosecutions began. As punishment became more possible, the motivation for murderous violence intensified.

The resulting pattern of violence defies easy explanation. In the Tennessee Valley, the Klan paraded widely, intimidating Republicans and occasionally ordering them out of their homes.[38] Whipping of voters and seizing guns from black veterans were common, even standard procedure. The political effect was obvious, with the Republican vote in the valley diminishing dramatically. Klansmen attacked suspect missionaries or denominations, especially where Republican meetings were held. Schools were torched and teachers attacked. The most prevalent targets were those identified with Republican politics, especially the hated Union Leagues. Black activists were central targets, and many officeholders experienced threats. Probate Judge William T. Blackford in Hale County reportedly received eleven written warnings.[39]

Most historians emphasize the political motivation. Seldom were Democrats targets, and violence normally spiked at ballot time. "Keep quiet until the present election is over," one notice warned. The movement was simultaneously political in the broader sense, punishing freedpeople for getting out of their place. Everything from "sass" to assault provided the pretext. Partisan terrorism could readily be turned against a host of social grievances. One freedman had night-riders shooting at him because they believed his wife was white.[40] Beyond this, Reconstruction politics touched imperative daily concerns of money and behavior. Emancipation challenged the racial order in various venues, and the night-riders repressed black freedom in all of them.

Violations of racial protocol could escalate. Outside Tuscaloosa the planter's sons Murchison Findley and his brother were returning home one night in April 1869. According to sympathetic accounts, they feigned abduction of an African American child. The men "were *not* in earnest about carrying off the little boy," one local explained, adding that they were half-drunk. The child's armed father and an uncle indicated displeasure, probably physically, leaving the horsemen begging for their lives. Later, Findley's friends returned to burn out the freedmen, but the alert targets killed Murk Findley and wounded two more. Now Klansmen mobilized in force, targeting the jailed father and his brother. As desperate freedmen wrote, "About forty came through town from North Port about 4 miles below town in pursuit of the man[,] they knock down and beat almost everybody they meet[,] they have killed 3 men to our knowledge in the last 24 hours and are in persuit of others yet."[41]

The Tuscaloosa raiders dispensed with disguises, as Klansmen sometimes did. Afterwards, nearly all the white young men in the vicinity reportedly fled the law, evidence of the extent of participation. The striking thing about this episode is that all the white observers blamed the freedmen. The nominally Republican sheriff called Findley a fine young man, blaming the freedmen's abuse for all the trouble. This demonstrated the normal dynamic: only the most pristine self-defense against the Klan won any toleration. Any resistance unified nearly all whites. Extremists could count on this gut response, and on the likely sequel that militarily experienced ex-Confederates would prevail.[42]

Apologists, at the time and later, highlighted the Klan's regulator function, crime control as a motive. The agricultural changes after emancipation do give the argument some substance. As Steven Hahn contended, livestock roamed through the unfenced woods, especially pigs, a major source of farmers' livelihoods.[43] Slaves, lacking guns or hunting dogs, could only occasionally appropriate them to their own use. Emancipation changed everything, and with the shift from gang labor to decentralized tenant farming supervision declined. Sharecroppers were thrown on their own resources to feed themselves, after several postwar years of ruinous crops and inconsistent pay. Planters complained the freedmen were pilfering from them. Partisans made these claims for public consumption, but they appear in diaries too. This motive for night-riding crossed class lines, because small landowners and tenants depended on pigs for their livelihood. Just as violence by the prewar patrols kept slaves near home, regulators exercised the same function.[44]

Octavia Otey, outside Huntsville, described the context for repeated Klan visits. She found negotiations with freedpeople stressful, bracing herself with opium at contract time, and she reluctantly rented them land. Otey then complained of disappearing hogs, and soon neighbors began inquiring too. After the 1868 presidential election, she was awakened one moonlit evening. The scene resembled a genteel night-rider Halloween: the hooded men requested a piano performance from her daughters, telling ghostly tales of their demise in battle. They disguised their voices, possibly for effect, but likely because they were neighbors. After a request for apples, the departing horsemen gave three cheers to the ladies. A subsequent visit revealed their harder edge. The Klansmen asked "if the negroes were humble and respectful," promising Otey protection. They sought one freedman, Jack, who fled for good reason; an accused thief nearby had just received two hundred lashes after a crossroads interrogation. Otey's diary described several Klan visits that winter, but they were not altogether unwelcome. The evident intent was to bolster the widow Otey and thus counteract a perceived neighborhood problem.[45]

Widespread support would have made Klan suppression difficult under any circumstances. Night-riders had such a spontaneous wealth of military experience, horses, and rifles that victims isolated in sharecroppers' cabins found them difficult to combat. Alabama's institutional vacuum exacerbated the problem, the confusion surrounding implementation of Reconstruction. When official vacancies occurred in the black belt, few experienced or educated men were able, or willing, to accept appointment at army hands. Required property bonds were tough to secure as well. Law enforcement positions like sheriff or solicitor remained vacant for months, awaiting action from Atlanta, and jurisdictional issues abounded. The outgoing legislature created ten new counties in its final 1866–67 session, which the advent of military rule upended.[46] For instance, Colbert County was formed in early 1867. The constitutional convention abolished it, the constitution's apparent defeat reestablished it, and then Alabama's readmission left the status unclear. Three sets of officers claimed position under the Reconstruction government, including holdover military appointees, in the Tennessee Valley where the Klan rampaged.[47] The dispute remained unresolved until 1870. In other counties boundary issues arose, or legal confusion about who ought to be in office.

Alabama's distinctive political limbo exacerbated lawlessness. The outcome of their boycott infuriated Democrats, and in several counties outgoing officials refused to cede their positions. This invited Klan intervention. Weeks or months of disorder followed, particularly in the plantation belt where white Republicans were few, and intimidation of incoming officials sometimes proved intense. Death threats induced Russell County's newly elected probate judge to resign.[48] In Clarke County, Republicans assumed some offices, but threats soon forced them out of the county seat. They requested authority to exercise their functions from another location. The governor disapproved on legal grounds but suggested no redress, so it remained their problem.[49]

Governor Smith's exactitude would prove less evident on other matters, but on this topic he was legalistic. In Athens, Silas Thurlow confronted a probate judge who clung to office, and he asked for instructions. Smith referred such inquirers to the judiciary, disregarding the practical issue of enforcing their writ, or he simply left the letters unanswered. Smith need not have troubled himself in this instance, since Thurlow soon died in the Huntsville Klan raid.[50] In Butler County, Probate Judge S. S. Gardner assumed office, but someone broke into his office and spread tar all over the records. Disguised men paraded nightly, the sheriff had resigned, and he had no protection: "On each side of the Court House but the front, there is a whiskey bar, and in these places men watch to see who comes and goes, until they find that I am alone. They will then send some drunken ruffian, who will make some pretext of business, and end by making a brutal assault." Rowdies reportedly took up a collection for the purpose. Gardner thought resistance would serve as pretext for his execution, and Democratic testimony suggests he was right.[51]

In Greene County, the Unionist planter and Probate Judge William Miller faced persecution, exacerbated by the Eutaw arrests. His predecessor legally contested removal, relinquished his position, and then attempted to regain it. A mob drove Miller from his office, raining abuse at every step. Yellow notices from the Great Grand Cyclops were placarded about, warning traitors to beware. Miller sent eleven missives that summer to the governor, pleading for a show of determination.[52] Smith again responded that enforcement was the courts' job; his office had no such authority. The governor endorsed most of Miller's letters "file," a bureaucratic death sentence. Finally installed, Miller remained powerless as the sole officeholder, without a sheriff or bailiff to collect taxes or serve processes.[53] No one would take the jobs, and the governor told Miller that no one could be appointed from outside. The obstruction looks strategic, because someone torched the courthouse. A Freedmen's Bureau report contended that it was done by planters, to forestall some eighteen hundred pending debt proceedings.[54]

Once civil government resumed, the army's legal authority diminished. Congressional Reconstruction had been premised on a swift resumption of normal rule, and no authority existed for continued oversight. But in many counties no legal machinery existed, just as army policing and courts disappeared. The reconstructed government had no militia, no state police to deploy, and Governor Smith had no desire to create them. Furthermore, Andrew Johnson's failed impeachment pushed the military toward inactivity, since the president was little disposed to aid the transition. Colonel O. L. Shepherd, upon being removed from command, warned of dire consequences if troops left precipitously, and Shepherd went outside the chain of command to alert superiors.[55] General Meade, commanding the district of the South, nonetheless determined to reduce the army's political profile, with an evident distaste for such complicated duties.[56] Dispersing troops was bad for discipline, he thought. In early August, just as local officials like Gardner and Miller were attempting to assume office, Meade ordered all troops withdrawn from central Alabama. Camps would remain in Mobile and Huntsville, safely away from the center of political agitation in Montgomery, as he observed. Meade reassured Republicans in Selma that help was just fifteen hours away by rail.[57] "The U.S. forces might as well be located in Maine," one horrified Republican wrote.[58] After stubborn resistance, Meade reversed his position following a riot in Georgia, but his initial inclination suggested the army would not be that helpful.

Perhaps nothing could have repressed Alabama's counter-revolution, but Governor Smith never really made the attempt. He knew full well the Klan's prevalence in his own vicinity, but his clarity diminished once he assumed office.[59] The problem facing his government was the lack of white support, especially from the elite of conservative inclination. Smith sought acceptability by resisting civil rights demands, and also by his own rhetoric of fiscal responsibility and bipartisanship. Nothing could antagonize the opposition more than mobilizing freedmen in self-defense. For this reason, Republican officials passed a merely nominal militia law. As one of Smith's intimates observed, "The state of our society is such that many of us fear the consequences of arming the blacks."[60]

The more forceful options available were admittedly double-edged. Remobilization of a now heavily black militia guaranteed racial polarization, but in the plantation belt, it could work to freedpeople's advantage. Terrorist activities looked so reckless in such areas that dominant opinion often discouraged them. But with balanced numbers, racial conflict threatened, as events demonstrated elsewhere. In western South Carolina, the white population rallied behind the Klan, to confront the state militia. But there were more sober options available: Tennessee's Unionist government established a mostly white, well-funded state force; two disciplined regiments were deployed to troubled areas to make arrests and protect witnesses.[61] The expense absorbed much of the state budget, but the policy did counteract the terrorists. In Arkansas, Governor Powell Clayton actually took the field with his state militia, defeating the Klan. Republican leaders took some action nearly everywhere, but Alabama's government pursued none of these options. President Grant himself noted the contrast: Smith was "sitting still and permitting these Ku Klux" to take his state away.[62]

Otherwise sympathetic observers deplored Smith's inactivity. The Montgomery *State Journal,* the administration's organ, urged that Klan lawlessness "be put down at once and by the strong hand."[63] But there was a chilling political logic to Smith's policy. If General Grant won, it would solidify Alabama's Reconstruction order, and security would improve once Republicans controlled the army. The saner opposition might then tire of lawlessness. In the meantime, Governor Smith disavowed disfranchisement. His school board mandated segregated education, and the state university would reopen on an all-white basis. Most importantly, he headed off legislators' attempt to call off the November election and cast Alabama's electoral vote themselves—as Florida did. Legislators grew exasperated, but Smith's political acumen was affirmed when he successfully lobbied President Johnson for more troops. Smith's bipartisanship won him praise in the press.[64]

The governor's strategy also made electoral sense, though in a perverse fashion. Klan or no, the freedmen voted heroically; only immediate danger deterred them. In 1868, Grant carried Alabama by 76,414 to 72,744, outpolling the Republican constitution by over 6,000. In eight Tennessee Valley counties the Republican vote declined over 40 percent between February and November 1868.[65] In the black belt, however, the Republican vote increased, suggesting that terrorism only solidified turnout in safer areas. In Dallas and Greene counties, Grant polled over a thousand more votes than the constitution had. The outcome proved Smith's electoral adroitness, but he traumatized his supporters. In at least twenty-six of Alabama's changing sixty-odd counties, Klan-style raids would be reported to Smith, and subsequent congressional testimony backed most of these statements. Less persuasive evidence named another half-a-dozen or more. Terrorist groups operated in most Alabama counties, at least briefly.

Throughout Smith's term, Klansmen rampaged across the Tennessee Valley.[66] They seldom ventured into the mountainous Unionist strongholds like Winston County, but they were active in the northern uplands nearly everywhere else, especially around Tuscaloosa and in Calhoun and Cherokee counties near the northeastern Georgia border. One agricultural feature united most of these northern counties, a large production of wheat, which may suggest that crop's episodic labor demands made workers more dispensable than on cotton plantations.[67] Beyond northern

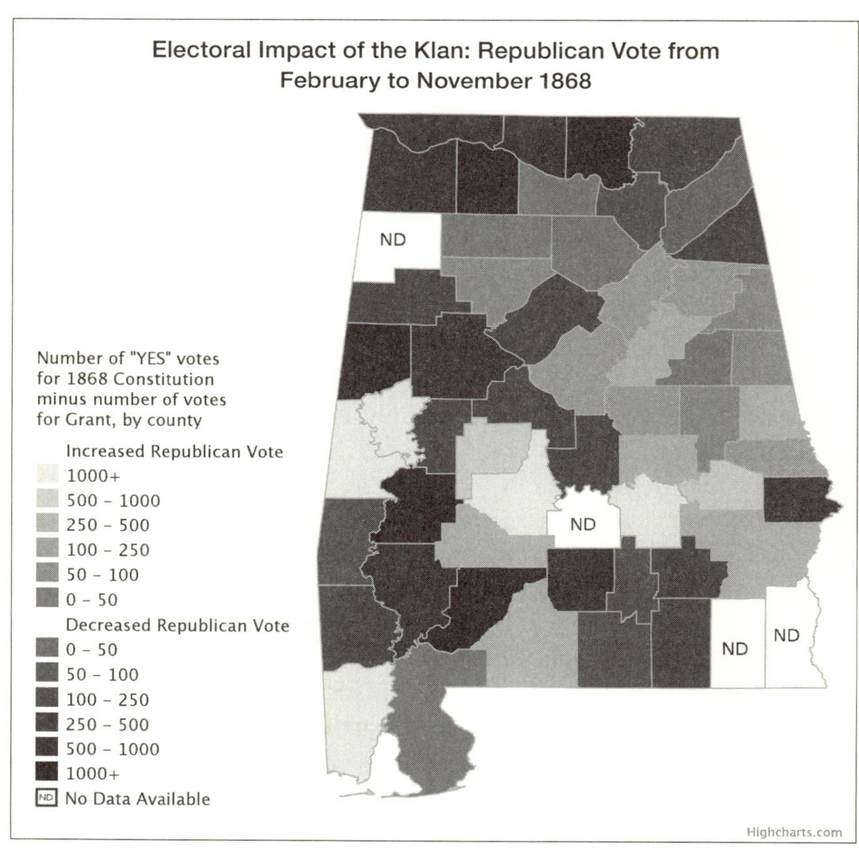

Alabama, the Klan terrorized the western black belt, like Greene County, and nearby Sumter and Pickens along the Mississippi border. Klan-style operations spread eccentrically across the northern and down the western part of the state, and in enclaves elsewhere, like Butler County in the south and around Tuskegee. In the southwestern river counties the Knights of the White Camellia functioned too. Statistically, little differentiates the terror-prone counties, save for mostly balanced racial proportions and, often, proximity to borders.[68]

Atrocities naturally focus historians' attention on the most violent areas, but the black belt in particular developed differently. From the spring through fall of 1868, Freedmen's Bureau officials reported few complaints of violence near Montgomery, no more than in the previous year. Selma and Dallas County, nearly four-fifths black, never saw much terrorist activity. This pattern intensified after Grant's election, as tenant farming spread and cotton profitability recovered. A Republican editor added nearby Hale, Marengo, and Perry counties to Dallas and Montgomery as places without terrorist violence—at least not during the fierce 1870 campaign. These were prewar Whig strongholds, and a conservative sensibility perhaps influenced them, though the huge black majorities mattered more.[69] Individual violence continued, but when circumstances demanded it racists could be flexible. Organized bands drove needed laborers away, and the central and eastern black belt saw little of them. This nonmarket force pushed laborers into the plantation belt, despite the fact that property-holding opportunities there were limited.[70] The region gained well over thirty thousand in black population between 1860 and 1870, the bulk of it after the war.[71] Given the labor shortage, this relocation process especially benefited wealthy landowners, whose superior land drew tenants.

Perry County offers an example of a relatively civil community. Bertis English contends it saw limited violence and that wealth, colleges, and prewar religious ties encouraged "Biracial Cooperation."[72] Southern Baptists here assisted in black church building and educational efforts. Lincoln Normal School—the predecessor of Alabama State—resulted in part from this collaboration. Southern Baptists favored independent black Baptist leaders over the area's AMA missionary, T. C. Stewart. Politically, Democrats preferred the Baptist leader Alexander H. Curtis to his white rival, Stewart, as well. In 1870, it seems, Republicans nominated their "most unexceptionable men," and Old Line Whig thought whites were "not much disposed to fight" their predominantly black ticket. Still, the threat of organized violence was held in reserve, sometimes explicitly. Decades later, Dr. G. P. L. Reed claimed the group he led never attacked anyone, but that he could have summoned a thousand men in four hours.[73]

Sometimes white leaders sought detente. In Hale County, the Webb shooting nearly provoked war in this three-quarters black county, and the Klan was active there during the 1868 campaign. But after Grant's election, John G. Harvey's Greensboro *Beacon* became the first non-Republican newspaper to editorialize against Klan lawlessness. This earned Harvey denunciations in the Tuscaloosa *Monitor* and elsewhere. Probate Judge W. T. Blackford had worked out a modus vivendi with elites, and in 1869 planters and overseers in rich southern Hale signed his official bond. He apparently reciprocated by fiscal restraint, his urging hard work on the freedmen, and by promoting railroad measures. Though the Klan existed in Hale, after 1868 it functioned less extensively than in neighboring areas. "Negroes have their own way in this county, but outside of this they 'walk a chalk line,'" one Klan sympathizer complained.[74]

Governor Smith highlighted such areas, which validated his restrained approach. He explained that "Exaggerated reports may have gone North about outrages, and the damage to Union men." He estimated that more than nine-tenths of the population was peaceably inclined.[75] In April 1869, Smith assured Washington it was "questionable" that the Ku Klux existed "in any form within the limits of Alabama."[76] Smith said he never felt personally threatened, and Smith traveled by rail constantly to his home in Randolph County. His ally, Senator Pennington, claimed that he never carried arms because a smart man could usually talk his way out of trouble.[77] The point may be broadly applicable to wealthy scalawags. Despite harsh social proscription, the Klan seldom killed or assaulted well-connected native officeholders or lawyers. William Miller in Eutaw was hated like S. S. Gardner in Greenville, but the planter scalawag survived, while the carpetbag reverend was bludgeoned and shot repeatedly. Some lingering social deference shielded even opportunistic scalawags, and their relative invulnerability colored the factional discourse. If freedmen and northern newcomers were the primary targets, they could be expected to resent inaction more.

Smith blamed the difficulties on his Radical detractors who benefited from trouble. Northerners who were gentlemen had no such problems, he thought.[78] As late as mid-1870, Smith denied that the people generally manifested a lawless disposition. No more than fifty Klan-style assassinations had been reported to him, he said, neglecting all the other forms of violence victims experienced. The laws had "been enforced without difficulty, wherever the proper officers have attempted to enforce them." The Democrats found such comments so useful they issued one of his speeches as a pamphlet.[79]

Smith's inaction did have one electoral advantage: it let Klan enthusiasts reveal themselves before the nation. During 1868, Alabama's opposition newspapers promoted, excused, or denied political violence. Future congressman P. M. Dox, a relative moderate, called for Democrats to recruit "every White boy old enough to carry a musket," organizing them like "a regiment of soldiers."[80] Alabama's martial tone echoed national Democratic discourse in unhelpful ways. Vice-presidential candidate Frank Blair talked about dispersing the Reconstruction governments at bayonet point, and General Nathan Bedford Forrest threatened Klan executions, in the press. In this context, Alabama's unchecked Klan effusions hurt. Randolph's editorials in the Tuscaloosa *Monitor* were problematic, especially his woodcuts predicting the murder of university administrators. Ohio Republicans reprinted his lynching images directed at Reverend A. S. Lakin, of Ohio. Here was history's first band of murderers with their own press, the New York *Tribune* observed. The state party disavowed Randolph, and editors conferred on how to quarantine him, sure sign of the damage he had done.[81]

One Freedmen's Bureau agent said that, even before the election, former Whigs came to his office to complain about the Democratic campaign, feeling rather threatened themselves.[82] Once Grant won, elements of the former political elite viewed their situation with fresh eyes. Alabama now faced four years of Republican rule in Washington. Conservatives who normally saw themselves as law-and-order men belatedly blamed sectional extremism. Prominent politicians announced their willingness to give the Grant administration a fair chance, recognizing Alabama's Reconstruction regime as the only legal government. In this context, disavowing the Klan seemed sensible. General Forrest officially disbanded the organization, repeatedly. This gesture encouraged some to conclude it no longer served any rational purpose. In Morgan and Lauderdale counties, in the Tennessee Valley, someone placarded disbandment notices. It seems that elite sanction of the organization diminished after early 1869; in Athens, an ex-Klan leader eventually issued an anonymous statement that things had gotten out of hand.[83] Leaders often distanced themselves to the extent of plausible denial.

Alabama experienced several months of diminishing violence in late 1868 and early 1869, save for the Tennessee Valley, where Klan raids continued.[84] Elsewhere Democrats were despondent, and Smith redoubled his conciliatory rhetoric, on the hopeful assumption that the Klan's day had passed. As a centrally directed organization, this had some truth, but the social movement and the method remained. The technique of disguising men and horses frustrated identification, as did attacks on isolated sharecroppers' cabins. So did the practice of calling in raiders from a distance, or from across state borders. Furthermore, sheriffs generally had to call out the posse when confronting outbreaks. They avoided summoning freedmen, so the results were farcical: either white Democrats ignored the demand, or they fulfilled their legal obligations by riding around pointlessly. If local officials meant business, suspects would likely get enough community warning to flee. Even if perpetrators were captured, redundant means existed to frustrate justice. Klansmen operated under obligation to alibi each other, and when on juries, to acquit. A grand jury might bring charges, but unanimous convictions were unlikely. Then there was the whole issue of intimidation of witnesses, or their elimination. Republicans frequently claimed there were no serious convictions at all, which is nearly accurate.[85] "They *laugh* at our civil authorities, and commit murder openly in sight of the Court House," one legislator wailed.[86]

Even Smith's conservative Republican supporters told him what this meant. The Montgomery *State Journal* pressed him: "If, under the present law, Governor Smith cannot raise militia to repress the bands of the Ku-Klux, he should make such a representation of the facts to the authorities at Washington. . . ."[87] As congressional elections approached in August 1869, Klan activities intensified, demonstrating that nothing had really changed. Republicans nonetheless carried four of the six congressional seats, losing only the two Klan-ridden northern districts. That year, Smith breasted waves of liberally underlined complaints. One Republican wrote from Tuscaloosa that law enforcement was hopeless "unless it is known that there is a power *here, of some kind,* which can and will protect the witnesses." Another Republican could name twenty men killed in that county, including Representative M. T. Crossland, waylaid with a colleague on his way to the legislature.[88] Complaints rained down from that unhappy vicinity. The son of Unionist Jacob Miller had been murdered by disguised men, the condition of the body indicating torture.

Young Miller had talked of using freedmen against the Klan. Freedmen witnessed the abduction but were frightened into silence. Afterwards, his father pelted the governor with pleading, then angry letters. "If thare is no chance for protection I am a going to kill and burn until I get satisfaction if they doant get me," Miller wrote. This threat apparently got Smith's attention to the extent of an investigation. Most complaints went unacknowledged, and much of the rest was handled by his secretary, Dalton. But public, truthful reports by critics became difficult to explain away. Widely reported outrages undercut Smith's denials.[89]

At first, Smith contended that he had no authority for local intervention, and he only gradually concluded that it was his problem. During 1869, Smith sought bipartisan solutions. On two occasions, he intervened to replace ineffective or unpopular Republican officials with moderate Democrats. In Greenville, freedmen saved the life of Judge Gardner repeatedly, at least one dying in the process. Smith sent Dalton and other trusted aides to negotiate his resignation with leading whites, in favor of sober Democrats. After yet more violence, Gardner reluctantly agreed on the condition that opponents admit his probity. Local lawyers then prosecuted terrorists with zeal enough to rein in the outbreak.[90] A similar errand to Tuscaloosa turned out worse. Dalton and associates induced the overwhelmed Republican sheriff to resign. Residents endorsed his Democratic successor by the hundreds, even Randolph himself, who editorialized that the time for violence had passed. These expressions made little impact in the surrounding countryside. The Democratic officials punished no one, and the former Republican officials complained they had forfeited their jobs for nothing.[91]

Troubled Sumter County illustrated the administration's attitude. Here Union League leader Gerard Chautteau confronted persecution. His plantation and cotton bales were torched in late 1868, after Klansmen had ordered family members out of the house. Chautteau sought safety in Livingston, but the Klan raided him the following year. A friend died defending his home, taking a disguised raider with him. Despite the lack of obvious provocation for such lethal attacks, Dalton emphasized Chautteau's unwholesome influence among the freedmen: "The Doctor (I understand) is a Frenchman, and is perhaps not sufficiently acquainted with our Institutions of Government, to comprehend the true American theory of differences of political opinion. I presume that it may be safely stated that he was not as tolerant toward people who differed from him as is contemplated by our Government." Chautteau was a Louisiana native, and a former large slaveholder at that, but Dalton somehow fit the episode into a narrative of carpetbagger insensitivity.[92]

Governor Smith sought responses least likely to antagonize the opposition. He hired secret detectives to send to affected areas, agents who privately contradicted his public statements. Smith posted rewards for informants in murder cases, which, as some pointed out, alerted perpetrators to beware. Smith also publicly exhorted sheriffs to use their power to make arrests. Sheriffs had only to call a posse, or ask for federal backup, and the governor would secure them. He explained at length why redress lay only with the courts, and why martial law was unconstitutional without invasion or rebellion. As Smith told desperate freedmen, "Before the Governor can do any thing, it must be shown that local authorities are either powerless or negligent."[93]

By 1870 several officials were incautious enough to provide him the needed proof. Probate Judge George Charlton killed a Klan leader, only to be assassinated after he got off the night train in Decatur.[94] In Greene County, in an ugly murder case, Klansmen killed a suspect's innocent father. Solicitor Alexander Boyd, the nephew of Judge Miller, vowed to jail the Klansmen. Dozens of disguised men then raided Boyd's hotel in Eutaw, riddling the solicitor with bullets. The lawyer William Cooper rejoiced at Boyd's death, pronouncing him "a *dog* of northern sympathies." He expressed equal joy that Judge Charlton died instantly, "what a blessing to this land." Yet at this very time, Smith's allies were urging him to hire Cooper, to prosecute Klan cases! And he agreed! Nothing could indicate more strongly the obstacles confronting law enforcement.[95]

Nuanced moves were not going to conciliate partisan Democrats, as another Klan sympathizer suggested. Eyre Damer worked at a rabid Eutaw newspaper. He described, even predicted, Klan murders, though "Nothing of that kind is put in the 'Whig,' and therefore . . . [was] not known outside of the county." Seeing Boyd's dead body at the inquest moved him to religious reflection. "[S]o long as the Radicals are in power, I feel I cannot be a consistent Christian," he wrote. His country—the South—needed assistance, and "when I see her trampled and insulted by her enemies, she has my aid in any work and her enemies my sincere and undying *hate.*" He longed for peace, but not under Radical rule, so *any* became the operative term. Even so, murder-prone allies troubled him. So did Smith's threat of mobilizing black militia with whites outnumbered, as Damer thought, five or eight to one.[96]

Violence was not all one-sided. Republicans took the law into their own hands, personally. Alabama Attorney General Josiah Morse came to office under indictment, having killed a Democratic editor in a street affray.[97] A Republican-connected university student, assisted by a faculty member, shot Ryland Randolph and then escaped jail.[98] Even law enforcement officials sought extralegal solutions. One solicitor said he killed a Klan leader. From jail, he asked the governor for another job since he had exhausted his usefulness in Marshall County.[99] In Fayette County, Sheriff Treadaway led Union veterans, "Mossy-backs," in retaliatory raids on the homes of Klan sympathizers.[100] Overawed officials only occasionally demonstrated this much zeal. Rumor frequently suggested that sheriffs or judicial officers drank to excess, perhaps to ease their discomfort. In Sumter County the governor appointed the nominal Republican lawyer A. W. Dillard as sheriff. Dillard soon quit in frustration, but more cynical placemen could fare better.[101] In this class-bound society, wealthier scalawags held office with a measure of white toleration. Pliant Republicans seeking a livable environment commonly worked out an accommodation. Sheriffs could go through the motions and pursue suspects with white posses. Trials might ensue on lesser charges, so long as everyone understood that no one would be punished that Democrats did not want punished. Some townspeople preferred to drive troublemakers away, so a measure of cooperation was possible.

This collaboration went to perplexing lengths. In strife-torn St. Clair County, the "Conservative Republican" Sheriff John C. Brown antagonized Representative Henry "Jack" Springfield, who exemplified Radical militancy. In the spring of 1870, Springfield fought Brown in the streets, reportedly over the sheriff's encouragement of a freedman's whipping after an altercation with a clerk.[102] It appears "the Democrats, or K.K." came to Sheriff Brown's aid, reportedly shooting two Springfields and other comrades in a general melee.[103] Months of retaliatory violence followed, as nearby black railroad workers assisted the Radical faction. In July, Jack Springfield returned to his home near Ashville with an escort, and an irregular posse composed of ex-Confederates gathered to disarm them. Two hundred besieged the home, but the defenders held and Sheriff Brown eventually negotiated a truce. When federal troops finally arrived, someone fired into their camp, and Jack Springfield, now a newly appointed federal marshal, was shot a second time. Afterward, someone killed one of the alleged posse participants, Frank Harrison, in town to attend a Democratic convention. St. Clair's confused turbulence defies allocation of responsibility, but Republican factionalism certainly contributed to the violence.[104]

Distinguishing between white mobs, legal posses, and Klansmen in civilian attire is not easy. At moments of conflict, Republican sheriffs seeking bipartisan cooperation were frequently surrounded by armed whites demanding action. Sheriffs often relinquished authority, with grim consequences for the freedmen and their Radical spokesmen. Overawed Republican officials often resisted the dispatch of federal troops, assuring the world everything was under control. Thus, in St. Clair County and elsewhere, Republicans resisted to prompt outside intervention. This drove the factionalism within Republican ranks, as freedmen sought leaders who would not scurry for cover. The legislator George Houston criticized a Sumter County sheriff who he thought shielded wrongdoers. Houston preferred Daniel Price, "the only white man in the county that took a real interest in the party," and perhaps the most outspoken Klan opponent in the state.[105]

Open confrontations intensified the pressure on Smith. Once Grant took office, the governor secured army assistance. Troops provided less inflammatory redress than martial law or forming local militias. Scholars frequently minimize the impact of the small occupation force in the southern states, but this misses a crucial aspect. Terrorists seldom risked confronting soldiers, so even a handful of infantrymen calmed local conflicts. General Samuel Crawford, the de facto commander for the state, moved troops and lobbied superiors on Smith's behalf, their close interaction rather violating the normal chain of command. Soldiers were permitted to accompany posses, and to guard prisoners and witnesses. But these measures only worked where law enforcement functioned. One official refused to summon a white posse because he could not trust which way they would shoot: "he would not dare to call for troops in his county. If he did, he could not live there, and that he had property there which he wished to look after."[106] Within a few weeks the soldiers would be needed elsewhere, and officeholders knew they would be on their own. After repeated deployments in Tuscaloosa, even Crawford had seen enough: he recommended withdrawing troops to force Smith to take action.[107]

The governor got similar feedback from other allies. Prosperous native whites dominated the Republican judicial apparatus, but their experience sobered them. David C. Humphreys privately urged the governor to mobilize the militia and decree martial law. Humphreys suggested keeping the courts in session longer, to intimidate lawbreakers and elicit more information. David P. Lewis disliked carpetbag Radicals, but he prosecuted Klan cases; he too urged mobilizing the militia, telling Smith it would assure his renomination.[108] Native Republicans often seemed moved by the violence. In 1870, Congressman Charles Hays persuaded two delegates to attend a Republican convention. Disguised men then killed Guilford Coleman and another Greene County freedman. Hays, guilt-stricken, pleaded for justice. Republicans in such violence-prone areas widely believed the governor sold them out.[109]

Feeble local law enforcement left only desperate options. It fell to rural Republicans to defend themselves or deter violence, somehow. In the Tennessee Valley, where the numbers were about even, self-defense efforts had mixed results, and in the upland region they fared worse. But in black-belt areas where African Americans predominated, they did much better. Just over half of the freedmen lived in counties where they were two-thirds of the population or more, the highest concentration in the South, a proportion which Steven Hahn contends inhibited terrorism. Over a third lived in counties where they constituted three-quarters of the populace, which offered protection according to Trelease's landmark account.[110] Neither proportion necessarily sufficed in carnage-prone western Alabama, but the concentration helped in most places.

Even in unpromising terrain, freedmen occasionally surprised night-riders. Near Courtland, Wash McDonald feared retaliation after winning a court dispute. His defenders shot one night-rider in disguise and injured others, the Klansmen managing to finish off one of their own. Whites returned the next day to retrieve the captured horses, threatening extermination, but the deputy sheriff told the freedmen they were on their own. They wrote an army officer, "we cannot do nothing without your help ple[a]s[e] send us some help jess as quick as you can." Perhaps the missive worked. The deputy sheriff allegedly relented and gathered ex-Confederate officers as a posse, preventing a bloodbath.[111] The consequences of fighting the Klan thus defied prediction. Successful self-defense risked horrific escalation, and in open firefights ex-Confederates generally did well. They had martial expertise, better arms, and superior mobility on horseback too. For ex-slaves, standing up to their late masters went against a lifetime of habit and training. No matter, freedmen and their white allies risked resistance whenever they had a chance.

But it was unusual to catch regulators in the act, and a different plotline normally prevailed. The Democratic press widely reported race scares or prospective riots, with the freedmen nearly always acting on the offensive. The newspapers conveniently omitted the underlying pattern: confrontational action by African Americans following regulator activity. Where the Klan was riding, it became evident when local law enforcement and white community sentiment would do nothing. That forced desperate responses, some display of retaliatory intent. Freedmen normally suspected who night-riders were, so confrontations often developed with presumed Klansmen in civilian garb. For example, Ryland Randolph himself was clubbed after he intervened in a fight between a fellow Klan participant and two freedmen.[112] In Cherokee and Calhoun counties, the Klan was riding for months, and after a street fight involving a Klan member, armed railroad workers came running to Cross Plains. They fired on the assailant while he exited church. A poor idea, as shall be evident, but Republicans could scarcely be whipped nightly without risking some response.

After outrages, freedmen often descended on the county seat, torches and guns in hand, demanding redress. Sometimes they went further. At Tuscumbia, when the Klan began riding before the 1868 election, freedmen talked through their response. One reportedly stated "that Captain Keller was Captain of the Ku-Klux, and he intended to put a man at his gate to bushwhack him."[113] This notion prompted disagreement, and they settled for torching the local women's school. The freedmen were arrested, and some reportedly testified; then three were lynched by disguised men.[114] Arson was employed elsewhere with better results, fire being difficult to trace and the threat being likely to gain the attention of men with property. After countryside school burnings and Klan threats, faculty at Talladega College readied for action, seeking guns from their missionary association. Prominent scalawags and town leaders then intervened, at one point dissuading a party of Klansmen on route. As the rejoicing principal reported, "Some colored people declared that if these buildings were burnt they would burn the town. [The teacher] Miss Beebe thinks this was the conclusive argument. . . ."[115]

Results were often unpredictable, as retaliatory actions risked everything. It often proceeded like Greek tragedy: some young whites started night-riding, freedmen began talking of arming or indiscriminate retaliation, a drink-fueled incident occurred, and ex-Confederates united for a shootout. If the numbers permitted, they would then normally win. Democrats knew the odds of battle and pressed their advantages. Several of the bigger confrontations at rallies or on election days had one-sided casualty counts. In the Eutaw riot of 1870, and the Eufaula riot in 1874, the margin was on the order of twenty to one.[116] When all-out battles occurred, racial pogrom proved the rule.[117]

Republicans, white and black, sought subtler options. If actual battle promised indeterminate results, the *threat* of force sometimes worked better, might give sober opponents pause. Private warning combined with public bluster became the preferred choice, the one most suited to reaching the conservative sensibility. This practice meant someone had to voice threats, hopefully someone with authority. As the moderate scalawag W. B. Jones warned, "Now Governor, it is not for my protection that I write to you, for I can paddle my own boat, but it is for the colored people who have appealed to me in thundering tone to write to you."[118] Fearing betrayal by their predominantly scalawag, moderate local officials, freedmen demanded a show of solidarity, and some embattled Republican leaders obliged. For black activists, Republican politics was bound up in notions of manhood, and silence seemed like cowardice. Some Republicans engaged in calibrated bluffing, while others sounded chillingly earnest. The trick was to suggest peril to bystanders or property without dying in the process.

Sumter County scalawag Daniel Price tried this tactic most blatantly. He once pressed a lukewarm Freedmen's Bureau official to protect a black ally, Yankee Ben Brown. Price threatened to "tell the white men that if Brown is killed the negroes would hang every man woman and child in the beat." Without troops at hand, such threats seemed the only recourse for protection. When the Klan subsequently murdered Brown, Price tried the governor. The freedmen were "greatly excited and it needs but a breath to start midnight murder by the wholesale." He said he had urged calm, because Smith would protect them if possible. In both instances, Price was being deliberately provocative in hope of securing action.[119]

Few Republican leaders talked like Price. The safer way was to warn of the enraged freedmen taking matters into their own hands. Embattled leaders issued fearful warnings to the white community, or to the press. The governor drew numbers of these frustrated threats. After the Boyd raid, W. B. Jones wrote, "Unless you come to the rescue, those sable Republicans . . . will rise up *en masse* and defend themselves." Republicans thus played upon images of racial barbarism, despite the prevalent evidence of actual restraint. "[W]hen these freedmen once taste blood," one Republican wrote, "God knows where it will end." Leaders frequently claimed they were losing control of their enraged followers. An anonymous letter warned, "The Negroes are now ready to burn the county but I do not believe nor do any of the [white] Republicans, in such measures, but Sir, we can not stand this much longer; let them make one more attempt then it will be 'War to the Knife' in Greene County." The ploys worked: Governor Smith increasingly bestirred himself to prevent race war.[120]

Tuskegee illustrated the process. In the eastern black-belt region with little night-riding, Macon County experienced unusual trouble: it even boasted a railroad engine called the "KuKlux." During 1870, there were Klan raids, including an attack on a church in which Republicans were meeting. Representative James H. Alston received threats, and a factional fight developed. A black Republican rival challenged his leadership, and later that night unknown parties fired into Alston's home, wounding him and his pregnant wife. Alston initially blamed his opponents, but later he claimed that Klansmen had either encouraged or performed the attack.[121] Whatever the truth, Alston concluded that nominally Republican officials like Sheriff J. J. Padgett "refused to give protection to republicans," saying the governor gave him no such power. Freedmen therefore posted sentinels in Alston's vicinity, but after several tense days, the sheriff confronted them. His white followers shot first, a firefight occurred with no one hurt, and whites picketed Tuskegee's outskirts to prevent entry by rural freedmen. Meanwhile, forty miles away in Montgomery, a company of freedmen readied themselves. They later claimed they mobilized at the request of the Republican sheriff there to act as a posse. As they got on the train, Democratic leader James Clanton confronted the squad at gunpoint, and finally alarmed, Governor Smith persuaded the freedmen to desist.

Governor Smith then boarded the train himself, as federal troops deployed in Tuskegee. Smith negotiated with Democratic leaders, sanctioning their armed patrols on their assurance that they followed his orders. Smith persuaded freedmen to let the legal machinery take its course. No one was ever convicted for the shooting, and Alston, several black allies, and one white Radical left town—on Democratic orders, Alston said. Interracial violence continued, but eventually elites tired of the turmoil. Some weeks after the Alston shooting, the local paper urged whites to avoid "mysterious terrorism," this at a time when the Klan received substantial press encouragement elsewhere. As the Tuskegee *News* observed, "It may be the work of thoughtless boys; if so, they should learn that their indiscretion may end in sorrow and remorse." Things finally settled down after the November election, and Republicans polled large majorities for years. Somehow Macon County survived the rest of Reconstruction in relative calm, to await Booker T. Washington and Tuskegee's subsequent destiny.[122]

These confrontations threatened Smith's reelection, and he finally admitted that his "uniform course of forbearance and conciliation" had miscarried.[123] In April 1870, after the Boyd killing, he announced he would organize militia for continuous service in Morgan, Greene, and Tuscaloosa counties. He never followed through, however. According to Justice Peters, the state possessed no arms nor had functional militia laws, and the legislature had not authorized martial law. The prewar laws, still on the books, barred black service. Lawmakers would have approved his anti-terrorist measures, but Smith resisted until too late. Still, after Smith's proclamation, violence declined for several months. And when the Cross Plains mass lynching occurred that summer, he hurried to the scene along with troops. Justice Peters elicited reams of proof in a marathon inquiry, concluding two-thirds of the area's young men were implicated. No jury would convict, but it was not for want of judicial effort: black pressure finally forced a serious prosecution by the state.[124]

In sum, threats of physical force or random retaliation seldom worked well, but Governor Smith's leadership left few other options. Sumter County offers a final illustration of the dynamic of bluff and escalation. Klan raids seldom persisted long in counties nearing 80 percent black, but Sumter and neighboring Greene were among the handful in the entire South.[125] The pattern defies easy explanation, but Sumter stretched along the Mississippi border for fifty miles, and it was on the rail line between chaotic Meridian and Klan-ridden Eutaw and Tuscaloosa. Sumter and Greene counties also suffered ruinously low cotton output, on the order of half, relative to the similar black-belt areas just to the east. Whether this was a cause or a consequence of pervasive raiding, the losses embittered the situation on plantations.[126]

Years of interruption in civil law exacerbated the situation. As of August 1868, some 147 criminal cases, from murder on down, had accumulated on the circuit-court docket. Perhaps for this reason, the Union League mobilization featured black drilling, self-defense rhetoric, and promotion of northern-origin and black leadership. All this galvanized a strong Klan response. In most places, such one-sided demographics yielded a measure of mutual restraint. In Sumter County, bullets flew.[127]

Even disregarding the night-riders, bloodletting was at exceptional levels. Bureau reports suggest an unusual number of escalating contract disputes. Crime existed on both sides, but racially motivated killing was one-sided. A twenty-two-year-old overseer's son, William J. Praytor, came to Livingston, drunkenly threatening to shoot any Republican available. Outside town he encountered Jerry Clark, who upon questioning avowed his politics. Praytor then killed him in front of an army of witnesses, and even the Livingston *Journal* called it a brutal murder. Some of the worst Sumter County violence was orchestrated by the Klan chieftain Steven Renfroe, eventually elected by the Democrats as sheriff. On one occasion, Renfroe and two undisguised associates killed freedmen for no apparent reason, after joking with the victims.[128]

A curious political situation compounded the disorder. Back in February 1868, Republicans had elected several northern Radicals and two African Americans to Sumter County positions. One of the latter, Richard Harris, could not secure the large property bond to assume office of sheriff, and the northern planters, now bankrupted, thought the constitution defeated and left.[129] This confusion left county offices in the hands of nominal Republicans, including a probate judge who did not wish to lose his reputation to assist Radicals. Thus freedmen always attended their meetings armed, some with Enfield military rifles. When Democrats attended a Republican meeting uninvited at Dr. Chautteau's plantation, one of them called him a liar. A freedman reportedly leveled a gun, but the whites started firing. Though no one was hurt, Klansmen hunted down the Republicans afterwards. The aforementioned Yankee Ben Brown was killed at his home, and his body lay out for days, the freedpeople fearing to bury it. Democrats staked out the roads to prevent witnesses from testifying in town. Afterwards, the disengaged bureau agent reported, "For the last ten or twelve days such occurrences & bad settlements are [occurring] daily," suggesting an interrelationship between crop disputes and the raids. Much of the black leadership experienced personal violence. Representative George Houston carried a Klan bullet in his body the rest of his life, displaying his wound before a congressional committee.[130]

Given their numbers, one wonders that the Sumter County freedmen did not seek open battle or engage in random retaliation. They apparently had little enthusiasm for actual race war, or confidence in their ability to prevail. Freedmen instead tried every combination of threat, blustering display, and self-defense imaginable. League leader Adam Kenard telegraphed the governor, "Killing freedmen has become so common in Sumter that there is no security[;] send us protection or we will fight."[131] Representative Richard Burke, an elderly minister, borrowed a gun from his ex-master to defend himself. The practice of carrying guns to meetings was a flash point; freedmen carried them if only to assure safe transit, but it provoked conflict repeatedly. On one occasion, whites warned freedmen not to come into Livingston for a rally. When they obediently dispersed, Representative Burke upbraided them for cowardice. He told them they had every right to carry their arms, but fifty disguised men killed him thereafter. His ex-master testified sadly that he could not understand slaying the harmless old man.[132] But Burke was not harmless: armed displays by freedpeople would transform the balance of power. White men generally carried guns on their person, both here and throughout the state. If freedmen could enforce their right to do the same, everything changed.

Former schoolteacher and now Circuit Clerk Daniel Price kept threatening resistance. After a Klan threat, he wrote, "I don't mind that, I am not afraid of the whole county I have a Brigade of Union Leaguers and am all right." On numerous occasions he urged self-defense, in the absence of functioning law enforcement. After a freedman was beaten by his ex-master, he warned: "You know very well that there is no possible redress for him, at present, from the courts. Now for your information, I will state that the members of the League are mutually bound to protect each other, and if it becomes necessary . . . to treat you or any one else with violence. . . . You whites who learned nothing from the war . . . will be *made* learn that there is a difference between whaling a freeman and pounding a slave. . . ." Price confronted an angry mob for this letter, but he said similar things on other occasions. Conservative Republicans, and the local bureau agent, thought him foolhardy, but, incredibly, he seems to have escaped violence.[133]

Even so, nothing Price and his diminishing cohort of allies tried worked. Price and other Radical leaders finally fled to Meridian in mid-1870. The Klan's triumph, however, had a surprising aftermath. Price sent word that wages were better near the prospering railroad crossing. Laborers started deserting contracts, and apparent Klansmen calling themselves deputies started after them across the state line. They functioned under the titular leadership of the former militant Adam Kenard, who had made terms with the Democrats. Price and his supporters beat Kenard, after which Klan raids began in earnest led by Steve Renfroe. As one conflicted resident observed, "people do not appear to be as much siveralized here as some places. . . . [W]e have had some fights here with the Negroes but the white people always comes off victorious. . . ."[134]

A riot followed. To simplify complicated Mississippi events, after terrorist killings someone set a fire in Meridian, and a trial resulted in March 1871. Activists were charged with disorderly conduct and incendiary speeches, and a trainload of Alabama Klan sympathizers attended. A courtroom firefight occurred, and Klansmen and other whites seized Meridian for three days. The intimidated Republican mayor sanctioned them as a posse and then fled. The mob executed perhaps ten freedmen, some while in custody. This confused episode became a national story, putting both Meridian and Sumter County into the midst of national discourse. The outrage facilitated federal legislation, the Ku Klux Act, which finally brought the Klan outbreak to an end.[135]

Daniel Price escaped again just before the riot, with official connivance, apparently to Arkansas.[136] His fate encapsulates the complexity of "paramilitary politics," as Steven Hahn termed the situation.[137] Even in this bloodbath, Republicans arguably accomplished something. The borderland confrontation helped precipitate the federal intervention which crushed the Klan. The Ku Klux Act also provided a leading issue in President Grant's reelection campaign. All the talk of retaliation always heightened the confrontation. The short-term results were seldom pleasant, but Republicans had to challenge the local dynamic of one-way violence without consequences. Governor Smith's calculated inattention left them few alternatives, thus strengthening the carpetbagger Radicals he so deplored. Smith's courtship of Democratic opinion explains why Klan repression assumed the dimensions it did, but historians have seldom noted an additional dimension. The governor's zeal for railroad promotion helps explain Alabama's violent Klan spasm.

8

Railroads, Race, and Reconstruction

The Curious Legacy of Governor William H. Smith

Indeed, it mattered not what party controlled the State, so that our railroads and other material interests were looked after.

—J. L. Pennington, Republican leader, October 1869

The relationship between Klan-style terrorism and the era's railroad boom has not been much emphasized in the Reconstruction literature, not in its partisan aspects.[1] In Alabama the political dimension seems clear: it shaped the priorities of Governor William H. Smith and his project of outreach to sober-minded opinion leaders. Anti-terrorist measures would antagonize the opponents he hoped to neutralize, but the pro-corporate ethos of the national Republican Party had some appeal for former Whigs and conservatives, if they could be induced to put those issues first. His quest for white respectability, however, had severe consequences: Alabama suffered a spectacular railroad meltdown under his leadership. Contemporary observers and Dunning-school historians after them generally blamed Reconstruction-era corruption on African American voters and their favored Radical leaders. In fact, Smith's troubled implementation of subsidy programs originated in his outreach to prosperous whites.

Several dimensions existed to such efforts. At the elite end of the social scale, Governor Smith courted conservatives as potential officeholders. He had unusual success: Alabama's prominent scalawags were prosperous before the war, relative to those elsewhere.[2] The former political class proved receptive to Smith's approaches, coming from a governor combating "carpetbag" influence. Alabama's readmission vacated numerous offices, and Grant's election confirmed that the Smith administration would be in place for years. For pragmatic individuals, a shift in approach suggested itself. Conservatives inclined toward law-and-order anyway, and Democratic extremism had backfired yet again. Even now, many states' rights hard-liners preferred not to recognize the Republican government as legal, to view its bonds and legislation as usurpations; some openly encouraged Klan-style violence. Unending disorder had limited appeal for those conservatives hoping to regain office quickly, or for those interested in business and outside investment. By backing the Smith administration, they could keep fiscal policy out of the hands of those they thought irresponsible—especially northern newcomers and the freedpeople they represented.

Then there was the simple fact that Congressional Reconstruction had expelled hundreds of officeholders. The Fourteenth Amendment now barred most prewar officials from regaining their positions—potentially ever. For those long employed as judges or local officials, this was a blow, but one that Congress could remedy. Former secessionists and partisan Democrats could expect little favor in Washington, but ex-Whigs and conservatives might fare better. For this reason, as Congress came back into session, a number of well-known conservatives petitioned to have their disabilities individually lifted. Some Democrats tried too, which added to the prevailing uncertainty. Any assertion of political flexibility in the future, of willingness to cooperate with the incoming administration, was likely to speed the process. "The folly of our people is past my comprehension," Alex McKinstry explained as he moved toward the Republicans.[3]

By early 1869, several high-profile politicians distanced themselves from the national Democratic Party, with indistinct intentions. Some early Reconstructionists who publicly defected during the ratification campaign returned, men like C. S. G. Doster and Joseph H. Speed.[4] More striking were the new Republican recruits of established reputation. Former Whig congressman Alexander White, for example, had been a racial intransigent. Now he approached Smith, and he privately circulated a statement calling for a "Union Conservative" third party to marginalize the ex-secessionists. Conservatives like W. M. Byrd asked Congress to encourage his movement by lifting officeholding disabilities.[5] The third-party initiative found few recruits, and White became an outright Republican. Others did too, notably former provisional governor Lewis Parsons, who over the years had taken every imaginable position. Some conversions appear inexplicable, motivated by opportunism or eccentricity. Former Supreme Court justice Samuel Rice had been a secessionist firebrand, but now he became a Smith administration intimate—and railroad enthusiast.[6]

Financial exigency encouraged conversions, especially among attorneys. One thought the constitution's debt ordinance would force all lawyers to go to farming or something equally unprofitable.[7] Now vacancies in judgeships and court officials permitted Governor Smith appointment opportunities. Native Republican officeholders of prominence tended to be planters and lawyers, particularly in the black belt; they had long political histories and generally had been prosperous before the war. Almost to a man, these officeholders had opposed Breckinridge and immediate secession, so there was an element of political consistency.[8] These new Republicans maintained a toehold in the white world of privilege and social acceptance. They had complex social loyalties, which distanced them from the bulk of black and white Republicans. For example, W. B. Jones was a combative fellow, but only a "political fool" could take the partisan abuse. "When a gentleman's social relations are assailed—when his family are compelled to seek enjoyments only at home," it was high time to quit.[9] But Jones had other problems: he had shot a man over an affair, apparently in self-defense, and he faced a Marengo County jury. Jones therefore defected in the most public manner possible by serving as an elector on the Democratic presidential ticket. Afterward, with the campaign over and his eventual acquittal, Jones resumed his sometime Republican loyalties.[10]

Sheer economic necessity pushed Jones toward the Republicans. He was the first planter in his area to rent land to freedmen, and when neighbors objected, he sought to arm his hands.[11] Despite his thousand acres of land, W. B. Jones underwent bankruptcy in the midst of his other travails. Financial troubles pushed other established political leaders toward the Republicans. Applications under the 1867 Federal Bankruptcy Law evidence this, given the prominent southern-born politicians declaring insolvency. Two of the three Supreme Court justices, Thomas M. Peters and Benjamin Saffold, declared themselves bankrupt in 1868. Saffold's brother Milton was having an equally difficult time finding work as a lobbyist in Washington. Education Commissioner Noah Cloud, a prominent agricultural reformer, and Alabama Attorney General Josiah Morse filed as well. Five of eleven Republicans on the first statewide ticket were recent bankrupts. Some Republicans owed large sums, like John Calvin Goodloe's fifty thousand.

Many prominent "scalawags" followed similar trajectories, men like Nicholas Davis of Huntsville. Judge J. McCaleb Wiley, another bankrupt, wanted his disabilities removed so that he could run for Congress, or, failing that, receive a judgeship. In at least eight cases, the career track into the legislature featured bankruptcy.[12] Northern migrants went bankrupt too, but they lacked the social profile of these native southern converts. Of twenty-eight prominent black-belt scalawags, at least six of them filed for bankruptcy at this time. Whatever their conservative inclinations, the evidence suggests financial troubles pushed these future officeholders toward the Republicans.[13]

The freedmen might have been uneasy about this movement into the party's higher leadership. But with Grant elected, and Klan activities temporarily abating, these prominent conversions looked like a good sign. The influx of familiar officeholders otherwise advanced Governor Smith's agenda. It helped staff the more technical positions in the legal system, where education and prewar experience were helpful, as was the cooperation of the legal fraternity. But recruiting conservative leaders had only limited appeal to the white electorate, and Smith's previous unconditional Unionist following repelled ex-Confederates. Smith needed a positive message for outreach, something consistent with the activist government promoted by President Grant. Public education had some appeal, but since the freedpeople disproportionately benefited, it was not the silver bullet. To shift the conversation away from race, he needed a positive message of social progress for whites.

Smith needed railroads politically, and, as it happened, personally.[14] His feckless actions on railroad matters were amply demonstrated to contemporaries, and they strain credulity today. Partisan opponents *ought* to have highlighted Smith as the prototypical corrupt scalawag, but their master narrative directed criticism elsewhere. Democrats understood Smith as the most racially conservative of the Reconstruction governors, so they embraced Smith's self-serving tales of carpetbagger corruption and black irresponsibility.

Conservative Republicans had few issues upon which to appeal to white voters without antagonizing their black constituency. State subsidies for railroad promotion threaded the partisan needle. Divisions among whites over public aid had deep roots in the antebellum political history of the state, because the Jacksonian party system emerged in conflict over banks and transportation policy. Aid was the core platform of the Whig Party, and by the prosperous 1850s, even many previously skeptical Democrats embraced railroads. Unfortunately for proponents, "American luddites roamed the hills," as J. Mills Thornton observed.[15] Alabama finally enacted a comprehensive subsidy plan just before secession, but the war interrupted implementation and then destroyed much of the existing infrastructure.

The obstruction frustrated opinion leaders because they long realized the economic potential of north Alabama. It possessed the South's best concentration of coal and iron, enough to supply the world for six hundred years, some boosters claimed.[16] At war's end, with agriculture in ruins, calls for dramatic restructuring of the economy resonated. Smith's predecessor, Governor Patton, worked feverishly to forestall default on Alabama's debt, and the Presidential Reconstruction legislature passed a general aid law, offering a state endorsement to the stock of nearly every railroad built in Alabama. Because investors feared governmental instability, nothing came of it at the moment, but aid was on the books awaiting implementation.

With Alabama's readmission, Wall Street and international markets opened up for the endorsed bonds of the Republican government. Patton seamlessly transitioned from governor to the president of one major project into the mountain region, a railroad running diagonally across the state from Chattanooga toward Meridian.[17] To his delight, Patton gained "the promise of the incoming Govr. Smith to arrange the state debt in any way he may recommend."[18] Both men also sought consolidation of a project in debt to the state, the North East & South West, with Patton's better-financed Wills Valley line. With this encouragement, ex-governor Patton approached northern capitalists, and the Republican legislature passed several bills to attract outside investors. The legislature replaced the complicated subsidy of $12,000 per mile, plus additional amounts depending on terrain, with a flat $16,000 state endorsement. This was "the only material amendment" in the policy approved under Governor Patton's conservative legislature, the aid provisions being copied nearly intact. The cost differential was small, as proponents argued, but it did demonstrate the supportive mood of the overwhelmingly Republican legislature.[19]

Patton interested a group of investors led by Daniel N. and John C. Stanton of Boston. They were railroad men of experience with a slightly shady past.[20] The brothers made repeated trips to Alabama and discovered several facts on the ground, or rather, in it. The iron and coal region had rich potential. Furthermore, the state guarantee, plus local resources, would be sufficient to fund much of the line. The Stantons were not fabulously wealthy men, as railroad promoters went, but they might not need to be. Unfortunately for Patton, the Stantons supplanted him by arguing for a Boston headquarters. Daniel N. Stanton became president of the new Alabama & Chattanooga (A&C), with his brother John as contractor. Patton's embitterment dovetailed into the rhetoric about "carpetbag" influence in state politics.[21] Patton soon departed the company board to lead the rival South & North line, which was also racing to penetrate the mountain region from Decatur to Montgomery.[22]

The Stantons promised investment would flow southward once Grant won. Prospects largely depended on Governor Smith because the project required numerous administrative interventions. He could largely determine which partially completed and combined fragments could be considered eligible for state aid. The Bostonians called on him to finalize the aforementioned consolidation arrangements in early November, just after the election. John Stanton urged, "Do not let any one prevent your selling the NE & SW Road. Keep me posted by telegraph." Stanton thought the sale would make title secure from previous debts, and the tone of this communication suggests the close ties between the two men. Governor Smith readily complied, and the consolidated A&C Railroad began building.[23]

Legislative support mattered too. The general aid law needed amendment to include their consolidated railroad, and numerous other obstructions loomed. Fortunately for the Stantons, their northern origins and Republican connections helped. If anything, they were unsettlingly successful in influencing legislation. Robert Jemison, of the absorbed line, observed:

> The facility & trifling cost of getting allmost any proposed measure through this Legislature has allmost frightened our Boston friends, to Bolt the track. They do not fear getting all they want, but it requires such constant & vigilant watching to prevent somebody from getting what they don't want. When they look upon the faces of those who compose the Legislature of the State, with all their radical notions they do not feel that there is much safety or security in trusting to Legislation here.

The hesitation is striking in view of the outsize role the Stantons would play in subsequent corruption. They finally concluded not to tamper with the existing subsidy laws, telling Governor Smith they trusted he would do what needed doing.[24]

Appropriations remained modest for the legislature's first three sessions, during the latter half of 1868. There were press allegations of bribery, but the scale seems small relative to subsequent developments. Jemison had objected specifically to aid to river improvement companies, and he singled out African American legislator James K. Green.[25] This characterization, if accurate, was unusual: black leaders almost never spearheaded subsidy initiatives. Benjamin Royal was the only black member in the entire Senate, the body which most indiscriminately voted aid. Even in the House, black leaders held no committee chairmanships, and they had no visible role in initiating the subsidy woes to come. The impetus came from elsewhere.

The fateful maneuvers are obscure, in part because the press ignored them. Late in 1868, someone in the legislature recognized the lucrative possibilities of Alabama's aid law, unusual in its automatic provisions.[26] The law on its face contained numerous safeguards; developers needed to demonstrate substantial means of their own before the state lent its credit. Still, once twenty miles of a line were built, at either end, the state subsidy would accrue for the portion already completed. This would allow more construction, and further endorsements of company stock would be granted as five-mile portions were completed. The promoters' task was to build the initial section, and additional means might be trusted to take care of themselves.

Amid the technicalities, the point is simple: if localities subscribed the funds for initial construction, promoters might stack grants to qualify for the state endorsement. Up to this time, local subsidies apparently required specific legislative authorization, but in December 1868, the legislature flatly validated all local aid grants. The law prescribed guidelines for mandatory city and county referenda upon demand of the railroad promoters. There had been such a proposal when the original general law passed during Presidential Reconstruction, but this new bill passed unnoticed. The enactment opened a Pandora's box, encouraging local officials to promote railroads with state credit. It gave them urgent motive, for fear rivals would take advantage before the aid law expired.[27]

County-level referenda were mandatory under the local endorsement law, to be repeated once if the voters initially demurred. Governor Smith aptly described the resulting tendency in a later message asking repeal: "So great is the desire for railroad facilities that counties and towns will readily vote subscriptions to aid them." As public policy, this created a time bomb. Because it was "only necessary to construct twenty miles of road to place it within reach of the State's endorsement," the inducement to act was nearly irresistible. Such measures, he thought, imperiled the state's credit. Generous aid might engender railroad construction in poorer areas where traffic would not justify it, or even pay running expenses once built. "Thus it will be seen that an entire road may be built upon public credit, and without the contribution of any private capital," Smith concluded.[28]

Well might Smith have come to this realization, because he pioneered the feat himself. On December 29, 1868, the governor signed legislation systematizing the initial stages of forming railroad corporations. That same day, Smith and his closest conservative Republican collaborator, Senator James L. Pennington, along with several other legislators, filed a company to take advantage of the law's provisions. Two days later, he signed the local aid authorization law.[29] The timing indicates Smith signed these bills knowing full well the implications. His Eufaula, Opelika, Oxford & Guntersville Railroad was projected to run from the black belt up the eastern border of the state, to connect with the Stantons' line at Oxford. The line was to pass through Smith's village of Wedowee, running not far from gold mines in which Smith was a prominent investor. "The Governor thinks their prospects for making a small fortune are very good," the Randolph *Enterprise* would observe.[30] The railroad's initial terminus was at Opelika, Pennington's home. He served as president, and most of the original directors were white Republican legislators then close to the governor. These included company treasurer George F. Harrington, the Speaker of the state house, and J. J. Hinds of Decatur.[31] Because the local aid law permitted the initial steps toward endorsement before the formation of a corporation, Treasurer Harrington opposed recruitment of outside investors, preferring to keep control close.[32] Harrington suggested that $100,000 in stock be issued to his comrades forthwith, in anticipation of federal land grants benefiting the company.

In justice, Governor Smith and State Senator Pennington could have been more incautious. They contented themselves with just the one railroad, and Smith turned down an eager offer of a one-fifth share in another project.[33] Some of his colleagues were less circumspect. State Senator Hinds appeared in the filings of no less than three railroad companies within the first week of January 1869. Four more Republican legislators filed two apiece on January 2, the personnel often overlapping. Justice Thomas M. Peters filed for two railroad ventures on that same day, despite his bankruptcy proceedings. None of the African American legislators participated. Indeed, this flurry of activity occurred as the legislature went out of session, to remain out of the capitol for most of 1869.

Neither the press at the time, nor historians afterwards, much noticed the flurry of corporation filings.[34]

Merely submitting incorporation paperwork cost individual legislators little, and few of these projects got very far. Governor Smith's consortium operated differently, because these insiders grasped that the opportunity would not persist. They sought local endorsements months before promoters of existing projects bestirred themselves. Smith's colleagues were diverse as to geographic origin, notably so in view of the governor's divisive anti-Yankee rhetoric to come. President Pennington, for example, was a recent arrival, a wartime Unionist editor from North Carolina; he became the spokesman for Smith's conciliatory policies toward white opponents.[35] Harrington and Hinds were northern newcomers. Hinds served in Senator Spencer's loyalist regiment during the war and would become one of his closest confidants.

Railroad concerns certainly shaped Smith's priorities. In early 1869, Governor Smith twice ventured to Washington, once to testify against Judge Busteed, and then to President Grant's inauguration. He sought patronage influence, reportedly in favor of one of his brothers, but he really wanted federal land grants.[36] In the 1850s, Congress had bestowed government land on railroad companies, with time limitations that had expired because of the war. Smith sought renewal of the technically forfeited grants. His own projected line was one potential beneficiary, as contemporaries noted. Still, the governor seems to have considered the fate of the railroad system more broadly, particularly the Stanton brothers' A&C. They had finalized the purchase on the assurance that, under Smith's Reconstruction government, Congress would restore the land grants.[37] The Stantons had already directed contributions to Smith, and there may have been other promises made, but Smith seems persuaded of the merits.[38] He had criticized the ex-secessionist leadership of most of Alabama's railroads.[39] This broadly applied to the Democratic-run South & North project, constructing slowly into the mountains. Governor Smith preferred their Boston-based and Republican-connected rivals, perhaps on principled grounds.

To the governor's dismay, Alabama's congressmen did not share Smith's priorities. Alabama's two senators, and five of the six House members, were recently from the northern states. None of them possessed obvious investments in Alabama railroad projects. Smith was naive in expecting much weight in Washington, or speed, and the A&C line encountered "a hitch."[40] Smith's frustration must have been exacerbated by State Senator

Hinds. He had secured lucrative postal contracts with the government, a pattern he pursued for decades, and he reportedly approached the Stantons to supply cross-ties as an independent contractor. This looks like a bribe solicitation, presumably in exchange for influence. The Stantons, in anger, exposed Hinds publicly.[41]

The railroad companies eventually got their renewals, over 100,000 acres—admittedly low-value at the moment—in the case of the A&C, but the episode had lasting consequences. Governor Smith previously had been on good terms with Alabama's delegation, including Senator Spencer. But after weeks of frustration in Washington, Smith erupted in rage, denouncing them to Grant himself for ignoring him on patronage.[42] "Gov. W. H. Smith will leave for home, perfectly disgusted with the state of affairs here," one reporter wrote. "The carpet-baggers treated him with the utmost neglect and contempt, and never consulted him in the least. . . ."[43] Smith vented on the train homeward, vowing exposure of Spencer's misdeeds.[44] Smith's divisive rhetoric escalated from this time, opening an entrée to opposition opinion.

While these events transpired, Pennington, as railroad president, busied himself with local government aid. He secured endorsements from Democratic newspapers and local leaders on the route. One public statement, from Pennington's Lee County, promised that the line would "ten times over pay the interest on the Bonds in reduced freight," and proponents predicted huge increases in land values.[45] Newspapers like the aptly named Opelika *Locomotive* rivaled each other in support. In the spring and summer of 1869, several of the counties along the proposed line approved substantial direct purchases of stock, on the order of $100,000 apiece.[46] These referenda mostly passed easily, aided by imaginative arguments. One statement contended that, once the company pocketed the state endorsement, they could return the county aid within months. Implausible promises abounded.[47]

Given partisan rancor, the Republican-laden project could not escape notice. Newspapers off the route occasionally criticized the Wild-Cat line, as the uninhibited Montgomery *Mail* called it. The editors denounced the governor for conflict of interest, fingering the reckless promoters who suggested the local bonds could always be repudiated.[48] The editors nonetheless conceded the futility of opposition: "We suppose the counties will vote aid, because the negroes will always vote that way, and because all those who live immediately on the line of the road will vote the same way. . . ."[49] This public criticism was conspicuous for its rarity. Urban boosterism was the default position of the Democratic press, while opposition seemed divisive. Newspapers promoting the railroad even cited the governor's connection favorably.[50] The Montgomery *Advertiser* initially praised it, advising there was "nothing in which East Alabama is more deeply or vitally interested."[51] The *Mail*'s opposition awakened more ill-feeling than the railroad itself. Alabama's aid policy antedated Radical Reconstruction, and many politicians and newspapers had pet projects. Thus only the most partisan of the "Democratic" wing of the Democratic and Conservative Party would dare undermine Alabama's credit.[52]

The bipartisan convergence over development had a dramatic illustration: the proposal to purchase west Florida. The legislature authorized it on December 30, in the midst of the flurry of railroad laws. In early 1869, Smith appointed Pennington and two colleagues to negotiate purchase for one million dollars. The partisan rationale is unclear, given the area's white majority, but the economic goal was: Pennington promised Floridians, "give us the harbor of Pensacola, and we will connect it by rail with our capital and our new system of railways in ninety days. . . ."[53] Pennington reported success, but a snag soon developed in the upright state auditor, R. M. Reynolds, who refused reimbursement for a suspicious expenditure of over ten thousand dollars. Governor Smith had to order payment from discretionary funds.[54] The explanation, as a Republican legislative committee would all but state, is that Pennington bribed the Floridians over the misgivings of his fellow delegates, but none of the major eastern Alabama newspapers saw much to criticize.[55] Purchase would have extended the general aid law to the Gulf Coast, a motive which overshadowed even partisan advantage.

The favorable reception of Smith's railroad initiatives dovetailed into his larger political needs. He found his duties taxing, and mail frequently went unacknowledged, even from prominent supporters. His letterbooks indicate he left the capitol a dozen times in a year, mostly for home.[56] Propelled by such concerns, Smith cultivated the more sober portion of the opposition, to gain white acceptance for his government. He faced dilemmas common to scalawags elsewhere. As Michael Perman observed, moderate Republican leaders reached out to conservative sectors of the opposition on development issues.[57] If Alabama is any indication, native southerners like Smith were prone to complicated railroad entanglements, far more than the Radical "carpetbaggers" he so reviled. Beyond this, there was one outstanding problem with Smith's approach, from the point of view of his black and Unionist following. Smith could hardly conciliate potential converts if he pursued measures against terrorism. In the absence of personal papers, it is difficult to evaluate how conscious Smith's inaction was. From his bipartisan political goals, to his enthusiasm for Alabama railroads, to the needs of his own railroad project specifically—all these various motives converged. Smith could not mobilize an interracial state militia or seek widespread arrests, certainly not in the places where he hoped to build his railroad.

One episode illustrates the theme, through a circumstantial but damning series of events. When Klan outbreaks occurred, Smith commonly sought federal troops. General Samuel Crawford was "in full accord with the conservative Republicans," so he generally honored Smith's requests.[58] In heavily white Calhoun and Cherokee counties, rural Klansmen attacked black laborers for the Selma, Rome & Dalton Railroad, which was laying track and constructing a permanent workshop. This provided the background for the Cross Plains or Patona episode. A missionary teacher in a company-sponsored black school, a Canadian, William Luke, received death threats. His railroad superiors, mostly northerners, encouraged employees to defend Luke and themselves. The army sent a detachment, but unfortunately the governor's projected railroad ran through Calhoun County. In late March 1870, Pennington and Smith arrived in Jacksonville to negotiate the consolidation of their line with a partially completed fragment.[59] General Crawford came as well, and the evidence indicates he participated in the railroad discussions.[60] Community leaders promised good behavior, but Crawford had witnessed Luke's harassment, so Smith and Pennington's persuasions left him unmoved.[61]

Elsewhere, Governor Smith threatened stern measures against the Klan at this very time. In Calhoun County, Pennington and he acted differently. Pennington soon returned to arrange for a county bond referendum.[62] He wrote Crawford's military superior in Atlanta, recommending departure of the troops, and then asked the governor to press the effort because removal would be "best, in more respects than one."[63] Smith complied, and a quid pro quo appears likely. Elite guarantees of good behavior may have been given in good faith, given the common interest in railroad promotion. Farmers in the countryside had other priorities, and night-riding resumed. According to the modern study, Klan meetings planned Luke's murder, while freedmen readied themselves with arms provided by the schoolteacher.[64] In this climate, the previously mentioned altercation at the railroad platform in Patona escalated. Freedmen shot at the white assailants, suspected Klansmen, while exiting church services. Though no one was hurt, the ill-timed response endangered churchgoers. Hundreds of Klansmen rode into town that night, removing from jail Luke and four freedmen, William Hall, Caesar Fredrick, Toney Cliff, and Berry Harris. They lynched them in leisurely fashion, letting Luke write a final letter home. It was a grim result for all the Republican governor's pains. Smith secured elite cooperation for his railroad, but what the freedmen got is less clear.[65]

The governor's inaction on the Klan generated ferocious Republican criticism. Freedpeople recognized his priorities, which pushed them toward the carpetbag leadership he so disdained. On civil rights and Klan-related issues, a Radical opposition formed in the legislature to oppose his conciliatory measures, and in Congress, Senator Spencer blasted the governor. The leadership of the Radical faction was mostly white, but black legislators and their constituents backed them most of the time. However, on the specific issue of the governor's development priorities, the issue is more complex. Modern revisionist scholars long downplayed the railroad issue, correctly judging it secondary to civil rights.[66] It complicated the rehabilitation of Reconstruction to emphasize development and the legislative corruption that subsidies bred. Still, Smith's behavior illuminates African American political agency in an unfamiliar venue. In Alabama, railroad issues were as important as anywhere else in the South, and they had ramifications for the repute of black politics. It is important to address the issue squarely: what did the freedpeople think about the railroads their dubious ally pursued?

Smith's railroad initiatives depended on local referenda, so the freedmen's preferences mattered. This was evident from the governor's own railroad project, the first to take advantage of state legislation. The Republican auspices of the proposal likely attracted freedmen. Smith and Pennington addressed interracial crowds repeatedly. From Chambers County, Pennington wrote: "Blacks all right and some of the whites will vote for subscription. I have two leading colored men at work now between Cusetta and Bluffton and send another up to-morrow. They will all marshall their forces and march them to LaFayette Saturday."[67] Pennington sought flags and a brass band. Barbeques occurred routinely, but such direct courtship of black voters was not typical, because the governor's project faced unusual partisan resistance.[68] Elsewhere, Democratic businessmen and planters spearheaded most major projects. These faced less criticism, and upland counties often voted subscription by wide margins. Of the five so-called "strangulated counties" that later defaulted, three had large white majorities.[69]

County votes often proved contentious, but not those of individual towns and cities. Here freedpeople's votes barely mattered because of the huge margins. Union Springs reportedly passed a proposal unanimously.[70] Greensboro passed another by 166 to 1.[71] In Selma, the postwar boomtown of the interior, the Republican legislature approved a charter which limited the vote on aid measures to property holders. One proposal still passed by a margin of 6 to 1.[72] Rarely did measures promising to bring a railroad to a city lack overwhelming white support, and some cities promoted measures recklessly. In 1871, with many companies collapsing, Talladega voted for a $50,000 endorsement, 232 to 2. Opelika voted two to one for a grant to Pennington's railroad, though the town lacked fire-fighting machinery for a year thereafter.[73]

Democrats often accused freedmen of indiscriminate support, an indictment sharpened by the eventual outcome. The Selma *Argus* suggested that black voters could always be bought for aid measures.[74] The evidence, though, reveals a complex pattern of local interest and racial accommodation. Reconstruction changed the geography of the electorate, both at the state level toward the black belt and toward the plantation districts within counties. One result was hotly contested elections to locate or move county courthouses, to be closer to the center of population, which was important for freedmen on foot who needed access to law enforcement.[75] The pattern in numerous votes was geographic, rural neighborhood by neighborhood. Railroad projects ran mostly through plantation areas, where wealth and population could provide traffic and freight. This gave planters and their labor force a common interest. It also gave freedmen the unusual opportunity to vote, in safety, along with their white neighbors, under circumstances where their participation would be welcomed.

Where detailed reports survive, the precinct returns suggest that freedpeople were more likely than whites to support pending aid measures. The stronger association, however, was with geography: proximity to the proposed lines correlated with support more than the proportion of black people.[76] The southern portion of Hale County, where the freedmen were concentrated, had a distinctively rich but impermeable soil that rains turned into an impassible grey goo.[77] Thus rich planters and their laborers both overwhelmingly supported aid. In Clarke County, the pattern is similar.[78] But freedpeople were not indiscriminate. Proponents sometimes called off votes at the last minute, fearing defeat, and Perry County reportedly turned down one proposal by five to one.[79] Dallas County, surrounding Selma, voted on two referenda in rapid succession. The initial attempt was defeated by precincts outside Selma. Supporters had promised a free wagon-and-foot bridge across the Alabama River, but this understanding had not been written into the bond measure. Even ballot-box shenanigans could not forestall the resulting defeat. Proponents then added these conditions, and it passed easily, even though voters trounced a proposal for another line at about the same time. Brass bands were beside the point: the outcome hinged upon the specifics of the proposal.[80]

Beyond casting their ballots, it is difficult to distinguish how the freedmen perceived the issue. Their leaders seldom addressed the topic in public forums, at least as reported in the press. Other issues mattered more than financial ones involving complex and technical matters in which voters had little direct experience. And, as the Democratic press endlessly repeated, few African Americans owned land, so they would not feel property taxes directly. Still, some rationale for support existed. Railroad subsidies were identified with their party. Once railroads were built, factories and mines would grow and provide an alternative to plantation labor. Freedpeople responded to the rhetoric of social transformation. Alderman Lawrence S. Berry of Mobile "wanted to keep pace with the march of improvement," and he expressed surprise that sensible men could oppose such measures.[81]

Railroads certainly hired vast numbers of temporary workers. The Atlanta *Constitution* reported that 14,000 railroad hands were at work during 1870, a substantial proportion of Alabama's paid labor force.[82] The A&C alone advertised for 4,000 workers at $1.50 per day, and it was unable to hire enough.[83] The company brought in hundreds of Chinese contract laborers, giving Alabamians fresh racial issues to ponder. Railroad construction sometimes provided troublesome jobs; there are reports of bankrupt companies leaving workers unpaid, of abusive work gangs, even of an occasional killing by white supervisors.[84] Still, the availability of railroad work helped freedmen. And, as Pennington promised, railroad jobs paid a dollar a day, in cash each month, a matter of concern for hard-pressed freedmen.[85] Railroad executives complained that rival companies bid up the cost of unskilled labor. The price of cotton was high in 1869 and most of 1870, and agricultural laborers and tenants did well in relative terms. The availability of short-term supplemental work enhanced their bargaining position.

The initial fruits of the railroad program looked favorable, even to most whites. Land values increased along the projected lines. In

Tuscaloosa, minister Charles Manly spoke with elite contacts after the A&C consolidation: "These men say they already consider their property worth 300 per cent now than they did a month ago." Senator Spencer took a jaundiced view of things Alabamian, but the economic prospects cheered him too. He wrote the railroad promoter Grenville Dodge, "The Decatur property I spoke of is an excellent bargain as the town is growing rapidly & we will soon have *five Rail Roads* there which must make it an important point. . . . All property in Alabama at present prices is bound to quadruple in the next eighteen months."[86]

Spencer exaggerated only slightly. Many towns experienced spectacular growth under the spur of real or projected railroad construction. Opelika reportedly had fifty buildings under construction, and locals predicted the population would double in a year. In Greensboro, a resident noted that the paint brush was much in demand.[87] Even in the countryside, the transition from "laborlord" to landlord made property improvements attractive. Railroad-inspired growth and change had a bipartisan appeal in a war-torn region, especially because most of the railroad companies were led by Alabamians, often by former Confederate generals. One partisan Democrat concluded a letter hopefully: "Alabama is being cut up with R. Roads now. Oh we may be something yet."[88]

Curious alliances spread during Reconstruction's heyday. Republicans pushed railroads because the issue so divided the opposition. Many whites, especially former Whigs and conservatives, overlooked the unwelcome auspices for long-desired subsidy measures. The freedpeople, in turn, warily accepted a range of collaborators. Perhaps the oddest of newfound allies was the former cavalry commander, Nathan Bedford Forrest. Widely reputed as the head of the Klan, in 1869 Forrest found new employment. He formed the Selma, Marion & Memphis Railroad from several scattered lines and came to Alabama as a promoter.

The Klansman's credentials might not seem ideal, but the Republican governor and he collaborated readily. Smith received requests for favors, even for shortcuts in legal requirements. Forrest once asked for endorsed bonds acknowledging he had no right to them yet.[89] Even more striking is the relationship between Forrest and the freedpeople, especially in the plantation counties through which his line ran. Perry and Dallas counties voted down aid to his line, overwhelmingly, which might have owed something to Forrest's reputation.[90] Forrest therefore went to lengths to conciliate freedpeople. He announced plans to exchange land for construction labor on his railroad.[91] He emphasized his black support, and he also authorized Mississippi legislator Robert Gleed and Alabama legislator James K. Green to give speeches on the railroad's behalf. Predictably, Ryland Randolph found fault: "We feel proud that Tuscaloosa has not yet seen fit to stoop to such stinking policy, nor do we apprehend that she ever will consent to flatter political niggers." His Tuscaloosa *Monitor* charged a betrayal of white supremacy, and it threatened violence if Green dared speak in the vicinity.[92]

Referenda debates seldom featured race-baiting, and one might have thought Forrest immune. The episode had a curious sequel, when Probate Judge W. T. Blackford refused to issue the bonds voted by the Hale County electorate. Congressional testimony indicates that Forrest then met privately with Blackford. Some accounts imply bribery, but if true, Blackford likely negotiated for protection from the Klansmen nearby as well. When Randolph again criticized Blackford, Forrest blasted the editor in a letter to the *State Journal,* Alabama's leading Republican paper. Forrest dissected the sorry war record of his onetime subordinate. The Democratic press winced at the airing of dirty laundry, while Republicans lauded Forrest as an entrepreneurial visionary.[93]

Forrest's visibility made him unique, but there are other examples of pragmatism trumping Klan enthusiasm. Take Robert Jemison, the cooperationist leader who went to the Confederate Senate as a conservative. War and emancipation cost him dearly, and only the half-built South West & North East Railroad project survived of his fortune. The Yankees stole his cotton, someone burnt his mill, and he had several ribs broken in a fight. He then lost his newly built mansion, pouring out his frustrations in bloodthirsty diatribes. One or the other race, he thought, "must be exterminated or expelled."[94] When the Klan began operations in Tuscaloosa, he envisioned race war with aplomb.

Railroad politics changed his mind. Two of his "colored friends" won election to the Reconstruction legislature, Shandy Jones and the famed bridge-builder Horace King. Jemison had helped King win his freedom decades before, and both legislators generously did him favors.[95] As the Stanton brothers maneuvered to buy his state-indebted railroad fragment, it dawned on him that Ryland Randolph's profile was unhelpful. After one Klan murder, Jemison wrote: "I do not know which many of our citizens dread most, an outbreak of the negroes, or the opening of the Batteries of the Monitor against them."[96] Jemison lobbied elites against him, both in Tuscaloosa and elsewhere. When Randolph won election to the legislature, Jemison warned that poor Tuscaloosa had "no agent at

Montgomery to watch the movement of Stanton & who . . . might have some influence & power to prevent it."[97]

Thus there was logic to black popular engagement with railroads. Freedmen always prioritized civil rights, and the courtship by railroad men made a favorable impression. Economic development was a secondary concern, but the freedpeople perceived aid measures as consistent with other goals. Such public-spirited endeavors expressed and even bolstered their claims for citizenship. When they backed subsidy measures, it was almost always along with planters and businessmen, informed grandees who presumably knew what they were doing. Freedmen miscalculated, beyond doubt, and their support for railroad projects would be seized on by racists later on. Still, the real failure was not with the electorate so much as the Republican leadership in Montgomery. There would be a state-level catastrophe, for which freedmen received disproportionate blame.[98]

Governor Smith led the way. By the summer of 1869, his railroad line had run into financial trouble. One county referendum wound up in court, to be overturned after years of litigation on technical grounds. In another county, aid would be rejected by a few votes, and in yet another, promoters delayed the vote in view of probable defeat. Pennington started construction up and down the line to impress local voters, but he could not complete the twenty consecutive miles required for state aid.[99] In August, Governor Smith was summoned to Boston on urgent business.[100] Smith reported that "Northern capitalists stand ready to take hold of the Road and help build it."[101] Testimony suggests that the backers provided some $80,000.[102] The Stantons aided in other ways, informing the shareholders of a bankrupt project, "*If you let Gov. Smith have the road it will be built.*"[103] The shareholders quickly offered to merge their project with the governor's. For his part, Smith reciprocated freely. He reportedly intervened to prevent a shakedown of the A&C, this time by his ally Harrington.[104] The point is that the governor could hardly interfere with the Stantons' legislative priorities. If Smith wanted his railroad built and to win reelection, he needed the A&C Railroad completed. Little else can account for his silence to come.

When the legislature reconvened in November 1869, the best-connected railroad heads conferred with Governor Smith, and then with legislative leaders, seeking additional aid. The resulting Railroad Omnibus proposal made a $3,000,000 favorable loan to the A&C and increased the state guarantees for another six lines, mostly to $20,000 per mile.[105] The political problem was that not all areas of the state benefited. In a marathon night session, the bill was amended to include every other project in the state, about thirty-five in all, effectively killing it.[106] Aid limited to stronger lines—along with Smith's included project—could not pass easily, so the A&C sought to pass its subsidy separately. In the resulting scramble, the rumors of corruption are so indiscriminate and partisan that finding the truth is difficult. Still, the press discourse suggests that accustomed influence-peddling segued into open purchase of votes.[107] Even the Republican *Journal* warned legislators against measures that "by their rottenness and corruption, would ruin any organization."[108]

The Stantons figured centrally, partly because they were high-rolling Bostonians and partly because their company had means. As outsiders, they disregarded Montgomery's customary legislative niceties. They hosted a posh Christmas inspection trip by legislators and administration officials, by one account including the governor himself. "The utmost unanimity prevailed and pledges were given of future state aid to the Road," an indiscreet attendee reported.[109] The Stantons' direction of the railroad had raised other concerns. They made various side investments, like the construction of a $125,000 hotel and land purchases near the terminal in Chattanooga.[110] They undertook shadowy land-option maneuvers, involving skullduggery in determining the crossing location of the A&C and the rival South & North. Outwitting the Bostonians figures prominently in the founding lore of Birmingham.[111] These side undertakings were common among railroad directors, but they blurred the distinction between corporate and private ventures, and presumably all were facilitated by diverted state aid.

In early 1870, lobbying became so complex as to defy ready explanation. The Stantons apparently turned against aid to any other lines.[112] State-endorsed company bonds had become so abundant as to depress the market, so they sought "straight" Alabama government bonds instead.[113] As the situation became clear, rival companies, communities distant from the line, and those that had completed roads rose up against them—joined by the House Democrats now united in opposition to the Alabama & Chattanooga grant. Since under the constitution aid measures required a two-thirds margin, passage was not guaranteed. A series of bipartisan mass rallies occurred in the capital, at which legislators denounced the three-million-dollar bill and other pending grants. White Republican opponents were the favored speakers. Auditor Reynolds observed that everyone at the meeting favored the subsidy principle, but "if we go on recklessly giving aid to railroads . . . we will become hopelessly involved in debt."[114] Among Republican critics, ideological conservatives and moderates predominated, mostly of native white origins, with the exception of those tied to the governor.

To add to the partisan confusion, numerous well-pedigreed Democrats backed the three-million loan. The only Democrat in the Senate spoke out for the bill. The future arch-segregationist US senator John T. Morgan served as company lawyer. He provided a learned rationale for the grant's legality, and he lobbied Selma legislators privately for passage. Ex–Supreme Court justice A. J. Walker, recently a member of Pennington's delegation to purchase west Florida, similarly represented the company. In the press, even the Tuscaloosa *Monitor* once editorialized for an A&C subsidy. There were other curious allies: the Montgomery *Mail* favored extension of the general aid law for another year. "The bill is so guarded that we think the State credit will suffer no detriment," the normally hyper-partisan paper concluded.[115]

The $3-million bill met defeat. Afterwards, newspapers charged that senators were literally in the lobby of the House, working the members.[116] A leading conservative Republican opponent of the bill, former justice Samuel F. Rice, mysteriously switched sides.[117] Finally, the House Committee on Internal Improvements was instructed to report back a bill in fifteen minutes.[118] The subsidy was reduced to $2 million, with enhanced provisions securing the state against loss.[119] After the Stantons got their aid, the other lines intensified their efforts too, with passage facilitated this time by Democratic support.[120] The already-built Mobile and Montgomery received a $2.5-million endorsement for improvement purposes, the narrow margin of passage secured by detaining opponents including Benjamin Royal, the sole African American in the Senate.[121] Democratic executives later admitted that they had bribed legislators on other bills.[122]

Democratic leaders helped pass numerous railroad measures, but the Republicans controlled the government. Republicans were certain to get the blame when things went wrong. Dissident leaders attested to the scale of corruption that winter. Representative Warren A. Brantley told contacts that gaining the last few votes in the House had cost the company dearly.[123] Rumors swirled around John Hardy, now chair of the House Internal Improvements Committee. After the South & North subsidy ran into a roadblock, one legislator said members were "well aware of the *motives* WHY the committee made the adverse report."[124] Thereafter, Hardy reportedly negotiated a $25,000 payment from the company, increasing it by $10,000 at the last moment, to the fury of the Democratic executives. Hardy allegedly doled out large sums to House members.[125] The rumored amounts, tens or even hundreds of thousands, defy credulity, but the reality must have been unedifying.[126] Pierce Burton, soon Republican nominee for lieutenant governor, wrote that "outsiders talk of buying and selling men at prices which would have been a disgrace to a slave before the war."[127]

Burton's racially suggestive language raises the issue of the role of the African American leadership. They were somewhat insulated from the corruption, if only because they did not chair committees. The Montgomery *Mail* observed, "The Railroad ring in the Legislature is composed principally of carpet-baggers. . . . The ring is strong in the Senate."[128] Blaming northern newcomers is a half-truth, but the point is that the freedmen were not even mentioned. Furthermore, white Republicans wholly dominated the railroad-friendly Alabama Senate.[129] At this very time, African American public meetings in Selma, led by future congressman Ben Turner, denounced the A&C proposal. Similar rallies occurred in Perry and Marengo counties.[130] Denouncing aid measures that ran counter to local interests was one way African Americans could conciliate white opponents, and Turner in particular enjoyed a reputation for honesty.

But black legislators ignored these constituent pleas. The substantial House contingent mostly backed the A&C bill from the start, even those from areas distant from the aided line.[131] Given what their white colleagues were doing, it would have been surprising had representatives of modest means held entirely aloof. Daniel N. Stanton lightheartedly minimized his own role by blaming them. He supposedly claimed he did not hand out money "except to '*nigger*' . . . *members of the Legislature, to whom he gave from fifty cents to cents to five dollars at a time*. . . ."[132] Perhaps the statement of future congressman Jeremiah Haralson reveals more. He had spoken to A&C agents who assured him the road was solid. Haralson also heard money talk from African American colleagues, and the Stantons entertained "about all the legislature" at their hotel. One agent "would carry members out of the room, one at a time, down a gangway, and stay a little, and the member would go off. . . ." Haralson, a former Democrat, had come to Montgomery opposing the bill, literally bearing the opposing resolutions from Selma. After two attempts he received fifty dollars "as a loan."[133] Haralson testified that several of his African American colleagues were so favored.

Haralson's sorry testimony at least suggests consideration of the bill's merits. The modest payments resemble tips for bills most representatives favored anyway. "I voted for Stanton's Railroad because I believed it a Republican measure, and I voted for it on principle," James K. Green recalled. Some representatives hotly denied having been bribed, like John Carraway on his deathbed.[134] These enactments involved a Republican-connected railroad, which was being constructed quickly and well. Completion would be a partisan coup, overshadowing the means. Besides, Democratic papers threatened assassination if the subsidy bills passed, which unified Republicans behind it.[135] Having reduced the Stantons' grant by a third, House members must have felt they had done their duty, and several African American holdouts changed their position for the final vote. It might have been better to have acted differently; they might have refused to vote aid under the circumstances, or supported it under protest. The public corruption of the Republican legislature damaged the moral luster of Reconstruction, but there were a host of other motivations pressing upon them. John Hardy, for example, was considered a reliable Radical legislative leader, while Republican critics were mostly moderate scalawags unsupportive on other issues. When a black leader tried to speak at an anti-aid rally in Montgomery, he was barred, according to the Tuscaloosa *Monitor*.[136] Sowing discord to benefit racists had little appeal, not over a secondary issue to their constituents.

The record was not good, but the decisive responsibility lies elsewhere. Governor Smith was closely identified with the A&C, but he did nothing to restrain the Stantons' behavior. He encouraged the giveaway climate surrounding the railroads, intensifying the partisan atmosphere by his neglect of the Klan outbreak. In March, Smith and Pennington visited the Stantons and had secured the use of A&C engines for the northern portion of their own railroad line once finished. By press accounts, their railroad hired J. C. Stanton as contractor.[137] Admittedly, Smith's inaction on the two-million-dollar bill may not have mattered. The Radicals were so antagonized by Smith that they may not have heeded anything he said, but he said next to nothing. Conservative Republican allies begged him to oppose the grant, and the Huntsville *Advocate* openly demanded his intervention.[138] Joseph P. Bradley urged a veto of the omnibus bill, because it would "be right & give you more character than any other act of your official life."[139] Democrats who had praised his racial policies and fiscal restraint puzzled over his silence.[140] So far as can be determined, the governor did nothing behind the scenes, nothing against the embarrassing display down the hall from his capitol office. Yet Smith was hardly inactive on other railroad issues. He appointed his ally, Speaker Harrington, as temporary mayor of Mobile, in part because the Board of Trade thought he would promote aid.[141] Governor Smith even signed the general aid extension, which he had cogently denounced as productive of reckless railroad projects.

None of this behavior looked salutary, but it was not necessarily fatal for Republicans. The railroad bills themselves were not unpopular with the electorate, and the Democratic press had to tread warily.[142] Had the Stantons' railroad been finished, or even had the bonds been administered honestly, political damage might have been mitigated. But the governor's prior behavior paled in comparison to his financial stewardship once the A&C bill passed. Smith's outgoing correspondence ledger contains numerous missing pages, but the outlines are clear. The general aid legislation carefully specified how the endorsed bonds were to be awarded. It also directed that second mortgage bonds were to be received in exchange as security. The two-million bill also contained numerous safeguards for the state's credit, but it appears that the governor's office surreptitiously disregarded provisions. The governor ordered the company's second mortgage bonds removed from the custody of the state auditor. He also delivered hundreds of thousands in endorsed bonds prematurely. This let the company pledge these as yet unauthorized bonds as security, to borrow money to finish the road.[143]

Worse followed. Governor Smith signed more bonds than the railroad would be entitled to even if the full length was finished. Smith signed over half a million in excess company bonds, unauthorized by the terms of the aid law and thus entirely illegal. Smith subsequently admitted it. In 1871, Smith and Pennington ventured to New York, shocked—shocked!—to discover that the Stantons were selling excess state-endorsed bonds. Smith assumed the blame: "If my genuine signature is . . . to a greater amount than four millions, it was an oversight."[144] In all, Smith acknowledged he had signed $5.3 million. He urged his successor not to "dwell too strenuously on technicalities," but simply to honor the endorsement, because the alternative was clearly ruinous. "I can only say that if you and the public judge me harshly, I shall have to bear it," he concluded. He was not the only state official to admit wrongdoing, at least tacitly. State Treasurer Arthur Bingham actually pled self-incrimination before a subcommittee, rather than testify about his knowledge of technical illegality involving other lines.[145]

Smith declared himself "astonished" at the excess bonds, which may not be entirely false.[146] His successor said Smith probably lost track of his signatures.[147] The flood of Alabama-endorsed securities depreciated them in European markets in the spring of 1870, and the A&C's overseas brokers pressed for speed, which encouraged forwarding signed bonds before legally due. Smith's statements seem culpable enough on their face, but on closer inspection they look even sorrier. The previous year, the governor's office concluded that the law did not authorize him to count the signed bonds, and, remarkably, so informed the company.[148] This was doubly curious because his office subsequently informed the state auditor that the governor was keeping track.[149] The length for the projected line was known, 295 miles, so at $16,000 per mile, simple multiplication would suggest the maximum amount to be issued, $4,720,000. Smith's office staff could scarcely lose track of numbered bonds being signed sequentially, in thousand-dollar denominations. Furthermore, the Democratic press questioned how bonds were being accounted for, and D. L. Dalton described the governor's exacting office procedures. New state bonds would be carefully counted, and "An accurate record will be made for permanent preservation in the proper office, showing the denominations, numbers and dates of the bonds."[150] Earlier correspondence suggests that both he and the governor had been logging the bonds issued to the A&C, the precise bonds later under dispute. Dalton took pains to keep accurate records, and these are hardly consistent with the governor's later pleas of incompetence.

In sum, the governor's priorities and malfeasance played the core role in Alabama's coming fiscal collapse, rather than black voters, corrupt Republicans in the legislature, or corrupt Democrats for that matter. All these revelations lay in the future, as Governor Smith approached reelection in 1870. If the details ever came out, it would likely destroy the state's credit and the half-completed railroad system along with it. If Smith won, and the railroad got built, these transactions might never see the light of day. Observers thought his prospects for reelection good. Republicans had carried the state in the last two elections, and Smith maintained a substantial following among opposition whites. As it proved, it was Smith's repute with the freedmen, and his ability to protect Republican voters, that would determine the economic future of the state.

9

Bipartisan Disaster
The Advent of Governor Robert Lindsay

[Smith] was elected governor by the republican party, but I don't know what his politics are.

—African American Representative Henry St. Clair

Night-riders rampaged throughout Governor Smith's term. But over time a more subtle countertrend became evident, one often overlooked in the literature on Reconstruction. Save for the eruption near the Mississippi border, historians broadly conclude that terrorist bands remained most persistent, and pervasive, in northern Alabama, especially in the hills and upper piedmont.[1] In this region, black labor was less necessary, and white farmers and tenants looked at them as rivals for jobs and rental lands. Railroad construction projects brought transient railroad workers into areas where few African Americans had been before. Farmers feared pilfering of their hogs and livestock, and they sometimes used night-riding to redistribute the labor force of successful neighbors. Beyond all this, the Klan movement enabled opportunistic lawlessness, seizure of arms, theft, even rape, by providing a racial rationale and palsying law enforcement. A sort of upcountry ethnic cleansing became evident early, overwhelming outnumbered victims. As one Tallapoosa Republican observed, "A great many of them [freedmen] left before I ever heard of the Klan. We had a black cavalry who ran a good many of them away soon after the surrender."[2]

The statement that Klan-style activities were deeply entrenched in some places has a corollary, or at least a suggestion, that things played out differently elsewhere. The grievances and motives fostering mayhem could not apply to all whites equally. Racial expulsion distanced those farmers who welcomed it from their more prosperous neighbors, who hired laborers freely. But the more dramatic contrast was with the plantation heartland. For sheer drama, Alabama's Klan nightmare overshadows everything else, but more benign processes emerged at the same time. Conflict in some locations jarringly coexisted with social gains elsewhere. In about half the state, preponderant black majorities fought, intimidated, or bluffed terrorists into relative inactivity.[3] Most freedpeople lived in areas that provided the numbers and influence for some self-protection, and whites dealt with them on a different basis. Thus, except at contentious election times, the freedpeople took quiet advantage of the lapse of racist legal predominance, just as economic recovery in the late 1860s and early 1870s opened possibilities. Returning prosperity gave the wealthier plantation owners and their laborers and tenants some interest in mutual accommodation, most of the time.

The spread of public education provides one example often overlooked in this context.[4] Before the war, Alabama established a public school system for whites, expanding it and centralizing funding in the 1850s, but schools remained primarily urban, financed by local aid and contributions. The antebellum system primarily funded private schools with state funds.[5] Under Republican Reconstruction, free schools for *all* represented a core goal, so no mandatory fees were permitted. The constitution of 1868 provided for a minimum of a fifth of state revenues earmarked to the schools, among other dedicated funding streams, and the Republican legislature appropriated much more. Schools operated under the centralized control of an elected state board and superintendent. County superintendents responsible to the state served along with neighborhood trustees, generally prosperous whites. School funding was provided after a census on a per-person basis. Over Governor Smith's apparent resistance, Superintendent Noah Cloud withheld funds from noncompliant counties, punishing racial obstruction.[6] On the other hand, the state board determined that all schools should be racially segregated unless both races agreed. This combination of carrot and stick encouraged acquiescence, while extending free public education for the freedpeople.[7]

Because Freedmen's Bureau education funding had ceased the previous fall, Republican officials rushed to reestablish schools. They therefore inaugurated the school system at a time many whites opposed anything the new government did. In Tuscumbia, Superintendent C P. Simmons soon resigned "to hunt for peace," and the initial 1868–69 term proved tumultuous.[8] The Reconstruction government only became operational in July 1868, which disrupted the fall's student census and funding allocations. Several counties overspent their eventual allotment, leaving teachers without their full pay.[9] Also, the constitutional convention had decreed that the state would honor the unpaid bureau and Patton-era commitments, among others. These overdue claims hamstrung local planning. There were also accusations of lax recordkeeping directed at Cloud, even by Republicans on an investigating committee. One unpaid teacher charged his clerking sons were "reckless drinking young men," and both were accused of embezzling thousands. Still, Noah Cloud had credentials as a prewar Whig agricultural reformer, and his Freedmen's Bureau colleagues approved his efforts. He persevered even if in an arbitrary fashion, and his records suggest something under a quarter of the public schooling funds went to African American children.[10]

After the August 1869 congressional elections, educational matters settled down and the system functioned more smoothly. In Hale County, the superintendent could not initially secure trustees he thought responsible, because of fears of integrated, Yankee-style schools, but that opposition had diminished.[11] Superintendent Arthur A. Smith had a tougher time in a Klan stronghold, Greene County. Night-riders torched schoolhouses, but the freedmen were mobilizing to rebuild and to defend themselves. Smith believed the better class of whites would identify the perpetrators, and he hoped for better times, with his trustees talking schools to Smith's satisfaction. Schoolhouses were targeted in the worst terrorist areas, but not normally elsewhere. Arson drove laborers away, while schools lured them into the densely populated plantation districts.[12]

Resistance diminished, especially where officials settled into a nonpartisan profile. As missionaries returned northward, native whites and African American teachers replaced them, both more acceptable to Democrats. In disorderly Sumter County, the white trustees reportedly avoided providing black schools, and the few native whites willing to teach betrayed little idealism. Still, the superintendent thought the system worked smoothly by the end of 1869.[13] In Russell County trustees served readily. The superintendent contended that schools would "satisfy, fix and locate" the workforce, this in a time of improving cotton prices and labor shortages. Cooperative planters presumably endorsed his belief that educated workers were "easier controlled," because schools improved their morals. The Freedmen's Bureau education officer for Alabama agreed that labor recruitment encouraged planters to cooperate.[14]

Antebellum Whigs made uplift arguments for the education of poor citizens, and now a similar logic assisted freed children. Black literacy did not threaten planters personally, and the freedmen were not demanding integrated schools. Democratic newspapers assailed the costs of administration, but they ceased denouncing education as a concept. To the Marion *Commonwealth,* "the only question for men of sense to consider is whether it is better they should be educated by friends or foes."[15] Republican leaders sold free public education as consistent with white self-interest, if only to capture tax money for dozens of schools per county.[16] A muted egalitarianism thus opened the schoolhouse doors to increasing numbers of emancipated youths. In 1870, nearly 16,000 African American children attended school, which would be just under 10 percent of the school-age population, as opposed to slightly over a third of the white population.[17] Community literacy let freedpeople decipher contracts, recalculate planters' ledgers, and even read the newspapers. Put another way, 16,000 compares bountifully to the 114 students, presumably Afro-Creole, officially reported in 1860. By 1880, a substantial minority of the younger generation would achieve basic literacy, and widespread public education would be one of the reforms that outlived Reconstruction's overthrow.

Segregated education suggested African American teachers, and black normal schools were established in Marion and Huntsville.[18] Once established, they commonly functioned without much harassment, though the AMA's Talladega College faced more. This sort of negative evidence of racial accommodation is evident elsewhere. The counties took over the bureau's responsibility for pauper relief, and the state took over the Freedmen's Bureau hospital as well. Alabama's well-regarded insane asylum increased its proportion of African Americans patients from 3.2 percent to 15.8 percent between 1865 and 1870, though housing them in a separate ward.[19] Progress occurred even on the more equality-freighted issue of jury composition. Scattered evidence suggests black jury service became common in the cotton belt. In Barbour County, for example, a white juror observed that freedmen served on the grand jury for the first time. They had done adequately, but their two-thirds preponderance he believed too high.[20]

Not all Lost Causes were worth fighting any longer. At least in the central plantation belt, this logic prevailed. By the late 1860s, cotton production recovered profitability, on the basis of self-selected work squads, and, increasingly, forms of tenant farming. The occasion for slavery-style coercion became less common. Between election upheavals, planters saw that the emancipation might not mean ruin. The Klan's existence perhaps bolstered this inclination, because to more restrained sympathizers, the mobilization looked like sensible self-defense, to be held in reserve as needed. The rampant Klan campaigns helped black-belt planters in quite another way: night-riding pushed laborers out of the piedmont and mountains into the plantation region. Average wealth was greater and better distributed for freedmen in these areas than in the black belt, where few acquired any land. It did not matter; freedpeople sought places where large majorities insured they could live and vote in peace.[21] The plantation region gained about eleven thousand in black population between 1860 and 1866, with another twenty-three thousand by 1870. This would be an increase of around 17 percent, most of it coming after the war.[22] The wealthiest planters gained willing laborers, which encouraged them to accommodate productive hands wherever easily done.

Reconstruction historians gravitate toward dramatic atrocities, but instructive things happened in quiet places too. The Tayloe family of Virginia owned an absentee empire across the western cotton belt, and after the war their managers warned of collapse.[23] W. H. Tayloe thought that even "the Yanks admit they can't make cotton with free labor. . . . We are faring as St. Domingo & Jamaica have done."[24] But cotton production eventually stabilized. One overseer observed that industrious freedmen resented gang labor, which left them subsidizing slack work; letting freedmen select their own work gangs worked better, leaving the less able to move on.[25] Another manager concluded he had to put up with freedwomen staying at home, burning his firewood, because he could not antagonize their husbands.[26] He could coax or hire married women into the fields in peak seasons, which sufficed.[27] Planters perpetually complained about theft but, in the western canebrake, postwar "no-fence" laws made it impossible to range hogs in the woods anyway. Planters could pen up livestock, letting tenants raise their own hogs and deal with resulting problems themselves.[28]

Planters shifted from compulsion to negotiation, or manipulation. In early 1867, H. A. Tayloe noticed the silver lining: "If it was not for the store I do not know what I should have done last year."[29] The plantation lost money, but his store made it back. As the shift to tenant farming proceeded, sharecroppers had to borrow supplies and buy food. Freedmen in the plantation belt made more cotton but kept less of their money on average than elsewhere.[30] Cash was there to be made. After one fine crop, business energized tiny Uniontown: "There are 5 or 6 large Jew stores & the amount of goods sold by them to Negroes is truly astonishing."[31] To settle their debts, tenant farmers picked and sold off their cotton at low prices each fall, which lifted middlemen's profits. Prices charged in Uniontown were reportedly double those back home in Virginia.[32] And in 1871, the legislature would make the landlord's lien on the crop superior to all others for advances made, thus inhibiting the competition from merchants and favoring planters with the means to lend money.[33]

The new system had drawbacks. Tenants slighted work that did not increase their share of the crop, contract provisions notwithstanding.[34] One overseer got a little work out of his squads on rainy days, by threatening to charge for their rations.[35] Some mourned the olden days, like T. T. Munford, who recalled slave children coming to his door requesting their "Kris-mas-gif."[36] Now, he found the silence at the holidays somber, but time moved on. One Selma cotton factor made three hundred bales with his African American overseer in 1870.[37] When Old Man Collins first rented and then left much of his estate to his black relations, planters groused about the "nice neighbors," but everyone apparently prospered and no one called in night-riders.[38] Similarly T. T. Munford's squads worked decently; "As a whole they are obedient & although not industrious, do very well by being watched."[39] H. A. Tayloe reported that his theft problem diminished once the new regime proved capable of jailing accused thieves.[40]

Planters and managers instead obsessed about their white neighbors. Planting was no longer a business for gentlemen, H. A. Tayloe wrote.[41] Irresponsible ex-overseers, now land renters, were outbidding him for workers, but even established planters followed suit. As T. T. Munford observed, "The negro's in this country are *wild with money* and crazy for mules & horses. Planters are renting them land and resorting to every devise to get them from one place to another."[42] Complaints that might have been directed solely at the freedmen were fixed on unscrupulous merchants. "Corn is the currency of this country," E. T. Tayloe observed. "The stores will buy any thing from a quart up. The consequence is Negroes are stealing everything."[43]

Some planters were giddy at success. In Marengo County, Rev. W. A. Stickney sold the 1869 cotton crop at twenty-two cents. He made $12,000, net, while his squads' share totaled $6,000. The proceeds worked out to from $234 to $259 per full hand, an impressive payout, as "Solomon drew $324.34!" Afterwards, Stickney's employees never questioned their share, and the existing terms suited them. The planter thus learned the lesson of flexibility, after a fashion. In extending his own credit to the employees, Stickney cautioned a merchant about their "African whims" of fair treatment. "Let there be no seeming constraint on them, to excite their suspicions," he warned.[44]

For over five years, from the spring of 1868 to mid-1873, cotton production mostly paid planters in the west-central cotton belt. If the Franco-Prussian War depressed cotton prices for the 1870 crop, it only interrupted an existing expectation of profitability. Planters found they could make free labor pay, and Reconstruction did not consistently violate their racial sensitivities. Planters disliked being governed by huge Republican majorities, but for all the denunciation of Radical "carpetbaggers," landowners seldom encountered them in positions of local authority. Wealthy planters could influence, or bar, unwelcome officeholders by refusing to endorse their required property bonds, or by withdrawing them. One exhaustive study found that, of white officeholders serving terms after the initial Republican sweep, fully 85 percent lived in Alabama before the war. Just 6 percent of officeholders were African American, often serving in the legislature rather than in local positions requiring bonds.[45]

In the black belt, most landowners simply acknowledged their limited political influence. For example, the partisan H. A. Tayloe saw no hope of winning elections in his vicinity, but then he lived in a Hale County precinct where freedmen predominated eighteen to one.[46] Provoking conflict was simply unthinkable, which colored his perceptions of what was happening elsewhere. In 1870, he understood that young Democrats were excitable, but somehow Republican speakers provoked the lopsided Eutaw riot. When disguised men killed a mail agent, Tayloe called it murder but still believed "it was done to excite the animosity of the Negroes and cause them to unite against the whites in the election."[47] These explanations were not credible, but they cushioned knowledge that did not comport with his placid reality.

For the freedpeople, the new situation offered fewer material gains. In the black belt, in five years after the war, almost none acquired any land, fewer than one household in fifty.[48] Somebody was making a lot of money, but not freedpeople, or at least they were not holding on to it. All the complaints about theft underscore their sense of grievance. Planters sounded so upbeat because they found commercial means to separate tenant farmers from their cash. Still, in the areas where freedmen concentrated, schools existed for their children, and possibilities were expanding for the strong, able, and lucky. Railroad construction projects were hiring all over the state, which gave them economic options and greater mobility. In all the Tayloe correspondence, there is little suggestion of coercion or debt peonage. The laws promoted equality, and employees left landlords and neighborhoods all the time.

Philip Pitts expressed the dominant tone: "I heard today the Hands some of them were dissatisfied with contract. Remember hereafter—Get in with Nelson, John Cook, Edmund and Joe—after that all will be well." He doled out twenty-five dollars to Cook, and concluded that such end-of-year tips to squad leaders were a fine idea. Contract disputes troubled him, but other changes he accommodated readily. He noted the sale of numerous plots in town, observing freedpeople bought many of them.[49] Pitts was not complaining, it was just how things were. By the early 1870s, widespread tenant farming distanced the freedpeople from the hated holdovers of the slavery regime. Freedwomen resisted field labor and rotated through domestic jobs. Poverty or no, much had changed in ways that freedpeople found gratifying. Children were not seeking out the big house at Christmastime, because they did not need what was being doled out. Old times were best forgotten, it would seem.

These favorable social processes intersected with the tumultuous 1870 election. Even in the black belt, political campaigns interrupted mutual accommodation, and Governor Smith's reelection canvass proved bitter. But the electoral process gave freedmen leverage, as activists became more adroit in using their numbers. Republican factionalism may not have helped the party electorally, but it enabled a challenge to Smith's conciliatory approach. It simultaneously eroded the white Republican monopoly of offices, a matter of importance to the black activists seeking a livelihood in politics.

If factionalism characterized Republican rule, the outsize personality of Senator George Spencer encouraged it. Elected at age thirty, he was the Senate's youngest member, with a talent for controversy.[50] As we have seen, Spencer had quarreled with his onetime protégé, Governor Smith, over the Busteed impeachment. Spencer soon added a sharper feud with his senatorial colleague. Willard Warner was a decade older than Spencer, a sitting Ohio legislator of some means who bought a plantation outside Montgomery. He claimed to have inherited and freed a slave before the war, but he was slow to embrace equal suffrage, denouncing Johnson's congressional critics well into 1866. Still, General Warner had a good military record and a reputation for financial honesty.[51] Supported by the powerful Sherman brothers, Warner expected influence. Spencer claimed he monopolized five-sixths of the federal patronage under Grant.[52]

"Of course," Spencer wrote, "when driven fairly to the wall, I am bound to show fight, and I will make it war to the knife and the knife to the hilt."[53] Patronage provided the conflict, but substantive issues mattered too. Senator Warner and Governor Smith cooperated, especially once it became clear that Smith did not seek Warner's Senate seat. Warner cautiously echoed Smith's assurances that the Klan was under control, though he favored federal anti-terrorist legislation. By contrast, Spencer scouted the rhetoric of conciliation, calling most Democrats the Klan's open sympathizers. Spencer feared giving "political thugs" more power, and he believed Warner simply wrong on granting amnesty to ex-officeholders.[54]

Warner scarcely veiled his contempt for Spencer: "We have in the southern States as much to fear from bad men in our own ranks as we have from the rebels themselves." In private, Warner was scathing.[55] Differences in approach separated the two senators, but there was a political motivation too. Republican moderates were likely to challenge Spencer's reelection in 1872. But both Warner and Smith had to undergo reelection in 1870, which suggested a preemptive move. Most freedmen, and many white Republicans, shared Spencer's gut response to the Ku Klux Klan. This provided the means, potentially, to deny his opponents renomination. The issue came to a head that spring, with a sharp spike in Klan episodes reported to the governor. The high-profile Klan assassinations of law-enforcement agents underscored the point.[56]

Flamboyant murders exposed the fatuity of Governor Smith's claims. Goaded to act, Smith announced he would authorize local militias in Tuscaloosa, Morgan, and Greene counties. Flaws in the long-neglected militia laws delayed him, and he feared political reverses or impeachment unless he followed the law precisely. One supporter suggested raising a volunteer regiment, "of white men if possible," but Smith apparently thought it too inflammatory.[57] Simply arming the freedmen to search out Klansmen around Eutaw, his initial threat, risked dangerous consequences.[58] In the end, he let his military options dwindle away.

Smith recovered his composure, hoping that his militia proclamation had calmed things. "Everything quiet in this section of the state," he wrote in an upbeat communication from his Randolph County home.[59] Smith sought other expedients, like sending an earnest detective to Eutaw, the future federal district attorney John A. Minnis. For his part, Senator Warner hailed the governor's initial turnabout, telegraphing, "let rebels be forgiven & murderers hung[,] amnesty & the halter will give us peace and safety."[60] But nothing really changed, and Republican frustration grew. "Unless something be done Gov. Smith can get no votes here and not only Smith but no other man of the Republican party," one Calhoun County supporter warned.[61] Even the moderate-dominated party press jabbed Smith. The Huntsville *Advocate* criticized his railroad enthusiasms and inaction on the Klan. Editor William Figures and the "scalawag" cluster around Joseph Bradley and D. C. Humphreys reviled the "carpetbaggers," but they refrained from endorsing Smith's reelection. David P. Lewis had warned against the militia, fearing what armed freedmen would do, but as a prosecutor of Klan cases he had seen enough. He now pleaded with the governor for drastic action out of sheer necessity.[62]

The Radical challenge emerged in Huntsville at a Republican county convention in June. One unanimous resolution "unqualifiedly" opposed renomination, while another scored him on the Klan. Not a soul dared defend the governor publicly. Radicals led by Representative Isaac D. Sibley dominated proceedings, and three of the five delegates chosen were African Americans. Appalled, editor Figures described a Tammany Hall scene, with freedmen pressing their leadership claims. For weeks, parties were "poisoning the minds of the colored citizens against Gov. Smith, and making him responsible for all the Ku Klux outrages, and the embodiment of traitorism, a second Moses, meaning thereby a native and not fit to be trusted."[63] For the Huntsville scalawag cohort, these were fighting words.

Given native white sensitivities, Smith knew just how to respond as he hurried to the scene. He declared open war with chosen Radicals in his coalition, thus validating years of Democratic rhetoric. The governor adroitly assailed the "carpetbagger" faction without directly antagonizing the black electorate. Representative Sibley, for example, had recently revealed Pennington's Florida-acquisition bribery and Smith's complicity. By highlighting men like Sibley and Spencer as irresponsible Radicals, Smith made it difficult for native white Republicans to oppose him. In the Tennessee Valley, leading scalawags knew better, but by speaking to their heartfelt grievances against the outside Radicals, the governor brought them in line.

Smith's invective established the tone of his remaining political career. He charged that, through constant use of the offensive term "Rebel," Spencer's supporters like Sibley and J. J. Hinds encouraged Klan violence. Thus Sibley hoped that continuing bloodshed would "furnish semblance of truth to Spencer's libels upon the people of the State generally."

Besides, the racial provocations were not all on one side: Smith blamed the Tuskegee troubles on the reckless comments of a carpetbag postmaster, who urged that freedmen come armed after the Alston shooting. Smith thus deserved reelection because he had defended the state from the Yankee harpies.[64]

Republican editors thought Smith's blast excessive and destructive of party unity.[65] Contemporaries predicted he could not be renominated, but incumbency mattered. One analysis concluded that Spencer had an urban following, but his opponents controlled the Republican press and the leadership in rural counties.[66] Conventions overrepresented officeholders, overwhelmingly scalawags, and they preferred a candidate that would not complicate their relationship with whites. Officials postponed the state convention repeatedly, giving Smith time to maneuver, as other scalawag aspirants like Bradley and Judge Peters endorsed him.[67] Alex White wrote, "If Gov. Smith is not re-nominated we have not the ghost of a chance[,] or if a colored candidate is put on our State ticket."[68] Besides, a disaffected Smith could wreak the party. The Democrats delayed their convention, and speculation swirled that they would nominate him, while the governor did nothing to disavow the rumors.[69] There were other subtleties. Smith's intimates defeated the renomination of his longtime ally, Congressman Robert Heflin, in favor of ex-congressman Benjamin Norris, whom Smith had long denounced as a carpetbagger. Smith thus bought off some Radical opponents before the state convention met in Selma in late August.[70]

Smith's supporters left little to chance. According to the infuriated Heflin, the Stanton brothers bribed delegates wholesale.[71] Smith claimed he had no idea of whatever the railroad men were doing, a curious inattention given that he was in Selma too.[72] Spencer's holdouts on the rules committee—all of them white—contested pro-Smith delegations, without success. Smith won renomination by a unanimous floor vote, but Radicals won concessions elsewhere. The nominee for lieutenant governor, Pierce Burton, opposed railroad corruption, and he was a northerner to boot. Then Nicholas Davis, a conservative scalawag rival of Smith, nominated James T. Rapier as secretary of state. After controversy the incumbent, Charles Miller, withdrew.[73] The governor's supporters feared an interracial ticket would undermine Smith's appeal. The Stantons allegedly offered ten thousand dollars if Rapier withdrew. If so, he spurned it.[74]

The freedmen do not seem to have rallied to Spencer's rebellion. One Perry County legislator, Matt Avery, wrote Smith before the convention, praising his anti-Klan talk. White contacts had approached Avery, all of whom backed Smith, and he was persuaded: "I believe that you suit both parties better than any other man we can get. If we were to get a one sided man it would ruin the party. You generally uses the means to overcome evil by doing good."[75] Such practical-minded black leaders must have concluded that Smith was the strongest candidate, and they consoled themselves with placing the college-educated Rapier on his ticket.

The bidding war enhanced freedmen's opportunities elsewhere. In the majority-black Mobile congressional district, Benjamin Turner won nomination for Congress over several white aspirants. Spencerites thus defeated the incumbent, A. E. Buck, who was aligned with Senator Warner. A Smith backer discerned poetic justice because "Buck and Reynolds were two who urged the Selma Convention to place a negro on the State Ticket, thinking that they would not ask for Congressional honors, for which they both contended. I guess they both have enough of the 'nigger' at last."[76] Treasurer Arthur Bingham's son relished their comeuppance. White politicians' scramble for office, combined with factional divisions, removed barriers in the biracial activist subculture.[77]

Smith's renomination surprised the Democrats. There was talk of postponing their convention, and hard-liners warned against dispiriting concessions on race.[78] Several Democratic newspapers preferred to run against the just-ratified Fifteenth Amendment guaranteeing equal voting rights. A Clarke County meeting supported "all measures advocating the supremacy of the white race" and rejected candidates who did not.[79] Such racial avowals suggested muscular means, and they came mostly from areas with active Klans. For example, the Eutaw *Whig* threatened bloodshed if freedmen dared attend party conventions armed.[80]

At the Democratic and Conservative Convention, however, caution prevailed; the delegates sought candidates who would appeal to north Alabama. The Montgomery platform promised to obey the laws, so long as they were on the books, pledging a fair ballot count. It avoided explicit reference to white supremacy, decrying carpetbaggers and corruption instead.[81] On the third ballot, the delegates nominated Robert Burns Lindsay for governor. A Scottish immigrant and former schoolteacher from Tuscumbia, Lindsay served in the 1850s as a Democratic legislator. A brother-in-law of "veto" governor Winston, Lindsay thus might be thought immune to corporate blandishments. In 1860, Lindsay served as a Douglas elector, and he opposed immediate secession. When Union forces overran the Tennessee Valley, he stayed on for a time. He then went into the Confederate Army in a staff position, but he never acquired much of a war record. After Grant's election, he flirted with the Republicans, and he mostly refrained from praising Klan-style violence.[82] Democrats thus appealed to anti-secession voters, and they avoided loading the ticket with men like John Jolly, with his Klan connections, for lieutenant governor. Some prominent Democrats remained ineligible to hold office, but neutralizing hotheads still was not easy. Republicans claimed there was an effort to remove James Clanton as party chair, and that he responded by attacking those—like Lindsay—who supinely sought the release of their officeholding disabilities.[83]

Democratic discretion owed much to the expectation that Governor Smith would be difficult to beat. However, the press had months to recant their praise. Newspapers called to mind his unconditional Unionist record, and also his postwar testimony before Congress demanding stronger Reconstruction measures. His anti-carpetbagger rhetoric turned against him, now that several were on his ticket. The most-emphasized issue, though, was race in the form of Rapier. Hecklers in white counties asked Smith if he intended to vote for him, and he eventually he had to answer, yes. Conservative Republicans complained constantly: Smith had better "sing Psalms to a dead horse" as run with Rapier in the wiregrass. One Republican spent half an hour nightly cursing the carpetbaggers, Rapier, and the troublemaker Nicholas Davis who nominated him.[84]

"The Negro ticket & the Patona affair, is all they have run on you," one supporter assured the governor.[85] None of this need have been decisive. Republicans won the two previous elections by several thousand votes each, despite large-scale Klan mobilizations. Given any protection, the freedmen would sustain the Republican candidates by overwhelming margins. In response, the Democrats would use the race issue to lift turnout, which would also enable voter suppression techniques, especially in the few terrorist-dominated counties with large black populations. Lindsay could run on the issues, while his followers in the Klan areas could do what was needed to win. Platform intimidation became the campaign mainstay. At Monroeville, candidate Ben Turner asked if he would be permitted to speak. Democratic leaders agreed that it was "politic" that they do so, but whites attended in force, which induced Turner to highlight his own southern origin. Freedmen found Turner's performance confusing. A Democratic leader shared his insight with party editors: whites should hear Turner wherever he spoke, "so as to keep him in the Carpet-bag-abusing track."[86]

Freedmen were unlikely to risk voting if the party had no public presence, and those not literate depended on public oratory. Unless he showed the flag, Smith heard, low turnout would doom his reelection. In the majority-white counties, Smith spoke in relative safety, but in the contested Klan areas, the pattern was different. Opponents could not let Republicans hold their meetings without risking the election. Democrats knew that their followers did well when shooting started, which sharpened their confrontational edge in negotiations. In the plantation region, towns were disproportionately white enclaves, prone to overreaction when freedmen arrived in arms, as they often did in violent places. Governor Smith, Senator Warner, and other prominent Republican politicians hoped that their exalted station would protect them. It was not entirely true.

In the western black belt, along the line of Stanton's railroad, the Klan dominated Tuscaloosa, Greene, and Sumter counties. In Tuscaloosa, things were finally settling down. As Shandy Jones wrote Smith, "The K.K.K. is very quiet, since one of their principals [Randolph] have lost a leg, and another his life. I am satisfied we can carry this county, if we can have it canvassed."[87] However, in neighboring Greene County, disguised night-riders recently murdered the county solicitor in Eutaw. Likewise, Sumter County had a constant stream of racial killings. In Sumter County, blacks numbered 78 percent of the population; in Greene County, 79 percent.[88] To operate in such unpromising demographic terrain, outside Klansmen had to flood the area, and the Mississippi border nearby assisted them. Day-tripping terrorists could ride the train, then return home with near legal impunity.[89]

In south Sumter County, Republicans gathered for a rally near Belmont on the fourth of July. According to W. B. Jones, armed Democrats heckled him, and one challenged him to a fight. Night-riding followed, and a white man was shot by a freedman defending a home. In response, one Collins, "a wild, reckless fellow," then rode either at the head of a small posse or undisguised Klansmen, though the "old-line whig" sheriff discouraged the attempt. At Zeke High's house, Collins was killed and his party repulsed, though one freedman died in the process. Now armed whites poured in, and about two hundred gathered on each side.[90] According to Republican Pierce Burton, who served as mediator: "The whites had lawyers to consult with and were acting as the Sheriff's posse. The blacks were assembled near Durden's Ferry and rather invited a contest saying they were willing to go out into an open field and 'fight it out.'"[91] The sheriff restrained his followers long enough to explain to the freedmen the legal consequences. After his assurances, they suddenly dispersed overnight.

The sequel proved clearer and more strategic. Sumter County whites were frustrated at the indecisive outcome, and when Republicans gathered for a convention, townspeople met them at the edge of Livingston ordering them to stack their guns. When they complied, Representative Richard Burke upbraided them, and there followed the killing of Burke.[92] This was the backstory when Governor Smith arrived, in the company of ex-governor Parsons and Senator Warner, who had traveled elsewhere without incident. Governor Smith was interrupted and insulted by well-armed whites. One man stood with "a large knife in his hand, drawn," while Senator Warner sat nearby and watched him intently, in hopes of intimidating him.[93] Smith's tense oration concluded, and the speakers managed to get away without further incident, heading, alas, for Eutaw. The party was joined by dozens of young men on the train, reportedly Klan sympathizers from Mississippi.[94]

After the Republicans had announced their meeting, Democrats summoned one at the same location, the Greene County courthouse, falsely advertising prominent speakers. Republicans offered a joint meeting, but Democratic leaders John Jolly and J. G. Pierce did not consider "the questions in the present political canvass debatable, either as to men or measures." To Republican leaders, all this portended trouble, and they secured troops who were stationed away from the scene. The Republicans met on the opposite side of the courthouse from the Democrats, with orators speaking from a table standing outside a window. When the Democratic rally ended, hundreds crowded in on either side of the Republican speakers, while others stationed themselves in the upstairs courthouse rooms. The freedmen predominated, but their opponents had revolvers, and in a pacific gesture some freedmen had stacked their guns. After heckling, Congressman Charles Hays got up to adjourn, and whites tripped him off the table. One shot rang out, perhaps as a signal, and a fusillade erupted from the hecklers. Some Democrats claimed Hays fired while falling, or that a freedman shot first, but Jolly himself testified that whites did nearly all the initial firing. Jolly's men occupied the circuit clerk's office, shooting over the speakers. One eyewitness in the room claimed they acted at Jolly's command.[95]

The casualty count suggests a planned operation. According to the ultra-Democratic Eutaw *Whig*, some twenty-five or thirty freedmen were shot, two fatally, with just two whites hurt. Another Democratic paper reported four dead and fifty wounded, all apparently black.[96] J. G. Pierce thought the firing was "all fun," purportedly not believing people were actually being shot all around him: "I got on the table, and laughed extravagantly at the way the negroes were flying and running about."[97] After the initial gunfire concluded, the sheriff reportedly prevented execution of the speakers. By the time freedmen regrouped, soldiers prevented them from returning to the scene. Admittedly, the Eutaw riot was atypical; it was the bloodiest such affair in the entire campaign. Senator Warner said it was the only place in the state in which he was molested, and immediately afterwards he spoke in Tuscaloosa without incident. Along the border, though, these events just before election day mattered.

Governor Smith was sick in his room during the riot, and he lost his zeal for further campaigning. He had other worries as well, one of them substantive. According to the constitution, the senators were to draw lots to determine who had to run for reelection after two years, but since all had been elected for four-year terms, the Senate decided to delay implementation for two more years. This dubious procedure inflamed the opposition, though the governor denounced the Senate's action. Senator Spencer added more confusion. After hesitation, Spencer formally endorsed the governor's reelection but sat out the campaign, and soon an allegedly purloined letter from one of Spencer's confidants appeared. During the war, it charged, Smith was "lounging, like a lazy, mangy dog, about our headquarters." Spencer's feigned irritation only confirmed the letter's authenticity. The evident intent was to remind Alabamians of his wartime Unionism, as Smith charged, and that he had accompanied Sherman's march.[98] Spencer's black constituency united behind Smith as the Republican nominee, but the senator's behavior suggested more trouble.

Lindsay and the Democrats had problems too. The nominee for treasurer, L. F. McCoy, had a previous defalcation. One Republican promised to "use him so rough" that he would never run for anything, and McCoy withdrew.[99] Lindsay had weightier problems, like opposing corruption without undermining the state's credit standing. Calibrating the Democrats' racial mobilization proved difficult. In black-belt Wilcox County, Democrats flexibly nominated an African American for the legislature. Democrats elsewhere complained that this did damage in the hill country, and they urged dropping him.[100] More broadly, the violence on the border lifted Republican intensity in the rest of the black belt. Nothing mobilized black voters anywhere like terrorism elsewhere. Violence also provided President Grant the political cover to send troops to guard the polls, which suppressed disorder on election day itself.

The manuscript returns showed Lindsay narrowly ahead by 79,628 to 78,196.[101] Smith ran better than most of the rest of Republican ticket by about 2,000 votes, from conservative whites who abstained from the other races.[102] Turnout in the black belt was very high, nearly 100 percent of the potential male electorate in several counties.[103] Republican majorities were huge in these densely populated plantation counties. Elsewhere, in the Tennessee Valley and in the upper piedmont and mountain region, turnout was much lower. Terrorist activities in the valley probably accounts for suppressed turnout among freedmen, but the more startling result is among white voters. Democrats carried the predominantly white counties by large margins, but not that many voted. Turnout was under 40 percent in Marion, under 45 percent in Blount County. If few whites preferred, or risked, voting for Smith's Republicans, a great many avoided the polls.[104]

Who actually won the election? The numbers would suggest the Klan won, especially in western Alabama. In Greene and Sumter counties, blacks were nearly four-fifths of the population, but Republicans lost both counties, narrowly in Greene, and by a substantial margin in Sumter. In the latter county, it appears that hundreds of freedmen voted Democratic, perhaps without direct coercion on election day. Either county alone tipped the statewide election. In addition, in Tuscaloosa, Republicans received 757 of 773 of their votes in the city itself, compelling evidence of rural intimidation.[105] In the leading Klan counties, the effect looks obvious. In Cherokee County, scene of the mass lynching, Republicans received just 8 percent. In such areas, freedmen largely avoided the polls. Republicans lost the entire Tennessee Valley, receiving just 13 percent of the vote in Colbert County, 14 percent in Marshall, again with low turnout. In the southeastern wiregrass, the freedpeople were so outnumbered and long intimidated that a terrorist campaign never emerged at all. This may reflect disillusionment at the failure of Republican officeholders to protect them, but even that could be ascribed to the terrorist campaign.[106]

Ryland Randolph underscored the point in his Tuscaloosa *Monitor*. Randolph decried the restraint shown by Selma's civic leaders during a street confrontation. Had Selma Democrats poured "volley after volley of lead" into the freedmen, killing and wounding "a few hundred," they would have won the subsequent election. Randolph pointed to the nearby example: "[S]uppose the Democrats of Eutaw, in the political riot there on the 25th ult., had foolishly folded their arms, and suffered the black and white Radicals to run roughshod over them—where, then, would Greene county be now? Why, she would be in the same condition with Dallas—Radical by an overwhelming majority." Randolph thus vindicated his intransigent approach, on the grounds that Democrats could not win without murder.[107]

Democrats made plausible accusations of Republican fraud too. Republicans carried Mobile County, which is possibly explained by urban-style repeat voting. Democrats alleged that the Stantons' railroad workers voted illegally, and the Republican numbers are indeed suspiciously high in Jefferson County. These anomalies might represent several hundred votes, in comparison to the thousands secured by previous Democratic intimidation. But election day itself passed with little disturbance. The army concentrated hundreds of troops from adjoining states, and General S. W. Crawford moved to Montgomery to exercise temporary command statewide. Companies were stationed in Eutaw and Livingston.[108] Democratic fraud does not seem pervasive, in view of Republican officials' control of the polls, though the votes for Russell and Baker were disallowed and the official returns disappeared in Washington County. On election day, more Democratic votes probably were cast, and barring obvious fraud, no real grounds existed to contest an election based on presumed voter preferences. The Klan swung the election, but not on voting day itself, and afterwards Republican newspapers and candidates conceded defeat.

All conceded, that is, except Governor Smith and Treasurer Arthur Bingham. Smith's vigorous response makes sense, given the railroad-bond irregularities. He expected to win reelection and believed he *had* won, and now exposure threatened ruin. His lawyers might find voting problems enough to prevail before the all-Republican judiciary. Surrendering office impeded this strategy, and retaining the state's records otherwise looked advisable. Treasurer Bingham testified he signed railroad bonds during his disputed occupancy, and the delay may also have facilitated cosmetic measures. The motivation is speculative, but railroad insiders believed the fear of exposure governed their actions. Smith and Bingham presumably thought whatever they were doing was worth some personal danger.[109]

Smith gathered his lawyers at the state capitol, and they debated strategy through the night. Lewis Parsons headed to Washington to seek federal court intervention, unsuccessfully. Just throwing out the vote as fraudulent in Klan-riddled plantation counties would not do, as it left the margins in predominantly white regions intact. In Montgomery, Smith's lawyers secured injunctions barring the count of the official returns when the new legislature met, and Senator Warner sought the restoration of General Crawford to command.[110] The situation grew tense: the Montgomery *Advertiser* called for restraint, but only because the plotters were "not worth the hemp it would take to hang them." The governor sought troops, fearing assassination, which Crawford encouraged his former subordinates to supply. The Grant administration disavowed these actions, and superiors in Atlanta ordered soldiers away from the capitol. Officers evaded the orders, stationing men two minutes away, and they even claimed a storm drove soldiers to shelter in the statehouse.[111] The military presence avoided entire reliance on African American volunteers. It appears Sheriff Barber, at the governor's request, used soldiers to bolster his posse, and perhaps to ease Democrats' movement in and out of offices on business. Freedmen rallied to defend the governor, who then disavowed them in the face of criticism. He denied that the posse protecting him even existed: a single black doorman had inspired all the alarm. For that matter, the governor denied asking for federal troops.[112]

The populace on both sides behaved with caution, a pattern generally in evidence in Montgomery. The freedmen had been drilling for years, but no one rushed to start shooting in this highly visible center. Otherwise, things were going badly for the governor. Republican editors questioned the electoral challenge and the martial moves, even the governor's own organ, the Montgomery *State Journal*. Attorney General Morse appeared at bipartisan protest rallies, as did Senator Spencer's spokesmen. The national Republican press offered little support either.[113] For their part, the Democrats feared a vigorous response might prompt federal intervention, whereas careful behavior might yet prevail. The pending reelection of Senator Warner before the newly seated legislature also inspired caution, because they hoped to peel off defectors. President Grant backed Warner, and every African American legislator fell in line. With the holdover Senate, Republicans enjoyed a several-vote majority on joint ballot. Over a dozen, mostly Spencer allies, held out for other Republican candidates hoping to force Warner's replacement. Suddenly, two Republican legislators bolted to the Democratic candidate, the northern-born lawyer George Goldthwaite, anti-secession but Confederate, who was elected by a majority of one vote.[114] Warner's allies contested the result in the US Senate tenaciously, but without success. Warner blamed Spencer's intrigues, and though outright proof is lacking, it seems probable. The outcome secured Spencer control of federal patronage in time for his re-election.[115]

Warner's defeat intensified the pressure on Smith. Democrats in the legislature inaugurated Lindsay, who proceeded to sign bills from the far end of the capitol building. John Jolly, fresh from his Eutaw triumph, acted as his emissary though Lindsay himself urged restraint. By preventing the counting of the ballots, Governor Smith forestalled the constitutional procedures for contesting fraudulent results.[116] Here was uncharted legal terrain, and judicial resolution suddenly materialized. Press reports claim that federal Judge Busteed brokered a way around the Republican-dominated judiciary. Busteed's old ally, former district attorney John Q. Smith, had long resented the governor. Both men recalled the governor's impeachment effort against Busteed. J. Q. Smith, now a state circuit judge, heard a plea from Lindsay's lawyers on December 7. The judge ordered Sheriff Barber to haul Governor Smith into court. At adjournment the judge ordered the sheriff to take possession of the governor's office. Smith finally capitulated to avoid "excitement, tumult, and, perhaps, an approach to anarchy."[117]

Alabama's Reconstruction era might logically have ended here, in December 1870. That pattern was the norm elsewhere, once the opposition won momentary power. Democratic control generally yielded recalibrated election laws to make it difficult to lose thereafter. However, in Alabama, the holdover Republican Senate delayed that outcome for some years, and more crucially, Governor Lindsay proved unable to handle the railroad mess his predecessor left behind. Lindsay's failures renewed partisan rivalry for years, as numbers of whites abandoned the Democrats. With their opponents in disarray, African Americans gained renewed political influence. The ultimate cost in black lives would be high when racist Redemption finally did occur. But in the meantime, the polity and the economic system functioned on the Reconstruction basis of legal equality, though under Democratic rule.

Smith's malfeasance became his successor's nightmare. Days before leaving office, Smith officially reported that he had endorsed—or guaranteed—Alabama & Chattanooga bonds for 250 miles of completed road. In fact, instead of $4.0 million, Smith actually endorsed bonds for all 295 miles, and more, $5.3 million. In all, 720 thousand-dollar bonds were prematurely issued, while about 500 more were entirely illegal. The railroad's bankers and brokers, especially Henry Clews & Co., presumably knew it. There were other more technical violations. None of this would have mattered, in practice, as long as the railroad paid the semiannual interest. Incoming governor Lindsay heard rumors of company default, but he assumed it was a bluff. No one anticipated nonpayment, but the Stantons had trouble borrowing money during the European war, and the election outcome deterred lenders. Investigators alleged they secured a loan to pay the interest, but that the Stantons diverted the money to finish the line. Whatever the reality, the company defaulted on both its endorsed bonds and the straight Alabama bonds received in the $2.0-million bill.[118]

"We have had a vast number of calls from astonished holders of the State obligations," Henry Clews wrote.[119] Governor Lindsay had to decide whether to honor the state endorsement, given the lack of records and his distrust of the company's agents. The sum required, about $250,000, represented a fifth of Alabama's budget. Clews and others implicated offered to front the money, but Lindsay claimed lack of legal authority. Lindsay probably should have paid off the less questionable bonds quickly, which would have been most of them. The impasse threatened all uncompleted railroads. "The interest must be met on the Stanton Bonds *promptly* or all is up" came the cry from New York. On the other hand, said F. M. Gilmer of the South & North, quick payment would make Alabama's credit even better than if the default had not occurred.[120]

Alabama would honor its just debts, Lindsay stated, but not before a full investigation, and one of his statements suggested not even then. He warned lawmakers that he would pay nothing without explicit legislation. One can easily imagine his desire for political cover, but Europeans barely knew where Alabama was, much less the distinction between various grades of state and corporate bonds. Bondholders demanded payment of all, and Clews inaccurately gave firm assurances based on a liberal translation of the governor's statements.[121] When Lindsay demurred, the *New York Times* denounced his partisan attitude as kin to repudiation.[122] Alabama was "suddenly placarded throughout Christendom as a defaulter," the governor lamented.[123]

If Lindsay expected lawmakers to help on financial matters, he soon learned otherwise. One ill-timed measure had the governor's full support, a dramatic reduction in the state's property taxes. According to Superintendent of Education Joseph Hodgson, the existing tax rate was insufficient to support the schools, much less the overdue interest.[124] As for the bonds, the Republican Senate sought immediate payment, while the House held lurid hearings on the passage of the railroad-aid legislation—especially on Stanton bribing Republicans, though they implicated Democratic railroaders too.[125] A good deal of intraparty jostling ensued, as much of the press urged wholesale repudiation.[126] Several lawmakers argued that the A&C corporate charter had technical flaws, so that none of the bonds need be honored. A majority of the Democratic House backed this position, to devastating effect on the uncompleted railroads.[127] General Forrest wired that, "unless the State pays interest promptly, irreparable ruin awaits the railroad and State credit." He couldn't borrow a dollar in New York for his interest payment.[128]

Lindsay eventually secured the authority in the Steele bill to investigate and pay legally issued bonds in the hands of innocent purchasers, over the vociferous objections of most Democratic legislators.[129] Numerous Alabama railroad contacts, including J. L. Pennington, then telegraphed him to come to New York.[130] To legislators' dismay, Lindsay hurried away, and even his relative, ex-governor Winston, thought financiers and fancy hotels influenced him.[131] Lindsay there met ex-governor Smith, who explained the situation and his efforts to get the company to pay off the excess secretly. Smith's public confession, presumably demanded by Lindsay, excused the Stantons by alleging illegality by those marketing their bonds. Smith thus enabled Lindsay to pay the legally issued portion, four million by his account, but the cesspool of revelations fed taxpayer demands to repudiate them all.[132]

These events coincided with the wider Democratic assumption of power, a complicated proceeding in its own right. A strange intermingling of venom and accommodation prevailed. For example, School Superintendent Joseph Hodgson often acted responsibly, and African American attendance increased early in his term, but he indulged in visceral rhetoric. "If necessary, to save Barbour County, and the white and colored schools from the supervision of the negro elected last Saturday, I will demand from him a bond of one million dollars," Hodgson pledged. He thus responded to the election of Ferdinand Smith, who had served time in the penitentiary on a Mobile debt matter. But Governor Patton had pardoned Reverend Smith on grounds of malicious prosecution. The real complaint was Smith holding a position of individual authority over whites. "Has it come to this, that our white teachers, male and female, are to be examined for licenses by an ignorant negro," Hodgson wrote. But ignorance was not the issue; the politics of gender and racial subordination mattered more.[133]

Racial tripwires notwithstanding, the Democrats pledged that terrorism would end. Several newspapers pressed the governor and the populace to punish Klan violence, in terms that sound unequivocal.[134] In most areas, Democrats were content for the time being. Some of their subsequent requests look benign. A Sumter County petition secured the pardon of a freedman who had been caught up in an indiscriminate group indictment, presumably during the recent troubles. After a shooting, he had feared violence if he turned himself in for a charge of resisting arrest. Pardoning him "would have a good effect on some of our best colored people," or so community notables thought.[135] In this Klan stronghold, some whites preferred to mend fences. Having won, elites often sought a return to more civil racial interaction. From Athens, an inexperienced lawyer sought a pardon because he had botched his client's defense. Besides, there was "a great prejudice here in 1869 against negroes generally, and I believe this was the cause of this man's conviction. . . . You know how helpless under present circumstances negroes are without friends or money and if I can do any thing for this one I desire to do it."[136]

In other places, Lindsay's role was that of a mediator negotiating the terms of a coup by his hard-line supporters. One elderly lawyer wrote from Eutaw, race relations were "never kinder in this County than they are now since we scouted a few dangerous radicals, white and black."[137] In Greene County, the purge was ongoing. John Jolly reportedly chose the governor's appointments, but Lindsay could not continuously please such unrestrained Democrats. Republican Probate Judge A. R. Davis fled, but he refused to resign for months. Nor did the governor move to force him out. Davis kept his position until assured that Governor Lindsay would pick a moderate replacement. Locals denounced Lindsay's action in the name of "*the white people & Democratic party of Greene, who helped secure your election. . . .*"[138]

A spasm of Klan raids drove officers out. In Marengo, all save one of the "carpetbaggers" resigned, and the Marion *Commonwealth* reported Klan appearances in Perry.[139] In Hale County, Probate Judge Blackford had conciliated local elites with his fiscal prudence, and the Greensboro *Beacon*, enjoying official advertising, bolstered him by denouncing the Klan. Militants within the county, and Klansmen in neighboring Greene and Tuscaloosa counties, resented Blackford's long invulnerability. After the election, a lawyer informed him that Lindsay's victory had settled the question. Dozens of disguised men rode into Greensboro, searching for the judge. A published letter from "K.W.C." warned that such Republicans would get "all they deserve, and perhaps a little more." After a week in the woods, sheltered by freedmen, Blackford fled to Montgomery, where Lindsay high-mindedly told Blackford he could not accept his resignation unless voluntary. He offered to write local notables and urge them to exert themselves. Blackford returned home, greeted by yet more threats. Blackford then sold his property to opponents, secured a statement that his books balanced, and departed. Lindsay avoided replacing him with Jolly's reported choice, instead picking a Democrat "as nearly acceptable to all parties as I could get."[140]

This pattern repeated itself in other trouble spots. Judge Luther R. Smith of Choctaw County was a conservative Republican. Public meetings in Sumter and elsewhere demanded his resignation, despite the lack of evidence of wrongdoing. The governor did nothing to help, and one of the judge's letters was endorsed "complaining generally." After Smith testified before Congress, repeated raids burned his fences and his expensive lumber mill. Finally he and his newlywed wife fled to Montgomery, though he stubbornly kept his post.[141] In all this, Governor Lindsay occupied a difficult position, and the threat of congressional action made his situation no easier. Summoned to Washington, Lindsay denied the existence of the Klan as an organization. Criminals adopted disguises occasionally, he conceded, but only as a temporary expedient. He did not think that "the Ku-Klux ever selected a victim because he belonged to any political party."[142] Indeed, never had a party so recognized the "freedom and purity of the ballot box" as did the Democrats on his election day.[143]

These fulsome denials increased pressure to act. Congressman Joseph Sloss warned, "We have much to contend with here, in protecting the character of our people against false charges, and I fear the result if any charge be proved to be true." Sloss heard that, in Fayette County, parading Klansmen had attended a Democratic meeting, outfitted. Sloss urged that someone be prosecuted under state authority.[144] Lindsay and much of the Democratic press issued public warnings against Klan activities, duly reported in northern newspapers. In Coosa County he exhorted a sheriff to act after a Klan-style beating.[145] With elections over, Lindsay could argue that these episodes were not politically motivated. By this time, it was becoming more true, as the partisan rationale dissolved while racial atrocities continued, in places becoming indiscriminate.[146] Democratic leaders were so widely complicit in previous activity that it complicated stopping it now.

The shift in white sentiment, combined with hundreds of federal prosecutions under the Enforcement acts, mostly brought the Klan mobilization to a close over 1871.[147] In one instance officials acted on Lindsay's urgings. The dissolute former guerilla chief Samuel M. Moore led a murderous Klan band composed substantially of planters' sons. They tortured an elderly Union man, Leonard Weir, for some workplace advice to freedmen. Limestone County officials gathered a posse and confronted the assailants, securing Weir's release. Afterwards, Democratic solicitor Daniel Coleman asked the governor to offer rewards, if only to drive them across the border. Moore then went to jail in lieu of $2,000 bond, and he eventually served a term in federal prison. Governor Lindsay did not order the local prosecutions, but he did establish the climate of opinion where they occurred.[148]

Between resolving the bond mess, temporarily, and damping down Democratic lawlessness, Lindsay placed the state on a less violent trajectory. Lindsay sought white supremacy, but his relative moderation might have mitigated the experience for African Americans. Had he succeeded, Redemption would have occurred without the White League spasm of 1874. Beyond saving lives, what difference this would have made in the long run is difficult to discern, as Alabama progressed toward its later destiny at Montgomery and Selma. Things might have been different, somehow. Instead, the railroad issue exploded Lindsay's government, giving Reconstruction a second life.

It reads like confusingly written fiction. In the spring of 1871, Daniel N. Stanton still had not completed his railroad, fearing that once finished the state would seize it. As long as that possibility existed, loans were scarce, so Stanton needed guarantees. When Governor Lindsay arrived in New York City, to investigate and pay the bonds, he had recently lost three children. His emotional stability always seemed questionable: a prewar credit report called him "a man of some sprightliness with many oddities."[149] Whatever the cause, Lindsay was befriended by one Nathaniel McKay, a locomotive builder with investment plans in Alabama. He showed off his fast carriages and allegedly introduced Lindsay to the city's dicier pleasures. Seeing an opportunity, McKay offered Stanton his assistance. They settled on a payment of $300,000 in dubious stock and bonds and $5,000 in cash. McKay then secured an ambiguously worded commitment from Lindsay not to seize the road.[150]

The Stantons were out of money, kiting checks to their infuriated Alabama lawyers.[151] When Lindsay had refused to honor the illegal bonds, the company paid the interest on them itself. Railroad hands went unpaid for months, and unsecured creditors began suing. Stanton might maintain control if Alabama paid the next interest payments, then left him unmolested until the railroad went into profitable operation. He thought he had bribed the governor, so he assured his contacts that his railroad was safe in his hands. The ex-Alabama financier P. D. Roddey heard rumors, and he went to Democratic leader James Clanton with the explosive news. Clanton challenged the governor, who disavowed everything and confronted McKay. Beyond this the facts are in dispute. Stanton later alleged that Lindsay must have known, while McKay and Lindsay agreed the governor knew nothing, McKay assuming the entire blame. But Governor Lindsay either knew of the bribe or should have suspected, and his intimacy with the confessedly corrupt McKay looks damning.

Daniel Stanton was right to fear completing the road, because once it was done, creditors descended. Bankruptcy suits occurred in Judge Busteed's federal court, while federal Judge W. B. Woods, Willard Warner's brother-in-law, intervened to keep the line out of Busteed's hands. From Chattanooga, J. C. Stanton defied court orders: his workers refused to let trains move, while sympathetic judges prevented removal of railroad property. Engineers had "turned, locked and spiked" the switches, and the city was "full to overflowing with negroes and white men all claiming their dues from the road."[152] At the line's other end, laborers seized an engine in Meridian, repeating the feat at Tuscaloosa. Stranded workers and residents along the line began suffering for provisions. When the company again defaulted on its interest payments in July, the state paid up, but it then seized the road under the terms of the endorsement legislation. Lindsay may have preferred to leave the Stantons in control, but once the bribery story started leaking, the governor could hardly leave them in possession. But because the railroad's connections lay outside of the state, in Chattanooga and Meridian, the state could not control this expensive economic asset.[153]

The governor's agent, John Gindrat, persuaded the strikers in Meridian that their chances of partial payment were best under state control. The workers restored a disabled engine, and Gindrat took formal possession of railroad property up the line, dispensing provisions as he went. Unfortunately, he then "found three trains of cars held under attachments issued out of the State of Georgia, and the road completely blocked." Creditors refused to allow traffic through Georgia's few miles of track, and in ten weeks, the hobbled road cost over fifty thousand dollars to run and repair.[154] To add to Lindsay's woes, the volatile Clanton suffered a miscommunication after confronting the Stanton's lawyers in court at Knoxville. Somehow a barroom invitation miscarried, aspersions against Clanton's courage followed, and the Democratic leader died in a street shootout.[155] Governor Lindsay thus lost an ally who supported seizing the railroad, who might have sheltered him from criticism.

Then again, perhaps nothing could have saved Lindsay. Daniel Stanton, after all, thought he had bribed the governor to keep possession, so Stanton felt betrayed. He published a detailed confession of the payments he made via McKay, laden with innuendo: McKay reportedly said he had taken the governor to places of amusement, "the character and names of which I will refrain from mentioning, but allow the people to judge." The governor became a laughingstock. "I suppose you have seen the villainous lying statements of D. N. Stanton," he wrote his secretary. Whether or not he received the money, Lindsay had only vaguely revealed the bribery attempt when confronted with the reports some weeks previously.[156] The governor's defenders were struck dumb at the revelations, and at McKay's subsequent statements that he had pocketed the sums himself. In an unrelated lawsuit, McKay later that year alleged he was defrauded out of fifty thousand dollars in company bonds, so the Lindsay episode did not hurt him much financially.[157] The administration organ, the Montgomery *Advertiser*, said next to nothing about the allegations. Only when a rival newspaper announced it would print four thousand copies of the Stanton revelations did editor Robert Tyler respond vigorously—against the offending Selma *Argus*.[158]

The railroad fiasco would go on and on, consuming the state's finances. Upon assuming office, Lindsay recommended cutting the state's property tax rate by up to a third. He saw himself as an anti-railroad budget cutter, and he resisted borrowing yet more money to defray the interest endorsement. But the interest payments absorbed nearly half the state's budget, which meant that all the other functions of government began shutting down. In May, School Superintendent Hodgson informed the governor that no funds were left to settle with several of the white counties, and that officials had left Montgomery dissatisfied. In August, he announced they would have to wait until the legislature met. As the Montgomery *Advertiser* pointed out, "There is no money in the Treasury to carry on our somewhat expensive Common School System for this current year."[159] The rest of the state's services fared similarly. In October, Superintendent Bryce wrote that he had nearly three hundred insane indigents on his hands. He had borrowed money to feed them, and the state was now out of funds. Lindsay only offered to seek a private loan, but around this time he had state financial agents, in secret, loan General Forrest $200,000 to meet his interest payment. By paying the bondholders, Lindsay diverted the state's revenue, leaving those holding state warrants—IOUs—without recourse until the state treasury had funds. Even then it was first come, first served.[160]

Everyone believed the railroad could be sold to recoup the state's investment. Instead, it turned out no one wanted a railroad embroiled in legal difficulties. The asset could not be unloaded. Eventually, the state bought the railroad itself for $320,000, a fraction of Alabama's endorsement, but then could not raise the purchase price to secure unquestioned possession. The state's meltdown continued unabated. Democratic critics of Lindsay launched an investigation with the aid of Senate Republicans. According to Representative B. B. Lewis, his ex parte committee had "no money, no fuel, no lights." He paid expenses out of his pocket, but the indictment proved devastating.[161] It silenced even the governor's strongest defenders. "His railroad policy is totally and hopelessly indefensible," the Tuscaloosa *Times* concluded.[162]

For the freedmen, the state's fiscal ruin had odd results. The collapse of the railroads cost thousands of laborers their wages, and the erosion of public schooling undermined a long-held dream. But the Democratic drive to eliminate freedmen from the political community miscarried. Alabama's competitive, biracial Reconstruction order persisted for years, especially in the black belt. Society functioned on the basis of something like equality before the law, at a time when cotton prices improved. Ironically, Reconstruction's promise came closest to reality during Lindsay's hobbled Democratic rule. The practices of plantation slavery became more distant. Free labor normalized over time, with market mechanisms and usury substituting for force. Politically, Democratic disarray combined with Republican factionalism to give African Americans influence, even jobs. The novelty of equal participation gave way to something more like modern ethnic-based politics, and black leaders became skilled at promoting individual and community interests. These benign processes became the reality of Reconstruction as President Grant's reelection campaign transfixed the nation.

10

False Dawn

The Promise of Reconstruction in the Early 1870s

The people here live pretty much as they did before the war. The most of them have their plantations left and they derive about as large incomes from them as they ever did.

—W. B. Young, Hale County, December 1870

In the long perspective, it is hard to see Radical Reconstruction as a success, and its place in the broader trajectory of civil rights is indistinct.[1] Yet Alabama gave real signs that society might move toward a lasting form of racial coexistence, on some modest level of civil equality. Surprisingly, the positive trends happened largely under the control of Reconstruction's opponents, weakened as they were by the railroad issue and the threat of federal intervention. For several years, political riots and organized violence diminished and then largely ceased. In Alabama, the distracted Democrats gave freedmen as positive a social environment as Reconstruction ever provided.

Gains grew out of the rising fortunes of the plantation economy, which in the early 1870s showed serious evidence of recovery. While the half-completed railroads faltered under Governor Lindsay, a thousand miles of track had been built in five years. This transformation opened up economic opportunity for nearby planters, enriched numerous interior towns, and encouraged mines and factories. The rail crossing of Birmingham had gone from zero to three or even four thousand people in eighteen months, making it thereafter Alabama's industrial "Magic City."[2] More crucially for planters, the European war ended and the price of cotton recovered in 1871 and 1872, approaching twice the prewar levels.[3] For landowners and agricultural laborers, good cotton prices overshadowed everything else. One Selma cotton factor reported that crops never looked better since surrender: "The negroes have worked well and it is the exception if we hear of a place that has not been well worked."[4]

Planters still complained of deteriorating maintenance, but anticipated profit transformed their mood.

Evidence comes from surprising places, like the letters of the Demopolis planter Samuel Strudwick. An ailing man, he vented at Radicals and freedpeople. Domestics left at whim, leaving his female relations to do their own cooking, sweeping, and milking. He once owned 130 slaves, but as of May 1871 just 3 laborers worked his plantation, and he concluded he would have to rent out his lands. Strudwick blamed landowners: "Cuffy is courted, flattered, patted on the shoulder and *caressed, by many, many, many* whom we once thought, could never be made to stoop so low."[5] Despite these grievances, Strudwick proved capable of surprising nuance: "The Negroes about us are civil and behave well. They doff their hats, call you '*Master*'—and are willing to lend a helping hand when required—no case of violence or outrage, has ever taken place in this neighborhood."[6]

Fears of labor shortage abounded. One man privately wrote that unscrupulous whites sent their own freedmen to entice away contract laborers with whiskey and fair promises.[7] At a time of high cotton prices, planters accommodated the former slaves. When a squad complained about their crowded housing, Henry Lyell, a business manager in Perry County, spent thousands on single-family quarters.[8] A Sumter County planter wrote that everyone was so afraid that neighbors would grow more cotton that they would hire any worthless laborer. With cotton at twenty-five cents, planters would give the hand half-share and take the "chances to cheat him out of enough to cover all losses."[9] Land rental became ever more prevalent, as holdouts mostly abandoned farming in squads, even self-selected ones. Despite what appear to be limited material gains in the black belt, freedpeople relished the changes in lifestyle and certainly spent more money. In marked contrast to the tumultuous implementation of black suffrage, by the early 1870s little collective labor protest occurred in cotton. Strikes were seldom reported, and northern reporters stopped hearing black-belt planters pine for slavery.[10]

Familiarity wore away some resentment at the changes that Reconstruction brought, especially when prosperous whites sought favors. For example, Congressman Benjamin Turner enjoyed a good reputation. In mid-1869, his Dun credit report said he was popular and had the confidence of the business community. A real estate developer praised Turner as "not more than half negro and a very sensible man." Congressman Turner's repute was not unique in Selma. One clerk wrote, "The negroes who hold office are sometimes preferable to the white men. The negro tax assessor of Dallas Co & negro clerk to one of the courts . . . appear quite respectable. . . ." As the white tax collector reportedly was a drunk, such comparisons somewhat reconciled Democrats to their black office-holders.[11]

With labor shortage as planters' obsession, Klan-style night-riding became localized in the more isolated hills and piedmont and more identified with poorer farmers. Larger landowners benefited from the presence of freedpeople, but their less prosperous neighbors resented the labor competition, especially with upland whites descending into the valley lands themselves.[12] Smaller farmers and tenants obsessively feared for their own hogs. Driving out black tenants, in sort of a hill-country ethnic expulsion, and simple mayhem further isolated the perpetrators. Under federal prosecution and Lindsay's discouragement, this violence dwindled in the early 1870s. The last major prosecution occurred in Tallapoosa and Coosa counties, with planters testifying against Klansmen who disrupted their operations. One made a practice of recruiting threatened laborers, and his testimony helped put several Klansmen in federal prison.[13]

Even where one might have expected racial violence, it materialized less often. In black-belt Wilcox County, the probate judge resigned in mid-1871, which placed the process of certifying official bonds in Democratic hands. This perhaps encouraged a subsequent confrontation as hundreds of freedmen mobilized to attend a rally, reportedly carrying guns to deter interruptions. When whites warned them not to march into McKinley, they reportedly responded "with gibes, with threats and with menaces." The Democrats feared former USCI veterans who had been "taught that it was right to have military organizations—to drill—be disciplined, and to bear arms." But with whites representing under a quarter of the population, no escalation followed: the Democratic governor instead requested federal troops who restored order. The bloodless pattern continued through subsequent confrontations. That fall, Republicans won all the Wilcox offices, but their sheriff could not secure the bond. Opponents feared "there may be some sort of fusion between the carpetbaggers and some Democrats," and so it proved. Throughout the decade, independent Democrats mostly governed, with some Republicans remaining in office, all of which infuriated the more partisan whites.[14]

The mixed outcome in Wilcox occurred because the lapse of terrorist violence made the route to full Democratic control indistinct. Governor Lindsay's woes undermined partisan unity, even at the county level. In the words of one hard-liner, Lindsay had hastened to the Wall Street financiers "to become a football for their ingenious handling." When Democrats tried to use their party machinery to maintain disciplined majorities, white voters resisted.[15] Voters wanted to retain some choice in traditionally less partisan local elections, especially where whites predominated. Electoral unity came more readily to the freedmen, which turned results to their advantage. In Tuscaloosa, Ryland Randolph's triumphant return to the legislature stopped cold; a conservative rival from one of his many duel imbroglios challenged him. Randolph withdrew, preventing a potential biracial alliance against him.[16]

All across Alabama, conventions and primaries yielded a crop of dissidents, running as independent Democrats or as fusion candidates with Republican support. In Opelika, a sympathetic newspaper described overlapping grievances: townspeople, former Whigs, and railroad supporters had all been frozen out at the Democratic convention. The independents were strong enough that fall to elect a sheriff.[17] Elsewhere the independents seem more backwoods and rural. The Republicans deliberately refrained from summoning nominating conventions in places where they were a minority.[18] In the fall of 1871, Democratic disarray yielded striking results. Republicans regained at least six counties they had carried the previous year while losing only one. In addition, "the regular Democratic nominees were beaten in six or eight counties by a fusion between the Union men and the Republicans."[19] These outcomes left Democrats scurrying for procedural redress. In Randolph County, Democrats complained that officials had thrown out several boxes for fraud, and they asked the governor to declare them victorious. For important offices, the common resort was for Democratic officials to reject official bonds, or preventing landowners from signing them through community pressure. This gambit did work—but not consistently.[20]

The fluid partisan situation served freedpeople well. After the bloody 1870 campaign, no major riots occurred in Alabama for well over three years. Freedmen served as local magistrates, which made them the first judicial stop for contract disputes. The numbers are obscure, but a Dallas County neighborhood complained that *one* of them had moved away and was thus ineligible.[21] From Eufaula came complaints that City Court Judge Elias Keils pursued minor complaints by freedpeople which were tried before his interracial juries. His grand jury even found a true bill against public officials for neglecting street maintenance.[22] With voting largely unchecked, freedmen could weigh in on local issues, like courthouse sites.[23] On neighborhood concerns, black voting often promoted the interests of the wealthier planters and intimidation proved rare.

African American influence at the ballot box often depended on deference to independent Democrats, but another venue allowed freer rein. Patronage demands always focused leadership attention. While officeholders and federal employees were predominantly white, the Republican electorate was not. The Democratic press broadcast black demands for office with opportunistic sympathy, in hope of encouraging factionalism. And Republican disputes were pervasive, because of the continuing rivalry between Senator Spencer and ex-senator Warner, and also President Grant's prospective renomination. The interlocking state and federal controversies invited black intervention on matters of practical moment, though primarily for the activists involved.

In this era of the spoils system, egalitarian beliefs intersected with the tangible issue of patronage jobs and racial exclusion. For white professionals in particular, prominence as Republicans inhibited other forms of economic activity and middle-class status, and they felt that their privations entitled them to preference. They formed an insular subculture: Judge Luther Smith's wife, Addie, described Republican women in Montgomery calling upon one another in proper Victorian fashion. Within a few days' time, she visited with the wives of ex-congressman Buckley, Assessor Reynolds, and Marshal Healy. They talked books, women's rights, and the fortunes of moderate Republicans.[24] Their racial views were not overtly retrograde, but presumably such all-white social networks looked out for their own first. Republican officeholders bridled at any diminution of their role. When James T. Rapier received an appointment as assessor, Judge James Corbin demanded his replacement with "some *white* Republican" from Dallas County. Corbin had backed Turner for Congress, but Rapier's appointment exhibited "too great a preponderance of the Negro Element" to suit him.[25]

Mobile's customhouse, with its scores of federal jobs, riveted the attention of those seeking a living in politics. With state government in Democratic hands, the racial politics of this repository of Republican employment became charged. Warner intended to contest the reelection of Senator Spencer, that "traitor and a debauched scoundrel."[26] Control of Alabama's patronage therefore was vital. Over Spencer's objections, President Grant removed the existing collector, the Unionist William Miller exiled from Greene County, and he installed Warner pending confirmation in the Senate. His predecessor initially had hired no black employees and even appointed some white Democrats, both on grounds of competency and business sentiment. This infuriated unemployed Republicans in the declining port city; it violated the norms of the spoils system and offended against Republican solidarity as well. Before a welcoming rally with a Creole brass band, Warner announced his intention of appointing only Republicans to office, greeted by applause. He then commenced what one might call affirmative-action measures, seeking the most qualified—and presentable—African American employees available. He chose Philip Joseph, an educated and freeborn Afro-Creole, for a conspicuous position in the office building.[27]

Warner's followers and opponents raced to show that they spoke for the masses, in the form of rival street rallies, petitions, and delegations to Washington. The customhouse contest energized grassroots politics, because what looked to some like color-blind equality looked to others like class exclusion. A factional bidding war for black popular loyalty ensued, reflecting well-articulated socioeconomic divisions within Alabama's one large commercial center. The prominent activists backing Warner were literate, propertied, and of mixed ancestry; they were generally free prewar residents of Mobile, often Afro-Creoles like Joseph and his relations. By contrast, Senator Spencer's activists were poorer, darker-complected, and often freedmen from the countryside. This pattern mirrored the broader division in this diverse seaport between longtime residents—free and slave—concentrated downtown and the freedpeople settling on the city's outskirts. For dockworkers and other laboring people, the issue was less about Warner or Spencer than about their own economic grievances in a declining port, and their own exclusion from federal employment.[28]

Numbers began to weigh against Warner's following. His faction was associated with "scalawag" moderates in city politics, while their Radical opponents were more heavily identified with the freedmen. Rallies became raucous, punctuated by fights: Spencer vowed, "look out for the flying of fur!"[29] Radicals mobilized a popular organization, the National Guard, supporting President Grant and measures against the Ku Klux Klan. Barred from the state militia, African Americans resorted to this paramilitary group, both in Mobile and in other centers of federal jobs, especially nearby the capital city of Montgomery. Diverse urban populations evidently were more prone to Republican factionalism than the freedpeople of the plantation hinterland.[30]

"Take away Mr. Warner and let us have peace," wrote Henry Europe, the father of a future jazz legend.[31] After removing Mobile officials in rapid succession, the president threw up his hands. "Grant is already scared and will soon do just what we want. . . . We must carry the war into Africa, and we will succeed," Spencer wrote.[32] The president finally withdrew Warner's appointment, which restored the position to Miller, who began hiring the senator's followers.[33] Clearly, the Warner-Spencer controversy empowered African American activists, breaking up the near-racial-monopoly on government jobs. Freedmen achieved this without antagonizing the Democratic public or press, which opportunistically applauded them. Republicans battled over the patronage issue, sometimes even physically, but never against the Democrats, so no one died. National politics similarly worked to the short-term advantage of black activists, with President Grant's reelection campaign. Once Grant's renomination became certain, critics formed a third party, running on the issues of civil-service reform and universal pardon. Embittered, Warner became a leader in this Liberal Republican movement which nominated the editor Horace Greeley in May. Prominent native Alabamians jumped on the bandwagon, especially lawyers and judges like Samuel Rice, W. J. Haralson, and W. S. Mudd. Most Republican editors initially concurred.[34]

In the flush of excitement, people expected the Liberal Republicans to transform politics. In Huntsville, Joseph Bradley and William Figure's faction reached out to sensible opponents. Nicholas Davis gushed that all the scalawags except officeholders would back the insurgent movement. If Grant's opponents united, they could win much of the black vote and a huge victory. Liberal Republicans like Davis hoped to dissolve old party loyalties, because to him the very name Democrat remained a synonym for calamity.[35] Such scalawags dreamed of consensus politics which would marginalize both ex-secessionists and Radical carpetbaggers, which had been the vision of conservatives in both parties all along.

Reality dashed these expectations. Democrats might back Greeley, but they were not disbanding, and freedmen distrusted a coalition that Democrats numerically dominated. Thus the most conservative Republican leaders conducted a self-purge, removing those most amenable to white social pressure. The Liberal Republican departure opened up positions to African American influence, and freedmen embraced Grant's signature issue, the Ku Klux Act. In Mobile the streets turned decisively against Warner. The National Guard deployed in earnest, mobilizing grassroots support for the president, who after all remained the hero of the Union war that freed them.[36] Warner's following in the African American and

Creole elite shriveled, and even his closest supporters refused to follow him against Grant. They eventually formed a separate black Republican offshoot under Philip Joseph's leadership, running their own factional candidates but losing consistently.

Factional divisions are normally not a positive sign for a party hoping to maintain power. Infighting might have seemed more dangerous had the opposition not looked so damaged. Nationally, the Democrats were weakened by three defeats in a row and the recent Tweed Ring revelations in New York City. Few pragmatists thought Democrats could take advantage of anti-Grant, anticorruption sentiment flying their own flag. National leaders concluded in 1871 to back a "New Departure" platform of accepting the postwar constitutional amendments, and then in 1872 to endorse the Liberal Republican candidate. "We cannot hope to elect a Democratic president," the ex-Confederate Leroy Pope Walker observed, "that possibility does not exist."[37] With Democratic support the Liberal Republicans would carry Alabama overwhelmingly, Walker thought, whereas a divided opposition could only reelect Grant.

For most white southerners tactical endorsement of the Fourteenth and Fifteenth amendments was a bitter dose. The *Shelby County Guide* claimed that only a single man in that county initially approved the New Departure.[38] Coalition with Liberal Republicans unsettled many, and then there was Horace Greeley personally. Over the years, the eccentric editor had endorsed nearly every social reform imaginable, from vegetarianism to utopian socialism—and, of course, abolition and Radical Reconstruction. He had even initially favored the Ku Klux Act.[39] A few conservatives were drawn to Greeley's message of interregional reconciliation and universal pardon. Still, one would have to search hard for a more distasteful candidate to Alabama Democrats. At the state convention, Democrats accepted a national coalition only after a fight. Editors and politicians swung behind Greeley with barely concealed reluctance. As Congressman P. M. Dox explained, "to cross the radical Gulf, I am ready to use any bridge."[40]

The continued meltdown of Governor Lindsay's administration only heightened the odds. In June, the state delayed on payment of all the endorsed railroad bonds, and the public schools ran on fumes. Some six railroads defaulted during Lindsay's term, at least eighteen million dollars' worth, mostly bearing state endorsement. Most would not be completed for decades.[41] Few Democrats ventured to defend Lindsay, even his fellow former Union men in his home region. Investigating committees demonstrated that Lindsay ignored laws wholesale to save the endorsed railroads.[42] Even the Montgomery *Advertiser,* Lindsay's longtime defender, conceded that he had been "deplorably, and even most culpably remiss. . . ."[43] Only deft maneuvering by the state convention chair reportedly avoided boos at his name.[44]

Forced into the Liberal Republican coalition at the national level, Democrats lurched in the opposite direction on the state ticket. According to the *New York Times* correspondent, Democrats refused to admit a single Liberal delegate. President Grant ironically facilitated the hard-liner takeover: at his urging, Congress repealed most of the remaining officeholding disabilities, which propelled Alabama's ex-secessionists back into the party's leadership. The nominee for governor, Thomas H. Herndon, was one of four immediate secessionists on the ticket. The Democrats also chose John Jolly for an at-large congressional seat, Klan affiliations and all. Jolly caused other problems; his delegates circulated stories that a rival, the hard-line editor Joseph Taylor, had fathered an illegitimate child of mixed ancestry.[45] Dismayed at the movement's profile, Warner concluded that "the Democrats have made a straight Ku Klux State ticket."[46] Some moderates like Congressman Dox thought concessions were in order, but others scoffed at the notion that they owed their partners anything more.[47] But of course, nothing forced the modest numbers of Liberal Republicans to back Herndon's Democratic state ticket, even if they voted for Greeley. According to a northern reporter, some of the original Liberals drifted back to the Republicans after the convention.[48]

Such perplexing struggles within the coalition continued all fall. In Mobile, for example, Democrats endorsed a Liberal Republican candidate for Congress, the Warner ally Frederick G. Bromberg. Despite this move, the hard-line Mobile *Register* resisted any formal coalition, and straight-out Democratic hecklers disrupted a Greeley club meeting with some reported violence.[49] Across the state, a lack of enthusiasm for the combined ticket was hard to miss. The Calhoun County paper complained of Democrats who could not make up their minds to vote for Greeley, even in this Klan stronghold.[50] From ex-secession Democrats to former Unionists in the hills, the Greeley-Herndon ticket had something to offend all their prospective voters in 1872.

Meanwhile, Senator Spencer led the Republicans on tiptoe. The Warner bolt solidified his control over the party, so he kept a low profile. There was some talk of nominating Robert Patton for governor, primarily for his financial expertise, but the politics pointed elsewhere. The Bohemian immigrant Paul Strobach wrote that Republicans agreed that "none of the so called 'carpetbaggers' should be put on the State's ticket," so they nominated only native Union men.[51] For the first time in three years the party was united. The consensus nominee for governor, David Lewis of Huntsville, emphasized the struggle "between unionists and secessionists for control of the State government."[52] The war was still too fresh in that region for voters to embrace south Alabama secessionist leadership. Lewis's ambivalent wartime record matched the region well: he had opposed secession but signed the ordinance reluctantly. He served briefly in the provisional Confederate Congress, but he disbanded his volunteer unit rather than go into the army for three years. He sought exemption from the Confederate draft first as a judge, and then as a miller, and finally he fled northward. Lewis backed the Reconstruction measures even though they disfranchised him, which left him out of office during the legislature's season of railroad corruption. He shared the Huntsville Unionists' venom for carpetbaggers, but he had prosecuted Klansmen. Given his later behavior, he likely agreed to back Spencer's reelection in exchange for the nomination.[53]

Freedmen had no reason to be enthusiastic about the Unionist-dominated ticket. Still, President Grant and the two black nominees for Congress, James T. Rapier and the incumbent Ben Turner, made up for it. Furthermore, the Republican resurgence facilitated local office gains in the black belt. One detailed count suggests that black numbers increased during the early 1870s.[54] The legislature lacked bonding requirements, and African Americans would win twenty of forty-five Republican seats in the House.[55] The curious electoral circumstances of 1872 encouraged this outcome. Because the whole Liberal Republican strategy was to look responsible, Democrats could not readily use open intimidation. Freedmen passed this election in unaccustomed peace. And at Senator Spencer's urging, the military presence increased in interior places like Sumter and Greene counties. Cavalry accompanied marshals who arrested suspected Klansmen or moonshiners, which Spencer's supporters reportedly calculated would keep terrorists away from the polls. One revenue official claimed he carried an intimidating stack of blank warrants. Whites were "more afraid of arrest by troops and trial by federal judges, than the negroes are of the supposed kuklux."[56]

Unaccustomed impunity allowed blacks a utopian season of open political discourse, often in the presence of Greeley spokesmen. Backing Greeley promoted good relationships with employers, Democrats contended, and that argument was difficult to dismiss. The Livingston *Journal* finally editorialized against bloodshed in earnest, promising Republicans they could meet unmolested. It also warned Sumter County freedmen to preserve the peace since Daniel Price and other Radicals fled. Two former Republican firebrands made the case at a Greeley barbecue: "John Little and Adam Kennard, both colored, then made able speeches to the colored people, telling them in plain and most forcible language some wholesome truths, and giving them convincing reasons why they should act with the white people of the South, and cultivate friendly relations to them, rather than to continue acting in such a way as will create hatred." In Sumter County, prior intimidation combined with current good behavior swayed some voters. Republicans carried the county that fall, but the numbers suggest hundreds of freedmen must have voted for Greeley without obvious coercion.[57]

Given the outcome of Reconstruction, one wonders what would have happened had these appeals worked elsewhere. But even in Klan-ridden counties, freedmen demurred. In Calhoun County, Democrats tried to sign up freedmen for a Greeley club. According to the Democratic paper, one speaker audaciously told the audience what he thought. George Woodward declared "that the negro would not vote for any man who had the support of the Democratic party, a party of which they were afraid." Orators might outtalk him, but then they had gone to college while he had been supporting them in the fields. The freedmen knew little of Greeley until lately, but they knew all about the Democrats: "One thing is certain, the colored men will all vote for Gen. Grant this time. Keep your Ku-Klux out of our houses with their masks and guns, saying they come from the far corner of the moon, and maybe by the next election we will begin to talk of voting with you. . . ."[58]

Whatever the eventual consequences, in this sole election where they could electioneer and vote safely, most freedmen found opposing Grant inconceivable. James T. Rapier estimated that statewide Greeley would not get fifty extra black votes. An African American acquaintance informed a horrified Democratic editor: "I am willing for Mr. Grant to be President as long as he lives, and I know of many colored men who think and feel as I do."[59] If the opposition made little headway among the freedmen, they had difficulty holding white support. J. L. Pennington sought pamphlets laden with choice Greeley quotations, thinking disaffected Democrats had a perverse curiosity about the rude things he had said about them.[60] The fall's northern-state elections indicated that Greeley would be crushed, which undermined tactical arguments.[61] The de-emphasis on racial rhetoric seemed to still Democratic enthusiasm. Ex-Confederates had difficulty bringing themselves to vote for anyone on a platform accepting the postwar amendments, while the stolid ex-soldier Grant irritated them less. Charles Hall wrote that "two thirds of those whom I have heard express themselves say they are bitterly opposed to Greeley & only voted for him because the Democratic convention nominated him." The son of a Democratic politician, he concluded that Grant was preferable.[62]

Election day was a wipeout. Grant carried the state by 90,272 to 79,444 for Greeley, a nearly 11,000-vote margin. Lewis beat Herndon for governor nearly as badly, 89,020 to 78,524.[63] Greeley deterred strong Democrats, Herndon repelled north Alabama, and the long odds demoralized everyone. Even so, Democratic numbers overall increased since 1870, with the county-level count surprisingly stable. Freedmen and white Unionists must have come out of hiding, 14,000 or so.[64] The lapse of intimidation by Democratic zealots emboldened other voters, black and white, in northern Alabama. In the Tennessee Valley, Republicans cut a 5,000 congressional district deficit to under 1,000 votes. In Lawrence County, according to a Democratic paper, the party was "routed horse, foot and dragoons—not by the Republicans, but by the Independents—all of whom are Greeley men."[65] Perhaps they were, but these independents would caucus with the Republicans. In the black belt, Republican vote totals increased consistently, ominously demonstrating that only force could defeat them. The only good Democratic news was from Mobile, where the Liberal Republican Frederick Bromberg defeated Congressman Turner. He was aided by the spoiler Republican candidacy of Warner's Afro-Creole spokesman, Philip Joseph, encouraged by five thousand dollars to remain in the race.[66]

Governor Lewis and his colleagues assumed office without challenge, and one might assume the victory meant a Republican senator too. "Our majority is too large to be trifled with," the Montgomery *Journal* predicted.[67] Not so, the state was going to undergo another disputed election. There were prior rumors of fraud, and in two black-belt counties Democrats rushed to seat their candidates.[68] Republican poll watchers at Eufaula turned up several minutes late when balloting began. Democrats secured an injunction against counting the heavily Republican box, allowing a momentary majority, and Barbour County officials sent the incomplete returns to Montgomery. The judge's rapid lifting of the injunction did not reverse the initial certification.[69] In Marengo County, voting officials at Demopolis claiming informality in registration threw out perhaps 1,000 votes. In Dayton, a ballot box got wet and disintegrated in the process of delivery, and officials barred the returns. The two boxes cost Republicans about 1,500 ballots, and Democrats claimed a narrow victory. In both cases, approval by the outgoing secretary of state gave Democrats prima facie possession, subject to challenge before the legislature. Given these counties' large black majorities and the statewide sweep, in all likelihood Republicans received more votes. But officials formally certified the Democratic candidates. If seated, even temporarily, they provided the margin needed to organize the legislature under Democratic control and defeat Senator Spencer.

The normal procedure would have been to seat those with certificates of election and then resolve the matter through an election contest. As Democrats pointed out, *someone* had to call a body into session, even on the basis of imperfect initial returns; otherwise, how could legislatures function? In practice, though, momentary recognition would have given Democrats the power to seat whomever they wished. Those challenged could help credential one another and prevail. Playing for time, federal marshals arrested aspiring legislators on the way to Montgomery for election fraud, spiriting the Marengo claimants to Mobile.[70] Republicans delayed until Governor Lewis took office, so the incoming secretary of state could certify Republican winners on the basis of the full returns from Barbour County. More dramatic moves were to follow. The constitution said the legislature had to meet in Montgomery, but not necessarily at the capitol, so Republicans withdrew to the federal courthouse. These members claimed a quorum by admitting the contested Republican claimants, and they unanimously reelected George Spencer to the Senate. Choosing anyone else would be "like a bomb," so scalawag rivals like Alexander White and Parsons backed Spencer in caucus and never waivered thereafter.[71]

For their part, the Democrats in the capitol claimed a quorum on the basis of the official certifications. They elected their own senator, the Unionist Francis W. Sykes. Sykes had been a racial liberal during Presidential Reconstruction and then a Republican; the hope in choosing him was to secure a few courthouse defectors. With rival legislatures now passing laws and governing the state, chaos loomed. The national public responded unenthusiastically to the Republican walkout, given Governor Smith's display two years previously. Still, Governor Lewis predicted the opposition would fade away. Another observer agreed Lewis held the high cards: the Republican courts would not overrule him, and "our Legislature cannot be long kept together without the ability to get the mileage & per diem of the members."[72]

After several days, the governor forced the issue by recognizing the courthouse legislature. The capitol body made impeachment moves, and there were rumors of Democratic volunteers on the march. The Livingston *Journal* warned that, if Lewis's followers were determined upon revolution, "*let them have it.*"[73] Sheriff Paul Strobach secured federal troops with the governor's endorsement.[74] A detachment arrived which camped nearby the capitol grounds. Superiors ordered the troops withdrawn, but President Grant countermanded the orders. On December 11, Governor Lewis demanded possession of the Senate, and hoping to prevent bloodshed, Strobach strode into the hall alone. The sergeant at arms arrested him, but relented when Strobach pointed out the window at the readying federal troops.[75] Here, as often, the Republicans threatened escalation to force outside intervention. If Lewis had been impeached or his subordinates arrested, he would have had to call out Strobach's posse, which threatened a fatal "alignment of race." In Lewis's words, only troops "prevented the effusion of blood, or perhaps the destruction of the city."[76]

On this point, Democrats agreed. Had Lewis called out the posse, the *Advertiser* observed, "certainly *one* man, before he had been thirty minutes older, would have been dangling at the end of a rope!" Such fearsome talk put some Democrats in the mood to negotiate. A mediation offer came from Washington, in the form of a lengthy telegram. Attorney General George Williams proposed that the absent legislators return to the capitol, and that all would be paid. The Republican claimants from Barbour County bearing certificates of election were to be seated, pending challenge, and the Democratic claimants from Marengo County and a disputed senate seat in Butler and Conecuh counties as well. None could vote on credentials until all challenges were resolved, and all the existing legislative officers were to resign. After considerable hesitation, the Democrats accepted the deal, the alternatives looking worse. The leadership put the best face on things possible. The Montgomery *Advertiser* claimed, "this is the most considerate and friendly act that has been exhibited by the Washington Administration to the people of Alabama since the war!"[77]

Or not. The attorney general may have intended a compromise, but the Republicans on the ground saw opportunity. In agreeing, and in proposing a bipartisan investigating committee, the Democratic leadership assumed it would retain control of the senate. Democrats quickly ceded the Barbour County contests, but they thought the Marengo County claims more solid. After all, the election officials were gentlemen, "incapable of the base conduct imputed to them."[78] Subsequent revelations suggested otherwise, and Republicans insisted on full investigation before the legislature organized. After some delay, local officials produced the missing registration books, which showed that nearly all the challenged voters were registered. They thus were legal voters, voting legally in Demopolis, and examination of the wet Dayton ballots revealed that most were legible—and Republican. The seating of the claimants left only a disputed Butler and Conecuh Senate seat between the Republicans and full control.[79]

While this transpired, five Democrats defected in the vote for Speaker of the House, which installed former governor Lewis Parsons. One might interpret this as a vote of no confidence in that party's leadership.[80] The Republicans acted with unaccustomed discipline. By returning to the capitol, they stopped any possibility of impeachment. But to maintain their claim of having been the legal legislature, the Republican body continued to transact business separately, and the governor recognized them until the pending contests were resolved. The US attorney general publicly disavowed their action, barring them from the federal courthouse, but the Republican legislators persisted, meeting and adjourning at an undisclosed location.[81]

Senator Spencer was not in Montgomery during the initial confrontation. But he encouraged Republican unity and Democratic disarray with tangible assets. Republicans had won at the ballot box, but prying reelection from the legislature required funds from the national party.[82] Spencer previously leaned on a protégé, Mobile postmaster George Putnam, for campaign funds. Putnam demurred, and Spencer had him removed. His successor, J. J. Moulton, was more accommodating, but Spencer proved unable or unwilling to repay a diversion of many thousands, and the authorities later arrested Moulton. Whatever the consequences, Spencer subsidized Republican legislators to stay near at hand because the treasury was not in condition to honor their pay warrants.[83]

Though several native white Republican leaders barely spoke to Spencer, Governor Lewis and his closest allies supported him. By report, the senator treated with the Democrats for control of the legislature in exchange for his reelection.[84] Aware it was Spencer or no one, Republicans united behind him.[85] If later Republican testimony before the Redeemer legislature can be credited, Spencer's supporters kept a hospitality room at a hotel, in which he supplied idled courthouse legislators with wine and cigars. "I kept it red-hot," the short-term host Mark Brainard recalled. The generosity went beyond refreshments, and according to ex-sheriff Robert Barber, "Most of the colored members would get loans" without expectation of repayment.[86] Allegedly some black leaders secured a few hundred dollars with a threat of backing an African American rival, but most did not need to be paid much to support the Republican incumbent. Several white Republicans did, mostly in the form of federal jobs. Testimony also suggests sums doled out to Democratic defectors to absent themselves from crucial votes.[87] A more dubious, later, tale had a key legislator drugged while playing cards.[88]

With Republicans sure of a majority in joint ballot, their senator from Sumter County suddenly died. To make up for it, the now-decisive Butler-Conecuh Senate contest revolved around a disagreement over printing ballots in part of newly created Escambia County; the issue was whether one or two separate tickets were required, and where the returns should be sent. On election day, Democratic officials counted only the ballots they deemed legally cast, which provided much of their margin of victory. The legitimate outcome is obscure.[89] At the end of January, after last-minute consultations with Washington, the Senate seated the Republican contestant, William Miller, by a sixteen-to-fourteen vote.[90] Democrats protested that a Republican senator voted dishonorably after having been "paired" with an absent Democrat. The hidden Republican suddenly appeared on the floor after handkerchief signals from the portico. Whatever the means, after a disputed ruling by Lieutenant Governor McKinstry cutting off reconsideration, the Senate had its permanent membership. With all the Republican claimants now seated, the courthouse gathering could claim a quorum all along, which retroactively validated Senator Spencer's reelection—no further vote deemed required.[91]

Democratic legislators were infuriated, but the caucus instructed their intransigents to submit. "I decline to begin a revolution in Alabama," one lawmaker disgustedly remarked.[92] The ousted senator from Barbour County, J. W. Mabry, clubbed a Republican legislator on the street after the final vote.[93] This rare outburst highlights the bloodless resolution of the protracted contest, even as Democrats saw their prospects slipping away. After the original confrontation in December, speeches featured martial rhetoric aplenty, but from the scene, ex-secessionist Senator C. C.

Clay predicted once troops arrived that the legislators would fold.[94] At no point did the army detachment number more than thirty men, and they never entered the capitol building. The courthouse legislature met unmolested. It appears that after the drubbing of Greeley and Herndon, Democratic voters were not seeking conflict. Nor did they want confrontation with Montgomery's freedmen, well organized as a potential posse. Democrats claimed that, during the decisive proceedings, armed Republicans were stationed in the galleries with ammunition distributed.[95] Here was the acid test of the civility of recent years, and it proved something that so protracted a controversy could be resolved in Republicans' favor without violence.

Fiscal disaster dictated this outcome, as less partisan Democrats deserted their leadership.[96] The impasse prevented fiscal legislation until the membership issue was resolved. Things had reached such a financial pass that it undermined Democratic resolve. Locked into low-tax pledges, Governor Lindsay seems to have simply thrown up his hands. He may have concluded that debt repudiation by his successor was unavoidable. The state had bought the bankrupt railroad, but Lindsay been unable to raise the price bid, which complicated sale. There was a potential buyer, a railroad consortium with English backing led by one G. Ingraham, but Lindsay insisted on the assumption of overdue interest payments, and the negotiations failed.[97] In July 1872, the state finally defaulted on its guarantee of the A&C bonds, which torpedoed the market for all state securities.[98] This assured that all other uncompleted railroads would be unable to pay their endorsed bonds. State obligations multiplied day by day.[99]

Upon assuming office, Republicans calculated that Lindsay left $600,000 in unpaid debts, besides the outstanding interest, and bankers holding bonds as collateral threatened to dump them.[100] The Democrats conceded that the school funds alone had $144,000 in unpaid warrants. For those Democrats who resisted repudiation, especially those connected to the railroads and finance, a stable Republican-led government might salvage things. Lewis recommended doubling property taxes, in part to reassure bond markets. Some Democrats favored tax increases, and urban elites feared partisan deadlock as yet another bond payment passed with year's end.[101]

"We never have had, and I am sure never will have, any party in Alabama favoring repudiation or anything tending that way," or so Governor Lewis said.[102] Many Democrats felt otherwise, returning to their Jacksonian roots by stiffing rich bondholders. The Selma *Argus* and its editor, Robert McKee, spoke for a number of small-town papers in endorsing outright repudiation. The *Argus* hoped that Lewis would wreck the state's finances, making extravagance impossible thereafter. "The state doesn't need credit," the paper concluded.[103] These more partisan Democrats had no intention of helping Governor Lewis improve his political standing. The normally restrained Montgomery *Advertiser* illustrated the conflicting pressures. The paper railed against repudiators like McKee, but during the legislative impasse it urged withholding tax payments, to deprive the Lewis government of means to pay his legislature.[104] As for the courthouse legislation, "We inform all parties plainly that the people of Alabama will not recognize these bonds at all." As the state's financial agent reported, no one would loan money under the circumstances, and the distinction between the bonds authorized by the courthouse legislature and other bonds confused investors.[105]

To some Democrats, these threats sounded mad. The situation looked bleak enough already, with every state-endorsed unfinished railroad plummeting toward insolvency. The debt totaled up to over $11,000,000 in direct liabilities and another $14,000,000 for endorsed bonds, giving a total contingent debt of $26,178,441.[106] Thus when Governor Lewis gained legislative majorities, many Democrats had tired of reckless partisanship, and they gave him a mandate to do something. Lewis indicated that he intended to honor all of Alabama's legitimate debts, and then some. To tide them over, Lewis and his treasurer, Arthur Bingham, turned to the A&C-connected financier Henry Clews, who alone was willing to loan $100,000, enough to meet Alabama's January interest on its own bonds.[107] In early 1873, Lewis passed most of his financial measures with bipartisan support, Republicans having given control of half-a-dozen Senate committees to cooperative Democrats. The legislature raised the state property tax rate by half, from 0.5 percent to 0.75 percent, by an emphatic House margin of sixty-five to twenty-four. The Montgomery *Advertiser* complained that the Democrats in the Senate had never agreed on anything, and that "too many *business* schemes" undermined party unity.[108] The governor encouraged this bipartisan inclination by appointing a Democratic friend, Robert Brickell, to the Supreme Court. The condition was that he accept the Unionist-friendly precedents of the Republican court and "not play the part of a bull in a China shop." "Davy" and "Bob" exchanged warm notes on his acceptance of this even-handed arrangement.[109]

Lewis anticipated that, if he could sell the railroad to someone able to assume the bond payments, the state's credit would recover enough to fund other unpaid obligations. The centerpiece fiscal proposal was to exchange state-endorsed but now-worthless railroad bonds for straight Alabama bonds, at a favorable ratio. In theory, the state would thus reduce up to $32,000,000 in contingent debt to $8,000,000, while giving the stricken companies means to complete their roads. Democrats in the legislature were split down the middle. The *Advertiser* itself opposed the bill but was unable to see "what particular damage could arise when obtaining *four* dollars of endorsed bonds in the place of *one* dollar of straight bonds!"[110] With sufficient borrowing to carry it out, and the railroad sold and paying its own interest, the state might dig its way out of trouble. The downside was that the direct state endorsement made repudiation even more difficult.[111]

Governor Lewis was optimistic that Alabama's creditors could be satisfied. Lewis even suggested that some settlement might be made of the half-million in excess bonds issued illegally by Governor Smith. Lewis was not acting like a man who thought the state's finances ruined. Upon assuming office, he vetoed a provision repealing free tuition at the long-troubled university, on grounds that other cuts could be found.[112] The bond substitution bill actually provided for *resumption* of the stalled railroad-aid policy, though under limited conditions.[113] That spring, he resurrected Governor Smith's proposal for purchasing west Florida for one million dollars. This was not a new question, and so he hoped "that public opinion is to a good degree ripe for action."[114] The purchase would have meant another eighty thousand dollars annually in interest payments. When one Florida source repeatedly suggested that bribing local newspaper editors might help, Lewis reluctantly talked to legislators and concluded that perhaps five or ten thousand might be secured for such lobbying.[115] Clearly, Governor Lewis intended investing in Alabama's future, and his Florida proposal passed by huge bipartisan margins.

To succeed, Lewis needed several things to fall into place, the A&C Railroad sale first among them. He came to terms with the Ingraham investors quickly. They agreed to pay off what the state owed on the bankruptcy purchase of the line, and to assume the future interest and repayment obligations.[116] Unfortunately for Lewis, obstructions appeared. Lewis heard "strange whisperings" of Judge Busteed's intentions, and the governor hurried sympathetic federal judges to the scene.[117] J. C. Stanton had been managing the trains under court direction, and the brothers now filed suit, on the basis of long-forgotten but un-cancelled mortgages of the A&C's predecessor companies. The frivolous lawsuit stalled the purchase long enough to have the deal fray, if the purchasers ever had sufficient means.[118] Lewis spent much energy denying inaccurate reports of his financial stewardship, and of that of Henry Clews.[119] Without a finalized purchase, the state had no money to do anything. As Lewis scribbled to German bondholders, "Unexpected difficulties in sale of Road renders postponement of payment of [interest] coupons unavoidable."[120] All obligations would be put on a sure basis, he hoped, "after a while."

Lewis needed cash to pay maturing interest payments so he could then sell yet more bonds at reasonable prices. After approving the issuance of a million and a half in bonds, the legislature unanimously voted that the unpaid school teachers be reimbursed before the bondholders, but the governor pocket-vetoed the bill.[121] While not formally shuttering the free schools, which were emphatically guaranteed in the constitution, he deferred payment of teachers indefinitely. The state already owed them over half a million, which let speculators centered in Montgomery buy pay warrants—good for tax payments—at a steep discount. As School Superintendent J. H. Speed later observed, teachers taught only listlessly when they doubted their full pay. Speed pleaded to keep school funds separate, first to the governor and then to legislative leaders, but the crisis of the state's finances proved too severe.[122]

The governor assumed that willingness to settle with bondholders would reopen financial markets to Alabama. In May, with the railroad-purchase agreement signed, Governor Lewis and Treasurer Bingham headed northward bearing half-a-dozen trunks' worth of state securities. News of the legal challenge undermined the effort, and not even Henry Clews would loan more money. Lewis hoped that bondholders would distinguish between the overdue state-endorsed railroad bonds and the still-inviolate straight bonds, but no luck. In his words, "Wall Street refused to recognize" compliance so long as "any coupon of an endorsed bond of the state was not provided for on maturity."[123] As one financier wrote, no prudent capitalist could invest without the railroad sold, and the legislature had not authorized enough bonds to pay off all the claims. After some weeks, the two returned with their unsold bonds. The Montgomery *Advertiser and Mail* gloated, "No money, and a law suit!"[124] The Selma *Argus* went further, contending that repudiation would sooner or later be a controlling issue in state politics. It was high time to disavow corruptly enacted debts to Republican- and Democratic-owned railroads alike.

At this juncture, Governor Lewis faced a challenge from restive African American legislators. They had submitted to an all-scalawag state ticket. They had backed Lewis in the winter's standoff. They then voted unanimously for all the governor's financial measures, including the tax increases. Now their Republican administration diverted resources from schools to bondholders. Republican rule offered little for their constituents, at least in the short term. Spending initiatives were off the table, and the Republicans never devised a plausible appeal to the class interests of poorer agriculturalists, which would have been difficult given their alliance with the national party anyway. Given the constraints, civil rights legislation looked like a positive alternative, giving supporters a reason to risk the polls. At the federal level, Senator Charles Sumner proposed outlawing racial discrimination in schools and public places, a demand which national leaders like Frederick Douglass embraced.

In Alabama, the freedpeople were unusually modest in their civil rights demands. At the constitutional convention, they had been satisfied with vague assurances of equal treatment and voting down explicit segregation guarantees. They had never much protested legally separate public schools, even as desegregation measures passed elsewhere. But by the early 1870s, racial exclusion from public places was becoming many private businesses' response to emancipation. The process was uneven, but black legislators saw it as widespread. In public transportation the issues of segregation, racial exclusion, and rude treatment came together. On Mobile's horse-drawn streetcars, for example, companies insisted that freedmen and freedwomen stand on the exterior platforms, while whites were seated inside. This rule intensified prewar exclusion, and legal challenges ensued as African Americans won political rights. Militants led streetcar occupations, with major riots occurring in 1867 and 1868, among lesser confrontations. The merits of legal redress vs. direct mass action divided Mobile's battling moderate and Radical Republican factions. Local enactments eventually forced some redress from the streetcar companies, and in the meantime Mobile's influential legislators pushed the issue into state politics.[125]

In February 1873, black leaders in the House introduced legislation outlawing racial distinction in all public businesses, and even schools. As Jere Haralson later explained, he did not expect it to pass, but he hoped to gain something. When Judiciary Committee Chair Alex White appeared to bury it, supporters forced consideration. The House then voted it down by a large margin, only seven whites voting for it.[126] Instead, White substituted a narrower transportation bill. Alabama's expanding railroad network projected such issues across the state, and the subsidy policy offered a convenient lever. Railway segregation was an odd blend of exclusion and insult in this era, a place where local custom and outside norms collided. By emerging practice white women and politely inclined white men rode in the first-class car, while all freedpeople were relegated to the second-class car. As Haralson explained, their white colleagues headed home in the nice ladies' car, while black senators and their wives rode in "a very inferior car, where white men come to smoke, drink whisky, and talk all sorts of ugly language. . . ."[127] Women traveling alone found the situation worrisome, especially given the additional issue of treatment in stations and hotels surrounding them. Unlike their constituents, lawmakers were in a position to do something about it. Now that they had a Republican government, they expected action.

Some white cooperation looked likely. One longtime conservative Republican, J. L. Pennington, opposed efforts to mandate separate first-class cars. Blacks rode alongside of whites peaceably in other southern states, he observed, and no one had the right to choose their companions in public anyway; this was not social—private—equality, which few legislators defended, but simple civility.[128] Several New Departure–style Democrats sought compromise. One Democratic senator "wanted the colored people to have a fair showing in traveling."[129] Most black legislators preferred full desegregation laws, but some might support measures providing for civil treatment in public places, something like a "separate but really equal" guarantee of first-class accommodations on railroads. In the spring of 1873, the Senate voted for such a measure by a large margin, and most Democrats reportedly either voted for it or absented themselves.[130] After holding fire tactically, their press roundly criticized them, perceiving an issue that would rouse their base.[131] The native Republican leadership in the House, especially Speaker Parsons and soon-to-be-congressman White, concluded that *any* measures on civil rights were dangerous. White warned of bloodshed, and he persuaded nearly every white Republican from northern Alabama to oppose the Senate bill. Though the Montgomery *Journal* expected enactment of a civil rights measure, Parsons and White made sure nothing passed before adjournment. White conveniently skipped the vote as he headed off to Congress.[132]

As Parsons and White understood, many north Alabama whites did not much care about the problems of planters in the black belt. Indeed, small farmers likely relished planters' permanent minority status, but the proposed measures made the race issue more immediate across Alabama. The political costs for white Republicans were real, but in giving such concerns priority, Republican leaders antagonized black allies. African American legislators had backed Speaker Parsons, and they had carefully refrained from holding up financial legislation for their own issue. Several black representatives backed a narrow approach focusing on transportation. Hales Ellsworth reportedly opposed a broader bill, because "It's got something about theaters and seminaries in it. I don't want to go where I am not wanted."[133]

Whether palliative measures would have satisfied most black leaders for long is unclear. But the scalawag leadership gave them nothing at all, after persuading them to focus on a narrow transportation bill. And, as one representative observed, "this had been a fight among Republicans alone. The Democrats had remained neutral throughout."[134] By stiff-arming the railroad legislation, and doing so through parliamentary stealth, Parsons and White assured a backlash. When one black colleague referred to such men as recognized party leaders, the militant Green Lewis denied that he had ever so considered them. "We will *think*, we will *speak*, we will *act* for ourselves, another spokesman emphasized."[135] Recall that both White and Parsons, as recently as 1868, had been emphatic proponents of racial supremacy. Legislative pragmatism had its virtues, but things had reached a tipping point when legislators so distrusted the native white leadership. There had been quite a range of views expressed during the debates, but now opinion solidified. It was hard to excuse perceived betrayal without looking foolish before attentive constituents, and few African American legislators tried.

"Have Our White Friends (?) Dealt Justly with Us," one editorial asked.[136] Civil rights advocacy became the signature issue of the younger, better-educated generation of leaders, and it also became a litmus test for which whites deserved trust. Green Lewis and others challenged the lawyers' claims of expertise, and he pointed out that Alexander White had sounded supportive of civil rights on the stump. Representative A. E. Williams reported that one of the Republican opponents of social equality had dined with him at an interracial party. Debate grew nasty, with hints about the interracial intimacies of individual Democratic opponents.[137] Growing numbers in the legislature gave African Americans a sense of rightful influence. By not biting the bullet early, Republicans guaranteed that the civil rights issue would remain in play throughout Governor Lewis's term. They could have passed something with a measure of bipartisan support. In less sensitive public venues, resistance to civil rights laws generally diminished once passed. Left unresolved, the grievance festered.

Representative L. J. Williams asked how much worse Democratic rule could be. He would have his answer right enough, but years of relative peace misled him.[138] Once the legislature adjourned, little could be done for the moment on civil rights laws, but patronage was another matter. "We have been in the past like dumb, driven cattle," W. V. Turner complained. African Americans were always doing the bidding of "traitorous, office-seeking Republicans."[139] Spencer's reelection had been smoothed by promises to a small army of white legislators. Of twenty-five Spencer lieutenants who subsequently received federal appointment, just four appear to have been African American.[140] Activists had fared better under Collector Warner. Philip Joseph, his former spokesman, suddenly went from moderate Republican to gadfly with a printing press. His peripatetic *Watchman* decried racism in varied forms. Joseph outed whites pursuing interracial relationships, generating threats and expensive lawsuits. He assured readers that black legislators would no longer be bought off by lobbyists and free railroad passes.[141]

"Not a single colored man in Alabama holds a position under the National Government of any prominence," a *Watchman* letter charged. In the state government "not a colored man sits at a desk." Joseph's paper exchanged racial barbs with the Montgomery *Journal* for weeks on end. The *Journal* accused the radicals of seeking a black man's party, while Joseph denounced it as a bastard sheet and its editor, Treasurer Arthur Bingham, as a "perfect blank." As freedmen became more literate, newspapers became more central to Republican infighting, and the Democratic press reprinted these juicy recriminations endlessly.[142]

Governor Lewis tried to respond to such complaints. For example, from Scottsboro, Republican leaders wrote him to recommend appointment of Robert Caver as constable. No white Republican would take the post, and Caver, a mixed-ancestry man of some property, had campaigned for the governor.[143] Lewis responded carefully: "I should have no hesitation in appointing a colored man to such an office where his official business had to be administered mainly among his own race." He knew of no reason to do so where blacks were a minority. Lewis instead sought some proper white person, of national sentiments and good character.[144] In the black belt, though, he indeed acted differently. On being told he had unknowingly appointed an illiterate to the Dallas County Commission, he responded that the man had been recommended as honest, which could "compensate for his literary deficiencies."[145]

Clearly threading the needle of conflicting Republican racial expectations was no mean feat. Raw race invective was somewhat new to Republican infighting, but the party had factional troubles before. The freedmen were not going to walk away lightly from the Lewis administration or their white Republican allies. The Democrats had divisions of their own. The more urgent matter confronting Lewis was the state's finances, on which all else depended. In July, one of Bingham's sons, his clerk, noted that "Pa returned from New York last Saturday, but failed to bring any of the 'wherewith' with him." Bingham was talking to bankers in Mobile, but at the moment "we are not actually getting in funds enough to pay the employees around the capital."[146] It was becoming difficult to find anyone who would accept Alabama bonds as collateral. Even so, with more tax revenue coming that fall, it was still possible that the situation might yet right itself. The governor was conceded to be honest, and he maintained belief in eventual success. As late as year's end, Lewis was still pursuing the Florida purchase.[147] Sooner or later the railroad would get sold, and Alabama's creditors might yet make concessions, given the alternative—disavowal of the railroad debt.

So it might have proved had national economic events not intervened. Republican prosperity came to a smashing end. In September 1873, the banking house of Jay Cooke, heavily invested in a transcontinental project, found itself unable to sell its railroad bonds. It suspended payments, and Alabama's banker Henry Clews and his foreign affiliates followed suit, leaving Wall Street in "very feverish and unsettled condition."[148] The Panic of 1873 swept the financial sector, and America entered five long years of depression, among the worst in the nation's history. The collapse uprooted the pattern of civil racial interaction, even in the heart of the plantation belt. The ground shifted with terrifying suddenness.

PART III

11

Beneath the White Banner

Depression and the Overthrow of Reconstruction

> [W]e say, no compromise . . . but a white man's rule, and a white man's government, or ruin and extermination.
>
> —Mobile *Register*

After Grant's reelection, the future looked brighter for plantation workers and tenants. Federal District Attorney J. A. Minnis boasted of the transformational results of his Klan prosecutions. Some freedpeople in the cotton belt had acquired "a little property, principally stock, a few even owned land," though he admitted not many. Blacks were better informed, they normally supported themselves, and even planters acknowledged they worked well. But in the fall of 1873 everything deteriorated, and Minnis wanted superiors to mark the rise of racial extremism. His explanation? Landowners had cut off credit, and the freedpeople had no food.[1]

Historians have emphasized the relationship between emancipation on the plantations and the political struggles of early Reconstruction.[2] But the era's final years receive far less attention, at least with respect to the plantation system. Scholars note the White League mobilization, the horrifying violence, and the sequence of northern retreats that marked Redemption. But these developments were rooted in the collapse of cotton production, in the places where racial coexistence had previously seemed possible. In Alabama, plantation disaster and labor turmoil helped eclipse the struggles that had divided whites since secession.

Agricultural dysfunction enabled the final overthrow of Reconstruction. The black belt suffered a wretched crop year in 1873. Heavy spring rains flooded the productive but lower-lying areas along rivers, delaying work and demoralizing the labor force. The rains left the crop more vulnerable. "The worms are thick all over this plantation and on many acres there is not a leaf of cotton to be seen," Henry Lyell wailed. Poor as his results were, he did better than his Perry County neighbors.[3] That year, fearful planters spent much money applying unfamiliar insecticides. "The stuff is the deadliest of poison and we fear there will be some dead 'Niggers' and white folks too, from the too careless handling of it," a factor crudely wrote. Planters were desperate enough to risk anything—or rather to have their hands do it.[4]

Tales of disaster came from across the black belt. On the eastern border, whole fields lay underwater.[5] In Hale County that spring, E. T. Tayloe saw only rain and weeds: "This whole country looks like one big grass patch. . . . Such a failure of crops were never known, not averaging over a Bale to the Head."[6] A nearby merchant agreed that few planters paid out.[7] The credit system broke down. The Selma *Argus* observed that indebted landowners delayed settling in hopes of higher prices, and in Montgomery merchants took out an advertisement begging planters to bring in their pledged cotton. These changes promised only hard times. As the *Argus* concluded, "Very many will of necessity next year do with fewer hands and fewer mules than heretofore."[8]

Losses inspired drastic remedies, and tenant farming occupied the central place in the litany of woe. Credit has been too cheap, one correspondent wrote to the Livingston *Journal*. Lazy whites without means would "rent out their lands for a small sum to a negro, who goes to a country merchant and gets him to buy him a mule, corn, meat, notions, & c. . . ." With a good crop and high cotton prices, everyone paid what they owed, but now the liabilities of the system became apparent to all, particularly merchants who borrowed outside capital and then absorbed losses.[9] But so long as the weather received some of the blame, landowners persevered. Planters traditionally farmed as much as available labor would permit, and cotton had been at the twenty-cent profitability threshold much of the time since the war. If planters continued to perceive a labor shortage, surplus freedmen remained a resource.

The Wall Street crash in September 1873 transformed everything, as heavily leveraged railroad projects and banking houses collapsed. Most Alabama banks suspended specie payments in the face of potential bank runs.[10] Credit disappeared. One Democratic paper warned Wall Street speculators that the "red flag of Communism may soon be flaunting in their faces."[11] These events played havoc just as planters and tenants were paying their year's debts. In Montgomery's Court Square, crowded with wagons of cotton, farmers found no one willing to buy except at a ruinous sacrifice.[12] The price there went from over seventeen cents a pound in September to under fourteen cents at Christmas.[13] Though sufficient by prewar standards, added to the year's previous woes this price meant ruin. "This Country & People are broke, ma[n]y can't keep up their places another year," E. T. Tayloe wrote.[14] The manager Henry Lyell discovered that he owed money to factors, leaving him initially unable to pay freedpeople their share.[15]

Every cent's decline diminished the laborers' leverage because "starvation" was "pushing the Negroes in for employment."[16] Multitudes instead headed westward. Lyell worried what their departure would mean, but excess workers looked expendable.[17] E. T. Tayloe reflected, "There is hardly anything left now for them to steal, I learn they are now commencing on the mules to run off with them."[18] A harsher logic beckoned, as newspapers widely hailed freedpeople's departure. Many planters questioned such advice, but labor shortage diminished as a concern.[19]

Problems with tenants that once seemed manageable looked intolerable. According to the Hayneville *Examiner,* renting was "bad for the landowner, worse for the tenant, and disastrous for the country."[20] When it became clear that tenants would emerge in debt, they had little incentive even to pick what cotton remained.[21] Furthermore, tenants slighted plantation maintenance which did not increase their take, like ditching and other unpleasant or unhealthy tasks. In good times, landowners could pay to have jobs done, but now plantations deteriorated, which made the flooding woes worse. Planters fantasized about paying cash wages and firing hands at will, but they were in no condition to borrow the necessary money. The business model for free labor plantations disintegrated. A Negro Labor convention met, with a subcommittee denouncing the squad-system and share-wage arrangements. It too recommended monthly wages in cash, to the end that laborers should buy small tracts of farmland. The Montgomery *Advertiser* dismissed such complaints, claiming planters had lost a hundred times as much as freedpeople that year.[22]

Harsh talk intensified. A freedman mounted the capitol steps and denounced whites and the government for not providing rations. The crowd allegedly cheered him. Outside Montgomery, planters met to settle on contract terms, while pledging to feed worthy laborers rather than evicting them. The planters also denounced petty thieving, which they proclaimed unbearably expensive. In response, freedmen demanded "a voice in setting the price of our labor, and the hours in which we shall work." At Livingston, a similar meeting demanded a dollar-a-day wage. The Montgomery *Advertiser* angrily warned such "dupes" they could not get along without employers. Years of labor peace evaporated. Particularly among hired fieldworkers, laborers confronted the largest planters most inclined toward racial coexistence.[23]

Agricultural columns bristled with complaint. The *Southern Cultivator* printed numerous articles on the practice of allowing stock to roam the woodlands. From Lowndes County, one large planter asked, "Is it true policy, to force the owners of land to fence the portion they cultivate, in order that the stock of those who own no land, shall pasture upon those of their neighbors?"[24] Complaints about livestock theft had declined, because planters raised less, and much of the black belt's western "canebreak" was already covered by "no-fence" legislation. Now, the pressing concern became pilfering of food and cotton by tenants who were not going to pay expenses that fall. Planters seldom articulated the underlying mechanism: when the crop failed, landowners cut off their advances. It made economic sense, but it engendered chaos. In Henry Lyell's observation, "there are hundreds of Negroes roving about that have been discharged on account of not having made enough to feed them, & many have gone to Mississippi."[25] Many felt they had been cheated.[26]

Recently moderate on racial issues, the Livingston *Journal* illustrated the punitive trend. Landowners were remiss in "allowing their farms to become *harbors* for idle and roguish negroes. Such live by theft, and are always prowling."[27] The paper advocated a state law to expel unemployed residents. Complaints of theft became all-pervasive, but only occasionally did the newspapers explain the social logic. One editorial observed that poorer tenants widely mortgaged their crops to merchants. They ran short of credit during the mid-summer, when the crop was "laid by" and work halted. Rather than abandon their crop, they appropriated enough to see them through until fall. Court dockets were crowded with petty larceny cases, but it did not deter anybody, according to the *Journal.* The solution appeared in repressing the crossroads stores that bought small lots of cotton or corn, especially in exchange for liquor.[28]

Though northern Alabama suffered too, flooding and cotton pests offered less trouble. "In many of the mountain counties, fine crops were made," while the cotton region looked "gloomy and discouraging in the extreme."[29] The emerging iron and coal industries were breathing life into the mountain region.[30] In six months time, Birmingham possessed ten "two story brick stores and about ten more under contract, and I suppose 60 frame houses." The boomtown suffered a disastrous cholera epidemic in 1873, but it still would grow dramatically in coming decades.[31] Farmers growing grain benefited, as a colony of German immigrants bought cheap land in what would become Cullman County. Railroad construction changed everything. Tiny "Blount Springs about the Depot is growing to be quite a village—Hotels—telegraph[,] Market house[,] Livery Stables & c & c." Land prices skyrocketed.[32]

Areas immersed in the cotton economy fared worst.[33] The emergence of the Grange movement in the black belt reinforced the point. Grangers are commonly viewed as restive small farmers, given their later association with Greenbacker third-party movements, in places like northern Alabama. In fact, planters' grievances largely determined the early agenda, often involving how tenants worked their land.[34] Anti-monopoly hostility to railroads, banking, and merchants, and demands for lower taxes shifted politics toward older Jacksonian values—though they also roiled the Democratic hierarchy as well. Agricultural crisis challenged racial coexistence precisely in the places it had become routine. And in 1874, flooding again inundated the richest river lands where the plantation economy normally prospered, and people had been functioning in relative peace. The poor crops eroded the patterns of civil interaction that had taken root, with harsh political implications.

The spring of 1873 had represented a high point of legislative bipartisanship. Alternatives to Lewis's financial measures frightened men rooted in commerce, for whom default represented public dishonor. The press remained divided over repudiation or enforced "scaling" of the endorsed railroad bonds, with the independent-minded Selma *Argus* and the party-establishment Montgomery *Advertiser* assailing each other. They disagreed on the moral legitimacy of party conventions, on party loyalty, and on the Grange agitation.[35] Almost in relief, the *Advertiser*'s editor, Robert Tyler, the state party chair, seized upon another issue. Both Tyler and his critic Robert McKee agreed on abandoning the Liberal Republican compromises, in favor of a "White Line" policy.[36] A racial monopoly of power became the official position. "Liberty, Law and Rights for All; But White Men Must Govern Alabama," read a careful *Advertiser* headline. Some accused the *Advertiser* of inconsistency, but most applauded the shift.[37]

Not everyone snapped to attention. Just that Easter day, an electoral confrontation in Colfax, Louisiana, ended in Reconstruction's worst atrocity, the mass execution of nearly a hundred captured freedmen. Federal prosecutions followed in the Cruikshank case, and for many conservatives armed extremism looked like folly. New Orleans moderates attempted to reach a compromise on civil rights in the short-lived Unification movement, and some Alabamians inclined similarly. Racism remained the premise, but many black-belt conservatives resisted open appeals to white solidarity. The Marion *Commonwealth* warned of the "danger which would threaten our every interest, by arraying the races in party opposition to each other."[38] Republicans sought a unified black vote, the Marengo *News* observed, so why help them?[39]

The Livingston *Journal* maintained this position most insistently.[40] Sumter County's Klan past induced some blacks to vote with sober Democrats. In February 1873, they won a special election, despite the presence of federal troops, and precinct returns suggested freedmen provided the margin.[41] That outcome regained Democrats a majority in the Senate.[42] Afterwards, the new senator William G. Little voted for the civil rights legislation on railroads, and the *Journal* become the only Democratic paper defending that position.[43] Some blacks would vote right, "unless we make the color of their skin an impediment to further political cooperation." A hostile stance would subject "twenty of our wealthiest counties to absolute negro domination," even if Democrats carried the state.[44] Editor Benjamin Herr privately lobbied editors against efforts to impose the White Line.[45]

Democrats outside the black belt rejected such caution. A legislator proclaimed the racial emphasis popular in the mountains as was the unabashed party label. "The Democratic party has ever been a whiteman's party," G. W. Hewitt emphasized. "It has never met negroes in Conventions, National or State."[46] The White Line won strong editorial endorsement in the northern half of the state. The Jacksonville *Republican* defended the new policy in unsettling terms: "the negroes will rule the counties where they predominate, let the issue be what it may." All the northern counties could do was win control of the state so they could mitigate the results elsewhere. This was not advice calculated to reassure the anxious planters of the black belt.[47] Thus plantation-belt conservatives and more partisan Democrats remained divided, over finance and race, much as they did in other Republican-ruled states like South Carolina and Louisiana. Had the impasse persisted, the habits of profitable coexistence in plantation districts might have been difficult to reverse, as slavery receded and as a more educated generation of African Americans matured. Instead, market collapse engendered extremism, in Alabama as throughout the deep South.

Depression shifted the terrain away from pragmatism. Governor Lewis was never going to find a buyer for the A&C Railroad that would assume its debts. Interest payments were going to pile up, and the schools would stay mostly closed. New York contacts offered help in refunding the debt, but that likely meant raising taxes.[48] Bipartisan cooperation on financial matters now looked less inviting. Furthermore, the crash marked a milestone in southern governance, upending the plausibility of Whiggish plans for economic development. State aid could not subsidize the transportation infrastructure, because outside investment was no longer forthcoming.[49] Besides, railroads now criss-crossed the mountain region. North-central Alabama would industrialize, and repudiation meant bondholders would pay the bill. Disregarding the indigenous origins of the aid policy, Democrats could blame blacks and corrupt carpetbaggers before a national audience vague on details. Alabama could resume its prewar Jacksonian values of small taxes and limited government, with nothing lost save commercial reputation. Intransigence might even force bondholder concessions and eventually set things right.

Conservatives had long fretted over racial extremism's effect on northern opinion. This had been the basis for the Liberal Republican demonstration that white southerners could be trusted. Though electorally unsuccessful, the show of sobriety eroded national resolve to repress terrorism. In early 1873, the Grant administration pardoned scores of recently convicted Alabama terrorists. Judge Busteed held court so infrequently that prosecutions stalled, and then impeachment proceedings forced the resignation of a judge who, for all his faults, imprisoned Klansmen.[50] With the Wall Street collapse that fall, Republicans suffered electoral losses, and the courts eroded anti-terrorist protection. In the Cruikshank case, Judge Joseph P. Bradley barred federal prosecutions of individual murderers by deeming it a state responsibility, a position the US Supreme Court later upheld. The "chains of the Ku-klux Act" had thus been "stricken from our oppressed limbs," the Mobile *Register* rejoiced.[51] Once Democrats perceived they could act without a northern reaction, everything changed. The popular constituency had long preferred rousing racial appeals, and now the economic collapse undermined skeptics.

When the legislature met late in 1873, the shift became clear. Governor Lewis's message invoked divine aid but offered little hope. Wall Street had neglected his good-faith payment efforts, the Ingraham purchase had fallen through, and litigation prevented efforts to sell a second bankrupt line.[52] As things stood, other state-endorsed lines were destined for courts and receivers, as "waifs for adventurous wreckers."[53] Unable to market its bonds, the state used them as collateral to secure what loans it could. The governor called for increased revenue and cutbacks. The educational system's benefits, Lewis thought, "were not in proportion to the great expense which attends it." Except on the finance bills, few legislators followed his guidance.[54]

Lewis offered African Americans little, and, by this point, black leaders had the numbers and self-confidence to speak for their constituents. Corruption became less of an issue, and representatives expressed themselves with more precision, at least as reported in the press. They offered more legislation, like Lawrence Speed, who simultaneously proposed hiring a physician for the destitute at Union Springs and a stronger laborers' lien on crops.[55] It was such men's misfortune to have come of age politically when the climate had turned so unforgiving. The plantation constituency of tenants and wage laborers had diverse economic needs, and a strapped Republican government could not offer much for the poor. Nor could the local stirrings of a labor movement suggest a wider solution, for that matter. Black leaders could block hostile legislation, but they could hardly ask their voters to risk death at the polls without a positive appeal. These realities made civil rights the fulcrum point of black politics. Even a bankrupt government could deliver such laws, and representatives still smarted at the common carrier rebuff of the previous spring. One House member reportedly "saw no reason why the Republicans should not stop the wheels of legislation" should Democrats oppose civil rights.[56] But James K. Green thought legislative retaliation irresponsible, and after some days of debate, Republicans tacitly agreed to let other bills proceed.

Democrats divided over the debt issue, and they reportedly did not caucus. Retrenchment measures found more favor. One Senate initiative was to cut legislators' travel reimbursement and the per diem from six to four dollars or less.[57] Jere Haralson provocatively proposed to raise it to ten, given their payment in depreciated warrants. Some Democrats agreed it was too aristocratic to cut legislative pay to the point of stringency, and given hotel prices they had a point.[58] Black representatives tended toward increasing candor, and among the most outspoken was Green S. W. Lewis of Perry County. Democratic county officials underassessed land, so he reportedly favored a state board of equalization in these words: "he wanted taxes raised to such a pitch that the large landowners would be compelled to sell their lands so that he, and others like him, could buy."[59] Colleagues joked that he had let the cat out of the bag, and the press thereafter hounded the Republicans as redistributionists.

Plantation turmoil infused the debates. Representative Alex E. Merriwether of Barbour County "hoped and prayed no more stock laws would be passed," and he blocked an expanded no-fence zone. His comrades had no desire to erode open-grazing rights further. The most contentious proposals involved prevention of theft. Democrats targeted "deadfall" country stores. Proponents generally acknowledged that hungry tenants were stealing mortgaged goods they had raised themselves, prompted by the failing crop, but they did not propose relief measures. Instead, the *Advertiser* editorialized, "The Legislature should make chicken-stealing a hanging matter, if it be necessary, to prevent stealing."[60] Despairing of catching people in the act, legislators wanted records kept of all nighttime sales of plantation produce. Speaker Parsons backed the proposal, urging that Republicans not shield thievery, and Democrats vented at black reluctance.[61]

Black leaders apparently held the deadfall legislation hostage for a civil rights bill or other concessions. James K. Green admitted that deadfall keepers were nuisances, and he believed they had "runners" who aided them in theft. Green thought legislation needed, but not this bill which made it too easy to misidentify sellers. Other Republicans instead critiqued the flaws of the share-wage and tenant system as a holdover of slavery.[62] Democratic defections in north Alabama doomed the deadfall proposal, and the civil rights bill narrowly failed as well. Only the governor's financial measures passed. One law substituted for warrants interest-paying obligations which could circulate like money, an anti-deflationary initiative of the governor. Strong partisans demurred: "It is strange how many Democrats can be found who are so anxious to help the present Radical Administration out of its financial strait!" Let them sink, the correspondent urged, along with their bondholder enablers. Democrats prevented an extension of the regular session, so the legislators headed home well before Christmas, not to meet again for nearly a year.[63]

With preparation for another season, access to credit contracted further. Alabama cotton acreage declined anywhere from 14 to 18 percent in 1874, which diminished demand for labor.[64] An editor wrote that he could not reprint all the accounts of the black-belt exodus westward.[65] Labor shortage receded in the planters' constellation of woes. For instance, Thomas T. Munford arrived to manage his money-pit Tayloe inheritance in the midst of "mud, *worry,* Negroes & hard times." Creditors threatened him with humiliating lawsuits for small sums.[66] Merchants would not advance money, despite vast family collateral, and a relation resorted to drink and opium. Munford fantasized about being a sea captain with a good crew, far away from worrying mail and telegrams.[67]

Losses hobbled arrangements for the new year. "I have been through a trying ordeal to day, and have had to do more talking than a Phila[delphia] lawyer to get the Negroes to sign our contract," Henry Lyell complained. "They wanted every thing, in fact they did not know what they wanted," an observation which makes sense when previous arrangements miscarried.[68] Frustration spread. A Cherokee County manager found not one of his tenants would rent on the existing terms.[69] From tenants to share-wage laborers and even those working for cash, everybody had failed, but the diversity of terms inhibited labor unity. Hired laborers made collective demands, but tenant farming balkanized the rest of the labor force. Civil rights became so prominent partly because of the difficulty of economic reforms, or even agreement on what was needed. One Opelika Republican testified that contract complaints consumed the freedmen: "There is scarcely any end to them. They keep coming day after day."[70]

Economic crisis suffused rural life. Near Huntsville, the indebted ex-senator C. C. Clay noted a neighbor's suicide. Clay felt too poor to replace a laborer's ragged shoes for fear he would use them to run off.[71] A Eufaula Democrat noted, "Everybody is broke and insolvent, or nearly so; and taxes amount to confiscation. We are all barely able to live."[72] For partisan Democrats, though, spreading despair held promise.[73] As a reverend wrote, "No party can long carry the odium of exorbitant taxation, financial paralysis, and demoralized labor, such as now prevail."[74] But could the Democratic and Conservative Party now unite? One fracture involved the political process, and the tendency to divide votes in local races. In predominantly white areas, Republicans generally backed whatever independents were available. This pattern had cost the Democrats dearly, and a similar result looked probable in 1874. In Sumter County, eight candidates announced for probate judge, subject to the Democratic Convention, and more as independents besides. Democrats could not count on quarantining local disputes. The *Shelby County Guide* observed that conventions alone could guarantee "union and harmony in the *white man's* party in the approaching campaign." The solution appeared to be rigorous party discipline, even in formerly nonpartisan races. They needed to freeze freedmen out, and this was the only practical way without legislative enactments. "In short, to win a man must be a flat-footed Democrat—pig, pig, all the time and never pup once," one paper vowed.[75]

Easier said than done. The remedy eliminated popular elections in favor of party meetings. But caucuses were distrusted as conclaves of shady lawyers and self-interested townspeople. Party endorsement would be tantamount to election in white strongholds, which did not suit Granger-minded farmers. Then there was the issue of timing, because early conventions empowered political professionals. It seemed undemocratic to cede so much power to party insiders, in areas with small black minorities. Democratic newspapers emphasized the public misgivings.[76] Editors proposed various reforms designed to assure full representation of farmers, and some raised the notion of primary elections.[77] Still, it was difficult for political hopefuls to abjure a direct appeal to white voters, and beyond procedural matters policy differences remained. Debt repudiation became ever more plausible. One Democrat wrote from Florence, "I stood alone here for a long time in opposition to paying the m[or]t[gage] on the R.R. swindle; now, 'tis hard to find a man who takes the other side."[78] The political class remained split, so such talk remained infrequent. Before the state convention, the Democratic Executive Committee committed the party to full repayment. The Montgomery *Advertiser* held the line of fiscal probity, while the Selma *Argus* accused the paper of self-important "sneering" at rivals.[79]

At this juncture, national developments fostered unity. President Grant's veto of the "inflation bill" all but guaranteed that credit stayed tight while the economy declined further.[80] Propertied party leaders distrusted making an issue of it, but Republican dissention favored them. Future congressman B. B. Lewis observed that Grant was right to veto the bill, on general principles, but deflation did the suffering South no favors.[81] The crucial congressional development in the spring of 1874 was the progress of federal civil rights legislation, and, after Senator Sumner's death, its approval by the Senate. The proposed legislation went beyond the transportation proposals under discussion in Alabama, to cover most public places. Even though the legislature buried modest civil rights proposals, the congressional measures emphasized the issue. As a legislator wrote from the Tennessee Valley, "I think now we can arouse our people and bring them out. They are more sensitive upon this question than all others."[82]

Within Republican ranks, African American politicians gained experience, and younger men with more education entered the leadership. Patronage had long been an activist concern, and civil rights talk heightened leverage against Republican incumbents. Governor Lewis's election on an all-white, all-native state ticket emphasized the issue. The situation often pitted native whites against insurgent freedmen and northerners willing to back their issues. No racial purge occurred, but local government did acquire more black representation. Aspirants became more confident, like Richard Harris in Sumter County, who noticed that probate judges antagonized whomever they ruled against—he concluded he could do as well himself.[83] Displaced officeholders felt aggrieved, and they often recovered caste standing by denouncing their successors as unqualified.

Occasionally African Americans achieved majority representation on Republican tickets, and these few examples received outsize attention. Dallas County won particular notice, nominating ten blacks and five whites for office that summer. Selma was the home of ex-congressman Turner and of Jeremiah Haralson, and white Republicans felt beleaguered. John Silsby, three-term clerk of the circuit court, warned that ignorance and corruption were more dangerous than open enemies. He that alleged his opponent, Tom Walker, "claimed his nomination on the ground that he was a colored man and in favor of mixed schools 'up to the handle.'" The former missionary Silsby said that officeholders under indictment scattered money about, and the opposition press broadcast his charges.[84]

Such talk enabled the Democratic narrative of combating corruption. The Dallas County Tax Payer's League formed that spring, under the auspices of the Grange and *Argus* editor Robert McKee. Taxpayers raised funds to prosecute delinquent local officials, with the threat of legal action restraining misbehavior.[85] Democrats pointed to the large increase in county receipts, though this mostly resulted from railroad endorsements. Selma's vicinity had a lavish prewar tradition of subsidies. No matter, "The plundered tax-payers of the large negro counties . . . have submitted to official peculation and robbery until resistance has become a duty."[86]

Democrats lumped social spending into the category of corruption, and local-governance specifics remain vague, then and now.[87] Republicans too accused factional rivals of profiteering, and there are clear cases of wrongdoing in Dallas County. Three former tax officials essentially confessed to embezzlement with one absconding, after having diverted an alleged forty-two thousand dollars.[88] In the absence of such proceedings elsewhere the prevalence remains indistinct—but much diminished with the depression. The freedmen did not seek tainted officeholders, but they only inconsistently regarded malfeasance as disqualifying otherwise acceptable candidates. John Hardy, for example, was a central figure in the 1870 legislative bribery episodes. He did not seek reelection, but Hardy returned to politics as Selma's Republican mayor. He wrote the city's history as a local notable, avoiding much reference to his own role.[89]

Fluid ethics similarly characterized Jeremiah Haralson. A former slave, he got his political start as a Democratic speaker, and in early 1871 he testified that the Stantons bribed him. But Haralson was an agile and earthy debater, flexibly devoted to civil rights, and his constituents sent him to Congress in 1874. One can hardly blame the freedmen too much for such choices, given that Governor Lewis surrounded himself with the suspect veterans of Governor Smith's administration. His state treasurer, Arthur Bingham, had pled the Fifth. Ex-governor Smith himself became an intimate of Lewis, who eventually appointed him as a circuit judge. The Republican bench was so thin that experienced officeholders were in demand, especially for technical positions.[90]

Given the scandals nationwide, clean-government issues dominated discourse. Democrats might have made taxation and retrenchment the centerpieces of their campaign. In South Carolina, taxpayers' clubs proliferated in 1874, a form of popular mobilization that minimized northern backlash. Alabama's Democrats could have touched the chords of race resentment with more subtlety; instead, the insurrectionary White Leagues of nearby Louisiana became their model. Financial measures and taxation divided their constituency, so Democrats would shout racial supremacy from the housetops. The federal civil rights proposals blurred the underlying premises, making it possible to use the issue without antagonizing northern opinion. Outrageous statements now passed without much notice. Much of the electorate saw black influence as the cause of taxes, corruption, bankruptcy. Most Democrats rejected previous compromises and sought racial confrontation, and even the Granger militants were driven back to the party fold.

Conservative holdouts still feared the White Line policy. At least eight journals opposed it outright. The *Wilcox News* thought it left Democrats in the black belt disarmed, with unclear prospects for social peace even in victory. The Livingston *Journal* called such a platform plank asinine, and the Greensboro *Beacon* persisted even after the state convention.[91] Extremism poured gasoline on the western black belt, hurting whatever chances remained for the crop, and open intimidation could well backfire. But racial polarization would maximize pressure on independents and the multitudes of nonparticipants—perhaps a quarter of the potential white electorate. The crucial constituency was the onetime cooperationists and wartime Union men in northern Alabama. Two years previously, such defections handed Governor Lewis victory. Democratic leaders needed to blunt the wartime loyalty issue, but with someone ex-secessionists could abide. There were several potential candidates, like the ex–Republican judge William Mudd of Jefferson County, and the repudiation-inclined former congressman C. C. Langdon. The available man proved to be George S. Houston, from Athens in the Tennessee Valley.

Houston's wartime record somewhat resembled that of Republican Governor Lewis. A longtime Democratic congressman, Houston opposed immediate secession vociferously, but he resigned his position afterwards. He supported the Confederacy early in the war, once traveling into the hill country to reconcile former Unionists.[92] He then "came home, closed his lips, allowed his sons to go into the Confederate service," but was thereafter publically "dead to all intents and purposes." He later said he had retained Confederate preferences even under Union occupation, and he apparently refused to take the wartime oath. "[I]f he was not loyal to the South, the North did not consider him very loyal to the stars and stripes," a reluctant apologist concluded.[93] He was elected to the US Senate under Presidential Reconstruction, but Congress never seated him, and he lapsed into inactivity. He bristled over unpaid claims for damage by the Union Army, and he battled the Freedmen's Bureau over an alleged political eviction.[94] He nonetheless prospered, assembling a fortune in land, and he had connections to the South & North Railroad through his law partner, Luke Prior. Republicans tried to recruit Houston, and partisan Democrats distrusted him. But the times demanded someone like him.[95]

Houston made ex-secessionists squirm. Major papers ignored his probable nomination, and party leaders critiqued his war record. R. K. Boyd found it disagreeable to nominate him because he was "popular with the tory element in north Alabama." C. C. Langdon complained that Houston, alas, was with the bondholders.[96] The Selma *Argus* acknowledged Houston's probable nomination, but it defied the consensus. Houston was understood to be in favor of supporting payment of the bonds, and to oppose injecting the issue into the canvass.[97] Still, Houston was acceptable. After victory, one McKee ally wrote, debt repudiation would likely come under a right-minded Democratic legislature, whatever Houston preferred.[98]

The Democratic state convention met in late July. The much-criticized party chair, Robert Tyler, had already lost his editorship, and he announced he would not serve again as chair. His priorities and candidate nonetheless prevailed.[99] The convention president, James L. Pugh, rhetorically soared: "We hear the roar of the black wave . . . but the glorious white cliffs of Caucasian supremacy, illuminated by eternal sunshine, will roll black this black sea and sink it forever. . . ."[100] The platform expressed itself less loftily, but it articulated the same themes. Black prejudice "made it necessary for the white people to unite and act, together, in self-defense, and for the preservation of white civilization." The militaristic overtones here may be literal, given the immediate sequel. Resolutions denounced the proposed civil rights bill as unconstitutional, forcing "an ignorant and barbarous race" into private realms. The platform welcomed white immigration, and promised retrenchment and honest government. Otherwise it said little, and the brief mention of the bond controversy was studiedly vague. It promised an investigation, pledging every dollar justly owed would be paid when possible. When and if that would occur remained indistinct. With the platform and candidates chosen, skeptics fell into line with whatever grace they could.[101]

"The Democratic ticket means war," Senator Spencer concluded.[102] Steven Hahn speaks of paramilitary politics, and in Alabama in 1874 the term looks apt. Days after the convention, the Mobile *Register* asked employers to give volunteers a day off for drilling and target practice. Two days later came a fearful observation: "The familiarity of the whites with the use of arms and the discipline which they learned in battle makes them equal to ten times their number of a negro rabble."[103] The Democrats did not adopt the White League name consistently; nor did they don sheets or uniforms. But reports of aggressive measures came from black-belt areas that had been quiet for years. Violence escalated in plantation districts with a history of Klan raids.[104] From Opelika an insurrection scare prompted the mayor's request for arms, and an inquiry about the legality of a "white militia company" arrived from Talladega.[105]

At Eufaula, Democrats had recently demonstrated what this meant. Barbour County possessed an official white militia, one of a number sanctioned by ex-governor Lindsay, and the contested election in 1872 remained on people's minds. Conflict revolved around the role of Elias M. Keils, an Alabama native whose position as city court judge once enjoyed bipartisan support.[106] Other Republican officials came to terms with Democrats, but Keils blasted the Klan.[107] Democrats broadcast allegations of corrupt behavior, not much burdened in his case with specifics, though he had little legal training. Keils complained that lawyers "voted for me when they believed they could use me for their selfish, or lawless purposes," but now they sought to have the legislature abolish his office.[108] An underlying issue was Keils's insistence that black complaints would be pursued by his court, which enjoyed wide jurisdiction. Democrats directed most of their hostility at his biracial juries, and at his reputation as a stickler for the law.[109]

A municipal election in February 1874 provided the spark. After years of relative peace, partisan officials under Mayor Wells Bray dominated a Eufaula polling place. Democratic challengers barred a mentally disabled voter, and his brother crossed under a rope to complain that he was a deaf-mute who knew signs. A Democrat ordered the brother out, followed by curses and then blows, and one of the black bystanders reportedly produced a knife. The challenger started firing, and other armed Democrats scattered the crowd. As freedmen regrouped, the official militia arrived. According to Judge Keils, some thirty shots were fired, none by freedmen, who were nearly all unarmed on his instructions. Armed whites dominated the streets for days, while fires broke out. Investigation suggested that the affray was not planned, and that the well-regarded militia officer had not ordered the shooting, so Governor Lewis determined that he lacked the authority to disband the company.[110] To the dismay of Republicans, command passed to the more partisan Captain G. L. Comer, part of a prominent Democratic family.

A paramilitary White Line emerged with the first prominent assassination of the campaign. The background appears to be a decision by Republicans, in the dangerous western black belt, to deemphasize public rallies in favor of private meetings. In Sumter County, lawyer Walter P. Billings among others operated through a fraternal society called the Friendly Brothers. As he neared home after a party meeting, thirty or so undisguised horsemen, probably led by Steve Renfroe and other former Klansmen, killed him. The recently arrived Billings had no personal enemies. Claims of theft as motive for the "mysterious affair" looked laughable, but editor Herr of the Livingston *Journal* became a full-throated apologist warning newspapers not to contradict his coverage. Governor Lewis himself acknowledged the scope of the terror. Calling out a white posse in Sumter County seemed ridiculous, and he never considered using freedmen. "What can we do, what ought we to do," he asked his congressional delegation. "It seems as if democrats intend to carry this election by assassination."[111]

The black leadership responded to spreading violence in a striking way. Modern historians identify with militant demands for racial equality, and as shall be evident there was no shortage of brave talk and resistance in 1874. Still, African American political behavior at this decisive juncture shows surprising nuance. Previously the momentum of a popular demand for civil rights legislation looked irresistible.[112] After Senate passage of the Sumner bill, it appeared that no open opponent could win nominations in the plantation belt. But black leaders began to reconsider how far they could push the issue. In late June, a statewide civil rights association gathered to set the agenda for the approaching Republican convention. Jere Haralson endorsed the principle of the civil rights bill, but his resolutions construed it somewhat inaccurately as not requiring racially mixed schools. His resolutions also disavowed social—private—equality as beyond the reach of law, adding that freedpeople only wanted their rights in public places.[113] Vigorous debate followed, as several members contended that seeking integrated schools would hurt in November. "We must work for the success of our party and not take up a club to break our own heads," one delegate observed.

"Some of my race seemed desirous of conceding this right to please the few white men in the party," W. H. Councill complained. The all-black conclave affirmed his stand, but at the state Republican Convention things proceeded differently. The death of Billings, combined with electoral defeats in other states, sobered black leaders. White officeholders exerted themselves procedurally too. The executive committee allocated delegates based on overall population, which overrepresented counties with few Republican voters. There were also efforts to pack local meetings, like the one in Mobile that rejected the militant Philip Joseph as delegate.[114] Behind the scenes, Senator Spencer and other congressmen reined in the delegates on the platform and nominations. White Republicans, particularly the native cohort from north Alabama, saw renominating Governor Lewis as their only hope. They crushed out a challenge by a rival candidate, the native southerner Adam Felder, a longtime moderate who ran as an advocate for the civil rights proposal.

The shift in direction stirred discord. Having finally resigned his position as federal judge, Richard Busteed attempted a comeback in Montgomery's factionalized politics, and he burnished his reputation with a railroad confrontation. In returning from a Selma meeting, his servant accompanied him into the first-class car. The conductor aided by whites ordered the man out, Busteed held them off with his pistol, and black delegates came to the rescue from the rear car.[115] Whether Busteed planned the episode or not, the erratic ex-judge won a following. At the state convention, however, Senator Spencer shut him down. Busteed "tried very hard to demagogue us on the Civil Rights bill[,] get a ticket & platform that would beat us. Everytime he would speak we would have him replied to by some Colored man." There was not a "grease spot" left, Spencer boasted.[116]

However strong the popular pressure for civil rights, at Alabama's decisive juncture, electoral pragmatism ruled. Without explicit repudiation of the civil rights bill, Congressman White warned, the work of the convention would be useless. And if the Democrats once gained power, they had the state forever. The delegates caved, even the recent militant Councill who "appealed to the negroes of the Convention, and said if the Republican party went down, the negroes went down with it." Delegates taunted him with his previous hard line, and some held out for a transportation bill, but these proposals died in committee.[117] Governor Lewis may not have even wanted renomination, but he received it unanimously, the delegates nominating all native whites except for one northerner.[118] Lewis's supporters got the platform statement they desired: "We want no social equality enforced by law." Every home was sacred, and in a free country every individual dictated his lines of social exclusion. Thus the Republican Party did not "desire mixed schools or mixed accommodations for the colored people" but only equal accommodations, and this was how the proposed congressional legislation should be read.[119] African Americans described these positions as a tactical retreat, but they were not easily achieved. Senator Spencer confided that the convention cost him a great deal of money. Perhaps the funds eased approval of the nominees—particularly Congressman White—and the resolutions he preferred. If so, it served as balm for distasteful positions.[120]

The *New York Times* thought the extreme Radicals had been buried.[121] One might instead discern realism as they looked down the barrel of a gun, and in dangerous areas, black candidates sometimes avoided civil rights talk. By election day, urban freedmen would be marching under banners declaring "No Social Equality" and "No Mixed Schools," for good or ill.[122] The counterpoint to Democratic racial extremism could not have been more strongly etched, but it did not much matter in western Alabama. Half-a-dozen contiguous counties exploded, as flooding along the Tombigbee and Alabama rivers provided the social spark. The damage was intense, to the point that Congressman Hays secured a relief bill.[123] Flooding disrupted crops and credit, loosing yet another wave of destitute migrants who found a ready refuge in the swollen swamps. Confronted with mobile freedpeople with nothing to lose, Democratic partisans had difficulty forcing an armed showdown on favorable terms.[124]

Conflict started in Sumter County, with the Mississippi border stretching on one side and the flooded Tombigbee on the other. Democrats claimed that clandestine black organizations were plotting violence. Private meetings did occur, likely to shield political organizing and secret endorsements, and labor grievances came under discussion too.[125] "We have for the last nine years been cheated out of everything that we have made," ran one complaint from neighboring Greene County.[126] In response, it appears, hard-liners started riding in the countryside to locate the meetings, and, often, to harass attendees afterwards. Democrats on a congressional investigating committee revealingly concluded: "[A]rmed bodies of white men" rode through the western region to "protect the whites against what was feared to be the evil designs of organized clubs of armed negroes."[127] The freedmen evidently had not *done* anything, but Republican officials could be pressured into sanctioning posses, so partisan Democrats rode.

Sumter Republicans tallied up a dead freedman a week, and Thomas L. Ivey reported that Democrats barred speakers. "I have had to keep twenty five or more men standing guard with me at my house," he wrote.[128] Ivey's wife recalled threats and that he slept in the woods for months, as did other black leaders. He publicly supported the proposed civil rights law, which even other black leaders thought too dangerous; Bob Reed once pulled him off a speakers' stand after hearing white bystanders threaten a riot. Ivey seldom went anywhere without armed escort, prompting complaints of frightening white women and children, and the Livingston *Journal* indistinctly menaced him. Late in August, while Ivey worked as a federal mail agent, undisguised gunmen flagged the train down and "put an end to his mad career," as the paper put it.[129]

With this second assassination, things started popping. The lines between night-riding, Democratic militias, and all-white posses blurred. The memoirs of Klansman John L. Hunnicutt suggest as much: he led illegal posses across the Mississippi border, in between episodes of drinking himself unconscious.[130] Simultaneous outbreaks complicate coherent narrative, suggestive of a blended metaphor of falling dominoes and hide-and-seek. In Clarke County, black religious gatherings inspired fear. "The negroes are expected to rise in arms tomorrow, to extinguish the whites," a wild telegram ran. Whatever actually happened, Democratic accounts said a "bad negro" had been killed. While this transpired, neighboring Choctaw County erupted. Republicans secretly endorsed an independent candidate, whites made threats, and it appears freedmen beat a defector for bearing tales. A posse summoned Jackson Turner and twenty followers to court, but when they came carrying their guns, shooting broke out. Freedmen spread incorrect reports of ten deaths, perhaps to prompt outside intervention. Turner arrived at the state convention with tales of blacks fleeing into the Tombigbee swamps. Even now, the three-odd weeks of tangled incidents defy retelling, but the events presage Jack Turner's notorious lynching during an insurrection hoax some years later.[131]

Jumpy people inhabited the region. Black families would "start like foxes for the fields as soon as they saw a white man coming, and leave their house vacant."[132] The threat of escalation was real. In Greene County, at the scene of the 1870 riot, freedpeople risked a mass meeting, surreptitiously importing guns by the wagonload. Upon discovery, a conservative Republican, A. W. Dillard, persuaded them to leave their arms outside Eutaw as he delivered a conciliatory speech. Nothing untoward happened, but Democrats were not mollified. The Eutaw *Whig* discerned "a crime against law" in entering town armed and frightening women. It more cogently warned that, if freedmen used force, it was "war to the knife and the knife to the hilt."[133]

As that scare wound down, more trouble erupted nearby. Representative Reed had been organizing Republican clubs at Belmont, in Sumter, for months.[134] Fearing insurrection, or claiming to, the sheriff gathered a posse of hundreds, scores from across the Mississippi border. They made arrests for—well—something like disturbing the peace. According to a Democratic leader, one participant joked, "All that want to kill Bob Reed, fall in."[135] Reed escaped, but the troubles again rattled Greene County as refugees crossed the river. There were reports of shootings by whites in Forkland Precinct outside Demopolis, which had a seven-to-one black preponderance. Freedmen then reportedly challenged the passing of horsemen after a Republican rally ended. Democrats claimed they killed a planter seeking parlay, Adrian Robinson, while blacks claimed they were fired upon first. An apparent posse arrived to make arrests, provoking another gun battle. The Livingston *Journal* quoted initial reports of three whites and fifteen blacks killed. It appears at least one black and one white actually died on or about September 15, with several more shot. Freedmen then petitioned for "a dividing line between the Republican partie & the Democract partie" because "we caint live together." Armed men on both sides poured in, with Reed remonstrating with officials while hidden on his side of the riverbank. Things eventually quieted as freedmen fled back across the river.[136]

That influx encouraged a last confrontation before federal troops stopped the chain reaction. It occurred at the rented farm of Warren Dew, candidate for the legislature. After the assassinations, officeholders huddled in fear like Probate Judge James Abrahams, who would be shot soon.[137] Despite this climate, Dew addressed public meetings, with his activities inflaming whites throughout northern Sumter County and Pickens County as well. Dew's armed bodyguards exchanged shots with white interlopers.[138] He told followers, "if there came up any company of disguised men to kill me, we must try to kill one out of the company."[139] After white neighbors complained, the county solicitor ordered his arrest. Dew offered to go to town to face charges, but negotiations broke down, and by the time the posse returned in force, many freedmen escaped. The fleeing Dew reportedly saw hundreds of white horsemen as he crossed the state border, all vowing his death. They reportedly sacked his home, clubbed his wife, and rampaged over neighbors' farms. The deputy sheriff arrested some eighteen freedmen. Dew and his comrades pleaded for troops, because "nearly all" the nearby whites participated in the raid.[140]

For all the turmoil, Democrats could not force the bloody firefight they apparently sought: armed Republicans now held their own, in the very portions of the black belt where the Klan had rampaged for years. In a sense, the freedmen proved their point, which spread panic throughout the white community. The alarm of women and children may been the standard pretext for posses, but it was genuine if Lucy Jackson's letters can be believed. She heard of a threatened massacre if Dew was hurt. Arson rumors induced a relative to stay in her home, buckshot at ready. After the mass arrest, there was a fresh report of freedmen marching on Gainesville to release the prisoners. White defenders turned out, some drunk, to Jackson's alarm. A neighbor came over to borrow her horse and guns, but she kept her last pistol: "He did not think there would be a fight, but they were getting all the rifles they could, so as to shoot at long range.

The Negroes only have shot-guns." It must have been an unsettling world, where elite women performed such calculations.[141]

The frightening confrontation along the western border may have deterred violence elsewhere. The remainder of Alabama passed the summer with less turmoil, but in Greenville, Adam Felder endorsed the civil rights bill, and crowd members pelted him with rotten eggs. Afterwards the two sides exchanged gunfire.[142] The resumption of Republican meetings precipitated scattered confrontations elsewhere. In Lee County, freedmen met secretly in a church, discussing the civil rights bill and labor grievances. Rumors spread that they were plotting to raid or burn the stores in Wacoochee Valley. After evacuating their families, armed whites confronted the freedmen one night. The Democratic press reported that 150 men rode, with 4 freedmen killed and two churches burned. Eyewitnesses testified freedmen were fired upon and beaten to reveal information. Afterwards, George Sharp had to speak as the Democrats wanted at a "peace" meeting, and afterwards "when our churches was burned we was done, we had nowhere else to go."[143]

Republicans pleaded for Governor Lewis to sanction their own militia bodies. He disregarded them, finally announcing that he had created no new units, black or white, during his term. He apparently ignored an offer from Louisiana officials to provide cannons for a memorial service in Mobile, even after repeated appeals by prominent Republicans. He also passed on a sales offer for Gatling guns. Lewis avoided provocative actions, but his decision had tangible consequences. As Marshal R. W. Healy observed: "The State militia is Rebel and in the hands of the Democrats. Gov. Lewis could do nothing."[144]

The governor's political strength was his north Alabama following, and arming blacks would not please them. He thus resisted acting even in circumstances where some response seemed obligatory. At riotous Eufaula, Mayor Bray found a freedman guilty of stealing a cow. Judge Keils issued a writ of habeas corpus and sent bailiffs to retrieve him. The mayor called out the police and then Captain Comer's militia to prevent it.[145] The governor marked the resulting Republican complaints, "File." After a more menacing riot in late August, the judge wrote for help. His witnesses were being murdered, and armed freedmen saved him from a Democratic mob. Other Republican officials scurried for cover, but Keils remained defiant even as his letter was interrupted by yet more reports of violence. "I have made up my mind to take the Bull by the horns," Keils wrote. "The law *shall* punish the guilty. The law *shall* protect the innocent."[146]

Attorney General Benjamin Gardner knew the local situation and lobbied the governor on Keils's behalf. The judge expected a sympathetic hearing, but he elicited an instructive response. Keils was "a fool" to think Lewis could declare martial law at whim. "I might & would provoke a war, the very thing that the public enemy wants," Lewis wrote. He advised Keils "to shut his mouth about my course, in respect to these disturbances." He even told Gardner to show Keils his letter.[147]

To be sure, Governor Lewis thought he had a better solution. Aided by Spencer and Republican representatives in Washington, Governor Lewis secured the troops which deployed in mid-September.[148] Federal detectives infiltrated the Sumter night-riders using old Klan passwords, and marshals halted a Democratic meeting to arrest Steve Renfroe and another accused killer of Billings, sending them off to Mobile for trial. They then surrounded forty-two members of the Belmont quasi-posse, along with the sheriff and the Democratic Party chair. The charge was detaining a mail agent and conspiracy to kill Bob Reed—along with federal detectives. "The swamp was full of white men expecting to be arrested," Reed recalled.[149] The army's intervention was equally dramatic in Lee and neighboring Barbour counties. At Eufaula, local officials had jailed Judge Keils for releasing prisoners, whereupon federal authorities briefly arrested Mayor Bray and seven other officials.[150] The press all but threatened Keils with murder, but Republican organizing resumed. The army presence stopped the bloodletting. There were no other prominent assassinations before election day, and Governor Lewis and Congressman White gave speeches relatively unmolested across northern Alabama, denouncing the civil rights act all the while.

Spencer professed confidence in victory with a fair election. "That is the trouble," he added, "we have fiends to deal with."[151] Republicans would indeed receive about the traditional black belt turnout. The real change occurred among white voters and nonvoters in north Alabama. Governor Lewis remained an attractive candidate for former Union men, and Democrats handled him gingerly, but the depression persuaded many that the old divisions over the war no longer mattered. Republicans never had devised a coherent economic appeal to Unionist small farmers; their party remained identified with big government, railroads, and high taxes. Governor Lewis failed at righting the state's finances, and European bondholders complained that he had stopped answering mail. Even the state's repossessed railroad remained unsold. Depression highlighted these very issues, and the military deployment and arrests only reinforced the intrusive federal presence. By nominating an emphatic anti-secessionist for governor, the "old Bald Eagle of the mountains," Democrats spread the red carpet wide. Ex-secessionists demonstrated that bygones would be bygones.[152]

In this context, appeals to racial unity prevailed. The ex-secessionist, ex-Confederate general John Morgan preached reconciliation to crowds composed of former Union men, some veterans.[153] He returned to Selma predicting triumph: "A great and mighty army marching beneath the white banner, and white to the core, is coming from the mountains to our relief."[154] He assured planters they would never again be abandoned to the governance of their black majorities. The collapse of the plantation economy made his listeners more receptive to such assurances.

"Our prospects are fair but not flattering," a Republican leader wrote.[155] In a depression year, with the state government bankrupt, the Republicans would have had difficulty winning. People were reduced almost to beggary, and only change could save them, one black-belt lawyer observed.[156] Economic issues still divided Democrats, but the civil rights bill united them: race was the overriding issue, and nothing else mattered. The misgivings of conservatives only emboldened whites elsewhere, given abiding resentment of rich black-belt planters. Governor Lewis emphasized that Alabama never passed a state civil rights bill, and the Republican convention disavowed it explicitly. But the bill's passage by the US Senate, and its eloquent advocacy by Congressman Rapier among others made the issue inescapable.[157]

White Republicans sought cover. A Blount County supporter used a financial metaphor, "Politics is *dead* here—the 'Civil Rights' goes to protest here." Unionists felt they had courted enough unpopularity without adding a fresh incitement. In Lawrence County, local leaders called a meeting of Republican opponents of the measure, to consider what to do. When the county convention met, the resolutions did not even mention the issue, to the derision of the local press.[158] Republican and independent candidates running in north Alabama generally denounced the bill.[159] The relentless racial emphasis, and the armed mobilization, made independent politics less viable. Democratic Congressman Joseph H. Sloss encountered this reality after he failed to be renominated in the Tennessee Valley. The moderate Sloss now ran as an independent Democrat. He reportedly expected to win, and he achieved some momentary renown when he shot his daughter's former suitor for bearing smutty tales. Sloss won praise for upholding family honor, and he escaped prosecution when the couple reconciled. But none of this goodwill would save Sloss in November.[160]

The civil rights proposal enabled the White Line, allowing Democrats to depict racial extremism as a defensive reaction. Suitable language taxed their imagination. Barbour County resolutions decried the "stubborn fanatical ignorance of the nature and wants of the negro" that inspired the legislation. The bill undermined "separate social freedom" in favor of racial amalgamation. Focusing on the civil rights bill allowed Democrats to channel all other white social grievances. Social pressure increased, both as a strategy and as a spontaneous response. The bill "loosed the flood-gates of passion here, and made the campaign bitter beyond all precedent."[161] The press threatened ostracism of the families of voters who did not proclaim themselves politically white. The Tuskegee *News* threatened to name individual Republicans and then called on individuals to take a stand. In the black belt, the effect looks devastating. One Eufaula physician's social invitations stopped, his practice dried up, and even his neutral father suffered isolation. He gave up and left.[162]

Republican survival depended on the willingness of the northern public to sustain them with laws and force. The administration was reluctant, but after the White League coup in New Orleans miscarried, Grant sent troops to Alabama. The issue was how the northern public would respond to the resulting arrests and trials. After a generation of Republican governance, it became more difficult to get anyone to listen to atrocity tales. In 1874, Republicans struggled against the headwind of depression, along with their own previous exaggerations and northerners' compassion fatigue, while Alabama contributed to the Republicans' declining national fortunes. Two issues mattered most, the lesser one being provision to food of flood victims. Congressman Hays urged an appropriation for the Tombigbee, Warrior, and Alabama rivers, the supplies starting to arrive as the crop ripened.[163] Republicans saw food distribution as a boon, as Governor Lewis journeyed to Washington in June. At his request Republican Congressmen hashed out distribution procedures, this at the same meeting where they finalized campaign plans.[164] Beyond the evident partisan overtones, there are claims of bribery, and allegations of issuing supplies to draw people to town for rallies or voting.

Rural distress seems genuine. The national press covered it that spring, along with well-publicized relief efforts. Democratic newspapers reported disastrous rains, but it was difficult to demonstrate the need from a distance once the water receded and the denials began.[165] Moreover, some of the distribution sites were outside the flooded district, which Democrats interpreted as an electoral ploy. One reporter thought it suspicious that those applying for "bacon" were overwhelmingly black, but who farmed along the rivers in the plantation counties? Regardless, the charges fit well with the narrative of Grant-era corruption, flood relief as a spoils system boondoggle.[166]

Efforts to publicize violence fared worse. With the White Line, Democrats proclaimed their intentions openly, and they made some jarring assertions. "We know here that no man has ever lost his life here in Alabama because of his affiliation with the republican party," stated the Selma *Argus* in a feat of editorial cynicism.[167] Northerners needed to understand the reality, so Congressman Hays sought the national conscience. He had just returned to Washington to lobby for troops, fearing danger after his vote for the civil rights bill.[168] According to his modern biographer, a congressional colleague suggested he write something, which he did quickly from available materials. Hays pulled out all the rhetorical stops. "Every midnight breeze brings to us the dying groans of some man," Hays wrote. He listed dozens of violent episodes, starting with the Billings and Ivey murders. His problem was that Alabama had no incontrovertible Louisiana-style pogroms, not just yet. So the congressman preferred quantity to quality, assembling his stories secondhand from press accounts and excited refugees. The Hays-Hawley letter initially had just the effect he wished. It won wide distribution as a campaign document.[169]

"The killing has all been on one side," Hays concluded. Perhaps not, but the characterization was ballpark accurate. Even so, the Hays letter could not withstand the scrutiny it received in the more skeptical 1874 environment. Some specifics were wrong, and several more could not be readily demonstrated. One man reported in the press as having been killed apparently turned up unhurt; another episode happened just across the Mississippi border. Ivey's body was not disfigured, as Hays claimed, it was merely "all shot to pieces." Witnesses also recanted earlier stories under pressure. A Sumter County hotelkeeper denied being beaten for a political motive: he had only been pistol-whipped for saying the Billings shooting had partisan intent, which Democrats somehow read as exoneration. Hays credited the exaggerated report of many dead in Choctaw County after talking with Jack Turner. Several high-minded Republicans witlessly enabled the Democrats with denials of trouble nearby, men like former district attorney J. A. Minnis writing from

Montgomery. John Silsby and other Republican officials in Selma said all was peaceful. These accurate statements served to contradict claims of violence elsewhere. Republican officeholder William B. Jones denied that anything was amiss at nearby Forkland, but then again Democrats had just nominated his brother to run against Congressman Hays. The New York *Tribune* labeled the Hays allegations "thrilling Alabama romances to fire the New England heart."[170]

Newspapers that had promoted Hays's statement backed off, and the congressman never attempted a rebuttal.[171] Meanwhile, northern reporters in Montgomery puzzled out what was happening in the countryside. One termed the two sides' newspaper accounts wholly inconsistent, and he judiciously split the difference, which he thought made the reality bad enough.[172] The Liberal Republican New York *Tribune* scored the decisive journalistic coup, by sending a reporter with much fanfare of objectivity. His post-election columns revealed he was not neutral, but the pose worked. By the time Z. L. White arrived, the army stopped most of the violence. Three days in Sumter County revealed nothing amiss save the posse members under arrest. His reporting actually had nuance; he conceded that Steve Renfroe had a bad reputation, that former Klansmen shot freedpeople with little provocation, and that some were riding about in arms. He even contradicted assertions that the Billings and Ivey assassinations were apolitical. But the *Tribune*'s editors headlined his statements, "Alabama at Peace" and "The Slandered State." Congressman Hays indicated their effectiveness by assaulting the reporter when he got off the train in Washington.[173]

On election day itself, polling mostly occurred without violence, with hundreds of federal election monitors on hand. Soldiers blanketed the western black belt. The situation emboldened plantation freedmen to vote unmolested. It seems that election-day intimidation was less common than in northern Alabama. There were, however, major outbreaks on election day, one in Mobile and two in Barbour County, which complicate the image of a fair ballot. Mobile's situation is morally confused. The city had witnessed several riots in which Democrats disrupted Republican rallies, and on election they displayed a cannon at the polls. On the other hand, urban Mobile had a Republican tradition of repeat voting, as several African American leaders later testified.[174] The city's Republican mayor expected trouble from armed bands and repeatedly telegraphed for troops.[175] Democrats massed on horseback, and when Republican activist Allen Alexander led freedmen from one crowded polling place to another one, the Democrats stopped them. Voters had the right to vote at any precinct, so barring passage was illegal, but a firefight broke out with at least one black killed and several more shot.[176]

In Barbour County, Democrats had armed themselves with breech-loading rifles. One quiet Republican testified the Democrats came door to door with a signature sheet, pledging that all whites would attend the polls.[177] At Eufaula, the Democratic version of what occurred is that freedmen taunted or attacked a sympathetic black voter coming out of the polling place. This was a recurrent cover story, and whatever basis it had here, Democrats were well prepared to escalate. A gleeful newspaper reported, "Big riot to-day. Several killed and many others hurt—some badly—but none of our friends among them. The white man's goose hangs high. Three cheers from Eufaula."[178] A federal deputy heard whites being ordered to fall in by companies, estimating six hundred shots in all. He saw no freedmen armed or firing, which would explain the lopsided casualty count. The excited estimates in the Democratic press vary from twenty to forty shot, nearly all black, and subsequent tallies doubled that. A day later, the deputy totaled up nine dead, the sole white victim a bystander in a buggy.[179]

The shooting at Spring Hill looks clearer still. Judge Keils had requested that the army stay near at hand, but the commander stationed his men three hundred yards away, on superiors' orders. Democrats who intercepted the messages then knew how little protection the army provided. Elsewhere soldiers provided safety, but here officers literally followed directions to intervene only to enforce court orders. When desperate Republicans manufactured a pretext, the ranking officer pulled down a dictionary, assessed the definition of "subpoena," and decided it did not qualify. With news of the Eufaula riot, Democratic leaders saw victory in reach. As officials counted ballots, Democrats burst in a back door, knocked out the lamps, and started shooting. They blasted the son of Judge Keils, not quite seventeen, who had come to protect him. Afterwards, several Comers, "the better class of Democrats," somehow got the judge out alive. The Eufaula *News* editorially apologized for the killing, after a fashion, because "all must know" the judge was the target and "no one desired to harm little Willie."[180]

Given the violence, did the Democrats actually win the election of 1874? Lewis actually gained four thousand votes on his 1872 total, the most any Republican candidate ever received, which complicates claims of widespread suppression. Comparing county Republican ballots, the total number mostly held constant. In the predominantly white mountain counties, Lewis's numbers are quite close, and he even picked up a few votes in several. The Republican equivocations on race likely preserved the white voters they already had. In the black belt, too, Lewis picked up raw votes in many areas and only lost marginally in others. In the contentious western border, Republicans actually gained in percentage terms. In Marengo County, scene of the election frauds in 1872, Republicans gained nearly two thousand votes. In Greene and Sumter counties, White Line politics handed Republicans a huge victory. Freedmen surged to the polls just as skeptical conservatives had feared.

But it did not matter: Democrats picked up over twenty-five thousand votes, an increase of nearly a third. In several counties the Republican vote stayed nearly the same while Democrats picked up hundreds. Hous-

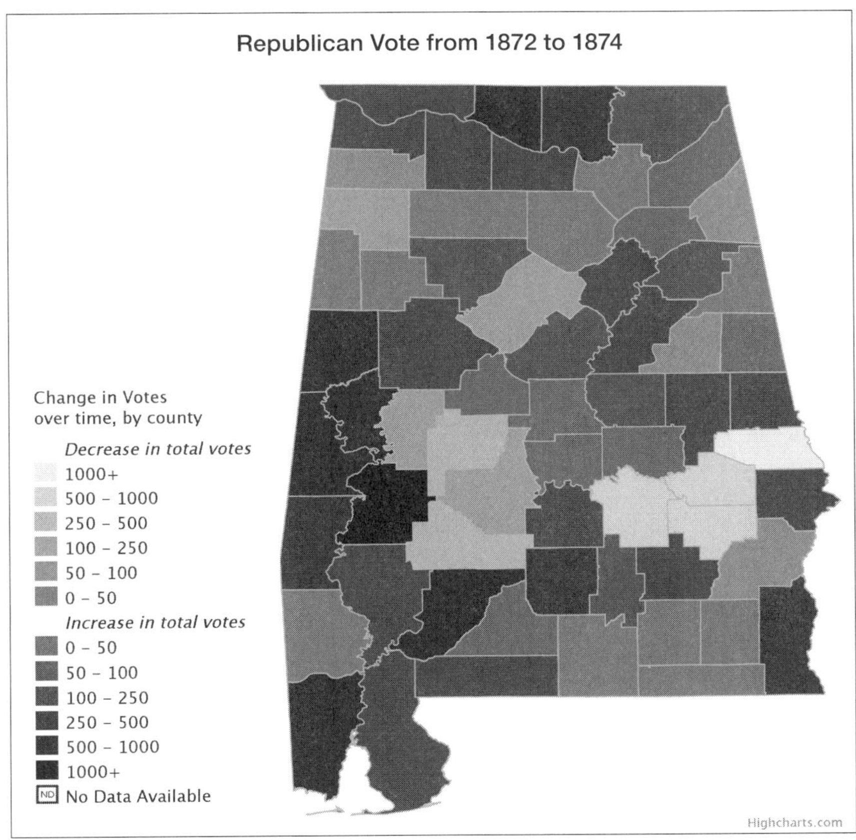

ton rolled up margins both in the Tennessee Valley and in the mountain region. In highland Walker County, Lewis gained fifty votes but Houston gained four hundred, turning a slight Democratic deficit into two-to-one majority. Several of these counties were far from the borders and railroads, with Republican voting officials. Ever since Reconstruction started, much of the white population of north Alabama did not vote, reflecting some combination of passive Unionism, distrust of planter elites, or backwoods indifference to the political process. Now fresh voters swelled the Democratic numbers, to back the anti-secessionist Houston and his platform of emphatic racial supremacy.

The official vote was 107,118 for Houston, 93,928 for Governor Lewis.[181] Republicans charged widespread fraud, sometimes even claiming enough votes to alter the result. In Barbour County, Democrats man-

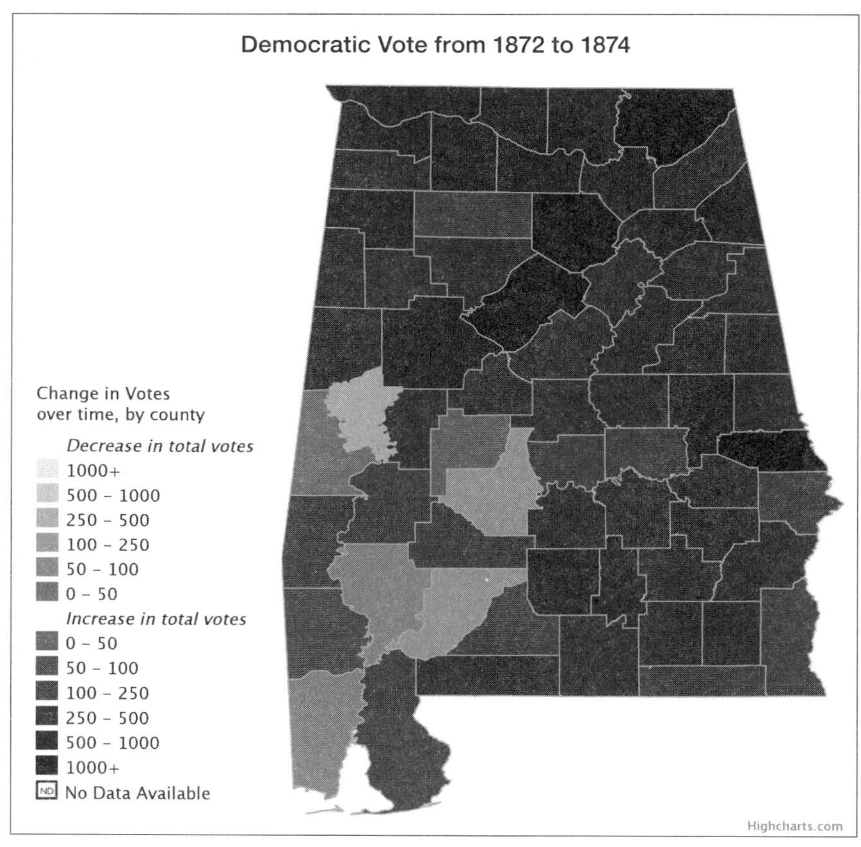

ufactured their margins out of lead. The Democratic totals look suspiciously large in several counties bordering Florida, and perhaps in some of the Tennessee River counties as well. In the Lee County boxes on the border, illegal voting by Georgians looks certain; investigating Democratic congressmen found the numbers "much too large."[182] These suspect gains perhaps account for several thousand ballots. But dramatic fraud would have been needed to create a 13,000-vote margin. Perhaps that much existed, but it seems likelier the Democrats won in ballots legally cast that day, if one disregards previous intimidation and massive social pressure. It would seem a decisive number of former Unionists fell into the welcoming arms of the ex-Confederate white majority.

Governor Lewis was honest. He might have saved the state's finances had good times continued. More than most southern states, Alabama's political elite had splintered over secession and war. Whites remained bitterly divided over railroad promotion and economic development, and in Alabama these matters rivaled race in political salience. So long as the state's finances seemed salvageable, and cotton production paid, many conservative planters and businessmen resisted White Line extremism. Circumstances might have kept the door open toward some level of racial coexistence. It had happened before; terrorist violence diminished as cotton profits bathed the plantations in hope. But ruinous crops, collapsing railroads, and the depression changed the situation. Financial disaster made it possible to blame Reconstruction for everything, uniting a diverse collection of former Unionists and conservatives behind the Democrats. Republican leaders, black and white, made errors enough, but nothing was going to save Reconstruction in the context of 1874. And once the Democrats momentarily regained full control, they solidified racist rule with surprising ease and equally surprising consequences.

12

"It Only Requires a Little More Figuring"

Redemption's Aftermath

Q. "What have they done to mistreat you?"
A. "The white people held me in slavery."
Q. "I mean since that time."
A. "Since that time it has been almost the same."

—Robert Ford, Montgomery

To hail Redemption, Virginia Clay dated a letter in French Revolution style, as "1 day White Jubilee 1874." Huntsville celebrated with rockets, Roman candles, and every prosperous home lit up. "The square was like a bee hive, & the streets like Br[oa]dway," she wrote. A grand procession carried a coffin with gilt letters proclaiming the death of Radicalism. Celebrants also bore caricatures of Senator Spencer, with a depiction of the carpetbagger scurrying homeward on spiderlike legs. "Better than all," Clay wrote, "West McCrary shot [US Marshal] Zack Thomas last night & 'tis said badly if not mortally!"[1]

Amid such venom, one might assume Alabama's Redemption would usher in unrestrained extremism. What occurred was more circumspect. Southern historians have long noted that the post-Redemption settlement empowered planters and urban boosters, leaving small farmers increasingly discontented. C. Vann Woodward emphasized the power of Whiggish New South promoters, but in Alabama things look different. Black-belt planters emerged in the driver's seat of the "Big Mule" coalition with an emerging industrial sector, a coalition which dominated the state in the New South era and beyond.[2] With Redemption, the tide set strongly in this direction, as White Liners empowered the most reactionary planter elements. Conservative misgivings proved misplaced: Governor Houston kept outside critics at bay, while racial solidarity legislatively delivered the black belt from majority rule. Whatever the previous prospects for some less harsh form of racial interaction, the White Line revolution enabled outright oppression of black laborers, and, increasingly, the white small farmers who had locked themselves out of power.

Ex-secessionists like Virginia Clay sought partisan payback, now that they had won. "The whipping-post should be restored to Alabama," Robert McKee's Selma *Argus* editorialized. Similarly Raphael Semmes challenged the Redeemers to show real backbone by denouncing the coming centennial exhibition.[3] The actual sequel proved more prudent. Governor Houston confronted the practical responsibilities of solidifying control while restoring the state's finances. Overt extremism contradicted his anti-secession background, and it also hurt with northern constituencies Houston needed for a debt settlement. Rhetoric of racial supremacy elected him, but national acceptance and continued tumult were incompatible. Redeemers thus proceeded with muffled oars. Unlike Alabama's civil rights–era governors, Houston flew beneath the radar of national scrutiny, and in this sense his leadership succeeded.

The immediate concern was to deliver black-belt constituents from permanent Republican majorities. Conservatives needed reassurance that Redemption would leave them in control locally. The Selma *Argus* suggested overturning the Greene and Sumter County legislative vote, on vague grounds that federal oversight made a fair election impossible.[4] But better options existed. Newly elected county executives had to put up property bonds, often tens of thousands of dollars, for those handling sums of money. Where Democratic officials could certify noncompliance, they simply turned officials out. Elsewhere, social ostracism proved effective. To hold office, native white Republicans normally relied on the financial backing of relations, friends, or potential business contacts, often Democrats, but in this heated climate that became less possible. Newspapers published the names of bond endorsers, calling on the public to indicate displeasure.[5] A published letter marveled that anyone should be so indifferent to white feelings as to bond an obnoxious official.[6] The process proved expedient: it conformed to existing law, and it could be defended as fiscal responsibility. It also respected conservative sensibilities in that it avoided lawlessness. With the offices left unfilled, the governor appointed replacements.

The strategy would take some months. In the weeks before leaving office, Governor Lewis reappointed some noncompliant Republican officials, buying them time. In Dallas County, where fiscally tainted Republicans failed to make bond, Lewis appointed a Democrat as sheriff and two white Republicans as tax collector and treasurer.[7] With Roderick B. Thomas elected in Selma as criminal-court judge, the Democrats reportedly offered the black lawyer several thousand dollars to resign.[8] He rebuffed them, so the legislators finally abolished his office. They tightened requirements elsewhere, requiring officeholders to run the bonding gauntlet repeatedly. "The integrity, honesty and capacity of these officials is not brought into question; it is purely a political matter," a Sumter County letter-writer explained. Local control tangibly mattered. To thwart federal election indictments, Eufaula's officials indicted witnesses on unrelated charges, jailing at least one. All lapsed into silence, and even Judge Keils fled, still stubbornly seeking witnesses against his son's killers.[9]

Expulsion often proved muscular. In Baldwin County, a Democratic official had reluctantly sworn in three county-board members, there being no bonding requirement. He examined his law books for a remedy. He sought help from the attorney general, claiming the recent election had been held a year early according to long-forgotten legislation. It was simply impossible to tolerate a black majority. The county commission would be "flooded with applications for the support of negro paupers," potentially absorbing half the county's taxation. Families sought burial appropriations, and if "those negroes had been seated they would have passed them. . . ." There is no malfeasance alleged, and no prospect that fraud would go undetected or unpunished. The issue was spending priorities, which somehow did not detract from the urgency of his demand: "Now what can be done about it?"[10]

Even in cases where the bonding laws were not in their favor, the victors pressed the point. "This is at present the highest trump in the Democratic pack, and if we fail to play it we had better retire," an editorial letter observed. In much of the black belt, Democrats achieved control of executive positions within a few months. In Macon County, the Republican probate judge barricaded himself to await the outcome of his legal challenge. Expulsion proved less contentious elsewhere. In Autauga County, the state solicitor resigned and was then employed to help void the local juries, to the fury of his former Republican allies.[11] Hale County's Judge James Garrett recalled that he never stuffed a ballot box, nor changed a ballot, but he boasted of eliminating Republican officials peacefully. A technicality allowed Hale's Republican tax collector to hold on until the spring, but lawyers wanted him replaced earlier. "We want to get the devils out as quickly as possible and know that you'll help us," one urged a legislator.[12]

While this quiet coup took place across the black belt—apparently without much resistance—the transition at the capitol proved jarring.

Governor Lewis's outgoing message denounced the states' rights Democrats, and he hoped that Alabama's residents would submit to the laws, finally. The incoming legislature refused to print his message.[13] Governor Houston assumed office before a crowd estimated at twenty thousand or more, including a statewide gathering of grey-clad companies. Despite the martial overtones, Houston sought oratorical conciliation. He repeated Lincoln's "with malice toward none, with charity for all" invocation, urging listeners to move past the recent acrimony. He pledged to safeguard rights without regard to race, color, or previous condition, under the rule of law, and he vaguely endorsed the principle of public education. One northern paper called it the most encouraging speech from the South in years; others noted the profusion of American flags. Houston lived up to these atmospherics, after a fashion; he would not spearhead racist legislation, though he risked nothing for blacks' benefit.[14]

In the legislature, trouble ensued. Democrats had a lengthy partisan agenda, from repealing Klan legislation to passing anti-theft laws to tightening voter-registration requirements. One suggestion was abolishing some county boards. The Montgomery *Advertiser* observed that "the tax paying people of the negro counties are wholly at the mercy of the most vicious and corrupt creatures in the state." The editors meant local officials, rather than constituents, but either way the solution was to place these counties under guardianship.[15]

Democrats enjoyed a substantial majority, and their constituents expected instant results, but these expectations proved unrealistic. Inexperienced Granger legislators, among them many "silent" farmers, met repeated frustration from opponents who knew the ropes and never left their seats. In the House of Representatives, African Americans outnumbered white Republicans two to one, so they dominated opposition discourse. They won notice for their infuriating command of parliamentary procedure, prompting complaints that they would "always imagine that any bill they cannot understand is aimed at their rights."[16] This belief had some excuse, and a deliberate pace limited invidious legislation and insured publicity. In early December, partisanship escalated over the troubles in Barbour County.[17] The outgoing secretary of state had certified Republican candidates, but a narrow majority expelled the three black legislators and seated the challengers, fresh from leadership in the recent bloodshed. Republicans then slowed the gears for everything except efforts to settle the debt. Existing rules favored them, requiring a four-fifths majority to force a quick vote.[18]

Montgomery's black community urged these tactics. Several large meetings were held, where leaders debated the options remaining with considerable heat; some endorsed emigration westward, others sought federal prosecutions.[19] Republicans hoped that the northern public might be sobered by the recent developments, as well as the rhetoric from nettled Democratic backbenchers. Besides, delay infuriated Democratic constituents, and House Speaker D. C. Anderson absorbed criticism for his impartial demeanor. Newspapers bewailed the expenditure of a thousand dollars a day.[20] The Mobile *Register* editorialized, "When you are dealing with lawless people the best way is to seize them at once by the throat and not waste words upon them."[21]

Only in the late winter and spring of 1875 did the Democratic legislative agenda bear fruit.[22] A statewide jury bill shifted the norm from competent voters to householders, eliminating most black jury service.[23] Rigorous municipal registration laws enabled the Democrats to sweep the Mobile elections in December, the Montgomery elections in May.[24] The much-debated "deadfall" law banning nighttime sales of agricultural goods also passed.[25] This was a "curiosity of legislation," as northern newspapers pointed out, and even the Selma *Argus* highlighted the harm to white civil liberties.[26] Some historians have emphasized that the law pursued social and political repression rather than primarily punishing theft.[27] While it accomplished that, it was not the main motive, not with alternative means being so plentiful. One Marengo letter claimed that two-thirds of laborers were stealing from the crops they raised, nearly nightly. Months after the bill passed, meetings continued denouncing illegal sales. Farmers outside Montgomery threatened "Judge L[ynch]" against violators, the courts being insufficient. The belief that crossroads storekeepers were buying stolen goods seems emphatically held.[28]

By the time the legislature adjourned in March, it had enacted over five hundred laws, all signed by the governor. Partisan and racial legislation predominated. Selma received a new charter and contracted its borders, both measures designed to give Democrats the majority, but they lost the mayor's office to an independent anyway.[29] The legislature stripped black-belt county governments of their duties, setting up rival boards of revenue. This eventually happened in Montgomery, Dallas, and Lowndes, becoming routine where the electorate proved stubborn.[30] At the ballot box, the decisive change was a requirement for voting only in one's home precinct. This sounded reasonable as an anti-fraud measure, but in Alabama it played out differently. Freedmen normally massed for safety in central locations where their votes were likely to be counted.

The new law opened the doors wide to intimidation and fraud in rural areas. Election officials could neglect to open ballot boxes in heavily Republican precincts. As the Montgomery *Advertiser* lightly observed after one such episode, "There is no law *compelling* them to open polls, if opening polls should chance to interfere with their wishes. . . ." Voters retained the legal option of opening polls themselves, a tall order for imperfectly literate voters.[31]

Republicans mustered one last counterblow before the nation. As Congress debated a federal election bill, pressed by Representative Alexander White, lengthy hearings occurred on the recent election. Republican legislators sent a timely memorial cataloging oppressive enactments and proposals.[32] The laundry list was infuriatingly accurate, forcing Democrats to scramble for denials and to vent at the "slimy reptile" who wrote it. They pressured several senators to recant their signatures, apparently threatening expulsion.[33] The failure to pass the enforcement act before Congress adjourned, however, left black voters at the mercy of the legislature. Congress did however pass the civil rights law, and black activists wasted no time in testing its penalties. Barring blacks from a visiting minstrel show in Montgomery wound up in federal court, eliciting perplexed discussions as to how best to comply with the law or evade its terms.[34]

The governor kept a low profile in these debates, even winning occasional praise in Alabama's Republican press.[35] The debt issue and the still-unsold A&C Railroad preoccupied him. He told his fiscal agents that he hoped to raise more revenue, thus appealing to commercial constituencies who preferred not to cut taxation levels. Depression realities undermined the chances: interest payments alone would absorb all existing tax revenue, suggesting the debt could never be paid fully.[36] Governor Houston proposed a commission to investigate and attempt a settlement with creditors. Recalling Lindsay's disastrous sojourns, Houston kept far from Wall Street and preferred shared responsibility. He served as one of the three commissioners, along with Levi Lawler and T. B. Bethea, which permitted him the decisive vote on a divided commission. The governor hoped that full disclosure of the state's insolvency would induce Alabama's creditors to forgive much of the debt. Houston was a wealthy landowner with railroad connections; he had little desire to disavow the debt, but he needed big concessions. For several months Houston declined comment to reporters, and he refused to commit to a payment plan. All the while repudiation talk strengthened his hand.[37]

White farmers had their own tax priorities. Before the war, a progressive tax structure had shielded them from property levies, but Reconstruction had changed things. "The people are poor—very poor—and they are not able to pay 75cts on the $100," a north Alabama editor observed. "They have not been able to pay it under radical rule;—they don't intend to pay it now." He joked that railroads were so unpopular that residents would flee if one was ever built.[38] Even the anti-repudiation Montgomery *Advertiser* warned of a wind from the mountains sweeping the debt away, if creditors offered no compromise. McKee's Selma *Argus* led a cohort of Grange supporters in promoting traditional Jacksonian views. He called for a whopping one-third reduction of the state tax rate, effective repudiation. Such editorials themselves undermined the state's credit, which he sometimes called desirable. The *Argus* disavowed all bonds emitted since Congressional Reconstruction began, including those issued under Democratic Governor Lindsay. Perhaps a tenth of the state debt involved obvious malfeasance—primarily the two-million-dollar bill, the half-million in excess bonds issued by Governor Smith, and the South & North special subsidy and other grants to Democratic-connected companies. The rest presumably were bona fide bond transactions passed with widespread support, to benefit mostly Alabama-led companies. No matter, the railroad debts were *all* void because the Reconstruction regime was illegitimate. Only the antebellum obligations need be honored.[39]

Dramatic remedies suggested themselves. One obvious possibility was replacing the current constitution, but congressional Democrats warned their southern allies to hold off. Influential editors opposed the proposal through the winter, and several sources identify the old conservative wing as the most resistant.[40] Some who still hoped for a debt settlement feared an agrarian-dominated convention. Skeptics warned another campaign would rouse the Republican masses, which might cause an embarrassing defeat. A black-belt paper predicted that twenty thousand conservatives would stay away from the polls. "Let us not invite extraordinary risks," the Livingston *Journal* urged.[41]

Perhaps conservatives felt that, having solidified their control, a degree of subordinate black participation facilitated stable rule. Open conflict had stopped with the election, and some wealthy planters were glad of it, especially those who had resisted the White Line emphasis. Black-belt pragmatists recognized that their interests had already been shielded from hostile Republican officials, so some cautiously preferred to leave well enough alone. Emphatic Democratic partisans instead preferred a policy of simply installing their nominees on whatever pretext they could. Monopoly of power implied continuing tumult, which appealed to White Liners flushed with victory and imbued with a Spartan racial ethic. Choking off all black input bolstered hard-liner predominance by deterring ad hoc interracial coalitions. That threat materialized occasionally, as in Wilcox County, where an independent-dominated interracial alliance maintained power for years. The hundred or more white supporters bonded officials, including some Republicans, to partisan Democrats' frustration.[42]

In the black belt, more normal weather conditions encouraged civility. "This year, so far, promises well, and a good crop would put both parties in good humor," a northern reporter wrote in May.[43] With the laws tilting in their favor, planters stopped railing about expelling workers, sometimes talking of recruiting more.[44] John Silsby, the missionary and Republican leader, found both blacks and whites more optimistic. While the price of cotton remained low, planters were growing less and borrowing less to do so. One Lowndes County farmer feared hired hands would become scarce, with good black laborers making enough money to buy mules and rent land. Repression deterred labor unrest, and strike talk became uncommon. No less than the Selma *Argus* praised the workforce with the end of carpetbagger interference. Freedmen had failed so badly on shares that they were now manageable and efficient, content to function as hired hands. "No free laborers in the world are doing better today than the negroes of Alabama," McKee concluded.[45]

Though cotton prices remained low, coexistence with a quiescent workforce had some appeal. A Perry County business manager, R. C. Moore, had poor crops in 1875 due to local flooding and hail. Cabins were damaged, and he urged his employer to build new ones quickly because the hands were threatening to leave. Moore was equally even-tempered over the loss of hogs, and he responded instructively through his series of losing seasons. The freedpeople were all in debt, but Moore asked permission to forgive their mortgages and let them keep the paltry corn they raised. This was what the neighbors were doing for hands that intended to stay, he explained.[46]

As depression deepened, political pressure for a new constitution grew, encouraged by the example of other Democratic states, like Arkansas. The governor acquiesced, because the debt commissioners determined upon a forced scaling of the railroad debt. As candidate, Houston declared Alabama honor-bound to pay up, and repudiators long distrusted him.[47] But Houston now concluded the intransigents were embarrassingly right: the entire debt could never be paid. Still, as fiscal agents warned, Alabama had to avoid the direct threat of compulsion. Even delay hurt the state's reputation.[48] If partial repudiation proved inevitable, expediency dictated targeting the most corruptly procured bonds of the most hated northern corporation. A new constitution would empower restive taxpayers, facilitating what the governor had to do.

Opposition collapse eased the decision. Republicans were in such disarray that they could not turn out their voters, the governor privately noted.[49] The party structure now immolated itself over fresh revelations surrounding Senator Spencer's 1872 reelection. The Democratic legislature held one-sided hearings, and Spencer had made so many promises that disaffected Republicans, including his former operatives, testified vividly.[50] While this transpired, Spencer's confidant and housemate, J. J. Hinds, was indicted in Washington for bribery in his plentiful mail contracts, this just after his momentary appointment as federal marshal.[51] Spencer found few defenders, and the accumulating details look damning enough, provoking national derision.[52] Alabama's leading native white Republicans disavowed him. Black leaders remained mostly silent, not trusting their motives, and all the old factional controversies reemerged over "carpetbag" patronage influence. The party's main remaining newspaper, the Montgomery *Journal,* had cautiously defended Spencer. Now the editors professed shock, tacitly crediting the allegations. Disorder would roil the party structure for years, making it incapable of resisting Democratic initiatives.[53]

Congress's adjournment eliminated the threat of federal legislation, and elite opinion solidified. Democrats in the state house endorsed a constitutional convention, with one dissenting vote.[54] Proponents disarmed critics. Democrats disavowed legislating people out of office, or disfranchising on property grounds, or eliminating the school system.[55] By taking the controversial issues off the table in the enabling legislation, the process looked more nonpartisan. The governor pledged to protect existing suffrage rights and prevent any educational or property requirement. "I would aid the disfranchised to defeat any such obnoxious principle or provision," he vowed.[56] Houston thus looked broadminded before the national press, who were unaware of facts on the ground and eager to forget Reconstruction entirely. The more subtle point was that revision could undermine bondholders' legal standing. A stripped-down government that forced scaling of the debt would be popular in north Alabama, whose recent support had provided victory.

Once the decision was made, Democratic and Conservative leaders fell in line. Only one conservative newspaper reportedly opposed it, the *Wilcox News*. No one recalled the Military Reconstruction process with pride, and the voters' oath to respect civil equality still rankled. Separating national and state elections would eliminate federal oversight of the ballot box, and new procedures might discourage black registration further. Though racial motives were overt, the complaints against the existing constitution ranged wide. The authorization of state subsidies for corporations now looked like folly. Certain offices could be dispensed with, like the lieutenant governor, some judgeships, and especially the board of education. While leaders disavowed school cuts, scattered supporters demanded them, and some such intention seems indicated, given what followed.[57] Small-government Democrats had ample grounds to oppose the existing constitution, and it had few conservative defenders on grounds other than expediency.

The weakened Republican party structure, still controlled by Spencer's beleaguered allies, barely mustered a response. There was no chance Republicans could win control: the convention bill gave each county a delegate, massively overrepresenting the sparsely populated white counties.[58] This, combined with the demoralization of Republicans, raised intricate tactical issues. A Spencerite meeting recommended voting *against* the convention, but *for* sympathetic Democrats as delegates. His holdover Republican state executive committee obligingly agreed to make no nominations, declaring it a nonpartisan issue. This let Republican rivals decry a sellout, calling instead for explicit party nominations.[59]

Some conciliatory party leaders took the opposite approach and endorsed the convention call. A handful of black spokesmen, like William V. Turner, thought the Democrats' pledge of a nondiscriminatory constitution sufficient.[60] Between the new precinct voting provisions, and the difficulty in explaining tactical moves, Republicans were sorely divided at the August election. Freedmen normally voted as a disciplined bloc, but they depended on an operative network to fund, print, and distribute tickets, and also to monitor the polls. These party functions failed, and several black-belt counties reported huge majorities *for* the convention. Corpse-strewn Barbour County endorsed by over twenty to one. Sumter County approved by 1,376 to 77, with the much-threatened Bob Reed returning to counsel nonparticipation. Even that display of his influence troubled the press.[61]

The delegate count demonstrated the extent of the party's collapse.

Republicans elected twelve delegates and helped elect another eight independents, mostly in the black belt, out of ninety-nine delegates. Just three were African American. The press proclaimed it the most peaceful election in memory, with not a fistfight to report. Despite the enfeebled opposition, the statewide count proved instructively close. The official vote was 77,763 to 59,928, the reality likely tighter, so a unified Republican vote might have defeated it.[62] Turnout was about a third below the previous election, which perhaps reflected white skepticism of a new constitution. Some feared the convention would repudiate the debt, others that it might not, and proponents were saying some unsettling things. One opposed elected judges, that "French red republicanism or communism engrafted on American democracy."[63] The White Line campaign had buried class and regional issues, but the continuing depression thrust them forward again. The reality was that, thus far, planters of the black belt had received most of Redemption's concrete benefits, and soon enough many poorer white farmers would rise in rebellion. The Republican constitution per se was not popular, but there were class-tinged provisions that had real white support. One newspaper extolled Alabama's "grandest system of free education that ever blessed the world. . . ." Now schools looked endangered with editorial letters calling Alabama too poor to support them. If the choice was closing schools to pay bondholders, "many of the poorer people favor the laws as they stand," as one editor wrote privately.[64]

The generous homestead exemption for debts, a thousand dollars and more, provided a sticking point. Many elite convention supporters opposed these provisions as unfair, arguing they inhibited further borrowing by those who needed supplies. But indebted farmers were not listening: protection from dispossession overrode everything. The Livingston *Journal* feared that the debt and school issues swayed mountaineers and others in the "ignorant and unreflective classes."[65] Since Democrats had pledged that their constitution would go to the voters for ratification, they had to draft a document that all whites would find acceptable, and one that would not galvanize black turnout. Besides, racial supremacy had been achieved at the local level, and no pressing need existed for redundant constitutional guarantees. North Alabama's farmers got what they wanted at the moment, a return to small-government and low-tax priorities. But white-solidarity rhetoric encouraged thoughtless concessions to the apparently vanquished black-belt planters, in practice guaranteed a reservoir of subject votes by the Fifteenth Amendment.

Everything promoted short-term discretion. Previous pledges, Houston's inclination, northern scrutiny, and the fears of an embarrassing defeat forced caution upon delegates. The overwhelming majority also made it easy for the Democratic leadership to restrain provocative behavior. Convention chair Leroy Pope Walker urged a drastic downsizing of governmental functions, but his other comments gained more attention. The war's outcome had eliminated all grounds for sectional controversy, so delegates should incorporate "National spirit and the National law" into their constitution and recognize the "perfect political and civil equality of all men." From a secessionist member of Jefferson Davis's cabinet, these were instructive words. Favorable commentary offered welcoming signs of how the national response would play out.[66]

Delegates outlawed slavery, declared all men "equally free and independent," and wrote into the bill of rights an explicit disavowal of secession. Bourbon newspapers grumbled about this last bit of eating "dirt," but the existing constitution had a more emphatic statement and delegates could hardly avoid it. Besides, former Union men would be pleased, and their support was crucial.[67] The secession stand attracted more favorable attention than anything else the convention did. *Harper's Weekly* called it "wise and manly," and even the *Times* of London thought it significant.[68] There were other striking features, like the emphatic assertion of the separation of church and state, and civil-libertarian provisions as well. Newspapers trumpeted the ban on imprisonment for debt, while few commented on the racial implications of the document. With a bloody White League campaign unfolding next door in Mississippi, Alabama's Redeemers exemplified restraint.[69]

Delegates enacted the constitution in record time, all the details being ironed out in caucus. The text disavowed educational or property qualifications for voting or holding office, along with all racial qualifications. On paper, arguably, the egalitarian guarantees exceeded those of the existing Reconstruction document.[70] The constitution also affirmed the principle of public education, though only committing to extending schools as means allowed. Even on the homestead exemption, caution prevailed. It stayed at one thousand dollars, save for allowing prospective borrowers to waive its protections—thus minimizing its future significance in practice. There had been delegate sentiment for an explicit disavowal of the railroad bonds, given "absolutely appalling" state finances in a committee's estimate. Houston headed such measures off with assurances that negotiations were proceeding to advantage.[71] Otherwise, the delegates contradicted the Republican predictions of a runaway convention.

The most dramatic changes involved state expenditures. Legislative extravagance was on people's minds, expressed in a one-third reduction in the representatives' per diem, a drastic cut in travel reimbursements, and a shift to biennial sessions. The state school board, the county school superintendents, and various other offices were abolished, with the remaining state officers getting a 25-percent reduction in pay. The constitution fixed state property-tax levels at current levels, 0.75 percent. Local taxation was limited as well, to a point that urban business leaders found counterproductive. Delegates adopted an outright ban on state and local governmental subsidies, part of the general rejection of Whig-Republican economic policies. Overall, the document prevented future legislatures from ever increasing the debt, as one paper pointed out. All this had dire implications for bondholders, as did the provision that the state could not be sued. McKee expressed satisfaction in an editorial entitled "Repudiation," declaring it "certain that the people do not intend to pay one dollar" of the millions of fraudulent bonds. Jacksonian inclinations were otherwise evident in detailed restrictions on banking and anticompetitive telegraph-company behavior. "The abuse of corporate power is pretty fully provided against," the *New York Times* concluded.[72]

While the constitution's enlightened racial tone agreeably disappointed the national press, some noted disquieting implications. Moving state elections to August eliminated the threat of federal oversight, which meant that local officials could inhibit voting. Such political changes escaped much criticism, but the school provisions fared differently. Governor Houston claimed school administration absorbed disproportionate funds, so that classroom cutbacks need not occur under more frugal laws. The Democratic school superintendent thought this unlikely; he doubted as well the provision guaranteeing that 96 percent of education funds go to teachers, virtually eliminating administrative oversight.[73] Convention delegates repealed the flat one-fifth guarantee for the schools, promising $100,000 from the legislature annually plus whatever else could be spared, in addition to other theoretical sources like the sparsely collected poll tax. The harsh implications would be demonstrated within weeks. The free schools were already hurting under Governor Lewis, given his debt preoccupation, and the new constitution halted the enrollment gains the Redeemers initially reported. Some critics saw school closings as inevitable. The Chicago *Tribune* decried that as "Southern Barbarism," a restoration of slavery.[74]

No one much troubled the black population for their opinion. Just as the convention met, residents of Calera, Shelby County, faced more immediate problems. They had schools and teachers, but "the White men did Beet them and Drove them from us." Their employer was not paying them in cash, they said, and "not onely him it is so all over this countery."[75] None of this made an impression at a distance. Outsiders found more to praise than blame in the constitution on racial issues, though tax provisions bothered editors more. Business interests realized that under the new limits the debt could never be repaid. Here too, the constitution's light touch served the Redeemers well, despite open talk of forcing a two-thirds reduction in debt. "So deftly is the purpose of repudiation concealed in this instrument that one may look through it carefully a dozen times and not find a hint of it," the *Journal of Commerce* complained.[76] A few papers professed outrage.[77] But the northern public cared little for the bondholders' fate, so outside financial circles the damage remained limited. There was no national backlash.

"The new constitution gives our people, generally, satisfaction."[78] So said W. L. Bragg, the state party chairman. Almost no criticism appeared in the Democratic press. A number of Republican leaders tacitly recommended letting ratification go by default, or even endorsed the revision outright. Ex-governors Lewis and Parsons did so. The holdover Republican state auditor R. T. Smith did as well, calculating the annual savings at a quarter-million dollars. Judge J. A. Minnis made the case for black acquiescence: "if you want peace, protection and prosperity, how can you vote against it?" Local practices under the existing constitution could hardly be worse, and there was advantage in having Democrats pledged to civil rights and equal schools, as John Silsby observed.[79] The state's fiscal straightjacket mattered little to freedmen in respect to government services they were not likely to receive. Also, debt scaling would help freedpeople as well as white farmers, as the insurgent Readjuster coalition would soon argue in Virginia.[80]

Whatever the demerits of the constitution, the Republicans were in no position to contest it.[81] Eventually both of the two contending Republican factions concluded that a token show of opposition would strengthen their position. The Spencerite state committee moved first; then ex-governor Smith weighed in with a public statement opposing ratification, adding that the existing constitution could be fixed by piecemeal amendments.[82] This intervention, however, seemed a matter of factional positioning rather than a serious effort to rouse the party's constituency. Few African American leaders spoke out, either way, and the constitution carried in a rout. It passed even in the white Unionist enclaves like Winston or Walker, and ratification carried most of the plantation belt as well. Eufaula voted 646 to 6 for ratification. In Sumter County, the vote was 1,662 to 2. Only Autauga, Lowndes, Macon, and Montgomery counties returned majorities against ratification. Thus the people had "almost silently" changed their constitution, "without one act of violence" to the governor's knowledge.[83]

Ratification's sequel was nonetheless harsh. The loss of the school earmark had dire consequences, at least in the short term. School officials stopped distributing funds under the terms of the old constitution, awaiting a legislative appropriation which never materialized. School commissioner J. M. McKleroy rose in denunciation: "I fear the result will be that in many townships there will be no schools for either race, while in many more there will be none for the colored race."[84] The system took years to recover. The new constitution had deadlier consequences for Alabama's prisoners. The convict lease existed before the war and expanded during Reconstruction, but it became racialized with emancipation. Whippings enabled a system of enforced labor, as prisoners headed into the mines and elsewhere, but the Redeemers made brutality a source of profit. New convict leases buoyed state budgets and allowed Governor Houston to tide the state over the debt settlement hurdle; he actually borrowed from the prospective lessees to do it. The prisons and jails became thereafter a financial mainstay of hard-pressed state and local governments. The death rates were enormous, and it would be decades before reformers moved to clean up the system.[85]

With the ratification of the constitution, and the elimination of Republicans as a political force, the Reconstruction era came to a definitive end.[86] Our story logically concludes here as well. Still, the Redeemers had loose ends, the major remaining one being the debt settlement. Governor Houston could now impose terms on bondholders, pointing to the tax limitations and governmental cuts in the new constitution. The commissioners determined upon the expedient plan of distinguishing between the various classes of railroad endorsements and Alabama's own bonds. The state would honor most straight state bonds and pay them at an initial rate of 2 percent, gradually rising thereafter to 5 percent. Missed interest payments were to be forgiven, and unhappy creditors could either take the terms or get nothing.[87]

Guaranteed railroad bonds fared worse, but even here the debt commissioners distinguished between the various Democratic-owned companies and the truly doomed Alabama & Chattanooga. These latter creditors were livid. Alabama reduced its overall debt by two-thirds, reportedly from about thirty to ten million dollars, and the A&C debt went from ten to a single million.[88] Though Alabama forced existing bondholders to accept its terms, under duress, fresh investors were unlikely to serve themselves up. One London banker observed, "this arrangement is *not satisfactory* to the Bondholders, and such being the case the Stock Exchange will be shut to any new loans & c of Alabama."[89] But that did not matter. If Alabama abandoned its Whiggish experiment in state-sponsored development and returned to its longstanding Jacksonian traditions, everything worked out. Proponents got their subsidies, the taxpayers escaped payment, and the carpetbaggers got the blame—along with their black supporters. Alabama had built its infrastructure at the expense of external moneymen. It lost only commercial reputation, which would not "hurt much" as one paper concluded. The state even unloaded the A&C Railroad to a consortium of the European bondholders, who feared losing everything otherwise. They wound up with a functioning, and eventually profitable, Alabama Great Southern Railroad through the state's industrial heartland.[90]

The political outcome was equally tidy. Governor Houston and his allies prospered through a discreet pursuit of white-supremacist ends.[91] The new constitution mandated state elections in August 1876, without federal oversight and under the new precinct-voting requirements. The timing proved fortuitous, as quarrelling Republicans sent rival delegations to the national convention. It resembled a patronage-infused War of the Roses, with black activists using Spencer's influence to maintain their toehold in federal employment.[92] Two Republican tickets appeared, with both withdrawn in favor of an independent ticket led by Selma's mayor, Noadiah Woodruff. Houston buried him by over forty thousand votes, with black-belt numbers dropping off dramatically. That fall, Senator Spencer privately urged a potential candidate for Congress not to bother: "It would do you personally no good and couldn't possibly result in anything but defeat for the party. This applies to any Republicans running."[93]

Republican totals improved a bit in the presidential election, holding the margin to 102,989 to 68,708, but it did not matter. Everyone knew the score. Future Democratic governor Joseph F. Johnson offered mock advice to a distant candidate: "Tell him if he a[i]n't elected to move to Ala & we'll give him 50000 maj[ority] in /78 for Gov. If he a[i]n't satisfied with that we'll make it 75000. It only requires a little more figgerin."[94] He had the numbers about right. The next Democratic candidate ran unopposed, and after the 1880 election Democrats held every Senate seat. Black officeholding disappeared. Elsewhere in the South, African Americans sometimes maintained some political influence, sometimes securing election in fusion arrangements as in Mississippi. In Alabama's plantation region it was more like exclusion: their entire irrelevance was punctuated only by Congress occasionally seating a Republican challenger. The voting guarantees in the new constitution benefited the planter elite. Equal access to the ballot was baked into the Redeemer's constitution, so thereafter captive votes could be tallied as circumstances dictated.[95]

The 1875 constitution decisively resolved the political contests of the Jacksonian era, just when they proved irrelevant. The wealthy abandoned

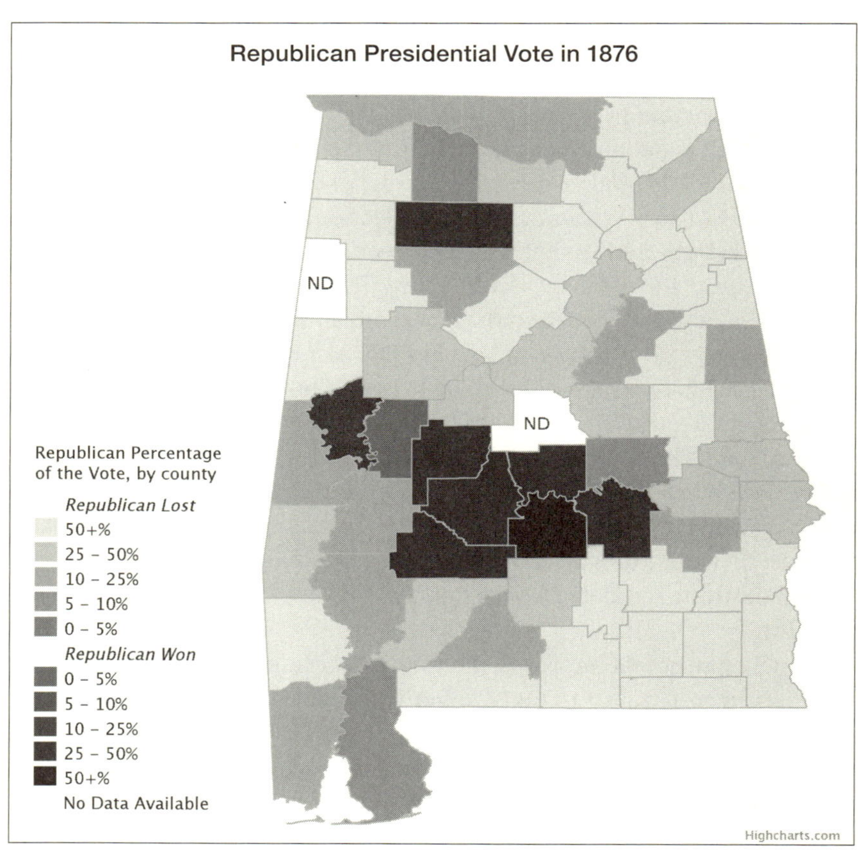

the social vision of the commercial sector and the great planters of the Whig-dominated plantation belt; the use of government subsidy to promote economic development diminished, and public education suffered badly as well. But with the railroad and financial infrastructure completed, black-belt elites no longer needed positive government. Circumstances proved they could live with a low-tax regime better than most anyone else. Similarly, the war era's struggles between conservatives and secessionists no longer mattered. The leadership reunited as "Bourbons" in support of a status quo that served them well. The Redemption settlement provided them both a huge reservoir of subject ballots to buttress their rule. The constitution allocated representation based on the whole population, which meant the black belt's few white voters enjoyed disproportionate legislative control. This allowed them to rewrite the debt, fence, and penal laws to suit themselves. Planters' dominance allowed them to coexist with their nominally free but legally fettered labor force with minimal concessions. All of sharecropping's shortcomings remained, but favorable laws allowed them to make money even in the midst of agricultural decline.[96]

The Civil War era dissidents mostly returned to their Democratic origins, their role in the race-drenched Redemption campaign marking their readmission into the South's consensus. Governor Houston's advent highlighted the symbolic concession of ex-secessionists to north Alabama's amalgam of anti-secession, cooperationist, and outright Unionist sentiment. Perhaps more crucially for the future, longstanding resentment of corporations and elites had encouraged debt repudiation, which forced a return to Jeffersonian-Jacksonian governance. Small farmers got what they wanted, but not what they needed in the modern world, as they became increasingly enmeshed in international markets—and debt. Ever larger numbers slid into tenancy. In an era of government-sponsored deflation, laissez-faire gave them no help in confronting banks, corporations, and a dollar so strong it would crush them all.

It did not take long to realize that something had gone amiss. Insurgent movements developed quickly, as Redemption brought no return of prosperity. In north Alabama, county-level uprisings against Democratic conventions and insiders proliferated.[97] A bewildering mix of Republicans, independent Democrats, and third-party "Greenbackers" contested for power. In the late 1870s, the Tennessee Valley elected a Greenbacker congressman, William Lowe, committed to relieving farmers' debts by reinflating the currency. In the 1880s, Farmer's Alliance agitation gave rise to the Populist revolt of the 1890s, the one mass movement for activist government in the nineteenth century. But the Redemption settlement of the mid-1870s let Bourbons beat back agrarian radicalism, with the moral capital and unassailable position the White Line had given them. The black votes of the plantation region voted down populism, voluntarily or not, or actually cast or not. In 1901, they would similarly be counted for an explicitly white supremacist constitution, which would finally disfranchise African Americans outright.[98] What remained behind was a snarl of resentments, which contributed to Alabama's explosive class-tinged response to the racial confrontations to come.

Where, then, did this leave the emancipated slaves and their descendents? Mercifully, the political killings mostly stopped in 1875, save in exceptional circumstances like Alabamians aiding Mississippi's White League campaign.[99] Mass violence in the form of lynching would reemerge, but it took some time. In scattered Alabama locations, especially cities, or at times of white disunity, blacks exercised some lingering political influence. In depressed Mobile, for example, black voters helped evict the Democrats in 1877. The legislature abolished and remade the city government, but the same thing happened again in 1884, as African Americans helped elect a business-led reform administration. In north Alabama, the white majorities were so large that dissidents dealt flexibly with the race issue as some blacks continued to vote. In other places, the black population at least got some consolation. Macon County Republicans finally surrendered legislative seats in exchange for a pledge of state funding for an industrial college. Booker T. Washington arrived to serve as the first principal of the new Tuskegee Institute, emerging as a national figure in the new, chilling climate of racial suppression.[100]

African Americans had lost most of what they had sought from Reconstruction, but they gained knowledge of the uses of state power and the ability to articulate it. One day, at places like Birmingham and Selma, with a different nation watching, that would matter—but not yet. After resigning his position in Barbour County to escape indictment, Judge Elias Keils relocated to Washington. He testified repeatedly to congressional committees, while his African American former supporters pelted him with pleas. "They don't give us any schools and try to crowd us down all they can because we won't vote with them for democrats," one wrote. "We would be better off in Africa than among these rebels." Others cited different grievances but had much the same conclusion: it was time to leave. "We are not allowed to have any colored men on the juries now; it takes no time to indict and convict republicans; if he is a colored republican, that is enough to convict him," another activist complained.[101]

Perhaps their final word rightly rests with the emancipated slave and onetime congressman, Jeremiah Haralson of Selma, who personally embodied the promise and failings of Reconstruction rule. Often brave and generally cynical, Haralson spoke with precision. Democrats had made no inroads into his constituency. Perhaps one in a hundred voted for the opposition, he thought, dismissing them as barbers and loungers around hotels. But it did not matter what the field hands preferred, because few white or literate black Republicans remained in the countryside to facilitate their voting. Democrats had many avenues of fraud: "they can make it so the only question would be what the majority would be. If they wanted to make it one hundred thousand, they could do it."

Haralson described a deteriorating climate in the black belt, once the center of racial coexistence: "I have seen most every democrat in the place around the polls on the day of election," prominent men laden with heavy canes and guns. From speakers' platforms, Haralson had warned that Democratic rule would reinstitute slavery in a new form, and now events justified his prediction. On Dallas County juries, blacks once had equal representation, but now few served besides the favored barbers. About the only place in his region where blacks could vote freely was Wilcox County; otherwise Democrats "count just as they please." Haralson empathized with white Republicans, swearing that he would never submit personally to the sort of political abuse they received. More surprisingly, he spoke warmly of conservatives who privately assured him they were uncomfortable with ex-secessionist rule and the sheer lawlessness of Redemption. They had a point: though black-belt planters' material interests would be served well, Whiggish beliefs in activist government, their distrust of Democratic extremism, mattered no longer.[102]

All that remained of Reconstruction was the struggle for the memory of the era: who to blame for its failings and how the era should be interpreted. A one-sided version dominated public discourse, as few Alabama whites had any interest in defending Reconstruction. States' rights, ex-secessionist Democrats appropriated its emotional legacy, to buttress party regularity, and, if necessary, to excuse stuffing ballot boxes and worse thereafter. Dominant opinion valorized Confederate loyalty and a racial hard line, and it subsumed dissenters within the restored racial consensus. Reconstruction thus lived as a memory of federal oppression, when irresponsible "carpetbaggers" led an illiterate electorate to bankrupt the state. There were enough shards of truth to make it plausible and convenient to the players who counted in the new, Redeemed, Alabama. The state's Hilary Herbert and a host of Democratic politicians promoted this vision to a new generation, nationwide, in *Why the Solid South?* (1890). And as professional scholarship of the era emerged, Walter Lynwood Fleming, in his *Civil War and Reconstruction in Alabama* (1905), buttressed the white-supremacist version to the point of defending the Ku Klux Klan.[103]

Redeemers could never have sold this narrative so effectively without native Republican assistance, and animosity to Senator Spencer provided the impetus. Through the end of his term in 1879, and beyond, the scalawag/carpetbagger rivalry lived on over federal patronage and public legitimacy. The remaining white Republicans depicted themselves as loyal Alabamians, within mainstream racial views, as opposed to the African Americans who remained Spencer's sole constituency. As should be evident, their depiction of Senator Spencer had truth. Peculation and political manipulation clung to him like glue. But Spencer and his coterie of federal officeholders had little to do with the fatal railroad subsidy program. The freedmen and their representatives were only secondary players. To embrace the Redeemers' version of Alabama's financial ruin meant forgetting the Whiggish origin of the subsidy policy before the war, its enactment during Presidential Reconstruction, and Governor Lindsay's colorful malfeasance.

Republican officials deserved blame too, but, implausibly, Republican ex-governor William H. Smith became the symbol of scalawag acceptance. Appointed a judge under Governor Lewis, he led the opposition to the "carpetbagger" faction, helping split the state party in two. He reportedly denied claims of Democratic fraud in 1876, saying "the election was fair and peaceable."[104] He served for years as federal district attorney, his racial regularity outweighing his shoddy record in the Alabama & Chattanooga fiasco. In 1896, Smith abandoned the national ticket, which won him praise in the Atlanta *Constitution* as "the cleanest" among his party.[105] The ex-governor and his numerous family members entrenched themselves in Birmingham, his son becoming a leader in the "lily white" Republican faction. When Governor Smith died in 1899, few Democrats troubled to recall the ruin he had brought their state. Why should they? Despite his Unionist politics, he and they agreed white supremacy was the core issue of Reconstruction. By then, Redeemers had embraced Smith's tidy narrative of carpetbagger profligacy and black corruption, even on railroad issues. As that version of history ran, native whites escaped almost scot-free—and those that by now were described as "the people" of Alabama appeared united against the interlopers on the natural order of things. A generous constructed memory served Democratic purposes better than an accurate accounting. Even so, it took a charitable amnesia for newspapers to proclaim the late governor "so admirable, so loveable a man."[106]

In all the memorials of Governor Smith's passing, there is no evidence of African American participation. They knew what made Smith "a right grand old man" in the disfranchisement era, and they saw little worth celebrating.[107] Scholars have analyzed the eventual emergence of a consensual national version of the Civil War. In the public discourse on Reconstruction, a sort of analogous, Alabama reconcilationist version offered qualified forgiveness to scalawags.[108] Governor Smith's rehabilitation suggested that among native whites, bitterly divided over secession and war, all agreed on racial subordination and resistance to outside interference. Unionism and opportunism could be forgiven, but apostasy on race, never. Governor Smith's story, while otherwise troublesome, fit the unifying narrative they now preferred. Thus the evident falsity of the story was irrelevant. It encapsulated their truth, the one that ultimately mattered.

Bolstered by scholarly benediction, this version won nearly universal assent among whites, and it informed public opinion thereafter. Unionist acceptance of emancipation and black people as electoral allies mostly dropped from sight, as did the surprising restraint of the black leadership on civil rights demands. Conservative misgivings over fanaticism, their pragmatic acceptance of shared prosperity with some notion of racial co-existence—all forgotten. The state's political leaders sailed into the Second Reconstruction, encouraged by simplistic lessons of heroic white resolve, and by the class animosity the Redemption settlement exacerbated. These legacies encouraged the wild intransigence that characterized Alabama's segregationists during the mid-century struggle. Ultimately, perhaps, their flawed understanding of Reconstruction hobbled their defense of Jim Crow.

Notes

Abbreviations

AC	Assistant Commissioner
ADAH	Alabama Department of Archives and History
ALPL	Abraham Lincoln Presidential Library and Museum
AMA	American Missionary Association
AU	Auburn University
BPL	Birmingham Public Library
BRFAL	Bureau of Refugees, Freedmen, and Abandoned Lands
DU	Duke University
FSSP	Freedmen and Southern Society Papers
GPO	General Printing Office
HU	Harvard University
IHS	Indiana Historical Society
KKK	"Testimony taken by the Joint Select Committee to Inquire into the Condition of Affairs in the Late Insurrectionary States"
LC	Library of Congress
LSU	Louisiana State University
MHS	Minnesota Historical Society
NA	National Archives, Washington D.C.
NA-CP	National Archives–College Park, MD
NARA	National Archives and Records Service
NY	New York
NYT	*New York Times*
OHS	Ohio Historical Society
OR	Official Records of the Rebellion
SAC	Sub Assistant Commissioner
SCC	Southern Claims Commission

SHC	Southern Historical Collection, University of North Carolina
SHSI-DM	State Historical Society of Iowa, Des Moines
SHSI-IC	State Historical Society of Iowa, Iowa City
UA	University of Alabama
UNC	University of North Carolina
USA	University of South Alabama
UVA	University of Virginia

Introduction

1. Walter L. Fleming, *Civil War and Reconstruction in Alabama* (NY: Columbia University Press, 1905), 210.

2. The book was "often labeled one of the best" of the Dunning studies, Allen Johnston Going observes. See *Bourbon Democracy in Alabama, 1874–1890* (1951; Tuscaloosa: UA Press, 1992), vii.

3. Fleming, *Civil War and Reconstruction in Alabama,* 378. On Fleming's work, see Michael W. Fitzgerald, "The Steel Frame of Walter Lynwood Fleming," in John David Smith and J. Vincent Lowery, eds., *The Dunning School: Historians, Race, and the Meaning of Reconstruction* (Lexington: University Press of Kentucky, 2013), 157–77. And for a similar Dunningite venture along less scholarly lines, see John Witherspoon DuBose, *Alabama's Tragic Decade: Ten Years of Alabama* (Birmingham, AL: Webb Book Co., 1940).

4. W. E. B. Du Bois, *Black Reconstruction: An Essay Toward a History of the Part Which Black Folk Played in the Attempt to Reconstruct Democracy in America* (NY: Russell and Russell, 1935), 720; Horace Mann Bond, *Negro Education in Alabama: A Study in Cotton and Steel* (NY: Atheneum, 1969).

5. Peter Kolchin, *First Freedom: The Responses of Alabama's Blacks to Emancipation and Reconstruction* (Westport, CT: Greenwood Press, 1972); Sarah W. Wiggins, *The Scalawag in Alabama Politics, 1865–1881* (University: UA Press, 1977).

6. Among the more influential more recent works on Alabama are Margaret M. Storey, *Loyalty and Loss: Alabama's Unionists in the Civil War and Reconstruction* (Baton Rouge: LSU Press, 2004); William Warren Rogers Jr., *Black Belt Scalawag: Charles Hays and the Southern Republicans in the Era of Reconstruction* (Athens: University of Georgia Press, 1993); and G. Ward Hubbs, *Searching for Freedom after the Civil War: Klansman, Carpetbagger, Scalawag and Freedman* (Tuscaloosa: UA Press, 2015).

7. Sarah Woolfolk Wiggins, introduction to Fleming, *Civil War and Reconstruction in Alabama* (Spartanburg, SC: Reprint Co., 1978), viii.

8. This has been a focus of the author's scholarship. See Fitzgerald, *The Union League Movement in the Deep South: Politics and Agricultural Change during Reconstruction* (Baton Rouge: LSU Press, 1989); and *Urban Emancipation: Popular Politics in Reconstruction Mobile, 1860–1890* (Baton Rouge: LSU Press, 2002), among other works.

9. Early examples of this large literature include Eric L. McKitrick, *Andrew Johnson and Reconstruction* (Chicago: University of Chicago Press, 1960); John Hope Franklin, *Reconstruction: After the Civil War* (Chicago: University of Chicago Press, 1961); and Kenneth Stampp, *The Era of Reconstruction, 1865–1877,* (NY: Knopf, 1965).

10. Sven Beckert, *Empire of Cotton: A Global History* (NY: Knopf, 2014); Edward E.

Baptist, *The Half Has Never Been Told: Slavery and the Making of American Capitalism* (NY: Basic Books, 2014).

11. The typicality issue is the bane of all state and local studies. Given the centrality of cotton production to the narrative to follow, it would seem that the findings would be most relevant to other Deep South states. That said, the trends look familiar elsewhere. See my *Splendid Failure: Postwar Reconstruction in the American South* (Chicago: Ivan R. Dee, 2007).

12. Fleming suggested his study was "a general history with especial reference to local conditions in Alabama" (*Civil War and Reconstruction in Alabama,* viii). Since Fleming, few scholars have made strong claims for the unique character of this "heart of Dixie."

13. Perhaps because the Dunning school emphasized the topic, revisionists paid little attention to the railroad program. The modern overview of the topic is Mark W. Summers, *Railroads, Reconstruction, and the Gospel of Prosperity: Aid under the Radical Republicans, 1865–1877* (Princeton, NJ: Princeton University Press, 1984). A subsequent examination is Scott Reynolds Nelson, *Iron Confederacies: Southern Railways, Klan Violence, and Reconstruction* (Chapel Hill: UNC Press, 1999).

14. One might view this as an extension of the insights of C. Vann Woodward in *Origins of the New South, 1877–1913* (Baton Rouge: LSU Press, 1951), which highlighted the business sector as the eventual winners of the Reconstruction settlement.

15. Michael Perman, *The Road to Redemption: Southern Politics, 1869–1879* (Chapel Hill: UNC Press, 1984).

16. J. Mills Thornton, "Fiscal Policy and the Failure of Radical Reconstruction in the Lower South," in J. Morgan Kousser and James M. McPherson, eds., *Region, Race and Reconstruction: Essays in Honor of C. Vann Woodward* (NY: Oxford University Press, 1982), 330–31, 366, 391.

17. Samuel L. Webb, "A Jacksonian Democrat in Postbellum Alabama: The Ideology and Influence of Journalist Robert McKee, 1869–1896," *Journal of Southern History* 62, no. 2 (1996): 239–74.

18. Eric Foner, *Reconstruction: America's Unfinished Revolution, 1863–1877* (NY: Harper & Row, 1988), 425, 433.

19. Foner, *Reconstruction,* 401, 405–6, and see the discussion of the previous several pages.

20. To qualify this statement with some care, there were several voting-related riots in the fall of 1870. After the election, Klan raids continued in many places in early 1871, diminishing over the course of the year. No large-scale armed confrontations resulted, as the Klan episode wound down that fall. The next serious riot was in Eufaula in February 1874, the harbinger of major confrontations that summer and fall.

21. Perman, *The Road to Redemption.* One instructive interpretive disagreement between Foner and Perman is over the role of "New Departure" conservatives in bringing the Klan to heel by mid-1871. Foner states that this contention "cannot be sustained by the evidence" (*Reconstruction,* 434).

22. Steven Hahn, *A Nation Under Our Feet: Black Political Struggles in the Rural South from Slavery to the Great Migration* (Cambridge, MA: Harvard University Press, 2003), 6, 261–2, 265.

23. The field's emphasis on the early postwar years reflects the influence of the ambitious series Freedom: A Documentary History of Emancipation, 1861–1867, published by Cambridge University Press and the University of North Carolina Press. These papers basically end with the initiation of Military Reconstruction. Both the published volumes and the massive files have been mined by Reconstruction scholars, and Steven Hahn and numerous other influential scholars served as editors. The effect of this

early tilt has been encouraged by the federal records themselves, since the Freedmen's Bureau mostly ceased functioning at the end of 1868. See Ira Berlin, Joseph P. Reidy, and Leslie S. Rowland, eds., *The Black Military Experience* (NY: Cambridge University Press, 1982), and subsequent postwar volumes of the Freedom: A Documentary History of Emancipation series.

24. The terms "sharecropper," or "tenant" and the like do not appear in Hahn's index; nor can I find any sustained discussion of the evolution of plantation production.

25. Foner, *Reconstruction*, xxv; Hahn, *A Nation Under Our Feet*, 1.

26. The terminology here causes confusion, because in Alabama the opposition to Reconstruction adopted the name "Democratic and Conservative Party," in part to bridge the divisions within its ranks. So, as shorthand, the term "conservative" is sometimes used as a synonym for Democrat, both at the time and by later historians. This work, however, will follow the narrow definition, using the term for the more restrained, legitimist wing of the opposition.

27. Richard Zuczek, *State of Rebellion: Reconstruction in South Carolina* (Columbia: University of South Carolina Press, 1996); see also Douglas R. Egerton, *The Wars of Reconstruction: The Brief, Violent History of America's Most Progressive Era* (NY: Bloomsbury Press, 2014).

28. Woodward, *Origins of the New South*, 75–106.

29. K. Stephen Prince, *Stories of the South: Race and the Reconstruction of Southern Identity, 1865–1915* (Chapel Hill: UNC Press, 2014); Carole Emberton, *Beyond Redemption: Race, Violence, and the American South after the Civil War* (Chicago: University of Chicago Press, 2013); Hannah Rosen, *Terror in the Heart of Freedom: Citizenship, Sexual Violence, and the Meaning of Race in the Postemancipation South* (Chapel Hill: UNC Press, 2009); Elaine Parsons, *Ku Klux: The Birth of the Klan during Reconstruction* (Chapel Hill: UNC Press, 2016).

Chapter One

Note to chapter epigraph: File of James Pugh, Case Files of Applications from former Confederates for Presidential Pardons ("Amnesty Papers"), 1865–67, roll 9, M 1003, NARA.

1. The use of "conservative" in Reconstruction writing is confusing, in that the term is sometimes used as shorthand for the postwar "Democratic and Conservative party," both by contemporaries and by historians. For the purposes of this book, this term describes only the more restrained, realist political tendency within the party, as opposed to the states' rights or secessionist majority.

2. For an analysis of the trajectory of southern Republican leaders, see James Alex Baggett, *The Scalawags: Southern Dissenters in the Civil War and Reconstruction* (Baton Rouge: LSU Press, 2003), 270–71.

3. Daniel S. Dupre, *Transforming the Cotton Frontier: Madison County, Alabama, 1800–1840* (Baton Rouge: LSU Press, 1997).

4. J. Mills Thornton, *Politics and Power in a Slave Society: Alabama, 1800–1860* (Baton Rouge: LSU Press, 1978), 238. This discussion draws on Thornton throughout.

5. For an examination of one such Whig reform hotspot, Tuscaloosa, see John W. Quist, *Restless Visionaries: The Social Roots of Antebellum Reform in Alabama and Michigan* (Baton Rouge: LSU Press, 1998), 11, 20–21.

6. Thornton, *Politics and Power in a Slave Society*, 181–86, 201–3.

7. J. W. Lapsley, *Prospectus of a Combined System of Railways* (NY: S. W. Green, 1870), 18; Thornton, *Politics and Power in a Slave Society*, 279.

8. Thornton, *Politics and Power in a Slave Society,* 328–30; Donna McPherson Castellano, "A Promise Delayed: The Politics of Banking, Railroad, and Mineral Development in Alabama, 1846–1860," MA thesis, UA, Huntsville, 2001.

9. Malcolm C. McMillan, *Constitutional Development in Alabama, 1798–1901: A Study in Politics, the Negro, and Sectionalism* (Chapel Hill: UNC Press, 1955), 87. For a denunciation of secessionist zealotry on the issue, see William R. Smith, *The History and Debates of the Convention of the People of Alabama* (Montgomery, AL: White, 1861), 285.

10. For county returns, see Lewy Dorman, *Party Politics in Alabama from 1850 through 1860* (1935; Tuscaloosa: UA Press, 1975), 176–77, 26. The victorious Abraham Lincoln and the Republicans received no popular votes at all, not fielding an Electoral College ticket.

11. Of the identified non-leadership Republicans testifying in the Southern Claims Commission records, some twenty-one reportedly voted for Douglas, sixteen for Bell, and two admitted voting for Breckinridge.

12. Dorman, *Party Politics in Alabama,* 158.

13. *NYT,* Feb. 25, 1869.

14. J. C. Goodloe to E. M. Stanton [Sept. 1862], and J. C. Goodloe to E. M. Stanton, Oct. 17, 1862, both filed as G-1062 (1862), Letters Received, Records of the Office of the Secretary of War, RG 107, NA [FSSP L-25].

15. Claim of James M. Masterson, Lawrence County, reel 20, M 2062 (microfilm), SCC Approved Claims, 1871–80, NARA; Quist, *Restless Visionaries,* 322–23; *KKK* 10: 1977; Wesley S. Thompson, *The Free State of Winston: A History of Winston County Alabama* (Winfield, AL: Pareil Press, 1968), 114–29. On Peters's prewar views, see Paul Horton, "Lightning Rod Scalawag: The Unlikely Political Career of Thomas Minott Peters," *Alabama Review* 64, no. 2 (2011): 116–42.

16. Huntsville *Advocate,* Oct. 3, 1866; see also William L. Barney, *The Secessionist Impulse: Alabama and Mississippi in 1860* (Tuscaloosa: UA Press, 1974), 239–45.

17. Turnout declined by 20 percent, and in several black belt counties secessionists ran unopposed. Barney, *The Secessionist Impulse,* 268, 317–18.

18. Dorman, *Party Politics in Alabama,* 194–95. The identified delegate count would include L. C. Allen, J. Brasher, James S. Clarke, J. P. Coman, N. Davis, J. Ford, D. P. Lewis, S. C. Posey, T. J. Russell, H. C. Sanford, C. C. Sheats, and R. S. Watkins. Jere Clemens, who promoted Reconstruction before his death, should be added to the list. Among other sources, see Margaret D. Storey, "Southern Ishmaelites: Wartime Unionism and Its Consequences in Alabama, 1860–1874," PhD diss., Emory University, 1999, appendices 2 and 3.

19. Thornton contends that, whether immediate secessionists or cooperationists, voters favored some form of secession "in virtually every case." The emphasis on a proslavery consensus may be correct, but the misgivings of coerced Confederates mattered for Reconstruction behavior (*Politics and Power in a Slave Society,* 347, 414). For a different view stressing conservative reluctance, see Barney, *The Secessionist Impulse,* 267–316.

20. Smith, *History and Debates of the Convention,* 80–81, 74.

21. H. L. Clay to C. C. Clay, Jan. 11, 1861, Clement Claiborne Clay Papers, reel 4, in Ira Berlin, ed., *Records of Southern Plantations from Emancipation to the Great Migration,* ser. A, pt. 1 (Bethesda, MD: University Publications of America, 2001).

22. Smith, *History and Debates of the Convention,* 118, 447.

23. *The Private Mary Chesnut: The Unpublished Civil War Diaries,* ed. C. Vann Woodward and Elisabeth Muhlenfeld (NY: Oxford University Press, 1984), 20, 28.

24. Col. John T. Morgan to C. C. Clay, Feb. 17, 1862, reel 4, in C. C. Clay Papers.

25. Smith, *History and Debates of the Convention,* 117; claim of Joseph P. Bradley, "Amnesty Papers," reel 2, M 1003, NARA; Philadelphia *Inquirer,* Mar. 31, 1864.

26. J. C. Bradley to Andrew Johnson, Mar. 8, 1861, *The Papers of Andrew Johnson,* ed. Leroy P. Graf et al. (Knoxville: University of Tennessee Press, 1986), vol. 4: 370–71.

27. J. C. Bradley to Andrew Johnson, Mar. 8, 1861, in *Papers of Andrew Johnson* 4: 370–71; Thomas M. Peters to Stephen A. Douglas, Jan. 16, 1861, Stephen Douglas Papers, University of Chicago.

28. Philadelphia *Christian Recorder,* July 13, 1861.

29. The estimate is that of Storey, who gives 15 percent as an upper estimate and 10 percent as more probable in 1861. These numbers seem plausible based on later election results. See Storey, *Loyalty and Loss,* 16.

30. Col. M. R. Kinsey to Gov. Shorter, Dec. 6, 1861, in Anne Kendrick Walker, ed., "Governor John Gill Shorter, Miscellaneous Papers, 1861–1863," *Alabama Review* 11, no. 2 (1958): 215–16; G. Goldthwaite to R. Jemison, Apr. 9, 1862, *OR,* ser. 1, vol. 52, pt. 2: 299–300; claim of Zacharias White, SCC Approved Claims, Walker County, reel 36, M 2062, NARA.

31. G. Goldthwaite to R. Jemison, Apr. 9, 1862, *OR,* ser. 1, vol. 52, pt. 2: 299–300; Jemison to Gov. Shorter, Mar. 10, 1862, Letterpress Book, Box 3571, Robert Jemison Papers, UA.

32. Jemison to Gov. Shorter, May 15, 1862; Jemison to Sheriff T. Enis, May 12, 1862; L. W. Jenkins to Jemison, June 18, 1862; T. Enis to Jemison, June 15, 1862, all Letterpress Book, Box 3571, Robert Jemison Papers, UA.

33. Jemison to Gov. Shorter, June 17, 24, 1862; B. H. Wilson to Jemison, Sept. 5, 1862, Letterpress Book, Box 3571, Robert Jemison Papers, UA.

34. Storey, *Loyalty and Loss,* 7; claim of Shadrach Bray, DeKalb County, reel 7, SCC Accepted Claims, M 2062, NARA. The use of "grassroots" here conveys that known Republican political aspirants were not included in these totals.

35. Claim of William Sanders, Jackson County, reel 14, Accepted Claims, SCC, NARA; Michael W. Fitzgerald, "'He Was Always Preaching the Union': The Wartime Origins of White Republicanism during Reconstruction," in Kenneth Noe, ed., *The Yellowhammer War: The Civil War and Reconstruction in Alabama* (Tuscaloosa: UA Press, 2013), 221–38; Michael W. Fitzgerald, "Radical Republicanism and the White Yeomanry During Alabama Reconstruction, 1865–1868," *Journal of Southern History* 56, no. 4 (Nov. 1988): 592–94.

36. Claim of John McBride, Limestone County, reel 23, Accepted Claims, SCC, M 2062, NARA.

37. Claim of John P. Blackwell, Walker County, Disallowed Claims, RG 233, SCC, NARA.

38. Claim of John V. Gross, Jackson County, reel 12, Accepted Claims, SCC, M 2062, NARA.

39. Claim of J. R. Jack, Cherokee County, reel 3, Accepted Claims, SCC, M 2062, NARA.

40. Claim of Amon McMillan; claim of Jesse Swindel, Tuscaloosa County, reel 31, Accepted Claims, SCC, M 2062, NARA.

41. For specifics, see Fitzgerald, "He Was Always Preaching the Union," 227–28.

42. Col. Bush Jones to Gov. Shorter, July 16, 1863; Dr. A. J. Kirksey to Gov. Shorter, July 18, 1863, Shorter Papers; Pardon Request for Louis D. Edwards, Gov. Robert M. Patton Papers, ADAH.

43. C. C. Clay to J. Davis, Jan. 22, 1863; Gov. Shorter to Gen. W. Mackall, May 18, 1863, both in *OR,* ser. 1, vol. 52, pt. 2: 411, 478–80; J. H. Clanton to L. Polk, May 9, 1864, *OR,* ser. 1, vol. 39, pt. 2: 588–89. For the career of one dissident legislator, see Allen W.

Jones, "Unionism and Disaffection in South Alabama: The Case of Alfred Holley," *Alabama Review* 24, no. 2 (1971): 114–32.

44. Thomas Armstrong to Gov. Shorter, July 3, 1863, Gov. Shorter Papers, ADAH.

45. Fitzgerald, "Radical Republicanism and the White Yeomanry," 592–94; Dorman, *Party Politics in Alabama,* 176, 194–95; Barney, *The Secessionist Impulse,* 317–18.

46. Pillow to J. A. Seddon, Mar. 19, 1863, *OR,* ser. 4, vol. 2: 442–46.

47. Pillow to J. A. Seddon, Sept. 21, Oct. 5, 1863, *OR,* ser. 4, vol. 2: 852–53, 819–20.

48. Pillow to S. Cooper, Sept. 13, 1863, *OR,* ser. 4, vol. 2: 805–6. On Pillow's exertions, see Nathaniel Cheairs Hughes Jr. and Roy P. Stonesifer Jr., *The Life and Wars of Gideon J. Pillow* (1993; Knoxville: University of Tennessee Press, 2011), 259–75.

49. Watts to P. D. Roddey, Feb. 14, 1865, Gov. Watts Papers, ADAH.

50. John Clisby to Gov. Shorter, July 22, 1863, Gov. Shorter Papers, ADAH.

51. Macon *Telegraph and Confederate,* Nov. 23, 1864; Philadelphia *Inquirer,* Mar. 8, 1865; Malcolm C. McMillan, *The Disintegration of a Confederate State: Three Governors and Alabama's Wartime Home Front* (Macon, GA: Mercer University Press, 1986), 68.

52. Willis Brewer, *Alabama: Her History, Resources, War Record, and Public Men* (Montgomery, AL: Barrett and Brown, 1872), 286; Joseph C. Bradley to Andrew Johnson, Sept. 28, 1865, in Gov. A. B. Moore File, "Amnesty Papers," reel 8, M 1003, NARA.

53. For a similar use of the term "conservative" in wartime Alabama, see Christine Dee, "Trying James Hickman: The Politics of Loyalty in a Civil War Community," *Alabama Review* 58, no. 2 (2005): 83–84. The anti-party Confederate ideology complicated the terminology; see George C. Rable, *The Confederate Republic: A Revolution Against Politics* (Chapel Hill: UNC Press, 1994).

54. Application of William B. Hall, "Amnesty Papers," reel 5, M 1003, NARA.

55. James H. Clanton to Gen. L. Polk, May 9, 1864, *OR,* ser. 1, vol. 39, pt. 2: 588–89.

56. Wilson Ashley to Watts, Aug. 15, 1864, Gov. Watts Papers, ADAH.

57. Gov. J. Shorter to Pres. J. Davis, Oct. 22, 1862, *OR,* ser. 1, vol. 52, pt. 2: 381.

58. L. Benton to Shorter, Aug. 7, 1863, Gov. Watts Papers, ADAH.

59. Richmond *Dispatch,* Nov. 5, 1864; US Census Office, Eighth Census, *Agriculture of the United States in 1860* (Washington, DC: GPO, 1864), 225. In 1860, the categories of slaveholders owning 20 slaves or more in Alabama totaled some 6,031, but by this point in the war the exemption threshold was 15 able bodied slaves, so the number might have been slightly larger.

60. Edmund Fowler to Abraham Lincoln, Oct. 27, 1863, Lincoln Papers, LC; Montgomery *Advertiser,* Aug. 9, 1865; Application of Milton Saffold, "Amnesty Papers," reel 10, M 1003, NARA.

61. H. W. Walter to Gen. Bragg, May 8, 1864, *OR,* ser. 4, vol. 3: 394.

62. J. A. Campbell to M. Saffold, June 19, 1863, *OR,* ser. 2, vol. 6, pt. 1: 30; New Haven *Palladium,* Apr. 1, 1864. In general, it is difficult to determine how far the covert peace proponents in Montgomery were willing to go. For a nuanced discussion of their plans, employing different terminology, see Christopher Lyle McIlwain Sr., *Civil War Alabama* (Tuscaloosa: UA Press, 2016), 120–27.

63. Watts to Gen. D. Maury, Aug. 16, 1864, Gov. Watts Papers, ADAH.

64. Atlanta *Intelligencer* qtd. in Philadelphia *Illustrated New Age,* Oct. 3, 1863; Richmond *Examiner,* Oct. 30, 1863.

65. Watts to Maury, Aug. 16, 1864, Gov. Watts Papers, ADAH.

66. After August 1863, an estimated 2,835 Alabama deserters took an oath of loyalty to the Union. See the extrapolation in Mark A. Weitz, *More Damning Than Slaughter: Desertion in the Confederate Army* (Lincoln: University of Nebraska Press, 2005), 131.

67. A. J. [Walker?] to Sir, [Aug. 1864?], Governor Watts Papers, ADAH.

68. J. E. Saunders to Gen. Joseph Wheeler, Jan. 30, 1864, *OR,* ser. 1, vol. 52, pt. 2: 613–14; Thompson, *The Free State of Winston,* 82–85, 92.

69. Judge of Probate B. W. Starke et al. to Watts, [early Sept. 1864], Gov. Watts Papers, ADAH; Richmond *Dispatch,* Sept. 14, 1864; G. T. Yelverton to M. A. Baldwin, Jan. 15, 1865, *OR,* ser. 4, vol. 3: 1043–44.

70. Capt. J. P. West to Watts, Sept. 9, 1864, and T. A. Davis to Watts, Sept. 4, 1864, Gov. Watts Papers, ADAH.

71. S. D. Cabaniss to Watts, Aug. 18, 1864, Gov. Watts Papers, ADAH.

72. W. S. Rosecrans to Major Rawlins, Aug. 29, 1862, *OR,* ser. 1, vol. 27, pt. 2: 191.

73. Gary Gallagher, *The Confederate War* (Cambridge, MA: Harvard University Press, 1997); Joseph W. Danielson, *War's Desolating Scourge: The Union's Occupation of North Alabama* (Lawrence: University Press of Kansas, 2012).

74. Montgomery *Mail* qtd. in Macon *Telegraph and Confederate,* Oct. 2, 1864; Augusta *Chronicle,* Oct. 7, 1864.

75. Philadelphia *Inquirer,* Oct. 31, 1864.

76. Montgomery *Mail,* Sept. 28, 30, Oct. 8, 1864; Augusta *Chronicle,* Oct. 15, 1864; Chicago *Tribune,* Oct. 29, 1864; *NYT,* Oct. 23, 29, 1864; *Jefferson Davis, Constitutionalist: His Letters, Papers, and Speeches,* ed. Dunbar Rowland (Jackson: Mississippi Dept. of Archives and History, 1923), vol. 6: 345–47; claim of David Carter, Montgomery County, reel 29, Microcopy M 2062, NARA; Mobile *Advertiser* qtd. in New Orleans *Tribune,* Oct. 21, 1864. Other peace-tinged resolutions promoting negotiations were under discussion; see Montgomery *Mail,* Oct. 4, 14, 1864. For a cogent recent discussion of the episode, see McIlwaine, *Civil War Alabama,* 212–18.

77. Macon *Telegraph and Confederate,* Oct. 15, 1864.

78. H. W. Walter to Gen. Bragg, May 8, 1864, *OR,* ser. 4, vol. 3: 394.

79. NY *Tribune,* Oct. 22, 1864.

80. New Haven *Palladium,* Apr. 1, 1864.

81. M. E. Fulenweeler to Watts, Dec. 18, 1864, Watts Papers, ADAH.

82. General Orders, No. 6, Dec. 7, 1864, and General Taylor to Wm. Brent, Dec. 14, 1864, *OR,* ser. 1, vol. 45, pt. 2: 568, 688–89.

83. Gov. I. Harris to Davis, Dec. 25, 1864, *OR,* ser. 1, vol. 45, pt. 2: 732; Gen. T. J. Wood to W. D. Whipple, Dec. 30, 1864, *OR,* ser. 1, vol. 45, pt. 2: 423–24.

84. Gen. T. J. Wood to W. D. Whipple, Dec. 30, 1864, *OR,* ser. 1, vol. 45, pt. 2: 423–24; Watts to G. W. Malone et al., Feb. 2, 1865, Watts Papers, ADAH.

85. Montgomery *Advertiser,* Mar. 3, 1865.

86. Watts to Capt. G. G. Holland, Mar. 11, 1865, Gov. Watts Papers, ADAH.

87. Joseph Bradley to A. B. Moore, Sept. 28, 1865, in A. B. Moore Application, "Amnesty Papers," reel 8, M 1003, NARA.

88. Col. Horner to Gen. G. Granger, Oct. 25, 1864, *OR,* ser. 1, vol. 49, pt. 3: 434–35.

89. Giers to Grant, Jan. 26 and Feb. 6, 1865, in *OR,* ser. 1, vol. 49: 590–92; Milwaukee *Sentinel,* Feb. 2, 1865; *NYT,* Feb. 10, 1865.

90. M. J. Turnley[?] to Watts, Mar. 14, 1865, Gov. Watts Papers, ADAH.

91. Seibels to Lincoln, Apr. 14, 1865, *Papers of Andrew Johnson* 7: 694–96.

Chapter Two

Note to chapter epigraph: *The Diary of James T. Ayers, Civil War Recruiter,* ed. John Hope Franklin (Springfield: Illinois State Historical Society, 1947), 6.

1. One example of this tendency is Chandra Manning, *What This Cruel War Was Over: Soldiers, Slavery, and the Civil War* (NY: Alfred A. Knopf, 2007), which con-

cludes decisively in the spring of 1865. On the other hand, Gregory P. Downs, *After Appomattox: Military Occupation and the Ends of War* (Cambridge, MA: Harvard University Press, 2015), essentially commences its coverage at that point.

2. For a different emphasis but agreement on the harsh nature of the army's activities, see Danielson, *War's Desolating Scourge.*

3. Ted and Hugh H. Genoways, *A Perfect Picture of Hell: Eyewitness Accounts by Civil War Prisoners from the 12th Iowa* (Iowa City: University of Iowa Press, 2001), 31, 99.

4. Mark Grimsley, *The Hard Hand of War: Union Military Policy toward Southern Civilians, 1861–1865* (Cambridge, UK: Cambridge University Press, 1995), 61–66, 78–85; Large to Father, July 7, 1862, John W. Large Papers, IHS.

5. John Beatty, *The Citizen-Soldier; Or, Memoirs of a Volunteer* (Cincinnati: Wilstach, Baldwin & Co., 1879), 138–39; R. D. Williams to Col. Heg, Aug. 29, 1863, *OR*, ser. 1, vol. 30, pt. 3: 972.

6. E. J. Wood to Jane Wood, Oct. 30, 1864, in *A Fierce, Wild Joy: The Civil War Letters of Colonel Edward J. Wood, 48th Indiana Volunteer Infantry Regiment*, ed. Stephen E. Towne (Knoxville: University of Tennessee Press, 2007), 207–9. This letter talks specifically about protecting Sherman's rail lines, but it presumably also reflects his experiences with guerillas while stationed at Huntsville.

7. Grimsley, *The Hard Hand of War*, 78–85; Large to Father, July 7, 1862, John W. Large Papers, IHS.

8. William Stuckey to Wife, July 17, 1862, William Stuckey Papers, IHS.

9. Andrew Johnson to Miss Julia, Aug. 8, 1862, Andrew Johnson Letter, ALPL; A. C. Weaver to Father and Mother, July 5, 1862,Weaver Papers, IHS.

10. Entry for June 5, 1862, William P. Moore Diary, digicoll.library.wisc.edu/1711.dl/WIWillMoore.

11. Athens *Democrat*, Jan. 22, 1861, qtd. in Faye A. Axford, ed., *The Jones-Donnell Papers* (n.p., [1994]), 99; O. M. Mitchel to Abraham Lincoln, May 2, 1862, box 42, entry 210, pt. 2, Records of the Division of Appointments, Applications and Recommendations for Positions in the Washington, D.C., Offices of the Treasury Department, 1830–1910, NA-CP.

12. George C. Bradley and Richard L. Dahlen, *From Conciliation to Conquest: The Sack of Athens and the Court-Martial of Colonel John B. Turchin* (Tuscaloosa: UA Press, 2006), 109–25, 208.

13. Statement of Col. Turchin, Records of the Judge Advocate General's Office, General Court Martials, KK-122, NA. Thanks to Stephen Chicoine for sharing this material with the author.

14. Stephen Chicoine, *John Basil Turchin and the Fight to Free the Slaves* (Westport, CT: Praeger, 2003), 63–68; Athens *Post*, June 6, 1867.

15. Joseph R. Reinhart, trans. and ed., *A German Hurrah! Civil War Letters of Friedrich Bertsch and William Stangle, 9th Ohio Infantry* (Kent, OH: Kent State University Press, 2010), 267–70; S. S. Canfield, *History of the 21st Regiment Ohio Volunteer Infantry, in the War of the Rebellion* (Toledo, OH: Vrooman, Anderson & Bateman, 1893), 47, 54.

16. Jenkins Jones, *An Artilleryman's Diary* (n.p.: Wisconsin History Commission, 1914), 202.

17. Charles Wright Wills, *Army Life of an Illinois Soldier . . . : Letters and Diary of the Late Charles W. Wills, Private and Sergeant 8th Illinois Infantry* (Washington, DC: Globe Print Co, 1906), 206.

18. E. W. Keil, *Thirty-Fifth Ohio, A Narrative of Service from August 1861 to 1864* (Fort Wayne, IN: Archer, Housh & Co, 1894), 79–80.

19. A. C. Weaver to Father and Mother, July 5, 1862, Weaver Papers, IHS; Wise to Brother, Mar. 14, 1864, in "Civil War Letters of George M. Wise," ed. Wilfred W. Black, *Ohio History* 65: 69.

20. Ayers, *Diary,* 1; letter from W. Lyon, June 8, 1864, William Penn Lyon, *Reminiscences of the Civil War* (San Jose, CA: Press of Muirson and Wright, 1907), 147.

21. Albert M. Williams to Friend Mernie, Mar. 27, 186[3], Union Soldiers' Letters, Filson Historical Society.

22. Letter from William Wheeler, Apr. 1, 1864, *Letters of William Wheeler of the Class of 1855* (privately published, 1875), 445; entry for Jan. 12, 1864, Walter Carpenter Diary, OHS; Geary to Mary, May 1, 1864, in *A Politician Goes to War: The Civil War Letters of John White Geary,* ed. William Alan Blair (University Park: Pennsylvania State University Press, 1995), 168.

23. C. Cook to Parents, Apr. 9, 1864, in Chauncy H. Cook, *Soldier Boy's Letters to His Father and Mother: 1861–1865* (n.p.: News Office, 1915), 62; E. J. Wood to Jane Wood, Dec. 18, 1863, July 10, 1864, in *A Fierce, Wild Joy: The Civil War Letters of Colonel Edward J. Wood,* ed. Stephen E. Towne, 151, 189.

24. William Sumner Dodge, *History of the Second Division, Army of the Cumberland* (Chicago: Church and Goodman, 1864), 276.

25. Thomas Davis to Wife, May 28, 1864, in Thomas P. Nanzig, *The Badax Tigers: From Shiloh to the Surrender with the 18th Wisconsin Volunteers* (Lanham, MD: Roman & Littlefield, 2002), 250–51; H. H. Maley to Parents, Feb. 8, Mar. 8, 1865, Henry H. Maley Letters, University of Notre Dame, www.rarebooks.nd.edu/digital/civil_war/letters/maley/.

26. Claire E. Swedberg, *Three Years with the 92d Illinois: The Civil War Diary of John M. King* (Mechanicsville, PA: Stackpole Books, 1999), 184–85.

27. Bella Zilfa Spencer, *Tried and True, Or, Love and Loyalty, A Story of the Great Rebellion* (Springfield, MA: W. J. Holland; 1866), xi; Spencer to Dodge, June 19, Aug. 4, 1864, Grenville Dodge Papers, SHSI-DM. For an incoming letter suggesting Spencer's active antislavery sympathy, see J. T. Harris to Spencer, July 3, 1864, Dodge Papers. And on his varied entrepreneurial pursuits, see the interview in Cincinnati *Enquirer,* Mar. 2, 1877.

28. Entry for June 5, 1865, Ichabod Frisbie Diary, Emory University; Ayers, *Diary,* 2, 5.

29. Brewer Mattocks to Mother, Aug. 4, 1862, Mattocks Papers, MHS.

30. E. E. C. Sheil[ds] to Fox, July 31, 1862, Joseph B. Fox Papers, Filson Historical Society.

31. C. Demby to Wife, June 27, 1862, Demby Papers, LC.

32. Entry for July 2, 1862, William H. Kemper Diary, OHS. See also the lengthy tirade in Ayres, *Diary,* 47–50.

33. John M. Eaton to Jacob Eaton, June 9, 1863, John M. Eaton Papers, Military History Institute Manuscript Collections, Carlisle Barracks, PA.

34. C. Cook to Mother, Mar. 23, 1863; Apr. 20, 1864; and Cook to Doe Cook, Sept. 10, 1864, in Cooke, *Soldier Boy's Letters to His Mother and Father,* 27, 63–64, 92–93.

35. James H. Meteer to Caleb Mills, Jan. 26, 1864, images.indianahistory.org/cdm/fullbrowser/collection/dc008/id/392/rv/compoundobject/cpd/396/rec/4.

36. Weitz, *More Damning than Slaughter,* 128.

37. Oscar Lawrence Jackson, *The Colonel's Diary: Journals Kept Before and During the Civil War* (n.p., 1922), 92.

38. Dodge to R. J. Oglesby, May 2, 1863, *OR,* ser. 1, vol. 23, pt. 1: 246.

39. Sherman to Gen. J. Logan, Dec. 21, 1863, in *Sherman's Civil War: Selected Correspondence of William T. Sherman, 1860–1865,* ed. Brooks D. Simpson and Jean V. Berlin (Chapel Hill: UNC Press, 1999), 575.

40. Sherman to Major R. M. Sawyer, Jan. 31, 1864, and Sherman to John Sherman, Apr. 11, 1864, in *Sherman's Civil War*, ed. Simpson and Berlin, 601, 620.

41. Sherman to Corse, Oct. 24, 1864, *OR*, ser. 1, vol. 39, pt. 3: 421.

42. William Newton Price, *One Year in the Civil War: A Diary of the Events from April 1st, 1864, to April 1st, 1865* (n.p., n.d.), 38.

43. Thomas C. Honnell to Friend Sallie, Oct. 26, 1864, Thomas C. Honnell Papers, OHS.

44. Randall Ross, "The March of a Day," in Benedict R. Maryniak and John Wesley Brinsfield Jr., comps. and eds., *The Spirit Divided: Memoirs of Civil War Chaplains—The Union* (Macon, GA: Mercer University Press, 2007), 173, 175.

45. Wills, *Army Life of an Illinois Soldier*, 314–16.

46. August Horstmann to Parents, Apr. 27, 1864, Walter D. Kamphoefner and Wolfgang Helbich, eds., *Germans in the Civil War: The Letters They Wrote Home*, trans. Susan Carter Vogel (Chapel Hill: UNC Press, 2006), 127.

47. Gus to Father, Feb. 13, 1864, Van Dyke Letters, IHS; Ayres, *Diary*, 35.

48. Claim of Nancy Jones, Madison County, reel 25, M 2062, NARA; claim of Millie Richardson, Limestone County, Accepted Claims, reel 23, M 2062, NARA.

49. Thomas to Wilson, Mar. 6, 1865, in *History of the Army of the Cumberland: Its Organization, Campaigns, and Battles* (Cincinnati: R. Clarke & Co, 1875), vol. 2: 484; G. H. Thomas to H. W. Halleck, Apr. 17, 1865, *OR*, ser. 1, vol. 49, pt. 2: 376; letter enclosed in J. J. Giers to Gen. G. H. Thomas, Dec. 13, 1865, [C-30], box 1, Unregistered Letters and Telegrams Received, Department of the Tennessee, ser. 928, pt. 1, RG 393, NA.

50. B. F. McGee, *History of the 72nd Indiana Volunteer Infantry* (Lafayette, IN: S. Vater & Co, 1882), 525. The largest raid assertion is from Edward G. Longacre, ed., "To Tuscaloosa and Beyond: A Union Cavalry Raider in Alabama, March–April 1865," *Alabama Historical Quarterly* 44 (Spring and Summer 1982): 109.

51. Given overwhelming Union numbers, Wilson could have seized the plantation belt, captured besieged Mobile from behind, and then opened up a supply line upriver to the interior. For a similar assessment, see Montgomery *Mail*, Apr. 7, 1865.

52. Wilson to Badeau, Apr. 22, 1865, in James P. Jones, ed., "'Your Left Arm': James H. Wilson's Letters to Adam Badeau, *Civil War History* 12, no. 3 (1966): 239. J. H. Wilson to E. M. McCook, Mar. 30, 1865; A. B. Hardcastle to J. Rawle, Apr. 11, 1865, *OR*, ser. 1, vol. 49, pt. 1: 419, 505–6.

53. Report of Col. E. Kitchell, Apr. 7, 1865, *OR*, ser. 1, vol. 49, pt. 1: 452; John Hardy, *Selma: Her Institutions and Her Men* (1879; Spartanburg, SC: Reprint Co., 1978), 51; James Harrison Wilson, *Under the Old Flag: Recollections of Military Operations in the War for the Union, the Spanish War, the Boxer Rebellion, Etc.* (NY: Appleton, 1912), vol. 2: 232; Ambrose Bierce, "'Way Down in Alabam," in *Phantoms of a Blood-Stained Period: The Complete Civil War Writings of Ambrose Bierce*, ed. Russell Duncan and David J. Klooster (Amherst: University of Massachusetts Press, 2002), 292.

54. Report of Gen. E. F. Winslow, Apr. 9, 1865, *OR*, ser. 1, vol. 49, pt. 1: 484; McGee, *History of the 72d Indiana Volunteer Infantry*, 484.

55. Entry for Apr. 5, 1865, Alva C. Griest, "Three Years in Dixie," typescript, IHS.

56. This would be the 137th United States Colored Infantry (USCI), organized on Apr. 8, 1865. Frederick H. Dyer, *A Compendium of the War of the Rebellion* (NY: Thomas Yoseloff, 1959), vol. 1: 253.

57. Entry for Apr. 11, 1865, Griest, "Three Years in Dixie"; Wales W. Wood, *A History of the Ninety-Fifth Regiment, Illinois Infantry Volunteers* (Chicago: Tribune, 1865), 185.

58. Macon *Telegraph and Confederate*, Apr. 14, 15, 1865; Chicago *Tribune*, May 18, 1865; Report of Francis Salter, [Apr. 7, 1865], *OR*, ser. 1, vol. 49, pt. 1: 406–7.

59. Mobile *News,* May 7, 1865. The statue apparently featured a slave holding a deer by a chain, and Union troops found it offensive enough to dump it into Bienville Square fountain.

60. Entry for Apr. 23, 1865, Charles Henry Snedeker Diary, AU Archives. Entry for Apr. 26, 1865, Elijah Evans Edwards diary, MHS; Joseph Manson to Dear Friends, May 9, 1865, Manson Papers, Emory University.

61. I. Jackson to unknown, [early May 1865], *"Some of the Boys . . .": The Civil War Letters of Isaac Jackson,* ed. Joseph Orville (Carbondale: Southern Illinois University Press, 1960), 247.

62. James E. Sefton, *The United States Army and Reconstruction, 1865–1877* (Baton Rouge: LSU Press, 1961), 261.

63. Downs in *After Appomattox,* 39–59, similarly endorses the occupation's utility in repressing racial violence, but the book is less critical of the army's overall conduct.

64. Entry for Apr. 22, 1865, Benjamin R. Hieronymous Papers, ALPL; entry for Apr. 22, 1865, Elijah E. Evans Papers, MHS; Greenville *Observer,* rpt. in Montgomery *Mail,* May 1, 1865.

65. Wyman Folsom to Parents, May 8, 1865, W. H. C. Folsom Papers, MHS.

66. Charles Turner to Wife, May 14, 1865, Charles Turner Papers, ALPL.

67. I. H. Rowland to Wife, May 12, 1865, Rowland-Shilladay Papers, IHS.

68. A. L. Towne to C. A. Towne, May 28, 1865, Albert Towne Papers, SHSI-IC.

69. John Scott, *Story of the Thirty Second Iowa Infantry Volunteers* (Nevada, IA: n.p., 1896), 345–47.

70. Entry for May 19, 1865, John W. Pratt Diary, University of Iowa, Iowa City.

71. Entry for May 8, 1865, Elijah Evans Edwards Diary, MHS.

72. Entry for July 11, 1865, Martin Hursh Diary, IHS; Joseph Manson to Wife, Sept. 17, 1865, Joseph Manson Papers, Emory University.

73. N. B. Middlebrook to "Sue," June 15, 1865, Nathan B. Middlebrook Collection, Military History Institute Manuscript Collections.

74. On fears of vengeance by loyalist troops, see G. W. Cary to Gen. Chrysler, July 18, 1865, folder 2, Petitions, Gov. Parsons Papers, ADAH.

75. Mitchel to Salmon Chase, Apr. 20, 1862, in *The Salmon P. Chase Papers,* ed. John Niven (Kent, OH: 1996), vol. 3: 178–81.

76. F. A. Mitchel, *Ormsby Macknight Mitchel: Astronomer and General: A Biographical Narrative* (Houghton Mifflin: Boston, 1887), 327. J. H. Clarke to T. Comstock, May 5, 1862, Don Carlos Buell Papers, Filson Historical Society. J. R. Paul to S. Sharp, May 4, 1862, Mitchel to Stanton, May 8, 1862; E. Kirby Smith to Buell, Aug. 6, 1862, and enclosures, both in *OR,* ser. 1, vol. 10, pt. 2: 637–40, 174. Henry Villard, *Memoirs of Henry Villard, Journalist and Financier, 1835–1900* (Boston: Houghton, 1904), vol. 1: 290.

77. For a short critical overview of this episode, see Richard W. Griffin, "Cotton Frauds and Confiscations in Alabama, 1863–1866," *Alabama Review* 7, no. 4 (1954): 265–76. Fleming devotes an entire chapter to the postwar cotton theft and frauds; see *Civil War and Reconstruction in Alabama,* 284–303. On the other hand, Downs's recent *After Appomattox* barely mentions the subject, despite its apparent relevance to enforcing emancipation.

78. James Q. Smith to James Speed, Oct. 14, 1865, reel 1, in Frederick S. Calhoun, ed., *Letters Received by the Attorney General, 1809–1870: Southern Law and Order* (microfilm, Bethesda, MD: University Publications of America, 1998).

79. *NYT,* June 2, 1866.

80. Entry for July 8, 14, 1865, Elijah Edwards Diary, MHS.

81. Spencer to G. Dodge, Aug. 1, Oct. 14, 1865, Dodge Papers, SHSI-DM; J. S. Kennedy to Parsons, Sept. 23, 1865, Governor Parsons Papers, ADAH.

82. *NYT*, June 2, 1866.

83. T. C. A. Dexter, Benjamin F. Flanders, and William A. Orr, Aug. 8, 1865, Cotton, Administrative Files, SG 022954, folder 3, Gov. Parsons Papers, ADAH.

84. T. M. Tomeny to [Andrew Johnson], Nov. 7, 1865, Hugh McCulloch Papers, LC.

85. Chandler to Busteed, Mar. 20, 1866, W. E. Chandler Papers, New Hampshire Historical Society, Concord; Whitelaw Reid, *After the War: A Tour of the Southern States, 1865–1866* (NY: Harper, 1965), 204. It appears the officer in question was Dexter (Montgomery *Advertiser*, Feb. 22, 1867).

86. W. H. Tayloe to H. A. Tayloe, Sept. 28, 1865, reel 22, Tayloe Family Papers, ser. M, pt. 1, in Kenneth Stampp et al., eds., *Records of Ante-Bellum Southern Plantations from the Revolution through the Civil War* (Frederick, MD: University Microfilms of America, 1985), hereafter Tayloe Papers.

87. [Illegible] to Parsons, Aug. 28, 1865, Administrative Files, Cotton, SG 022954, folder 3, Governor Parsons Papers, ADAH.

88. A. Dunham to Brothers, July 29, 1865, Abner Dunham Letters, SHSI-IC.

89. Entry for July 20, 1865, A. H. Kerr Diary, MHS.

90. Bierce, "'Way Down in Alabam,'" 291, 293, 296; Roy Morris Jr., *Ambrose Bierce: Alone and in Bad Company* (NY: Crown, 1995), 97–102; Bert Hitchcock, "The Alabama-Bierce Connections," *Alabama Review* 38, no. 3 (July 1985): 222–38.

91. F. Reed to Mother, Sept. 4, 1865, Franklin B. Reed Papers, SHSI-IC.

92. With respect to both the cotton trade and the behavior of Federal officials, Fleming and his colleagues paid these topics considerable attention, perhaps because they illustrated preferred Dunningite themes. Modern scholars, on the other hand, have given these issues little sustained attention. In Alabama, however, these distractions clearly complicated the military function of repressing racial violence.

93. Lewis Parsons, Joseph C. Bradley and James Q. Smith to Johnson, May 15, 1865, *Papers of Andrew Johnson* 8: 75.

94. James Q. Smith to Johnson, Oct. 23, 1865, *Papers of Andrew Johnson* 9: 272–75.

95. See Downs, *After Appomattox*, 39–60, for a concurring account.

96. Entry for May 2, 1865, John W. Schlagle Diary, IHS.

97. One plantation memoirist viewed any outward joy as a "dangerous" indiscretion; see Eliza Walker, "Other Days," *Alabama Historical Quarterly* 5 (Summer 1943): 217; entry for May 16, 1865, Benjamin Hieronymous Diary, May 16, 1865, ALPL.

98. Entry for May 14, 1865, Lemuel Burke Diary, ALPL; entry for May 14, 1865, Charles Snedeker Diary, AU. For a physician's testimony, see "Message of the President," 39th Congress, 1st Sess., Senate Executive Doc. 2 (Serial Set 1237), 70–71.

99. Contracts dated June 26, 30, 1865; John H. Parrish to Henry Watson, June 19, 25, July 30, 1865, and J. A. Wemyss to Watson, July 14, 1865, Watson Papers, reel 2, ser. A., pt. 1, in Berlin, ed., *Records of Southern Plantations* (hereafter Watson Papers).

100. H. N. Herrick to Anne Herrick, May 18, 29, 1865, Herrick Papers, MHS.

101. H. N. Herrick to Anne Herrick, May 29, 1865, Herrick Papers, MHS.

102. Henry N. Herrick Diary, May 15, 1865, and H. Herrick to Anne Herrick, June 3, 22, 26, 1865, Herrick Papers, MHS.

103. See map in Downs, *After Appomattox*, 24.

104. P. J. Osterhaus to T. W. Conway, Apr. 15, 1865; C. T. Christensen to T. W. Conway, May 22, 1865; T. W. Conway to C. T. Christensen, June 3, 1865, all in *OR*, ser. 1, vol. 49, pt. 2: 363, 880, 954. T. Conway to Howard, June 5, 1865; T. Conway to Har-

mont, June 21, 1865, Letters Sent, Records of the Assistant Commissioner for the State of Louisiana, M 1027, reel 1, NARA.

105. Thomas W. Conway, *The Freedmen of Louisiana: Final Report of the Bureau of Free Labor, Department of the Gulf* (New Orleans: Times Book and Job Office, 1865), 24–25; Conway to S. S. Gardner, June 20, 1865, reel 1, M 1027, RG 105, NARA.

106. S. S. Gardner to T. W. Conway, June 12, July 3, 1865, reel 15, Letters Received, BRFAL, M 752, RG 105, NARA.

107. On this topic, see Michael W. Fitzgerald, "Emancipation and Military Pacification: The Freedmen's Bureau and Social Control in Alabama," in Paul A. Cimbala and Randall M. Miller, eds., *The Freedmen's Bureau and Reconstruction: Reconsiderations* (NY: Fordham University Press, 1999), 46–66.

108. Montgomery *Advertiser*, Aug. 3, 1865; Chicago *Tribune*, Oct. 25, 1865; C. W. Buckley to Conway, June 1, 11, 1865, reel 14, Letters Received, BRFAL, M 752, RG 105, NARA; C. W. Buckley to C. Cadle, Oct. 7, 1865, reel 5, Letters Received by the Assistant Commissioner for Alabama, BRFAL, M 809, NARA.

109. F. Reed to Mother, May 3, 1865, Franklin B. Reed Papers, SHSI-IC.

110. Wyman Folsom to Parents, May 13, 26, 1865, Folsom Family Papers, MHS.

111. George Harmont to T. W. Conway, May 30, 1865, vol. 108, Letters Sent, Mobile Subassistant Commissioner, BRFAL, RG 105, NA.

112. Martha V. Schroeder to G. Schroeder, Apr. 1865, H. A. Schroeder Papers, City of Mobile Museum, Mobile, AL.

113. C. Turner to Wife, May 28, June 7, 1865, Charles Turner Papers, ALPL. See Turner's stern orders against squatters and the pass system referenced in Montgomery *Mail*, May 16, 1865.

114. D. H. Whittle to O. O. Howard, June 8, 1865, reel 18, M 752, RG 105, NARA.

115. Col. L. F. Hubbard, HQ Demopolis, May 25, 1865, Letters Sent, 2nd Brigade, 1st Div., 16th A. C., [entry 6196], RG 393, pt. 2, NA; James to Sis Cathy, June 30, 1865, Cole-Taylor Family Papers, SHC.

116. Jonathan M. Wiener, *Social Origins of the New South: Alabama, 1860–1885* (Baton Rouge: LSU Press, 1981), 51; William S. McFeely, *Yankee Stepfather: General O. O. Howard and the Freedmen* (New Haven, CT: Yale University Press, 1968), 78–79.

117. Kenneth B. White, "Wager Swayne: Racist or Realist?" *Alabama Review* 31, no. 2 (Apr. 1978): 106, 109. For a sympathetic recent account, see Jason J. Battles, "Labor, Law, and the Freedmen's Bureau in Alabama, 1865–1867," in Noe, ed., *The Yellowhammer War*, 240–57.

118. Swayne to Howard, Sept. 11, 18, 1865, reel 17, M 752; Swayne to G. D. Robinson, Sept. 13, 1865; and Swayne to L. James, Aug. 1, 1865, reel 1, M 809, RG 105, NARA.

119. General Orders, No. 12, Aug. 30, 1865, reel 17, M 809, RG 105, NARA; Swayne to Howard, Jan. 31, 1866, reel 2, M 809, RG 105, NARA.

120. The army occupation that summer was heavily concentrated in the black belt and around Huntsville in the Tennessee Valley, so soldiers were well located to oversee emancipation. See Downs, *After Appomattox*, 24, 48.

Chapter Three

Note to chapter epigraph: Milton Saffold, "Letter of M. J. Saffold, 'Southern Aristocratic Republic! Versus Southern Democratic Republic'" (Montgomery, AL, 1866), 11.

1. Montgomery *Advertiser*, July 28, 1865.

2. For a broad usage of "Unionist," see Wiggins, *The Scalawag in Alabama Politics,* 5–17, and for the opposite tendency, Storey, *Loyalty and Loss.*

3. On the varied characteristics of Union occupation, see Steven V. Ashe, *When the Yankees Came: Conflict and Chaos in the Occupied South, 1861–1865* (Chapel Hill: UNC Press, 1995).

4. Jefferson Davis to Varina Davis, Dec. 15, 1862, in *The Papers of Jefferson Davis,* ed. Lynda Lasswell Crist (Baton Rouge: LSU Press, 1995), vol. 8: 549.

5. Braxton Bragg to Davis, Jan. 17, 1863, *Papers of Jefferson Davis* 9: 29.

6. Jere Clemens to Johnson, [Sept. 1863], *Papers of Andrew Johnson* 6: 346–47; Dee, "Trying James Hickman," 83–112, and more broadly, Christine Doyle Dee, "Land Worth Fighting For: Scioto County, Ohio, and Madison County, Alabama, during the American Civil War," PhD diss., Harvard University, 2002. Dee contends that around Huntsville the major division was between effectively neutral "conservatives" and the secessionist—emphatically Confederate—minority who demanded some show of symbolic or physical defiance. The conservatives defended Hickman to affirm their own pragmatism under occupation.

7. *NYT,* Jan. 28, 1861; Smith, *History and Debates of the Convention,* 117; Jere Clemens and Nick Davis to W. B. Figures, Jan. 11, 1861, qtd. in Huntsville *Southern Advocate,* Jan. 16, 1861; Louisville *Journal,* Nov. 9, 1861.

8. Deposition of R. S. Tharin, Oct. 3, 1862, Abraham Lincoln Papers, LC. Clemens's brief Confederate conversion was emphatic; he suggested hanging Judge Lane for accepting appointment at Lincoln's hands; see Clemens to Secretary of War, Apr. 4, 1861, *OR,* ser. 1, vol. 49, pt. 2: 34–35.

9. Jere Clemens, *Tobias Wilson: A Tale of the Great Rebellion* (Philadelphia: J. B. Lippincott, 1865). On his literary politics, see Wallace T. Hettle, "Curing the 'Sir Walter Disease': The Politics and Fiction of Jeremiah Clemens," *Alabama Review* 52, no. 3 (1999): 163–91.

10. Robert Seymour Symmes Tharin, *Arbitrary Arrests in the South; Or, Scenes from the Experience of an Alabama Unionist* (NY: John Bradburn, 1863), 14–16; Deposition of R. S. Tharin, Oct. 3, 1862, Abraham Lincoln Papers, LC; *NYT,* Sept. 25, 1863.

11. R. S. Tharin to Caleb Smith, Aug. 18, 1862, and Caleb Smith to Lincoln, Oct. 3, 1862, Abraham Lincoln Papers, LC; NY *Herald,* June 4, 1863; Tharin, *Arbitrary Arrests in the South;* R. S. Tharin to W. A. Stickney, Jan. 17, 1865, Faunsdale Collection, BPL.

12. Sherman to Major R. M. Sawyer, Jan. 31, 1864, and Sherman to John Sherman, Apr. 11, 1864, in *Sherman's Civil War,* ed. Simpson and Berlin, 601, 620.

13. The four counties mostly north of the Tennessee River reported 8.4 percent of the white population in 1860 (US Census, *A Compendium of the Ninth Census, 1870* [Washington, DC: GPO, 1872], 24).

14. Nashville *Union,* Mar. 2, 25, 26, 1864; Chicago *Tribune,* Mar. 17, 20, 1864; *NYT,* Mar. 14, 1864. There had been a preliminary gathering in Larkinsville, Jackson County.

15. NY *Tribune,* Mar. 24, 1864.

16. R. S. Granger to G. Thomas, Nov. 27, 1864, *OR,* ser. 1, vol. 45, pt. 1: 1099.

17. Lincoln to Stanton, Nov. 16, 1864, in *Collected Works of Abraham Lincoln,* ed. Roy Basler (Springfield, IL: Abraham Lincoln Association, 1953), vol. 8: 112; Giers to Clemens, Dec. 17, 1864, included in Clemens to William H. Seward, Dec. 22, 1864, reel 86, William Seward Papers, LC; J. J. Giers to U. S. Grant, Jan. 26 and Feb. 6, 1865, in *OR,* ser. 1, vol. 49, pt. 1: 590–92, 659.

18. Levy Dysinger to Harriet Dysinger, Apr. 6, 1865, Dysinger Collection, Huntsville Madison Public Library, digitalarchives.hmcpl.org/cdm/compoundobject/collection/p15431c01111/id/3/rec/11.

19. Storey, *Loyalty and Loss*; on the subset of Unionists who became Republicans, see Fitzgerald, "He Was Always Preaching the Union," 221–39; for the estimate of Union recruitment, see Richard Nelson Current, *Lincoln's Loyalists: Union Soldiers from the Confederacy* (Boston: Northeastern University Press, 1992), 103–7, 217.

20. Shorter to J. A. Seddon, May 8, 1863, in *OR*, ser. 2, vol. 5, 946–47.

21. William Stanley Hoole, *Alabama Tories: The First Alabama Cavalry, U.S.A., 1862–1865* (Tuscaloosa, AL: Confederate Publishing Co., 1960), 16.

22. George Spencer et al., to Johnson, May 17, 1865, reel 14, Andrew Johnson Papers, LC; Spencer to Dodge, May 20, 1865, Dodge Papers, SHSI-DM; Montgomery *Journal*, Oct. 16, 1874; Marylyn Davis Barefield, comp., *Historical Records of Randolph County, Alabama, 1832–1900* (n.p., 1985), 83–84. One brother's arrest precipitated the family flight; see R. T. Smith to Parsons, Aug. 3, 1865, Gov. Parsons Papers, ADAH.

23. NY *Tribune*, Oct. 22, 1864.

24. Selma *Times and Messenger*, Aug. 15, 1868.

25. Speech of Congressman J. H. Caldwell, *Congressional Record*, 43rd Congress, 2nd Sess., Appendix, 153–54; "Letter of M. J. Saffold, Southern Aristocratic Republic! versus Southern Democratic Republic," 7; NY *Tribune*, Mar. 24, 1864.

26. Claim of Washington Patterson, in Morgan County, reel 30, M 2062; NARA; J. Clemens to Johnson, Nov. 19, 1864, reel 12, Andrew Johnson Papers, LC.

27. *Papers of Andrew Johnson* 7: 545, 583.

28. Gen. G. Thomas to C. A. Dana, Jan. 21, 1865, *OR*, ser. 1, vol. 45, pt: 2: 622.

29. D. S. Stanley to Whipple, Feb. 15, 1865, and G. H. Thomas to Citizens of Morgan, Marshall, Lawrence Counties, & C. [Apr. 1865], in *OR*, ser. 1, vol. 49, pt. 1: 718–19, 506; J. J. Giers to Johnson, Apr. 27, May 14, 1865, and Morgan County Resolutions, May 13, 1865, in reel 14, Andrew Johnson Papers, LC.

30. Clemens to Johnson, Apr. 21, 1865, reel 13, Andrew Johnson Papers, LC; *NYT*, May 19, 1865.

31. Clemens to Johnson, Apr. 21, 1865, reel 13, Andrew Johnson Papers, LC.

32. Edmund Fowler to Abraham Lincoln, Oct. 27, 1863, Lincoln Papers, LC; Montgomery *Advertiser*, Aug. 9, 1865.

33. Montgomery *Advertiser*, Mar. 3, 1865.

34. Chicago *Tribune*, May 18, 1865; Montgomery *Advertiser*, Apr. 18, 1865.

35. Siebels to Lincoln, Apr. 14, 1865, *Papers of Andrew Johnson* 7, 694–96.

36. Montgomery *Mail*, Apr. 22, 29, 1865; J. D. Phelan et al. to Gen. F. Steele, May 1, 1865, Andrew Johnson Papers, reel 14, LC; Steele to C. T. Christianson, May 1, 1865, Frederick Steele Papers, Stanford University.

37. Montgomery *Advertiser*, Dec. 23, 1865. On the contending viewpoints, see Montgomery *Mail*, May 1, 1865.

38. Huntsville *Advocate*, Oct. 3, 1866; New Orleans *Times*, May 18, 1865; Bradley et al. to Johnson, May 8, 1865, reel 14, Andrew Johnson Papers, LC. Bradley and Parsons eventually signed both, though theirs were the last two signatures on the second petition.

39. New Orleans *Times*, June 14, 1865.

40. Manchester *Guardian*, May 13, 1865; Clipping, [Nashville] Press, May 31, 1865, in Lewis E. Parsons Papers, ADAH; Nashville *Union*, June 1, 1865.

41. L. E. Parsons and J. C. Bradley to Johnson, June 10, 1865, reel 15, Andrew Johnson Papers, LC; F. C. Taylor to Jemison, June 28, 1865, Jemison Papers, UA; Montgomery *Mail*, June 19, 1865.

42. D. H. Bingham to Johnson, May 4, 1865, Andrew Johnson Papers, reel 14, LC;

printed pamphlet by D. H. Bingham and J. Larcombe, June 27, 1865, alplm-cdi.com/chroniclingillinois/items/show/20752.

43. James S. Clark and F. W. Sykes to Johnson, May 21, 1865, and David P. Lewis to Johnson, May 21, 1865, Andrew Johnson Papers, reel 14, LC; Col. W. P. Lyon to Sam Kneeland, Dec. 21, 1864, *OR,* ser. 1, vol. 45, pt. 1: 638.

44. George E. Spencer to Dodge, May 20, 1865, Dodge Papers, SHSI-DM; J. W. Smith et al. to Johnson, May 16, 1865, reel 14, and G. L. Godfrey to Johnson, June 2, 1865, reel 15, Andrew Johnson Papers, LC.

45. Statement enclosed in J. J. Giers to Gen. G. H. Thomas, Dec. 13, 1865, Unregistered Letters and Telegrams Received, ser. 928, Military Division of the Tennessee, Records of US Army Continental Commands, RG 393, Pt. 1, NA [FSSP C-30]; L. E. Parsons and J. C. Bradley to Johnson, June 10, 1865, reel 15, Andrew Johnson Papers, LC. Bradley somehow headed petitions for both Seibels and Parsons, within days of each other.

46. Bradley to Seibels, July 22, 1865, Parsons Papers, ADAH.

47. H. W. Walter to Gen. Bragg, May 8, 1864, *OR*, ser. 4, vol. 3: 394.

48. "Record of Governor Parsons, of Alabama; Alabama Governors, and Alabama Slave Code" (n.p., 1866), 2; US Congress, "Report of the Joint Committee on Reconstruction," 39th Congress, 1st Sess., pt. 3: 60; claim of David Carter, Montgomery County, reel 29, SCC, M 2062, NARA.

49. Chicago *Tribune,* July 7, 1865; *Journal of the Proceedings of Convention of the State of Alabama Held in the City of Montgomery, on Tuesday, September 12, 1865* (Montgomery, AL: Gibson & Whitfield, 1865), 3, 9.

50. Paul H. Bergeron, *Andrew Johnson's Civil War and Reconstruction* (Knoxville: University of Tennessee Press, 2011), 74–76.

51. Montgomery *Advertiser,* July 26, 27, 1865.

52. Bradley to Johnson, Aug. 24, 1865; Application of A. S. Garner, "Amnesty Papers," roll 4, M 1003, NARA.

53. Bradley to Parsons, Aug. 30 and 31, 1865, Gov. Parsons Papers, ADAH; Bradley to Parsons, Aug. 31, 1865, Case of Steven B. Severe, "Amnesty Papers," reel 10, M 1003, NARA.

54. John H. Chisholm to Parsons, July 28, 1865, Gov. Parsons Papers, ADAH; Montgomery *Advertiser,* July 25, 1865; New Orleans *Picayune,* Sept. 27, 30, 1865.

55. Milton Saffold to O. O. Howard, May 23, June 17, and July 1, 1867, O. O. Howard Papers, Bowdoin College Library; entry for Nov. 28, 1865, Frank Gurley Diary, Huntsville Madison County Public Library, digitalarchives.hmcpl.org/cdm/ref/collection/p16458c01118/id/21/rec/22.

56. Joseph Bradley to Parsons, Aug. 18, 1865, in Septimus Cabaniss Application, "Amnesty Papers," reel 2, M 1003, NARA.

57. Joseph Bradley to Parsons, Aug. 11, 1865, William Powers Application, "Amnesty Papers," reel 8, M 1003, NARA.

58. John White to Parsons, July 25, 1865, Gov. Parsons Papers, ADAH.

59. Montgomery *Advertiser,* July 26, 1865.

60. Case of Eli Shorter, "Amnesty Papers," reel 10, M 1003, NARA. See Parsons to Johnson, Aug. 10, 1865.

61. Case of Robert Ware, "Amnesty Papers," reel 12, M 1003, NARA.

62. Parsons to James Speed, Aug. 22, 1865, in Case of Robert Ware, Amnesty Papers, reel 12, M 1003, NARA; Chicago *Tribune,* Sept. 8, 1865; Macon *Telegraph,* Sept. 8, 1865.

63. Mobile *Advertiser and Register,* July 23, 25, 27, 28, 30, Aug. 1, 2, 5, 1865; Parsons

to Johnson, Aug. 24, 1865, *Papers of Andrew Johnson* 8: 468; Parsons to Johnson, Oct. 2, 1865, in "Provisional Governors of States," 39th Congress, 1st Sess., House Executive Doc. 26, 97–98. In theory, all holdover officials had to take a loyalty oath, and those requiring individual pardons remained ineligible for the time being.

64. E. Herbert to Parsons, July 28, 1865, W. C. Hunter et al. to Gov. Parsons, [July 1865], folder 34, Gov. Parsons Papers, ADAH.

65. A. C. Wood et al. to Parsons, Aug. 2, 1865; E. B. West and D. P. Smith to Parsons, Aug. 26, 1865, Appointment Papers, Gov. Parsons Papers, ADAH.

66. W. H. Smith to Parsons, Sept. 5, 1865; J. T. Heflin to Parsons, Aug. 9, 1865; and M. Cruikshank to Parsons, Dec. 1, 1865, Gov. Parsons Papers, ADAH. See also John T. Heflin et al. to Patton [Apr. 1866], in Pardons File, Gov. Patton Papers.

67. M. Saffold to Parsons, Aug. 10, 1865, Parsons Papers, ADAH; A. W. Dillard to Col. Seibels, July 31, 1865, Applications for Sumter County, Gov. Parsons Papers, ADAH.

68. Bradley to Parsons, July 15, 1865; D. C. Humphreys and Joseph Bradley to Parsons, Aug. 14, 1865; Bradley to Parsons, July 13, 1865, all in Appointment Papers, Gov. Parsons Papers, ADAH.

69. Bradley to Parsons, Aug. 17, 1865, Gov. Parsons Papers, ADAH.

70. Gen. A. McArthur to Gov. Parsons, July 30, 1865, Gov. Parsons Papers, ADAH.

71. W. M. Byrd to Parsons, July 24, 1865, Gov. Parsons Papers, ADAH.

72. Montgomery *Advertiser,* Sept. 30, 1865; Wilmer to W. A. Stickney, Oct. 5, 1865, Faunsdale Collection, BPL.

73. *A Wisconsin Boy in Dixie: The Selected Letters of James K. Newton,* ed. Stephen E. Ambrose (Madison: University of Wisconsin Press, 1961), 164–65; R. L. Howard, *History of the 124th Regiment* (Springfield, IL: H. W. Rokker, 1880), 364–67.

74. B. F. Porter to Parsons, July 21, 1865, Gov. Parsons Papers, ADAH.

75. Alabama, "Journal of the Proceedings of Convention of the State of Alabama" (Montgomery: Gibson and Whitfield, 1865), 43.

76. Benjamin Arnett to Parsons, Sept. 27, 1865, Gov. Parsons Papers, ADAH.

77. S. S. Houston to Parsons, Aug. 29, 1865, Gov. Parsons Papers, ADAH. Bureau records contain much specific evidence backing this characterization of the southwestern river region. See "Message of the President," 39th Congress, 1st Sess., Senate Executive Doc. 2 (Serial Set 1237), 73.

78. T. Conway to W. Swayne, Aug. 31, 1865, reel 1, M 1027, NARA.

79. General Orders, No. 7, Aug. 4, 1865, in Swayne to T. M. Owen, Jan. 7, 1902, Wager Swayne Papers, ADAH; Swayne to Howard, Aug. 21, 1865, reel 2, M 809, RG 105, NARA.

80. Montgomery *Advertiser,* Oct. 28, 1865.

81. Philadelphia *North American and United States Gazette,* Sept. 5, 1865; Swayne to Parsons, July 29, 1865, and other memos on black testimony, folder 34, Parsons Papers; Parsons to Magistrates and Judges, Aug. 18, 1865, reel 16, M 752, RG 105, NARA.

82. Fitzgerald, *Urban Emancipation,* 45.

83. Chicago *Tribune,* Oct. 25, 1865.

84. Swayne to Howard, Aug. 21, Sept. 4, 18, 1865, reel 2, M 809, NARA.

85. Milwaukee *Sentinel,* Sept. 11, 1865.

86. Schurz to Johnson, Aug. 21, 1865, in Leroy P. Graf, ed., *Advice after Appomattox: Letters to Andrew Johnson* (Knoxville: University of Tennessee Press, 1987), 101.

87. Mobile *Advertiser and Register,* July 23, 27, 1865.

88. NY *Herald,* Sept. 22, 1865; Montgomery *Advertiser,* Sept. 15, 21, 1865.

89. *NYT,* Oct. 15, 1865.

90. McMillan, *Constitutional Development in Alabama,* 91; Montgomery *Adver-*

tiser, Sept. 21, 1865; *Journal of the Proceedings of Convention of the State of Alabama Held in the City of Montgomery, on Tuesday, September 12, 1865,* 39. An 1867 voter registration report lists 29,338 as the 1865 vote; see W. H. Smith Report, Aug. 22, 1867, [SS-707], 3rd Military District, pt. 1, box 1, NA.

91. Montgomery *Advertiser,* Aug. 20, 1865; New Orleans *Picayune,* July 30, 1865.

92. Philadelphia *North American,* Sept. 19, 1865; Montgomery *Advertiser,* Aug. 27, 1865.

93. Montgomery *Mail,* May 1, 1865; Montgomery *Advertiser,* Aug. 5, 1865.

94. S. Forwood to W. S. Forwood, Sept. 17, 1865, William Stump Forwood Papers, SHC.

95. *NYT,* Sept. 25, 1865. In his "Politics in the Lower South during Presidential Reconstruction, April to November 1865," PhD diss., University of California, 1963, 158, Donald Hubert Breese attempts to verify the prewar background, but he found only ten ex-Whigs and fifteen ex-Democrats. The actual proportion is thus difficult to gauge, but the reported profusion of Bell voters suggests former Whigs were plentiful.

96. Montgomery *Advertiser,* Sept. 29, Oct. 1, 1865; Mobile *Times,* Oct. 1, 1865. The editor of the *Advertiser* indicated that this had been a "carefully prepared tabular statement of the Convention."

97. *NYT,* Aug. 21, 1865.

98. *NYT,* Oct. 15, 1865.

99. Breese, "Politics in the Lower South," 164. Breese notes the concentration of strong Unionists in the Alabama convention, which was unusual in the South as a whole.

100. *Journal of the Proceedings of Convention of the State of Alabama, 1865,"* 42; McMillan, *Constitutional Development in Alabama,* 104; Montgomery *Advertiser,* Sept. 27, 1865.

101. *Journal of the Proceedings of Convention of the State of Alabama, 1865,"* 69; McMillan, *Constitutional Development in Alabama,* 104.

102. Philadelphia *Inquirer,* Sept. 18, 1865; Philadelphia *North American,* Sept. 19, 1865; Albany *Evening Journal,* Sept. 23, 1865; *NYT,* Sept. 17, 30, Oct 15, 1865; *Papers of Andrew Johnson* 9, 255–56; F. W. Sykes et al. to Parsons and B. Fitzpatrick, Sept. 19, 1865, reel 17, Andrew Johnson Papers, LC; Bradley to Johnson, Oct. 13, 1865, reel 18, Andrew Johnson Papers, LC.

103. *Journal of the Proceedings of Convention of the State of Alabama, 1865,* 17. The best account of the proceedings is McMillan, *Constitutional Development in Alabama,* 90–109.

104. Montgomery *Advertiser,* Sept. 22, 1865.

105. Montgomery *Advertiser,* Sept. 22, 1865; Charles Pelham to Governor Parsons, Sept. 17, 1865, Gov. Parsons Papers, ADAH.

106. New Orleans *Picayune,* Sept. 27, 1865; *NYT,* Sept. 30, Oct. 15, 1865.

107. Montgomery *Advertiser,* Sept. 20, 24, 26, 27, 1865.

108. *NYT,* Sept. 24, 1865.

109. Milwaukee *Sentinel,* Sept. 26, 1865; NY *Tribune,* Sept. 26, 1865.

110. *NYT,* Oct. 15, 1865; Parsons to Johnson, Oct. 2, 1865, in "Provisional Governors of States," 39th Congress, 1st Sess., House Executive Doc. 26, 98; Swayne to Howard, Dec. 3, 1865, M 809, reel 2, RG 105, NARA.

111. Parsons to Johnson, Sept. 13, 1865, *Papers of Andrew Johnson* 9: 75–76.

112. Parsons to Johnson, Aug. 30, 1865, *Papers of Andrew Johnson* 8: 682.

113. Parsons to Johnson, Sept. 1, 1865, *Papers of Andrew Johnson* 9: 12.

114. General Orders, No. 26, May 26, 1865, HQ 16th Army Corps, RG 393, pt. 2, NA.

115. "Instructions to the Officers," 39th Congress, 1st Sess., House Executive Doc. 26, 108–9; F. Titcomb to Gov. Parsons, Oct. 13, 1865, and Parsons to Col. F. Hobson, Nov. 14, 1865, Gov. Parsons Papers, ADAH. It appears Parsons organized the militia, but did not generally call it into active service, lacking arms and means.

116. W. Garrett to Parsons, Sept. 18, 1865, Gov. Parsons Papers, ADAH.

117. R. A. Hardaway to Parsons, Oct. 15, 1865, Gov. Parsons Papers, ADAH.

118. Johnson to Parsons, Oct. 2, 1865, *Papers of Andrew Johnson* 9: 167–73.

119. Swayne to Howard, Sept. 25, Oct. 2, 9, 1865, reel 2, M 809, NARA.

120. Boston *Advertiser,* Sept. 30, 1865; Johnson to Parsons, Oct. 3, 1865, *Papers of Andrew Johnson* 9: 182.

121. Swayne to Howard, Oct. 2, 9, 1865, reel 2, M 809, RG 105, NARA; Tuscumbia *North Alabamian,* Nov. 17, 1865; *The Liberator,* Dec. 1, 1865.

122. US Congress, "Report of the Joint Committee on Reconstruction," pt. 3: 6.

123. J. C. Parsons to Daughter, Nov. 3, 1865, Jeannette Hepburn Parsons Papers, ADAH.

124. Bradley to Johnson, Sept. 8, 1865, reel 18, Andrew Johnson Papers, LC.

125. Bradley to Johnson, Oct. 13, 1865, reel 18, Andrew Johnson Papers, LC.

126. In Unionist stronghold Winston County, in the fall of 1865, twenty-four ex-Confederate soldiers were indicted for murder, for executing draft evaders under orders. See H. C. [Spruke] to Patton, Sept. 7, 1867, Patton Papers, ADAH.

127. Bradley to Johnson, Oct. 13, 1865, reel 18, Andrew Johnson Papers, LC.

128. D. J. Burke to Parsons, Oct. 4, 1865; D. H. Blackman to Parsons, Sept. 7, 1865, Parsons Papers, ADAH.

129. US Congress, "Report of the Joint Committee on Reconstruction," pt. 3: 60.

130. Gov. Parsons to W. H. Crenshaw, Oct. 25, 1865, Gov. Parsons Papers, ADAH.

131. State of Alabama, *Senate Journal, 1865–1866* (Montgomery, AL: Reid & Screws, 1866), 28–31.

132. Bradley to Johnson, Nov. 15, 1865, *Andrew Johnson Papers* 9: 383. For a misreading of the figures, see Breese, "Politics in the Lower South," 238. If ex-Confederates dominated the new legislature, ex-secessionists still did not according to one future Republican, C. S. G. Doster (*NYT,* Nov. 25, 1867).

133. Bradley to Johnson, Sept. 8, 1865, reel 18, Andrew Johnson Papers, LC; Montgomery *Advertiser,* Sept. 13, 1865; Huntsville *Advocate,* Nov. 9, 1865. My calculation is that the black percentage of population by precinct is correlated with the vote for Humphreys by -0.502.

134. Mobile *Advertiser and Register,* Nov. 18, 1865; US Congress, "Report of the Joint Committee on Reconstruction," pt. 3: 11, 14.

135. W. H. Smith testimony, US Congress, House Judiciary Committee, "Busteed Impeachment Investigation," 40th Congress, 3rd Sess. (Washington, DC: GPO, 1869), 183. Winston County had a large Union majority, and in Randolph, the Radical R. S. Heflin was elected probate judge by a vote of 918 to 357 ("May 1866 Election Returns," SG 2475, Secretary of State Papers, ADAH).

136. US Congress, "Report of the Joint Committee on Reconstruction," pt. 3: 12.

137. Montgomery *Advertiser,* Apr. 28, 1871. Even Parsons's associate Cruikshank was appalled at the secessionist resurgence. See Cruikshank to Parsons, Nov. 12, 1865, Parsons Papers, ADAH.

138. T. M. Goodfellow to C. Fisk, Sept. 20, 1865, reel 25, T-142, NARA; J. Bradley to [Johnson], Sept. 28, 1865, in A. B. Moore Application, "Amnesty Papers," reel 8, M 1003, NARA.

139. Bradley to Johnson, Oct. 13, 1865, reel 18, Andrew Johnson Papers, LC.

140. Huntsville *Independent,* Feb. 10, Mar. 7, 1866.

141. US Congress, "Report of the Joint Committee on Reconstruction," pt. 3: 11, 66, 15, 61, 8–10. Strikingly, whites provided all of the congressional testimony criticizing Presidential Reconstruction in Alabama that winter.

142. Governor Patton decried the damage Unionists were doing, suggesting from Washington that it was "worth while to watch all such men." See Patton to J. Donnell, Mar. 15, 1866, in Axford, ed., *The Jones-Donnell Papers,* 116–17.

143. Mrs. M. C. Mulligan to S. Hurt, July 31, 1866, reel 1, AMA Papers; for specifics, see Fitzgerald, "Radical Republicanism and the White Yeomanry," 572–73.

144. Capt. W. H. H. Peck to Patton, July 14, 1866, Gov. Patton Papers, ADAH; C. Cadle to Capt. A. Nininger, July 28, 1866, reel 1, M 809, NARA.

145. Sheriff John S. Ogletree to Gov. Patton, Jan. 3, 1866, Gov. Patton Papers, ADAH.

146. S. A. M. Wood, to Gov. Patton, Feb. 13, 1866, Gov. Patton Papers, ADAH.

147. J. N. Settle to Col. G. W. Bruer, Sept. 24, 1866, Gov. Patton Papers, ADAH.

148. J. F. McGogy to Conyngham, Mar. 27, 1867, reel 29, M 1900, RG 105, NARA.

149. Sheriff G. B. Hall to Patton, June 1, 1866, Gov. Patton Papers, ADAH.

150. W. B. Wood to Patton, Nov. 3, 1866, Gov. Patton, ADAH; Montgomery *Advertiser,* Nov. 21, 1867.

151. A. P. Jones to Patton, Apr. 5, 1867, Patton Papers, ADAH.

152. C. Cadle to Capt. A. Nininger, July 28, 1866, reel 1, M 809, RG 105, NARA.

153. Anonymous to Governor Patton, July 21, 31, 1866, Gov. Patton Papers, ADAH; [R Theune] to C. Cadle, July 26, 1866, reel 31, M 1900, NARA.

154. M. H. Cruikshank to Patton, July 29, 1866, and B. T. Pope to Patton, Sept. 5, 1866, Gov. Patton Papers, ADAH.

155. A. M. Gibson and J. W. Moore to Patton, Aug. 16, 1866, Gov. Patton Papers, ADAH.

156. G. W. Jones to Patton, Apr. 8, 20, May 20, and [mid-May 1867]; G. W. Ash to Patton, May 27, 1867; James Forman to Patton, June 3, 1867, Gov. Patton Papers, ADAH. T. J. Moody to G. G. Meade, Feb. 8, 1868, box 2, District of Alabama, 1867–68, RG 393, pt. 2, NA.

157. F. L. Cramer to A. Hough, Nov. 21, 1866, and G. H. Thomas to Gov. Patton, Nov. 23, 1866, RG 393, pt. 2, District of Alabama, Letters Received, 1865–67, box 1, NA.

158. W. B. Occleston to J. F. Conyingham, Apr. 14, 1867, RG 393, pt. 2, District of Alabama, Letters Received, 1865–67, box 1, NA.

159. Copy of General Orders, No. 11, Sept. 27, 1865, in deposition of Green D. Bager, June 26, 1867, Letters Received, 1865–67, box 1, District of Alabama, RG 393, pt. 2, NA.

Chapter Four

Note to chapter epigraph: Gov. R. M. Patton to W. M. Connell, May 22, 1867, Patton Letterbooks, Gov. Patton Papers, ADAH.

1. The literature on Patton is rather sparse, but the short account by Dan T. Carter contextualized him well among his peers. See *When the War Was Over: The Failure of Self-Reconstruction in the South, 1865-1867* (Baton Rouge: LSU Press, 1985), esp. 45–47.

2. Mobile *Advertiser and Register,* Dec. 15, 1865; Swayne to Howard, [Nov.] 1865, reel 2, M 809, RG 105, NARA.

3. "Provisional Governors of States," 39th Congress, 1st Sess., House Executive Doc. 26, 109, 247–48.

4. Thomas McAdory Owen, *History of Alabama and Dictionary of Alabama Biography* (Chicago: S. J. Clarke Publishing Co., 1921), vol. 4: 1327–28; US Census, Population Schedule, 1860, Lauderdale County, 23, and Slave Schedule, 1860, 6.

5. Thornton, *Politics and Power in a Slave Society,* 279, 330, 359.

6. Ann Robinson King, "The Political Career of Robert Miller Patton," MA thesis, Samford University, 1972, 30–41, 47–48; Patton to P. [Beiune?], Jan. 20, 1868, Septimus Cabaniss Papers, Duke University; *Frank Leslie's Illustrated Newspaper,* Feb. 23, 1867, 359; Application of Robert M. Patton, "Amnesty Papers," reel 8, M 1003, NARA; Montgomery *Advertiser,* Oct. 14, 1865.

7. R. Patton to G. P. [Beirne?], Jan. 20, 1868, Cabaniss Papers.

8. Montgomery *Advertiser,* Oct. 15, 1865; Feb. 16, 1866.

9. William Garrett, *Reminiscences of Public Men in Alabama for Thirty Years* (Atlanta: Plantation Publishing Co., 1872), 738; *Frank Leslie's Illustrated Newspaper,* Feb. 23, 1867, 359.

10. Columbus *Inquirer,* Oct. 2, 1866.

11. Robert M. Patton, "The New Era of Southern Manufactures," *DeBow's Review,* After the War series, vol. 3 (Jan. 1867): 60.

12. Huntsville *Advocate,* Aug. 13, 1866; Columbus *Sun,* Aug. 7, 1866.

13. Patton, "The New Era of Southern Manufactures," 60.

14. Thomas Pearsall to Patton, Aug. 17, 1866, Gov. Patton Papers, ADAH. He added the word "probably" above "not" in the sentence, possibly fantasizing that slavery might be salvaged yet.

15. Bradley to Johnson, Nov. 15, 1865, *Andrew Johnson Papers* 9: 383.

16. Mobile *Advertiser and Register,* Dec. 15, 19, 1865; Montgomery *Advertiser,* Dec. 15, 16, 1865.

17. W. A. McClure to Gov. Parsons, Dec. [2], 1865, Gov. Parsons Papers, ADAH.

18. Swayne to Howard, Oct. 9, 1865, reel 2, M 809, RG 105, NARA; BRFAL, "Report of the Assistant Commissioner for Alabama for 1866" (Montgomery, AL: Barrett and Brown, 1866), 5.

19. John C. Burris et al. to Patton, Dec. 17, 1865, Gov. Patton Papers, ADAH.

20. Mobile *Advertiser and Register,* Dec. 23, 1865.

21. Sefton, *The United States Army and Reconstruction,* 261.

22. Mobile *Advertiser and Register,* Dec. 23, 24, 1865; Lieut. W. B. Cheetham to G. D. Robinson, 21 Nov. 1865, filed with T(D)-14 (1866), Letters Received Relating to Military Discipline and Control, ser. 22, Records of the Headquarters of the Army, RG 108, NARA [FSSP S-18]; Swayne to Howard, Oct. 2, 1865, reel 2, and Major Charles A. Miller to Swayne, Sept. 25, 1865, reel 19, in M 809, RG 105, NARA.

23. Swayne to J. S. Fullerton, June 13, 1866, reel 1, M 809, RG 105, NARA. For a discussion of Swayne's policies at more length, see Michael W. Fitzgerald, "Wager Swayne, the Freedmen's Bureau, and the Politics of Reconstruction in Alabama," *Alabama Review* 48, no. 3 (1995): 188–218.

24. Swayne to Howard, [Nov.] 1865, Dec. 22, 1865, reel 2, M 809, RG 105, NARA.

25. Swayne to Howard, Dec. 22, 1865, reel 2, M 809, RG 105, NARA.

26. Montgomery *Advertiser,* Jan. 17, 19, 1866.

27. Montgomery *Advertiser,* Jan. 2, 1866. Grant countermanded Patton and Thomas's request. See endorsement on Gov. Patton to Gen. Thomas, Dec. 30, 1865, in *The Papers of Ulysses S. Grant,* ed. John Y. Simon and John F. Marszalek (Carbondale: Southern Illinois University Press, 1967–), vol. 16: 54.

28. Montgomery *Advertiser,* Feb. 16, 1866.

29. Gainesville *North Sumter News,* Jan. 27, 1866.

30. Montgomery *Advertiser,* Jan. 17, 1866.

31. Montgomery *Advertiser,* Jan. 24, 1866; Huntsville *Independent,* Feb. 1, 1866; S. A. M. Wood to Patton, Jan. 31, 1866, Gov. Patton Papers, ADAH. See also J. Mills Thornton, "Alabama's Presidential Reconstruction Legislature," in *A Political Nation: New Directions in Mid-Nineteenth Century Political History,* ed. Gary W. Gallagher and Rachel A. Sheldon (Charlottesville: University of Virginia Press, 2012), 175–79.

32. Montgomery *Advertiser,* Jan. 14, 1866; US Congress, "Report of the Joint Committee on Reconstruction," pt. 3: 141. The state's caution on Black Codes is well established. "Alabama took moderate action compared to her sister states," one critical study observed. See Daniel A. Novak, *The Wheel of Servitude: Black Forced Labor after Slavery* (Lexington: University Press of Kentucky, 1978), 5–6.

33. Huntsville *Advocate,* Dec. 7, 1865; BRFAL, "Report of the Assistant Commissioner, 1866," 6.

34. Montgomery *Advertiser,* Jan. 17, 1866; S. Thomas to W. Swayne, June 19, 1866, box 1, District of Alabama, Letters Received, 1865–67, RG 393, pt. 2, NA.

35. M. H. Cruikshank to Judge of Probate for Winston County, Jan. 16, 1866, and Statement by Agent Benjamin Long, July 1868, Butler County, Supplies for Destitute, Administrative Files, SG 023024, Gov. Patton Papers, ADAH.

36. BRFAL, "Report of the Assistant Commissioner, 1866," 14, and Wager Swayne, "Report of the Assistant Commissioner for Alabama, 1867" (Montgomery, AL: Barrett and Brown, 1867): 5.

37. Montgomery *Advertiser,* Feb. 28, 1866.

38. Montgomery *Advertiser,* Jan. 17, 1866.

39. R. L. Walker to Patton, Apr. 23, 1866, Gov. Patton Papers, ADAH; BRFAL, "Report of the Assistant Commissioner, 1866," 12.

40. C. W. Gazzam, Bank of Mobile, to Patton, July 30, 1866, Financial Records, SG 023025, Gov. Patton Papers, ADAH; Sheffield & Weith [to Patton], May 31, 1866, SG 023025, Gov. Patton Papers, ADAH.

41. Patton to R. M. Reynolds, Nov. 11, 1867; James Robb to Patton, Aug. 18, 1866; C. W. Gazzam to Patton, July 30, 1866, all in Financial Records, SG 023025, Gov. Patton Papers, ADAH.

42. Patton to R. M. Reynolds, Nov. 11, 1867, SG 023025, Gov. Patton Papers, ADAH.

43. Montgomery *Advertiser,* Jan. 17, 1866.

44. Lawrence N. Powell, *New Masters: Northern Planters during the Civil War and Reconstruction* (New Haven, CT: Yale University Press, 1980), 157; Powell's estimates would suggest two to five thousand northerners engaged in planting in Alabama, though most lost heavily and soon returned home. The Macon *Telegraph,* Feb. 23, 1866, estimated five thousand settlers, and in 1868, the Montgomery *Mail* estimated that six thousand northerners had arrived since the war (*Harpers Weekly,* Apr. 18, 1868, 243).

45. Patton, "The New Era of Southern Manufactures," 60.

46. "Report of the Committee of the Alabama Association upon the Relation of the Colored Members to the Churches with the Speech of I. T. Tichenor, D. D." (Montgomery, AL: Barrett and Brown, 1865), 6; [R. Theune] to Kinsman, July 8, 1866, reel 31, M 1900, RG 105, NARA.

47. W. W. Garth to Patton, Aug. 10, 1866, Gov. Patton Papers, ADAH.

48. *Christian Advocate,* Oct. 18, 1866.

49. Fitzgerald, *Urban Emancipation,* 59–60, 72–73; W. H. Peck to O. D. Kinsman, Oct. 9, 1866, Letters Sent, SAC Tuscaloosa, reel 33, M 1900, RG 105, NARA.

50. J. F. McGogy to O. D. Kinsman, June 20, 1866, reel 8, M 809, RG 105, NARA.

51. B. F. Porter to J. F. McGogy, Aug. 18, 1866, reel 12, M 1900, RG 105, NARA.

52. Mobile *Times,* July 11, June 9, 1866.

53. C. C. Langdon to Patton, May 12, 1866; A. P. Gage to Patton, Aug. 30, 1866, Gov. Patton Papers, ADAH. Pendleton Colson to Semmes, May 17, 1866; William Knox to Semmes, May 18, 1866; Swayne to Semmes, Aug. 28, 1866, Raphael Semmes Papers, ADAH.

54. L. E. Parsons to Patton, Apr. 13, 1866, Gov. Patton Papers, ADAH.

55. A. W. Spies to Patton, Nov. 30, 1866, Gov. Patton Papers, ADAH.

56. Columbus *Sun,* Oct. 2, 1866; Swayne to Howard, June 25, 1866, reel 1, M 809, RG 105, NARA.

57. Mobile *Times,* May 29, 1866.

58. Swayne to O. O. Howard, Aug. 23, 1866, O. O. Howard Papers, Bowdoin College Library.

59. Patton to Andrew Johnson, Sept. 13, 1866, reel 37, M 752, RG 105, NARA.

60. Swayne to Howard, Sept. 14, 1866, reel 1, M 809, RG 105, NARA; Swayne to O. O. Howard, Sept. 21, 1866, O. O. Howard Papers, Bowdoin College Library.

61. Patton to Swayne, July 24, 1866, reel 8, M 809, RG 105, NARA; James Robb to Patton, Dec. 6, 1866, Gov. Patton Papers, ADAH.

62. Jacksonville *Republican,* Jan. 12, 1867; *NYT,* Jan. 14, 23, 1867.

63. *NYT,* Jan. 16, 1867; Gov. Patton to Dalton, Dec. 28, 1866, Gov. Patton Papers, ADAH.

64. Montgomery *Advertiser,* Dec. 27, 1866; Jan. 15, 22, 1867. Montgomery *Mail,* Apr. 17, 1867.

65. Calculated from *The Statistics of the Population of the United States,* Ninth Census, (Washington, DC: GPO, 1872), vol. 1: 619.

66. NY *Tribune,* Feb. 1, 1867. *NYT,* Dec. 22, 1866; Jan. 19, 1867.

67. NY *Tribune,* Dec. 28, 1866.

68. On the congressional debates, see Michael Les Benedict, *A Compromise of Principle: Congressional Republicans and Reconstruction, 1863–1869* (NY: Norton, 1974), 228–40.

69. Baltimore *Sun,* Feb. 15, 1867; Montgomery *Mail,* Nov. 24, 1867; J. J. Giers to R. M. Patton, Feb. 14, 1867, Gov. Patton Papers, ADAH; Memo by "G," [Feb. 1870], Gov. Smith Papers, ADAH; *Congressional Globe* (Feb. 12, 1867), 39th Congress, 2nd Sess., vol. 37, pt. 2: 1171. Smith's motivation for dissent is not altogether clear, because the bill had other provisions, and he was spoken of for appointment as provisional governor.

70. W. H. Smith to O. O. Howard, Dec. 20, 1866, reel 44, M 752, RG 105, NARA; Swayne to Howard, Jan. 24, 1867, reel 1, M 809, RG 105, NARA. Governor Patton and other Alabama officials rushed to Swayne's support (Gov. Patton et al. to E. M. Stanton, [Jan. 1867], reel 41, M 752, RG 105, NARA).

71. Montgomery *Advertiser,* Dec. 7, 1866; William Veitch to Patton, Nov. 27, 1866; A. W. Spies to Patton, Nov. 30, 1866; Patton to Dalton, Dec. 28, 1866; L. F. Mellen to Patton, Jan. 29, 1867, all in Gov. Patton Papers, ADAH.

72. Jemison to Cole, Dec. 6, 1866, box 1581, Jemison Papers, UA; Swayne to S. Chase, Dec. 10, 1866, Salmon Chase Papers, LC.

73. Swayne to Howard, Dec. 15, 1866, reel 37, M 752, RG 105, NARA.

74. Montgomery *Advertiser,* Dec. 8, 15, 1866; Huntsville *Advocate,* May 10, 1867; Johnson to Parsons, Jan. 17, 1867, *Papers of Andrew Johnson* 9: 611.

75. S. C. Posey to Patton, Feb. 26, 1867, Gov. Patton Papers, ADAH.

76. Montgomery *Advertiser,* Dec. 13, 11, 1866.

77. C. C. Clay to Virginia Clay, Dec. 12, 1866, reel 7, C. C. Clay Papers, in Berlin, ed., *Records of Southern Plantations,* ser. A, pt. 1.

78. Montgomery *Advertiser,* Dec. 30, 1866, and Jan. 1, 1867.

79. Montgomery *Advertiser,* Nov. 13, 1866; S. K. Rayburn to Patton, Jan. 28, 1867, Gov. Patton Papers, ADAH.

80. B. R. Tardy to Gov. Patton, Jan. 28, 1867, Gov. Patton Papers, ADAH; James A. Raynor to Patton, Feb. 11, 1867, Financial Records, SG 023025, Patton Papers, ADAH.

81. Patton to J. D. Coffee, Feb. 8, 1867, Coffee-Patton Papers, Tennessee State Library and Archives; Neander Rice to Patton, Feb. 18, 1867, Gov. Patton Papers, ADAH.

82. Patton to "Coffee," Aug. 7, 1867, Coffee-Patton Papers, Tennessee State Library and Archives.

83. Patton to Coffee, Feb. 8, 1867, Coffee-Patton Papers, Tennessee State Library and Archives; T. O. Glascock to C. Sumner, Mar. 17, 1867, reel 17, *The Papers of Charles Sumner* (microfilm, Alexandria, VA: Chadwick-Healey, 1988).

84. James A. Raynor to Patton, Nov. 11, 1867, and Jan. 23, 1868; Raynor and Williams to Patton, Jan. 29, 1868, Financial Papers, SG 023025, Gov. Patton Papers, ADAH.

85. Willis G. Clark, *History of Education in Alabama, 1702–1889* (Washington, DC: GPO, 1889), 243–44.

86. Patton to W. G. Clark, May 30, 1867, Secretary's Letterbook, 1867, Gov. Patton Papers, ADAH.

87. Robert Jemison to C. Waddell, Aug. 20, Sept. 1, 1867, Letterbooks, box 3572, 1864–68, Robert M. Jemison Papers, UA.

88. Patton to J. A. Raynor, May 16, 1867, Secretary's Letterbook, 1867, Gov. Patton Papers, ADAH.

89. Patton to James A. Raynor, May 13, 1867, Secretary's Letterbook, 1867, Gov. Patton Papers, ADAH.

90. Patton to William S. Williams, May 14, 1867, Secretary's Letterbook, 1867, Gov. Patton Papers, ADAH.

91. Jemison to "Ma," June 28, July 4, 19, 21, 1868; Jemison to "Gent.," [Sept. 1868], Robert Jemison Papers, AU.

Chapter Five

Note to chapter epigraph: Gainesville *North Sumter County News,* Feb. 9, 1867.

1. Hahn, *A Nation Under Our Feet,* 5.

2. Hahn, *A Nation Under Our Feet,* 13–61.

3. George P. Rawick, ed., *The American Slave: A Composite Autobiography* (Westport, CT: Greenwood Press, 1972), vol. 6: 46, 103–4.

4. Calculated from US Census, *A Compendium of the Ninth Census, 1870,* 457, 554.

5. Daniel R. Hundley, *Social Relations in Our Southern States* (1860; rev. ed., Baton Rouge: LSU Press, 1979), 352.

6. Rawick, ed., *The American Slave* 6: 46, 173.

7. Rawick, ed., *The American Slave* 6: 329.

8. Sara Wood, "To the Cleveland Freedmen's Union Commission: A Report of the Progress of Education among the Freedmen of Alabama" (Montgomery, AL, 1866), 3.

9. Walter L. Fleming, ed., *Documentary History of Reconstruction: Political, Military, Social, Religious, Educational & Industrial, 1865 to the Present Time* (Cleveland: Arthur H. Clark Co., 1906), vol. 1: 92.

10. The figure comes to 91.2 percent, calculated from US Census, *A Compendium of the Ninth Census, 1870,* 548–50.

11. Calculated from US Census, *A Compendium of the Ninth Census, 1870,* 24–25.

12. The statistic is based on a 1 percent sample of the population census, as prepared for the Integrated Public Use Microdata Series, version 5.0 (machine-readable database, Minneapolis: University of Minnesota, 2010), by Steven Ruggles, J. Trent Alexander, Katie Genadek, Ronald Goeken, Matthew B. Schroeder, and Matthew Sobek, with the assistance of St. Olaf College's Professor Paul Roback and students Thomas Hegland, Eric King, and Charlotte Sivanich, hereafter cited as IPUMS.

13. Fitzgerald, *Urban Emancipation,* 15.

14. James Benson Sellers, *Slavery in Alabama* (1950; 2nd ed., University: UA Press, 1964), 363.

15. See "Petitions to Become Slaves," Records of the Probate Court of Mobile County, Mobile County Courthouse.

16. Mobile *Nationalis*t, Apr. 26, 1866.

17. D. H. Maury to S. Cooper, Nov. 7, 1863, *OR,* ser. 4, vol. 2: 941.

18. Some sixteen of forty-five, or 35 percent, were free before war's end. Of a larger sample located, some forty-four of ninety-two, almost half, were described as mulattoes. One suspects some upwards bias, but they are dramatic figures nonetheless. These numbers were derived by tabulating the Alabama officeholders and activists identified in Eric Foner's biographical dictionary, but omitting the local policemen and adding some additional information from my research. See Eric Foner, *Freedom's Lawmakers: A Directory of Black Officeholders During Reconstruction* (rev. ed., Baton Rouge: LSU Press, 1996); Richard Bailey, *Neither Carpetbaggers Nor Scalawags: Black Officeholders during the Reconstruction of Alabama, 1867–1878* (5th ed., Montgomery, AL: New South Books, 2010), 356–67.

19. Loren Schweninger, *James T. Rapier and Reconstruction* (Chicago: University of Chicago Press, 1978), 18–19, 30; Fitzgerald, *Urban Emancipation,* 12–13, 16.

20. Ophelia Taylor Pinkard and Barbara Clayton Clark, *Descendants of Shandy Wesley Jones and Evalina Love Jones: The Story of an African American Family of Tuscaloosa, Alabama* (Baltimore: Gateway Press, 1993), 5, 123, 188. Also see Hubbs, *Searching for Freedom after the Civil War,* 98–157.

21. John S. Lupold and Thomas L. French Jr., *Bridging Deep South Rivers: The Life and Legend of Horace King* (Athens: University of Georgia Press, 2004), 123–28.

22. Charles O. Boothe, *Cyclopedia of the Colored Baptists of Alabama, Their Leaders and their Work* (Birmingham: Alabama Publishing Co., 1895), 138–39.

23. Claim of Benjamin Sterling Turner, reel 6, Dallas County, SCC, M 2062, NARA.

24. Charles A. Brown, "John Dozier: A Member of the General Assembly of Alabama, 1872–1873 and 1873–1874," *Negro History Bulletin* 26, no. 3 (Dec. 1962): 113–14; Charles A. Brown, "Reconstruction Legislators in Alabama," *Negro History Bulletin* 26, no. 6 (Mar. 1962): 198–99; Charles A. Brown, "Lloyd Leftwich, Alabama State Senator," *Negro History Bulletin* 25, no. 6 (Feb. 1963): 161–62; Charles A. Brown, "A. H. Curtis: An Alabama Legislator 1870–1876, with Glimpses into Reconstruction," *Negro History Bulletin* 25, no. 5 (Feb. 1962): 99–101.

25. Hardy, *Selma,* 76; *"Fear God and Walk Humbly": The Agricultural Journal of James Mallory, 1843–1877,* ed. Grady McWhiney, Warner O. Moore Jr., and Robert F. Pace (Tuscaloosa: UA Press, 1997), 274–75.

26. Entries for May 21–31, 1861, Daniel R. Hundley Diary, UA. One free black suffered torture and coerced re-enslavement, then tried to collect restitution after the war (A. Patterson to J. B. Callis, Feb. 11, 1866, Letters Received SAC Huntsville, reel 14, M 1900, RG 105, NARA).

27. Claim of Margaret Butler, reel 31, Shelby County, M 2062, NARA.

28. Rawick, ed., *The American Slave* 6: 53, 338, 340–41.

29. Claim of John H. Berry, reel 24, Madison County, M 2062, NARA. For other assertions of emphatic loyalty, see claim of Henry Hall, reel 6, Dallas County; claim of Henry Slaughter, reel 3, Morgan County; and claim of Ellen Pinson, reel 3, Cherokee County, M 2062, NARA.

30. Claim of Thomas McFarland, reel 26, Madison County, M 2062, NARA.

31. Claim of John H. Berry, reel 24, Madison County, M 2062, NARA.

32. Claim of Edgar Watkins, reel 20, Lawrence County; claims of Ogden and Haynes, and claim of Archibald Steele, reel 26, Madison County, all in M 2062, NARA.

33. Claims of Ogden and Haynes, and Thomas McFarland, reel 26, Madison County, M 2062, NARA.

34. Berlin et al., eds., *The Black Military Experience*, 12.

35. Claim of Henry Hall, reel 6, Dallas County, M 2062, NARA.

36. Claim of Henry Hall, reel 6, Dallas County, M 2062, NARA.

37. *OR*, ser. 1, vol. 52, pt. 2: 352.

38. Letter to Mother, Dec. 22, 1862, George Doherty Johnson Papers, UA; Ira Berlin, Barbara J. Fields, Thavolia Glymph, Joseph P. Reidy, and Leslie S. Rowland, eds., *The Destruction of Slavery*, Freedom: A Documentary History of Emancipation, 1861–1867, ser. 1, vol. 1 (NY: Cambridge University Press, 1985), 756–58.

39. Berlin et al., eds., *The Destruction of Slavery*, 722, 738–41; Fitzgerald, *Urban Emancipation*, 20.

40. Walter J. Morris to Lieut. Col. E. Surget, Nov. 9, 1864, #1677 (1864), Letters and Telegrams Received, ser. 93, Department of Alabama, Mississippi, and East Louisiana, Records of Military Commands, War Department Collection of Confederate Records, RG 109, NA [FSSP F-208].

41. Montgomery *Mail*, Apr. 8, 1865.

42. Lt. Col. J. Strickton to Col. Hough, May 31, 1865, reel 24, M 1900, NARA.

43. H. E. Sterkx, "William C. Jordan and Reconstruction in Bullock County, Alabama," *Alabama Review* 15, no. 1 (1962): 64–65.

44. Walker, "Other Days," 217.

45. R. Jemison to Col. Thomas, June 21, 1865, Letterbook, box 3572, Jemison Papers, UA.

46. Maria [Walker?] to Augusta H. Rice, May 15, 1865, Rice Family Papers, Mississippi State University, Starkville.

47. Montgomery *Mail*, May 26, 1865; H. Traber to Sister, June 25, 1865, Henry J. Traber Papers, Wisconsin Historical Society. W. H. Tayloe to "Henry," June 22, 1865, reel 22, Tayloe Papers, Stampp, ed., *Records of Ante-bellum Southern Plantations*, ser. M, pt. 1.

48. J. A. Wemyss to Watson, July 14, 1865, Watson Papers.

49. Entry for June 3, 1865, Diary of Joshua Burns Moore, ADAH.

50. Contract dated June 17, 1865, Labor Records, 765.5.19, Faunsdale Papers, BPL.

51. J. Manson to Wife, Aug. 7, 1865, Joseph Manson Papers, Emory University.

52. This is becoming the standard view; see Anthony E. Kaye, *Joining Places: Slave Neighborhoods in the Old South* (Chapel Hill: UNC Press, 2007), 52–61.

53. On the general pattern of behavior after emancipation, see Leon F. Litwack, *Been in the Storm So Long: The Aftermath of Slavery* (NY: Random House, 1979).

54. C. Gayle to Mr. Watson, Oct. 28, 1865, Watson Papers.

55. George Shorkley to Maj. Kinsman, June 4, 1867, reel 28, M 1900, RG 105, NARA.

56. Pierce to Swayne, Oct. 25, 1866, reel 9, M 1900, RG 105, NARA.

57. Gainesville *North Sumter News*, June 6, 1866.

58. Swayne to Clay, Dec. 15, 1866, reel 7, C. C. Clay Papers.

59. Columbus *Enquirer,* Sept. 8, 1865; Swayne to M. Meigs, Jan. 3, 1866, reel 1, M 809, RG 105, NARA.

60. Steven Hahn, Steven F. Miller, Susan E. O'Donovan, John C. Rodrigue, and Leslie S. Rowland, eds., *Land and Labor, 1865,* Freedom: A Documentary History of Emancipation, 1861–1867, ser. 3, vol. 1 (Chapel Hill: UNC Press, 2008), 386–87.

61. C. Fisk to O. O. Howard, Sept. 2, 1865, reel 14, M 752, RG 105, NARA; W. H. Tayloe to H. A. Tayloe, Oct. 21, 1865, reel 22, Tayloe Papers.

62. N. A. Matheson to Swayne, Oct. 11, 1866, and Thomas L. Bevill to C. W. Pierce, May 29, 1866, in René Hayden, Anthony E. Kaye, Kate Masur, Steven F. Miller, Susan E. O'Donovan, Leslie S. Rowland, and Stephen A. West, eds., *Land and Labor, 1866–1867,* Freedom: A Documentary History of Emancipation, 1861–1867, ser. 3, vol. 2 (Chapel Hill: UNC Press, 2013), 166–67, 139–40.

63. General Orders, No. 12, Aug. 30, 1865, reel 17, M 809, RG 105, NARA; Swayne to Howard, Jan. 31, 1866, reel 2, M 809, RG 105, NARA.

64. Crydenwise to Parents and All, June 25, Aug. 7, 1865, Henry Crydenwise Papers, Emory University.

65. Hahn et al., eds., *Land and Labor, 1865,* 304–5.

66. Montgomery *Advertiser,* Aug. 3, 1865; L. Brown to C. Cadle, [early] Dec. 1865, reel 11, M 1900, RG 105, NARA.

67. T. W. Moysten to C. Cadle, Dec. 21, 1865, reel 11, M 1900, RG 105, NARA.

68. Swayne to Howard, Oct. 8, 1865, reel 2, M 809, RG 105, NARA.

69. Hahn et al., eds., *Land and Labor, 1865,* 811–13.

70. James H. Clanton to Gov. Parsons, Oct. 20, 1865, Gov. Parsons Papers, ADAH.

71. C. Gayle to Mr. Watson, Oct. 28, 1865, Watson Papers.

72. Swayne to C. R. Woods, Dec. 28, 1865; Swayne to "Commanding Officer of the Militia in Lowndes County," Dec. 28, 1865, reel 1; and Swayne to Howard, Jan 31, 1866, reel 2, M 809, RG 105, NARA. Montgomery *Advertiser,* Sept. 5, 1865. T. B. Cooper to Patton, Jan. 5, 1866, Gov. Patton Papers, ADAH.

73. See Grant's endorsement on Gov. Patton to Gen. Thomas, Dec. 30, 1865, *Papers of Ulysses S. Grant* 16: 54.

74. Mobile *Nationalist,* Feb. 15, 1866.

75. Chaplain W. C. Kephart to Tappan, May 9, 1864, reel 1, AMA Papers.

76. I. T. Tichenor, "Speech of I. T. Tichenor upon the Adoption of the Report" (Montgomery, AL: Barrett and Brown, 1865), 6.

77. *NYT,* Oct. 22, 1865; *American Baptist,* June 16, 1868; W. Stanley Hoole, ed., "The Diary of Dr. Basil Manley, 1858–1867," *Alabama Review* 2, no. 2 (1952): 152.

78. J. B. F. Hill to J. P. Durbin, Aug. 2, 1866, James F. Chalfant Correspondence, Woodruff Library, Atlanta University.

79. The two African Methodist denominations were not on friendly terms either. See *Christian Recorder,* Mar. 17, 1866.

80. J. Silsby to E. R. Smith, June 20, 1866, and J. Silsby to G. Whipple, Sept. 14, 1866, reel 1, AMA Papers; Mobile *Nationalist,* Nov. 22, 1866. Swayne, by contrast, suspected "men of principle" used southern rhetoric to shield humanitarian intent (BRFAL, "Report of the Assistant Commissioner, 1866," 19).

81. Philadelphia *Christian Recorder,* Mar. 17, June 23, Aug. 4, 1866; F. Mossbach to O. D. Kinsman, June 16, 1866, reel 55, M 1903, NARA; Swayne to C. C. Sibley, May 4, 1867, reel 2, M 809, RG 105, NARA; I. Parker to Chalfant, Sept. 19, 1867, Chalfant Correspondence, Woodruff Library, Atlanta University; Mobile *Nationalist,* July 12, 1866.

82. Elliot Whipple to E. P. Smith, July 18, 1867, reel 1, AMA Papers.

83. Howard to Swayne, June 24, 1867, reel 3, M 742, RG 105, NARA.

84. Black church criticism of their educational efforts would become a longstanding complaint of northern missionaries. See T. C. Steward to Cravath, Oct. 24, 1870; E. W. Bassett to Miss Cook, Mar. 12, 1871, reel 1, AMA Papers.

85. Entries for Oct. 28, Dec. 4, 1865, Council Minutes, reel 1, Selma City Records, AU Library.

86. US Census, *A Compendium of the Ninth Census, 1870,* 112, 115.

87. Berlin et al., eds., *The Black Military Experience,* 744–45; Fitzgerald, *Urban Emancipation,* 73–74.

88. Fitzgerald, *Urban Emancipation,* 61–62.

89. Mobile *Nationalist,* Jan. 18, 1866.

90. Marion *Commonwealth,* Apr. 4, 1867.

91. Fitzgerald, *Urban Emancipation,* 49–85.

92. Fitzgerald, *The Union League Movement in the Deep South,* 35.

93. Mobile, *Nationalist,* Mar. 22, 1866.

94. W. H. Peck to O. D. Kinsman, Oct. 9, 1866, SAC Tuscaloosa, M 1900, reel 33, NARA.

95. Mobile *Nationalist,* Nov. 29, 1866.

96. Mobile *Nationalist,* Aug. 23, 1866; J. D. Williams to Gov. Patton, Sept. 11, 1866, Gov. Patton Papers, ADAH.

97. Lee W. Formwalt, "The Origins of African-American Politics in Southwest Georgia: A Case Study of Black Political Organization during Presidential Reconstruction, 1865–1867," *Journal of Negro History* 77, no. 4 (1992): 211–22; Mobile *Nationalist,* Nov. 22, 1866. Lawrence Speed's leadership in Georgia did not turn out well, as he was accused of embezzling money from his association.

98. Pierce to Swayne, Dec. 3, 1866, reel 9, M 1900, RG 105, NARA.

99. J. L. Sheffield to Gov. Patton, Mar. 25, 1867, Administrative File, SG 20034, Gov. Patton Papers, ADAH.

100. Rich. Randolph to "Friend," Apr. 16, 1866, Sydingham Moore Papers, ADAH.

101. Agent R. H. Brewer to Capt. L. J. Whiting, Oct. 24, 1866, reel 26, M 1900, RG 105, NARA; Roger L. Ransom, *One Kind of Freedom: The Economic Consequences of Emancipation* (2nd ed., Cambridge, UK: Cambridge University Press, 2001), 44–46 and Appendix C.

102. W. W. Gwaltmey to W. A. Tayloe, June 10, Sept. 10, 1866; Mary Gwaltmey to [W. A. Tayloe], Dec. 27, 1866, reel 14, Tayloe Papers.

103. Entry for Jan. 3, 1866, entries from Jan. to Mar. 1867, and Jan. 8, 17, and Feb. 7, 8, 1868, reel 11, Octavia Otey Diary, ser. J, pt. 7, in Stampp et al., eds., *Records of Ante-Bellum Southern Plantations.*

104. E. T. Tayloe to W. H. Tayloe, Nov. 19, 1866, reel 20, Tayloe Papers.

105. H. Watson to W. A. & G. A. Maxwell & Co., Apr. 12, 1867, Watson Papers.

106. Downs, *After Appomattox,* 262–63; P. Burton to Sumner, Feb. 20, 1867, reel 38, Sumner Papers; J. H. Speed to Shorkley, Aug. 7, 1867, Letters Received, SAC Selma, reel 29, M 1900, RG 105, NARA.

107. J. H. Speed to Shorkley, Aug. 7, 1867, reel 29, Letters Received, SAC Selma, and R. A. Wilson to John Stelzig, Aug. 27, 1868, reel 9, Letters Received, SAC Demopolis, M 1900, RG 105, NARA.

108. Hayden et al., eds., *Land and Labor, 1866–1867,* 687–89.

109. On the prevalence of the bad rental scenario, see J. S. Williams to G. Shorkley, Oct. 29, 1867, reel 29, M 1900, RG 105; Pierce to Swayne, Jan. 2, 1867, reel 9, M 1900, RG 105, NARA.

110. The Freedmen's Bureau officer in Selma kept a complaint log in the late summer and fall of 1866, and freedpeople's complaints increased in the fall. The bulk of them,

at least twenty-three of thirty-one total, were from within surrounding Dallas County, and almost all were plantation disputes. Of complaints listed from July 19 through October 23, at least twenty-two of the thirty-one involved employers as perpetrators, with one involving an overseer as well. Twelve involved work disputes, five reportedly grew out of contract issues, and another two involved property disputes. Most of the seven episodes of violence involved the same sort of issues, as did the numerous episodes of threats, which often involved driving laborers off a plantation. Over a third of the cases, twelve in all, involved freedwomen as among the victims (my research, conducted with the assistance of a student assistant, Cynthia J. Zapata of St. Olaf College). One logical explanation for this extensive record—in so short a period—might be that, especially after the war, ex-slaveholders had difficulty overcoming their habit of threats and beatings, given the agricultural losses and frustrations they experienced with free laborers.

111. Given what happened after Redemption, the fears for enhancing great planters' influence had a point.

112. J. Mills Thornton, "Class Conflict and Black Enfranchisement in Alabama," *Journal of the Historical Society* 11, no. 3 (2012): 235–40; Thornton, "Alabama's Presidential Reconstruction Legislature," 181–83; Mobile *Nationalist,* Oct. 23, 1866.

113. W. Swayne to Comly, June 17, 1867, James M. Comly Papers, OHS.

114. Lieut. 45th USCI, SAC Montgomery, to Col. Kinsman, June 29, 1867, reel 23, M 1900, NARA.

115. *NYT,* Dec. 16, 1867; J. Callis to R. Schenck, Aug. 19, 1867, reel 13, M 1900, RG 105, NARA; Fleming, ed., *Documentary History of Reconstruction* 2: 13–19.

116. Mobile *Nationalist,* Mar. 28, 1867.

117. Thomas Haughey to John Keffer, July 12, 1867, Swayne Papers, ADAH.

118. A. G. Bennett to Patton, July 29, 1867, Patton Papers, ADAH.

119. J. J. Bailey to Patton, Sept. 16, 1867, Gov. Patton Papers, ADAH.

120. [Jared] H. Young to Jeniral [*sic*] Swaine, July 27, 1867, Swayne Papers, ADAH.

121. Charles C. Colton and M. G. Candee, to F. T. Adams, [mid-July 1867], Swayne Papers, ADAH.

122. Swayne to William D. Whipple, Feb. 8, 1867, reel 1, M 809, RG 105, NARA.

123. On this general tendency, see Hahn, *A Nation Under Our Feet,* 174–77.

124. Thomas Haughey to W. H. Smith, May 5, 1867, Swayne Papers, ADAH.

125. John H. Parrish to Henry Watson, May 20, Aug. 6, 13, 1867, Watson Papers; S. Forwood to W. S. Forwood, July 21, 1867, William S. Forwood Papers, SHC; J. J. Bailey to [Gov. Patton], Sept. 16, 1867, Gov. Patton Papers, ADAH.

126. John Parrish to Henry Watson, Dec. 19, 1867, Watson Papers.

127. Fitzgerald, *The Union League Movement in the Deep South,* 153–59; Union Springs *Times,* Sept. 25, 1867; Wm. Bining to S. C. Greene, Oct. 1, 1867, Letters Received, box 1, District of Alabama, RG 393, pt. 2, NARA.

128. Greenville *Advocate,* Sept. 19, 1867; Montgomery *State Sentinel,* Dec. 13, 1867; R T. Smith to Kinsman, Dec. 7, 1867, reel 27, M 1900, RG 105, NARA; Cincinnati *Gazette,* Dec. 5, 1867; Washington *National Intelligencer,* Dec. 17, 1867; Union Springs *Times,* Dec. 21, 1867.

129. After the shooting, Orrick fled to Mexico and Honduras before winding up in Texas. He changed his name to George Arrington and became notorious as a hang-'em-high lawman. See www.texasranger.org/dispatch/8/Arrington.htm and www.tshaonline.org/handbook/online/articles/AA/far20.html.

130. Mobile *Times,* June 20, 1867; Mayor Dormand to Swayne, June 14, 1867, Swayne Papers, ADAH; John Parrish to Henry Watson, June 20, 1867, Watson Papers.

131. Pierce to Swayne, June 14, 30, 1867, reel 9, M 1900, RG 105, NARA; C. W. Pierce

to Swayne, June 28, 1867, A1794 (1867), Letters Received, ser. 5782, Bureau of Civil Affairs, 3rd Military District, Records of US Army Continental Commands, RG 393 Pt. 1, NA [FSSP SS-684].

132. [Parrish] to Watson, [May 28, 1867], Watson Papers.

133. W. O'Berry to Paul Cameron, Aug. 11, 1867, Cameron Family Papers, SHC.

134. E. T. Tayloe to W. H. Tayloe, Jan. 7, 1868, reel 20, Tayloe Papers.

135. J. R. John to Col. Tayloe, Oct. 24, 1867, reel 15, Tayloe Papers.

136. J. C. Hamson to J. B. Hendrix, Mar. 3, 1868, reel 25, M 1900, RG 105, NARA. See also entry for Jan. 8, 1868, P. B. Cabell Notebook, box 48, Cabell Papers, UVA, NARA.

137. S. S. Gardener to O. D. Kinsman, Dec. 20, 24, 1867, reel 11, M 1900, RG 105, NARA.

138. George Shorkley to J. P. D. Carmichael, Dec. 28, 1867, reel 28, M 1900, RG 105.

139. J. R. John to Col. Tayloe, Sept. 28, 1867, reel 15, Tayloe Papers.

140. J. A. Wemyss to Watson, Oct. 10, 1867, Watson Papers.

141. H. A. Tayloe to Brother, Jan. 8, 1868, reel 21, Tayloe Papers.

142. A. S. Bennett to George Shorkley, Jan. 31, 1868, reel 9, M 1900, RG 105, NARA.

143. Circular Number 7, Feb. 5, 1868, reel 17, M 809, RG 105, NARA.

144. Geo. Shorkley to Col. O. L. Kinsman, Dec. 27, 1867, reel 28, M 1900, RG 105, NARA.

145. J. C. Hendrix to O. D. Kinsman, Dec. 31, 1867, Montgomery, reel 23, and Jan. 6, 1868, reel 26, M 1900, RG 105, NARA; Mobile *Nationalist,* Jan. 30, 1868.

146. E. T. Tayloe to W. H. Tayloe, Feb. 14, 1868, reel 20, Tayloe Papers.

147. J. A. Wemyss to John Watson, Jan. 11, 1868 and Mar. 4, 1868, Watson Papers.

148. J. A. Yordy to C. W. Pierce, May 22, 1868, Letters Received, SAC, Demopolis, RG 105, NA.

149. Union Springs *Times* qtd. in Mobile *Register,* Mar. 16, 1868.

150. A. C. Jones to Paul Cameron, Oct. 6, 1869, Cameron Family Papers, SHC; Greensboro *Beacon,* Feb. 26, 1870.

151. F. P. Clingman to "Cousin," May 17, 1867, Jarratt-Puryear Family Papers, reel 20, in Berlin, ed., *Records of Southern Plantations,* ser. A, pt. 1.

152. H. A. Tayloe to Brother, Mar. 28, 1870, reel 21, Tayloe Papers.

153. Union Springs *Times* qtd. in Mobile *Register,* Mar. 16, 1868.

154. An interpretive difference suggests itself with Hahn, whose work broadly parallels this discussion. Hahn places little emphasis on the transition to widespread sharecropping, but it seems important in black-belt planters' turn toward coexistence. See the discussion in Hahn, *A Nation Under Our Feet,* 201–33.

155. J. A. Wemyss to Watson, Nov. 24, 1868, Watson Papers.

156. Calculated from the IPUMS 1 percent sample of the census. The precise figure is that 3.63 percent of Alabama's black heads of households in 1870 reported land, and 19.59 percent reported other property over the fifty-dollar reporting threshold. The real property figure would be accurate, but the census was taken in August, before freedpeople were paid off annually. This may suggest they normally had more in personal property.

157. Gainesville *News* qtd. in Montgomery *Journal,* Jan. 23, 1869.

Chapter Six

Note to chapter epigraph: D. H. Bingham to Steven, Oct. 23, 1867, reel 6, *The Thaddeus Stevens Papers,* ed. Beverly Wilson Palmer et al. (Wilmington, DE: Scholarly Resources, 1994).

1. Montgomery *Advertiser,* Jan. 1, 1867.

2. S. C. Posey to Swayne, Apr. 25, 1867, Swayne Papers, ADAH.

3. H. Barton et al. to Swayne, Aug. 5, 1867, Swayne Papers, ADAH; Talladega Resolutions, Aug. 23, 1867, Swayne Papers, ADAH.

4. Huntsville *Advocate,* June 16, 1867; J. W. Moore to Patton, Apr. 9, 1867, Gov. Patton Papers, ADAH.

5. Spencer to Keffer, July 12, 1867, Gov. Swayne Papers, ADAH; R. T. Smith to Kinsman, June 29, 1867, Letters Sent SAC Opelika, reel 27, M 1900, NARA.

6. Jonathan Truman Dorris, *Pardon and Amnesty under Lincoln and Johnson: The Restoration of the Confederates to Their Rights and Privileges, 1861–1898* (Chapel Hill: UNC Press, 1953), 363–65.

7. Thomas O. Glascock to Sumner, Mar. 17, 1867, reel 38, *Papers of Charles Sumner.*

8. Spencer to Dodge, July 1, 1867, Dodge Papers, SHSI-DM.

9. J. Alvord to Howard, Jan. 1, 1867, reel 1, and Swayne to Howard, Jan. 22, 1867, reel 8, M 803, NARA; Swayne to Howard, Feb. 14, 1867, reel 41, M 752; BRFAL, "Report of the Assistant Commissioner, 1867," 13.

10. C. W. Pierce to Kinsman, June 21, 1867, reel 9, M 1900, RG 105, NARA; Swayne to Howard, Apr. 4, 1867, O. O. Howard Papers, Bowdoin College Library, Bowdoin, ME.

11. F. D. Powell to Howard, May 4, 1867, reel 44, M 752, RG 105, NARA.

12. Swayne to D. L. Dalton, July 25, 1867, Gov. Patton Papers, ADAH; Swayne to Comly, June 17, 1867, reel 1, James M. Comly Papers, OHS.

13. William Franklin Gore Shields, *Personal Recollection of Distinguished Generals* (NY: Harper and Brothers, 1866), 331.

14. J. Silsby to E. P. Smith, Mar. 23, 1867, reel 1, AMA Papers; BRFAL, "Report of the Assistant Commissioner," 1867, 13.

15. C. W. Buckley to J. H. Chapire, Aug. 1867, reel 1, M 810; Swayne to Howard, June 18, Dec. 24, 1867, reel 2, M 809, RG 105, NARA.

16. C. W. Buckley to C. Wheeler, Oct. 4, 1867, reel 15, M 809, RG 105, NARA.

17. Patton to [illegible], Aug. 7, 1867, Letterbook, Gov. Patton Papers, ADAH.

18. Gov. R. M. Patton to S. A. M. Wood, July 20, 1867, Letterbook, Gov. Patton Papers, ADAH. Patton estimated thirty to forty thousand for all the Reconstructed states, which would make the Alabama figure perhaps five thousand.

19. Gov. R. M. Patton to Br. Tardy, May 17, 1867, Letterbook, Governor Patton Papers, ADAH.

20. Galveston (TX) *Flake's Bulletin,* June 6, 1867.

21. Thomas C. Lanier to Patton, June 25, 1867, Patton Papers, ADAH.

22. A. B. Moore to Patton, June 1, 1867, Patton Papers, ADAH.

23. US House, "Busteed Impeachment Investigation," 157.

24. Selma *Messenger,* June 6, 1867; Swayne to Howard, Feb. 2, 1867, reel 1, M 809, RG 105, NARA. His conflict with Busteed is a major theme of Swayne's correspondence for the previous year.

25. Swayne to Salmon Chase, June 3, 1867, Salmon Chase Papers, LC; Swayne to Hugh McCulloch, Dec. 2, 1867, reel 2, M 809, RG 105, NARA.

26. NY *Herald,* June 20, 1867.

27. Testimony of W. Swayne, US House, "Busteed Impeachment Investigation," 167–69; Columbus *Enquirer,* Mar. 26, 1867.

28. Boston *Journal,* June 5, 1867; Montgomery *Advertiser,* June 5, 1867.

29. NY *Herald,* June 7, 1867; NY *Commercial Advertiser,* June 10, 1867.

30. Montgomery *State Sentinel,* June 5, 1867.

31. D. H. Williams to Dr. A. M. Anderson, June 9, 1867, and Swayne to G. Horton,

June 10, 1867, Letters Sent, HQ District of Alabama, entry 3218, RG 393, pt. 2, NA; Swayne to Chase, June 28, 1867, Chase Papers, LC; Montgomery *Advertiser*, June 9, 1867; Swayne to Howard, June 8, 1867, O. O. Howard Papers; Mobile *Times*, June 6, 20, 1867.

32. Swayne to Howard, June 18, 1867, O. O. Howard Papers, Bowdoin College Library, Bowdoin, ME.

33. Swayne to Chase, June 28, 1867, Chase Papers, LC. Swayne thought their concentration in the more populous black-belt counties favored them legislatively.

34. Cincinnati *Enquirer*, June 6, 1867.

35. NY *Herald*, Apr. 8, 1867.

36. Since no one actually counted how many were disfranchised under the Reconstruction acts, the estimates are guesswork. But Governor Patton once suggested it was 3,500, and the ultraconservative Montgomery *Mail* claimed 3,000 petty officials were covered by similar provisions in the Republican constitution. These numbers seem at wide variance with the tens of thousands often claimed (Montgomery *Mail*, Feb. 4, 1868).

37. D. L. Dalton to J. McCaleb Wiley, June 18, 1867, Letterbooks, Governor Patton Papers, ADAH.

38. Patton to Thomas M. Peters, Aug. 5, 1867, Letterbooks, Governor Patton Papers, ADAH; Patton to Pope, June 11, 1867, Records of the 3rd Military District, Letters Received, 1867, Box 1, RG 393, NA.

39. D. H. Williams to Dr. A. M. Anderson, June 9, 1867, and Swayne to G. Horton, June 10, 1867, Letters Sent, HQ District of Alabama, entry 3218, RG 393, pt. 2, NA; Swayne to Chase, June 28, 1867, Chase Papers, LC.

40. General Orders, No. 20, 3rd Military District, May 21, 1867, in *American Annual Cyclopedia for 1867* (NY: Appleton & Co., 1868), 7.

41. Pope to Grant, Apr. 24, 1867, *Papers of Ulysses S. Grant* 17: 118.

42. Keffer to Smith, Apr. 13, 1867, Swayne Papers, ADAH.

43. Swayne to Howard, Apr. 30, 1867, reel 41, M 752, RG 105, NARA.

44. Swayne to SACs, June 12, 1867, and Kinsman to Howard, Aug. 6, 1867, reel 2, M 809, RG 105; Whittlesley to Swayne, Aug. 1, 1867, reel 3, M 742, RG 105, NARA.

45. Swayne to Howard, July 11, 1867, O. O. Howard Papers, Bowdoin College Library, Bowdoin, ME.

46. Pierce to O. L. Kinsman, July 24, Sept. 16, 1867; Pierce to Mayor of Eutaw and Pierce to J. B. F. Hill, both July 31, 1867, reel 9, M 1900, NARA.

47. Baltimore *Sun*, May 16, 1867; Fitzgerald, *Urban Emancipation*, 97–99. Both generals Pope and Grant thought the talk of black city-council members premature.

48. Pope to Grant, Sept. 4, 1867, *Papers of Ulysses S. Grant* 17: 266–67; J. Hayden to J. F. Meline, Jan. 15, 1868, box 5, Dept. of Civil Affairs, 3rd Military District, [A 2701] RG 393, NA. The numbers remain obscure. Civil officials estimated an adult white male population of around 110,000, but only about 90,000 had voted in the heated 1860 presidential election. If one assumes that the recent demographic estimates of 13 percent of military-age white men died across the South holds true, and are valid for Alabama, then the results are not far from the lower estimates for those disfranchised in 1867. For the estimates, see J. David Hacker, "A Census Count of the Civil War Dead," *Civil War History* 57, no. 4 (2011): 341–42.

49. Entry for Oct. 7, 1867, William Cooper Diary, Emory University.

50. J. H. Clanton to W. Lowe, June 22, 1867, Buchanan and McClellan Family Papers, SHC.

51. Montgomery *State Sentinel*, Sept. 5, 1867.

52. Montgomery *Mail,* Aug. 16, 1867. One later account claimed that thirteen black delegates were in attendance, and that one had served on the resolution committee. All, allegedly, joined the Union League before leaving town. See Selma *Argus,* Aug. 28, 1874.

53. Montgomery *Mail,* Sept. 10, 1867; Montgomery *State Sentinel,* Sept. 5, 1867; NY *Herald,* Sept. 6, 1867.

54. Montgomery *State Sentinel,* Sept. 5, 1867. On Thompson, see Howard N. Rabinowitz, "Holland Thompson and Black Political Participation in Montgomery, Alabama," in *Southern Black Leaders of the Reconstruction Era,* ed. Rabinowitz (Urbana: University of Illinois Press, 1982), 249–80.

55. Montgomery *State Sentinel,* Sept. 7, 1867; Montgomery *Mail,* Sept. 7, 1867; Montgomery *Advertiser,* Sept. 6, 1867; NY *Herald,* Sept. 6, 1867; New Orleans *Picayune,* Sept. 15, 1867.

56. Patton to J. C. Bradley, Aug. 5, 1867; Dalton to J. Wiley, July 10, 1867; R. M. Patton to S. A. M. Wood, July 20, 1867, Letterbooks, Gov. Patton Papers, ADAH.

57. Gov. Patton to S. A. M. Wood, July 20, 1867, Letterbooks, Gov. Patton Papers, ADAH.

58. Gov. R. M. Patton to E. Richardson, June 12, 1867, Letterbooks, Gov. Patton Papers, ADAH.

59. Pope to Grant, July 24, 1867, *Papers of Ulysses S. Grant* 17: 261.

60. NY *Tribune,* Aug. 22, 1867; Montgomery *Mail,* Oct. 8, 1867; Mobile *Nationalist,* Oct. 24, 1867; Hayneville *Examiner,* Apr. 9, 1868.

61. Entry for Aug. 23, 1867, William Cooper Diary, Emory University; *NYT,* Apr. 1, 1868.

62. Pope to Grant, July 6, 1867, *Papers of Ulysses S. Grant* 17: 207.

63. Pope to Grant, Aug. 17, 1867, *Papers of Ulysses S. Grant* 17: 262–64.

64. J. Forsyth to M. Marble, Dec. 17, 1867, Manton Marble Papers, LC.

65. Moulton *Union,* Sept. 7, 1867.

66. US House, "Busteed Impeachment Investigation," 78; G. Horton to Swayne, Aug. 11, 1867, Division of the South, Letters Sent, Selma, entry 1190, RG 393, pt. 4, NA.

67. Swayne to Pope, Dec. 16, 1867, Records of the Third Military District, Telegrams Received, vol. 27, RG 393, pt. 1, NA; Mobile *Times,* Dec. 25, 1867, Jan. 7, 1868; Chicago *Tribune,* Jan. 24, 1868.

68. L. V. B. Martin to Henry Stanbery, [mid-July 1867], reel 1, in Calhoun, ed., *Letters Received by the Attorney General, 1809–1870*; Swayne to Pope, Dec. 16, 20, 21, 1867, entry 5740, Telegrams Received, 1867, Third Military District, vol. 27, RG 393, pt. 1, NA; Eliza Horton to Son, Jan. 8, 1868, Gustavus Horton Papers, Museum of Mobile.

69. Selma *Messenger,* Nov. 5, 1867.

70. G. T. Yelverton to C. W. Buckley, July 2, 1867, reel 3, M 810, RG 105, NARA.

71. Selma *Press,* Sept. 30, 1867.

72. Richard L. Hume, *Blacks, Carpetbaggers, and Scalawags: The Constitutional Conventions of Radical Reconstruction* (Baton Rouge: LSU Press, 2008), 78.

73. Bartlett to "Father," Sept. 29, 1867, C. C. Bartlett Papers, ADAH.

74. *NYT,* Jan. 23, 1867; Montgomery *Advertiser,* Feb. 5, 12, 1867.

75. W. B. Figures, memo, [Apr. 13, 1867], Swayne Papers, ADAH.

76. A. S. Lakin to Chalfant, May 29, 1867, Chalfant Correspondence, Atlanta University; Wm. B. Occleston to J. F. Conyngham, May 7, 1867, District of Alabama, Letters Received, Box 1, RG 393, pt. 2, NA.

77. Wiggins, *The Scalawag in Alabama Politics.*

78. J. W. Cantwell to C. J. Kipp, Apr. 10, 1867, Swayne Papers, ADAH.

79. Charles Pelham to Smith, Sept. 19, 1867, Swayne Papers, ADAH.

80. Tuscaloosa *Reconstructionist,* Oct. 3, 1867; Charles C. Bartlett to "Father," Nov. 17, 1867, C. C. Bartlett Papers, ADAH.

81. Election Returns, District of Alabama, vols. 23 and 24, RG 393, NA; Pope to Grant, Oct. 9, 1867, *Papers of Ulysses S. Grant* 17: 266–67, 366; NY *Tribune,* Oct. 8, 1867. The precise-sounding 18,553 figure is from Pope's office, but the evidence provides no indication of how it was derived. Smith's registration correspondence does not indicate that the votes were to be tallied by race. Still, Pope's number is probably not far off. The county returns suggest a much larger number of white supporters than in the ratification election four months later.

82. Swayne to Howard, Oct. 12, 1867, O. O. Howard Papers, Bowdoin College Library, Bowdoin, ME.

83. D. H. Bingham to Steven, Oct. 23, 1867, reel 6, *Thaddeus Stevens Papers.*

84. Michael Les Benedict, "The Rout of Radicalism: Republicans and the Elections of 1867," in Benedict, *Preserving the Constitution: Essays on Politics and the Constitution in the Reconstruction Era* (NY: Fordham University Press, 2006), 23–31.

85. J. Gillette to O. D. Kinsman, Oct. 24, 1867, Letters Sent, vol. 108, SAC Mobile, RG 105, NA; G. E. Spencer to G. Dodge, Oct. 22, 1867, Dodge Papers, SHSI-DM.

86. *KKK* 10: 1850; Cincinnati *Gazette,* Dec. 9, 1867.

87. Cincinnati *Gazette,* Nov. 15, 1867.

88. Alabama Constitutional Convention, *Official Journal of the Constitutional Convention of the State of Alabama, Held in the City of Montgomery, Commencing on Tuesday, November 5th, A.D. 1867* (Montgomery, AL: Barrett and Brown, 1868), 13–14; Cincinnati *Gazette,* Nov. 15, 16, 20, 1867; NY *Herald,* Nov. 15, 25, 1867. The Cincinnati *Gazette* coverage, though sympathetic, offers the best inside account of what was happening.

89. *Official Journal of the Constitutional Convention of the State of Alabama, 1867,* 16–17.

90. *Official Journal of the Constitutional Convention of the State of Alabama, 1867,* 31–32, 36, 71; Columbus *Enquirer,* Nov. 16, 1867.

91. *NYT,* Nov. 13, 18, 1867.

92. Cincinnati *Gazette,* Nov. 20, 1867; Boston *Journal,* Nov. 19, 1867.

93. *Official Journal of the Constitutional Convention of the State of Alabama, 1867,* 22; entry for Nov. 14, 1867, in *The Journals of Josiah Gorgas, 1857–1878,* ed. Sarah Woolfolk Wiggins (Tuscaloosa: UA Press, 1995), 217.

94. *NYT,* Nov. 15, 1867; NY *World,* Nov. 20, 29, 1867.

95. Alabama was the first of the Congressional Reconstruction conventions to meet, which presumably made it the first legislative body with substantial African American participation.

96. NY *World,* Nov. 18, 1867; NY *Herald,* Nov. 29, 1867.

97. Boston *Advertiser,* Dec. 10, 1867.

98. NY *Commercial Advertiser,* Dec. 6, 1867; NY *Herald,* Nov. 11, 1867. A certain cautiousness by new lawmakers makes sense. For a recent examination of the limits that legal practice posed for Reconstruction policymakers, see Laura F. Edwards, *A Legal History of the Civil War and Reconstruction: A Nation of Rights* (NY: Cambridge University Press, 2015), 149–53.

99. This number has been variously given, both at the time and by historians since. This count is from the most careful recent study. See Hume, *Blacks, Carpetbaggers, and Scalawags,* appendix C. Montgomery *Journal,* Nov. 13, 1875, gives the same figure.

100. Hume, *Blacks, Carpetbaggers, and Scalawags,* appendix C.

101. NY *Herald,* Nov. 21, 1867; Columbus *Enquirer,* Nov. 22, 1867; Cincinnati *Enquirer,* Dec. 4, 1867.

102. See the enthusiastic praise in Franklin, *Reconstruction,* 89–90, 106–7.

103. Montgomery *Sentinel,* Nov. 16, 1867; Cincinnati *Gazette,* Nov. 14, 1867.

104. *NYT,* Nov. 11, 1867.

105. Special Orders No. 71, Oct. 30, 1867, reel 17, M 809, RG 105, NARA.

106. Cincinnati *Gazette,* Dec. 2, 1867.

107. Harper to J. W. Alvord, Nov. 2, 1868, reel 3, M 809, RG 105, NARA. On the fairly substantial increases in property taxes these changes required, see Thornton, "Fiscal Policy and the Failure of Radical Reconstruction in the Lower South," 361, 368, 372.

108. Wm. Mudd to P. A. Fitts, Nov. 21, 1867, A. C. Hargrove Papers, UA; NY *Herald,* Nov. 12, 1867.

109. D. L. Dalton to Patton, Nov. 30, 1867, Gov. Patton Papers, ADAH.

110. Montgomery *State Sentinel,* Sept. 4, 1867; "H. C. Semple, Speech at Prattville Ala to Whites & Negroes against the Adoption of the Constitution, 1867," H. C. Semple Papers, ADAH.

111. Memphis *Avalanche,* Dec. 3, 1867; Cincinnati *Commercial,* Dec. 9, 1867; Cincinnati *Gazette,* Dec. 5, 1867.

112. *Official Journal of the Constitutional Convention of the State of Alabama, 1867,* 61; NY *Herald,* Nov. 15, 17, 1867; Cincinnati *Gazette,* Nov. 18, 1867.

113. Cincinnati *Gazette,* Nov. 25, 27, 1867. Keffer's initiative may have originated in Swayne's frustration with black support for Bingham's faction on disfranchisement. The delegates do seem to have abandoned Bingham in the subsequent vote for governor.

114. Cincinnati *Gazette,* Dec. 6, 1867.

115. *Official Journal of the Constitutional Convention of the State of Alabama, 1867,* 265; *American Annual Cyclopedia for 1867,* 30; BRFAL, "Report of the Assistant Commissioner, 1867," 19; Jacksonville *Republican,* Nov. 29, 1867; *NYT,* Nov. 14, 1867.

116. Cincinnati *Gazette,* Nov. 29, 1867.

117. Cincinnati *Gazette,* Nov. 11, 1867; Columbus *Enquirer,* Nov. 11, 1867; *NYT,* Dec. 12, 1867.

118. NY *Tribune,* Nov. 15, Dec. 7, 1867.

119. Boston *Journal,* Nov. 19, 1867; Memphis *Avalanche,* Dec. 8, 1867.

120. Boston *Advertiser,* Dec. 24, 1867; Central City [Colorado] *Miners' Register,* Dec. 24, 1867.

121. G. W. Graves to Patton, Dec. 20, 1867, Gov. Patton Papers, ADAH; Montgomery *Mail,* Dec. 4, 1867.

122. Cincinnati *Gazette,* Nov. 21, Dec. 6, 1867; Demopolis *Southern Republican,* July 20, 1870; J. J. McDonald to Dalton, Dec. 7, 1867, and Dalton to Patton, Dec. 1, 1867, Gov. Patton Papers, ADAH. Smith later claimed to have stoutly opposed disfranchisement; see "Letter from William H. Smith in Defense of his Administration" (Montgomery, AL: Barrett and Brown, 1870), 5.

123. *Official Journal of the Constitutional Convention of the State of Alabama, 1867,* 239; McMillan, *Constitutional Development in Alabama,* 151; Cincinnati *Gazette,* Dec. 7, 10, 1867; Savannah *News and Herald,* Dec. 18, 1867.

124. Qtd. in John Tyler Jr. to Andrew Johnson, Dec. 30, 1867, *Papers of Andrew Johnson* 13: 385.

125. New Orleans *Tribune,* Dec. 19, 1867; Macon *Telegraph,* Jan. 10, 1868; Pope to Grant, Dec. 27, 1867, vol. 1, Letters Sent, 3rd Military District, #5730, RG 393 pt. 1, NA.

126. John Forsyth to Johnson, Dec. 12, 1867, *Papers of Andrew Johnson* 13: 327.

127. Chicago *Tribune,* Jan. 24, 1868; Dalton to Patton, Jan. 2, 1868, Gov. Patton Papers, ADAH.

128. Hayden to Meade, Mar. 18, 1868, [entry 5786], box 5, Bureau of Civil Affairs, Third Military District, RG 393, pt. 1, RG 105, NA.

129. Howard to J. Hayden, Feb. 12, 1868, reel 14, M 809, RG 105, NARA; Meade to Grant, Feb. 23, 1868, Letters Sent, 1868, Third Military District, [entry 5730], vol. 2, RG 393, pt. 1, NA.

130. J. Hayden to O. O. Howard, Jan. 27, 1868; Shorkley to Hayden, Feb. 3, 1868; and Hayden to J. B. Healy, Feb. 1, 1868, reel 2, M 809, RG 105, NARA. W. T. Hatchett to Samuel [Leofley?], Jan. 18, 1868, and W. T. Hatchett to N. P. Williams, Jan. 30, 1868, Deposition of Holland Thompson, Feb. 17, 1868, reel 9, *George Gordon Meade Collection* (Wilmington, DE: Scholarly Resources, 1998).

131. Raleigh [NC] *Register,* Dec. 31, 1867; Huntsville *Advocate,* Jan. 10, 1868; Mobile *Nationalist,* Jan. 30, 1868; Ralph Erskine Parnell, "The Administration of William Hugh Smith: Governor of Alabama, 1868–1870," PhD diss., AU, 1958, 13; NY *Tribune,* Jan. 13, 1868.

132. Cincinnati *Enquirer,* Jan. 9, 1868; Burke to Meade, Mar. 15, 1868, reel 9, *George Gordon Meade Collection*; O. O. Howard to Henry Wilson, Jan. 13, 1868, O. O. Howard Papers, Bowdoin College.

133. Wiggins, *The Scalawag in Alabama Politics,* 147, 136. Wiggins's depiction of officeholders is strongly echoed by a detailed study of 2,700 Republican activists. Some 85 percent of the whites initially elected lived in Alabama by 1860. See William McKinley Cash, "Alabama Republicans during Reconstruction: Personal Characteristics, Motivations, and Political Activity of Party Activists, 1867–1880," PhD diss., UA, 1973, 111.

134. Montgomery *Mail,* Jan. 14, 1868.

135. The perception of predominance by northern-origin officeholders is misleading. In 1875, the head of the state's Grand Army of the Republic, a Union veterans' organization tied to the Republican Party, reported 150 northern veterans. This he thought an approximation of the "carpetbagger" population over the previous several years. See *Congressional Record,* 43rd Congress, 2nd Sess., 1902. On the larger question of northern numbers in the electorate, the Montgomery *Advertiser,* Aug. 21, 1870, estimated white Republican voters at 7,000 natives and 500 "carpetbaggers," which if remotely accurate would suggest over a ten-to-one proportion.

136. Thomas Molloy to Patton, Nov. 5, 1867; James M. Morton to Patton, Mar. 15, 1868; A. A. Summers to Patton, May 14, 1868; E. P. Jones to Patton, May 16, 1868, Gov. Patton Papers, ADAH. On vote totals, see Fitzgerald, "Radical Republicanism and the White Yeomanry," 594.

137. NY *Herald,* Dec. 22, 1867; Macon *Telegraph,* Dec. 20, 1867; Washington *National Intelligencer,* Feb. 18, 1868; Savannah *News and Herald,* Feb. 19, 1868; Jacksonville *Republican,* Dec. 21, 1867; W. P. Chilton to Meade, early Jan. 1868, reel 9, *George Gordon Meade Collection*; H. A. Tayloe to Brother, Jan. 8, 1868, reel 21, Tayloe Papers, Stampp, ed., *Records of Ante-bellum Southern Plantations,* ser. M, pt. 1.

138. The wording of the Second Reconstruction Act suggests, but does not quite say, that if the numerical provisions were not met the constitution would not be forwarded for congressional consideration.

139. The later election victories occurred in the face of a rampant Klan, which suggests a substantial Republican majority existed before the terror emerged.

140. Mobile *Advertiser* and Boston *Journal,* Jan. 17, 1868, qtd. in Milwaukee *Sentinel,* Dec. 16, 1867.

141. Memphis *Avalanche,* Jan. 22, 1868.

142. Several accounts of Clanton's statement exist. See Swayne to H. C. Wood, Jan. 6, 1868, Letters Received, 1868, 3rd Military District, [SS-529], RG 393, NA; S. S. Gardner to S. C. Greene, Dec. 25, 1867, reel 11, M 1900, RG 105, NARA; NY *Tribune,* Jan. 1, 1868. For the tense context after a police shooting, see Greenville *Advocate,* Jan. 2, 1868.

143. Montgomery *Mail,* Jan. 8, 1868; Mobile *Register,* Feb. 2, 1868; Mobile *Tribune* qtd. in NY *Tribune,* Feb. 11, 1868.

144. Washington *National Intelligencer,* Jan. 29, 1868.

145. Bangor *Whig & Courier,* Jan. 22, 1868.

146. Convention Minutes, Jan. 14 and 15, 1868, reel 5, Robert McKee Papers, ADAH.

147. Memphis *Avalanche,* Jan. 22, 1868.

148. Montgomery *Advertiser,* Jan. 21, 1869.

149. "Alabama Election," 40th Congress, 2nd Sess., House Executive Doc. 238, 2. Meade's conclusion on the vote cast is probably correct; at least it is not obviously flawed.

150. Blount, Tallapoosa, and Walker lost over half the previous pro-Reconstruction vote, which indicates a large reduction in white support (Election Returns, District of Alabama, vols. 23 and 24, RG 393, NA).

151. Report of Meade, 40th Congress, 3rd Sess., House Executive Doc. 1, 97; Fitzgerald, "Radical Republicanism and the White Yeomanry," 565–96, esp. 595.

152. G. H. Yancey to Ham Yancey, Feb. 15, 1868, B. C. Yancey Papers, SHC.

153. J. A. Yordy to A. S. Bennett, Feb. 15, 1868, Letters Received, SAC Demopolis, box 27, RG 105, NA.

154. S. Moore to Meade, Mar. 3, 1868, reel 9, *George Gordon Meade Collection.*

155. Patton to Hayden, Mar. 6, 1868, reel 9, *George Gordon Meade Collection.*

156. M. D. Brainard to Thaddeus Stevens, May 2, 1868, box 11, 40A-H21.1, RG 233, NARA; J. L. Pennington to C. Sumner, Feb. 9, 1868, reel 41, *Papers of Charles Sumner.*

157. Parnell, "The Administration of William Hugh Smith," 14–15; Spencer to Dodge, May 3, 1868, Dodge Papers, SHSI-DM.

158. 40th Congress, 2nd Sess., House Misc. Doc. 111, "Election in Alabama," 33.

159. Wetumpka *Elmore Standard,* Feb. 1, 1868, qtd. in 40th Congress, 2nd Sess., House Misc. Doc. 111, "Election in Alabama," 38–39; Hayden to Howard, Mar. 7, 1868, reel 52, M 752, RG 105, NARA.

160. 40th Congress, 2nd Sess., House Misc. Doc. 111, "Election in Alabama," 1–46.

161. 40th Congress, 2nd Sess., House Misc. Doc. 111, "Election in Alabama," 30–31.

162. NY *Tribune,* Feb. 15, 1868; *NYT,* Feb. 15, 19, 1868.

163. 40th Congress, 2nd Sess., House Report 22, 1. Admitting Alabama after the apparently successful boycott was termed illegal by Democrats and sympathetic historians. It may, however, have been within the discretion of Congress. The Reconstruction Act outlined what would happen if the constitution vote met numerical requirements; technically, it said nothing about what would happen otherwise. According to lawyer-historian Christopher McIlwain, "Congress had the exclusive power to decide whether to admit Alabama's new congressional delegation, and therefore to impose whatever conditions on admission it believed were proper" (McIlwain to author, Jan. 15, 2016).

164. NY *Herald,* June 20, 1867; Parnell, "The Administration of William Hugh Smith," 4–5.

165. Receipt for Secret Service, 1863, box 63, and G. Spencer to G. Dodge, May 20, 1865, Dodge Papers, SHSI-DM; *OR,* ser. 4, vol. 2: 87, 258; US Congress, "Report of the Joint Committee on Reconstruction," pt. 3: 11–12.

166. W. H. Smith testimony, US House, "Busteed Impeachment Investigation," 182–83; Eliza Horton to F. L. Horton, Jan. 25, 1869, Horton Family Papers, Museum of Mobile.

167. George E. Spencer testimony, US House, "Busteed Impeachment Investigation," 44, 47; Smith to Semple, July 2, 1868, and Memo from Gov. Smith, [1868], Henry C. Semple Papers, ADAH; Smith to Dalton, Jan. 24, 1869, Smith Papers, ADAH.

168. Montgomery *Advertiser,* July 15, Aug. 8, 14, 1868. The electoral college bill was suggested initially by Republicans in Washington, among them senators Spencer and Warner.

169. Fleming, *Civil War and Reconstruction in Alabama,* 747.

Chapter Seven

Note to chapter epigraph: Ziegler Chapman to Gov. Smith, Oct. 3, 1868, Gov. Smith Papers, ADAH.

1. Emberton, *Beyond Redemption*; Parsons, *Ku Klux*; Rosen, *Terror in the Heart of Freedom*; Kidada E. Williams, *They Left Great Marks on Me: African American Testimonies of Racial Injustice from Emancipation to World War I* (NY: New York University Press, 2012). These comments of course include the host of similar organizations operating during the period.

2. Bertram Wyatt-Brown, *Honor and Violence in the Old South* (Oxford, UK: Oxford University Press, 1986).

3. Diane Summerville, *Rape and Race in the Nineteenth Century South* (Chapel Hill: UNC Press, 2004).

4. Philip Gosse, *Letters from Alabama Chiefly Relating to Natural History* (London: Morgan and Chase, 1859), 250, 278, 251.

5. George P. Rawick, Jan Hillegas, and Ken Lawrence, eds., *The American Slave,* Supplement Series 1: *Alabama Narratives* (Westport, CT, 1977), 297–302.

6. Sally E. Hadden, *Slave Patrols: Law and Violence in Virginia and the Carolinas* (Cambridge, MA: Harvard University Press, 2001), 99–104, 211–15.

7. Claim of Ebenezer Leath, Southern Claims Commission Approved Claims, 1871–80, Cherokee County, reel 3, M 2062, NARA.

8. J. M. McArthur, to Lt. Col. J. Hough, June 9, 1865, *OR.*, ser. 1, vol. 49, pt. 1: 975–76.

9. Nearby Moore, the Klansman Parks Townsend was either the guerilla sympathizer federal spies identified or his cousin. See Notebook in Edward F. Reid Papers, IHS.

10. Allen W. Trelease, *White Terror: The Ku Klux Klan Conspiracy and Southern Reconstruction* (NY: Harper and Row, 1971), 21, 81–84; "The Klan in the Tennessee Valley," *Old Morgan County: History and Stories of the Tennessee Valley* (Decatur, AL: Great Southern Publishing, ca. 1996–97), no. 18: 12.

11. General Thomas H. Ruger to R. C. Drum, Nov. 1, 1868, Letters Sent, District of Alabama, RG 393, pt. 2, NA.

12. *KKK* 5: 505–6; Alabama General Assembly, *Report of Joint Committee on Outrages* (Montgomery, AL: Jno. G. Stokes & Co., 1868), 11–13.

13. A. S. Lakin to J. P. Chalfant, Mar. 13, Aug. 24, 1866; J. Talley to Chalfant, Aug. 6, 1867, Chalfant Correspondence, Atlanta University.

14. Gov. Patton to Gen. Thomas, Dec. 30, 1865, *Papers of Ulysses S. Grant* 16: 54.

15. *Christian Advocate,* Jan. 27, Sept. 5, 1866; W. Garrett to Parsons, Sept. 18, 1865, Gov. Parsons Papers, ADAH; O. D. Kinsman to F. Mossbach, June 18, 1866, reel 1, M

809, RG 105, NARA; W. Stansell to J. Chalfant, June 30, 1867, Chalfant Correspondence, Atlanta University.

16. Swayne to Gen. W. D. Whipple, Feb. 12, 1867, filed as A-43 (1867), Letters Received, ser. 4720, Dept. of the Tennessee, Records of US Army Continental Commands, RG 393 Pt. 1, NA [FSSP C-2029]; A. J. Abbott to Swayne, n.d. [1865], Unregistered Letters Received, ser. 9, Alabama Assistant Commissioner, RG 105, NA [FSSP A-1618]. An "organized band of villains" was reported in Autauga County too, disarming freedpeople and preventing them from seeking new farms; see Kinsman to J. M. Smith, [1866], reel 1, M 809, RG 105, NARA.

17. On the urgent fear of white "indiscretion" provoking racial conflict, see Sidney Lanier to R. S. Lanier, Jan. 21, 1868, in *Sidney Lanier: Letters, 1857–1868, Centennial Edition,* ed. Charles R. Anderson and Aubrey H. Starke (Baltimore: Johns Hopkins Press, 1945), vol. 7: 372.

18. Fleming, *Civil War and Reconstruction in Alabama,* 668, 690–93; Foner, *Reconstruction,* 425, 432–33.

19. *NYT,* Apr. 7, 1868; J. H. McDonald to Patton, Feb. 24, 1868; J. K. Henry to Patton, Feb. 21, 1868, Patton Papers, ADAH.

20. Thomas Chalmers McCorvey, *Alabama Historical Sketches* (Charlottesville: University of Virginia Press, 1960), 170–73; Population Schedules, Limestone County, 1860 and 1870 Census; Susan Lawrence Davis, *Authentic History, Ku Klux Klan, 1865–1877* (NY: American Library Service, 1924), 35–43.

21. Alabama General Assembly, *Report of Joint Committee on Outrages,* 7; Tuscumbia *North Alabamian,* Jan. 4, 1906.

22. R. Randolph to Fleming, Aug. 21, 23, 1901, Walter L. Fleming Papers, New York Public Library; R. Randolph to Katie Withers, Apr. 12, 1869, and Jan. 20, 1870, Ryland Randolph Papers, Samford University.

23. For an exploration of Randolph, see Hubbs, *Searching for Freedom after the Civil War,* 9–56; and for his outlandish record of challenges and duels, see Sarah Woolfolk Wiggins, "The Life of Ryland Randolph as Seen through His Letters to John W. DuBose," *Alabama Historical Quarterly* 30 (Fall and Winter 1968): 145–80.

24. It was possible to locate some 200 in one or more decennial years. One cannot readily determine if they were actual Klansmen, but they were implicated enough in regulator operations to be among the few caught. The bulk were convicted under federal antiterrorist legislation after 1871; others were recognized by victims or named by anonymous informants. A few were identified by fellow Klan members or even killed in Klan garb. Witnesses took their lives in their hands, so people seldom named names lightly. The socioeconomic biases in the statistics seemingly balanced out, for if well-off men had better information and opportunities to escape, they abandoned more property if they fled.

25. Some 135 of the 600 identified Klansmen could be located in the 1870 census, and 25 of them were described as hired laborers or similar modest categories.

26. Michael W. Fitzgerald, "The Ku Klux Klan: Property Crime and the Plantation System in Reconstruction Alabama," *Agricultural History* 71, no. 2 (1997): 186–206. According to IPUMS's 1 percent sample for 1870, the average wealth for white households in 1870 was $1,323 and the median was $400.

27. For a longer discussion of the technique, with less complete numbers, see Michael W. Fitzgerald, "Ex-Slaveholders and the Ku Klux Klan: Exploring the Motivations of Terrorist Violence," in Bruce E. Baker and Brian Kelly, eds., *After Slavery: Race, Labor, and Citizenship in the Reconstruction South* (Gainesville: University Press of Florida, 2013), 153–68.

28. The prewar standing of these families would be less biased by any class-related differences in fleeing capture, as might be reflected in the postwar census.

29. Some 80 of the 147 appear as owners in the 1860 census, a significant majority. This understates the number, because 4 more live adjacent to grandparents with slaves, and another 4 families appear as slaveholders in the previous census.

30. The 51 names appear in 265 distinct episodes of collective violence, including lynchings. See Fitzgerald, "Ex-Slaveholders and the Ku Klux Klan," 149–50.

31. A. F. Posey to Schurz, Apr. 29, 1870, reel 4, Carl Schurz Papers, LC.

32. Tuscaloosa *Monitor,* Mar. 25, 1868. U. S. Grant to Meade, May 2, 1868; U. S. Grant to Meade, May 4, 1868; Meade to R. Busteed, May 11, 1868; Meade to Clark and Jolly, May 16, 1868, reel 10, *George Gordon Meade Collection.*

33. Telegraph from Cotton Factors Kirksey & Carpenter, May 5, 1868, and J. T. Brodnax to E. F. Golson, July 6, 1868, box 1, Golson Brothers Papers, Hill Library, LSU. On Jolly's Klan participation, see *Reconstruction in West Alabama: The Memoirs of John L. Hunnicutt,* ed. William Stanley Hoole (Tuscaloosa, AL: Confederate Publishing Co., [1959]), 56.

34. *KKK* 1: 25.

35. For example, see Montgomery *Mail,* Mar. 19, 22, 25, 1868.

36. "Mary" to J. R. Buford, Apr. 24, 1868; [Anne?] to J. R. Buford, [Mar. 1868], Confederadoes Collection, Draughon Library, AU. I have located such statements by ex-Confederate sympathizers elsewhere, but no condemnations of the Klan's initial activities. For an outright endorsement of Klan violence, see W. C. Pickens to Brother, Apr. 19, 1868, and I. Pickens to Brother, May 1, 1868, Pickens Papers, University of South Alabama.

37. NY *Herald,* June 28, 29, 1871.

38. According to the local press, in September 1868 locals heard the Klan would ride into downtown Athens, and then a party actually did so. See Faye Acton Axford, *Limestone County after Appomattox* (Athens, AL: n.p., [1985]), 35. See also Athens *Post,* Jan. 9, 1869.

39. *KKK* 9: 1278.

40. Letter to J. R. Conn, [1870], Ku Klux Klan Collection, Archives and Special Collections, Ball State University; H. R. Starkweather to Smith, Dec. 13, 1869, Smith Papers, ADAH.

41. Montgomery *Journal,* May 22, 1869. Tuscaloosa *Monitor,* Apr. 27, 1869. Sheriff T. P. Lewis to Smith, May 5, 1869; W. Miller to Smith, May 3, 1869; Freedmen to Smith, Apr. 22, 1869, Gov. Smith Papers, ADAH.

42. Livingston *Journal,* May 27, 1869; "Respectfully Yours" to Smith, May 1, 1870, Gov. Smith Papers, ADAH.

43. Steven Hahn, *The Roots of Southern Populism: Yeoman Farmers and the Transformation of the Georgia Upcountry, 1850–1890* (NY: Oxford University Press, 1983), 58–63, 67.

44. Fitzgerald, "The Ku Klux Klan," 186–206.

45. Entries for Nov. 29, Dec. 6, 1868; Jan. 19, Feb. 1, Apr. 10, May 9, 1869, Octavia Otey diary, reel 11, ser. J, pt. 7, in Stampp et al., eds., *Records of Ante-Bellum Southern Plantations.* See also US Census, Population Schedules for 1860 and 1870, Madison County.

46. Montgomery *Advertiser,* Feb. 24, 1867.

47. C. P. Simmons to Smith, Sept. 3, 1868, and C. Womble to Smith, Sept. 7, 1868, Gov. Smith Papers, ADAH; D. L. Dalton to C. Womble, Sept. 10, 1868, Letterbook, Smith Papers, ADAH.

48. T. L. Appleby to Smith, Sept. 1, 1868, Smith Papers, ADAH.

49. B. R. Wilson to Smith, n.d.; Smith to Wilson, Sept. 3, 1868, Letterbook 1868–69, Smith Papers, ADAH.

50. Silas Thurlow to Smith, Sept. 3, 1868, Smith Papers, ADAH.

51. S. S. Gardner to Smith, Sept. 3, 1868, Smith Papers, ADAH; Alabama General Assembly, *Report of Joint Committee on Outrages,* 15–17, 24.

52. Miller to Smith, July 22, 25, 28, 30, 31, Aug. 14, 17, 22, 25, 31, Sept. 1, 1868, Gov. Smith Papers, ADAH; J. A. Yordy to R. A. Wilson, Sept. 1, 1868, box 27, Letters Received, SAC Demopolis, RG 105, NARA.

53. Smith to Miller, Aug. 1, Sept. 25, 1868, Letterbook, 1868–69, Smith Papers, ADAH.

54. R. A. Wilson to T. H. Ruger, Aug. 31, 186[8], reel 18, M 809, RG 105, NARA; Miller to Smith, Sept. 22, 1868, Gov. Smith Papers, ADAH. For previous local agitation of the issue, see Mobile *Advertiser and Register,* Oct. 19, 1866.

55. O. L. Shepherd to General R. C. Drum, July 29, 1868, Letters Sent, District of Alabama, RG 393, pt. 2, NA; O. L. Shipherd to Howard, Aug. 13, 1868, and R. D. Harper to Howard, Aug. 14, 1868, O. O. Howard Papers, Bowdoin College.

56. NY *Tribune,* Aug. 4, 1868. Meade was the recipient of harsh personal gossip in the Democratic press; see R. Jemison to Ma, July 4, 1868, Jemison Papers, UA.

57. Meade to Secretary of War, Aug. 5, 1868, Meade to E. D. Townsend, Aug. 24, 1868, reel 10, George Gordon Meade Papers.

58. Charles A. Miller to O. O. Howard, Aug. 1, 1868, reel 57, M 752, RG 105, NARA.

59. W. H. Smith to Gen. G. G. Meade, Apr. 14, 1868, enclosed in E. T. Belcher to R. C. Drum, Apr. 17, 1868, B-162 (1868), Letters Received, ser. 5738, 3rd Military District, Records of US Army Continental Commands, RG 393, pt. 1, NA [FSSP SS-534].

60. Charles A. Miller to O. O. Howard, Aug. 1, 1868, reel 57, M 752, RG 105, NARA.

61. Ben Severance, *Tennessee's Radical Army: The State Guard and Its Role in Reconstruction, 1867–1869* (Knoxville: University of Tennessee Press, 2005).

62. Downs, *After Appomattox,* 216; William Woods Holden, *Memoirs of W. W. Holden* (Durham, NC: Seeman Printery, 1911), 194. Grant included North Carolina's governor in his reported criticism.

63. Montgomery *Journal,* Jan. 14, 1869.

64. Alabama, *Journal of the Senate of the State of Alabama, during the Sessions Commencing in July, September and November 1868* (Montgomery, AL: Stokes, 1868), 124–26, 164–66.

65. Records of 3rd Military District, Election Returns, District of Alabama, vol. 23, entry 5787, RG 393, pt. 1, NA; Jacksonville *Republican,* Nov. 28, 1868; Wiggins, *The Scalawag in Alabama Politics,* 42. The number is variously given. Klan-stricken Colbert County went from 640 votes for the constitution to a mere 39 votes for Grant.

66. To take one vivid instance, the previously apologist Athens *Post* began covering disguised Klan raids nearby in 1869. See Athens *Post,* Jan. 9, Feb. 13, Mar. 6, and July 2, 1869. A September 10 editorial conceded that "bands of men in disguise are continually prowling this section of country" representing themselves as Ku Klux Klan. The paper then concluded that it was time for these spurious Klansmen to be arrested (Athens *Post,* Nov. 19, 1869).

67. The two leading wheat-producing counties, Calhoun and Cherokee, were centers of unusually harsh Klan activity. Talladega and Tallapoosa counties also had strong Klan outbreaks, and both grew about 50,000 bushels apiece. In fact, most of the piedmont and Tennessee Valley counties with Klan episodes grew tens of thousands of bushels, and nearly all the large producers had Klan outbreaks (US Census, *A Compendium*

of the Ninth Census, 1870, 712–13). On the distinctive seasonality of labor demands in wheat, see Max Grivno, *Gleanings of Freedom: Free and Slave Labor along the Mason-Dixon Line* (Urbana: University of Illinois Press, 2011), 93–97. See also the labor-demand charts illustrating the contrast between wheat and cotton in Gavin Wright, "The Economics and Politics of Slavery and Freedom in the U.S. South," in Frank McGlynn and Seymour Dresher, eds., *The Meaning of Freedom: Economics, Politics, and Culture after Slavery* (Pittsburgh: University of Pittsburgh Press, 1992), 101, 103.

68. In December 1868, a legislative committee recommended five counties for martial law, Madison and Lauderdale in the Tennessee Valley, Pickens, Tuscaloosa, and Butler. Three of the five were on the state's borders (Alabama General Assembly, *Report of Joint Committee on Outrages,* 6).

69. [SAC at Montgomery] to Edward Beecher, Reports from Mar. to Oct. 31, 1868, reel 26, M 1900, RG 105, NARA. Demopolis *Southern Republican,* Nov. 16, 1870; Dorman, *Party Politics in Alabama,* 218, 223, 224.

70. Regional estimates in 1870 prepared by IPUMS. Black household wealth in the black belt averaged $30.86, in the piedmont region $45.90, and in the mountains $125.20.

71. This would be an approximation, given boundary changes, but the increase looks noticeable, around 17 percent in a decade. The estimate follows the regional boundaries and 1866 calculations of Kolchin, *First Freedom,* 13–14, in comparison with US Census, *A Compendium of the Ninth Census, 1870,* 25.

72. Bertis English, "Freedom's Church: Sociocultural Construction, Reconstruction, and Post-Reconstruction in Perry County, Alabama's African American Churches," in Noe, ed., *The Yellowhammer War,* 258–79; English, "A Black Belt Anomaly: Biracial Cooperation in Reconstruction-Era Perry County, 1865–1874," *Alabama Review* 62, no. 1 (2009): 3–36; English, "Civil Wars and Civil Beings: Violence, Religion, Race, Politics, Education, Culture, and Agrarianism in Perry County, Alabama, 1860–1875," PhD diss., AU, 2006.

73. Montgomery *Advertiser,* Aug. 1, 1869; Montgomery *Mail,* Oct. 30, 1870; G. P. L. Reed to Fleming, n.d., Walter L. Fleming Papers, New York Public Library. It appears Dr. Reed, of Marion, led a mostly independent group, though perhaps connected with the Knights of the White Camellia. By the early 1870s, even AMA missionaries were achieving a measure of local acceptance; see William Warren Rogers Jr., "'The Prospect Before Us': A Massachusetts Congregationalist in Reconstruction Alabama," *Alabama Review* 60, no. 1 (2007): 3–28.

74. Bond for W. T. Blackford, Apr. 7, 1869, Hale County, Secretary of State, Elections, and Registration Division, Bond Book, 1868–83, ADAH. Greensboro *Beacon,* Nov. 6, Dec. 4, 11, 1869; Apr. 9, 1870. Tuscaloosa *Monitor,* Oct. 19, 1869; Feb. 14, 1871. Blackford to Smith, Dec. 20, 1868, Gov. Smith Papers, ADAH. W. C. Pickens to I. Pickens, Sept. 1, 1870, Pickens Papers, USA. On the Klan's limited sway in Hale, see Michael W. Fitzgerald, "Extralegal Violence and the Planter Class: The Ku Klux Klan in the Alabama Black Belt During Reconstruction," in Christopher Waldrep and Donald G. Nieman, eds., *Local Matters: Race, Crime, and Justice in the Nineteenth-Century South* (Athens: University of Georgia Press, 2001), 155–71.

75. Bellefonte (PA) *Democratic Watchman,* Nov. 13, 1868; NY *Herald,* Oct. 26, 1868; Smith to A. Ducal, Dec. 11, 1868, Gov. Smith Papers, ADAH.

76. Smith to H. Fish, Apr. 28, 1869, Secretary's Letterbook, Gov. Smith Papers, ADAH.

77. Montgomery *Advertiser and Mail,* Mar. 2, 1873.

78. Huntsville *Advocate,* July 1, 1870; Demopolis *Southern Republican,* July 20, 1870.

79. "Letter from William H. Smith, Governor of Alabama, in Defense of His Administration," 6, 15; Jacksonville *Republican,* July 23, 1870.

80. P. M. Dox to S. D. Cabaniss, Aug. 18, 1868, Cabaniss Papers, Duke University.

81. Tuscaloosa *Monitor,* Sept. 1, Oct. 6, 1868; Montgomery *Mail,* Sept. 26, 1868; NY *Tribune,* Oct. 8, 1868; H. M. Somerville to R. McKee, Oct. 3, 1868, reel 1, Robert McKee Papers, ADAH.

82. Stelzig to Wilson, Sept. 24, 1868, reel 20, M 1900, RG 105, NARA.

83. N. Rice to Smith, Mar. 1, 1869, Gov. Smith Papers, ADAH. Montgomery *Journal,* Nov. 16, 1868; Feb. 22, 1869. Huntsville *Advocate,* Mar. 12, 1869. Athens *Post,* Nov. 19, 1869.

84. J. Williams to Smith, Feb. 6, 1869; A. C. Beard to Smith, Feb. 8, 1869, Gov. Smith Papers, ADAH.

85. There is at least one example, an instance of three disguised men being convicted of arson under the Ku Klux statute (Moulton *Advertiser,* June 25, 1869).

86. J. Richards to Smith, June 10, 1869, Gov. Smith Papers, ADAH.

87. Montgomery *State Journal,* Jan. 14, 1869.

88. J. C. Loomis to Smith, May 11, 1870; D. Woodruff to D. L. Dalton, June 4, 1869, Gov. Smith Papers, ADAH. R. Blair to E. Beecher, Nov. 15, 1868, reel 14, M 809, RG 105, NARA.

89. Miller to Smith, June 20, 1869, Gov. Smith Papers, ADAH. Miller kept trying to prosecute for the next half-dozen years and more, and he still threatened violence; see Miller to L. Parsons, Dec. 12, 1875, Lewis Parsons Papers, ADAH.

90. D. L. Dalton to J. A. Minnis, Jan. 31, 1869, and D. L. Dalton to S. S. Gardner, Jan. 31, 1869, Letterbooks; W. Seawell to Smith, May 2, July 4, Oct. 10, 1869, and Gardner to Smith, Nov. 21, 1869, all Gov. Smith Papers, ADAH.

91. D. L. Dalton to J. C. Loomis, May 17, 1869, Letterbooks; Sheriff J. J. Pegues to Dalton, June 22, 1869, and clipping, "Let Murder Cease," [June 1869], all Gov. Smith Papers, ADAH.

92. Gainesville *News,* Aug. 19, 1869; D. L. Dalton to Gov. John L. Palmer of Illinois, Oct. 11, 1869, Secretary's Letterbook, Governor Smith Papers, ADAH; G. Chautteau to Smith, Nov. 14, 1868, Sumter County File, Gov. Smith Papers, ADAH.

93. William Warren Rogers Sr. and Ruth Pruitt, *Alabama's Outlaw Sheriff: Stephen S. Renfroe* (1972; Tuscaloosa: UA Press, 2005), 33; G. Houston to Smith, Aug. 13, 1869, Gov. Smith Papers, ADAH; Gov. William H. Smith to Adam Kenard, Oct. 6, 1868, Letterbooks, Gov. Smith Papers, ADAH.

94. *KKK* 8: 132, 611; 9: 774.

95. Entries for Mar. 18, Apr. 16, 1870, William Cooper Diary, Emory University; D. C. Humphries to Smith, May 9, 1870, Gov. Smith Papers, ADAH.

96. Damer to Israel Pickens, Mar. 8, 30, Apr. 14, 1870, Pickens Papers, USA; Eyre Damer, *When the Klan Rode* (NY: Neale Publishing Co., 1912).

97. Montgomery *Mail,* June 19, 1868.

98. J. G. A. Smith to Gov. Smith, Apr. 16, 1870, Gov. Smith Papers, ADAH; Tuscaloosa *Monitor,* Nov. 8, 1870; Tuscaloosa *Observer,* Apr. 15, 1871.

99. W. T. [Bain?] to Smith, July 25, 1869, Gov. Smith Papers, ADAH.

100. *KKK* 9: 1229; J. A. Minnis to A. Akerman, Oct. 13, 1871, reel 1, M 1356, "Letters Received by the Department of Justice from the State of Alabama," NARA; Trelease, *White Terror,* 268–70.

101. A. W. Dillard to Smith, Aug. 14, 1869, Sumter County Files, folder 57, Gov. Smith Papers, ADAH.

102. Jacksonville *Republican,* Apr. 16, 1870; Columbus *Enquirer,* Apr. 20, 1870;

Huntsville *Democrat,* Aug. 1, 15, 1870; H. J. Springfield to Smith, July 3, 1870, Ku Klux Klan File, folder 20, Gov. Smith Papers, ADAH.

103. Montgomery *Mail,* July 14, 1870, quoting Chattanooga *Times,* and July 19, 1870 quoting Gadsden *Times;* H. J. Springfield to Smith, Apr. 18, 1870, Gov. Smith Papers, ADAH.

104. *Southern Railroad Man: Conductor N. J. Bell's Recollections of the Civil War Era,* ed. James A. Ward (DeKalb: Northern Illinois University Press, 1993), 53. J. W. Inzer to Smith, Aug. 3, 1870; Capt. [M. Frank Gallagher] to Lt. James Miller, July 12, 1870; Lieut. G. H. McLaughlin to Lieut. J. Miller, July 31, 1870, all Gov. Smith Papers, ADAH. Huntsville *Democrat,* July 11, Aug. 2, 1870. Mobile *Register,* Aug. 23, 1870. Montgomery *Journal,* Sept. 2, 1870. *KKK* 9: 1217–23, 1241.

105. *KKK* 9: 1003, 998.

106. Gen. Alfred Terry to Smith, July 31, 1870, S. W. Crawford to Smith, July 20, 1870, Gov. Smith Papers, ADAH.

107. S. W. Crawford to Smith, Apr. 6, 1870, and Report of Crawford to Terry, Feb. 14, 1870, both in Gov. Smith Papers, ADAH.

108. D. Lewis to Smith, July 13, 1870, Miscellaneous File, and T. Peters to Smith, Aug. 24, 1868, Gov. Smith Papers, ADAH.

109. C. Hays to Willard Warner, Sept. 15, 1870, Gov. Smith Papers, ADAH; for a similar evaluation of Hays's state, see Rogers, *Black Belt Scalawag,* 70.

110. Calculated from US Census, *A Compendium of the Ninth Census, 1870,* 24–25; Hahn, *A Nation Under Our Feet,* 282; Trelease, *White Terror,* 64.

111. Irving Allen to [J. Wager?], Aug. 15, 1870, and J. Wager to Smith, Aug. 16, 1870, Smith Papers, ADAH; Huntsville *Democrat,* Aug. 15, 19, 1870; *KKK* 9: 1223–27.

112. Hubbs, *Searching for Freedom after the Civil War,* 33.

113. Tuscumbia *Alabamian* qtd. in Memphis *Avalanche,* Oct. 2, 1868.

114. Montgomery *Advertiser,* Sept. 25, 1868; Macon [GA] *Telegraph,* Oct. 2, 1868; *KKK* 8: 179.

115. J. N. Brown to E. M. Cravath, Sept. 19, 26, 1870, reel 1, AMA Papers. The town's mayor sold insurance, eventually to the college, which may account for the elite interest in damping down the confrontation (A. A. Saffold to Cravath, Oct. 19, 1871, reel 1, AMA Papers).

116. Eutaw *Whig* qtd. in Jacksonville *Republican,* Nov. 5, 1870.

117. See also the discussion in chapter 11 of the casualty count in Barbour County election riots in 1874.

118. W. B. Jones to Smith, July 6, 1870; Price to Smith, Oct. 7, 1868, Gov. Smith Papers, ADAH.

119. Daniel Price to C. W. Pierce, June 12, 1868, Letters Received, SAC, Demopolis, box 27, RG 105, NA; D. Price to Smith, Oct. 7, 1868, Gov. Smith Papers, ADAH.

120. W. B. Jones to Smith, Apr. 3, 1870, Gov. Smith Papers, ADAH; C. C. Colton to B. F. Butler, Apr. 10, 1868, Butler Papers, LC; Republican to Smith, Apr. 9, 1870, [Eutaw], Gov. Smith Papers, ADAH.

121. 42nd Congress, 2nd Sess., House Committee on Elections, Misc. Doc. 15, "Contested Election: Norris vs. Handley, Alabama," 52–55, 68, 70–72, additional Record-Evidence, 70, on subsequent elections.

122. *KKK* 9: 1023; 8: 229; 9: 1061. F. S. Ferguson to Smith, June 13, 1870, Gov. Smith Papers, ADAH. Montgomery *Journal,* June 17, 1870. Tuskegee *News* qtd. in Montgomery *Mail,* June 8, 9, and June 15, 1870. Jacksonville *Republican,* June 18, 1870. Hayneville *Examiner,* June 29, Oct. 12, 1870; July 12, 1871. Tuskegee *News* qtd. in Montgomery *Journal,* Aug. 19, 1870. On Tuskegee's subsequent history, see Robert J.

Norrell, *Reaping the Whirlwind: The Civil Rights Movement in Tuskegee* (NY: Random House, 1985), 3–18.

123. Montgomery *Mail,* Apr. 13, 1870.

124. Thomas Peters to Gen. S. W. Crawford, July 28, 1870, Letters Received, District of Alabama, RG 393, pt. 1, NA; Peters to Smith, Sept. 5, 1870, Luke File, folder 28, Gov. Smith Papers, ADAH. For Smith and Peters's exertions, see Gene L. Howard, *Death at Cross Plains: An Alabama Reconstruction Tragedy* (Tuscaloosa: UA Press, 1984), 93–119.

125. Trelease, *White Terror,* 64.

126. In 1870, Sumter reported 11,646 bales, Greene 9,910; this as compared to their substantially less violent neighbors Hale at 18,573 bales and Marengo at 23,614. Demographically and otherwise, little else separates these counties. US Census, *A Compendium of the Ninth Census, 1870,* 712–13.

127. Trelease, *White Terror,* 64; J. L. Stelzig to Wilson, Aug. 25, 1868, reel 20, M 1900, RG 105, NARA.

128. R. A. Wilson to Stelzig, Aug. 13, 1868; J. L. Stelzig to Wilson, Aug. 5, 11, 1868, reel 20, M 1900, RG 105, NARA. Livingston *Journal,* Aug. 14, 1868. George Houston to Smith, Aug. 17, 1868, Sumter County File, Gov. Smith Papers, ADAH. On Renfroe's violent career, see Rogers and Pruitt, *Alabama's Outlaw Sheriff,* especially 34.

129. J. C. Gillespie to Patton, June 6, 1868, Gov. Patton Papers, ADAH; *KKK* 10: 1664.

130. G. Chautteau to Smith, Nov. 14, 1868, Sumter County File, folder 57, Gov. Smith Papers, ADAH; Stelzig to Wilson, Oct. 2, 6, 8, 1868, reel 20, M 1900, RG 105, NARA; Price to Smith, Oct. 7, 1868, Gov. Smith Papers, ADAH; *KKK* 8: 1003.

131. Kenard to Smith, Oct. 9, 1868, Sumter File, folder 57, Gov. Smith Papers, ADAH.

132. Demopolis *Southern Republican,* Aug. 31, 1870; *KKK* 8: 334.

133. D. Price to C. W. Pierce, May 1, June 12, 1868, Letters Received, Demopolis SAC, box 27, RG 105, NARA; Livingston *Journal,* July 17, 1868.

134. Demopolis *Southern Republican,* Aug. 31, 1870; *KKK* 11: 8, 14, 51; R. C. Merryman to Ella Merryman, Sept. 5, 1870, Ella Merryman Papers, Virginia Historical Society.

135. William C. Harris, *Day of the Carpetbagger: Republican Reconstruction in Mississippi* (Baton Rouge: LSU Press, 1979), 395–98.

136. The census matches perfectly for his family. See 1880 manuscript census, page 12, Franklin, Little River County, Arkansas, and the 1870 census for Livingston, Sumter County.

137. Hahn, *A Nation Under Our Feet,* 265.

Chapter Eight

Note to chapter epigraph: Montgomery *Mail,* Oct. 5, 1869.

1. For the conflict along railroad lines under construction, a pattern much in evidence in Alabama, see Nelson, *Iron Confederacies,* 4–5, 95–138. Mark W. Summers provides the modern study of the railroad program, with a revealing chapter on the Alabama & Chattanooga "catastrophe." But Summers's study does not much explore Smith's own railroad project, nor its relevance to racial politics or Klan suppression. See Summers, *Railroads, Reconstruction, and the Gospel of Prosperity,* 213–36.

2. Baggett finds that Alabama's sixty-five leading scalawags were unusually prosper-

ous in 1860, relative to their counterparts elsewhere and their Democratic opponents. See *The Scalawags*, tables 3 and 4.

3. A. McKinstry to F. W. Kellogg, Jan. 13, 1869, file 13021, HR 40-HR21.R, Records of the Select Committee on Reconstruction, RG 233, NA. He is specifically talking about the press abuse he received, but it fits the general attitude too.

4. Montgomery *Journal*, July 12, 1871.

5. Alexander White to Smith, Dec. 14, 1868, Gov. Smith Papers, ADAH; White to Moren, Dec. 11, 1868, and "To the Old Union Men of Alabama," (n.p., n.d.), in E. H. Moren Papers, ADAH.

6. W. H. Smith to Dalton, Sept. 16, 1869, Gov. Smith Papers, ADAH; *KKK* 8: 506, 519.

7. J. McDavis to Dalton, Dec. 7, 1867; J. McCaleb Wiley to Patton, Nov. 13, 1867, Gov. Patton Papers, ADAH.

8. Wiggins, *The Scalawag in Alabama Politics,* 128–31; Cash, "Alabama Republicans during Reconstruction," 129–30.

9. W. B. Jones to Smith, Aug. 17, 1868, Gov. Smith Papers, ADAH.

10. *KKK* 8: 1451–52, 1459–60; Jones to Smith, Oct. 28, 1869, Smith Papers, ADAH.

11. C. W. Pierce to Jones, May 5, 1866, reel 10, M 1900, RG 105, NARA.

12. J. McCaleb Wiley to Patton, Nov. 13, 1867, Gov. Patton Papers, ADAH. In 1868, these bankrupts include Wyatt Golson and J. A. Farden of Autauga, J. T. Foster of Choctaw, and W. W. Glass of Macon. Other insolvent legislators were Green T. McAfee of Talladega County, Justin Ronayne of Madison, and Alexander McKinstry of Mobile, a future lieutenant governor.

13. Thomas M. Peters, Case 820; B. F. Saffold, Case 1264; Noah B. Cloud, Case 1467; Joshua Morse, Case 1467; Case 1618; J. C. Goodloe, Case 888; Green T. McAfee, Case 1226; Justin Ronayne, Case 711; Gustavus Horton, Case 140, John C. Keffer, Case 235, all in Bankruptcy Records, Atlanta Branch, NARA. Wiggins, *The Scalawag in Alabama Politics,* 128, has the list, and B. Saffold, N. Cloud, J. Morse, C. C. Crowe, W. B. Jones, and J. T. Foster are among them. Of course numerous Democrats went bankrupt too; the point here is that many prominent Republican converts were in dire financial difficulty.

14. Summers, *Railroads, Reconstruction, and the Gospel of Prosperity,* 246.

15. Thornton, *Politics and Power in a Slave Society,* 321.

16. Macon *Georgia Weekly Telegraph,* June 10, July 29, 1873.

17. The evidence suggests that the two roles overlapped late in Governor Patton's administration. See D. N. Stanton to Patton, Apr. 11, 1868, and D. N. and J. C. Stanton to Patton, Apr. 22, 1868, Patton Papers, ADAH.

18. Robert Jemison to "My Dear Ma," June 28, 1868, Jemison Papers, Hoole Library, UA.

19. Benjamin Gardner to Gov. Lewis, Dec. 19, 1873, Gov. Lewis Papers, ADAH. Even the Democratic press later admitted the aid bill was not materially altered by the Republicans. See Mobile *Register* qtd. in St. Louis *Globe-Democrat,* Dec. 14, 1875.

20. Patton to J. H. Fitts, Aug. 8, 1868, Jemison Papers, UA; entry for J. C. and D. N. Stanton, Nov. 16, 1867, vol. 8, Suffolk County, MA, Dun Credit Records, Baker Library, Harvard University.

21. Montgomery *Journal,* Dec. 18, 1868; "Review of the Testimony Taken by the Investigating Committee of the Alabama House of Representatives" (Tuscaloosa, AL: Observer, 1871).

22. Elements of the Alabama & Chattanooga Railroad scandal, and Governor Smith's connection to it, have been noted in a number of older studies. See A. B. Moore,

"Railroad Building in Alabama During the Reconstruction Period," *Journal of Southern History* 1, no. 4 (1935): 422–41; John Ralph Scudder Jr., "The Alabama and Chattanooga Railroad Company," MA thesis, UA, 1951. However, no modern study has yet put together the story in full political and racial context.

23. Montgomery *Journal,* Oct. 21, 1868; Montgomery *Advertiser,* Nov. 6, 1868; St. Louis *Globe-Democrat,* Dec. 14, 1875; D. L. Dalton to Porter King et al., June 1, 1869, Letterbooks, and John C. Stanton to Smith, Nov. 6, 1868, all in Gov. Smith Papers, ADAH.

24. Jemison to Cole Hargrave, Nov. 13, 15, 1868, Scrapbook, Jemison Papers, UA; D. N. Stanton to Smith, Nov. 19, 1868, Smith Papers, ADAH.

25. Montgomery *Journal,* Nov. 21, Dec. 10, 11, 1868; Jemison to Cole Hargrave, Nov. 15, 1868, Jemison Papers, UA.

26. Summers, *Railroads, Reconstruction, and the Gospel of Prosperity,* 43.

27. Fleming, *Civil War and Reconstruction in Alabama,* 604.

28. Montgomery *Advertiser,* Nov. 16, 1869.

29. Montgomery *Mail,* Dec. 31, 1868; Jan. 3, 1869. "An Act to Provide for the Creation and Regulation of Railroad Companies . . . ," approved Dec. 29, 1868, 462; "An Act to Authorize the Several Counties and Towns," approved Dec. 31, 1868, 514, both in State of Alabama, General Assembly, *Acts, 1868.*

30. Randolph *Enterprise* qtd. in Montgomery *Journal,* May 15, 1872; see Lewis S. Dean, "The Prospecting Career of William Hugh Smith," *Alabama Review* 40, no. 2 (1987): 95–110.

31. Montgomery *Mail,* May 16, 1869.

32. Harrington to Smith, Feb. 28, 1869, Smith Papers, ADAH.

33. P. D. Roddey to Smith, Feb. 11, 1869, Railroad Files, folder 38, Smith Papers, ADAH.

34. Several of these lines were projected to link up with the A&C in the mountain region. Secretary of State, Corporations Division, Corporation Record, SS-45-1 A, G 4895, ADAH.

35. *NYT,* Aug. 16, 1869.

36. D. N. Stanton to Smith, Jan. 4, 1869, Smith Papers, ADAH.

37. Selma *Press,* Feb. 13, 1869.

38. J. L. Pennington and W. H. Smith to J. C. Stanton, Oct. 8, 1868, W. E. Chandler Papers, LC.

39. W. H. Smith to O. O. Howard, Dec. 20, 1866, reel 44, M 752, RG 105, NARA.

40. Harrington to Smith, Feb. 28, 1869, Smith Papers, ADAH.

41. Montgomery *Mail,* Apr. 6, July 14, 1869; for evidence of Spencer's longstanding ties to Hinds, see NY *Tribune,* Feb. 12, 1876.

42. Smith to Grant, Mar. 13, 1869, *Papers of Ulysses S. Grant* 19: 377–78.

43. Huntsville *Democrat* qtd. in Montgomery *Advertiser,* Apr. 3, 1869; see also Huntsville *Advocate,* Apr. 2, 1869.

44. Montgomery *Mail,* Feb. 23, 1869.

45. Montgomery *Journal,* Mar. 4, 1869; Montgomery *Advertiser,* Mar. 28, Apr. 20, 1869.

46. Montgomery *Mail,* May 16, 1869; Montgomery *Advertiser,* May 24, 1869.

47. Opelika *East Alabama Monitor,* Mar. 26, 1869.

48. Montgomery *Mail,* May 6, 16, 23, 1869.

49. Montgomery *Mail,* May 16, 1869.

50. Opelika *Recorder* qtd. in Columbus *Enquirer,* Apr. 2, 1870.

51. Montgomery *Advertiser,* Mar. 4, 1869.

52. Montgomery *Mail,* Aug. 19, 1869; Perman, *The Road to Redemption,* 87–107.

53. Hugh C. Bailey, "Alabama and West Florida Annexation," *Journal of Florida History* 35, no. 3 (1957): 221–22.

54. J. A. Yordy to Smith, Dec. 14, 1869, "Annexation of West Florida," folder 58, Smith Papers, ADAH; J. L. Pennington, A. J. Walker, and Charles A. Miller to Smith, July 1869, Smith Papers, ADAH; Mobile *Register,* Feb. 4, 11, 1870.

55. State of Alabama, *Senate Journal, 1869–70* (Montgomery, AL: Stokes, 1870), 234–44. Even the partisan *Mail* approved the purchase. See Montgomery *Mail,* Dec. 21, 1868, May 26, 1869.

56. Counted from the secretary of state's letterbooks, about twelve absences from Montgomery from August 1868 to August 1869, totaling nearly three months in a year's time (Alabama Governor's Papers, Secretary's Letters, June 1868–Aug. 1869, ADAH).

57. Perman, *The Road to Redemption,* 99.

58. Smith to Dalton, July 25, 1870, Smith Papers, ADAH.

59. Jacksonville *Republican,* Apr. 2, May 21, June 18, 1870.

60. Louis Wythe to Smith, Mar. 19, 1870, Railroad Files, folder 41, Smith Papers, ADAH; H. E. Brown to [Wm. H. Gilbert], July 13, 1870, Gilbert Cheever Papers, Yale University.

61. Jacksonville *Republican,* Apr. 2, 1870; *KKK* 9: 1219–20.

62. Jacksonville *Republican,* May 21, June 18, 1870. The county called an election in June, but after a narrow defeat in a neighboring country, the promoters delayed the election indefinitely.

63. J. L. Pennington to W. H. Smith, May 31, 1870, Forney to Smith, June 16, 1870, Smith Papers, ADAH.

64. Jacksonville *Republican,* June 11, 23, 1870; James F. DeCamp to Smith, June 29, 1870, Smith Papers, ADAH.

65. J. N. Brown to E. M. Cravath, Nov. 14, 1870, reel 1, AMA Papers. For a modern account of this episode, see Howard, *Death at Cross Plains.*

66. Summers, *Railroads, Reconstruction, and the Gospel of Prosperity,* surprisingly is still the only modern study of the topic, but even this work does not address black motivation in a sustained fashion.

67. J. L. Pennington to Smith, Apr. 26, 29, 1869, Gov. Smith Papers, ADAH.

68. Opelika *Monitor,* Apr. 2, 1869.

69. Fleming, *Civil War and Reconstruction in Alabama,* 605; Montgomery *Advertiser,* Aug. 11, 28, Dec. 16, 1869; Montgomery *State Journal,* June 2, 1869.

70. Montgomery *Advertiser,* Apr. 17, 1869.

71. Greensboro *Beacon,* July 3, 1869.

72. Selma *Press,* May 8, 1869.

73. Montgomery *Advertiser and Mail,* July 7, 1871; Columbus *Enquirer,* Nov. 25, 1871, Jan. 14, 1873.

74. Selma *Southern Argus,* Mar. 24, 1870.

75. Even hostile whites conceded this motive; see Demopolis *New Era,* Nov. 27, 1867, and E. T. Tayloe to W. H. Tayloe, Nov. 20, 1868, reel 20, Tayloe Papers, Stampp, ed., *Records of Ante-bellum Southern Plantations,* ser. M, pt. 1. For a perceptive elaboration of this theme, see William Warren Rogers Jr., "'For the Destruction of Radicalism': A Reconstruction Case Study," *Alabama Review* 62, no. 3 (2009): 190–210.

76. Because voters could cast their ballots at any poll, the results are not conclusive; in theory, the freedmen could have marched across the county to vote. But since these campaigns seldom featured violence, and since Hale County in particular had little Klan activity at this time, the geographic pattern seems genuine.

77. G. Ward Hubbs, *Guarding Greensboro: A Confederate Company in the Making of a Southern Community* (Athens: University of Georgia Press, 2003), 8.

78. In Hale County, polling-place proximity to the projected line is correlated with percentage yes vote by a relatively high +.642. This is substantially better than the correlations with percentage black, which is +.482, and with the anti-Democratic vote in August 1869, an almost identical +.488. Overall, the Hale County figures suggest the centrality of geography in the outcome. The pattern in Clarke County is more difficult to interpret. Proximity to the line is only mildly correlated with the yes vote, +.284, which is almost identical to the correlation with percentage black, +.277. There is a midrange correlation, however, between the railroad yes percentage and the total vote cast by precinct, +.483. This might suggest that outnumbered freedmen in smaller precincts were heading to town to vote, in a region with a terrorist presence.

79. Selma *Press,* Aug. 6, 1870.

80. Selma *Press,* June 4, July 23, Aug. 13, 1870.

81. Mobile *Register,* May 28, 1869.

82. Atlanta *Constitution,* June 12, 1870.

83. Huntsville *Democrat,* Jan. 11, 1870.

84. For an account of managerial violence, see Bell, *Southern Railroad Man,* 50–60.

85. Opelika *Monitor,* Apr. 2, 1869; "Proceedings of the Twenty-Second Annual Meeting of the Stockholders of the Mobile and Ohio Railroad Co. Held in Mobile, May 17, 1870" (Mobile, AL: n.p., 1870), 15.

86. Charles Manly to Parents, Oct. 5, 1868, Manly Family Papers, UA; Geo. E. Spencer to Dodge, July 11, 1869, Dodge Papers, SHSI-DM.

87. Columbus *Enquirer,* May 21, 1870; Baltimore *Sun,* May 7, 1869; A. C. Jones to Harry Watson, June 7, 1870, Watson Papers.

88. Harold D. Woodman, *New South, New Law: The Legal Foundations of Credit and Labor Relations in the Postbellum Agricultural South* (Baton Rouge: LSU Press, 1995); R. S. Hart to James Buford, June 18, 1869, Confederadoes Collection, AU.

89. Forrest to D. L. Dalton, July 11, Aug. 13, 1869, Gov. Smith Papers, ADAH.

90. Republican editorial accounts suggest this; see Selma *Press,* July 9, 23, Aug. 6, 1870.

91. Montgomery *State Journal,* Sept. 21, 1869.

92. *KKK* 12: 724–25; Montgomery *Mail,* July 20, 1869; Tuscaloosa *Monitor,* July 6, 1869.

93. Montgomery *Journal,* Sept. 24, Oct. 7, 1869; Tuscaloosa *Monitor,* Sept. 28, 1869; Montgomery *Mail,* Oct. 1, 1869; NY *Tribune,* Oct. 7, 1869; *KKK* 1: 18. On the implication of bribery, see John C. Jay, "General N. B. Forrest as a Railroad Builder in Alabama," *Alabama Historical Quarterly* 24, no. 1 (1962): 20–22.

94. R. Jemison to Maj. B. F. Fecklin, Aug. 28, 1865; R. Jemison to J. T. Taylor, June 18, 19, 1865, Jemison Papers, UA.

95. Jemison to W. A. C. Jones, Aug. 14, 1868, and Jemison to Tom Scott, Apr. 17, 1868, Jemison Papers, UA.

96. R. Jemison to E. A. Pettus, Sept. 13, 1868, Jemison Papers, UA.

97. Jemison to Tom Scott, Mar. 29, Apr. 17, 1868; Jemison to "Ma," Sept. 26, 1868; Jemison to Cole Hargrave, Dec. 19, 1869, Jemison Papers, UA.

98. Summers, *Railroads, Reconstruction, and the Gospel of Prosperity,* 213.

99. Pennington to Smith, July [1], 1869; W. L. Brown to Smith, July 2, 1869, Gov. Smith Papers, ADAH; Montgomery *Advertiser,* May 7, 1871.

100. D. L. Dalton to J. H. Speed, Aug. 10, 1869, Secretary's Letters, Gov. Smith Papers, ADAH.

101. Montgomery *Advertiser,* Sept. 3, 1869.

102. Columbiana *Shelby County Guide,* Feb. 8, 1872; Macon *Telegraph,* Apr. 26, 1870; Chattanooga *Republican,* July 24, 1869.

103. R. B. Kyle to Smith, Nov. 8, 1869, Gov. Smith Papers, ADAH.

104. Montgomery *Mail,* Jan. 21, 1870.

105. Mobile *Register,* Nov. 23, 1869; Montgomery *Mail,* Dec. 15, 30, 1869.

106. Huntsville *Advocate,* Dec. 14, 17, 21, 1869; Montgomery *Mail,* Dec. 16, 1869.

107. Montgomery *Advertiser,* Dec. 15, 1869; Montgomery *Mail,* Dec. 22, 1869; Mobile *Register,* Jan. 27, 28, 1870.

108. Montgomery *Journal,* Dec. 30, 1869.

109. Montgomery *Advertiser,* Dec. 28, 1869; also Montgomery *Mail,* Dec 29, 1869.

110. Dun Credit Ledgers, Tennessee, vol. 14: 7, Baker Library, Harvard University; Atlanta *Constitution,* June 18, 1870.

111. Ethel Armes, *The Story of Coal and Iron in Alabama* (Birmingham, AL: Chamber of Commerce, 1910), 218–21. There is a great deal of evidence of land speculation in anticipation of the railroad crossing; see Thomas Peters to S. H. Woodward, Mar. 31, Apr. 10, May 11, Sept. 10, 1869; Sept. 1, 21, 1870, Woodward Family Papers, UA.

112. Montgomery *Mail,* Jan. 21, 1870; Feb. 6, 1870.

113. Montgomery *Mail,* Mar. 9, 1870.

114. Montgomery *Mail,* Jan. 26, 27, 1870.

115. Montgomery *Mail,* Nov. 18, 1869; Feb. 16, 20, 1870. Tuscaloosa *Monitor,* Dec. 21, 1869.

116. Montgomery *Mail,* Jan. 29, Feb. 5, 1870; Huntsville *Democrat,* May 7, 1870.

117. Montgomery *Mail,* Feb. 8, 1870.

118. Montgomery *Mail,* Feb. 5, 8, 1870.

119. State of Alabama, General Assembly, *Acts, 1869–70* (Montgomery, AL: Stokes, 1870), 89–92.

120. Montgomery *Advertiser,* Jan. 25, 1871; State of Alabama, General Assembly, *Acts, 1869–70,* 149–57, 374.

121. State of Alabama, General Assembly, *Acts, 1869–70,* 175–79; Montgomery *Mail,* Feb. 15, 16, 1870.

122. DuBose, *Alabama's Tragic Decade,* 157–58.

123. Selma *Southern Argus,* Feb. 17, 1870.

124. Montgomery *Mail,* Mar. 4, Apr. 24, 1870; *KKK* 8: 231–32.

125. *KKK* 1: 319; Armes, *The Story of Coal and Iron,* 216.

126. Selma *Southern Argus,* Nov. 4, 1870, Feb. 10, 1871.

127. Montgomery *Mail,* Feb. 18, 1870.

128. Montgomery *Mail,* Jan. 25, 1870.

129. Montgomery *Mail,* Jan. 25, 1870.

130. Montgomery *Journal,* Jan. 1, 1870; Selma *Southern Argus,* Feb. 10, 1870.

131. Selma *Southern Argus,* Feb. 17, 1870.

132. Selma *Southern Argus,* Aug. 26, 1870; see also Montgomery *Advertiser,* Oct. 30, 1870.

133. *KKK* 1: 320–21.

134. Jacksonville *Republican,* Mar. 1, 1873; Fitzgerald, *Urban Emancipation,* 169. Carraway may be the legislator who allegedly had fifty dollars reluctantly thrust upon him; see *KKK* 8: 232.

135. Selma *Southern Argus,* Feb. 10, 17, 1870; Mobile *Register,* Jan. 23, 1870.

136. Tuscaloosa *Monitor,* Feb. 1, 1870.

137. Opelika *Recorder* qtd. in Columbus *Enquirer,* Apr. 2, 1870; Cherokee *Advertiser* qtd. in Huntsville *Democrat,* May 13, 1870; Macon *Telegraph,* Apr. 26, 1870.

138. Huntsville *Advocate,* Dec. 17, 1869.

139. Bradley to Smith, Jan. 11, 1870, Robert McKee Papers, reel 1, ADAH; see also L. B. Cooper to Dalton, Feb. 17, 1870, Gov. Smith Papers.

140. Mobile *Tribune* qtd. in Montgomery *Mail,* Mar. 2, 1870.

141. Fitzgerald, *Urban Emancipation,* 147–50.

142. Montgomery *Mail,* Mar. 16, 1870; Montgomery *Journal,* July 22, 1870.

143. R. M. Reynolds to Dalton, Oct. 6, 1869, Railroad folder 38, Gov. Smith Papers, ADAH.

144. Montgomery *Advertiser,* Apr. 16, 30, 1871; *KKK* 8: 194.

145. Montgomery *Advance,* Nov. 4, 1872; *KKK* 1: 319.

146. Montgomery *Advertiser,* Apr. 30, 1871.

147. *KKK* 8: 196.

148. D. L. Dalton to Albert F. Thayer, Secretary, Alabama & Chattanooga RR, in Boston, June 15, 1869, Secretary's Letterbook, 1869–70, Gov. Smith Papers, ADAH.

149. Dalton to R. M. Reynolds, July 30, 1869, Secretary's Letters, 1869–70, Gov. Smith Papers, ADAH.

150. Montgomery *Mail,* Mar. 26, 1870. Dalton technically made this statement in reference to the new state bonds issued to Stanton's railroad. Still, Dalton suggested that an overissue could never happen unintentionally, around the time when it occurred with the A&C's endorsed bonds.

Chapter Nine

Note to chapter epigraph: 42nd Congress, 2nd Sess., House Committee on Elections, Misc. Doc. 15, "Contested Election: Norris vs. Handley, Alabama," 78.

1. Trelease believes that Klan activity was more widespread and virulent in 1869 and 1870 in Alabama than nearly anywhere in the South, centrally involving half the state. He identifies northern Alabama and the western black belt, with the north as "the larger area" of night-riding. Fleming made a tabulation of violence reported in the congressional Klan testimony, and his count is broadly consistent. (Trelease, *White Terror,* 246, 247–73; Fleming, *Civil War and Reconstruction in Alabama,* 703).

2. 42nd Congress, 2nd Sess., House Committee on Elections, Misc. Doc. 15, "Contested Election: Norris vs. Handley, Alabama," 210.

3. Fleming provides a count of Klan episodes in congressional testimony, apparently tabulated from the index. He finds that episodes were reported in twenty-nine of sixty-four then existing Alabama counties, with murders in twenty-one of them. If accurately conveyed, it is surely an undercount of the real number, but the pattern suggests the range of experience across the state. Fleming's commentary on this evidence is revealing in its own right (*Civil War and Reconstruction in Alabama,* 703–5).

4. The relationship between public schools and the wider currents of Reconstruction politics remains indistinct in the literature, at least for Alabama. For a recent examination of the politics of schools in Mobile, see Hilary Green's *Educational Reconstruction: African American Schools in the Urban South, 1865–1890* (NY: Fordham University Press, 2015).

5. T. T. Edmunds to N. Cloud, Dec. 1, 1869, SG 15916, Correspondence of State Superintendent of Education, 1869–70, ADAH; Thornton, *Politics and Power in a Slave Society,* 292–94. For an accessible discussion of this topic, see Thornton's 2004 legal deposition: knightsims.com/pdf/04_05_10/Dr_Thornton_Deposition.pdf.

6. Clark, *History of Education in Alabama*, 241–45. Silsby to Smith, June 15, 1869, Smith Papers, ADAH. E. Beecher to J. Alvord, July 13, 1869; Jan. 5, 1870, reel 15, M 803, RG 105, NARA. Montgomery *Advertiser*, June 16, 1869. On Cloud, see Hubbs, *Searching for Freedom after the Civil War*, 98–131.

7. The state school board decreed separate schools the initial day it met. See "School Laws of the State of Alabama" (Montgomery, AL: Stokes and Co., 1870), 15.

8. C. P. Simmons to Smith, Dec. 24, 1869, Gov. Smith Papers, ADAH.

9. Huntsville *Advocate*, July 13, 1869; W. M. Loftin to N. Cloud, Oct. 1, 1869, SG 15916, Correspondence of State Superintendent of Education, 1869–70, ADAH.

10. Finis Smith to Gov. Smith, Aug. 10, 1870, Gov. Smith Papers, ADAH; Montgomery *Advertiser*, Jan. 17, 1871; E. Beecher to J. Alvord, Jan. 5, 1870, reel 15, and Beecher to Alvord, Jan. 26, Mar. 17, 1870, reel 10, M 803, RG 105, NARA; Noah Cloud, "Report of the Superintendent of Public Instruction" (Montgomery: Stokes and Co., 1869), 28–29. Democrats pursued Cloud as a substantial defaulter after he left office, with what justification being unclear; it may have been related to a controversy over Mobile's rival school boards. See entry for Noah B. Cloud, vol. 20, Montgomery County, Alabama, Dun Credit Ledgers, Baker Library, Harvard University. For a favorable assessment of Cloud's Whiggish career, see Hubbs, *Searching for Freedom after the Civil War*, 99–131. Finally, in Alabama, none of the Republican officials' alleged diversions of funds rival the gigantic theft by an absconding Democratic state treasurer after Reconstruction ended. See *NYT*, Feb. 1–6, 1883; July 28, 1887.

11. J. A. Yordy to Cloud, Dec. 4, 1869, SG 15916, Correspondence of State Superintendent of Education, 1869–70, ADAH.

12. A. A. Smith to Luther Smith, July 22, Aug. 3, 1869, Luther Smith Papers, Missouri History Museum Library, St. Louis; *KKK* 8: 52.

13. Superintendent R. Bradshaw to Cloud, Dec. 8, 1869, SG 15916, Correspondence of State Superintendent of Education, 1869–70, ADAH; Daniel Price and George W. Houston to O. O. Howard, May 2, 1869, reel 6, M 803, RG 105, NARA.

14. G. M. T. Gibson to Cloud, Nov. 8, 1869, and T. T. Edmunds to N. Cloud, Dec. 1, 1869, SG 15916, Correspondence of State Superintendent of Education, 1869–70, ADAH; E. Beecher to J. Alvord, July 13, 1869, Jan. 5, 1870, reel 15, M 803, RG 105, NARA.

15. Marion *Commonwealth*, Jan. 26, 1871.

16. T. T. Edmunds to N. Cloud, Dec. 1, 1869, SG 15916, Correspondence of State Superintendent of Education, 1869–70, ADAH.

17. US Census, *A Compendium of the Ninth Census, 1870*, 453–54.

18. Clark, *History of Education in Alabama*, 254–55.

19. State of Alabama, "Annual Report of the Officers of the Alabama Insane Hospital at Tuscaloosa" (Montgomery, AL, 1869), 8; and John S. Hughes, "Labeling and Treating Black Mental Illness in Alabama, 1861–1910," *Journal of Southern History* 58, no. 3 (1992): 445; "Report of the Secretary of the Board of Trustees, Freedmen's Hospital" (Montgomery, AL, 1869), 1, 18; Going, *Bourbon Democracy in Alabama*, 195.

20. Eufaula *Bluff City Times*, June 30, 1870.

21. Regional estimates in 1870 prepared through IPUMS. Black household wealth in the black belt averaged $30.86, in the piedmont region $45.90, and in the mountains $125.20. In terms of landownership, the pattern is similar, 1.9 percent in the black belt, 3.7 percent in the piedmont, and 19.4 percent in the mountain region.

22. This is an approximation necessitated by county boundary changes, using Kolchin's definition of the black-belt region. Dallas and Wilcox counties, with unchanged borders, showed increases even larger (Kolchin, *First Freedom*, 13; US Census, *A Compendium of the Ninth Census, 1870*, 24–25).

23. W. W. Gwaltmey to Tayloe, Aug. 10, 1867, reel 14, Tayloe Papers, Stampp, ed., *Records of Ante-bellum Southern Plantations*, ser. M, pt. 1.

24. Henry A. Tayloe to Brother, Feb. 7, 1867, reel 21, Tayloe Papers.

25. W. W. Gwaltmey to Tayloe, Aug. 25, 1867, reel 14, Tayloe Papers.

26. T. T. Mumford to [W. H. Tayloe], Jan. 30, 1869, reel 17, Tayloe Papers.

27. T. T. Munford to Tayloe, Mar. 2, 1869, reel 17, Tayloe Papers.

28. T. T. Munford to Tayloe, Jan. 8, 1870, reel 17, Tayloe Papers.

29. H. A. Tayloe to Brother, Feb. 7, 1867, reel 21, Tayloe Papers.

30. See note 22, above.

31. Robert W. Nicolson to "Cousin" W. H. Tayloe, Oct. 29, 1869, reel 17, Tayloe Papers.

32. Thomas T. Munford to Tayloe, Jan. 8, 1868, reel 17, Tayloe Papers.

33. Novak, *The Wheel of Servitude*, 25.

34. H. A. Tayloe to Brother, July 16, 1870, Apr. 4, 1871, reel 21, Tayloe Papers.

35. T. T. Munford to Tayloe, 24 Mar. [n.d.], reel 17, Tayloe Papers.

36. T. T. Munford to Tayloe, Dec. 29, [1870], reel 17, Tayloe Papers.

37. H. A. Stollenwerck & Bros., to W. H. Tayloe, Mar. 2, 1871, reel 26, Tayloe Papers.

38. W. W. Gwaltmey to Tayloe, Aug. 5, 1867, reel 14; H. A. Tayloe to Brother, June 24, July 10, 1867, reel 21, both in Tayloe Papers.

39. John Munford to [William Henry] Tayloe, Oct. 29, 1869, reel 17, Tayloe Papers.

40. H. A. Tayloe to Brother, Apr. 17, 1869, reel 21, Tayloe Papers.

41. H. A. Tayloe to Brother, Mar. 28, 1870, reel 21, Tayloe Papers.

42. Thomas J. Munford to Tayloe, Dec. 8, 186[9], reel 17, Tayloe Papers.

43. E. T. Tayloe to W. H. Tayloe, [Nov. 1868], reel 20, Tayloe Papers.

44. W. A. Stickney to Louisa Starkey, Feb. 25, Mar. 30, 1870; W. A. Stickney to I. Adler and Bros., Jan. 31, 1872, Faunsdale Collection, BPL.

45. Cash, "Alabama Republicans during Reconstruction," 111.

46. H. A. Tayloe to Brother, July 16, 1870, reel 21, Tayloe Papers; US Census, *A Compendium of the Ninth Census, 1870*, 113.

47. Montgomery *Advertiser*, Sept. 2, 1870. H. A. Tayloe to Brother, Nov. 4, 1870; Apr. 4, 1871, reel 21, Tayloe Papers.

48. Analysis of the IPUMS sample for 1870 reveals that only 1.9 percent of black heads of households reported owning lands, as opposed to 3.7 percent in the piedmont, and 19.4 percent in the mountains. The pattern for personal property is similar.

49. Entries for Jan. 8, 10, Sept. 17, 1870, reel 7, Philip H. Pitts Papers, ser. J, pt. 7, in Stampp et al., eds., *Records of Ante-Bellum Southern Plantations*.

50. On Spencer's background, see Terry L. Seip, "Of Ambition and Enterprise: The Making of Carpetbagger George E. Spencer," in Noe, ed., *The Yellowhammer War*, 191–219.

51. Warner to Willard Warner II, Dec. 27, 1865, Warner Papers, Tennessee State Library and Archives; Warner to John Sherman, Apr. 22, 1866, Sherman Papers, LC; NY *Tribune*, July 24, 1871.

52. Spencer to Grant, July 6, 1871, Records of the Division of Appointments, Records Relating to Custom Service Appointments, General Records of the Dept. of the Treasury, RG 56, NA.

53. Jacksonville *Republican*, July 6, 1872; Spencer to Logan, July 25, 1871, John A. Logan Papers, LC.

54. *Congressional Globe*, 41st Congress, 2nd Sess., Mar. 17, 1870, 2018–19.

55. *Congressional Globe*, 41st Congress, 2nd Sess., Apr. 19, 1870, 2812–13; W. Warner to W. Reid, Jan. 8, 1870, reel 189, Whitelaw Reid Paper, LC.

56. Sheriff H. G. Thomas to Smith, May 30, 1870, Smith Papers, ADAH.

57. T. M. Peters to S. M. Crawford, July 28, 1870, apparently misfiled in entry 102, Letters Received, Dept. of Alabama, 1865–66, RG 393, pt. 1, NA; Montgomery *Mail,* Apr. 13, 1870; J. A. Minnis to Smith, May 5, 1870, Gov. Smith Papers, ADAH.

58. Montgomery *Journal,* Aug. 12, 1870.

59. Smith to Dalton, May 24, 1870, Smith Papers, ADAH.

60. Minnis to Smith, May 5, 7, 25, 1870, Smith Papers, ADAH; Warner to Smith, Apr. 14, 1870, Smith Papers, ADAH.

61. H. C. Sanford to Dalton, July 7, 1870, Smith Papers, ADAH.

62. D. P. Lewis to Smith, June 29, 1869, and Lewis to Smith, July 13, 1870, Misc. Correspondence, folder 2, Smith Papers, ADAH.

63. Huntsville *Advocate,* June 24, 1870. The reference here is to arch-villain Andrew Johnson, who once famously called himself the slaves' Moses.

64. Huntsville *Advocate,* July 1, 1870.

65. Montgomery *State Journal,* July 15, 1870.

66. Hayneville *Examiner* qtd. in Montgomery *Mail,* July 8, 1870.

67. Montgomery *State Journal,* July 15, 1870; Montgomery *Mail,* July 26, 1870.

68. Alexander White to Dalton, Aug. 9, 1870, Smith Papers, ADAH.

69. Huntsville *Advocate,* July 8, 1870.

70. Montgomery *Advertiser,* Aug. 30, 1870.

71. Opelika *Locomotive,* Sept. 3, 1870; Montgomery *Mail,* Sept. 1, 7, 1870.

72. Mobile *Register,* Aug. 31, 1870; Montgomery *Advertiser,* Sept. 3, 1870; Huntsville *Advocate,* Sept. 23, 1870.

73. Montgomery *Journal,* Sept. 2, 1870.

74. Montgomery *Mail,* Sept. 3, 4, 1870; Huntsville *Democrat,* Oct. 29, 1870; Mobile *Register,* Nov. 1, 1870. On Rapier's nomination, see Schweninger, *James T. Rapier and Reconstruction,* 68–82.

75. Matt Avery to Gov. Smith, June 22, 1870, Smith Papers, ADAH.

76. [S. R. Bingham] to D. P. Smith, Sept. 21, 1870, Alabama State Treasurer, Record of Railroad Valuation and Bonds, 1866–73, SG 8087, ADAH. On Buck, see Shyam Krishna Bhurtel, "Alfred Eliab Buck: Carpetbagger in Alabama and Georgia," PhD diss., AU, 1981.

77. Selma *Argus,* Sept. 23, 1870.

78. Montgomery *Mail,* Aug. 26, 1870; Mobile *Register,* Sept. 2, 1870.

79. Montgomery *Mail,* Aug. 20, 23, 1870.

80. Montgomery *Mail,* Aug. 30, 1870.

81. Montgomery *Advertiser,* Sept. 3, 1870.

82. Huntsville *Democrat,* Aug. 27, 1870; Huntsville *Advocate,* Oct. 21, 1870. For an apparent endorsement of intimidating voters, see Mobile *Register,* Sept. 6, 1870.

83. Montgomery *Mail,* Sept. 25, 1870; Huntsville *Advocate,* Sept. 9, 1870.

84. J. McCaleb Wiley to Dalton, Sept. 27, 1870, Smith Papers, ADAH.

85. W. L. Cain to Smith, Oct. 8, 1870, Gov. Smith Papers, ADAH.

86. W. B. H. Howard to McKee, Oct. 17, 1870, reel 1, Robert McKee Papers, ADAH.

87. Shandy Jones to Smith, Sept. 21, 1870, Gov. Smith Papers, ADAH.

88. US Census, *A Compendium of the Ninth Census, 1870,* 24–25.

89. The train tactic seldom worked in reverse; when black railroad laborers wanted to aid the Springfields in St. Clair County, supervisors talked many out of it, but white Democrats reportedly rode in and out of the troubled area unmolested. See Bell, *Southern Railroad Man,* 53.

90. W. B. Jones to Smith, July 6, 1870, Smith Papers, ADAH. *KKK* 9: 1359–60; 10: 1452, 1580, 1622. Greensboro *Beacon,* Aug. 6, 1870. Livingston *Journal,* Aug. 5, 1870,

qtd. in *KKK* 10: 1666–68. According to his widow after his jailhouse lynching, High had come to Jones's defense when threatened at the rally, and he was harassed afterwards.

91. Pierce Burton to Smith, Aug. 4, 1870, Sumter County File, Smith Papers, ADAH; Meridian *Gazette,* Aug. 4, 1870.

92. *KKK* 8: 334–35.

93. *KKK* 8: 26; Huntsville *Advocate,* Nov. 4, 1870.

94. Selma *Argus,* Nov. 4, 1870.

95. *KKK* 8: 268–69, 44–45. On the episode, see Melinda Meek Hennessey, "Political Terrorism in the Black Belt: The Eutaw Riot," *Alabama Review* 33, no. 1 (Jan. 1980): 35–48.

96. Eutaw *Whig* qtd. in Montgomery *Mail,* Oct. 30, 1870, and Selma *Times* qtd. in Montgomery *Mail,* Oct. 29, 1870.

97. *KKK* 8: 26–30, 268–70, 301–2; Eutaw *Whig* qtd. in Montgomery *Mail,* Oct. 30, 1870; Montgomery *Journal,* Nov. 1, 3, 1870; Montgomery *Advertiser,* Aug. 4, 1871; Huntsville *Advocate,* Nov. 4, 1870.

98. Sarah Woolfolk Wiggins, "The Role of the Scalawag in Alabama Reconstruction," PhD diss., LSU, 1965, 143; Huntsville *Democrat,* Mar. 3, 1870; Selma *Argus,* Oct. 14, 1870; Montgomery *Mail,* Oct. 9, 1870; Huntsville *Advocate,* Oct. 21, 1870; G. Spencer to W. Chandler, Sept. 9, 1870, W. E. Chandler Paper, LC.

99. [S. R. Bingham] to D. P. Smith, Sept. 21, 1870, Alabama State Treasurer, Record of Railroad Valuation and Bonds, 1866–73, SG 8087 C, ADAH.

100. J. T. Heflin to Hall, Sept. 29, 1870, Bolling Hall Papers, ADAH.

101. Manuscript returns compiled from Secretary of State's Records, by Norwood A. Kerr, ADAH.

102. Hayneville *Examiner,* Nov. 30, 1870. Freedmen almost never split their tickets, so this seems certain.

103. Turnout was 98 percent of the census count in Montgomery County, 99 percent in Perry and Barbour, and 102 percent in Dallas, somehow. The reported census undercount of blacks may explain these high figures.

104. Rapier's presence on the ticket probably hurt in former Unionist strongholds. He ran far behind Governor Smith in the mountains; for example, Smith carried Winston County with 298 votes, while Rapier received just 36. See the returns in Schweninger, *James T. Rapier and Reconstruction,* 82, compared to Wiggins, "The Role of the Scalawag in Alabama Reconstruction," 299.

105. Tuscaloosa *Monitor,* Nov. 15, 1870.

106. Cincinnati *Commercial,* Nov. 29, 1870.

107. Tuscaloosa *Monitor,* Nov. 15, 1870; Montgomery *Advertiser,* May 25, 1871; *NYT,* Nov. 6, 1871. The Selma episode involved freedmen seizing a murder suspect from police and beating him nearly to death. Armed Democratic leaders left the assailants to punishment by the courts. For an explanation of this relative restraint, see testimony by Edmund J. Pettus in *KKK* 8: 375.

108. J. H. Taylor to Gen. Alfred H. Terry, Oct. 26, 1870; J. H. Taylor to AAG [Assistant Adjutant General], US Army, Oct. 15, 1870; J. H. Taylor to Gen. S. W. Crawford, Nov. 2, 3, 1870, all in Department of the South, RG 393, pt. 1, entry 4091, vol. 3, NA.

109. Robert Jemison to A. J. Walker, Dec. 1, 1870, Letterbook, box 3572, Jemison Papers, UA; Montgomery *Advertiser,* Feb. 10, 1870; Hayneville *Examiner,* Nov. 30, 1871; *KKK* 8: 197; School Superintendent Cloud briefly also contested his result based on a vague duel challenge his opponent recently issued (NY *Herald,* Dec. 2, 1870).

110. Warner to Grant, Nov. 17, 1870, and Smith to Grant, Nov. 18, 1870, *Papers of Ulysses S. Grant* 21: 18–19; Hayneville *Examiner,* Nov. 23, 30, 1870.

111. B. B. Keeler to S. W. Crawford, Nov. 21, 1870; J. H. Taylor to Gov. A. H. Terry, Nov. 26, 27, 29, 30, Dec. 1, 1870; J. H. Taylor to Gov. S. W. Crawford, Dec. 2, 1870; J. H. Taylor to Gen. Terry, Dec. 1, 1870; J. H. Taylor to Capt. Drum, Nov. 29, 1870, Letters Sent, Department of the South, RG 393, pt. 1, entry 4091, vol. 3 of 13, NA. Capt. E. W. Smith to J. H. Taylor, Dec. 1, 1870, box 4, Letters Received 1869–74, Military Division of the South, box 4, Letters Received 1869–74, entry 4406, RG 393, NA.

112. Cincinnati *Commercial,* Dec. 2, 1870; Montgomery *Mail,* Nov. 27, 1870; Montgomery *Advertiser,* Nov. 27, 29, 30, Dec. 1, 1870.

113. Huntsville *Advocate,* Dec. 2, 16, 1870; Cincinnati *Commercial,* Dec. 17, 1870.

114. Grant to C. W. Buckley, Nov. 21, 1870, *Papers of Ulysses S. Grant* 21: 18; NY *Herald,* Dec. 7, 8, 1870.

115. Grant to C. W. Buckley, Nov. 23, 1870, *Papers of Ulysses S. Grant* 21: 18; Montgomery *Mail,* Dec. 8, 1870; Huntsville *Democrat,* Dec. 21, 1870; Hayneville *Examiner,* Jan. 25, 1871.

116. Montgomery *Mail,* Dec. 2, 1870.

117. Montgomery *Mail,* Dec. 10, 11, 1870. On Busteed and Smith's role, see J. Minnis to A. Akerman, May 29, 1871, reel 1, M 1356, NARA.

118. B. B. Lewis to R. McKee, Dec. 31, 1871, reel 1, McKee Papers, ADAH; entry for A&C Railroad, Dec. 10, 1872, vol. 372, NY City, Dun Credit Reports, Baker Library, Harvard University.

119. Clews to Lindsay, Jan. 6, 1871, Henry Clews folder, Gov. Lindsay Papers, ADAH.

120. Montgomery *Advertiser,* Apr. 30, 1871; F. M. Gilmer to B. Hall, Jan. 12, 1871, Bolling Hall Papers, ADAH.

121. Tuscaloosa *Observer,* Feb. 4, 1871; Clews & Habicht & Co. to Lindsay, Jan. 17, 1871, and H. Clews to Lindsay, Feb. 9, 1871, both Gov. Lindsay Papers, ADAH.

122. *NYT,* Jan. 6, 7, 21; Feb. 1, 10, 1871.

123. Montgomery *Advertiser,* Jan. 25, 1871.

124. State of Alabama, *Journal of the Session of 1870–71 of the Senate of Alabama* (Montgomery: Screws, 1871), 84; Joseph Hodgson to R. McKee, Apr. 25, 1873, reel 1, R. McKee Papers, ADAH.

125. Montgomery *Advertiser,* Feb. 8, 1871.

126. Joseph Taylor to R. McKee, Apr. 5, 1871, reel 1, Robert McKee Papers, ADAH.

127. Montgomery *Advertiser,* Feb. 4, 1871.

128. Montgomery *Advertiser,* Feb. 12, Mar. 23, 1871; N. B. Forrest to Lindsay, Feb. 17, 1871, Gov. Lindsay Papers, ADAH.

129. B. B. Lewis to R. McKee, May 6, 1871, reel 1, Robert McKee Papers, ADAH.

130. G. F. Lewis to Lindsay, Mar. 14, 1871; J. L. Pennington to Lindsay, Mar. 20, 1871; P. D. Roddey to Gindrat, Mar. 17, 20, 1871, all in Lindsay Papers, ADAH.

131. John Winston to R. McKee, May 12, 1871, reel 1, McKee Papers, ADAH.

132. Montgomery *Advertiser,* Apr. 11, 16, 30, 1871; Columbiana *Shelby County Guide,* Dec. 7, 1871.

133. T. C. Stewart to E. M. Cravath, Feb. 8, 23, 1871, reel 2, AMA Papers; Columbus *Enquirer,* Mar. 15, 1871; Manhattan [Kansas] *Nationalist,* Apr. 14, 1871; Fitzgerald, *Urban Emancipation,* 59–61.

134. One upcountry newspaper reported the sabering of a Klansman by a freedman, without apparent dismay. Columbiana *Shelby County Guide,* Jan. 19, Aug. 10, 1871.

135. Thomas Cobbs to Lindsay, [Oct. 1871], and E. W. Smith to Lindsay, Oct. 18, 1871, Gov. Lindsay Papers, ADAH.

136. Robert A. McClellan to Gov. Lindsay, Aug. 31, 1871, Governor Lindsay Papers, ADAH.

137. Joseph H. Sloss to Gov. Lindsay, Apr. 12, 1871, Gov. Lindsay Papers, ADAH; J. B. Clark to Luther Smith, Mar. 27, 1871, Luther R. Smith Papers, Missouri Historical Society.

138. G. B. Mobley to W. V. Chardavoyne, Aug. 30, 1871; Samuel W. Dunlap to Lindsay, May 15, June 25, 1872, Gov. Lindsay Papers, ADAH.

139. A. Y. Sharpe to "Aunt," July 13, 1871, William Dunlap Simpson Papers, Duke University; T. C. Stewart to Cravath, Apr. 3, 1871, and Helen Leonard to Smith, May 29, 1871, reel 2, AMA Papers; Marion *Commonwealth*, Jan. 19, 26, 1871.

140. The letter's reference is to the Knights of the White Camellia, another terrorist group. Tuscaloosa *Monitor*, May 11, 1869. Thomas Seay to A. A. Coleman, Mar. 3, 1871; E. W. Rucker to J. G. Randolph, Mar. 6, 1871, both in Gov. Lindsay Papers, ADAH. Selma *Argus*, Feb. 3, 1871. *KKK* 8: 176–77; 10: 1272–76.

141. Livingston *Journal*, Feb. 24, 1871, and Apr. 10, 1872. Endorsement in Smith to Lindsay, Apr. 13, 1871; Smith to Lindsay, Nov. 17, 1871, and Feb. 9, 1872; and D. C. Hodo to Lindsay, Apr. 5, 1871, Gov. Lindsay Papers, ADAH. *KKK* 8: 107.

142. *KKK* 8: 165, 170–71.

143. Columbus *Enquirer*, Apr. 7, 1871.

144. Joseph H. Sloss to John A. Steele, Feb. 23, 1871; Sloss to Lindsay, Apr. 12, 1871, Gov. Lindsay Papers, ADAH. On the episode itself, see Tuscaloosa *Observer*, Apr. 22, 1871.

145. Huntsville *Democrat*, Dec. 5, 6, 1870; *NYT*, Jan. 25, 1871.

146. It appears the spasm of local political expulsions after the election encouraged wider mayhem. Several of the outrages listed in the Alabama Klan testimony occurred in 1871, mostly early in the year. See *KKK* 8: li–lii.

147. Trelease notes the "really marked decline in violence" in the summer and fall of 1871 (*White Terror*, 310). On the federal trials, see Christopher Lyle McIlwain, "United States District Judge Richard Busteed and the Alabama Klan Trials of 1872," *Alabama Review* 65, no. 2 (2012): 263–89.

148. Fitzgerald, "The Ku Klux Klan," 198–99. *KKK* 9: 646–49. J. A. Minnis to A. Akerman, Sept. 19, 1871, reel 1, M 1356, NARA. Daniel Coleman to Lindsay, Aug. 14, 26, Sept. 29, Oct. 12, 14, 21, 1871, Gov. Lindsay Papers, ADAH.

149. R. Lindsay report, 1855, Franklin County, Dun Credit Records, Baker Library, Harvard University.

150. NY *Herald*, May 4, 1871; Macon *Telegraph*, Aug. 29, 1871; Montgomery *Advertiser and Mail*, Aug. 26, 1871.

151. Rice & Chilton to J. C. Stanton, June 23, July 7, 1871, Letterbook of Rice & Chilton, Williams Collection, UA.

152. Montgomery *Advertiser and Mail*, June 9, 10, 16, 17, 1871.

153. Montgomery *Advertiser*, June 20, 25, 26, July 7, 29, 1871; Tuscaloosa *Observer*, Aug. 5, 1871.

154. J. Gindrat to Lindsay, Aug. 5, 1871, Gov. Lindsay Papers, ADAH; Montgomery *Advertiser*, Aug. 5, 1871; "Report of John H. Gindrat, Receiver of the Alabama & Chattanooga Railroad, to the Governor" (Montgomery, AL: W. W. Screws, 1871), 3–4, 6; Tuscaloosa *Observer*, Oct. 1, 1871.

155. Livingston *Journal*, Sept. 1, 1871; Hayneville *Examiner*, Sept. 20, 1871; Cincinnati *Commercial*, Aug. 3, 1871; Columbus *Enquirer*, Sept. 29, 1871; Record for J. H. Clanton, Montgomery County, Dun Credit Records, Harvard University.

156. NY *Tribune*, Aug. 15, 1871; Lindsay to Chardavoyne, Aug. 19, 1871, Gov. Lindsay Papers, ADAH; Montgomery *Advertiser and Mail*, Aug. 5, 1871.

157. *NYT*, Aug. 24, 1873. It would appear the two men remained in contact on rail-

road matters even after the disclosures. See N. McKay to Lindsay, July 18, 1871, and the telegram from "N.M." to Lindsay, Sept. 7, 1871, Gov. Lindsay Papers, ADAH.

158. Montgomery *Advertiser,* Aug. 4, 23, 24, 26, 1871.

159. Columbus *Enquirer,* Jan. 27, 1871; Hayneville *Examiner,* June 19, 1871; Hodgson to Lindsay, May 22, 1871, Gov. Lindsay Papers, ADAH; Montgomery *Advertiser,* Aug. 24, 1871.

160. Bryce to Lindsay, Oct. 12, 1871; Lindsay to Bryce, Oct. 17, 1871; published report of Lehman Durr to Lindsay, Dec. 21, 187[1], folder 29, all in Gov. Lindsay Papers, ADAH.

161. B. B. Lewis to R. McKee, Dec. 31, 1871, and Jan. 30, 1873, reel 1, Robert McKee Papers, ADAH.

162. Columbiana *Shelby County Guide,* Feb. 29, 1871; Tuscaloosa *Times,* Feb. 21, 1872.

Chapter Ten

Note to chapter epigraph: W. B. Young to "Aunt," Dec. 4, 1870, William Dunlap Simpson Papers, Duke University.

1. For an example of a wholesale reconsideration, see Adam Fairclough, "Was the Grant of Black Suffrage a Political Error? Reconsidering the Views of John W. Burgess, William A. Dunning, and Eric Foner on Congressional Reconstruction," *Journal of the Historical Society* 12, no. 2 (June 2012): 155–88.

2. Mobile *Register,* Nov. 26, 1872; Atlanta *Sun,* Jan. 25, 1873.

3. Richard Sutch et al., *Historical Statistics of the United States, Millennial Edition* (Cambridge, UK: Cambridge University Press, 2006), vol. 3: 209.

4. H. A. Stollenwerck to H. Watson, June 14, 1872, Watson Papers.

5. S. Strudwick to Pattie, June 18, 1870, and S. Strudwick to Pattie and Mary, May 31, 1872, Samuel Strudwick Papers, ADAH.

6. S. Strudwick to My Dear Sledge, May 19, 1871, Samuel Strudwick Papers, ADAH.

7. Ben Grey to R. McKee, Feb. 4, 1870, reel 1, Robert McKee Papers, ADAH.

8. Henry Lyell to Henry A. Tayloe, Feb. 5, Mar. 5, 1872; Mar. 22, 1873, reel 47, Tayloe Papers, Stampp, ed., *Records of Ante-bellum Southern Plantations,* ser. M, pt. 1.

9. *Southern Cultivator,* May 1870, 141.

10. *NYT,* Aug. 9, 1873. I have found no instances of strikes of cotton hands or tenants during the early 1870s.

11. Entry for Benjamin Turner, July 24, 1869, Dallas County, AL, vol. 10, R. G. Dun Credit Ledgers, Baker Library, Harvard University; T. Peters to S. H. Woodward, Dec. 19, 1870, Woodward Family Papers, UA; Frederick Watson to Arthur Watson, Oct. 30, 1872, Watson Papers.

12. See Robert Arthur Gilmour, "The Other Emancipation: Studies in the Society and Economy of Alabama Whites During Reconstruction," PhD diss., Johns Hopkins University, 1972, 64–66, 74–75.

13. Julius C. Greene, "Reminiscence of Julius C. Greene," unpublished manuscript, 4, UA; *KKK* 9: 1125–27.

14. Lindsay to J. J. Parker, July 11, 1871; W. T. Abrahams to Gov. Lindsay, Oct. 19, 1871; J. Y. Kilpatrick to Lindsay, Nov. 19, 1871; J. Y. Kilpatrick to Gov. Lindsay, Jan. 30, 1872, all Gov. Lindsay Papers, ADAH. Livingston *Journal,* Oct. 11, 1872. See also Cynthia Griggs Fleming, *In the Shadow of Selma: The Continuing Struggle for Civil Rights in the Rural South* (Lanham, MD: Rowman and Littlefield, 2004), 9–13.

15. Columbiana *Shelby County Guide,* May 25, Sept. 14, Oct. 5, 12, 1871; May 28, 1872.

16. Montgomery *Advertiser,* Mar. 12, 1869; Selma *Argus,* Oct. 10, 1873; W. S. Wyman to Lindsay, May 12, 1871, Gov. Lindsay Papers, ADAH; Tuscaloosa *Observer,* Mar. 25, June 17, Aug. 5, 1871. Randolph's opponent, John M. Martin, was the son-in-law of Supreme Court Judge E. W. Peck. See Hubbs, *Searching for Freedom after the Civil War,* 45, 50.

17. Opelika *Era and Whig,* Sept. 8, 15, 22, Dec. 1, 1871.

18. Columbiana *Shelby County Guide,* Sept. 21, Oct. 5, 1871.

19. W. Warner to W. Reid, Nov. 22, 1871, reel 189, Whitelaw Reid Papers, LC.

20. G. D. Cunningham et al. to Lindsay, Dec. 15, 1871; W. L. Heflin to R. B. Lindsay, Nov. 15, 1871; J. W. Suttle to R. B. Lindsay, Dec. 2, 1871, all Gov. Lindsay Papers, ADAH. Marion *Commonwealth,* Oct. 26, 1871.

21. Committee to Gov. Lindsay, [Dec. 1871], Gov. Lindsay Papers, ADAH. Also, the Hayneville *Examiner,* Nov. 29, 1871, refers to several African Americans filing their bonds as magistrates.

22. Henry County *Register,* May 14, 1870; Eufaula *Bluff City Times,* June 22, 29, Dec. 21, 1871.

23. For an examination of this topic, see Rogers, "For the Destruction of Radicalism."

24. Addie Smith to Luther Smith, Nov. 1, 7, 8, 1871, Luther Smith Papers, Missouri Historical Society.

25. John S. Corbin to Genl. Pleasanton, Mar. 18, [1871], Selma, Division of Appointment Records, Records Relating to IRS Assessors, Applications for Positions as Internal Revenue Collectors & Assessors, entry 258, box 1, RG 56, NA-CP.

26. W. Warner to W. Reid, Jan. 8, 1870, reel 189, Whitelaw Reid Papers, LC.

27. Fitzgerald, *Urban Emancipation,* 180–81.

28. For an extended discussion, see Fitzgerald, *Urban Emancipation,* 168–96, and on the Radical leader Allen Alexander, 233–38.

29. G. Spencer to Logan, July 25, 1871, John A. Logan Papers, LC.

30. J. A. Minnis to A. Akerman, Oct. 31, 1871, reel 1, M 1356, NARA. On the rising factionalism in Montgomery, see Rabinowitz, "Holland Thompson and Black Political Participation in Montgomery, Alabama," 261–64.

31. Henry Europe to G. Boutwell, July 15, 1871, Records of the Division of Appointments, Records Relating to Customs Service Appointments, Applications for Appointments as Customs Service Officers, 1833–1910, RG 56, NA-CP.

32. G. E. Spencer to G. L. Putnam, Aug. 12, 1871, qtd. in Alabama General Assembly, *Report of the Joint Committee of the General Assembly of Alabama, in Regard to the Alleged Election of Geo. E. Spencer* (Montgomery, AL: W. W. Screws, 1875), 16, lviii.

33. Alabama General Assembly, *Report of the Joint Committee . . . in Regard to the Alleged Election of Geo. E. Spencer,* lvi–lviii; B. W. Norris to A. A. Smith, Feb. 3, 1872, Luther Smith Papers, Missouri Historical Society.

34. Wiggins, "The Role of the Scalawag in Alabama Reconstruction," 168.

35. N. Davis to F. P. Blair, Apr. 17, 1872, reel 7, Carl Schurz Papers, LC.

36. Miller to Boutwell, July 27, 1872, box 4, General Records of the Department of the Treasury, Records of the Division of Appointments, Records Relating to Customs Service Appointments, "Records Relating to 'Customhouse Nominations,' 1833–1910," [entry 246], RG 56, NA-CP.

37. L. P. Walker to Marble, May 9, 1872, Manton Marble Papers, LC.

38. Columbiana *Shelby County Guide,* Aug. 31, 1871.

39. See Mitchell Snay, *Horace Greeley and the Politics of Reform in Nineteenth Century America* (Lanham, MD: Roman and Littlefield, 2011).

40. P. M. Dox to Cabaniss, June 3, 1872, S. D. Cabaniss Papers, Duke University.

41. Compiled from Newspaper Cuttings File of the Council of Foreign Bondholders, reel 219, Stanford University. For uncompleted lines, see the map in Going, *Bourbon Democracy in Alabama,* 129.

42. Columbiana *Shelby County Guide,* Jan. 13, 1872.

43. Montgomery *Advertiser* qtd. in Columbiana *Shelby County Guide,* Feb. 29, 1872.

44. Montgomery *State Journal,* June 11, 1872.

45. Mobile *Tribune,* Aug. 8, 1872; *NYT,* Aug. 13, 1872; Jacksonville *Republican,* Sept. 14, 1872; J. G. Harris to R. McKee, July 9, 1872, and J. Taylor to R. McKee, Aug. 24, 1872, reel 1, Robert McKee Papers, ADAH.

46. Warner to C. Schurz, July 22, 1872, reel 8, Carl Schurz Papers, LC.

47. P. M. Dox to Cabaniss, June 3, 1872, S. D. Cabaniss Papers, Duke University; Huntsville *Democrat,* Aug. 2, 1872; Jacksonville *Republican,* July 6, 1872.

48. *NYT,* July 1, 1872.

49. Mobile *Tribune,* Aug. 9, 11, 29, 30, 1872.

50. Jacksonville *Republican,* Aug. 24, Sept. 7, 1872.

51. Paul Strobach to Chandler, Aug. 18, 1872, W. E. Chandler Papers, LC.

52. D. C. Whiting to Chandler, Aug. 9, 1872, and James T. Rapier to Chandler, Aug. 30, 1872, W. E. Chandler Papers, LC; Jacksonville *Republican,* Sept. 21, 1872.

53. David P. Lewis Application, "Amnesty Papers," reel 7, M 1003, NARA; D. P. Lewis to Swayne, July 5, 1867, Swayne Papers, ADAH.

54. See Cash, "Alabama Republicans during Reconstruction," 111. Cash undertook an exhaustive search for the social origins of Republican officeholders, to find that African Americans were only 6 percent of the original cohort elected in 1868. Though he does not follow this logic, simple arithmetic suggests a significantly higher number in the early 1870s to reach his 11 percent figure for the Reconstruction era as a whole.

55. Calculated from the table in Wiggins, *The Scalawag in Alabama Politics,* 150.

56. J. H. Taylor to [illegible], Oct. 29, 1872, and A. H. Terry to J. W. Taylor, Nov. 4, 1872, Headquarters Department of the South, [entry 4091], RG 393, pt. 1, NARA; G. Spencer to Robert Barber, Oct. 22, 1872, qtd. in Alabama General Assembly, *Report of the Joint Committee . . . in Regard to the Alleged Election of Geo. E. Spencer,* 50, xlii–xliv.

57. Livingston *Journal,* July 5, Aug. 2, 23, Sept. 20, Nov. 1, 1872.

58. Jacksonville *Republican,* Aug. 24, 1872.

59. Washington *New National Era,* June 29, 1872; Montgomery *Advance,* Nov. 4, 1872.

60. J. L. Pennington to Chandler, Aug. 20, 1872, W. E. Chandler Papers, LC.

61. Wm. F. Samford to Ben. C. Yancey, Sept. 18, 1872, B. C. Yancey Paper, SHC.

62. Charles Hall to Bolling Hall, Dec. 1, 1872, Bolling Hall Papers, ADAH.

63. Montgomery *Journal,* Nov. 22, 1872.

64. In Shelby County, for example, the Democrats lost eight votes while the Republicans gained nearly three hundred; in overwhelmingly white Winston County, Democrats lost two while Republicans gained over one hundred. The largest Republican gains seem to be accounted for in northern Alabama areas where freedmen could now vote. In Madison County alone, they gained nearly a thousand votes, in Colbert over six hundred more.

65. Moulton *Advertiser,* Nov. 6, 1872. For a visual sense of the outcome, see the maps in Going, *Bourbon Democracy in Alabama,* 214–17.

66. Mobile *Register,* July 20, 1877; Fitzgerald, *Urban Emancipation,* 189–90.

67. Montgomery *Journal,* Nov. 6, 1872.

68. *NYT,* Dec. 9, 1872; Hearing rumors of planned fraud in Russell County, near Barbour County, Republicans dispatched federal District Attorney J. T. Minnis to the scene, and nothing of the sort occurred there.

69. Montgomery *Journal,* Nov. 22, 1872. For a version of these complex events assuming the legitimacy of the Democratic count, see Charles M. Crook, "The Barbour County Background to the Election of 1872 and Alabama's Dual Legislatures," *Alabama Review* 56, no. 4 (2003): 242–77.

70. Alabama General Assembly, *Report of the Joint Committee . . . in Regard to the Alleged Election of Geo. E. Spencer,* xcix; Columbiana *Shelby County Guide,* Nov. 21, 1872. The timeline and Democratic argument are well laid out in the speech of Senator W. T. Hamilton, *Congressional Record,* 43rd Congress, 1st Sess., Appendix, 323–31.

71. US Congress, Senate, "Election of George E. Spencer," 44th Congress, 1st Sess., Report No. 331: 168–69, 193, 197–99.

72. R. W. Walker to Cabaniss, Nov. 23, 1872, S. D. Cabaniss Papers, Duke University.

73. Livingston *Journal,* Dec. 13, 1872.

74. P. Strobach to Gov. Lewis, Nov. 29, 1872, in Strobach to Chandler, Dec. 6, 1872, W. E. Chandler Papers, LC; Lewis to Col. T. B. Wier, Nov. 30, 1872, SG 023238, Gov. Lewis Papers, ADAH. .

75. Paul Strobach to W. E. Chandler, Dec. 6, 1872, W. E. Chandler Papers, LC; Paul Strobach to Son, 1900, Paul Strobach letter, ADAH; Huntsville *Democrat,* Dec. 15, 1872.

76. David P. Lewis to Grant, Nov. 30, 1872 and subsequent documents in *Papers of Ulysses S. Grant* 23: 459; Gen. Alfred H. Terry to [illegible], Dec. 9, 1872, Letters Sent, HQ Dept. of the South, RG 393, NARA; Montgomery *Advertiser and Mail,* Nov. 24, 30, Dec. 12, 1872.

77. Livingston *Journal,* Dec. 20, 1872; Montgomery *Advertiser and Mail,* Dec. 14, 15, 1872.

78. Montgomery *Advertiser and Mail,* Dec. 6, 22, 1872.

79. Montgomery *Journal,* Dec. 27, 1872.

80. Montgomery *Advertiser and Mail,* Dec. 22, 1872; Livingston *Journal,* Dec. 27, 1872; Selma *Argus,* Jan. 17, 1873. See also Chicago *Inter-Ocean,* Jan. 11, 1876.

81. Cincinnati *Commercial,* Jan. 10, 15, 1873; P. Hamilton et al. to G. H. Williams, Dec. 23, 1872, reel 1, M 1356, NARA.

82. Alabama General Assembly, *Report of the Joint Committee . . . in Regard to the Alleged Election of Geo. E. Spencer,* clvi–clviii; George E. Spencer to Chandler, Nov. 27, 1872, W. E. Chandler Papers, LC.

83. Alabama General Assembly, *Report of the Joint Committee . . . in Regard to the Alleged Election of Geo. E. Spencer,* xxii–xxv, xxxiv, cxxxviii, cxlvii–clvi; Montgomery *Advertiser and Mail,* Jan. 12, 22, 1873; Montgomery *Journal,* Feb. 9, 1873; Fitzgerald, *Urban Emancipation,* 193.

84. George Spencer to R. Barber, Oct. 16, 1872, in Alabama General Assembly, *Report of the Joint Committee . . . in Regard to the Alleged Election of Geo. E. Spencer,* 50, xcv–xcvi, cxx, cxxii. Here as elsewhere, there is room to wonder what the later Democratic investigating committee left out about their own members' conduct, given the Republican near-boycott of the proceedings.

85. Montgomery *Advertiser and Mail,* Jan. 14, 1873; Alabama General Assembly, *Report of the Joint Committee . . . in Regard to the Alleged Election of Geo. E. Spencer,* lxii, clvii; Fitzgerald, *Urban Emancipation,* 192–93.

86. Alabama General Assembly, *Report of the Joint Committee . . . in Regard to the Alleged Election of Geo. E. Spencer,* lxxii, lxxxviii, cxxxv, clxxxi.

87. Alabama General Assembly, *Report of the Joint Committee . . . in Regard to the Alleged Election of Geo. E. Spencer,* xciv, xxvii, xxxv–xli, lxxii, cviii–cix, cxxxv, cxxxvii; Columbiana *Shelby County Guide,* Feb. 20, 1873.

88. Alabama General Assembly, *Report of the Joint Committee . . . in Regard to the Alleged Election of Geo. E. Spencer,* clxvii, lxxxviii, xcii.

89. *NYT,* Jan. 13, 1873; Montgomery *Advertiser and Mail,* Jan. 30, 1873.

90. Parsons to Chandler, Jan. 29, 1873, W. E. Chandler Papers, LC.

91. Alabama General Assembly, *Report of the Joint Committee . . . in Regard to the Alleged Election of Geo. E. Spencer,* lxxi, cxxxlii.

92. Columbiana *Shelby County Guide,* Feb. 13, 1872; Selma *Argus,* Feb. 7, 1873.

93. Montgomery *Journal,* Feb. 13, 1873; Columbiana *Shelby County Guide,* Feb. 20, 27, 1873; Ashville *Southern Aegis,* Feb. 20, 1873.

94. NY *Herald,* qtd. in Montgomery *Advertiser,* Dec. 6, 1872; C. C. Clay to Virginia Clay, Dec. 4, 1872, reel 9, C. C. Clay Papers, in Berlin, ed., *Records of Southern Plantations,* ser. A, pt. 1.

95. Columbiana *Shelby County Guide,* Jan. 30, 1873; *NYT,* Feb. 1, 1873; Alabama General Assembly, *Report of the Joint Committee . . . in Regard to the Alleged Election of Geo. E. Spencer,* lxx.

96. Montgomery *Advertiser and Mail,* Jan. 28, 1873.

97. Montgomery *Advertiser* qtd. in Macon *Georgia Weekly Telegraph,* Feb. 11, 1873.

98. Montgomery *Advertiser and Mail,* July 18, 1872.

99. Montgomery *Advertiser and Mail,* Apr. 13, 15, 1873.

100. Selma *Argus,* Jan. 3, 1873; Montgomery *Advertiser and Mail,* Jan. 3, 1873.

101. Montgomery *Advertiser and Mail,* Apr. 27, 1873; Jacksonville *Republican,* Jan. 18, 1873; P. Hamilton to Lewis, Dec. 2, 1873, SG 023238, Gov. Lewis Papers, ADAH.

102. *NYT,* Jan. 7, 1873.

103. Selma *Argus,* Jan. 3, 1873. On McKee, see Webb, "A Jacksonian Democrat in Postbellum Alabama," 239–74.

104. Montgomery *Advertiser and Mail,* Dec. 10, 1872; Jan. 29, 1873.

105. Montgomery *Advertiser and Mail,* Dec. 22, 27, 1872; Montgomery *Journal,* Feb. 9, 1872; Ashville *Southern Aegis,* Jan. 30, 1873; *NYT,* Jan. 13, 1873; E. R. Mitchell to Lewis, Jan. 13, 1873, folder 13, Letters on Financial Matters, Gov. Lewis Papers, ADAH.

106. Montgomery *Advertiser and Mail,* Jan. 3, 1873.

107. Selma *Argus,* Feb. 7, 21, 1873.

108. Montgomery *Advertiser and Mail,* Feb. 14, Mar. 4, May 2, 6, 1873.

109. Lewis to "Bob" [Brickell], May 21, 1873, Gov. Lewis Papers, ADAH. Lewis's initial choice, a Republican from Selma, withdrew his application (John White to Lewis, May 18, 1873, Appointment Papers, SG 023238, Gov. Lewis Papers, ADAH).

110. *NYT,* Apr. 13, 1873; Montgomery *Advertiser and Mail,* May 14, 1873; Going, *Bourbon Democracy in Alabama,* 64.

111. The Selma *Argus,* for one, decried any further recognition of tainted endorsements (Apr. 4, 1873).

112. Lewis to J. H. Speed, Dec. 7, 1872, Correspondence, SG 023238, Gov. Lewis Papers, ADAH.

113. Selma *Argus,* Apr. 25, 1873.

114. Lewis to Gov. O. Hart, Apr. 11, 1873, Gov. Lewis Papers, ADAH.

115. W. J. Purman to Lewis, Apr. 21, 1873, and Lewis to Purman, Apr. 1873, Gov. Lewis Papers, ADAH.

116. Selma *Argus,* Feb. 14, Apr. 11, 1873. In theory the strategy had merit; later in the decade English bondholders took over the bankrupt line and developed the mineral re-

sources of the land grant. By 1879, despite depression, the road was reportedly worth four to five million; it was "more than paying running expenses & is in good cr[edit]." See entry for Alabama & Great Southern Railroad, Chattanooga, Tennessee, in Dun Credit Records, vol. 14: 166, Baker Library, Harvard University.

117. Lewis to Judge W. B. Woods, Mar. 31, 1873; Woods to Lewis, Apr. 7, 1873, Railroad Folders, Gov. Lewis Papers, ADAH.

118. Selma *Argus,* May 16, 1873.

119. Montgomery *Advertiser and Mail,* May 18, 1873; *NYT,* Mar. 23, 1873; Lewis to Clews, Mar. 19, 1873, Railroad Folders, Gov. Lewis Papers, ADAH.

120. Endorsement on Seligman et al. to Lewis, Mar. 26, 1873, Railroad Folders, Gov. Lewis Papers, ADAH.

121. Montgomery *Advertiser and Mail,* May 3, 1873.

122. J. H. Speed to Gov. Smith, Mar. 1, 1873, and J. H. Speed to L. E. Parsons, Apr. 5, 1873, Gov. Lewis Papers, ADAH; Speed to Lewis, Sept. 30, 1874, School Report, SG 023238, Gov. Lewis Papers, ADAH.

123. Selma *Argus,* Nov. 21, 1873.

124. Selma *Argus,* May 23, 30, 1873; Montgomery *Advertiser and Mail,* May 3, 28, 1873; Abraham Hewett to Lewis, June 16, 1873, Gov. Smith Papers, ADAH.

125. Fitzgerald, *Urban Emancipation,* 93–94, 122–25, 152–53. On the broader pattern, see Barbara Welke, *Recasting American Liberty: Gender, Race, Law, and the Railroad Revolution, 1865–1920* (Cambridge, UK: Cambridge University Press, 2001), 253–57.

126. Montgomery *Advertiser and Mail,* Feb. 20, Mar. 7, 1873; Selma *Argus,* Mar. 14, 1873.

127. Montgomery *Journal,* Mar. 14, 1873.

128. Montgomery *Journal,* Mar. 7, 1873.

129. Montgomery *Advertiser and Mail,* Mar. 6, 1873.

130. Livingston *Journal,* Apr. 25, May 30, 1871; Columbiana *Shelby County Guide,* Apr. 10, 17, 1873.

131. Selma *Argus,* Mar. 14, 21, 1873.

132. Columbiana *Shelby County Guide,* Mar. 13, 1873; Selma *Argus,* Mar. 14, 1873; Montgomery *Journal,* Mar. 15, 1873; Mobile *Watchman* qtd. in Montgomery *Advertiser and Mail,* Sept. 3, 1873.

133. Montgomery *Advertiser and Mail,* Mar. 6, 7, 1871; Jacksonville *Republican,* Mar. 1, 1873.

134. Montgomery *Advertiser and Mail,* Mar. 1, 1873.

135. Selma *Argus,* Feb. 14, 1873; Montgomery *Advertiser and Mail,* Mar. 1, 1873; Mobile *Watchman,* July 19, 1873.

136. Mobile *Watchman* qtd. in Montgomery *Advertiser and Mail,* Aug. 2, 1873. It appears this letter, signed "W.H.C.," was authored by the educator William H. Councill, ironically a future conservative rival of Booker T. Washington.

137. Montgomery *Advertiser and Mail,* Mar. 1, 1873.

138. Columbiana *Shelby County Guide,* Sept. 11, 1873.

139. Mobile *Watchman,* Aug. 30, 1873.

140. Alabama General Assembly, *Report of the Joint Committee . . . in Regard to the Alleged Election of Geo. E. Spencer,* clxxiv.

141. Alabama General Assembly, *Report of the Joint Committee . . . in Regard to the Alleged Election of Geo. E. Spencer,* clxxiii–clxxiv; [Montgomery] *Watchman* qtd. in Columbiana *Shelby County Guide,* Feb. 20, 1873.

142. Mobile *Watchman,* July 19, Aug. 30, 1873; Mobile *Watchman* qtd. in Montgomery *Advertiser and Mail,* Aug. 2, Sept. 18, 1873.

143. L. C. Coulson to Lewis, Aug. 13 and 14, 1872, Gov. Lewis Papers, ADAH.

144. Gov. Lewis to Coulson et al., Aug. 19, 1873, Gov. Lewis Papers, ADAH. Gov. Lewis directed that a copy of his response be kept.

145. Gov. Lewis to E. H. Saltiel, Jan. 9, 1873, Gov. Lewis Papers, ADAH. An Oscar Hunter appears in the 1870 census for Dallas County as a sixty-seven-year-old African American farm laborer with $250 in personal property.

146. J. A. Bingham to R. P. Baker, July 4, 1873, Letterbook, SG 5911, Alabama State Treasurer, ADAH.

147. Lewis to Parsons, Goodloe and Cobb, Oct. 20, 1873, and Lewis to R. W. Ruter, Dec. 29, 1873, Gov. Lewis Papers, ADAH.

148. Richard White, *Railroaded: The Transcontinentals and the Making of Modern America* (NY: Norton, 2011), 47–87; NY *Sun* qtd. in Selma *Argus,* Oct. 3, 1873.

Chapter Eleven

Note to chapter epigraph: Mobile *Register,* June 25, 1874, qtd. in Montgomery *Journal,* Sept. 25, 1874.

1. J. A. Minnis to G. H. Williams, July 18, Oct. 16, 1873, reel 3, M 1356, NARA.

2. This is an animating insight in the work of Foner and Hahn, among others, and the ambitious Freedom: A Documentary History of Emancipation, 1861–1867, documentary series is primarily devoted to the topic.

3. Greensboro *Beacon,* Sept. 18, 1873; Northport *Spectator,* Sept. 23, 1873; Henry Lyell to Henry A. Tayloe, Dec. 13, 1873, reel 47, Tayloe Papers, Stampp, ed., *Records of Ante-bellum Southern Plantations,* ser. M, pt. 1.

4. A. Beuners to Watson, July 23, 1873, and W. S. Schlieffelin & Co. to Watson, Aug. 12, 1876, Watson Papers, and T. S. Fry & Co. to S. O. Wood, Dixon's Mills, Aug. 2, 1873, Samuel O. Wood Papers, reel 1, in Berlin, ed., *Records of Southern Plantations.*

5. Montgomery *Advertiser and Mail,* June 27, 1873; Jacksonville *Republican,* July 5, 1873.

6. E. T. Tayloe to Henry A. Tayloe, June 29, Oct. 14, 1873; Feb. 22, 1874, reel 49, Tayloe Papers.

7. H. A. Stollenwerck to H. A. Tayloe, Dec. 29, 1873, reel 50, Tayloe Papers.

8. Selma *Argus,* Sept. 5, 19, 1873; Montgomery *Advertiser and Mail,* Oct. 9, 1873; Jacksonville *Republican,* Nov. 15, 1873.

9. Livingston *Journal,* Sept. 12, 1873.

10. Ashville *Southern Aegis,* Sept. 24, Oct. 29, 1873; Livingston *Journal,* Oct. 3, 1873.

11. Jacksonville *Republican,* Oct. 4, 1873.

12. Montgomery *Advertiser and Mail,* Sept. 26, 1873.

13. Montgomery *Advertiser and Mail,* Sept. 15, Dec. 25, 1873. The price for low middling grade cotton went from 17¼ to 13¾ cents a pound.

14. E. T. Tayloe to Henry A. Tayloe, Oct. 14, 1873, reel 49, Tayloe Papers.

15. Henry Lyell to Henry A. Tayloe, Aug. 6, Oct. 7, Nov. 29, 1873, reel 47, Tayloe Papers.

16. John E. Wallace to J. Bragg, Sept. 27, 1873, John Bragg Papers, SHC.

17. Henry Lyell to Henry A. Tayloe, Dec. 13, 1873, reel 47, Tayloe Papers.

18. E. T. Tayloe to Henry A. Tayloe, Oct. 14, 1873, reel 49, Tayloe Papers.

19. *NYT,* Nov. 1, 1873; Mobile *Register,* Jan. 13, 14, 1874.

20. Qtd. in Selma *Argus,* Dec. 19, 1873.

21. W. C. Pickens to S. Pickens, Oct. 3, 1873, Pickens Papers, USA.

22. Montgomery *Advertiser and Mail,* Nov. 13, Oct. 9, 1873.

23. Montgomery *Advertiser and Mail,* Oct. 9, 28, Nov. 4, 1873; Livingston *Journal,* Nov. 7, 1873. For a somewhat unsympathetic account of the destitution in Montgomery, see Edward King, *The Great South: A Record of Journeys in Louisiana, Texas, Alabama and Maryland* (Hartford, CT: American Publishing Co., 1879), 331–34.

24. *Southern Cultivator,* July 1873, 245–46, and Dec. 1873, 451–52.

25. A. Beuners to H. Watson, July 5, 1874, Watson Papers; J. A. Minnis to G. H. Williams, Oct. 16, 1873, reel 3, M 1356, NARA; Henry Lyell to Henry A. Tayloe, Oct. 7, 1873, reel 47, Tayloe Papers.

26. J. A. Minnis to G. H. Williams, July 18, Oct. 16, 1873, reel 3, M 1356, NARA.

27. Livingston *Journal,* Oct. 17, 1873.

28. Livingston *Journal,* Oct. 24, 1873.

29. Selma *Argus,* Sept. 12, 1873.

30. *NYT,* Sept. 15, 1873.

31. Thomas Peters to S. H. Woodward, Nov. 24, 1871, Woodward Family Papers, UA.

32. A. Beuners to H. Watson, July 5, 1874, Watson Papers.

33. Marion *Alabama Baptist,* Apr. 7, 1874.

34. Late in 1873, some 98 of 284 subordinate Alabama Granges were located in the black belt, which meant that whites there were overrepresented. The rest were concentrated in surrounding areas of southern Alabama, rather than in the northern half of the state (Selma *Argus,* Dec. 5, 1873).

35. Selma *Argus,* June 13, 1873.

36. Selma *Argus,* Aug. 15, 1873.

37. Columbiana *Shelby County Guide,* Feb. 13, 1873.

38. Abbeville *Henry County Democrat,* Aug. 15, 1873; Montgomery *Advertiser and Mail,* July 9, 1873.

39. Livingston *Journal,* Sept. 5, 1873.

40. Livingston *Journal,* Sept. 12, 1873; Camden *Wilcox News & Pacificator,* May 20, 1874.

41. Livingston *Journal,* Nov. 8, 1872; Feb. 8, 28, 1873. Comparing the November presidential election with the February results, the turnout is similar, but Democrats did six hundred votes better and Republicans five hundred votes worse. Much of the difference occurred in the smaller precincts, where numbers of freedmen seem to have voted for the Democratic candidate. The *Journal* claimed a quarter did.

42. Selma *Argus,* Mar. 7, 1873.

43. Livingston *Journal,* Apr. 25, May 30, 1873.

44. Livingston *Journal,* Aug. 8, 15, 1873.

45. B. Herr to R. McKee, July 22, Aug. 6, 1873, reel 1, McKee Papers, ADAH.

46. Montgomery *Advertiser and Mail,* Jan. 14, 1873; G. W. Hewett to McKee, Sept. 24, 1873, reel 1, McKee Papers, ADAH.

47. Jacksonville *Republican,* Aug. 2, 16, 1873.

48. Henry Clews & Co. to Arthur Bingham, Apr. 24, 1874; A. Goettel & Co. to Gov. Lewis, Nov. 10, 1873; E. Soloman to Gov. Lewis, Nov. 14, 1873; and Edward Bayer to Gov. Lewis, Nov. 15, 1873, all in Governor Lewis Papers, ADAH.

49. Chicago *Tribune,* Dec. 10, 1873; Aug. 14, 1874.

50. J. L. Pennington to Attorney General, Aug. 8, 1873, reel 1, M 1356, NARA.

51. Mobile *Register,* July 9, 15, 1874.

52. Montgomery *Advertiser and Mail,* Nov. 18, 1873; Montgomery *Journal,* Nov. 12, 1873.

53. Lewis to General Assembly, Dec. 16, 1873, Gov. Lewis Papers, ADAH.

54. Montgomery *Advertiser and Mail,* Dec. 6, 18, 1873.

55. Montgomery *Advertiser and Mail,* Nov. 19, 1873.

56. Montgomery *Advertiser and Mail,* Nov. 20, 21, Dec. 3, 1873.

57. Montgomery *Advertiser and Mail,* Nov. 22, 26, 1873.

58. Montgomery *Advertiser and Mail,* Nov. 22, 26, 1873; Columbiana *Shelby County Guide,* June 8, Aug. 24, 1871. Earlier in the decade, two hotels in town charged four dollars daily for room and board.

59. Montgomery *Advertiser and Mail,* Dec. 5, 1873. Under-assessment seems a valid concern: Governor Lewis's Democratic successor decried the "inexcusable inequality"; see "Message of George S. Houston, Governor of Alabama, to the General Assembly, Submitted Dec. 28th, 1875" (Montgomery, AL: W. W. Screws, 1875), 10.

60. Montgomery *Advertiser and Mail,* Dec. 17, Nov. 26, 1873.

61. Montgomery *Advertiser and Mail,* Dec. 17, Nov. 26, 1873.

62. Montgomery *Advertiser and Mail,* Nov. 25, 26, 1873.

63. Jacksonville *Republican,* Nov. 29, Dec. 6, 13, 1873; St. Louis *Globe-Democrat,* Nov. 26, 1875.

64. Mobile *Register,* July 6, 1874; Chicago *Tribune,* May 31, June 16, 1874.

65. J. E. Wallace to J. Bragg, Dec. 24, 1873, John Bragg Papers, SHC; Raymond (MS) *Hinds County Gazette,* Jan. 14, 21, 1874; Jacksonville *Republican,* Jan. 10, 1874.

66. T. T. Munford to H. A. Tayloe, Dec. 6, 24, 1873, reel 47, Tayloe Papers.

67. T. T. Munford to H. A. Tayloe, [Dec.] 1873; Jan. 6, 14, 1874, reel 47, Tayloe Papers.

68. Henry Lyell to Henry A. Tayloe, Jan. 5, 1874, reel 47, Tayloe Papers.

69. John Long to B. C. Yancey, Sept. 26, 1873, B. C. Yancey Papers, SHC.

70. Testimony of Isaac Heyman, 43rd Congress, 2nd Sess., House Report 262, February 23, 1875, House Select Committee on the Condition of Political Affairs in Alabama, "Affairs in Alabama," 56–57.

71. J. J. B. Hillard to Virginia Clay, Jan. 1, 1874; A. H. Colquitt to Virginia Clay, Jan. 15, 1874; C. C. Clay to Virginia Clay, Jan. 23, Apr. 14, and May 31, 1874, reel 10, C. C. Clay Papers, in Berlin, ed., *Records of Southern Plantations,* ser. A, pt. 1.

72. J. M. Buford to J. R. Buford, Apr. 10, 1874, Confederadoes Collection, AU.

73. R. K. Boyd to R. McKee, Apr. 29, 1874, reel 1, McKee Papers, ADAH.

74. Columbiana *Shelby County Guide,* Nov. 6, 1873.

75. Mobile *Register,* Apr. 29, 1874; Columbiana *Shelby County Guide,* Apr. 30, 1874; Jacksonville *Republican,* Apr. 18, 1874.

76. Selma *Argus,* Mar. 6, 1874; Columbiana *Shelby County Guide,* Apr. 30, 1874; Jacksonville *Republican,* June 24, July 11, 25, Aug. 11, 1874; Camden *Wilcox News & Pacificator,* May 20, 1874.

77. Selma *Argus,* Feb. 13, 1874.

78. H. G. Jones to R. McKee, Jan. 26, 1874, reel 1, Robert McKee Papers, ADAH.

79. Mobile *Register,* May 17, 19, 1874; Columbiana *Shelby County Guide,* Apr. 16, 1874; Selma *Argus,* Mar. 13, 1874.

80. Walter T. K. Nugent, *The Money Question during Reconstruction* (NY: Norton, 1967), 93–94; Irwin Unger, *The Greenback Era: A Social and Political History of American Finance, 1865–1879* (Princeton, NJ: Princeton University Press, 1964), 213–45.

81. Mobile *Register,* May 3, 1874; B. B. Lewis to R. McKee, May 14, 1874, reel 1, Robert McKee Papers, ADAH.

82. R. K. Boyd to R. McKee, June 1, 1874, reel 1, Robert McKee Papers, ADAH.

83. Mobile *Register,* June 5, 1874.

84. Mobile *Register,* June 27, 1874; Selma *Argus,* Aug. 21, 28, Sept. 18, 1874. On Silsby's upright tone, see J. Silsby to Lewis, Apr. 10, 1873, Gov. Lewis Papers, ADAH.

85. Selma *Argus,* May 29, 1874; Mobile *Register,* May 17, 1874.

86. Hardy, *Selma,* 68–77, 94; Selma *Echo* qtd. in Selma *Argus,* Aug. 28, 1874; Selma *Argus,* May 29, 1874.

87. Most local studies of Reconstruction politics date back to the Dunning school, or they were done by amateur historians following similar precepts. Thus the details of Alabama's local governance remain obscure, the claims of excess spending difficult to evaluate. Even-handed studies of grassroots Reconstruction by modern scholars remain needed.

88. W. M. Brooks to Lewis, May 9, 1874, Gov. Lewis Papers, ADAH.

89. Hardy, *Selma.*

90. 44th Congress, 1st Sess., House Committee on Elections, Misc. Doc. 47, "Contested Election: Bromberg vs. Haralson, Alabama," 172; J. L. Pennington to D. Lewis, July 28, 1873, Gov. Lewis Papers, ADAH.

91. Camden *Wilcox News & Pacificator,* May 20, 1874; Livingston *Journal,* June 26, 1874; Greensboro *Beacon,* July 25, Aug. 15, 1874; Demopolis *News* qtd. in Montgomery *Journal,* June 6, 1874.

92. G. S. Houston to A. B. Moore, Aug. 1, 27, 1861, copies in Alabama Political Figures Papers, Hoole Library, UA.

93. General G. S. Stanley to W. D. Whipple, Feb. 15, 1865, *OR,* ser. 1, vol. 49, pt. 1: 718–19; US Congress, "Report of the Joint Committee on Reconstruction," pt. 3: 75–76; Mobile *Register,* Aug. 4, 1874; W. Brewer to R. McKee, May 10, 1874, reel 1, Robert McKee Papers, ADAH. For a view of his conflicted loyalties, see McIlwain, *Civil War Alabama,* 168.

94. J. B. Callis to J. Danforth, July 31, 1867; Burnet Houston to G. S. Houston, Aug. 3, 1867; G. S. Houston to Swayne, Sept. 15, 1867, G. S. Houston Papers, Duke University.

95. Thomas Peters to Houston, Jan. 8, 1874, G. S. Houston Papers, Duke University; W. H. Chambers to R. McKee, May 11, 1874, reel 1, McKee Papers, ADAH; Bond, *Negro Education in Alabama,* 55.

96. W. Brewer to McKee, May 10, 23, 1874; R. K. Boyd to McKee, Apr. 29, May 16, 1874, reel 1, McKee Papers, ADAH.

97. Selma *Argus,* May 20, 1874.

98. B. B. Lewis to R. McKee, June 3, 1874, reel 1, McKee Papers, ADAH.

99. Livingston *Journal,* June 12, 1874; Montgomery *Journal,* June 17, 1874.

100. Selma *Argus,* Aug. 7, 1874.

101. NY *Tribune* qtd. in Montgomery *Journal,* Aug. 9, 1874; Mobile *Register,* May 30, 1874; Selma *Argus,* Aug. 7, 1874; Livingston *Journal,* Aug. 7, 1874; Montgomery *Journal,* Sept. 25, 1874.

102. G. Spencer to W. E. Chandler, July 31, 1874, W. E. Chandler Papers, LC.

103. Mobile *Register,* Aug. 5, 7, 1874.

104. James A. Stevens et al. to Lewis, Aug. 6, 1874; W. H. Black to Lewis, Aug. 25, 1874, Gov. Lewis Papers, ADAH. C. Mayer to G. H. Williams, Sept. 1, 1874, reel 6, M 1356, NARA.

105. J. Murphy to Lewis, Aug. 22, 1874; J. H. Speed to D. Lewis, July 25, 1874; J. A Pace to Lewis, Aug. 18, 1874; Alonzo Scaggs et al. to Lewis, Sept. 4, 1874, Gov. Lewis Papers, ADAH.

106. Eufaula *Bluff City Times,* Mar. 3, 17, 1870.

107. Eufaula *Bluff City Times,* June 15, 22, 29, 1871. For an older interpretation of Keils, see Harry P. Owens, "The Eufaula Riot of 1874," *Alabama Review* 16, no. 3 (1963): 222–37.

108. E. Keils to Lewis, Dec. 3, 1873, Gov. Lewis Papers, ADAH.

109. Eufaula *Bluff City Times,* Dec. 21, 1871.

110. Abbeville *Henry County Register,* Feb. 27, 1874; testimony of Henry Frasier, R. Lock, L. H. Brown, in Adjutant General's Office, Administrative Files, Eufaula Election Riot of 1874, SG 15148, ADAH.

111. Montgomery *Journal,* Aug. 9, 11, 13, 16, 18, 27, 29, 1874; testimony of E. H. Saltiel, US House Select Committee, "Affairs in Alabama," 1123; Mobile *Register,* Aug. 22, 1874; Livingston *Journal,* June 12, Aug. 14, 21, Sept. 4, 1874; D. Lewis to A. White, Aug. 13, 1874, Gov. Lewis Papers, ADAH.

112. Scholars have generally emphasized the strength of demands for civil rights across the South, even their inevitability. In Alabama, however, we see something different, of the brakes being applied by black leaders for tactical reasons.

113. Mobile *Register,* June 30, July 2, 1874; Montgomery *Journal,* June 21, 27, July 9, 1874 .

114. Mobile *Register,* Aug. 5, 1874.

115. Mobile *Register,* Aug. 18, 25, 1874; Jacksonville *Republican,* Aug. 22, 1874; *NYT,* Aug. 20, 1874.

116. G. Spencer to Chandler, Aug. 23, 1874, W. E. Chandler Papers, LC; Livingston *Journal,* Sept. 4, 1874.

117. Montgomery *Journal,* Aug. 11, 1874; Mobile *Register,* Aug. 25, 1874.

118. Montgomery *Journal,* Aug. 22, 1874; R. M Williamson to D. Lewis, July 7, 1874, Gov. Lewis Papers, ADAH.

119. Mobile *Register,* Aug. 23, 1874; Montgomery *Journal,* Aug. 25, 1874.

120. Spencer to Chandler, Sept. 17, 1874, W. E. Chandler Papers, LC.

121. *NYT,* Sept. 9, 1874.

122. *NYT,* Sept. 9, 1874; Fitzgerald, *Urban Emancipation,* 212.

123. Columbiana *Shelby County Guide,* May 28, 1874.

124. This discussion is enabled by comparison with Natchez after Redemption, where black militias were backed up against the Mississippi River, with fatal consequences. See Justin Behrend, *Reconstructing Democracy: Grassroots Black Politics in the Deep South after the Civil War* (Athens: University of Georgia Press, 2015), 218–21.

125. Livingston *Journal,* June 12, Sept. 11, 1874; testimony of Cato Jackson, US House Select Committee, "Affairs in Alabama," 709–10.

126. Republican Citizens to U. S. Grant, Oct. 3, 1874, *Papers of Ulysses S. Grant* 25: 197.

127. US House Select Committee, "Affairs in Alabama," lxiii.

128. Montgomery *Journal,* Aug. 30, Sept. 10, 1874; Thomas Ivey to Gov. Lewis, Aug. 5, 1874, Gov. Lewis Papers, ADAH.

129. Testimony of Maria Ivey, US Congress, Senate Report No. 704, "Alabama in 1874, 1875 and 1876," 44th Congress, 2nd Sess., 510–13; testimony of Robert Reed, US House Select Committee, "Affairs in Alabama," 17; Montgomery *Journal,* Aug. 19, 1874; Mobile *Register,* Sept. 2, 1874; Livingston *Journal,* Aug. 14, Sept. 4, 1874.

130. Hunnicutt, *Reconstruction in West Alabama,* 79–92,

131. Montgomery *Journal,* Aug. 19, 23, 26, Sept. 16, 1874; testimony of W. O. Winston, US House Select Committee, "Affairs in Alabama," 631; Mobile *Register,* Aug. 7, 8, 14, 18, 23, 26, Sept. 5, 1874; Livingston *Journal,* Aug. 21, 26, Sept. 18, 28, 1874; Carrollton *West Alabamian,* Aug. 19, 1874; Demopolis *News-Journal,* Aug. 23, 1874; testimony of William B. Jones, US House Select Committee, "Affairs in Alabama," 638; Edmund and Jack Turner to D. Lewis, Aug. 21, 1874, Gov. Lewis Papers, ADAH. There is a judicious modern account of the conflict, William Warren Rogers and Robert David Ward,

August Reckoning: Jack Turner and Racism in Post–Civil War Alabama (Baton Rouge: LSU Press, 1973), 24–54.

132. Testimony of J. N. Beach, US House Select Committee, "Affairs in Alabama," 1189.

133. Mobile *Register,* Sept. 10, 11, 16, 1874; Montgomery *Journal,* Sept. 13, 20, 1874; Carrollton *West Alabamian,* Sept. 16, 23, 1874; Eutaw *Whig* qtd. in Selma *Argus,* Sept. 18, 1874; testimony of F. M. Kirksey, US House Select Committee, "Affairs in Alabama," 536.

134. Testimony of Bob Reed, US House Select Committee, "Affairs in Alabama," 17.

135. Montgomery *Journal,* Sept. 22, 1874; NY *Tribune,* Oct. 31, 1874; testimony of Thomas Wetmore, 920, and testimony of J. Beach, 1186, both in US House Select Committee, "Affairs in Alabama."

136. Livingston *Journal,* Sept. 18, 25, 1874; Demopolis *News Journal,* Sept. 19, 1874; Jacksonville *Republican,* Sept. 19, 1874; Montgomery *Journal,* Sept. 17, 20, 1874; G. Cole to D. Lewis, Sept. 21, 1874, Gov. Lewis Papers, ADAH; Republican Citizens of Forkland Beat to [G. H. Williams], Oct. 3, 1874, reel 6, M 1356, NARA; testimony of W. B. Jones, and testimony of W. A. Glover, US House Select Committee, "Affairs in Alabama," 639 and 907–8; Selma *Argus,* Oct. 2, 1874. See also the account of this episode and its aftermath in Mary Ellen Curtin, *Black Prisoners and Their World: Alabama, 1865–1900* (Charlottesville: University Press of Virginia, 2000), 12–27.

137. *Papers of Ulysses S. Grant* 25: 195–96.

138. Livingston *Journal,* Sept. 18, 1874; Montgomery *Advertiser,* Sept. 17, 1874. Because the Mobile *Register* appeared daily, it often reported these events before local Democratic apologists could perfect and print their version. The correspondent reporting the Dew episode from the scene unwittingly indicated the freedpeople were acting on the defensive against night-riders. See Mobile *Register,* Sept. 17, 1874.

139. Testimony of Warren Dew, US House Select Committee, "Affairs in Alabama," 914–16.

140. Montgomery *Journal* qtd. in Cincinnati *Times,* Sept. 25, 1874; Livingston *Journal,* Sept. 18, 1874; Warren Dew et al. to Gov. Lewis, Sept. 15, 1874, Gov. Lewis Papers, ADAH.

141. Montgomery *Journal,* Sept. 17, 1874; US House Select Committee, "Affairs in Alabama," 632; Lucy Jackson to Husband, Sept. 12, 1874, Susalee Smith Papers, University of West Alabama.

142. Greenville *Advocate,* July 23, 1874; Livingston *Journal,* July 24, 1874.

143. Columbus *Enquirer,* Aug. 29, 1874; Montgomery *Journal,* Sept. 1, 1874; testimony of Isaac Campbell, 43–44, 48; testimony of J. F. Powledge, 190; testimony of George Sharp, 77; testimony of Nathan Griffin, 85–86; all in US House Select Committee, "Affairs in Alabama."

144. C. J. Atkinson to W. L. Bragg, Sept. 7, 1874; E. T. Welles to D. Lewis, June 5, 1874, Gov. Lewis Papers, ADAH. Fitzgerald, *Urban Emancipation,* 142.

145. A. E. Williams to B. Gardner, July 3, 1874, Gov. Lewis Papers, ADAH; Montgomery *Journal,* Sept. 1, 2, 1874.

146. Eufaula *News,* July 4, 9, 1874. E. M. Keils to Gov. Lewis, Aug. 8, 1874; E. M. Keils to B. Gardner, Aug. 25, 1874, Gov. Lewis Papers, ADAH. Others warned that Keils would be killed; see Marshal R. W. Healy to G. H. Williams, Sept. 7, 1874, reel 1, M 1356, NARA.

147. B. Gardner to Gov. Lewis, July 6, 1874; Gov. Lewis to B. Gardner, July 9, 1874; E. M. Keils to Lewis, Aug. 8, 1874; Keils to Gardner, Aug. 25, 1874; Gov. Lewis to Gardner, Sept. 4, 1874, Gov. Lewis Papers, ADAH.

148. NY *Tribune,* Sept. 3, 1874; G. Spencer to W. E. Chandler, Sept. 8, 1874, W. E. Chandler Papers, LC; G. H. Williams to Z. E. Thomas, Sept. 30, 1874, reel 6, M 1356, NARA.

149. Chicago *Tribune,* Oct. 24, 1874; NY *Tribune,* Oct. 14, 1874; R. W. Healy to G. H. Williams, Oct. 16, 1874, reel 3, M 1356, NARA; testimony of Bob Reed, US House Select Committee, "Affairs in Alabama," 25.

150. Columbus *Enquirer,* Aug. 29, 1874.

151. G. Spencer to W. E. Chandler, Sept. 17, 1874, W. E. Chandler Papers, LC.

152. E. Hazlewood to D. Lewis, July 13, 1874; E. A. Crandall to Gov. Lewis, June 8, 1874, Gov. Lewis Papers, ADAH. Mobile *Register,* Aug. 4, 1874. Northport *Spectator,* Sept. 26, 1874.

153. Montgomery *Advertiser* qtd. in Mobile *Register,* Oct. 2, 1874.

154. Selma *Argus* qtd. in Mobile *Register,* Oct. 4, 1874.

155. T. U. Greene to D. Lewis, Sept. 25, 1874, Pardon Files, Gov. Lewis Papers, ADAH.

156. R. H. Dawson to R. Jones, Oct. 21, 1874, Wheeler Family Papers, ADAH.

157. Schweninger, *James T. Rapier and Reconstruction,* 126–27.

158. J. M. Wooten to Gov. Lewis, June 12, 1874, Lands File, Gov. Lewis Papers, ADAH; Moulton *Advertiser,* July 24, 1874.

159. Moulton *Advertiser,* Aug. 28, 1874; Montgomery *Journal,* Sept. 15, 1874.

160. Moulton *Advertiser,* July 31, 1874.

161. Eufaula *News,* July 11, 1874; Cincinnati *Commercial,* Oct. 1, 1874.

162. Tuskegee *News,* Sept. 3, 1874, qtd. in US House Select Committee, "Affairs in Alabama," 1131, and testimony of Z. T. Daniel, 1064.

163. Augusta *Chronicle,* May 19, 1874.

164. M. Candee to D. Lewis, May 21, 1874; D. Lewis to C. J. Atkinson, June 20, 1874; Alex White to D. Lewis, June 28, 1874, SG 023238, Gov. Lewis Papers, ADAH.

165. *NYT,* Apr. 29, 1874.

166. Cincinnati *Commercial,* Sept. 30, 1874.

167. Selma *Argus,* Sept. 4, 1874.

168. Testimony of John G. Stokes, US House Select Committee, "Affairs in Alabama," 1073.

169. Boston *Advertiser,* Sept. 16, 1874. See the even-handed account in Rogers, *Black Belt Scalawag,* 105–20.

170. Testimony of Maria Ivey, US Senate Report No. 704, "Alabama in 1874, 1875 and 1876," 511; J. A. Minnis to G. H. Williams, Sept. 21, 1874, US House Select Committee, "Affairs in Alabama," 1230; Montgomery *Journal,* Sept. 11, 17, 19, 1874; Livingston *Journal,* Sept. 4, 18, 1874; NY *Tribune,* Oct. 7, 8, 9, 1874. For a nuanced evaluation of Hays's letter, see Rogers, *Black Belt Scalawag,* 105–20.

171. Hartford *Courant,* Oct. 1, 9, 1874.

172. Cincinnati *Commercial,* Sept. 30, Oct. 1, 1874.

173. NY *Tribune,* Oct. 8, 12, 17, 22, 27, Nov. 2, 1874; Boston *Advertiser,* Nov. 16, 1874; Testimony of Z. L. White, US House Select Committee, "Affairs in Alabama," 1084.

174. 44th Congress, 1st Sess., House Committee on Elections, Misc. Doc. 47, "Contested Election: Bromberg vs. Haralson, Alabama," 9, 15, 31–31.

175. C. F. Moulton to G. H. Williams, Oct. 30, Nov. 2, 1874, reel 6, M 1356, NARA.

176. Speech of Alexander White, *Congressional Record,* 43rd Congress, 2nd Sess., Appendix, 18.

177. E. M. Keils to "Sir," Oct. 2, 1874, reel 3, M 1356, NARA; testimony of Z. T. Daniel, US House Select Committee, "Affairs in Alabama," 1064.

178. Testimony of James D. Williford, 427–28; testimony of W. J. Turner, 599, both in US House Select Committee, "Affairs in Alabama." Eufaula *News,* Nov. 5, 1874. Montgomery *News,* Nov. 4, 1874, qtd. in *Congressional Record,* 42nd Congress, 2nd Sess., 1902.

179. See clippings in R. W. Healy to G. H. Williams, Nov. 4, 1874, reel 3, M 1356, NARA. Newspaper clipping in E. M. Keils to Houston, Dec. 1, 1874, Rewards Files, NSG 006410, folder 1, Gov. Houston Papers, ADAH. Testimony of Elias Keils, 3, 6; testimony of W. J. Turner, 599, both in US House Select Committee, "Affairs in Alabama."

180. R. W. Healy to G. H. Williams, Nov. 4, 1874, reel 6, M 1356, NARA; newspaper clipping in E. M. Keils to Houston, Dec. 1, 1874, Rewards Files, SG 006410, folder 1, Gov. Houston Papers, ADAH; speech of Alexander White, *Congressional Record,* 43rd Congress, 2nd Sess., Appendix, 18.

181. Going, *Bourbon Democracy in Alabama,* 213.

182. US House Select Committee, "Affairs in Alabama," lxvii.

Chapter Twelve

Note to chapter epigraph: *Congressional Record,* 42nd Congress, 2nd Sess., 1841.

1. Virginia Clay to C. C. Clay, Nov. 7, 1874, reel 10, C. C. Clay Papers, in Berlin, ed., *Records of Southern Plantations,* ser. A, pt. 1.

2. On the black-belt planters' dominant power, see Wiener, *Social Origins of the New South,* esp. 186–211; also see the muted dissent from Woodward's thesis in the revised introduction to Going, *Bourbon Democracy in Alabama,* x. Going's 1951 book overall echoes the Dunning view of Reconstruction, but his treatment of the Redeemers' economic policy is more nuanced.

3. Montgomery *Advertiser and Mail,* Aug. 22, 1875; Selma *Argus,* Nov. 27, 1874; Montgomery *Journal,* Apr. 2, 1875. On McKee's animus toward the Democratic leadership, see Webb, "A Jacksonian Democrat in Postbellum Alabama," 239–74.

4. Selma *Argus,* Nov. 27, 1874.

5. Selma *Argus,* May 21, Apr. 16, 1875.

6. Eutaw *Whig and Observer,* Nov. 19, Dec. 31, 1874.

7. Mobile *Register,* Nov. 20, 1874; Selma *Argus,* Nov. 27, 1874; Montgomery *Advertiser and Mail,* Nov. 26, 1874.

8. Selma *Argus,* Feb. 5, 1875; Montgomery *Advertiser and Mail,* Mar. 6, 1875.

9. Eutaw *Whig and Observer,* Nov. 26, 1874; Livingston *Journal,* Jan. 8, 15, 1875; E. M. Keils to Hillard Miles, Aug. 23, 1875, Rewards Files, folder 1, SG 006410, Gov. Houston Papers, ADAH.

10. W. H. Gasyin[?] to J. D. Dreisbach, Dec. 2, 1874, Gov. Lewis Papers, ADAH. Black activists seem well aware of their inability to secure white backing for bonds, with some suggesting that nominations for the non-bonded offices by right belonged to them. See Montgomery *Republican Sentinel,* Oct. 5, 1878.

11. Montgomery *Advertiser and Mail,* Apr. 24, May 1, 1875.

12. [James Garrett], "Manuscript History of the Garrett Family of Birmingham and Alabama," Williams Collection, UA. Montgomery *Advertiser and Mail,* Nov. 19, 1874. J. T. Walker to J. M. Martin, Nov. 26, 1874; J. M. Hobson, Deposition, Nov. 20, 1874; John White to Gov. Lewis, Nov. 20, 1874, all in Gov. Lewis Papers, ADAH.

13. Mobile *Register,* Nov. 20, 1874; Montgomery *Advertiser and Mail,* Nov. 18, 29, 1874.

14. Mobile *Register,* Nov. 26, 1874; Lowell *Citizen and News,* Dec. 1, 1874; NY *Herald,* Nov. 25, 1874; Providence *Press,* Nov. 25, 1874.

15. Montgomery *Advertiser and Mail,* Nov. 22, 1874.

16. Going, *Bourbon Democracy in Alabama,* 47; Jacksonville *Republican,* Dec. 26, 1874; Greenville *Advocate,* Feb. 4, 1875; Wiggins, *The Scalawag in Alabama Politics,* 150–51; Montgomery *Advertiser and Mail,* Jan. 27, 1875; Mobile *Register,* Nov. 20, 1874.

17. Montgomery *Advertiser and Mail,* Dec. 5, 1874.

18. Montgomery *Advertiser and Mail,* Nov. 29, Dec. 5, 15, 1874.

19. 43rd Congress, 2nd Sess., House Executive Doc. 45, "Civil Rights in Alabama," 1, 9, 10.

20. Selma *Argus,* Nov. 27, 1874; Jan. 29, 1875. Montgomery *Advertiser and Mail,* Nov. 22, 1874; Jan. 10, 22, 1875.

21. Mobile *Register,* Nov. 24, Dec. 5, 1874; Montgomery *Advertiser and Mail,* Nov. 22, 1874.

22. Montgomery *Advertiser and Mail,* Feb. 3, 1875; Selma *Argus,* Jan. 14, 1876.

23. Arrington and Tomkins to Houston, Jan. 8, 1875, Governor G. S. Houston Papers, ADAH; Selma *Argus,* July 30, 1875.

24. Fitzgerald, *Urban Emancipation,* 214–15; Moulton *Advertiser,* May 14, 1875.

25. Selma *Argus,* Feb. 26, 1875.

26. Boston *Advertiser,* Feb. 26, 1875; Selma *Argus,* Feb. 26, 1875.

27. Curtin, *Black Prisoners and Their World,* 53–56.

28. Montgomery *Advertiser and Mail,* Dec. 10, 1874; Aug. 24, 1875. Eutaw *Whig and Observer,* Nov. 11, 1875.

29. Selma *Argus,* Mar. 26, May 14, 28, 1875.

30. Montgomery *Advertiser and Mail,* Mar. 13, 1875; R. H. Dawson to McKee, Sept. 13, 1876, McKee Papers, ADAH.

31. Jacksonville *Republican,* Mar. 6, 1875; Montgomery *Advertiser and Mail,* June 6, 1875.

32. 43rd Congress, 2nd Sess., House Misc. Doc. 107, "Memorial of the Republican Members," 1–11.

33. *NYT,* Feb. 17, 1875; Montgomery *Advertiser and Mail,* Mar. 6, 20, 1875; Jacksonville *Republican,* Mar. 6, 1875; Livingston *Journal,* Feb. 26, Apr. 2, 1875; Montgomery *Journal,* July 9, 1875.

34. Montgomery *Advertiser and Mail,* Mar. 13, 14, 1875; Selma *Argus,* Mar. 19, 1875.

35. Montgomery *Journal,* June 25, 1875.

36. J. Bragg to [T. B. Bethea], Jan. 1, 1875; G. S. Houston to [Duncan], Jan. 14, 1875; Houston, Lawler and Bethea to Duncan, Sherman & Co., Jan. 25, 1875, all in Governor Houston Papers, ADAH. According to official statements, treasury receipts for the year ending Sept. 30, 1874, totaled about $1,870,000. At 6 percent, servicing a $31,000,000 debt would take nearly every penny (Montgomery *Advertiser and Mail,* Mar. 18, 1875).

37. Selma *Argus,* Apr. 16, 1875; Jacksonville *Republican,* Jan. 23, 1875; R. M. Patton to Houston, Feb. 25, 1875, Gov. Houston Papers, ADAH. It appears the repudiationists continued to distrust Houston. For example, the Selma *Argus* barely mentioned the governor's name editorially in 1875.

38. Thornton, "Fiscal Policy and the Failure of Radical Reconstruction in the Lower South," 349–94, esp. 361, 368, 372; Moulton *Advertiser,* Dec. 4, 1874.

39. Selma *Argus,* Nov. 27, Dec. 11, 1874; Apr. 16, May 28, 1875.

40. Montgomery *Advertiser and Mail,* Mar. 5, 1875; Selma *Argus,* Feb. 19, 26, 1875; Livingston *Journal,* Feb. 5, 1875; Moulton *Advertiser,* Jan. 22, Feb. 19, 1875.

41. W. Brewer to McKee, Feb. 13, 1875, McKee Papers, ADAH; Livingston *Journal,* Jan. 22, Mar. 19, 1875.

42. Montgomery *Advertiser and Mail,* June 13, Aug. 25, 1875; J. F. Hagler to Houston, May 22, 1876, Houston Papers, ADAH; R. H. Dawson to McKee, Sept. 13, 1876,

McKee Papers, ADAH; 44th Congress, 1st Sess., House Committee on Elections, Misc. Doc. 47, "Contested Election: Bromberg vs. Haralson, Alabama," 142.

43. Charles Nordhoff, *The Cotton States in the Spring and Summer of 1875* (1876; rpt. NY: Burt Franklin, n.d.), 93. See also Carrollton *West Alabamian,* May 5, 1875.

44. J. Bragg to [B. Bethea], Jan. 1, 1875, Gov. Houston Papers, ADAH.

45. J. Silsby to M. E. Strieby, July 7, 1875, reel 4, AMA Papers; Greenville *Advocate,* June 24, 1875; Montgomery, *Advertiser and Mail,* July 30, 1875; Selma *Argus,* May 14, 1875.

46. Joseph Taylor to H. A. Tayloe, July 3, 1875, reel 49; R. C. Moore to H. A. Tayloe, May 25, Oct. 12, Dec. 25, 1875, June 3, Nov. 8, 1876, Jan. 2, Feb. 21, 1877, reel 47, Tayloe Papers, Stampp, ed., *Records of Ante-bellum Southern Plantations,* ser. M, pt. 1.

47. C. C. Langdon to R. McKee, May 16, 1874, McKee Papers, ADAH. McKee's contacts mostly concurred with this evaluation of candidate Houston, as did the editor himself.

48. W. Bush Duncan to G. S. Houston, Jan. 20, 1875, and Houston, Lawler, and Bethea, Commissioners, to Duncan, Sherman & Co., Jan. 25, Mar. 28, 1875, Gov. Houston Papers, ADAH.

49. Houston to T. B. Bethea, Mar. 31, 1875, Gov. Houston Papers, ADAH.

50. Alabama General Assembly, *Report of the Joint Committee . . . in Regard to the Alleged Election of Geo. E. Spencer.*

51. P. Strobach to Spencer, May 14, 1875; W. E. Chandler Papers, LC; Montgomery *Advertiser and Mail,* Apr. 7, 20, 1875; Montgomery *Journal,* Apr. 25, 1875; Washington *National Republican,* Apr. 16, 1875.

52. *The Nation,* May 20, 1875, 337; *NYT,* Mar. 21, May 13, 1875; Chicago *Tribune,* May 14, 1875; NY *Tribune,* May 13, 1875. Some Democratic legislators apparently resisted pressing the campaign, fearing to reveal their own dirty laundry in 1872. See Chicago *Inter-Ocean,* Jan. 11, 1876.

53. Montgomery *State Journal,* May 14, 1875; *NYT,* July 5, 1875; and on the long-lasting factional dispute, see Wiggins, *The Scalawag in Alabama Politics,* 108–27, and more broadly throughout.

54. Montgomery *Advertiser and Mail,* Mar. 16, 1875.

55. Selma *Argus,* July 9, 1875.

56. Livingston *Journal,* May 28, 1875.

57. Selma *Argus,* June 25, Sept. 3, 1875; Moulton *Advertiser,* June 11, 1875; Jacksonville *Republican,* Jan. 23, 1875.

58. Montgomery *Advertiser and Mail,* Apr. 1, 1875; Going, *Bourbon Democracy in Alabama, 1874–1890,* 20.

59. Montgomery *Advertiser and Mail,* May 28, June 16, 26, 30, July 16, 1875; Selma *Argus,* July 2, 1875.

60. Montgomery *Advertiser and Mail,* July 3, 1875.

61. Montgomery *Advertiser and Mail,* Aug. 11, 1875; Livingston *Journal,* Aug. 20, 1875.

62. Montgomery *Advertiser and Mail,* Aug. 15, 19, 20, 24, 1875; Livingston *Journal,* Aug. 20, 1875; Wiggins, *The Scalawag in Alabama Politics,* 153. The reportedly belated Wilcox County returns were not counted, but initial published counts reported a majority of 2,500 against.

63. Selma *Argus,* June 11, 18, 1875.

64. Montgomery *Advertiser and Mail,* Sept. 12, 21, 1875; Moulton *Advertiser,* June 18, 25, 1875; W. Brewer to R. McKee, Feb. 13, 1875, McKee Papers, ADAH.

65. Livingston *Journal,* July 22, 1875.

66. Alabama Constitutional Convention, *Journal of the Constitutional Convention of the State of Alabama, Assembled in the City of Montgomery, Sept. 6th, 1875* (Montgomery, AL: W. W. Screws, 1875), 5; *NYT,* Sept. 7, 1875; Philadelphia *American and Gazette,* Sept. 20, 1875.

67. *NYT,* Sept. 18, 23, Oct. 9, 1875; Montgomery *Advertiser and Mail,* Sept. 25, 1875; Washington *Republic,* Nov. 1, 1875.

68. *Harper's Weekly,* Oct. 9, 1875, 815; London *Times,* Oct. 4, 1875.

69. Montgomery *Advertiser and Mail,* Oct. 7, 1875. The constitution actually forbade state subsidy of denominational schools; see Article VIII, Section 8.

70. One exception would be the explicit guarantee of separate schools, not present in the previous constitution. See Selma *Argus,* Oct. 8, 1875.

71. *Journal of the Proceedings of Convention of the State of Alabama, 1865,* 35; *NYT,* Sept. 15, Oct. 30, 1875; Selma *Argus,* Dec. 10, 1875; Montgomery *Advertiser and Mail,* Dec. 21, 1875.

72. Webb, "A Jacksonian Democrat in Postbellum Alabama," 239–74; McMillan, *Constitutional Development in Alabama,* 198, 202, 205–8; Selma *Argus,* Oct. 8, 28, 1875; Montgomery *Advertiser and Mail,* Oct. 10, 1875; *NYT,* Oct. 9, 10, 1875.

73. Montgomery *Advertiser and Mail,* Oct. 6, 16, 17, 1875.

74. Montgomery *Advertiser,* Oct. 5, 1875; *NYT,* Sept. 27, 1875; Chicago *Tribune,* Oct. 15, 21, 25, 1875.

75. G. Miligan to Grant, Sept. 18, 1875, in *Papers of Ulysses S. Grant* 26: 525.

76. Montgomery *Advertiser,* Oct. 12, 1875; Livingston *Journal,* Nov. 12, 1875.

77. Chicago *Tribune,* Oct. 15, 21, 25, 1875.

78. W. L. Bragg to J. Wheeler, Oct. 12, 1875, Wheeler Family Papers, ADAH.

79. *NYT,* Oct. 24, 1875; Montgomery *Advertiser and Mail,* Oct. 23, 24, Nov. 6, 13, 1875; J. Silsby to M. E. Strieby, Oct. [27], 1875, reel 4, AMA Papers.

80. On the racial politics of the Readjusters, see Jane Dailey, *Before Jim Crow: The Politics of Race in Postemancipation Virginia* (Chapel Hill: UNC Press, 2000).

81. Montgomery *Advertiser and Mail,* Oct. 30, 1875.

82. Montgomery *Advertiser and Mail,* Nov. 5, 1875.

83. *NYT,* Nov. 17, 1875; Livingston *Journal,* Nov. 19, 1875; Montgomery *Advertiser and Mail,* Dec. 1, 1875; "Message of George S. Houston, Governor of Alabama, to the General Assembly, Submitted Dec. 28th, 1875," 4.

84. US Senate Report No. 704, "Alabama in 1874, 1875 and 1876," 684.

85. Curtin, *Black Prisoners and Their World,* 66–68.

86. In Alabama, Foner's contention that Redemption marked a decisive turning point seems obviously correct. See Foner, *Reconstruction,* 602, 604.

87. Montgomery *Advertiser and Mail,* Dec. 9, 1875. Demands for more dramatic repudiation continued apace; see Selma *Argus,* Dec. 10, 1875, and Webb, "A Jacksonian Democrat in Postbellum Alabama," 264–67.

88. The specifics remain in dispute depending on assumptions employed, and the debt owed to the educational endowment defies easy characterization. Going contends the Democratic leadership exaggerated repudiation amounts, for political reasons. See *Bourbon Democracy in Alabama,* 62–69, 72–74.

89. Montgomery *Advertiser and Mail,* Oct. 10, 1875; Jan. 20, 1876. *NYT,* Mar. 13, 1875. Levi Lawler to Butler, Duncan, Oct. 2, 1875; Edward Hazlewood to Houston, Lawler, and Bethea, Mar. 3, 1876, both in Gov. Houston Papers, ADAH.

90. London *Times,* Dec. 25, 1875. Jacksonville *Republican* qtd. in Selma *Argus,* Jan. 7, 1876; Mar. 31, 1876. *NYT,* Sept. 24, 1875; May 3, 1876. Going, *Bourbon Democracy in Alabama,* 72–74.

91. The deft performance of Houston, and other southern leaders like him, eased the national retreat from Reconstruction. This may have mattered; historians increasingly contend that northern Republicans only grudgingly accommodated to the overthrow of constitutional guarantees in the South. See Charles W. Calhoun, *Conceiving a New Republic: The Republican Party and the Southern Question, 1869–1900* (Lawrence: University of Kansas Press, 2006; Xi Wang, *The Trial of Democracy: Black Suffrage and Northern Republicans, 1860–1910* (Athens: University of Georgia Press, 1997). Legal scholars are even making similar arguments about the Supreme Court; see Edwards, *A Legal History of the Civil War and Reconstruction*, 161–62.

92. *Official Proceedings of the National Republican Conventions of 1868, 1872, 1876, and 1880* (Minneapolis: Charles W. Johnson, 1903), 264–66. On the endless factional struggle, see Wiggins, *The Scalawag in Alabama Politics*, 91–127.

93. Spencer to Dustan, Sept. 28, 1876, Dustan Papers, ADAH. Spencer thought the better strategy was running independent Democrats, which might break down the Democratic monopoly and make the party more respectable.

94. J. F. Johnston to [illegible], [1876], Joseph F. Johnston Papers, ADAH.

95. Going, *Bourbon Democracy in Alabama*, 213, 226.

96. Going, *Bourbon Democracy in Alabama*, 95–99; it took some decades, but William Cohen contends that, by the Jim Crow era, the legislators of Alabama and other southern states "had come remarkably close to reenacting the black codes." See Cohen, *At Freedom's Edge: Black Mobility and the Southern White Quest for Racial Control, 1861–1915* (Baton Rouge: LSU Press, 1991), 247.

97. Samuel L. Webb, *Two-Party Politics in the One-Party South: Alabama's Hill Country, 1874–1920* (Tuscaloosa: UA Press, 1997).

98. William Warren Rogers, *The One-Gallused Rebellion: Agrarianism in Alabama, 1865–1896* (Baton Rouge: LSU Press, 1970); Glenn Feldman, *The Disfranchisement Myth: Poor Whites and Suffrage Restriction* (Athens: University of Georgia Press, 2004), tables 4, 6, 9, 12; R. Volney Riser, *Defying Disfranchisement: Black Voting Rights Activism in the Jim Crow South, 1890–1908* (Baton Rouge: LSU Press, 2010).

99. Alabamans participated in a major riot in Aberdeen and were present in Columbus and elsewhere in eastern Mississippi, from Pickens County in particular. See US Congress, Senate Report No. 527, pt. 2, "Mississippi in 1875," 44th Congress, 1st Sess., 56, 66, 71, 166, 812–13, 1027, 1029, 1031, 1100, 1104–5, 1176, 1182.

100. Fitzgerald, *Urban Emancipation*, 198–267; Norrell, *Reaping the Whirlwind*, 3–18.

101. US Senate Report No. 704, "Alabama in 1874, 1875 and 1876," 606.

102. US Senate Report No. 704, "Alabama in 1874, 1875 and 1876," 149, 150, 155, 156, 168, 173; *NYT*, June 5, 1876.

103. Hilary Abner Herbert, *Why the Solid South? Or, Reconstruction and Its Results* (Baltimore: R. H. Woodward and Co., 1890).

104. Concord *New Hampshire Patriot*, Sept. 13, 1876.

105. Atlanta *Constitution*, June 24, 1896.

106. Birmingham *Age Herald*, Jan. 3, 1899. See also Montgomery *Advertiser*, Jan. 3, 4, 1899; Roanoke *Randolph Herald*, Jan. 6, 1899; Randolph *The Leader*, Jan. 4, 1899.

107. Birmingham *Age Herald*, Jan. 1, 1899.

108. David W. Blight, *Race and Reunion: The Civil War in American Memory* (Cambridge, MA: Harvard University Press, 2001); Bruce E. Baker, *What Reconstruction Meant: Historical Memory in the American South* (Charlottesville: University Press of Virginia, 2007), 76.

Select Bibliography

Manuscript Collections

Alabama Department of Archives and History, Montgomery

C. C. Bartlett Papers.
Charles Dustin Papers.
Bolling Hall Papers.
Governor George S. Houston Papers.
Joseph F. Johnston Papers.
Governor David Lindsay Papers.
Manly Family Papers.
Robert McKee Papers.
Joshua Burns Moore Diary.
Sydingham Moore Diary.
E. H. Moren Papers.
Governor Lewis E. Parsons Papers.
Governor Robert M. Patton Papers.
Raphael Semmes Papers.
H. C. Semple Papers.
Governor John Gill Shorter Papers.
Governor William H. Smith Papers.
Paul Strobach Letter.
Samuel Strudwick Papers.
Wager Swayne Papers.
Governor Thomas H. Watts Papers.
Wheeler Family Papers.

Atlanta University Center Woodruff Library, ITC Gammon Seminary Archives

James F. Chalfant (Freedmen's Aid Society) Correspondence.

Auburn University, Draughon Library

City Council Minutes, Selma, Alabama.
Confederadoes Collection.
Charles Henry Snedeker Diary.

Ball State University, Muncie, Indiana

Ku Klux Klan Collection.

Birmingham Public Library

Faunsdale Collection.

Bowdoin College Library, Bowdoin, Maine

O. O. Howard Papers.

Dillard University, Amistad Research Center, New Orleans

American Missionary Association Manuscripts, Alabama.

Duke University, Perkins Library

Septimus D. Cabaniss Papers.
George S. Houston Papers.
William Dunlop Simpson Papers.

Emory University, Woodruff Library

William Cooper Diary.
Henry Crydenwise Papers.
Ichibod Frisbie Diary.
Joseph Manson Papers.

Filson Historical Society, Louisville, Kentucky

Joseph B. Fox Papers.

Harvard University, Baker Library, Cambridge, Massachusetts

Dun Credit Ledgers.

Huntsville Madison County Public Library

Dysinger Collection.
Frank Gurley Diary.

Indiana Historical Society, Indianapolis

James M. Comly Papers.
Alva C. Griest, "Three Years in Dixie." Typescript.
Benjamin R. Hieronymous Papers.

Martin Hurst Papers.
John W. Large Papers.
Edward F. Reid Papers.
Rowland-Shilladay Papers.
John W. Schlagle Diary.
William Stuckey Papers.
Augustus M. Van Dyke Papers.
Amos C. Weaver Letters.

Library of Congress, Washington, DC

B. F. Butler Papers.
W. E. Chandler Papers.
Salmon P. Chase Papers.
Demby Family Papers.
U. S. Grant Papers.
Andrew Johnson Papers.
Abraham Lincoln Papers.
John A. Logan Papers.
Manton Marble Papers.
Whitelaw Reid Papers.
Carl Schurz Papers.
John Sherman Papers.

Abraham Lincoln Presidential Library and Museum, Springfield, Illinois

Lemuel Burke Diary.
Andrew Johnson Letter.
Charles Turner Papers.

Louisiana State University, Hill Library, Baton Rouge

Golson Brothers Papers.

Minnesota Historical Society, St. Paul

Elijah E. Evans Papers.
W. H. C. Folsom and Family Papers.
Henry N. Herrick and Family Papers.
A. H. Kerr Diary.
Ebenezer Brewer Mattocks and Family Papers.

Mississippi State University, Starkville

Rice Family Papers.

Missouri Historical Society, St. Louis

Luther Smith Papers.

MOBILE COUNTY PROBATE COURT, MOBILE COUNTY COURTHOUSE

"Petitions to Become Slaves."

NATIONAL ARCHIVES AND RECORDS SERVICE, WASHINGTON, DC

Case files of Applications from former Confederates for Presidential Pardons ("Amnesty Papers"), 1865–67, Alabama, in Records of the Adjutant General's Office, 1780s–1917, Record Group 94.

Records of the Bureau of Refugees, Freedmen and Abandoned Lands, RG 105.

Records of the Judge Advocate General's Office, General Court Martials, KK-122, RG 153.

Records of the Southern Claims Commission, Accepted Claims, Alabama, RG 217.

Records of the Southern Claims Commission, Disallowed and Barred Claims, Alabama, RG 233.

Records of US Army Continental Commands, RG 393.

NATIONAL ARCHIVES, COLLEGE PARK

Records of the Division of Appointments, Applications and Recommendations for Positions in the Washington, DC, Offices of the Treasury Department, 1830–1910, RG 56.

NEW HAMPSHIRE HISTORICAL SOCIETY, CONCORD

W. E. Chandler Papers.

NEW YORK PUBLIC LIBRARY

Walter L. Fleming Papers.

OHIO HISTORICAL SOCIETY, COLUMBUS

Thomas H. Honnell Papers.

William H. Kemper Papers.

SAMFORD UNIVERSITY, BIRMINGHAM

Ryland Randolph Papers.

STANFORD UNIVERSITY, PALO ALTO, CALIFORNIA

Frederick Steele Papers.

STATE HISTORICAL SOCIETY OF IOWA, DES MOINES

Grenville Dodge Papers.

STATE HISTORICAL SOCIETY OF IOWA, IOWA CITY

Franklin B. Reed Papers.

Albert Towne Papers.

Tennessee State Library and Archives, Nashville

Coffee-Patton Papers.
Willard Warner Papers.

University of Alabama, Hoole Library

"Reminiscence of Julius C. Greene."
Daniel R. Hundley Diary.
Robert Jemison Papers.
George Doherty Johnson Papers.
Woodward Family Papers.

University of Alabama, Williams Collection

"Manuscript History of the Garrett Family of Birmingham and Alabama."
Rice & Chilton Papers.

University of Iowa, Iowa City

John W. Pratt Diary.

University of North Carolina, Southern Historical Collection

John Bragg Papers.
Buchanan and McClellan Family Papers.
Cameron Family Papers.
Cole-Taylor Family Papers.
William Stump Forwood Papers.
B. C. Yancey Papers.

University of Notre Dame, South Bend, Indiana

Henry H. Maley Papers.

University of South Alabama, Mobile, McCall Collection

Pickens Family Papers.

University of Virginia, Alderman Library

Cabell Family Papers.

University of West Alabama, Livingston

Susalee Smith Papers.

Virginia Historical Society, Richmond

Ella Merryman Papers.

WISCONSIN HISTORICAL SOCIETY, MADISON

William P. Moore Diary.
Henry J. Traber Papers.

US MILITARY HISTORY INSTITUTE MANUSCRIPT COLLECTIONS, CARLISLE BARRACKS, PENNSYLVANIA

John M. Eaton Papers.
Nathan B. Middlebrook Collection.

YALE UNIVERSITY, NEW HAVEN, CONNECTICUT

Gilbert Cheever Papers.

Alabama Newspapers

Abbeville *Henry County Register,* 1870, 1873.
Ashville *Southern Aegis,* 1873.
Athens *Post,* 1867–69.
Camden *Wilcox News and Pacificator,* 1874.
Carrollton *West Alabamian,* 1874–75.
Columbiana *Shelby County Guide,* 1870–74.
Demopolis *Marengo News-Journal,* 1873–74.
Demopolis *Southern Republican,* [1870].
Eufaula *Bluff City Times,* 1870–72.
Eufaula *News,* 1874.
Eutaw *Whig and Observer,* 1874.
Gainesville *North Sumter News,* 1866–67.
Greensboro *Beacon,* 1869–70, 1873–75.
Greenville *Advocate,* 1868, 1874.
Grove Hill *Clarke County Democrat,* 1872.
Hayneville *Examiner,* 1868–72.
Huntsville *Advocate,* 1866–72.
Huntsville *Democrat,* 1870–72.
Huntsville *Independent,* 1866.
Jacksonville *Republican,* 1867–76.
Livingston *Journal,* 1868, 1872–75.
Marion *Commonwealth,* 1867–71.
Mobile *Advertiser and Register,* 1865–67.
Mobile *Nationalist,* 1865–69.
Mobile *Register,* 1868–77.
Mobile *Times,* 1865–66.
Mobile *Tribune,* 1872.
Mobile *Watchman,* 1873–74.
Montgomery *Advance,* 1871–72.

Montgomery *Advertiser,* 1865–71.
Montgomery *Advertiser and Mail,* 1871–75.
Montgomery *Alabama State Journal,* 1868–76.
Montgomery *Mail,* 1864, 1868–70.
Montgomery *State Sentinel,* 1867.
Moulton *Advertiser,* 1869, 1874–75.
Opelika *East Alabama Monitor,* 1869.
Opelika *Era and Whig,* 1871.
Opelika *Locomotive,* [1870].
Selma *Argus,* 1869–76.
Selma *Messenger,* 1867.
Selma *Press,* 1869–70.
Selma *Times and Messenger,* 1868.
Tuscaloosa *Monitor,* 1868–71.
Tuscaloosa *Observer,* 1871–72.
Tuscaloosa *Reconstructionist,* [1867].
Tuscaloosa *Times,* 1872.
Tuscumbia *North Alabamian,* [1865].
Union Springs *Times,* 1867.
Wetumpka *Elmore Standard,* 1867.

Selected Non-Alabama Newspapers

Atlanta *Constitution,* 1865–76.
Chattanooga *Republican,* 1869.
Chicago *Tribune,* 1861–77.
Cincinnati *Gazette,* 1867.
Columbus (GA) *Enquirer,* [1868–74].
Manhattan (KS) *Nationalist,* [1871].
Nashville *Union,* [1864–65].
New Orleans *Tribune,* [1865].
NY *Herald,* 1867.
NY *Times,* 1861–76.
NY *Tribune,* 1861–76.
NY *World,* 1867.
Philadelphia *Enquirer,* [1864].

Periodicals

Christian Advocate, 1861–77.
DeBow's Review, 1865–75.
Harper's Weekly, 1865–76.
The Liberator, 1865.

Published Primary Sources

American Annual Cyclopedia for 1867. NY: Appleton & Co., 1868.

Ayers, James T. *The Diary of James T. Ayers: Civil War Recruiter.* Ed. John Hope Franklin. Springfield: Printed by authority of the State of Illinois, 1947.

Axford, Faye A., ed. *The Jones-Donnell Papers.* N.p., [1994].

Beatty, John. *The Citizen-Soldier; Or, Memoirs of a Volunteer.* Cincinnati: Wilstach, Baldwin & Co., 1879.

Bell, N. J. *Southern Railroad Man: Conductor N. J. Bell's Recollections of the Civil War Era.* Ed. James Arthur Ward. DeKalb: Northern Illinois University Press, 1994.

Benners, Augustus, Glenn M. Linden, and Virginia Linden. *Disunion, War, Defeat, and Recovery in Alabama: The Journal of Augustus Benners, 1850–1885.* Macon, GA: Mercer University Press, 2007.

Berlin, Ira, ed. *Records of the Southern Plantations from Emancipation to the Great Migration.* Microfilm. Ser. A, pt. 1. Bethesda, MD: University Publications of America, 2001.

Bierce, Ambrose. *Phantoms of a Blood-Stained Period: The Complete Civil War Writings of Ambrose Bierce.* Ed. Russell Duncan and David J. Klooster. Amherst: University of Massachusetts Press, 2002.

Calhoun, Frederick S., ed. *Letters Received by the Attorney General, 1809–1870: Southern Law and Order.* Microfilm. Bethesda, MD: University Publications of America, 1998.

Chase, Salmon P. *The Salmon P. Chase Papers.* Ed. John Niven. Kent, OH: Kent State University Press, 1996.

Chesnut, Mary. *The Private Mary Chesnut: The Unpublished Civil War Diaries.* Ed. C. Vann Woodward and Elisabeth Muhlenfeld. NY: Oxford University Press, 1984.

Clay-Clopton, Virginia. *A Belle of the Fifties: Memoirs of Mrs. Clay, of Alabama, Covering Social and Political Life in Washington and the South, 1853–66.* Ed. Ada Sterling. NY: Doubleday, Page & Co., 1905.

Clemens, Jeremiah. *Tobias Wilson: A Tale of the Great Rebellion.* Philadelphia: J. B. Lippincott, 1865.

Conway, Thomas W. *The Freedmen of Louisiana: Final Report of the Bureau of Free Labor, Department of the Gulf.* New Orleans: Times Book and Job Office, 1865.

Cook, Chauncy H. *Soldier Boy's Letters to His Father and Mother: 1861–1865.* N.p.: News Office, 1915.

Davis, Jefferson. *Jefferson Davis, Constitutionalist: His Letters, Papers, and Speeches.* Ed. Rowland Dunbar. Jackson: Mississippi Dept. of Archives and History, 1923.

———. *The Papers of Jefferson Davis.* Ed. Lynda Lasswell Crist. Baton Rouge: LSU Press, 1995.

Dennett, John Richard. *The South as It Is: 1865–1866.* Ed. Caroline E. Janney. Tuscaloosa: UA Press, 2010.

Dickinson, Anna E. *A Tour of Reconstruction: Travel Letters of 1875.* Ed. Matthew Gallman. Lexington: University Press of Kentucky, 2011.

Geary, John White. *A Politician Goes to War: The Civil War Letters of John White Geary.* Ed. William Alan Blair. University Park: Pennsylvania State University Press, 1995.

Gorgas, Josiah. *The Journals of Josiah Gorgas, 1857–1878.* Ed. Sarah Woolfolk Wiggins. Tuscaloosa: UA Press, 1995.

Gosse, Philip. *Letters from Alabama Chiefly Relating to Natural History.* London: Morgan and Chase, 1859.

Grant, Ulysses S. *The Papers of Ulysses S. Grant.* Ed. John Y. Simon and John F. Marszalek. Carbondale: Southern Illinois University Press, 1967–.

Hood, John Bell. *Advance and Retreat: Personal Experiences in the United States and Confederate States Armies.* New Orleans: Hood Orphan Memorial Fund, 1880.

Howard, R. L. *History of the 124th Regiment.* Springfield, IL: H. W. Rokker, 1880.

Hundley, Daniel R. *Social Relations in Our Southern States.* Ed. William J. Cooper Jr. 1860. Rev. ed. Baton Rouge: LSU Press, 1979.

Jackson, Isaac. *"Some of the Boys . . .": The Civil War Letters of Isaac Jackson.* Ed. Joseph Orville. Carbondale: Southern Illinois University Press, 1960.

Jackson, Oscar Lawrence. *The Colonel's Diary: Journals Kept Before and During the Civil War.* N.p., 1922.

Johnson, Andrew. *The Papers of Andrew Johnson.* Ed. LeRoy P. Graf et al. Knoxville: University of Tennessee Press, 1967–.

Jones, Jenkins. *An Artilleryman's Diary.* N.p.: Wisconsin History Commission, 1914.

Kamphoefner, Walter D., and Wolfgang Helbich, eds. *Germans in the Civil War: The Letters They Wrote Home.* Trans. Susan Carter Vogel. Chapel Hill: UNC Press, 2006.

King, Edward. *The Great South: A Record of Journeys in Louisiana, Texas, Alabama and Maryland.* Hartford, CT: American Publishing Co, 1879.

Lapsley, J. W. *Prospectus of a Combined System of Railways.* NY: S. W. Green, 1870.

Longacre, Edward G., ed. "To Tuscaloosa and Beyond: A Union Cavalry Raider in Alabama, March–April 1865." *Alabama Historical Quarterly* 44 (Spring and Summer 1982): 109–22.

Lyon, William Penn. *Reminiscences of the Civil War.* San Jose, CA: Press of Muirson and Wright, 1907.

Mallory, James. *"Fear God and Walk Humbly": The Agricultural Journal of James Mallory, 1843–1877.* Ed. Grady McWhiney, Warner O. Moore Jr., and Robert F. Pace. Tuscaloosa: UA Press, 1997.

Maryniak, Benedict R., and John Wesley Brinsfield Jr., comps. and eds. *The Spirit*

Divided: Memoirs of Civil War Chaplains—The Union, Macon, GA: Mercer University Press, 2007.

McClellan, William Cowan. *Welcome the Hour of Conflict: William Cowan McClellan and the 9th Alabama.* Ed. John C. Carter. Tuscaloosa: UA Press, 2007.

McMillan, Malcolm C., ed. *The Alabama Confederate Reader.* Tuscaloosa: UA Press, 1992.

Meade, George Gordon. *George Gordon Meade Collection.* Microfilm. Wilmington, DE: Scholarly Resources, 1998.

Newton, James K., *A Wisconsin Boy in Dixie: The Selected Letters of James K. Newton.* Ed. Stephen E. Ambrose. Madison: University of Wisconsin Press, 1961.

Nordhoff, Charles. *The Cotton States in the Spring and Summer of 1875.* 1876. Rpt. NY: Burt Franklin, n.d.

Patton, Robert M. "The New Era of Southern Manufactures." *DeBow's Review.* After the War series, vol. 3 (Jan. 1867): 56–112.

Phillips, John R. "The Diary of a Union Soldier from Alabama." *Alabama Heritage* 28 (1993): 20–25.

Price, William Newton. *One Year in the Civil War: A Diary of the Events from April 1st, 1864, to April 1st, 1865.* N.p., n.d.

"Review of the Testimony Taken by the Investigating Committee of the Alabama House of Representatives." Tuscaloosa, AL: Observer, 1871.

Saffold, Milton. "Letter of M. J. Saffold, 'Southern Aristocratic Republic! Versus Southern Democratic Republic.'" Montgomery, AL, 1866.

Shaw, Nate. *All God's Dangers: The Life of Nate Shaw.* Ed. Theodore Rosengarten. NY: Knopf, 1974.

Sherman, William T. *Sherman's Civil War: Selected Correspondence of William T. Sherman, 1860–1865.* Ed. Brooks D. Simpson and Jean V. Berlin. Chapel Hill: UNC Press, 1999.

Smith, William H. "Letter from William H. Smith in Defense of his Administration." Montgomery, AL: Barrett and Brown, 1870.

Smith, William Russell. *The History and Debates of the Convention of the People of Alabama.* Montgomery, AL: White, 1861.

Somers, Robert. *The Southern States since the War, 1870–71.* University: UA Press, 1965.

Spencer, Bella Zilfa. *Tried and True, Or, Love and Loyalty, A Story of the Great Rebellion.* Springfield, MA: W. J. Holland; 1866.

Stampp, Kenneth M., Randolph Boehm, Martin Paul Schipper, and Manuscript Division Library of Congress, eds. *Records of Ante-Bellum Southern Plantations from the Revolution through the Civil War.* Frederick, MD: University Microfilms of America, 1985.

Stevens, Thaddeus. *The Thaddeus Stevens Papers.* Ed. Beverly Wilson Palmer and Holly Byers Ochoa. 12 microfilm reels; 35 mm. vols. Wilmington, DE: Scholarly Resources Inc., 1993.

Sumner, Charles. *The Papers of Charles Sumner.* Ed. Beverly Wilson Palmer. 85 microfilm reels; 35 mm vols. Alexandria, VA: Chadwyck-Healey, 1988.

———. *The Selected Letters of Charles Sumner.* Ed. Beverly Wilson Palmer. Boston: Northeastern University Press, 1990.

Swedberg, Claire E. *Three Years with the 92d Illinois: The Civil War Diary of John M. King.* Mechanicsville, PA: Stackpole Books, 1999.

Taylor, Grant. *This Cruel War: The Civil War Letters of Grant and Malinda Taylor, 1862–1865.* Ed. Malinda J. Slaughter Taylor, Ann Kicker Blomquist, and Robert A. Taylor. Macon, GA: Mercer University Press, 2000.

Taylor, Richard. *Destruction and Reconstruction: Personal Experiences of the Late War.* NY: Longmans, Green, 1955.

Tharin, Robert Seymour Symmes. *Arbitrary Arrests in the South or, Scenes from the Experience of an Alabama Unionist.* NY: J. Bradburn, 1863.

United States Bureau of Refugees Freedmen and Abandoned Lands. *Records of the Assistant Commissioner for the State of Alabama, Bureau of Refugees, Freedmen and Abandoned Lands, 1865–1870: M809, RG 105.* Washington, DC: National Archives and Records Service, 1968.

———. Education Division. *Records of the Education Division of the Bureau of Refugees, Freedmen, and Abandoned Lands, 1865–1871: M803, RG 105.* Washington: National Archives and Records Service, 1983.

Villard, Henry. *Memoirs of Henry Villard, Journalist and Financier, 1835–1900.* Boston: Houghton, 1904.

Walker, Eliza. "Other Days." *Alabama Historical Quarterly* 5 (Summer 1943): 209–33.

Wheeler, William. *Letters of William Wheeler of the Class of 1855.* Privately published, 1875.

Wills, Charles Wright. *Army Life of an Illinois Soldier . . . : Letters and Diary of the Late Charles W. Wills, Private and Sergeant 8th Illinois Infantry.* Washington, DC: Globe Print Co, 1906.

Wilson, James Harrison. *Under the Old Flag: Recollections of Military Operations in the War for the Union, the Spanish War, the Boxer Rebellion, Etc.* NY: Appleton, 1912.

Wise, George M. "Civil War Letters of George M. Wise." Ed. Wilfred W. Black. *Ohio History* 65: 53–81.

Wood, Edward J. *A Fierce, Wild Joy: The Civil War Letters of Colonel Edward J. Wood, 48th Indiana Volunteer Infantry Regiment.* Ed. Stephen E. Towne. Knoxville: University of Tennessee Press, 2007.

Wood, Sara. "To the Cleveland Freedmen's Union Commission. A Report of the Progress of Education among the Freedmen of Alabama." Montgomery, AL, 1866.

Wood, Wales W. *A History of the Ninety-Fifth Regiment, Illinois Infantry Volunteers* Chicago: Tribune, 1865.

Articles

Amos, Harriet E. "Religious Reconstruction in Microcosm at Faunsdale Plantation." *Alabama Review* 42, no. 4 (1989): 243–69.

Bailey, Hugh C. "Disaffection in the Alabama Hill Country, 1861." *Civil War History* 4, no. 2 (1958): 183–94.

Benedict, Michael Les. "Preserving the Constitution: The Conservative Basis of Radical Reconstruction." *Journal of American History* 61, no. 1 (1974): 65–90.

Bethel, Elizabeth. "The Freedmen's Bureau in Alabama." *Journal of Southern History* 14, no. 1 (1948): 49–92.

Bridges, Edwin C. "Juliet Opie Hopkins and Alabama's Civil War Hospitals in Richmond, Virginia." *Alabama Review* 53, no. 2 (2000): 83.

Brown, Charles A. "A. H. Curtis: An Alabama Legislator 1870–1876, with Glimpses into Reconstruction." *Negro History Bulletin* 25, no. 5 (1962): 99–101.

Crook, Charles M. "The Barbour County Background to the Election of 1872 and Alabama's Dual Legislatures." *Alabama Review* 56, no. 4 (2003): 242–77.

Daniel, Michael J. "Samuel Spring Gardner, a Maine Parson in Alabama." *Maine Historical Society Quarterly* 23, no. 4 (1984): 151–76.

Dee, Christine. "Trying James Hickman: The Politics of Loyalty in a Civil War Community." *Alabama Review* 58, no. 2 (2005): 83–112.

Derbes, Brett J. "The Production of Military Supplies at the Alabama State Penitentiary During the Civil War." *Alabama Review* 67, no. 2 (2014): 131–60.

Eckinger, Helen. "The Militarization of the University of Alabama." *Alabama Review* 66, no. 3 (2013): 163–85.

Fairclough, Adam. "Was the Grant of Black Suffrage a Political Error? Reconsidering the Views of John W. Burgess, William A. Dunning, and Eric Foner on Congressional Reconstruction." *Journal of the Historical Society* 12, no. 2 (June 2012): 155–88.

Fitzgerald, Michael W. "Another Kind of Glory: Black Participation and Its Consequences in the Campaign for Confederate Mobile." *Alabama Review* 54, no. 4 (2001): 243–75.

———. "From Unionists to Scalawags: Elite Dissent in Civil War Mobile." *Alabama Review* 55, no. 2 (2002): 106–21.

———. "The Ku Klux Klan: Property Crime and the Plantation System in Reconstruction Alabama." *Agricultural History* 71, no. 2 (1997): 186–206.

———. "Radical Republicanism and the White Yeomanry During Alabama Reconstruction, 1865–1868." *Journal of Southern History* 54, no. 4 (1988): 565–96.

———. "Railroad Subsidies and Black Aspirations: The Politics of Economic Development in Reconstruction Mobile, 1865–1879." *Civil War History* 39, no. 3 (1993): 240–56.

———. "Republican Factionalism and Black Empowerment: The Spencer-Warner Controversy and Alabama Reconstruction, 1868–1880." *The Journal of Southern History* 64, no. 3 (1998): 473–94.

———. "'To Give Our Votes to the Party': Black Political Agitation and Agricultural Change in Alabama, 1865–1870." *Journal of American History* 76, no. 2 (1989): 489–505.

———. "Wager Swayne, the Freedmen's Bureau, and the Politics of Reconstruction in Alabama." *Alabama Review* 48, no. 3 (1995): 188–218.

Formwalt, Lee W. "Notes and Documents: A Case of Interracial Marriage During Reconstruction." *Alabama Review* 45, no. 3 (1992): 216–24.

———. "The Origins of African-American Politics in Southwest Georgia: A Case Study of Black Political Organization during Presidential Reconstruction, 1865–1867." *Journal of Negro History* 77, no. 4 (1992): 211–22.

Griffin, Richard W. "Cotton Frauds and Confiscations in Alabama, 1863–1866." *Alabama Review* 7, no. 4 (Oct. 1954): 265–76.

Hettle, Wallace T. "Curing the 'Sir Walter Disease': The Politics and Fiction of Jeremiah Clemens." *Alabama Review* 52, no. 3 (1999): 163–91.

Horton, Paul. "Lightning Rod Scalawag: The Unlikely Political Career of Thomas Minott Peters." *Alabama Review* 64, no. 2 (2011): 116–42.

———. "Submitting to the 'Shadow of Slavery': The Secession Crisis and Civil War in Alabama's Lawrence County." *Civil War History* 44, no. 2 (1998): 111–36.

Hughes, John S. "Labeling and Treating Black Mental Illness in Alabama, 1861–1910." *Journal of Southern History* 58, no. 3 (1992): 435–60.

Jones, Allen W. "Unionism and Disaffection in South Alabama: The Case of Alfred Holley." *Alabama Review* 24, no. 2 (1971): 114–32.

Jones, James P., ed. "'Your Left Arm': James H. Wilson's Letters to Adam Badeau." *Civil War History* 12, no. 3 (1966): 230–45.

Kitchens, Joel D. "E. W. Peck: Alabama's First Scalawag Chief Justice." *Alabama Review* 54, no. 1 (2001): 3–32.

Krebs, Sylvia. "The Chinese Labor Question: A Note on the Attitudes of Two Alabama Republicans." *Alabama Historical Quarterly* 38, no. 3 (1976): 214–17.

Kyriakoudes, Louis M. "The Rise of Merchants and Market Towns in Reconstruction-Era Alabama." *Alabama Review* 49, no. 2 (1996): 83–107.

McIlwain, Christopher Lyle, Sr. "United States District Judge Richard Busteed and the Alabama Klan Trials of 1872." *Alabama Review* 65, no. 4 (2012): 263–89.

Mills, Gary B. "Miscegenation and the Free Negro in Antebellum 'Anglo' Alabama: A Reexamination of Southern Race Relations." *Journal of American History* 68, no. 1 (1981): 16–34.

Moore, A. B. "Railroad Building in Alabama During the Reconstruction Period." *Journal of Southern History* 1, no. 4 (1935): 421–41.

Ottens, Allen J., and Daniel W. Stowell. "Forging Loyalty: The Curious Case of Williamson R. W. Cobb." *Manuscripts* 63, no. 3 (2011): 185–98.

Phillips, John R. "The Diary of a Union Soldier from Alabama." *Alabama Heritage* 28 (1993): 20–25.

Ritchey, David. "Williamson R. W. Cobb: Rattler of Tinware and Crockery for Peace." *Alabama Historical Quarterly* 36, no. 2 (1974): 112–20.

Robinson, Stephen R. "Rethinking Black Urban Politics in the 1880s: The Case of William Gaston in Post-Reconstruction Alabama." *Alabama Review* 66, no. 1 (2013): 3–29.

Rogers, William Warren. "Agrarian Distress in the Seventies: The Mulberry Agricultural Club Versus Governor David P. Lewis." *Alabama Historical Quarterly* 33, no. 3/4 (1971): 169–76.

———. "The Boyd Incident: Black Belt Violence During Reconstruction." *Civil War History* 21, no. 4 (1975): 309–29.

———. "The Eutaw Prisoners: Federal Confrontation with Violence in Reconstruction Alabama." *Alabama Review* 43, no. 2 (1990): 98–121.

———. "'Politics Is Mighty Uncertain': Charles Hays Goes to Congress." *Alabama Review* 30, no. 3 (1977): 163–90.

Rogers, William Warren, Jr. "'For the Destruction of Radicalism': A Reconstruction Case Study." *Alabama Review* 62, no. 3 (2009): 190–209.

———. "'The Prospect before Us': A Massachusetts Congregationalist in Reconstruction Alabama." *Alabama Review* 60, no. 1 (2007): 3–28.

Schweninger, Loren. "Black Citizenship and the Republican Party in Reconstruction Alabama." *Alabama Review* 29, no. 2 (1976): 83–103.

Sterkx, H. E. "William C. Jordan and Reconstruction in Bullock County, Alabama." *Alabama Review* 15, no. 1 (1962): 61–73.

Thornton, J. Mills. "Class Conflict and Black Enfranchisement in Alabama." *Journal of the Historical Society* 11, no. 3 (Sept. 2012): 235–40.

Walker, Anne Kendrick, ed. "Governor John Gill Shorter, Miscellaneous Papers, 1861–1863." *Alabama Review* 11, no. 2 and 3 (1958): 208–32, 267–85.

Webb, Samuel L. "A Jacksonian Democrat in Postbellum Alabama: The Ideology and Influence of Journalist Robert McKee, 1869–1896." *Journal of Southern History* 62, no. 2 (1996): 239–74.

White, Kenneth B. "The Alabama Freedmen's Bureau and Black Education: The Myth of Opportunity." *Alabama Review* 34, no. 2 (1981): 107–24.

———. "Wager Swayne: Racist or Realist?" *Alabama Review* 31, no. 2 (Apr. 1978): 92–109.

Wiggins, Sarah Woolfolk. "Ostracism of White Republicans in Alabama During Reconstruction." *Alabama Review* 27, no. 1 (1974): 52–64.

———. "The "Pig Iron" Kelley Riot in Mobile, May 14, 1867." *Alabama Review* 23, no. 1 (1970): 45–55.

———. "Press Reaction in Alabama to the Attempted Assassination of Judge Richard Busteed." *Alabama Review* 21, no. 3 (1968): 211–19.

Books

Abbott, Richard H. *The Republican Party and the South, 1855–1877: The First Southern Strategy*. Chapel Hill: UNC Press, 1986.

Amos Doss, Harriet E. *Cotton City: Urban Development in Antebellum Mobile.* University: UA Press, 1985.

Armes, Ethel. *The Story of Coal and Iron in Alabama.* Birmingham, AL: Chamber of Commerce, 1910.

Ashe, Steven V. *When the Yankees Came: Conflict and Chaos in the Occupied South, 1861–1865.* Chapel Hill: UNC Press, 1995.

Baggett, James Alex. *The Scalawags: Southern Dissenters in the Civil War and Reconstruction.* Baton Rouge: LSU Press, 2003.

Bailey, Richard. *Neither Carpetbaggers Nor Scalawags: Black Officeholders during the Reconstruction of Alabama, 1867–1878.* 5th ed. Montgomery, AL: New South Books, 2010.

Baker, Bruce E. *What Reconstruction Meant: Historical Memory in the American South.* Charlottesville: University of Virginia Press, 2007.

Bardaglio, Peter Winthrop. *Reconstructing the Household : Families, Sex, and the Law in the Nineteenth-Century South.* Chapel Hill: UNC Press, 1995.

Barney, William L. *The Secessionist Impulse: Alabama and Mississippi in 1860.* Princeton, NJ: Princeton University Press, 1974.

Benedict, Michael Les. *The Impeachment and Trial of Andrew Johnson.* NY: Norton, 1973.

Bergeron, Paul H. *Andrew Johnson's Civil War and Reconstruction.* Knoxville: University of Tennessee Press, 2011.

Blight, David W. *Race and Reunion: The Civil War in American Memory.* Cambridge, MA: Harvard University Press, 2001.

———. *A Slave No More : Two Men Who Escaped to Freedom: Including Their Own Narratives of Emancipation.* Boston: Harcourt, 2007.

Bond, Horace Mann. *Negro Education in Alabama: A Study in Cotton and Steel.* NY: Atheneum, 1969.

Bradley, George C., and Richard L. Dahlen. *From Conciliation to Conquest: The Sack of Athens and the Court-Martial of Colonel John B. Turchin.* Tuscaloosa: UA Press, 2006.

Brasher, John Lawrence. *The Sanctified South: John Lakin Brasher and the Holiness Movement.* Urbana: University of Illinois Press, 1994.

Brewer, Willis. *Alabama: Her History, Resources, War Record, and Public Men, from 1540 to 1872.* Montgomery, AL: Barrett and Brown, 1872.

Burnett, Lonnie A. *The Pen Makes a Good Sword: John Forsyth of the Mobile Register.* Tuscaloosa: UA Press, 2006.

Butchart, Ronald E. *Northern Schools, Southern Blacks, and Reconstruction: Freedmen's Education, 1862–1875.* Westport, CT: Greenwood Press, 1980.

Calhoun, Charles W. *Conceiving a New Republic: The Republican Party and the Southern Question, 1869–1900.* Lawrence: University Press of Kansas, 2006.

Canfield, S. S., *History of the 21st Regiment Ohio Volunteer Infantry, in the War of the Rebellion.* Toledo, OH: Vrooman, Anderson & Bateman, 1893.

Carmer, Carl. *Stars Fell on Alabama.* NY: Blue Ribbon Books, 1934.

Carter, Dan T. *When the War Was Over: The Failure of Self-Reconstruction in the South, 1865–1867.* Baton Rouge: LSU Press, 1985.

Censer, Jane Turner. *The Reconstruction of White Southern Womanhood, 1865–1895.* Baton Rouge: LSU Press, 2003.

Chicoine, Stephen. *John Basil Turchin and the Fight to Free the Slaves* (Westport, CT: Praeger, 2003.

Cimbala, Paul A. *Under the Guardianship of the Nation: The Freedman's Bureau and the Reconstruction of Georgia, 1865–1870.* Athens: University of Georgia Press, 1997.

Clark, Willis G. *History of Education in Alabama, 1702–1889.* Washington, DC: GPO, 1889.

Cox, LaWanda C. Fenlason. *Politics, Principle, and Prejudice, 1865–1866: Dilemma of Reconstruction America.* Ed. John H. Cox. NY: Free Press of Glencoe, 1963.

———, and Donald G. Nieman. *Freedom, Racism, and Reconstruction: Collected Writings of Lawanda Cox.* Athens: University of Georgia Press, 1997.

Crofts, Daniel W. *Reluctant Confederates: Upper South Unionists in the Secession Crisis.* Chapel Hill: UNC Press, 1989.

Current, Richard Nelson. *Lincoln's Loyalists: Union Soldiers from the Confederacy.* Boston: Northeastern University Press, 1992.

Curtin, Mary Ellen. *Black Prisoners and Their World: Alabama, 1865–1900.* Charlottesville: University Press of Virginia, 2000.

Damer, Eyre. *When the Klan Rode.* NY: Neale Publishing Co., 1912.

Danielson, Joseph Wesley. *War's Desolating Scourge: The Union's Occupation of North Alabama.* Lawrence: University Press of Kansas, 2012.

Davis, William C. *A Government of Our Own: The Making of the Confederacy.* NY: Free Press, 1994.

Dawsey, Cyrus B., and James M. Dawsey. *The Confederados: Old South Immigrants in Brazil.* Tuscaloosa: UA Press, 1995.

Dew, Charles B. *Apostles of Disunion: Southern Secession Commissioners and the Causes of the Civil War.* Charlottesville: University Press of Virginia, 2001.

Diouf, Sylviane A. *Dreams of Africa in Alabama: The Slave Ship Clotilda and the Story of the Last Africans Brought to America.* NY: Oxford University Press, 2007.

Dodge, William Sumner. *History of the Second Division, Army of the Cumberland.* Chicago: Church and Goodman, 1864.

Dorman, Lewy. *Party Politics in Alabama from 1850 through 1860.* 1935. Tuscaloosa: UA Press, 1975.

Dorris, Jonathan Truman. *Pardon and Amnesty under Lincoln and Johnson: The Restoration of the Confederates to Their Rights and Privileges, 1861–1898.* UNC Press: Chapel Hill, 1953.

Downs, Gregory P. *After Appomattox: Military Occupation and the Ends of War.* Cambridge, MA: Harvard University Press, 2015.

———. *Declarations of Dependence: The Long Reconstruction of Popular Politics in the South, 1861–1908.* Chapel Hill: UNC Press, 2011.

———, and Kate Masur, eds. *The World the Civil War Made.* Chapel Hill: UNC Press, 2015.

DuBois, Ellen Carol. *Feminism and Suffrage : The Emergence of an Independent Women's Movement in America, 1848–1869.* Ithaca, NY: Cornell University Press, 1978.

Du Bois, W. E. B. *Black Reconstruction: An Essay Toward a History of the Part Which Black Folk Played in the Attempt to Reconstruct Democracy in America, 1860–1880.* NY: Russell and Russell, 1935.

DuBose, John Witherspoon. *Alabama's Tragic Decade: Ten Years of Alabama, 1865–1874.* Ed. James K. Greer. Birmingham, AL: Webb Book Co., 1940.

Dunning, William Archibald. *Reconstruction, Political and Economic, 1865–1877.* NY: Harper & Brothers, 1907.

Dupre, Daniel S. *Transforming the Cotton Frontier: Madison County, Alabama, 1800–1840.* Baton Rouge: LSU Press, 1997.

Durham, David I. *A Southern Moderate in Radical Times: Henry Washington Hilliard, 1808–1892.* Baton Rouge: LSU Press, 2008.

Dyer, Frederick H. *A Compendium of the War of the Rebellion.* NY: Thomas Yoseloff, 1959.

Edwards, Laura F. *Gendered Strife & Confusion: The Political Culture of Reconstruction.* Urbana: University of Illinois Press, 1997.

———. *A Legal History of the Civil War and Reconstruction: A Nation of Rights.* NY: Cambridge University Press, 2015.

Egerton, Douglas R. *The Wars of Reconstruction: The Brief, Violent History of America's Most Progressive Era.* NY: Bloomsbury, 2014.

Elliott, Carl, Nelson Foot Smith, Don Dodd, Wynelle S. Dodd, and John Martin Dombhart. *Annals of Northwest Alabama.* Tuscaloosa: n.p., 1958–.

Emberton, Carole. *Beyond Redemption: Race, Violence, and the American South after the Civil War.* Chicago: University of Chicago Press, 2013.

Evans, Curtis J. *The Conquest of Labor: Daniel Pratt and Southern Industrialization.* Baton Rouge: LSU Press, 2001.

Fitts, Alston. *Selma: Queen City of the Blackbelt.* Selma, AL: Clairmont, 1989.

Fitzgerald, Michael W. *Splendid Failure: Postwar Reconstruction in the American South.* Chicago: Ivan R. Dee, 2007.

———. *The Union League Movement in the Deep South: Politics and Agricultural Change During Reconstruction.* Baton Rouge: LSU Press, 1989.

———. *Urban Emancipation: Popular Politics in Reconstruction Mobile, 1860–1890.* Baton Rouge: LSU Press, 2002.

Fleming, Cynthia Griggs. *In the Shadow of Selma: The Continuing Struggle for Civil Rights in the Rural South.* Lanham, MD: Rowman and Littlefield, 2004.

Fleming, Walter L. *Civil War and Reconstruction in Alabama.* NY: Columbia University Press, 1905.

——, ed. *Documentary History of Reconstruction: Political, Military, Social, Religious, Educational & Industrial, 1865 to the Present Time.* Cleveland: Arthur H. Clark Co., 1906.

Flynt, Wayne. *Alabama Baptists: Southern Baptists in the Heart of Dixie.* Tuscaloosa: UA Press, 1998.

——. *Poor but Proud: Alabama's Poor Whites.* Tuscaloosa: UA Press, 1989.

Foner, Eric. *The Fiery Trial: Abraham Lincoln and American Slavery.* NY: W. W. Norton, 2010.

——. *Freedom's Lawmakers: A Directory of Black Officeholders During Reconstruction.* Rev. ed. Baton Rouge: LSU Press, 1996.

——. *Nothing but Freedom: Emancipation and Its Legacy.* Baton Rouge: LSU Press, 1983.

——. *Reconstruction: America's Unfinished Revolution, 1863–1877.* NY: Harper & Row, 1988.

Franklin, John Hope. *Reconstruction: After the Civil War.* Chicago: University of Chicago Press, 1961.

Gallagher, Gary. *The Confederate War.* Cambridge, MA: Harvard University Press, 1997.

Garrett, William. *Reminiscences of Public Men in Alabama for Thirty Years.* Atlanta: Plantation Publishing Co., 1872.

Genoways, Ted and Hugh H. *A Perfect Picture of Hell: Eyewitness Accounts by Civil War Prisoners from the 12th Iowa.* Iowa City: University of Iowa Press, 2001.

Going, Allen. *Bourbon Democracy in Alabama, 1874–1890.* 1951. Rev. ed. Tuscaloosa: UA Press, 1992.

Green, Hilary. *Educational Reconstruction: African American Schools in the Urban South, 1865–1890.* NY: Fordham University Press, 2015.

Grimsley, Mark. *The Hard Hand of War: Union Military Policy toward Southern Civilians, 1861–1865.* Cambridge, UK: Cambridge University Press, 1995.

Hadden, Sally E. *Slave Patrols: Law and Violence in Virginia and the Carolinas.* Cambridge, MA: Harvard University Press, 2001.

Hahn, Steven. *A Nation Under Our Feet: Black Political Struggles in the Rural South from Slavery to the Great Migration.* Cambridge, MA: Harvard University Press, 2003.

Hardy, John. *Selma: Her Institutions and Her Men.* 1879. Spartanburg, SC: Reprint Co., 1978.

Harris, Carl Vernon. *Political Power in Birmingham, 1871–1921.* Knoxville: University of Tennessee Press, 1977.

Herbert, Hilary Abner. *Why the Solid South? Or, Reconstruction and Its Results.* Baltimore: R. H. Woodward and Col, 1890.

Hildebrand, Reginald Francis. *The Times Were Strange and Stirring: Methodist Preachers and the Crisis of Emancipation.* Durham, NC: Duke University Press, 1995.

History of the Army of the Cumberland: Its Organization, Campaigns, and Battles, Written at the Request of Major-General George H. Thomas Chiefly from His Private Military Journal and Official and other Documents Furnished by Him. Cincinnati: R. Clarke & Co, 1875.

Holt, Thomas C. *Black over White: Negro Political Leadership in South Carolina During Reconstruction.* Urbana: University of Illinois Press, 1977.

Hoogenboom, Ari Arthur. *Rutherford B. Hayes: Warrior and President.* Lawrence: University Press of Kansas, 1995.

Hoole, William Stanley. *Alabama Tories: The First Alabama Cavalry, U.S.A.* Tuscaloosa, AL: Confederate Publishing Co., 1960.

Howard, Gene L. *Death at Cross Plains: An Alabama Reconstruction Tragedy.* Tuscaloosa: UA Press, 1984.

Hubbs, G. Ward. *Guarding Greensboro: A Confederate Company in the Making of a Southern Community.* Athens: University of Georgia Press, 2003.

———. *Searching for Freedom after the Civil War: Klansman, Carpetbagger, Scalawag and Freedman.* Tuscaloosa: UA Press, 2015.

Hughes, Nathaniel Cheairs, Jr., and Roy P. Stonesifer Jr. *The Life and Wars of Gideon J. Pillow.* 1993. Knoxville: University of Tennessee Press, 2011.

Hume, Richard L. *Blacks, Carpetbaggers, and Scalawags: The Constitutional Conventions of Radical Reconstruction.* Ed. Jerry B. Gough. Baton Rouge: LSU Press, 2008.

Hunnicutt, John L. *Reconstruction in West Alabama: The Memoirs of John L. Hunnicutt.* Ed. William Stanley Hoole. Tuscaloosa, AL: Confederate Publishing Co., [1959].

Hunt, Robert Eno. *The Good Men Who Won the War: Army of the Cumberland Veterans and Emancipation Memory.* Tuscaloosa: UA Press, 2010.

Hyman, Michael R. *The Anti-Redeemers: Hill-Country Political Dissenters in the Lower South from Redemption to Populism.* Baton Rouge: LSU Press, 1990.

Johnson, Michael P. *Toward a Patriarchal Republic: The Secession of Georgia.* Baton Rouge: LSU Press, 1977.

Jones, Jacqueline. *Labor of Love, Labor of Sorrow: Black Women, Work, and the Family from Slavery to the Present.* NY: Basic Books, 1985.

Jones, James Pickett. *Yankee Blitzkrieg: Wilson's Raid through Alabama and Georgia.* Athens: University of Georgia Press, 1976.

Jones, Jenkins, *An Artilleryman's Diary.* N.p.: Wisconsin History Commission, 1914.

Jones, Maxine, and Joe M. Richardson. *Talladega College: The First Century.* Tuscaloosa: UA Press, 1990.

Kelley, Robin D. G. *Hammer and Hoe: Alabama Communists During the Great Depression.* Chapel Hill: UNC Press, 1990.

Kolchin, Peter. *First Freedom: The Responses of Alabama's Blacks to Emancipation and Reconstruction.* Westport, CT: Greenwood Press, 1972.

LaFantasie, Glenn W. *Gettysburg Requiem: The Life and Lost Causes of Confederate Colonel William C. Oates*. Oxford, UK: Oxford University Press, 2006.

Letwin, Daniel. *The Challenge of Interracial Unionism : Alabama Coal Miners, 1878–1921*. Chapel Hill: UNC Press, 1998.

Levine, Bruce C. *Confederate Emancipation: Southern Plans to Free and Arm Slaves During the Civil War*. Oxford, UK: Oxford University Press, 2006.

Lewis, W. David. *Sloss Furnaces and the Rise of the Birmingham District: An Industrial Epic*. Tuscaloosa: UA Press, 1994.

Litwack, Leon F. *Been in the Storm So Long: The Aftermath of Slavery*. NY: Random House, 1979.

Lupold, John S., and Thomas L. French Jr. *Bridging Deep South Rivers: The Life and Legend of Horace King*. Athens: University of Georgia Press, 2004.

Manning, Chandra. *What This Cruel War Was Over: Soldiers, Slavery, and the Civil War*. NY: Alfred A. Knopf, 2007.

McClellan, William Cowan, and John C. Carter. *Welcome the Hour of Conflict: William Cowan McClellan and the 9th Alabama*. Tuscaloosa: UA Press, 2007.

McCorvey, Thomas Chalmers. *Alabama Historical Sketches*. Charlottesville: University of Virginia Press, 1960.

McCurry, Stephanie. *Masters of Small Worlds: Yeoman Households, Gender Relations, and the Political Culture of the Antebellum South Carolina Low Country*. NY: Oxford University Press, 1995.

McFeely, William S. *Yankee Stepfather: General O. O. Howard and the Freedmen*. New Haven, CT: Yale University Press, 1968.

McGee, B. F., *History of the 72nd Indiana Volunteer Infantry*. Lafayette, IN: S. Vater & Co, 1882.

McIlwain, Christopher Lyle, Sr. *Civil War Alabama*. Tuscaloosa: UA Press, 2016.

McKitrick, Eric L. *Andrew Johnson and Reconstruction*. Chicago: University of Chicago Press, 1960.

McMillan, Malcolm Cook. *Constitutional Development in Alabama, 1798–1901: A Study in Politics, the Negro, and Sectionalism*. Chapel Hill: UNC Press, 1955.

———. *The Disintegration of a Confederate State: Three Governors and Alabama's Wartime Home Front, 1861–1865*. Macon, GA: Mercer University Press, 1986.

Miller, Brian Craig. *John Bell Hood and the Fight for Civil War Memory*. Knoxville: University of Tennessee Press, 2010.

Mitchel, F. A. *Ormsby Macknight Mitchel, Astronomer and General: A Biographical Narrative*. Boston: Houghton Mifflin, 1887.

Moneyhon, Carl H. *The Impact of the Civil War and Reconstruction on Arkansas: Persistence in the Midst of Ruin*. Baton Rogue: LSU Press, 1994.

Morris, Robert Charles. *Reading, 'Riting, and Reconstruction: The Education of Freedmen in the South, 1861–1870*. Chicago: University of Chicago Press, 1981.

Nanzig, Thomas P. *The Badax Tigers: From Shiloh to the Surrender with the 18th Wisconsin Volunteers*. Lanham, MD: Roman & Littlefield, 2002.

Nelson, Scott Reynolds. *Iron Confederacies: Southern Railways, Klan Violence, and Reconstruction*. Chapel Hill: UNC Press, 1999.

Nieman, Donald G. *To Set the Law in Motion: The Freedmen's Bureau and the Legal Rights of Blacks, 1865–1868*. Millwood, NY: KTO Press, 1979.

Norrell, Robert J. *Reaping the Whirlwind: The Civil Rights Movement in Tuskegee*. NY: Random House, 1985.

Novak, Daniel A. *The Wheel of Servitude: Black Forced Labor after Slavery*. Lexington: University Press of Kentucky, 1978.

Nugent, Walter T. K. *The Money Question during Reconstruction*. NY: Norton, 1967.

Owen, Thomas McAdory. *History of Alabama and Dictionary of Alabama Biography*. Chicago: S. J. Clarke Publishing Co., 1921.

Parsons, Elaine. *Ku Klux: The Birth of the Klan during Reconstruction*. Chapel Hill, UNC Press, 2016.

Perman, Michael. *Reunion without Compromise: The South and Reconstruction: 1865–1868*. Cambridge, UK: Cambridge University Press, 1973.

———. *The Road to Redemption: Southern Politics, 1869–1879*. Chapel Hill: UNC Press, 1984.

Pinkard, Ophelia Taylor, and Barbara Clayton Clark. *Descendants of Shandy Wesley Jones and Evalina Love Jones: The Story of an African American Family of Tuscaloosa, Alabama*. Baltimore: Gateway Press, 1993.

Powell, Lawrence N. *New Masters: Northern Planters during the Civil War and Reconstruction*. New Haven, CT: Yale University Press, 1980.

Prince, K. Stephen. *Stories of the South: Race and the Reconstruction of Southern Identity, 1865–1915*. Chapel Hill: UNC Press, 2014.

Pruitt, Paul M., Jr. *Taming Alabama: Lawyers and Reformers, 1804–1929*. Tuscaloosa: UA Press, 2010.

Quist, John W. *Restless Visionaries: The Social Roots of Antebellum Reform in Alabama and Michigan*. Baton Rouge: LSU Press, 1998.

Rable, George C. *But There Was No Peace: The Role of Violence in the Politics of Reconstruction*. Athens: University of Georgia Press, 1984.

———. *The Confederate Republic: A Revolution against Politics*. Chapel Hill: UNC Press, 1994.

Ransom, Roger L. *One Kind of Freedom: The Economic Consequences of Emancipation*. Ed. Richard Sutch. 2nd ed. Cambridge, UK: Cambridge University Press, 2001.

Reid, Whitelaw. *After the War: A Tour of the Southern States, 1865–1866*. NY: Harper, 1965.

Richardson, Heather Cox. *The Death of Reconstruction: Race, Labor, and Politics in the Post-Civil War North, 1865–1901*. Cambridge, MA: Harvard University Press, 2004.

———. *West from Appomattox: The Reconstruction of America after the Civil War*. New Haven: Yale University Press, 2007.

Richardson, Joe Martin. *Christian Reconstruction: The American Missionary Association and Southern Blacks, 1861–1890.* Athens: University of Georgia Press, 1986.

Roark, James L. *Masters without Slaves: Southern Planters in the Civil War and Reconstruction.* NY: Norton, 1977.

Robinson, Armstead L. *Bitter Fruits of Bondage: The Demise of Slavery and the Collapse of the Confederacy, 1861–1865.* Charlottesville: University of Virginia Press, 2005.

Rogers, William Warren, and Robert David Ward. *August Reckoning: Jack Turner and Racism in Post–Civil War Alabama.* Baton Rouge: LSU Press, 1973.

——. *The One-Gallused Rebellion: Agrarianism in Alabama, 1865–1896.* Baton Rouge: LSU Press, 1970.

——, and Ruth Pruitt. *Alabama's Outlaw Sheriff: Stephen S. Renfroe.* 1972. Tuscaloosa: UA Press, 2005.

Rogers, William Warren, Jr. *Black Belt Scalawag: Charles Hays and the Southern Republicans in the Era of Reconstruction.* Athens: University of Georgia Press, 1993.

——. *Confederate Home Front: Montgomery During the Civil War.* Tuscaloosa: UA Press, 1999.

Rosen, Hannah. *Terror in the Heart of Freedom: Citizenship, Sexual Violence, and the Meaning of Race in the Postemancipation South.* Chapel Hill: UNC Press, 2009.

Royce, Edward Cary. *The Origins of Southern Sharecropping.* Philadelphia: Temple University Press, 1993.

Rubin, Anne S. *A Shattered Nation: The Rise and Fall of the Confederacy, 1861–1868.* Chapel Hill: UNC Press, 2005.

Saville, Julie. *The Work of Reconstruction: From Slave to Wage Laborer in South Carolina, 1860–1870.* Cambridge, UK: Cambridge University Press, 1994.

Schweninger, Loren. *James T. Rapier and Reconstruction.* Chicago: University of Chicago Press, 1978.

Sefton, James E. *The United States Army and Reconstruction, 1865–1877.* Baton Rouge: LSU Press, 1961.

Sellers, James Benson. *Slavery in Alabama.* 1950. 2nd ed. University: UA Press, 1964.

Severance, Ben H. *Tennessee's Radical Army: The State Guard and Its Role in Reconstruction, 1867–1869.* Knoxville: University of Tennessee Press, 2005.

Simpson, Brooks D. *Let Us Have Peace: Ulysses S. Grant and the Politics of War and Reconstruction, 1861–1868.* Chapel Hill: UNC Press, 1991.

Singletary, Otis A. *Negro Militia and Reconstruction.* NY: McGraw-Hill, 1963.

Slap, Andrew L. *The Doom of Reconstruction: The Liberal Republicans in the Civil War Era.* NY: Fordham University Press, 2006.

Snay, Mitchell. *Gospel of Disunion: Religion and Separatism in the Antebellum South.* NY: Cambridge University Press, 1993.

Stampp, Kenneth M. *The Era of Reconstruction, 1865–1877.* NY: Knopf, 1965.

———. *Reconstruction: An Anthology of Revisionist Writings.* Ed. Leon F Litwack. Baton Rouge: LSU Press, 1969.

Storey, Margaret M. *Loyalty and Loss: Alabama's Unionists in the Civil War and Reconstruction.* Baton Rouge: LSU Press, 2004.

Stowell, Daniel W. *Rebuilding Zion: The Religious Reconstruction of the South, 1863–1877.* NY: Oxford University Press, 1998.

Summers, Mark W. *A Dangerous Stir: Fear, Paranoia, and the Making of Reconstruction.* Chapel Hill: UNC Press, 2009.

———. *The Era of Good Stealings.* NY: Oxford University Press, 1993.

———. *The Ordeal of the Reunion: A New History of Reconstruction.* Chapel Hill: UNC Press, 2014.

———. *Railroads, Reconstruction, and the Gospel of Prosperity: Aid under the Radical Republicans, 1865–1877.* Princeton, NJ: Princeton University Press, 1984.

Thompson, C. Mildred. *Reconstruction in Georgia: Economic, Social, Political, 1865–1872.* NY: Columbia University Press, 1915.

Thompson, Elizabeth Lee. *The Reconstruction of Southern Debtors: Bankruptcy after the Civil War.* Athens: University of Georgia Press, 2004.

Thompson, Wesley S. *The Free State of Winston: A History of Winston County Alabama,* Winfield, AL: Pareil Press, 1968.

Thornton, J. Mills. *Politics and Power in a Slave Society: Alabama, 1800–1860.* Baton Rouge: LSU Press, 1978.

Trefousse, Hans L. *Andrew Johnson: A Biography.* NY: Norton, 1989.

Trelease, Allen W. *White Terror: The Ku Klux Klan Conspiracy and Southern Reconstruction.* NY: Harper & Row, 1971.

Waldrep, Christopher. *Roots of Disorder: Race and Criminal Justice in the American South, 1817–80.* Urbana: University of Illinois Press, 1998.

Walker, Clarence Earl. *A Rock in a Weary Land: The African Methodist Episcopal Church During the Civil War and Reconstruction.* Baton Rouge: LSU Press, 1982.

Wallenstein, Peter. *From Slave South to New South: Public Policy in Nineteenth-Century Georgia.* Chapel Hill: UNC Press, 1987.

Walther, Eric H. *William Lowndes Yancey and the Coming of the Civil War.* Chapel Hill: UNC Press, 2006.

Wang, Xi. *The Trial of Democracy: Black Suffrage and Northern Republicans, 1860–1910.* Athens: University of Georgia Press, 1997.

Webb, Samuel L. *Two-Party Politics in the One-Party South: Alabama's Hill Country, 1874–1920.* Tuscaloosa: UA Press, 1997.

Weitz, Mark A. *More Damning Than Slaughter: Desertion in the Confederate Army.* Lincoln: University of Nebraska Press, 2005.

Welke, Barbara. *Recasting American Liberty: Gender, Race, Law, and the Railroad Revolution, 1865–1920.* Cambridge, UK: Cambridge University Press, 2001.

Wetherington, Mark V. *Plain Folk's Fight: The Civil War and Reconstruction in*

Piney Woods Georgia. Chapel Hill: UNC Press, 2005.

Wiener, Jonathan M. *Social Origins of the New South: Alabama, 1860–1885.* Baton Rouge: LSU Press, 1981.

Wiggins, Sarah Woolfolk. *The Scalawag in Alabama Reconstruction, 1865–1881.* Tuscaloosa: UA Press, 1977.

Williams, Kidada E. *They Left Great Marks on Me: African American Testimonies of Racial Violence from Emancipation to World War I.* NY: New York University Press, 2012.

Wilson, Kirt H. *The Reconstruction Desegregation Debate: The Politics of Equality and the Rhetoric of Place, 1870–1875.* East Lansing: Michigan State University Press, 2002.

Wood, Wales W. *A History of the Ninety-Fifth Regiment, Illinois Infantry Volunteers* Chicago: Tribune, 1865.

Woodman, Harold D. *New South, New Law: The Legal Foundations of Credit and Labor Relations in the Postbellum Agricultural South,* Baton Rouge: LSU Press, 1995.

Woodward, C. Vann. *Origins of the New South, 1877–1913.* Baton Rouge: LSU Press, 1951.

———. *Reunion and Reaction: The Compromise of 1877 and the End of Reconstruction.* Boston: Little, Brown, 1951.

———. *The Strange Career of Jim Crow.* NY: Oxford University Press, 1955.

Ziegler, Edith. *Schools in the Landscape: Localism, Cultural Tradition, and the Development of Alabama's Public Education System, 1865–1915.* Tuscaloosa: UA Press, 2010.

Zuczek, Richard. *State of Rebellion: Reconstruction in South Carolina.* Columbia: University of South Carolina Press, 1996.

Edited Books

Baker, Bruce E., and Brian Kelly, eds. *After Slavery: Race, Labor, and Citizenship in the Reconstruction South.* Gainesville: University Press of Florida, 2013.

Barefield, Marylyn Davis, comp. *Historical Records of Randolph County, Alabama, 1832–1900.* N.p., 1985.

Berlin, Ira, Joseph P. Reidy, and Leslie S. Rowland, eds. *The Black Military Experience.* Freedom: A Documentary History of Emancipation, 1861–1867, ser. 2. NY: Cambridge University Press, 1982.

Berlin, Ira, Barbara J. Fields, Thavolia Glymph, Joseph P. Reidy, and Leslie S. Rowland, eds. *The Destruction of Slavery.* Freedom: A Documentary History of Emancipation, 1861–1867, ser. 1, vol. 1. NY: Cambridge University Press, 1985.

Berlin, Ira, and Leslie S. Rowland, eds. *Families and Freedom: A Documentary History of African American Kinship in the Civil War.* NY: New Press, 1997.

Cimbala, Paul A., and Randall M. Miller, eds. *The Freedmen's Bureau and Reconstruction: Reconsiderations.* NY: Fordham University Press, 1999.

——, ed. *The Great Task Remaining before Us: Reconstruction as America's Continuing Civil War.* NY: Fordham University Press, 2010.

Gallagher, Gary W., and Rachel A. Sheldon, eds. *A Political Nation: New Directions in Mid-Nineteenth Century Political History.* Charlottesville: University of Virginia Press, 2012.

Hahn, Steven, Steven F. Miller, Susan E. O'Donovan, John C. Rodrigue, and Leslie S. Rowland, eds. *Land and Labor, 1865.* Freedom: A Documentary History of Emancipation, 1861–1867, ser. 3, vol. 1. Chapel Hill: UNC Press, 2008.

Hayden, René, Anthony E. Kaye, Kate Masur, Steven F. Miller, Susan E. O'Donovan, Leslie S. Rowland, and Stephen A. West, eds. *Land and Labor, 1866–1867.* Freedom: A Documentary History of Emancipation, 1861–1867, ser. 3, vol. 2. Chapel Hill: UNC Press, 2013.

Kousser, J. Morgan, and James M. McPherson., eds. *Region, Race, and Reconstruction: Essays in Honor of C. Vann Woodward.* NY: Oxford University Press, 1982.

Noe, Kenneth W., ed. *The Yellowhammer War: The Civil War and Reconstruction in Alabama.* Tuscaloosa: UA Press, 2013.

Rabinowitz, Howard N., ed. *Southern Black Leaders of the Reconstruction Era.* Urbana: University of Illinois Press, 1982.

Rawick, George P., ed. *The American Slave: A Composite Autobiography.* Westport, CT: Greenwood Press, 1972.

——, Jan Hillegas, and Ken Lawrence, eds. *The American Slave.* Supplement Series 1: *Alabama Narratives.* Westport, CT, 1977.

Remington, W. Craig, and Thomas J. Kallsen, eds. *Historical Atlas of Alabama.* Dept. of Geography, College of Arts and Sciences, UA, 1999.

Smith, John David, J. Vincent Lowery, and Eric Foner, eds. *The Dunning School: Historians, Race, and the Meaning of Reconstruction.* Lexington: University Press of Kentucky, 2013.

Sykes, Francis W., George Eliphaz Spencer, John Tyler Morgan, Edward Asbury O'Neal, and Alabama Supreme Court., eds. *In the Matter of the Contest before the Senate between Francis W. Sykes and George E. Spencer.* Washington, DC: Judd & Detweiler Printers, 1875.

Waldrep, Christopher, and Donald G. Nieman, eds. *Local Matters: Race, Crime, and Justice in the Nineteenth-Century South.* Athens: University of Georgia Press, 2001.

Theses and Dissertations

Bailey, Richard. "Black Legislators During the Reconstruction of Alabama, 1867–1878." Ph. D., University of Kansas, 1986.

Bhurtel, Shyam Krishna. "Alfred Eliab Buck: Carpetbagger in Alabama and Georgia." PhD diss., AU, 1981.

Breese, Donald Hubert. "Politics in the Lower South during Presidential Reconstruction, April to November 1865." PhD diss., University of California, 1963.

Cash, William McKinley. "Alabama Republicans During Reconstruction: Personal Characteristics, Motivations, and Political Activity of Party Activists, 1867–1880." PhD diss., UA, 1973.

Castellano, Donna McPherson. "A Promise Delayed: The Politics of Banking, Railroad, and Mineral Development in Alabama, 1846–1860." MA thesis, UA, Huntsville, 2001.

Dannelly, Hermione. "The Life and Times of Robert Jemison, Jr. During the Civil War and Reconstruction." MA thesis, UA, 1942.

Dee, Christine Doyle. "Land Worth Fighting For: Scioto County, Ohio and Madison County, Alabama During the American Civil War." PhD diss., Harvard University, 2002.

English, Bertis Deon. "Civil Wars and Civil Beings: Violence, Religion, Race, Politics, Education, Culture, and Agrarianism in Perry County, Alabama, 1860–1875." PhD diss., AU. ProQuest Dissertations Publishing, 2006.

Gilmour, Robert Arthur. "The Other Emancipation: Studies in the Society and Economy of Alabama Whites During Reconstruction." PhD diss., Johns Hopkins University, 1972.

Hasson, Gail Snowden. "The Medical Activities of the Freedmen's Bureau in Reconstruction Alabama, 1865–1868." PhD diss., UA, 1982.

King, Ann Robinson. "The Political Career of Robert Miller Patton." MA thesis, Samford University, 1972.

Myers, John B. "Black Human Capital: The Freedmen and the Reconstruction of Labor in Alabama, 1860–1880." PhD diss., Florida State University, 1974.

Parnell, Ralph Erskine. "The Administration of William Hugh Smith: Governor of Alabama, 1868–1870." PhD diss., AU, 1958.

Smith, Louis Roycraft, Jr. "A History of Sumter County, Alabama, through 1886." 1990.

Speirs, Jennifer Kaye. "Educating Blacks in Reconstruction Alabama: John Silsby, the American Missionary Association, and the Freedmen's Bureau." MA thesis, AU, 1991.

Storey, Margaret D. "Southern Ishmaelites: Wartime Unionism and Its Consequences in Alabama, 1860–1874." PhD diss., Emory University, 1999.

Wiggins, Sarah Woolfolk. "The Role of the Scalawag in Alabama Reconstruction." PhD diss., LSU, 1965.

Government Documents

[Alabama.] *Journal of the Proceedings of Convention of the State of Alabama Held in the City of Montgomery, on Tuesday, September 12, 1865.* Montgomery, AL: Gibson & Whitfield, 1865.

Alabama Constitutional Convention. *Journal of the Constitutional Convention of the State of Alabama, Assembled in the City of Montgomery, Sept. 6th, 1875.* Montgomery, AL: W. W. Screws, 1875.

———. *Official Journal of the Constitutional Convention of the State of Alabama, Held in the City of Montgomery, Commencing on Tuesday, November 5th, A.D. 1867.* Montgomery, AL: Barrett & Brown, 1868.

Alabama General Assembly. *Report of Joint Committee on Outrages.* Montgomery, AL: Jno. G. Stokes & Co., 1868.

———. *Report of the Joint Committee of the General Assembly of Alabama, in Regard to the Alleged Election of Geo. E. Spencer.* Montgomery, AL: W. W. Screws, 1875.

Houston, George S. "Message of George S. Houston, Governor of Alabama, to the General Assembly, Submitted Dec. 28th, 1875." Montgomery, AL: W. W. Screws, 1875.

Morgan, John Tyler, Alabama Attorney General, and US Senate Committee on Privileges and Elections. *Argument of John T. Morgan, Attorney for the State of Alabama, in the Matter of Charges against George E. Spencer, before the Committee on Privileges and Elections of the Senate of the United States.* Montgomery, AL: n.p., 1874.

———. *Charges and Specifications Proffered by the State of Alabama against George E. Spencer, and Submitted to the Senate Committee on Privileges and Elections.* Montgomery, AL: n.p., 1874.

United States Census Office. *A Compendium of the Ninth Census, 1870.* Washington, DC: GPO, 1872.

United States Congress. House. Committee on Elections. "Civil Rights in Alabama." 43rd Congress, 2nd Sess. Executive Doc. 45.

———. "Contested Election: Bromberg vs. Haralson, Alabama." 44th Congress, 1st Sess., Misc. Doc. 47.

———. "Contested Election: Norris vs. Handley, Alabama." 42nd Congress, 2nd Sess., Misc. Doc. 15.

———. "Election in Alabama: Affidavits of Discharge from Employment in Alabama for Voting. March 26, 1868." 40th Congress, 2nd Sess., Misc. Doc. 111.

———. "Election in Alabama. Letter from the Secretary of War, Transmitting a Communication from the General of the Army, with a Report by Major General Meade, Commanding 3d Military District, Relative to the Recent Election in Alabama, Supplemental to His Report Sent to the House on the Twenty-Seventh of March Last. June 3, 1868." 40th Congress, 2nd Sess., Exec. Doc. 303.

———. House. Freedmen's Bureau. "Message from the President of the United States, Transmitting Report of the Commissioner of the Bureau of Refugees, Freedmen, and Abandoned Lands. December 19, 1865." 39th Congress, 1st Sess., Ex. Doc. 11.

———. Joint Committee on Reconstruction. "Report of the Joint Committee on Reconstruction, at the First Session Thirty-Ninth Congress." 1866.

———. Joint Select Committee to Inquire into the Condition of the Late Insurrectionary States. "Testimony Taken by the Joint Select Committee to Inquire into the Condition of Affairs in the Late Insurrectionary States. Alabama." Vols. 8, 9, 10. 1872.

———. Judiciary Committee. "Busteed Impeachment Investigation." 40th Congress, 3rd Sess. Washington, DC: GPO, 1869.

———. Select Committee on the Condition of Political Affairs in Alabama. "Affairs in Alabama." 43rd Congress, 2nd Sess. House Report 262, February 23, 1875.

United States Congress. Senate. "Alabama in 1874, 1875 and 1876." 44th Congress, 2nd Sess. Senate Report 704.

———. Committee on Privileges. "In the Senate of the United States. March 3, 1877.—The Subcommittee of the Committee on Privileges and Elections to Inquire and Report Whether in Any of the Elections in the State of Alabama in the Elections of 1874, 1875, and 1876 the Right of Male Inhabitants of Said State, Being Twenty-One Years of Age and Citizens of the United States, to Vote Had Been Denied or Abridged, & C.." 1877.

———. "Election of George E. Spencer." 44th Congress, 1st Sess. Report 331.

———. Senate. "Memorial of the Republican Members of the Legislature of Alabama, Asking the Enactment of Stringent Laws for the Protection of All Citizens of the United States. February 25, 1875." 43rd Congress, 2nd Sess., Misc. Doc. 107.

Index

1860 election, 17–18
1863 election, 26–27
1866 election, 95
1867 Federal Bankruptcy Law, 207
1868 Constitution, 166–69
1868 election, 173, 187–88
1870 election, 241–48
1872 election, 266–72, 313–14, 324
1874 election, 300, 313–14
1875 constitution, 324–27, 332–33
1876 election, 331
1880 election, 332

abolition, 38–39
Abrahams, James, 306
Adams-Onis Treaty, 109–10
African Methodist Episcopal Church, 93, 118–19, 366n79. *See also* black churches
African Methodist Episcopal Zion Church, 118, 366n79. *See also* black churches
agriculture: crop yields, 93, 121, 165, 285; flooding and, 93, 289; wartime damage and, 93
Alabama & Chattanooga Railroad, 101, 210, 213–14, 222–28, 248–49, 253–56, 273, 275–76, 321, 385–86n22, 386n34, 390n150
AMA missionaries, 381n73
American Missionary Association (AMA), 119–20
Applegate, Andrew J., 162
Arkansas, 187
arson, 110–11, 198, 231, 382n85
Athens, 35
Avery, Matt, 239

bankruptcies, 207–8, 254, 385n13
Beatty, John, 34
Bell, John, 17, 26, 357n95
Berry, Lawrence S., 120–21, 219
Billings, Walter P., 307, 310
Bingham, Arthur, 240, 297
Bingham, Daniel H., 35, 57, 62, 97, 155, 374n113
black belt: army occupation of, 352n120; black majority of, 316, 318; Civil War loss and, 22; conservatives of, 290; demographics of, 14; description of, 14; devastating crops of, 285–86; Ku Klux Klan and, 305; peace societies and, 27; pragmatism of, 322; Republican majority of, 317; secession and, 19; Union invasion of, 32; weakened county government of, 320
Black Cavalry, 74, 93, 177, 229
black churches, 115. *See also* African Methodist Episcopal Church and African Methodist Episcopal Zion Church
Black Codes: in Alabama, 361n32; D. C. Humphreys and, 59; Fourteenth Amendment, 95; Robert M. Patton and, 88; Wager Swayne and, 89; Walter Lynwood Fleming and, 1–2
black suffrage: agency and, 7–8; army oversight of, 100, 144; big government and, 3; Constitutional Convention and, 155, 164; economic development and, 83; First Military Reconstruction Act and, 143; perceptions of, 1–3; Radical Reconstruction and, 107; Reconstruction and, 32; retention of, 324; reunion and, 124, 166; riots and, 341n20; Robert M. Patton and, 100; support for, 97; taxation and, 3; Unionists and, 266; Union Leagues and, 124–28; violence and, 5–6; voter suppression and, 241; voter turnout and, 399n64; voter turnout of, 358n133; voting results of, 388n78; Wager Swayne and, 125; white control of, 124, 144, 147, 153, 163
black testimony, 70, 74
Blount County, 376n150

Bond, Horace Mann, 2
bonding laws, 318
Boyd, Alexander, killing of, 194, 199, 201
Bradley, Joseph C., 18, 21, 27, 31, 56, 60–62, 65, 67, 154, 263
Bragg, Braxton, 25, 56
Bragg, W. L., 329
Brainard, Mark D., 169
Brantley, Warren A., 224
Bray, Wells, 300, 307
Breckinridge, John C., 17–18, 25
Breese, Donald Hubert, 357n95
bribery, 70, 221, 224–26, 238–39, 297, 309, 315
Brown, Yankee Ben, 199, 202
Buck, A. E., 240
Buckley, C. W., 51, 117, 146, 164
Buell, Don Carlos, 34
Bulger, M. J., 77, 150
Bull Run, 22
Burke, J. W., 164
Burke, Richard, 203, 243
Burton, Pierce, 224, 239, 242
bushwhacking, 34, 61, 82, 198
Busteed, Richard, 88, 147, 152–53, 172, 180, 248, 291, 301–2
Butler County, 381n68

Calhoun County, 154, 380–81n67
Callis, John, 164
Campbell, John A., 28
canal project, 14
Canfield, S. S., 36
carpetbaggers, 7–8, 37, 68, 375n135
Carraway, John, 147, 160
cavalry, 25–26
census data, 353n13, 369n156, 371n48
certificates of election, 269–70, 317–18
Cheatham, W. B., 87
Cherokee County, 380–81n67
Chinese railroad workers, 219–20
civil rights, 7, 79, 277–80, 292, 301–2, 306–9, 407n112
Civil War: abuse of civilians after, 34–36; class differences and, 27–28; dissatisfaction of Union soldiers after, 36–38, 69; end of, 27–28; guerrilla warfare and, 23; negotiations to end, 29–32; neutrality and, 22; raids and, 29–31; regional divisions about, 22; start of, 22; Union occupation of Alabama during, 34–36, 39, 43–45; Union raids and, 23; Union soldiers' dissatisfaction with, 44–45
Clanton, James, 163, 200
Clarke County, 388n78
class struggles, 13–14
Clay, C. C., 26, 99, 294
Clay, Henry, 18
Clemens, Jeremiah, 21, 57–58, 60
Cloud, Noah, 162, 207, 230–31
Cobb, Williamson R. W., 26
Compromise of 1850, 16
Congressional Reconstruction, 186, 206
Congressional Reconstruction convention, 98, 372n52, 373n95
conscriptions: evaders of, 22–25, 29, 56, 59; Ku Klux Klan and, 175–76; legal avoiding of, 27
conservative, 13, 17, 27, 297, 342n1, 345n52, 353n6
Constitutional Convention of 1867: back pay for freedmen, 160; black suffrage and, 155, 164, 166; boycott and, 166–69; boycotting of, 177; delegates of, 71, 153, 158–61; disfranchisement and, 156–57; disunion and, 72; economic recovery and, 161; efficiency of, 162; factions within, 153–54; freedmen and, 73, 158–61; grants and, 161; John Pope and, 163; Lewis Parsons and, 71–72; loyalty oaths and, 71, 166; northerners and, 164; officeholders barred by, 155–56, 166; opposition to, 165; pardons and, 71; passage of constitution by, 155–56; ratification of constitution, 166–69; reunion and, 150, 166; Robert M. Patton and, 84, 165; salary of delegates and, 162; school funding and, 146; schools and, 159, 164; segregation and, 160, 165–66; slave owner compensation and, 73; slavery and, 71–73; state debts and, 72; successes of, 75, 165; suffrage and, 159; Supreme Court and, 162; taxation and, 72; Wager Swayne and, 163
Constitutional Union Party, 17
contraband camps, 37, 41, 51, 112
Cooper, William, 194
cooperationists, 19–21, 23, 26, 45, 57, 154, 221, 298, 333, 343n19
cotton belt. *See* black belt
cotton industry: postwar thefts of, 45–47, 221, 341n11, 350n77, 351n92; profitably of, 4–5, 85, 129, 219, 232–35, 257–58, 289, 293–94, 323; strikes of workers of, 258, 397n10
Councill, W. H., 301
courts: biracial juries of, 334–35; bonding provision of, 123; circuit, 76; civilian, 49; fees, 64–65; freedmen and, 69–70, 151;

grand juries and, 76; juries and, 151; lawlessness and, 152; mob law and, 81; treason trials and, 64–65
Crawford, Samuel, 216, 245–46
"Creoles," 109, 262, 268
crime, 81, 202, 320
Cruikshank, Marcus, 63, 80, 90
Curry, J. L. M., 119
Curtis, Alexander H., 189

Davis, Jefferson, 22, 25, 56
Davis, Nicholas, 18, 20–21, 62, 154, 207
deadfall legislation, 293, 320
Democratic and Conservative Party: 1863 election and, 26; 1875 constitution and, 324–27, 329–30; agenda of, 319–20, 324; in Baldwin County, 318; Compromise of 1850 and, 16; convention of, 240, 299; disarray of, 260, 294–95; ethics and, 297; factions within, 353n6; Fifteenth Amendment and, 240; freedmen and, 279–80; Jacksonian democracy and, 273–74; Liberal Republicans and, 264–65; pragmatism of, 264; race and, 277–81; removal of elected officials by, 317–18; Republican Party rally and, 242–44; social spending and, 296–97; Southern Rights Democrats and, 17; states' rights and, 16; success of, 14; terminology of, 342n1, 342n26; voter suppression and, 241–42; Whigs and, 17
Dew, Warren, 305, 408n138
Dexter, T. C. A., 46
Dillard, A. W., 66, 304
Dodge, Grenville, 40
Doster, C. S. G., 206
Douglas, Stephen, 16, 18, 26
Dozier, John, 110
Du Bois, W. E. B., 2
Dunning school, 1–2, 45, 124–25, 340n2, 341n13

economic depressions, 5, 286–88, 291, 294, 321–22, 326, 401–2n116
economic recovery: 1875 constitution and, 327–28; agriculture and, 93; cotton industry and, 85, 129; Fourteenth Amendment and, 98; Ku Klux Klan and, 177–78; land values and, 129, 219–20; under Military Reconstruction, 101; mining and, 86, 101, 209, 212; northern investment and, 95–96; prison labor and, 92; railroads and, 86, 92–93, 96, 102–3, 222–28, 257, 289; reunion and, 99–100; riots and, 95; Robert M. Patton and, 90; schools and, 92; state auditors and, 227–28; state bonds and, 91, 226–28; state debts and, 91, 96, 99–100, 144, 165, 209, 226–28; textiles and, 85; William H. Smith and, 222–28
educational endowment, 90–91, 413n88
Electoral College, 343n10, 377n168
Ellsworth, Hales, 279
emancipation, 2–3, 39–40, 47, 49–50, 62, 110, 116, 285
Emancipation Proclamation, 56, 160
Episcopal Church, 68

Fayette County, 23
Felder, Adam, 301, 306
Fifteenth Amendment, 240, 326–27
Figures, William, 67, 154, 238
First Alabama Cavalry, 58, 62, 79
First Florida Cavalry, 25
First Military Reconstruction Act, 97, 143
Fleming, Walter Lynwood, 1–2, 124–25, 340n2, 351n92, 390n1, 390n3
Florida, 19, 215, 275
Foner, Eric, 4–6, 403n2
food distributions, 80, 90–91
food supplies, 39–40, 80
Forrest, Nathan Bedford, *142*, 220–21, 256
Forsyth, John, 152
Fort Donelson, 23
Fort Henry, 23, 33
Fort Sumter, 22
"forty acres and a mule," 53, 87, 116, 125
Fourteenth Amendment: Black Codes and, 90, 95–97; disfranchisement and, 146, 371n48; First Military Reconstruction Act and, 144; Joseph C. Bradley and, 78–79; loyalty oath and, 146; officeholders barred by, 152, 166, 206; ratification of, 144; reunion and, 144; slaveholding threshold of, 345n59; southern rejection of, 124
freedmen: 1875 constitution and, 324–26; as armed militias, 126; arms and, 304; black belt labor shortage and, 189; in cities, 51–52; civil rights and, 302; Constitutional Convention and, 158–61; continued control over, 113–14; David P. Lewis and, 277–80; Democratic and Conservative Party and, 279–80; demographics of, 107, 364n18, 369n156; disputes of, 367–68n110; domestic workers and, 115; fear of, 113–14, 127, 174, 303–4; field hands and, 115; firearms and, 203; food distributions for, 287; gender norms and, 115, 122, 236; insurrection of, 116–17; on juries, 334–35; Ku Klux Klan and, 189, 201–

freedmen (*continued*)
3, 230, 267; labor contracts and, 113–14, 117–18; land for labor, 220; literacy and, 231–32; marriage and, 114; movements of, 51–52, 232–33; Nathan Bedford Forrest and, 220; newspapers and, 120–21; as officeholders, 110, 121, 148, 153–54, 164, 202, 211, 225–26, 235, 301, 332; officeholders and, 364n18, 399n54; personal wealth of, 235, 323, 391n21, 392n48, 403n145; planters and, 113–14, 122–23, 127; politics of, 6–7; railroads and, 195, 217–20, 222, 235; redistribution of lands and, 53, 87, 107, 116–17, 125; as renters, 130; Republican Party and, 7, 147–48; resistance of, 120–23; rural, 121; schools for, 93–94, 115, 118–19, 151, 230–32, 235; schools of, 250–51; sharecropping and, 130–32; as skilled labor, 107–8, 115; support of, 112, 118; surnames and, 114; tenant farming and, 130–32, 233; travel of, 113–14; treatment of, 58–59; Unionists and, 82, 96–97; Union Leagues and, 146; Union soldiers' attitude about, 52; violence against, 43–44, 48–49, 116, 127, 145, 153, 301, 303–4; voter turnout and, 399n64; as a voting bloc, 150; Wilcox County rally of, 259–60; work habits of, 128
Freedmen's Bureau: beginnings in Alabama, 50–51; confiscated land and, 69; Constitutional Convention and, 159; decline of, 341–42n23; food distributions of, 90–91, 97, 122; funding of, 69, 75; goals of, 76; labor contracts and, 113; land values and, 129; leadership of, 97; perceptions of, 53; Robert M. Patton and, 103; Union Leagues and, 149; Wager Swayne and, 67

Gardner, S. S., 51, 129, 185, 190
Garrett, William, 26
Garrison, William C., 156
Garth, W.W., 93
General Order No. 12, 53, 115
General Order No. 49, 152
Gettysburg, 26
Giers, J. J., 31–32, 60, 62, 96–97
Gleed, Robert, 220–21
global capitalism, 2
Goldthwaite, George, 247
Goodloe, Calvin, 18
Granges, 404n34
Grant, U. S., 33, 148, 173, 187, 205, 262, 265
Greeley, Horace, 162, 263, 265
Green, James K., 211, 220–21, 292–93
Greenbacker party, 289
Gregory, Ovid, 147
Griffin, Albert, 120, 124
guerrilla warfare, 23, 34, 36, 39, 57, 176
Gwaltmey, W. W., 122

Hahn, Steven, 5–6, 107, 341–42n23, 369n154, 403n2
Hale County, 388n78
Haralson, Jeremiah, *141*, 225–26, 277–78, 292, 296–97, 301, 334
Haralson, W. J., 263, 292, 297, 301
"hard war" policy, 34, 40–43, 176
Hardy, John, 47, 147, 224, 226, 297
Harrington, George F., 212
Hatchett, W .T., 164
Haughey, Thomas, 126, 156
Hayden, Julius, 163
Hays, Charles, 18, 243, 309–11
Herrick, Henry N., 49–50
Hewitt, G. W., 290
Hildreth, Ben, 94
Hill, J. B. F., 118, 180
Hinds, J. J., 213–14, 238
Hodgson, Joseph, 250
"home guards," 39
Hood, J. B., 30–31
Horton, Gustavus, 152
Houston, George S., 62, *140*, 298, 319, 331
Howard, O. O., 53, 90
Humphreys, D. C., 18, 21, 57–58, 62, 65, 77, 79, 196–97
Huntsville, 37, 57, 238

inflation bill, 295
Ingraham purchase, 291
Ivey, Thomas L., 303, 310

Jacksonian democracy: Alabama as a, 14–15, 331–33; class differences and, 24, 59, 89–90; government appointments and, 159; Grange and, 322; public subsidies and, 3; railroads and, 208; regional divisions and, 161; tenets of, 79, 289, 291, 328
Jemison, Robert, 23, 101, 113, 221
Johnson, Andrew, 30, 46, 59, 62–63, 65, 94
Jolly, John, 181, 243, 247, 251, 265
Jones, Shandy, 121, 221
Joseph, Philip, 110
journalism, 120
jury bill, 320

Keffer, John, 127, 157
Keils, Elias, 300, 307, 334

Kenard, Adam, 203–4, 267
King, Horace, 221
Knights of the White Camellia, 178, 381n73
Know-Nothings, 16
Kolchin, Peter, 2
Ku Klux Act, 263–64, 319
Ku Klux Klan: 1870 election and, 241–42, 245–46; antecedents of, 174; appearance of, *133*, 174–76, 178, 192; army presence and, 186, 196; arson and, 382n85; balloting time and, 182; in the black belt, 189, 305; black militias and, 186–87; black railway laborers and, 216–17; black suffrage and, 5; Calhoun County and, 380–81n67; causes of, 174; Cherokee County and, 380–81n67; in Choctaw County, 252; Congressional Reconstruction and, 186; conscriptions and, 175–76; convictions of, 378n24; in Dallas County, 189; demographics of, 179, 188–89; difficult in prosecuting, 192–93; duels and, 179; early history of, 35–36; economic recovery and, 177–78, 180; in Fayette County, 252; forcing elected officials out, 251–52; freedmen and, 197–98, 201–3, 230, 232–33, 267; George E. Spencer and, 238–39; in Greene County, 242; guerrilla warfare and, 176; in Hale County, 189–90; "hard war" policy and, 176; identification of, 378n24; increased activity by, 390n1; increasing violence of, 181–83; labor shortage and, 189, 232–33, 258–59; lack of law enforcement and, 184–85, 193, 200; in Lauderdale County, 191; lawlessness and, 229; local support of, 180–81; in Macon County, 200–201; in Marengo County, 189, 251–52; martial law and, 194, 196–97; membership of, 177–79; militias and, 237; in Morgan County, 191; newspapers and, 181, 191, 194, 380n66; night-riding and, 176; origins of, 93–94, 170, 174; in Perry County, 189; personal wealth and, 179–80; the planter class and, 4; political campaigns and, 191; political vacuum and, 175–76, 185, 201–2; Presidential Reconstruction and, 176; prosecution of, 253–54; punishments of, 378n24; racial killings by, 242; raids of, 299; railroads and, 215–17, 384n1; range of, 188–89, 229; reasons for, 174–82; recruitment for, 191; Republican Party and, 195–96; resistance to, 174, 183, 197–98, 230; retaliations and, 201; schools and, 182, 231; in Selma County, 189; sharecropping and, 183–84; slave patrols and, 175; study of, 174; in Sumter County, 202–3, 242, 251; support of, 238, 254, 379n36; suppression of, 193–94; Talladega County and, 380–81n67; Tallapoosa County and, 380–81n67; targets of, 189–193; tenant farming and, 183–84; threats of violence and, 189–90, 199–201; in Tuscaloosa County, 242; Union Leagues and, 177, 193; U. S. Grant and, 262; vigilantism and, 174–77; violence of, 300, 378n24, 379n36, 380n66, 390n1; voter suppression by, 170, 182, 191, 198, 241–42, 245–46, 290; voting riots and, 341n20; Walter Lynwood Fleming and, 1–2; in Wilcox County, 259; William H. Smith and, 186–87, 190–93, 196, 204, 215–17, 229; witness intimidation by, 202. *See also* Black Cavalry; Knights of the White Camellia

labor codes, 50–51, 53
labor contracts: Black Codes and, 89; breaking of, 122–23; chain gangs and, 116; civil officials and, 116; conditions of, 51, 53, 116; disputes about, 122–23, 236; for the family, 115–16; forced, 52, 86, 122; Freedmen's Bureau and, 113–14; violence and, 116, 122–23; Wager Swayne and, 89, 116
labor movement, 292
labor shortages, 189, 232–33, 258–59, 286, 323
laissez-faire government, 333
Lakin, Aram S., 118
Langdon, C.C., 298
Lauderdale County, 381n68
Lee, Thomas, 157
Lee County, 214
Lewis, David P.: abuse of railroad subsidies by, 315; election of, 295–96; freedmen and, 277–80; impeachment and, 269–70; militias and, 238, 306–7; platform of, 302; Republican Party and, 269–70; state debts and, 274–75; Unionists and, 21
Lewis, Green S. W., 292
Liberal Republican, 263–65, 268
Lincoln, Abraham, 35, 44, 59, 343n10
Lindsay, Robert Burns: abuse of aid and, 249–50, 253–56; background of, 240–41; failures of, 264–65, 321; Ku Klux Klan and, 252; picture of, *139*; white supremacy and, 253
Little, William G., 290
livestock, 233, 288, 293
looting, 25
Louisiana, 96–97, 297
Louisiana Purchase, 109–10

loyalty oaths, 34, 39, 67, 70–71, 146, 155–57, 166, 345n66
Lyell, Henry, 288
lynching, 1–2, 25, 198, 201, 217, 304, 393–94n90

Mabry, J. W., 272
Madison County, 381n68
manumissions, 109
Marion County, 23
martial law, 196–97, 381n68
Martin, L. V. B., 152
McClellan, George B., 30
McKay, Nathaniel, 253–54
McKleroy, J. M., 330
Meade, George Gordon, 163, 170, 380n56
Merriwether, Alex E., 293
Methodist Episcopal Church, 118
Mexican War, 15–16
Military Reconstruction, 91, 101, 103, 126, 145, 154, 156
Militia Laws, 28
Miller, William, 272
mining, 16, 42, 86, 101, 209, 212
Minnis, J.A., 285, 310, 329
miscegenation, 37, 39, 108–9
Mississippi, 19, 204, 220–21, 303, 334
Mitchel, O. M., 33–34, 45
Mobile and Ohio Railroad, 16
Mobile *Nationalist*, 120–21, 124, 128
Montgomery *Advertiser*, 247
Montgomery County, 394n103
Montgomery *State Journal*, 247
Moore, A. B., 18–19, 146
Moore, Samuel M., 253
Morgan, John T., 21, 112, 308
Morse, Josiah, 59
mountain region, 14–15
mulattoes, 37, 108–9, 364n18
Munford, Thomas T., 293

Negro Labor Convention, 287
night-riding, 229, 390n1, 408n138
North Carolina, 62
North East & South West Railroad, 101, 210, 221, 298

open-grazing rights, 293
Orrick, John C., 128, 368n129

pardons, 62–65, 71, 90, 97
Parsons, Lewis: black testimony and, 70; bribery scandal and, 70; Constitutional Convention and, 71–72, 75; critiques of, 76; education and, 70; goals of, 67; influence of, 27; Joseph C. Bradley and, 67; law enforcement and, 74; pardons and, 71; perceptions of, 70, 75–76; reunion and, 30, 60–63; Robert M. Patton and, 83; picture of, *138;* secessionists and, 66–67; slavery and, 70; as Speaker of the House, 271; Stephen Douglas and, 18; successes of, 75–76; Wager Swayne and, 69–70, 75–76; William H. Smith and, 243
pass system, 113
Patton, Robert M.: background of, 77, 84; black suffrage and, 100; Constitutional Convention and, 84, 165; Daniel N. Stanton and, 209–10; disfranchisement of, 160; economic policies of, 99; Fourteenth Amendment and, 98; Freedmen's Bureau and, 95; influence of, 80; John C. Stanton and, 209–10; Lewis Parsons and, 83; motivations of, 101; personal wealth of, 101; picture of, *137*; policy priorities of, 85; politics of, 84; pragmatism of, 151; railroads and, 16–17; railroad subsidies and, 99; re-election of, 100; reunion and, 146; Unionists and, 144; Wager Swayne and, 88, 95, 100–101, 146
peace societies, 27
Peck, E. W., 18, 156
Pennington, J.L., 169, 212, 250, 278
personal wealth, 375n26q, 391n21, 392n48, 403n145
Peters, Thomas M., 18, 21, 159, 212
Pickens County, 381n68
Pierce, Charles, 121
Pierce, J. G., 243
Pillow, Gideon, 25
Pope, John, 145, 149, 163
Populist revolt, 333–34
Posey, S. C., 144
presidential pardons, 62–63
Presidential Reconstruction, 62–65, 68–69, 79–80, 82, 101, 112–13, 176, 211, 298
Price, Daniel, 196, 199, 203
Pugh, James L., 299

racial supremacy, 4
racial violence, 4–5
racism, 3–4
Radical Reconstruction, 2, 37, 107, 215, 257
Radical Republicans, 145
raids, 23, 29–31, 299
railroads: abuse of aid and, 212–13, 222–28, 295; benefits of, 219–20; black laborers and, 195, 216–17; bonds and, 401–2n116;

building of, 92–93, 156; in Chambers County, 217; Chinese laborers and, 219; in Clarke County, 218; conflicts along, 384n1; corruption and, 212–13; in Dallas County, 218–20; Dunning school and, 341n13; economic recovery and, 4–5, 86, 92–93, 96, 209, 257, 289; federal intervention and, 257; freedmen and, 217–20, 222, 235; in Hale County, 218; insolvency of, 273–75; Ku Klux Klan and, 215–17, 384n1; land grants and, 213; land values and, 219–20; meltdown of, 205; merging of, 222; mining and, 16, 212; northern investment and, 209–10; in Perry County, 218, 220; public subsidies for, 3, 17, 99, 390n150, 401–2n116; rebuilding of, 34, 156; Republican Party and, 220, 224–25; segregation and, 277–79; in Selma County, 218–19; Smith and, 384n1; state bonds and, 209–11, 291; state debts and, 223–28, 330–31; state purchase of, 273; subsidy programs for, 205, 208–10; in Talladega County, 218; wartime damage and, 208–9; white support of, 218; William H. Smith and, 208; William Tecumseh Sherman and, 347n6
Randolph, Ryland, 150–51, 178–80, 193, 195, 198, 220–21, 245–46
Rapier, James T., 110, 159
Reconstruction Act, 376n163
Redeemer, 271–72, 317, 327–30, 336, 410n2
Redemption: 1872 election and, 324; 1875 constitution and, 324–27, 332–33; black belt and, 320, 322, black militias and, 407n124; Booker T. Washington and, 334; conservatives and, 317–19; cotton industry and, 323; Democratic and Conservative Party and, 319–20, 324–27, 329–330; economic depressions and, 321–22, 326; Eric Foner and, 413n86; freedmen and, 323, 334–35; George E. Spencer and, 324, 336; Granges and, 322; Jacksonian democracy and, 322; John Silsby and, 323; labor shortages and, 323; laissez-faire government and, 333; lasting results of, 316, 332–37; Populist revolt and, 333–34; Republican majorities and, 317–19; Republican Party and, 321, 324, 328–29; sharecropping and, 333; state debts and, 321–22, 324, 330–31; tenant farming and, 333; violence against freedmen and, 248, 285; White Line campaign and, 253, 285, 316–317; William H. Smith and, 322, 336–37
Reed, Bob, 304, 307, 325
Renfroe, Steve, 203–4, 300
Republican Party: 1875 constitution and, 324–29; in black belt, 317–18; candidates of, 264–66; certificates of election and, 317–18; convention of, 146–48; conversions to, 207–8; demographics of, 23–25; disarray of, 325; ethics and, 297; factions within, 146–47, 238, 261–64, 324; failures of, 317; freedmen and, 7, 146–48, 264; gains in, 260; George E. Spencer and, 271–72; Liberal Republican movement and, 263–64; personal debts and, 208; race and, 277–81; Radical Republicans and, 316; Radicals and, 145; railroads and, 220; rally of, 242–44; removal of elected officials, 317–18; repression of, 24; resistance by, 320–21; schools and, 147; slavery and, 18; successes of, 267–68; taxation and, 147; violence and, 273
Revisionists, 2, 9, 33, 45, 341n13
Reynolds, R. M., 215
Rice, Samuel, 206
riots, 242–44, 277, 341n20
Roddey, P. D., 31
Royal, Benjamin, 211
runaways, 49

Saffold, Benjamin, 153, 163, 207
Saffold, Milton, 27, 60–62, 65, 68, 77, 97
scalawags, 17, 57
schools: African Methodist Episcopal Church and, 367n84; African Methodist Episcopal Zion Church and, 367n84; Constitutional Convention and, 164; for freedmen, 93–94, 115, 118–19, 151, 235, 250–51; Freedmen's Bureau and, 230–31; funding of, 146, 151, 156, 230–31, 327–332, 413n69; integration of, 7; Ku Klux Klan and, 231; Reconstruction politics and, 390n4; Republican Party and, 147; segregation and, 160, 172, 187, 230; segregation of, 92
Schurz, Carl, 70
secession: class differences and, 19; factions within, 19; regional divisions of, 19; reluctance about, 21–22; slavery and, 18; timing of, 19; Whigs and, 19
Second Reconstruction Act, 2, 375n138
Seibels, J.H., 27, 32, 60–61, 65–66, 68
Selma, 42–43
Selma, Marion & Memphis Railroad, 220
Selma, Rome & Dalton Railroad, 216
Semmes, Raphael, 94, 317
Semple, Henry C., 160, 172
sexual assaults, 35, 38

sharecropping, 4, 130–32, 183–84, 232–34, 236, 333, 342n24, 369n154
Sheats, Christopher C., 21
Shelby County, 30
Sherman, William T., 40, 116–17
Sherman's March to the Sea, 28–31
Shiloh, 33
Shorter, John Gill, 22–23, 26, 58, 65, 127–28
Sibley, Isaac D., 238
Silsby, John, 120, 296, 323
slaveholding rates, 345n59, 379n29
slavery: broken families and, 113–14; Constitutional Convention and, 72–73; continuation of, 41, 62, 73; discipline and, 108–9; domestic workers and, 108–9, 115; emancipation and, 39–40, 47; field hands and, 108–10, 115; gang system, 108; gender norms and, 108; global capitalism and, 2–3; literacy and, 107, 109; Republican Party and, 18; resistance and, 107–8; secession and, 18; slave owner compensation and, 73; states' rights and, 78; support of, 13
slaves, 38–39
smallpox, 120
Smith, Arthur A., 231
Smith, Ferdinand, 250–51
Smith, James Q., 64, 152
Smith, William H.: abuse of railroad subsidies by, 212–14, 222–28, 243, 246, 248–50, 322, 336–37; administration of, 206; Alabama & Chattanooga Railroad and, 226–27; background of, 171; congressional testimony of, 79; disfranchisement and, 172, 187; draft and, 171; duties of, 215–16; escape of, 58; First Alabama Cavalry and, 62; freedmen and, 200; as judge, 66; Ku Klux Klan and, 186–87, 190–93, 196, 204, 215–17, 229; legacy of, 336–37; militias and, 237; Nathan Bedford Forrest and, 220; public office and, 169; railroad corporations of, 212–14, 222–28; railroad of, 384n1, 385–86n22; railroads and, 208; reelection of, 228, 239–43, 246–47; Republican Party and, 147; Robert M. Patton and, 101; Stephen Douglas and, 18; voter registration and, 149; Wager Swayne and, 97; wartime activities of, 171; west Florida and, 275
Smith, W. R., 77
South Carolina, 18, 187, 297
Southern Baptists, 68, 118–19, 210
Southern Methodists, 68, 118
Southern Republican Association, 96
Southern Rights Democrats, 17
Speed, J. H., 146, 206
Speed, Lawrence, 121
Spencer, George E.: reunion and, 169; 1872 election and, 271; Andrew Johnson and, 62; background of, 236; black suffrage and, 236; as carpetbagger, 58; cotton industry and, 46; Democratic and Conservative Party and, 299; picture of, *136*; redistribution of lands and, 144; reelection of, 324; Republican Party and, 237, 271–72, 336; Richard Busteed and, 147, 301–2; wartime record of, 79; Willard Warner and, 237, 261
Springfield, Jack, 144, 195
Stanton, Daniel N., 209–10, 221, 223–26, 253–56, 390n150
Stanton, John C., 209–10, 221, 223–26, 253–56
state bank, 14
state bonds, 91, 100–101, 211, 243, 248–50, 253–56, 274–75, 292, 330–31
state debts, 62, 72, 91, 100–101, 165, 209, 211, 243, 248–50, 253–56, 274–75, 321–22, 324, 330–31
states' rights, 2, 78
St. Clair County, 25, 81–82, 144, 195
Stevens, Thaddeus, 155
Stewart, T. C., 189
Sumter County, 272
Supreme Court, 162
Swayne, Wager: background of, 88; Black Codes and, 89; black suffrage and, 125, 374n113; black testimony and, 74; Constitutional Convention and, 155, 163; food distributions of, 80, 90–91, 97; Freedmen's Bureau and, 67, 75; labor contracts and, 53, 89, 116; Lewis Parsons and, 69–70, 75–76; picture of, *135*; policies of, 53; pragmatism of, 88; redistribution of lands and, 87; replacements for, 163; Robert M. Patton and, 88, 95, 100–101, 146; Union Leagues and, 125; voter registration and, 149; William H. Smith and, 97
Sykes, Francis W., 269

Talladega College, 119, 145–46, 198
Talladega County, 380–81n67
Tallapoosa County, 376n150, 380–81n67
Tammany Hall, 238
taxation, 3, 72, 82, 101, 144, 147
Tayloe, E. T., 287
Tayloe family, 233
Taylor, Joseph W., 150

Taylor, Richard, 43, 61
tenant farming, 4, 130–32, 183–84, 232–34, 236, 286, 333, 342n24
Tennessee River Valley: Civil War loss and, 22; conditions of, 40–41; decline of slavery in, 112; demographics of, 353n13; fear of freedmen and, 111; returning soldiers and, 31; secession and, 19–20; slave population of, 41, 111; treatment of civilians and, 34–36, 39–41; Union occupation of, 34–36, 39
Third Reconstruction Act, 146, 151
Thomas, George H., 41, 60
Thomas, Roderick B., 317
Thompson, Holland, 122
Thornton, J. Mills, 3, 208
Tomeny, T. M., 46
Towles, Tollifer, 74
Turner, Benjamin, 110, 121, *134*, 240–41, 266, 296
Turner, Henry M., 125
Turner, Jack, 304, 310
Tuscaloosa County, 381n68
Tuscaloosa *Monitor*, 245–46
Tuscumbia, 40
Tyler, Robert, 163, 299

Uncle Tom's Cabin, 39
Unionists: Compromise of 1850 and, 16; Congressional Republicans and, 80; demographics of, 24–25; disunity of, 56; in Fayette County, 23; food distributions and, 80; Fourteenth Amendment and, 96; freedmen and, 60, 82, 96–97; loss of power by, 77–78; in Marion County, 23; Presidential Reconstruction and, 79–80; raids on, 57; Robert M. Patton and, 144; secessionists and, 78; terminology of, 55–56, 61, 353n2; in Winston County, 23
Union Leagues: black suffrage and, 124–28; Congressional Reconstruction convention and, 372n52; freedmen and, 80–81, 146; Ku Klux Klan and, 177, 193; meetings of, 127; planters and, 127–28; purpose of, 125–26; spread of, 126
University of Alabama, 42, 92

vagrancy laws, 86, 89, 116–17, 120, 145
Vicksburg, 26
violence, 149, 153
voting: 1866 election and, 95; army oversight of, 266; boycotting of, 166–69; election results of, 404n41; Ku Klux Klan and, 182, 387n76; regulations for, 387n76; reunion and, 150; on secession, 19–21; voter intimidation and, 170, 198; voter registration and, 149; voter turnout and, 70–71, 77, 168, 187–88, 245–46, 311–14, 326, 343n17, 344n29, 358n133, 371n48, 394n103

Walker, Leroy Pope, 264, 327
Walker County, 19, 376n150
Wall Street collapse, 286, 291
Warner, Willard, 172, 237, 243, 247, 261–62, 265
Washington, Booker T., 334
Watts, Thomas, 22, 28, 31
Webb, Alexander, 128
Weir, Leonard, 253
West, A. A., 30
West Virginia, 22
Whigs, 17, 19, 26, 78, 84, 99, 206, 316, 357n95
White, Alexander, 18, 59, 73, 167, 206
White League, 253, 285, 299
White Line campaign, 5, 297–98, 300, 309–10, 316, 326
white supremacy, 58–59, 220–21, 253, 299, 336–37
Wiggins, Sarah, 2
Wild-Cat line, 214
Wills Valley line, 101, 209
Wilmer, Richard, 68
Wilson, Henry, 162
Wilson, James, 42, 53–54, 59, 349n51
Wilson's raid, 60–61, 90, 112, 349n51
Winston County, 23, 358n126
Wood, Edward, 34
Wood, W. B., 81
Woodruff, Noadiah, 331
Woodward, C. Vann, 316

Yancey, William, 17, 19–20